FREE SPEECH

AND

ASSOCIATION

FREE SPEECH

AND

ASSOCIATION

The Supreme Court and the First Amendment

Edited by
PHILIP B. KURLAND

THE UNIVERSITY OF CHICAGO PRESS
CHICAGO AND LONDON

The University of Chicago Press, Chicago 60637
The University of Chicago Press, Ltd., London

Printed in the United States of America

ISBN: 0-226-46403-2

TO

JEAN AND BERNIE MELTZER,

for teaching by example the
meaning of kindness and
civility

CONTENTS

PREFACE

In a period of political and social quiescence, the guarantees of the First Amendment are essentially hortatory. When society is sure of its goals and its means for attaining them, it is easy to tolerate the lone voice crying in the wilderness, for it is often thought to afford amusement if not education. When a society is deeply riven, as the American society has been for a quarter-century, the constitutional provisions for freedom of speech take on added significance. With the dropping of the iron curtain, and with the exacerbation of racial conflicts, and with a war on foreign soil that sundered the American social and political fabric, the United States became deeply troubled in its attempt to meet its felt needs and, at the same time, to abide its conscience. Gone were the truths of yesteryear. The spirit of fraternity, which never had a great hold on Americans, dissolved into hateful factions. Toward the end of this period, even the cement of economic well-being disintegrated. It is once more a time for the testing of men's souls and, thus, once more a time for the testing of the veritudes of First Amendment free speech doctrine.

Constitutional doctrines do not live through judicial decisions alone. But, in giving some protection to the multitude of voices expressing the views of every minority however constituted, the Supreme Court has provided a leadership that has proved the worth to a democratic society of an undemocratic system of judicial review. This is not to say that all the Supreme Court decisions in this area are to be considered worthy of the Court's role of America's censor. One has to be suspect, for example, of the heavy investment of the Court's time and effort in its concern over pornography. It is true, of course, that these decisions highlighted the fact that we pay in civility for the opportunities for diversity. But civility is a debased coin in contemporary America and the Court is partly responsible for its debasement.

The work of academic critics of the Court in the free speech area was led by the late Professor Harry Kalven, Jr., whose voice is so frequently recorded in the pages of this volume, in both his own articles and those written by others. Kalven was a direct intellectual descendant of Professor Zechariah Chafee and Professor Alexander Meiklejohn. And it was in this great tradition that most of the essays contained herein were composed. For them, it was not enough that the "right" results were reached. The concept of Freedom of Speech emerged from the Age of Reason (and may well die with it). It is necessary, therefore, to provide a rational argument based on a recognition of the competing demands of the contemporary scene and history, on the competing demands of the principles of democracy and constitutionalism, which are not the same, on the need for the majority to tolerate the minority, but also of the minority to understand the limits of tolerance if law is to remain the viable alternative to force.

This nation has not yet emerged from the darkness that has engulfed it. The Supreme Court's decisions analyzed in this book afford some light for the upward, if tortuous, path that will return us to common purpose, to civility, to tolerance, to all those things for which individual freedom is a means.

PHILIP B. KURLAND

ALEXANDER MEIKLEJOHN

THE FIRST AMENDMENT IS AN ABSOLUTE

Forty-two years ago the *Schenck* opinion,[1] written by Mr. Justice Holmes for a unanimous Court, opened a judicial controversy that still rages. It has taken many forms. In recent years it has divided the Supreme Court Justices into two groups which seem unable to understand each other well enough to formulate with clarity the issue about which they differ. Their discussion of that issue, which is indicated by the title of this paper, has been unclear because the contending parties have not been able to agree on the sense in which the word "absolute" shall be used.

The first portions of this paper will seek a needed clarification of the issue in controversy. For that purpose it will use Mr. Justice Black's recent James Madison Lecture, *The Bill of Rights*[2] and that section of Mr. Justice Harlan's *Konigsberg*[3] opinion which discusses theoretically the meaning of the First Amendment. Relevant opinions of Justices Holmes and Frankfurter will also be taken into account. I shall then attempt an expression of my own thesis.[4]

Alexander Meiklejohn, former President of Amherst College, is Professor Emeritus of Philosophy, University of Wisconsin.

1 Schenck v. United States, 249 U.S. 47 (1919).

2 35 N.Y.U.L. Rev. 882 (1960).

3 Konigsberg v. State Bar, 366 U.S. 36, 49–56 (1961).

4 For several reasons, much of this paper is written in the first person.
First, in his *Konigsberg* dissent, 366 U.S. at 56, Mr. Justice Black, taking the

I. Mr. Justice Black's Position

Mr. Justice Black's absolutist thesis is stated by his lecture in one sentence: "I take no law abridging to mean *no law abridging*."[5] With that general statement in mind, he examined and interpreted, one by one, the ten provisions of the Bill of Rights. And, on historical and philosophical grounds, he found them all to be "absolutes" in the sense that "they mean what they say." It should be noted, however, that this assertion does not imply that in all respects they say fully and clearly what they mean. The Framers of the Constitution suffered from the same semantic difficulties as do its present-day interpreters. The following quotations illustrate the point at issue.

Concerning the Eighth Amendment, Mr. Justice Black said:[6]

> The Eighth Amendment forbids "excessive bail," "excessive fines," or the infliction of "cruel or unusual punishments."

---

absolutist position, speaks of "some people" of the same school whose view of the First Amendment differs from his own. And, in an appended note, he mentions me as one of them. *Id.* at 65 n. 19, referring to: Meiklejohn, *What Does the First Amendment Mean?* 20 U. Chi. L. Rev. 461 (1953). In the words which follow, I must, therefore, speak not for absolutism in all its forms, but only for my own version of it.

Second, my book *Free Speech and Its Relation to Self-Government* (1948) has a closing chapter entitled "Reflections" that begins: "No argument about principles is, I suppose, ever finished. But the argument of these lectures seems to the writer of them, peculiarly incomplete. They constitute, it seems to me, not an inquiry, but only the beginning of an inquiry. Even if it be agreed that the 'clear and present danger' formula denies rather than expresses the meaning of the Constitution, even if we are convinced that the guarantee of the freedom of public discussion which is provided by the First Amendment admits of no exceptions, we are, because of those very conclusions, plunged at once into a multitude of bewildering questions. Those questions relate both to theory and to practice. And this book makes no pretense of having specifically dealt with them." *Id.* at 92. That frankly acknowledged incompleteness has often been called to my attention and I need, in reply, to say about it whatever a non-lawyer can say.

Third, the writing of this paper is largely due to the friendly insistence of Professor Harry Kalven, Jr., of the Law School of the University of Chicago. He and I have had, in recent years, a continuing exchange of ideas. Professor Kalven tells me that he is not sure that my interpretation of the First Amendment can stand the test of lawyer-like application to the many specific situations which the courts must handle. In response to that challenge, I cannot presume to offer fully specific answers to specific problems. I can only suggest principles, bringing them as near as I can to the actual issues with which the courts deal.

5 Black, *supra* note 2.

6 *Id.* at 871–72.

> This is one of the less precise provisions. The courts are required to determine the meaning of such general terms as "excessive" and "unusual." But surely that does not mean that admittedly "excessive bail," "excessive fines," or "cruel punishments" could be justified on the ground of "competing" public interest in carrying out some generally granted power like that given Congress to regulate commerce.

And part of his discussion of the Fourth Amendment was as follows:[7]

> The use of the word "unreasonable" in this Amendment means, of course, that not *all* searches and seizures are prohibited. Only those which are *unreasonable* are unlawful. There may be much difference of opinion about whether a particular search or seizure is unreasonable and therefore forbidden by this Amendment. But if it *is* unreasonable, it is absolutely prohibited.

About the Fifth Amendment he said:[8] "There has been much controversy about the meaning of 'due process of law.' Whatever its meaning, however, there can be no doubt that it must be granted." And, finally, as he declared the First Amendment to be absolute, Mr. Justice Black supported his assertion by singling out only one phrase of that very complicated statement: "The phrase 'Congress shall make no law' is composed of plain words, easily understood."[9]

With regard to the ambiguity of other phrases of the Amendment, he was not explicit, as he was in dealing with the Eighth and Fourth and Fifth Amendments. But it may, I think, be taken for granted that the words "abridging the freedom of speech, of the press; or the right of the people peaceably to assemble, and to petition the Government for a redress of their grievances" are not "plain words, easily understood." Together with such expressions as "excessive fines" or "cruel or unusual punishments" or "due process of law," they have been subject to "much controversy." We have inherited them from ages of bitter conflict over civil liberties. "The courts are required to determine [their] meaning."[10]

---

[7] *Id.* at 873.

[8] *Ibid.*

[9] *Id.* at 874.

[10] *Id.* at 871. I am not sure that Mr. Justice Black will accept this reading of what he means.

That constitutional effect of a combination of absolutist language with terms of partial ambiguity, Mr. Justice Black summed up in this statement:[11]

> To my way of thinking, at least, the history and language of the Constitution and the Bill of Rights, which I have discussed with you, make it plain that one of the primary purposes of the Constitution with its amendments was to withdraw from the Government *all* power to act in certain areas—*whatever the scope of those areas may be.*

It is clear, I think, that Mr. Justice Black, as an absolutist, is here saying, and is saying only, that the provisions of the Bill of Rights are "universal" statements. In affirmative form they say "all are"; when negative, they say: "none are." And such statements are "not open to exceptions." As universals, they refer, validly or invalidly, clearly or unclearly, to every member of the class which their terms designate. If you believe that "all are," it is nonsense to say that "some are not." If you believe that "none are," you thereby believe, whether you know it or not, that "some are" is false. The "absolute" assertion, like every other intelligible assertion "means what it says" or, at least, what it tries to say.

II. Mr. Justice Harlan's Rejection of the Black Position

As one reads the opinions of the "non-absolutists," "balancers," or "operationalists" who undertake to refute the thesis that Mr. Justice Black advocated in his lecture, one is amazed at the extent to which they substitute caricature for refutation. A striking example of this intellectual irrelevance may be found in the opening words of Mr. Justice Harlan's discussion of the constitutional issue in his *Konigsberg* opinion:[12]

> At the outset we reject the view that freedom of speech and association . . . , as protected by the First and Fourteenth Amendments are "absolutes," not only in the undoubted sense that where the constitutional protection exists it must prevail, but also in the sense that the scope of that protection must be gathered solely from a literal reading of the First Amendment. Throughout its history this Court has consistently rec-

---

[11] *Id.* at 874–75. (Emphasis added.)

[12] 366 U.S. at 49–50.

> ognized at least two ways in which constitutionally protected freedom of speech is narrower than an unlimited license to talk. . . .

That statement not only flatly rejected the absolutist theory but also gave two different accounts of what that theory is. The first of these two accounts might be accepted by any absolutist as a clear and accurate statement of his belief about the First Amendment. But, in sharp contrast, the second was a caricature which, for forty-two years since Mr. Justice Holmes, in *Schenck*, initiated and then discarded it, has confused and defeated the intention of the Court to confer reasonably about what the First Amendment means to say.

As he drew the caricature which made possible an easy victory over his opponent, Mr. Justice Harlan claimed the support of Mr. Justice Holmes, who had said of the provisions of the Constitution:[13] "Their significance is vital not formal; it is to be gathered not simply by taking the words and a dictionary, but by considering their origin and the line of their growth." He might also have quoted from Mr. Justice Frankfurter's concurring opinion in *Dennis v. United States*,[14] where the same accusation of historical illiteracy was made:[15] "The language of the First Amendment is to be read not as barren words found in a dictionary but as symbols of historic experience illumined by the presuppositions of those who employed them." But Mr. Justice Harlan's own misunderstanding of his opponent goes further than that of his predecessors. His words misconstrue not only the methods of absolutist thinking but also the conclusion at which such thinking arrives. To the accusation that his opponent relies "solely" on a dictionary, he now adds the charge that he interprets the First Amendment as establishing "an unlimited license to talk."

The absolutist interpretation, when it is thus misstated, is, of course, easily destroyed. The supposed belief in "an unlimited license to talk" is casually refuted by a footnote observation that it "cannot be reconciled with the law relating to libel, slander, mis-

---

[13] Gompers v. United States, 233 U.S. 604, 610 (1914), quoted at 366 U.S. at 50 n. 10.

[14] 341 U.S. 494, 517 (1951).

[15] *Id.* at 523.

representation, obscenity, perjury, false advertising, solicitation of crime, complicity by encouragement, conspiracy, and the like. . . ."[16] But who, among Mr. Justice Harlan's colleagues, believes in "an unlimited license to talk"? Who interprets the words of the First Amendment without "considering their origin or the line of their growth"? Who reads the text as "barren words found in a dictionary" rather than as "symbols of historic experience"?

The records of judicial debate, including Mr. Justice Black's lecture, show these allegations to be mere irrelevancies. Mr. Justice Harlan could not have made them if he had kept in mind what Mr. Justice Holmes wrote in the *Frohwerk* case in 1919:[17] "The First Amendment . . . obviously was not intended to give immunity for every possible use of language. . . . We venture to believe that neither Hamilton nor Madison, nor any other competent person then or later, ever supposed that to make criminal the counselling of a murder . . . would be an unconstitutional interference with free speech." In these words, Mr. Justice Holmes effectively told us that the notion of "an unlimited license to talk" is not worthy of serious consideration. No "competent" person accepts it.

This section cannot, however, be closed without noting that other "balancers" have similarly caricatured the absolutist contention. This is especially true of Mr. Justice Frankfurter in his *Dennis* opinion, where he referred to my book on free speech.[18] He there described an "absolute" as "a sonorous formula which is in fact only a euphemistic disguise for an unresolved conflict."[19] He also represented it as claiming to be "self-defining and self-enforcing."[20] And he further characterized absolute statements as "dogmas too inflexible for the non-Euclidean problems to be solved."[21]

In relation to these inaccurate characterizations, Mr. Justice Black has said that his "absolutes" are not "self-defining"; they make use of terms whose meanings must be "determined by the courts."[22] Nor are they "self-enforcing." No general principle,

---

16 366 U.S. at 49 n. 10.

17 Frohwerk v. United States, 249 U.S. 204, 206 (1919).

18 341 U.S. at 524 n. 5.

19 *Id.* at 519.

20 *Id.* at 523.

21 *Id.* at 525.

22 See text *supra,* at note 10.

whether absolute or not, is enforced except as it is found to "fit the facts." The generalizing and particularizing elements in any intellectual activity must always join forces if they are to be effective. To think without facts is as ineffectual as to think without principles. Again, the absolute provisions are not "inflexible." Mr. Justice Black knows, as well as do his antagonists, that the Constitution did not exist two centuries ago. It provides for its own amendment and, through the courts, for its reinterpretation. How long it will last and how it may be changed no one knows. And, finally, absolute statements are not in themselves "dogmas." They may be either true or false, certain or uncertain, wise or foolish. For example, an assertion that "Congress has unlimited authority to abridge political freedom" is absolute in exactly the same sense as is the assertion that "Congress has no authority to abridge political freedom." Their only relevant difference is that one of these propositions is supported by the Constitution, while the other is repudiated by it.

III. Mr. Justice Harlan's Position

Having refuted an assertion which Mr. Justice Black did not make, Mr. Justice Harlan might next be reasonably expected to attempt to refute the assertion which his opponent did make. But at that point the *Konigsberg* opinion branches off in another direction. It offered a new and more theoretical version of the "balancing" doctrine:[23]

> On the one hand certain forms of speech, or speech in certain contexts, has [*sic*] been considered outside the scope of constitutional protection. . . . On the other hand, general regulatory statutes, not intended to control the content of speech but incidentally limiting its unfettered exercise, have not been regarded as the type of law the First or Fourteenth Amendment forbade Congress or the States to pass, when they have been found justified by subordinating valid governmental interests, a prerequisite to constitutionality which has necessarily involved a weighing of the governmental interest involved.

These words have interest for this inquiry because in his restatement of the "balancing" doctrine, Mr. Justice Harlan used "contrast" terms which, by implication, suggest the positive meaning of

---

[23] 366 U.S. at 50–51.

the First Amendment. "Regulatory" suggests, by contrast, "prohibitory"; "not intended to control the content of thought" suggests "intended to control the content of thought"; "incidentally" suggests "by deliberate intention." Here are the elements which, properly fused, might tell us what the First Amendment forbids. But more immediately relevant to the present discussion is the fact that Mr. Justice Harlan here turned from the consideration of "the abridgment of the freedom of speech" to a study of the "regulation of speech." And he did so without determining the relation between "regulation" and "abridgment of freedom." Are these two terms identical? I think not. Nor are freedoms and regulation antithetical. For example, a man may be denied the privilege of speaking at a meeting because someone else "has the floor." But the freedom of discussion is not thereby abridged. Members of Congress are guaranteed freedom "on the floor of either House." But their speaking is regulated under "rules of order." A citizen has authority to "petition" Congress or the Supreme Court. But the time, place, circumstances, and manner of the presentation are determined, not by his own choice, but by carefully prescribed regulations. In 1953 I wrote:[24] "Speech, as a form of human action, is subject to regulation in exactly the same sense as is walking, or lighting a fire, or shooting a gun. To interpret the First Amendment as forbidding such regulation is to so misconceive its meaning as to reduce it to nonsense." In the intervening years I have found no reason to change that assertion.

The freedom that the First Amendment protects is not, then, an absence of regulation. It is the presence of self-government. Our argument now proceeds to define, as clearly as it can, the intention of the Constitutional provision that begins with the words: "Congress shall make no law abridging. . . ."

IV. "Rational Principles To Mark the Limits of Constitutional Protection"

In his *Free Speech in the United States*[25] Professor Chafee stated the dilemma which confronts our inquiry and which divides

---

[24] Hearings before the Subcommittee on Constitutional Rights of the Senate Committee on the Judiciary, 84th Cong., 2d Sess., at p. 17 (1955).

[25] 15 (1941).

the Supreme Court so evenly: "The question whether such perplexing cases are within the First Amendment or not cannot be solved by the multiplication of obvious examples, but only by the development of a rational principle to mark the limits of constitutional protection." Professor Chafee was too much involved in the complexities of balancing to formulate the needed principle of which absolutists speak. But he indicated the goal toward which every interpreter of the First Amendment should now be trying to make his way.[26] We are looking for a principle which is not in conflict with any other provision of the Constitution, a principle which, as it now stands, is "absolute" in the sense of being "not open to exceptions," but a principle which also is subject to interpretation, to change, or to abolition, as the necessities of a precarious world may require.

Apart from the First Amendment itself, the passages of the Constitution which most directly clarify its meaning are the Preamble, the Tenth Amendment, and Section 2 of Article I. All four provisions must be considered in their historical setting, not only in relation to one another but, even more important, in relation to the intention and structure of the Constitution as a whole. Out of such consideration the following principles seem to emerge:

1. All constitutional authority to govern the people of the United States belongs to the people themselves, acting as members of a corporate body politic. They are, it is true, "the governed." But

---

[26] That Chafee was, in 1942, a "balancer" is shown by the first chapter of his book to which I already have made reference. There he said in summation: "That is, in technical language, there are individual interests and social interests, which must be balanced against each other, if they conflict, in order to determine which interest shall be sacrificed under the circumstances and which shall be protected and become the foundation of a legal right." *Id.* at 32. On the other hand, his absolutist demand for a "rational principle" was never fully abandoned, though never fully satisfied. It reappears in tentative form in a personal letter to Ernest Angell: "Penning a longhand letter from a hospital bed in 1953, he [Chafee] wrote: 'In court cases fine lines have to be drawn—it's unavoidable once you get that far. Yet Meiklejohn is right in a way—things ought never to have got to this pass where freedom of thought and expression depend on distinctions as thin as a hair.' And: 'The upshot of all this is that I see little prospect of a recovery of freedom and sanity through any particular court decision. There will have to be a real repudiation of the whole darned business—but by whom? Or else, which seems more probable, it will die out because people are sick of it, the way censorship expired in 1695 in England.'" Angell, *Zechariah Chafee, Jr.—Individual Freedoms*, 70 HARV. L. REV. 1341, 1343 (1957).

they are also "the governors." Political freedom is not the absence of government. It is self-government.

2. By means of the Constitution, the people establish subordinate agencies, such as the legislature, the executive, the judiciary, and delegate to each of them such specific and limited powers as are deemed necessary for the doing of its assigned governing. These agencies have no other powers.

3. The people do not delegate all their sovereign powers. The Tenth Amendment speaks of powers that are reserved "to the people," as well as of powers "reserved to the States."

4. Article I, § 2, speaks of a reserved power which the people have decided to exercise by their own direct activity: "The House of Representatives shall be composed of members chosen every second year by the people of the several States. . . ." Here is established the voting power through which the people, as an electorate, actively participate in governing both themselves, as subjects of the laws, and their agencies, as the makers, administrators, and interpreters of the laws. In today's government, the scope of direct electoral action is wider than the provisions made when Article I, § 2, was adopted, but the constitutional principle or intention is the same.

5. The revolutionary intent of the First Amendment is, then, to deny to all subordinate agencies authority to abridge the freedom of the electoral power of the people.

For the understanding of these principles it is essential to keep clear the crucial difference between "the rights" of the governed and "the powers" of the governors. And at this point, the title "Bill of Rights" is lamentably inaccurate as a designation of the first ten amendments. They are not a "Bill of Rights" but a "Bill of Powers and Rights." The Second through the Ninth Amendments limit the powers of the subordinate agencies in order that due regard shall be paid to the private "rights of the governed." The First and Tenth Amendments protect the governing "powers" of the people from abridgment by the agencies which are established as their servants. In the field of our "rights," each one of us can claim "due process of law." In the field of our governing "powers," the notion of "due process" is irrelevant.

V. The Freedom of Thought and Communication by Which We Govern

The preceding section may be summed up thus: The First Amendment does not protect a "freedom to speak." It protects the freedom of those activities of thought and communication by which we "govern." It is concerned, not with a private right, but with a public power, a governmental responsibility.

In the specific language of the Constitution, the governing activities of the people appear only in terms of casting a ballot. But in the deeper meaning of the Constitution, voting is merely the external expression of a wide and diverse number of activities by means of which citizens attempt to meet the responsibilities of making judgments, which that freedom to govern lays upon them. That freedom implies and requires what we call "the dignity of the individual." Self-government can exist only insofar as the voters acquire the intelligence, integrity, sensitivity, and generous devotion to the general welfare that, in theory, casting a ballot is assumed to express.

The responsibilities mentioned are of three kinds. We, the people who govern, must try to understand the issues which, incident by incident, face the nation. We must pass judgment upon the decisions which our agents make upon those issues. And, further, we must share in devising methods by which those decisions can be made wise and effective or, if need be, supplanted by others which promise greater wisdom and effectiveness. Now it is these activities, in all their diversity, whose freedom fills up "the scope of the First Amendment." These are the activities to whose freedom it gives its unqualified protection. And it must be recognized that the literal text of the Amendment falls far short of expressing the intent and the scope of that protection. I have previously tried to express that inadequacy:[27]

> We must also note that, though the intention of the Amendment is sharp and resolute, the sentence which expresses that intention is awkward and ill-constructed. Evidently, it was hard to write and is, therefore, hard to interpret. Within its meaning are summed up centuries of social passion

[27] Meiklejohn, *supra* note 4, at 463.

> and intellectual controversy, in this country and in others. As one reads it, one feels that its writers could not agree, either within themselves or with each other, upon a single formula which would define for them the paradoxical relation between free men and their legislative agents. Apparently, all that they could make their words do was to link together five separate demands which had been sharpened by ages of conflict and were being popularly urged in the name of the "Freedom of the People." And yet, those demands were, and were felt to be, varied forms of a single demand. They were attempts to express, each in its own way, the revolutionary idea which, in the slowly advancing fight for freedom, has given to the American experiment in self-government its dominating significance for the modern world.

What I have said is that the First Amendment, as seen in its constitutional setting, forbids Congress to abridge the freedom of a citizen's speech, press, peaceable assembly, or petition, whenever those activities are utilized for the governing of the nation. In these respects, the Constitution gives to all "the people" the same protection of freedom which, in Article I, § 6(1), it provides for their legislative agents: "and for any speech or debate in either House, they shall not be questioned in any other place." Just as our agents must be free in their use of their delegated powers, so the people must be free in the exercise of their reserved powers.

What other activities, then, in addition to speech, press, assembly, and petition, must be included within the scope of the First Amendment? First of all, the freedom to "vote," the official expression of a self-governing man's judgment on issues of public policy, must be absolutely protected. None of his subordinate agencies may bring pressure upon him to drive his balloting this way or that. None of them may require him to tell how he has voted; none may inquire by compulsory process into his political beliefs or associations. In that area, the citizen has constitutional authority and his agents have not.

Second, there are many forms of thought and expression within the range of human communications from which the voter derives the knowledge, intelligence, sensitivity to human values: the capacity for sane and objective judgment which, so far as possible, a ballot should express. These, too, must suffer no abridgment of their freedom. I list four of them below.

1. Education, in all its phases, is the attempt to so inform and cultivate the mind and will of a citizen that he shall have the wisdom, the independence, and, therefore, the dignity of a governing citizen. Freedom of education is, thus, as we all recognize, a basic postulate in the planning of a free society.

2. The achievements of philosophy and the sciences in creating knowledge and understanding of men and their world must be made available, without abridgment, to every citizen.

3. Literature and the arts must be protected by the First Amendment. They lead the way toward sensitive and informed appreciation and response to the values out of which the riches of the general welfare are created.

4. Public discussions of public issues, together with the spreading of information and opinion bearing on those issues, must have a freedom unabridged by our agents. Though they govern us, we, in a deeper sense, govern them. Over our governing, they have no power. Over their governing we have sovereign power.

VI. A Paradox

Out of the argument thus far stated, two apparently contradictory statements emerge. Congress may, in ways carefully limited, "regulate" the activities by which the citizens govern the nation. But no regulation may abridge the freedom of those governing activities. I am sure that the two statements are not contradictory. But their combination is, to say the least, paradoxical. It is that paradox that I must now face as I try to respond to Professor Kalven's challenge.[28] As a non-lawyer, I shall not discuss in detail the difficulties and puzzlements with which the courts must deal. I can only suggest that, here and there, seeming contradictions are not real.

First. A distinction must be drawn between belief and communication in their relations to Congressional authority. A citizen may be told when and where and in what manner he may or may not speak, write, assemble, and so on. On the other hand, he may not be told what he shall or shall not believe. In that realm each citizen is sovereign. He exercises powers that the body politic reserves for

---

[28] See *supra* note 4.

its own members. In 1953, testifying before the Senate Committee on Constitutional Rights, I said:[29]

> . . . our First Amendment freedom forbids that any citizen be required, under threat of penality, to take an oath, or make an affirmation, as to beliefs which he holds or rejects. Every citizen, it is true, may be required and should be required, to pledge loyalty, and to practice loyalty, to the nation. He must agree to support the Constitution. But he may never be required to *believe* in the Constitution. His loyalty may never be tested on grounds of adherence to, or rejection of, any *belief*. Loyalty does not imply conformity of opinion. Every citizen of the United States has Constitutional authority to approve or to condemn any laws enacted by the Legislature, any actions taken by the Executive, any judgments rendered by the judiciary, any principles established by the Constitution. All these enactments which, as men who are governed, we must obey, are subject to our approval or disapproval, as we govern. With respect to all of them we, who are free men, are sovereign. We are "The People." We govern the United States.

However far our practice falls short of the intention expressed by those words, they provide the standard by which our practice must be justified or condemned.

Second. We must recognize that there are many forms of communication which, since they are not being used as activities of governing, are wholly outside the scope of the First Amendment. Mr. Justice Holmes has told us about these, giving such vivid illustrations as "persuasion to murder"[30] and "falsely shouting fire in a theatre and causing a panic."[31] And Mr. Justice Harlan, referring to Holmes and following his lead, gave a more extensive list:[32] "libel, slander, misrepresentation, obscenity, perjury, false advertising, solicitation of crime, complicity by encouragement, conspiracy. . . ." Why are these communications not protected by the First Amendment? Mr. Justice Holmes suggested an explanation when he said of the First Amendment in *Schenck*:[33] "It does not

---

29 *Supra* note 24, at p. 20.

30 Abrams v. United States, 250 U.S. 616, 627 (1919).

31 Schenck v. United States, 249 U.S. 47, 52 (1919).

32 366 U.S. at 49 n. 10.

33 249 U.S. at 52.

even protect a man from an injunction against uttering words that may have all the effect of force."

Now it may be agreed that the uttering of words cannot be forbidden by legislation, nor punished on conviction, unless damage has been done by them to some individual or to the wider society. But that statement does not justify the imputation that all "words that may have all the effect of force" are denied the First Amendment's protection. The man who falsely shouts "Fire!" in a theatre is subject to prosecution under validly enacted legislation. But the army officer who, in command of a firing squad, shouts "Fire!" and thus ends a life, cannot be prosecuted for murder. He acts as an agent of the government. And, in fact, all governing communications are intended to have, more or less directly, "the effect of force." When a voter casts his ballot for a tax levy, he intends that someone shall be deprived of property. But his voting is not therefore outside the scope of the First Amendment. His voting must be free.

The principle here at stake can be seen in our libel laws. In cases of private defamation, one individual does damage to another by tongue or pen; the person so injured in reputation or property may sue for damages. But, in that case, the First Amendment gives no protection to the person sued. His verbal attack has no relation to the business of governing. If, however, the same verbal attack is made in order to show the unfitness of a candidate for governmental office, the act is properly regarded as a citizen's participation in government. It is, therefore, protected by the First Amendment. And the same principle holds good if a citizen attacks, by words of disapproval and condemnation, the policies of the government, or even the structure of the Constitution. These are "public" issues concerning which, under our form of government, he has authority, and is assumed to have competence, to judge. Though private libel is subject to legislative control, political or seditious libel is not.

Third. In discussions of the First Amendment too little attention has been given to the regulatory word "peaceable" in relation to "assembly." It suggests principles of limitation which apply also to speech, press, petition, and to the other forms of communication which support them. This limitation is significant in demonstrating that a citizen's governing is often both "regulated" and "free."

Peaceableness in governing may serve either one or both of two purposes. It provides protection for an assembly against external violation of rules of public order. It also seeks to ensure that relations within the assembly shall succeed in serving the governing function which warrants its protection by the First Amendment. The first of these purposes has to do with relations between the assembly and "outsiders" who, disagreeing with its ideas and intentions, may seek to disrupt the discussion and, in various ways, to render it ineffectual. In this situation, both the local authorities which have authority to "regulate" and the police who seek to apply the regulations are held responsible by the intention of the First and Fourteenth Amendments. No ordinance may be based upon disapproval of policies to be discussed or decreed by the assembly. And the police must, to the limit of their power, defend the meeting from interruption or interference by its enemies. But basically more important are the conditions of peaceableness within an assembly itself. It is, of course, impossible that everyone should be allowed to express his point of view whenever and however he chooses. In a meeting for discussion, as contrasted with a lecture, however, no one may be "denied the floor" on the ground of disapproval of what he is saying or would say. And, if the interests of a self-governing society are to be served, vituperation which fixes attention on the defects of an opponent's character or intelligence and thereby distracts attention from the question of policy under discussion may be forbidden as a deadly enemy of peaceable assembly. Anyone who persists in it should be expelled from the meeting, and, if need be, the police should give help in getting it done.

I cannot, however, leave those words on record without noting how inadequate, to the degree of non-existence, are our public provisions for active discussions among the members of our self-governing society. As we try to create and enlarge freedom, such universal discussion is imperative. In every village, in every district of every town or city, there should be established at public expense cultural centers inviting all citizens, as they may choose, to meet together for the consideration of public policy. And conditions must be provided under which such meetings could be happily and successfully conducted. I am not thinking of such lunatic-fringe activities as those in Hyde Park in London. I am thinking of a self-governing body politic, whose freedom of individual expression should be cultivated, not merely because it serves to prevent outbursts of violence which would result from suppression, but for the positive purpose of bringing every citizen into active and intelligent sharing in the government of his country.

Fourth. Largely because of our failure to make adequate provision for free and unhindered public discussion, the courts are called upon to judge the constitutionality of local ordinances which forbid or limit the holding of public meetings in public places. Such ordinances come into effect when individuals or groups assemble in such a way as to interfere with other interests of the community or of its members. The most striking and perplexing cases of this kind occur when meetings are held on the public streets or in parks whose primary use is, in the opinion of the authorities, blocked or hindered to a degree demanding action. Now if such ordinances are based upon official disapproval of the ideas to be presented at the meeting, they clearly violate the First Amendment. But if no such abridgment of freedom is expressed or implied, regulation or prohibition on other grounds may be enacted and enforced.

It must not be assumed that every governmental regulation of a public meeting is, under current conditions, destructive of political freedom. Conditions of traffic on a city street are very different from those in the relatively open spaces of a country village. Parks may be needed for rest, quiet, and release from excitement and strain. Just as an individual, seeking to advocate some public policy may not do so, without consent, by interrupting a church service, or a classroom, or a sickroom, or a session of Congress or of the Supreme Court, or by ringing a doorbell and demanding to be heard, so meetings must conform to the necessities of the community, with respect to time, place, circumstance, and manner of procedure. And, unless those considerations are dishonestly used as a cover for unconstitutional discrimination against this idea or that, there is no First Amendment complaint against the ordinances which express them. The Amendment, I repeat, does not establish an "unlimited right to talk."

It must further be noted that in "emergency" situations, when something must be said and no other time, place, circumstance, or manner of speech will serve for the saying of it, a citizen may be justified in "taking the law into his own hands." In the famous example of Mr. Justice Holmes, a man is not allowed to shout "Fire!" *falsely* in a theatre. But, if, during a performance in a theatre, a person sees a fire which threatens to spread, he is not only allowed, he is duty-bound, to try to find some way of informing others so that a panic may not ensue with its disastrous consequences. The distinction between "falsely" and "truly" is here fundamental to an understanding of what freedom is.

Fifth. In the current discussions as to whether or not "obscenity" in literature and the arts is protected by the First Amendment, the basic principle is, I think, that literature and the arts are protected because they have a "social importance" which I have called a "governing" importance. For example, the novel is at present a powerful determinative of our views of what human beings are, how they can be influenced, in what directions they should be influenced by many forces, including, especially, their own judgments and appreciations. But the novel, like all the other creations of literature and the arts, may be produced wisely or unwisely, sensitively or coarsely, for the building up of a way of life which we treasure or for tearing it down. Shall the government establish a censorship to distinguish between "good" novels and "bad" ones? And, more specifically, shall it forbid the publication of novels which portray sexual experiences with a frankness that, to the prevailing conventions of our society, seems "obscene"?

The First Amendment seems to me to answer that question with an unequivocal "no." Here, as elsewhere, the authority of citizens to decide what they shall write and, more fundamental, what they shall read and see, has not been delegated to any of the subordinate branches of government. It is "reserved to the people," each deciding for himself to whom he will listen, whom he will read, what portrayal of the human scene he finds worthy of his attention. And at this point I feel compelled to disagree with Professor Kalven's interpretation of what I have tried to say. In his recent article on obscenity, he wrote:[34]

> The classic defense of John Stuart Mill and the modern defense of Alexander Meiklejohn do not help much when the question is why the novel, the poem, the painting, the drama, or the piece of sculpture falls within the protection of the First Amendment. Nor do the famous opinions of Hand, Holmes, and Brandeis. The emphasis is all on truth winning out in a fair fight between competing ideas. The emphasis is clearest in Meiklejohn's argument that free speech is indis-

[34] Kalven, *Metaphysics of the Law of Obscenity*, 1960 Sup. Ct. Rev. 1, 15–16.

> pensable to the informed citizenry required to make democratic self-government work. The people need free speech because they vote. As a result his argument distinguishes sharply between public and private speech. Not all communications are relevant to the political process. The people do not need novels or dramas or paintings or poems because they will be called upon to vote. Art and belles-lettres do not deal in such ideas—at least not good art or belles-lettres. . . .

In reply to that friendly interpretation, I must, at two points, record a friendly disavowal. I have never been able to share the Miltonian faith that in a fair fight between truth and error, truth is sure to win. And if one had that faith, it would be hard to reconcile it with the sheer stupidity of the policies of this nation—and of other nations—now driving humanity to the very edge of final destruction. In my view, "the people need free speech" because they have decided, in adopting, maintaining and interpreting their Constitution, to govern themselves rather than to be governed by others. And, in order to make that self-government a reality rather than an illusion, in order that it may become as wise and efficient as its responsibilities require, the judgment-making of the people must be self-educated in the ways of freedom. That is, I think, the positive purpose to which the negative words of the First Amendment gave a constitutional expression. Moreover, as against Professor Kalven's interpretation, I believe, as a teacher, that the people do need novels and dramas and paintings and poems, "because they will be called upon to vote." The primary social fact which blocks and hinders the success of our experiment in self-government is that our citizens are not educated for self-government. We are terrified by ideas, rather than challenged and stimulated by them. Our dominant mood is not the courage of people who dare to think. It is the timidity of those who fear and hate whenever conventions are questioned.

VII. Conclusion

Professor Leonard W. Levy, in a stimulating book,[35] has recently given strong evidence that the Framers of the Constitution were not, for the most part, explicitly concerned with those aspects of the First Amendment's meaning and application which now

---

[35] Legacy of Suppression (1960).

especially concern us. If we assume that his thesis has been established, what bearing does it have upon the contentions of this paper?

In answer to that question, two different statements can be made which properly supplement each other. First, the Framers initiated a political revolution whose development is still in process throughout the world. Second, like most revolutionaries, the Framers could not foresee the specific issues which would arise as their "novel idea" exercised its domination over the governing activities of a rapidly developing nation in a rapidly and fundamentally changing world. In that sense, the Framers did not know what they were doing. And in the same sense, it is still true that, after two centuries of experience, we do not know what they were doing, or what we ourselves are now doing.

In a more abstract and more significant sense, however, both they and we have been aware that the adoption of the principle of self-government by "The People" of this nation set loose upon us and upon the world at large an idea which is still transforming men's conceptions of what they are and how they may best be governed. Wherever it goes, that idea is demanding—and slowly securing—a recognition that, with respect to human dignity, women have the same status as men, that people of all races and colors and creeds must be treated as equals, that the poor are at least the equals of the rich. In popular language the idea finds expression in such phrases as "the land of the free," or "government by consent of the governed," or "government of the people, by the people, for the people shall not perish from the earth."

In our discussions of the Constitution, we commonly think that the clearest and most compelling expression of the "idea" of political freedom is given by the First Amendment. But in theory, and perhaps in practice, more penetrating insights are given by the Preamble's declaration that "We, the people of the United States . . . do ordain and establish this Constitution . . . ," or by the Tenth Amendment's assertion that, while we have delegated some limited governing powers to our agents, we have reserved other powers to ourselves, or, finally, by the provision of Article I, Section 2, that we have authority to exercise direct governing power in electing our representatives.

If what we are saying here is true, then *Robertson v. Baldwin* seems to me to contain the most disastrous judicial pronouncement that I have found:[36] "The law is perfectly well settled that the first ten amendments to the Constitution, commonly known as the Bill of Rights, were not intended to lay down any novel principles of government, but simply to embody certain guaranties and immunities which we had inherited from our English ancestors. . . ." In 1951, in his opinion in *Dennis*, Mr. Justice Frankfurter, in quoting that statement, said of it,[37] "That this represents the authentic view of the Bill of Rights and the spirit in which it must be construed has been recognized again and again in cases that have come here within the last fifty years."

In 1953, in a comment on that concurring opinion,[38] I quoted that dictum and criticized it. To sum up what I have been trying to say in this paper, I wish to repeat some part of that criticism. Mr. Justice Frankfurter, it must be noted, does not here speak as one expressing his own opinion. He is telling us of a contention which has prevailed for a long time in the Court. Is that contention valid? Is it true, for example, that the religion clause of the First Amendment was "inherited" from a nation which had, and still has, an established church? However that may be, a ringing dissent by the first Mr. Justice Harlan in *Robertson v. Baldwin* seems to me to cut into meaningless bits the assertion that no "novel principles of government" were in mind when the Bill of Rights was adopted. Arguing, in his dissent, about the constitutionality of involuntary servitude, he said:[39] "Nor, I submit, is any light thrown upon the question by the history of legislation in Great Britain. The powers of the British Parliament furnish no test for the powers that may be exercised by the Congress of the United States." The distinctive feature of our Constitution, he declared, that marks it off from British political institutions, is that it is established, not by the legislature, but by the people. And he summed up the novelty of our system:[40] "No such powers have been or can be exercised by any legislative body under the American system. Absolute, arbitrary

[36] 165 U.S. 275, 281 (1897).

[37] 341 U.S. at 524.

[38] Meiklejohn, *supra* note 4.

[39] 165 U.S. at 296.

[40] *Ibid.*

power exists nowhere in this free land. The authority for the exercise of power by the Congress of the United States must be found in the Constitution. Whatever it does in excess of the powers granted it, or in violation of the injunctions of the supreme law of the land, is a nullity, and may be so treated by every person." To a teacher of freedom in the United States that seems to be good law. I wish it would seem so to those who now have authority to determine what good law is.

DAVID FELLMAN

CONSTITUTIONAL RIGHTS OF ASSOCIATION

If freedom of association is indispensable to a constitutional democracy, it is nonetheless true that no such right is even mentioned in American constitutional documents, which speak only in the more limited terms of a "right of assembly." Until very recently the idea that rights of association are entitled to the constitutional protection afforded such traditional rights as freedom of religion and freedom of speech was almost unknown to American law. But the courts have begun to recognize the concept and to spell out its limits, although the process is yet in its early stages. That rights of association have already achieved a place in our public law is reflected in the work of the Supreme Court during the 1960 Term. Indeed, if any single issue dominates the Court's efforts for that Term, it is the question of defining the significant aspects of these rights.

In May, 1961, the Supreme Court held unconstitutional two Louisiana statutes that required the state chapter of the NAACP to file a list of the names and addresses of all its officers and members as well as affidavits that none of the officers of any group with which the NAACP chapter had affiliated was subversive.[1] It is now well established, said Mr. Justice Douglas, that where "disclosure of membership lists results in reprisals against and hostility to the mem-

---

David Fellman is Professor of Political Science, University of Wisconsin.

[1] Louisiana *ex rel.* Gremillion v. NAACP, 366 U.S. 293 (1961).

bers, disclosure is not required."[2] In this area, he added, "any regulation must be highly selective in order to survive challenge under the First Amendment."[3] And he closed with the observation that "regulatory measures . . . no matter how sophisticated, cannot be employed in purpose or in effect to stifle, penalize, or curb the exercise of First Amendment rights."[4]

While the Supreme Court during the 1960–61 Term thus protected the right of association as it related to the disclosure of membership in the NAACP, it also rendered several decisions that drew the line in favor of the public interest in disclosure in cases involving membership in the Communist Party. In two important cases it again held punishable as contempt the refusal of a witness to tell a congressional committee whether he was a member of the Communist Party.[5] In two other cases the Court held that a state did not deny due process where, because of refusal to answer questions including some concerning membership in the Communist Party, it denied admission to the bar.[6] The Court stated that the public interest in determining the fitness of men to practice law outweighed the interest in associational freedom. Indeed, since bar committee interrogations are conducted in private, it could see "no likelihood that deterrence of association may result from foreseeable private action."[7] In still another case the Court finally upheld an order under the Subversive Activities Control Act.[8] Speaking for the Court, Mr. Justice Frankfurter ruled that "rational interests high in the scale of national concern"[9] justified the regulation,

---

2 *Id.* at 296.

3 *Ibid.*

4 *Id.* at 297.

5 Wilkinson v. United States, 365 U.S. 399 (1961); Braden v. United States, 365 U.S. 431 (1961). The vote in both these cases was five to four.

6 Konigsberg v. State Bar of California, 366 U.S. 36 (1961); *In re* Anastaplo, 366 U.S. 82 (1961). The Court was divided five to four in both cases. In Cohen v. Hurley, 366 U.S. 117 (1961), the Court sustained the disbarment of an attorney who refused on grounds of self-incrimination to answer questions in an investigation of professional misconduct taking the form of "ambulance-chasing." In Lathrop v. Donohue, 367 U.S. 820 (1961), the Court ruled that a state may constitutionally require all lawyers to belong to an integrated bar association. See also Machinists v. Street, considered *supra*, at pp. 49–73.

7 366 U.S. at 52.

8 Communist Party v. Subversive Activities Control Board, 367 U.S. 1 (1961).

9 *Id.* at 102.

which ordered the registration of an association found by Congress to be a foreign-directed conspiracy against the safety of constitutional government.

Most significant of all the cases decided in the spring of 1961 was *Scales v. United States*,[10] in which the Court upheld, by a five-to-four vote, the constitutionality of the clause of the Smith Act that makes it a felony to acquire or hold knowing membership in any organization that advocates the overthrow of the government by force or violence. Scales was convicted of belonging to the Communist Party when he knew of its illegal purpose. The Court emphasized that the trial judge had properly construed the statute as requiring proof that the Communist Party advocated violent action to overthrow the government, and that the defendant must be shown to have been an active member who knew about the Party's illegal intent and advocacy of violent overthrow as soon as circumstances would permit. A combination promoting criminal activity is not the sort of association, the Court ruled, that is protected by the First Amendment.

I. Historical Origins

"In no country in the world," Tocqueville wrote in his celebrated book on American democracy, "has the principle of association been more successfully used or applied to a greater multitude of objects than in America."[11] What was true over a century ago is even more true today. Many have drawn attention to the extraordinary multiplicity of interest groups in the United States, to the American insistence upon voluntary group action by private citizens, and indeed, to the American passion for being a joiner.[12] It is

---

10 367 U.S. 203 (1961). In Noto v. United States, 367 U.S. 290 (1961), the Court set aside a conviction under the membership clause of the Smith Act because of insufficiency of evidence.

11 1 Tocqueville, Democracy in America 191 (Bradley ed. 1948).

12 See, *e.g.*, Wirtz, *Government by Private Groups*, 13 La. L. Rev. 440 (1953); Schlesinger, *Biography of a Nation of Joiners*, 50 Am. Hist. Rev. 1 (1944), reprinted in Paths to the Present ch. 2 (1949); Gellhorn, American Rights ch. 9 (1960); Merz, The Great American Band-Wagon (1928).

"There are at least 200,000 organizations, associations, clubs, societies, lodges and fraternities in the United States, along with innumerable social groups and *ad hoc* committees formed for specific causes. . . . This prodigious array of volunteer citizens . . . is unique in the world." Editors of Fortune, U.S.A., The Permanent Revolution 131–32 (1951).

not surprising, therefore, that, however ill-defined they may be, the rights of association have a definite place in American constitutional law.[13] In fact, among American associations many may be found that exercise the right of association for the specific purpose of protecting the right to have rights.[14]

Tocqueville emphasized the liberty of political association, which had become "a necessary guarantee against the tyranny of the majority," especially needed in democracies to prevent the abuse of political power.[15] He noted that the right of political association involves, first, a number of individuals who give public assent to certain doctrines; second, the power of meeting; and third, the union of partisans to choose delegates to represent them in a central assembly. In his view, therefore, association becomes, in effect, a government within the government. He concluded:[16]

> The most natural privilege of man, next to the right of acting for himself, is that of combining his exertions with those of his fellow creatures and of acting in common with them. The right of association therefore appears to me almost as inalienable in its nature as the right of personal liberty. No legislator can attack it without impairing the foundations of society.

Tocqueville also drew attention to the fact that political associations may be dangerous, as in Europe, where they were weapons of conflict and direct action. In fact, he might have pointed out, every type of association has at some time been regarded as subversive: the dissenting churches of the sixteenth and seventeenth centuries, labor unions in the eighteenth and nineteenth centuries, and various fraternal groups throughout modern history.[17] But Tocqueville

---

[13] See ABERNATHY, THE RIGHT OF ASSEMBLY AND ASSOCIATION (1961); HORN, GROUPS AND THE CONSTITUTION (1956); Abernathy, *The Right of Association*, 6 S.C.L.Q. 32 (1953); Wyzanski, *The Open Window and the Open Door*, 35 CALIF. L. REV. 336 (1947).

[14] See Robison, *Organizations Promoting Civil Rights and Liberties*, 275 ANNALS 18 (May 1951); Vose, *Litigation as a Form of Pressure Group Activity*, 319 ANNALS 20 (Sept. 1958); Note, *Class Actions: A Study of Group-Interest Litigation*, 1 RACE REL. L. REP. 991 (1956).

[15] 1 TOCQUEVILLE, *op. cit. supra* note 11, at 194–95.

[16] *Id.* at 196.

[17] See HORN, *op. cit. supra* note 13, at 122–24. The Star Chamber regarded as illegal any unlicensed combination of men whose purposes were considered contrary to

thought that in America private political associations were salutary —their intentions were peaceful and they employed strictly legal methods. He suggested that universal suffrage made a difference, since associations knew that they did not represent the majority of the nation.

The Supreme Court once took the position that the right of the people to assemble for lawful purposes existed long before the adoption of the Constitution. Speaking for the Court in the famous Reconstruction case, *United States v. Cruikshank*,[18] Mr. Chief Justice Waite wrote: "The very idea of a government, republican in form, implies a right on the part of its citizens to meet peaceably for consultation in respect to public affairs and to petition for a redress of grievances." Accordingly, the Court ruled that the right of assembly did not owe its origin to the Constitution, and that the purpose of the constitutional provision on the subject was simply to secure a pre-existing right against invasion by the national government.

Rights of association as such, as already noted, are not mentioned in the national or state constitutions. The First Amendment states that Congress shall make no law abridging "the right of the people peaceably to assemble, and to petition the Government for a redress of grievances." The broader rights of association have developed partially from the right of assembly and partially from due-process concepts. Historically, the right of assembly is closely connected with the right of petition. Mentioned as early as Magna Carta,[19]

---

public policy by the judges, even though the acts involved were neither tortious nor indictable crimes. 8 HOLDSWORTH, A HISTORY OF ENGLISH LAW 382 (1926). Thomas Hobbes wrote: "Leagues of the Subjects of one and the same Common-wealth, where every one may obtain his right by means of the Soveraign Power, are unnecessary to the maintaining of Peace and Justice, and (in case the designe of them be evill, or Unknown to the Common-wealth) unlawfull. For all uniting of strength by private men, is, if for evill intent, unjust; if for intent unknown, dangerous to the Publique, and unjustly concealed." LEVIATHAN 200–201 (Everyman's Am. ed. 1950).

18 92 U.S. 542, 552 (1876).

19 Ch. 61: "That if, we, our justiciary, our bailiffs, or any of our officers, shall in any circumstances have failed in the performance of them toward any person, or shall have broken through any of these articles of peace and security, and the offence be notified to four barons chosen out of the five-and-twenty before mentioned, the said four barons shall repair to us, or our justiciary, if we are out of the realm, and laying open the grievance, shall petition to have it redressed without delay." See MCKECHNIE, MAGNA CARTA 465–77 (2d ed. 1914).

the right of petition is important in English constitutional history because it first enabled the barons and commons in Parliament to assert the right to assume the initiative in legislation.[20] As the King summoned Parliament to supply funds for the support of government, Parliament, especially the Commons, quickly got into the habit of petitioning the Crown for a redress of grievances as the condition for voting the money. In addition, Parliament, as a court of justice, received petitions from many different sources, individuals and communities, for remedies not within the province of the regular courts.

Gradually the petition evolved into the legislative bill, so that by 1414 the Commons were able to assert to the King "that there should no statute or law be made unless they gave thereto their assent," since they were "as well assenters as petitioners."[21] The King agreed not to alter the petitions of the Commons. In 1669 the Commons resolved:[22]

> That it is an inherent right of every commoner of England to prepare and present Petitions to the house of commons in case of grievances, and the house of commons to receive the same. . . .
>
> That it is the undoubted right and privilege of the commons to judge and determine concerning the nature and matter of such Petitions, how far they are fit or unfit to be received. . . .
>
> That no court whatsoever hath power to judge or censure any Petition presented to the house of commons, and received by them, unless transmitted from thence, or the matter complained of by them. . . .

The right of petition received its classic modern formulation in the Bill of Rights of 1689, which declared "That it is the right of the subjects to petition the king and all commitments and prosecutions for such petitioning are illegal."[23]

---

20 See POLLARD, THE EVOLUTION OF PARLIAMENT 329–31 (1920).

21 For the text, see ADAMS & STEPHENS, SELECT DOCUMENTS OF ENGLISH CONSTITUTIONAL HISTORY 181–82 (1916). Down to Tudor times the words "petition" and "bill" were regarded as synonymous in common speech. MCILWAIN, THE HIGH COURT OF PARLIAMENT 211 (1910).

22 4 PARL. DEB. (1st ser. Cobbett) 432–33 (1669). See Smellie, *Right of Petition*, 12 ENCYC. SOC. SCI. 99 (1934).

23 ADAMS & STEPHENS, *op. cit. supra* note 21, at 464.

While historically the right of peaceable assembly is regarded as a by-product of the right of petition, and was so once described by the Supreme Court,[24] it is now regarded, as Mr. Chief Justice Hughes said in 1937, as:[25]

> cognate to those of free speech and free press and is equally fundamental. . . . [T]he right is one that cannot be denied without violating those fundamental principles of liberty and justice which lie at the base of all civil and political institutions. . . . The greater the importance of safeguarding the community from incitements to the overthrow of our institutions by force and violence, the more imperative is the need to preserve inviolate the constitutional rights of free speech, free press and free assembly in order to maintain the opportunity for free political discussion, to the end that government may be responsive to the will of the people and that changes, if desired, may be obtained by peaceful means. Therein lies the security of the Republic, the very foundation of constitutional government.

That the rights of peaceable assembly and petition have deep roots in the American experience is reflected in the frequency with which they were asserted in the formative period of American history. Thus, the Stamp Act Congress of 1765 asserted "That it is the right of the British subjects in these colonies to petition the King or either House of Parliament."[26] The First Continental Congress, on October 14, 1774, adopted a "Declaration and Resolves" that, among other things, asserted that Americans "have a right peaceably to assemble, consider their grievances, and petition the King; and that all prosecutions, prohibitory proclamations, and commitments for the same, are illegal."[27] The Declaration of Independence recited that "In every stage of these Oppressions We have Petitioned for Redress in the most humble terms. Our repeated Petitions have been answered only by repeated injury."[28] Four of the revolutionary states' constitutions spelled out a guaranty of rights to assemble and petition. Thus, the North Carolina Constitu-

---

[24] See United States v. Cruikshank, 92 U.S. 542, 552 (1876).

[25] De Jonge v. Oregon, 299 U.S. 353, 364–65 (1937).

[26] SOURCES OF OUR LIBERTIES 271 (Perry ed. 1959).

[27] *Id.* at 288.

[28] *Id.* at 321.

tion of 1776 declared: "That the people have a right to assemble together, to consult for their common good, to instruct their Representatives, and to apply to the Legislature, for redress of grievances."[29]

The constitutional convention of 1787 did not include a bill of rights in its finished document. When Richard Henry Lee tried, without success, to attach a bill of rights, he included the right of assembly.[30] When the states ratified the Constitution, four of them formulated amendments to include a guaranty of rights of assembly and petition.[31] After ratification of the Constitution, James Madison's proposed bill of rights included the following: "The people shall not be restrained from peaceably assembling and consulting for their common good: nor from applying to the Legislature by petitions, or remonstrances, for redress of their grievances."[32] When the amendments were reported by the select committee on July 28, 1789, the provision had taken this form: "The freedom of speech, and of the press, and the right of the people peaceably to assemble and consult for their common good, and to apply to the government for redress of grievances, shall not be infringed."[33] This amendment passed the House of Representatives in this form on August 24, 1789.

This did not occur, however, until after debate in the House on Saturday, August 15, and Monday, August 17.[34] The debate on Saturday centered on a proposal made by Sedgwick of Massachusetts to delete the words "assemble and" from the clause, on the ground that the inclusion of the right of assembly with the rights of

---

29 N. C. CONST. art. 18 (1776); *cf.* PA. CONST. art. IX, § 20 (1790): "That the citizens have a right, in a peaceable manner, to assemble together for their common good, and to apply to those invested with the powers of governments for redress of grievances, or other proper purposes, by petition, address, or remonstrance." On this subject the Massachusetts and New Hampshire constitutions were almost identical: "The people have a right in an orderly and peaceable manner, to assemble to consult upon the common good. . . ." MASS. CONST. art. 19 (1780); N.H. CONST. art. 32 (1784).

30 See 2 LETTERS OF RICHARD HENRY LEE 439, 442–44 (1911–14).

31 The texts of the state proposals for amending the Constitution are conveniently collected in DUMBAULD, THE BILL OF RIGHTS 173–205 (1957).

32 *Id.* at 207.

33 *Id.* at 210.

34 For the best available account, see 1 ANNALS OF CONGRESS 731–47 (1789).

speech and press was improper and unwise because the former is too trifling and obvious. "If people freely converse together, they meet to assemble for that purpose; it is a self-evident, inalienable right which the people possess; it is certainly a thing that never would be called in question." He said that it was like listing the right to put on your hat, and insisted that "it is derogatory to the dignity of the House to descend to such minutiae."[35] But several members of the House opposed Sedgwick's motion. Benson of New York thought it wise to secure an inherent right of the people against infringement by government. Tucker of South Carolina expressed the hope that the words would not be stricken, and both Gerry of Massachusetts and Hartley of Pennsylvania called attention to the fact that the right of assembly was included in several state constitutions. Vining of Delaware stated that incorporation of these words would gratify the states. Page of Virginia called attention to the fact that the right of people to assemble together on lawful occasions had been violated in the past and ought to be safeguarded. "If the people could be deprived of the power of assembling under any pretext whatsoever," he declared, "they might be deprived of every other privilege contained in the clause." The record of Congress shows that following this brief debate, the motion to strike the words "assemble and" failed "by a considerable majority."[36]

The rest of the debate on the right-of-assembly clause centered on a motion by Tucker to add the words "to instruct their representatives." The right of the people to instruct their legislative representatives having deep roots in colonial practice,[37] the Tucker motion touched off an interesting debate on the theory of the function of the representative. Hartley argued vigorously against the motion on the ground that representatives should be presumed to know the interests and circumstances of their constituents and to have their confidence. He also doubted whether the people of a locality would be sufficiently well informed to understand the needs of the nation as a whole, and he feared that if a representative listened to all the voices in his constituency, he would find it impos-

---

35 *Id.* at 731.

36 *Id.* at 733.

37 See Phillips, The Development of a Residential Qualification for Representatives in Colonial Legislatures (1921).

sible to accommodate so many different desires.[38] In reply, Page argued that without the power to instruct their representatives, the people would be unable to consult for the common good. He made the point, then widely held, that instruction and representation were inseparable. Gerry maintained that even if the right of instruction were specifically spelled out in the Constitution, the representative would still be at liberty to act as he pleased; but he could see no harm in including it if only to encourage people, particularly the diffident, "to come forward with their instructions, which will form a fund of useful information for the Legislature."[39] But the contrary view prevailed. Madison argued that the added words could do no "real good" because the people already had the right to communicate their sentiments and wishes to their representatives. William L. Smith of South Carolina thought that Tucker's proposal would be a partial inconvenience to the more distant states, and Stone of Maryland went so far as to assert that it would change government entirely from a representative system to a "democracy of singular properties."[40] Perhaps the most telling argument was that if the representatives adopted laws that were not satisfactory to the people, the people had it within their power to withdraw their support and vote for others.

A clause guaranteeing the rights of assembly and petition is found today not only in the national Constitution, but also in all but four state constitutions.[41] That such guaranty is not out of style is reflected in the new constitutions of Alaska and Hawaii.[42] A clause in the Texas Constitution includes most of the stock phrases:[43] "The citizens shall have the right, in a peaceable manner, to assemble together for their common good; and apply to those invested with the powers of government for redress of grievances or other purposes, by petition, address or remonstrance." Almost all state constitutional clauses on this subject speak of "peaceful" or "orderly" assembly, or the right to assemble "peaceably." The vast

---

38 1 ANNALS OF CONGRESS 733–35 (1789).

39 *Id.* at 737.

40 *Id.* at 739.

41 Maryland, Minnesota, New Mexico, and Virginia do not make constitutional provision for this subject.

42 ALASKA CONST. art. I, § 6; HAWAII CONST. art. I, § 3.

43 TEXAS CONST. art. I, § 27.

majority also speak of the purpose of assembly, whether "to consult for the common good," or "to apply to the state government," or "to instruct their representatives." Finally, a large majority describe the method of redress to be used, generally by "petition," though such phrases as "remonstrance" and "redress" are also used.

II. Unlawful Assembly

Like other fundamental rights, the right of assembly does not and cannot exist without limitation. "Although the rights of free speech and assembly are fundamental," Mr. Justice Brandeis once wrote, "they are not in their nature absolute. Their exercise is subject to restriction, if the particular restriction proposed is required in order to protect the State from destruction or from serious injury, political, economic or moral."[44] Thus, the doctrine of freedom of association does not apply to an alliance for crime; and one who knowingly joins an association with criminal purposes may be punished as a criminal.[45] The law of conspiracy limits the freedom of association.[46] The right to assemble and petition may be limited by the requirements of public order and public peace. The leaders of General Coxey's famous march of the unemployed on Washington in 1894 were arrested for walking on the grass of the Capitol. Similarly, the camps of the veterans who marched on Washington in 1932 demanding bonus legislation were destroyed by the army as public nuisances.[47] Breach of the peace, riot, and use of unlawful force are all considerations that set limits to the right of assembly.

Above all, the right of assembly is qualified by the concept of unlawful assembly. It has been emphasized by American courts that to sustain the charge of unlawful assembly, it must be alleged and proved, first, that the defendants "assembled together," and, second,

---

44 Whitney v. California, 274 U.S. 357, 373 (1927) (concurring opinion). See Comment, *Limitations on the Right of Assembly*, 23 Calif. L. Rev. 180 (1935); Chafee, *Right of Assembly*, 2 Encyc. Soc. Sci. 275 (1930–1935).

45 See, *e.g.*, United States v. Socony-Vacuum Oil Co., 310 U.S. 150 (1940); United States v. Crimmins, 123 F.2d 271 (2d Cir. 1941); Momand v. Universal Film Exchange, 6 F.R.D. 409 (D. Mass. 1947).

46 See Perkins, Criminal Law 546–48 (1957); Clark & Marshall, A Treatise on the Law of Crimes 489–522 (6th ed. Wingersky 1958).

47 See Schlesinger, The Crisis of the Old Order 257–65 (1957).

that they intended to do an unlawful act or a lawful act in a violent, boisterous, or tumultuous manner.[48] Intimidation and threats are unlawful acts,[49] as are urging boycotts and making personal attacks.[50] Furthermore, there may be an unlawful assembly even though those who assembled did not intend to act unlawfully; unlawfulness may depend solely upon the numbers involved and their demeanor, so that the illegal purpose may have developed after the act of assembling.[51]

In 1891, in *People v. Most*,[52] the New York Court of Appeals went about as far as American courts have been willing to go. At a meeting held to protest the execution of ten Chicago anarchists who had been involved in the celebrated Haymarket affair, Most had made a speech in which he glorified the deeds of the anarchists, denounced and threatened with death the officers connected with the case, and called upon his listeners to arm themselves and resist the authorities. The people in the assembly indicated their agreement by applause. The Court of Appeals sustained a conviction for unlawful assembly under a statute that defined the offense as any attempt or threat on the part of three or more persons to do any act "tending towards a breach of the peace or an injury to person or property, or any unlawful act."[53] The Court held that the statute was violated although only one man in the assembly had spoken; the requisite of the crime is met if two or more other people indicated agreement in some fashion. Furthermore, the court held, the purpose of such speeches is no less illegal merely because the speaker asserts that the time is not yet ripe for action. No one, said the court, can foresee the consequences of using incendiary language before a crowd of ignorant and misguided men.

On the other hand, it is clear, according to the state courts, that a meeting cannot be prohibited merely because shocking or unpopu-

---

48 See State v. Woolman, 84 Utah 23 (1934); Aron v. Wausau, 98 Wis. 592 (1898).

49 See State v. Gennis, 41 N.M. 453 (1937).

50 See American League of the Friends of the New Germany of Hudson County v. Eastmead, 174 Atl. 156 (N.J. Chan. 1934).

51 See People v. Kerrick, 86 Cal. App. 542 (1927).

52 128 N.Y. 108 (1891) (Andrews, J.).

53 *Id.* at 113.

lar ideas may be advocated.[54] The right of public assembly for the "free and open discussion of public questions" at stake in an election may not be denied where there is no disturbance and troops are present to maintain order.[55] Workers on strike may demonstrate, holding processions and public meetings, within the protection of "the rights to meet and discuss and petition," so long as there is no violence or intent to commit acts of violence or breaches of the peace, even though the object of the demonstration is to protest publicly action taken by the police.[56] Deeply rooted are the rights of the people "to meet in public places to discuss in an open and public manner all questions affecting their substantial welfare and to vent their grievances, to protest against oppression, economic or otherwise, and to petition for the amelioration of their condition, and to discuss the ways and means of attaining that end. . . ."[57]

The Supreme Court of Colorado recently upheld as legal the picketing of the Governor's mansion by a group that chanted grievances and carried signs; no profane or offensive language was used and no one complained to the authorities.[58] In the absence of violence, or tumultuous or offensive conduct, the court could find no warrant for a conviction for the offense of "disturbing the peace of others." The court took the view that the right of the community to peace and quiet must be balanced against the constitutional right to appeal to the authorities for a redress of grievances. "It would seem," it observed, "that what the public endures for the sake of sports, it should be able to endure in the assertion of fundamental rights. That is part of the price of our freedoms."[59]

In contrast with the British, American courts do not look with favor upon the view that the police may forbid a public meeting merely because they have reasonable grounds to believe that public disorder will result if the meeting is held, although there are deci-

---

[54] See American League of the Friends of the New Germany of Hudson County v. Eastmead, 174 Atl. 156 (N.J. Chan. 1934).

[55] Neelley v. Farr, 61 Colo. 485 (1916).

[56] State v. Butterworth, 104 N.J.L. 579 (1928).

[57] *Id.* at 581.

[58] Flores v. Denver, 122 Colo. 71 (1950).

[59] *Id.* at 78.

sions that the police do not have to wait until disorder occurs.[60] Nevertheless, the latitude of police discretion is bound to be great. A resourceful police chief determined to prevent a meeting has many weapons available, such as calling in the building inspectors to find flaws in the building. Police harassment in this area is one of the familiar facts of life.

While the First Amendment protection of the right of assembly by its language applies only to the national government, the Supreme Court has taken the view, since the late nineteen twenties, that it is one of the basic rights of liberty that the Due Process Clause of the Fourteenth Amendment protects against invasion by the states. This means, of course, that in the Supreme Court's view the right of assembly is fundamental to any system of ordered liberty. Thus, while the Court sustained a conviction for violation of the California Criminal Syndicalism Act in *Whitney v. California*,[61] it proceeded on the explicit assumption that rights of assembly and association were within the protection of the Due Process Clause. In 1937, in *De Jonge v. Oregon*,[62] a unanimous Court ruled that a state statute was repugnant to due process which punished participation in a meeting for lawful discussion of public issues because the meeting was held under the auspices of the Communist Party. "Peaceable assembly for lawful discussion," Mr. Chief Justice Hughes declared, "cannot be made a crime. The holding of meetings for peaceable political action cannot be proscribed. Those who assist in the conduct of such meetings cannot be branded as criminals on that score."[63] The right to take part in a peaceable assembly is a personal right. No matter who sponsored the meeting, "[t]he defendant was none the less entitled to discuss the public issues of the day and thus in a lawful manner, without incitement to violence or crime, to seek redress of alleged grievances. That was of the essence of his guaranteed personal liberty."[64]

Similarly, the Court ruled in 1939, in *Hague v. C.I.O.*,[65] and again

---

60 See, *e.g.*, Commonwealth v. Benjamin, 10 Pa. D. & C. 775 (Q. Sess. Phila. Co. 1928). The court held that police are specially qualified by training and experience to know the conditions and anticipate the probable results of a public meeting.

61 274 U.S. 357 (1927). See also Stromberg v. California, 283 U.S. 359 (1931).

62 299 U.S. 353

63 *Id.* at 365.

64 *Id.* at 366.

65 307 U.S. 496.

in 1945, in *Thomas v. Collins*,[66] that the right of unions to hold public meetings was protected against improper state interference. In the latter case Mr. Justice Rutledge observed that "it was not by accident or coincidence that the rights to freedom in speech and press were coupled in a single guaranty with the rights of the people peaceably to assemble and to petition for redress of grievances. All these, though not identical, are inseparable. They are cognate rights . . . and therefore are united in the First Article's assurance."[67] In *Thomas* it was decisive that "the assembly was entirely peaceable, and had no other than a wholly lawful purpose."[68] And Mr. Justice Rutledge concluded his opinion with the observation that the right in question "is a national right, federally guaranteed. There is some modicum of freedom of thought, speech and assembly which all citizens of the Republic may exercise throughout its length and breadth, which no State, nor all together, nor the Nation itself, can prohibit, restrain or impede."[69]

III. Meetings in Streets and Other Public Places

Since earliest times, meetings have been held in streets, parks, and other public places. Such meetings often create serious problems of disorder and breach of the peace. The primary function of streets is to afford passage. Parks are primarily for repose and recreation. Accordingly, American law has long been concerned with the problems created by the holding of meetings in public places.[70] But if street and park meetings are properly subject to regulation, they may not be altogether prohibited. A short answer to the familiar observation that if one wants to make a speech he ought to "hire a hall" is that halls cost money that the speaker may not have, or the right hall may not be available. Furthermore, those who stage street meetings often count on capturing the attention of passers-by and

---

66 323 U.S. 516.

67 *Id.* at 530.

68 *Id.* at 536.

69 *Id.* at 543.

70 See Abernathy, *Assemblies in the Public Streets*, 5 S.C.L.Q. 384 (1953); Saulson, *Municipal Control of Public Streets and Parks as Affecting Freedom of Speech and Assembly*, 49 Mich. L. Rev. 1185 (1951); Comment, *Public Order and the Right of Assembly in England and the United States: A Comparative Study*, 47 Yale L.J. 404 (1938); Comment, *Municipal Regulation of Free Speech in the Streets and Parks*, 46 Ill. L. Rev. 489 (1951).

bringing to their attention views and facts that might otherwise escape them.

The right to hold a street meeting ends at the point where unlawful assembly and riot begin. And the police may interfere where a breach of the peace or disorderly conduct has occurred.[71] Two types of municipal ordinances, however, are primarily utilized for handling the problems arising from street meetings: those forbidding obstructions of the streets and those requiring a permit for such activities.

There is no doubt of the constitutionality of an ordinance that functions to keep street traffic free from obstruction. In a leading case decided in 1929 by the highest court of Massachusetts,[72] Chief Justice Rugg recognized that the right of peaceable assembly is secured by the state constitution and is to be scrupulously protected by the judiciary. Nevertheless, he declared:[73]

> [It] cannot be exercised at times and places and in circumstances in conflict with the enjoyment of other well recognized rights of individuals or the public. . . . The easement of passage for the public acquired by the layout of a highway includes reasonable means of transportation for persons and commodities and of transmission of intelligence. Whatever interferes with the exercise of this easement is a nuisance, even

---

71 For example, the New York Penal Law provides that one is guilty of disorderly conduct if he "congregates with others on a public street and refuses to move on when ordered by the police" or "by his actions causes a crowd to collect, except when lawfully addressing such a crowd." N.Y. PENAL LAW § 722. Convictions have been sustained by the New York courts under this statute over the objection that it interfered with the constitutional right of assembly. People *ex rel.* Neiman v. McWilliams, 22 N.Y.S.2d 571 (Mag. Ct. N.Y. City 1940), *rev'd on other grounds,* 31 N.Y.S.2d 37 (Sp. Sess. 1941); People v. Hussock, 23 N.Y.S.2d 520 (Sp. Sess. 1940), *cert. denied,* 312 U.S. 659 (1941); People *ex rel.* Whelan v. Friedman, 14 N.Y.S.2d 389 (Mag. Ct. N.Y. City 1939). In People v. Kieran, 26 N.Y.S.2d 291 (Co. Ct. Nass. Co. 1941), involving a procession of fourteen Jehovah's Witnesses, the court concluded that the defendants were not guilty of disorderly conduct.

72 Commonwealth v. Surridge, 265 Mass. 425 (1929).

73 *Id.* at 427. See also Harwood v. Trembley, 97 N.J.L. 173 (1922); Barker v. Commonwealth, 19 Pa. 412 (1852); Tacoma v. Roe, 190 Wash. 444 (1937); *Ex parte* Bodkin, 86 Cal. App.2d 208 (1948); Louisville v. Lougher, 209 Ky. 299 (1925); People v. Pierce, 85 App. Div. 125 (3d Dept. 1903). Evidence of obstruction was held to be insufficient by the court in People v. De Cecca, 29 N.Y.S.2d 524 (Sp. Sess. N.Y. Co. 1941), involving a group of Jehovah's Witnesses.

> though no inconvenience or delay to public travel actually takes place.

The court held that it was immaterial that defendant had a permit, since it was beyond the ordinance-making power of the city to grant a permit that authorized obstruction of a public way.

Similarly, it has been held that police are not given illegal power where an ordinance authorizes them to break up a meeting obstructing street traffic.[74] The police are obliged to act reasonably; in protecting traffic from obstruction they have a broad discretion to view the public safety and convenience in the light of such factors as time, place, and conditions of traffic.[75]

It is important to note, however, that making a speech in a street is not a nuisance *per se*. Any rule declaring it so "is scarcely suited to the genius of our people or to the character of their institutions, and would lead to the repression of many usages of the people now tolerated as harmless, if not necessary."[76] So, too, an ordinance forbidding all processions and parades calculated to attract a crowd on the streets is unreasonable, since "a crowd of people is one of the most ordinary incidents of every-day life in any city of considerable size in this country."[77] Many years ago the Kansas Supreme

---

[74] State v. Sugarman, 126 Minn. 477 (1914).

[75] Burkitt v. Beggans, 103 N.J. Eq. 7, 10 (1928): "The public streets and highways are not places where any person may claim an unqualified right to be for the purpose of addressing assemblages gathered as audiences; they are intended for passage and traffic and not for assemblage. Sound public policy forbids that courts should interpose by injunctive process to hamper or thwart the power and discretion of the police touching the performance of the duties which the law has cast upon or entrusted to them pertaining to the public weal."

[76] Fairbanks v. Kerr, 70 Pa. 86, 92 (1872). See also Anderson v. Tedford, 80 Fla. 376 (1920).

[77] Anderson v. Wellington, 40 Kan. 173, 178 (1888). See *In re* Gribben, 5 Okla. 379, 391–92 (1897): "A city implies a large aggregation of people. The use of its streets contemplates, not quietude and repose, but the noise, bustle and confusion, incident to the transaction of the lawful business of the people and their lawful and harmless amusements and recreations, pleasures and devotions. These are but incidents of a city's life.

"The tendency of American thought and action is towards association for the accomplishment of good purposes; hence, we see a large portion of our people associated in the various organizations for the promotion of public good, the betterment of mankind and the alleviation of its miseries. Every city has its charitable, benevolent, and religious associations, to say nothing of the great political organizations. . . ."

Court declared that it is "an abridgement of the rights of the people" to prohibit all street parades, since[78]

> it represses associated effort and action. It discourages united effort to attract public attention, and challenges public examination and criticism of the associated purposes. It discourages unity of feeling and expression on great public questions, economic, religious, and political. It practically destroys these great public demonstrations that are the most natural product of common aims and kindred purposes.

In fact, courts have taken a more tolerant attitude toward street parades than toward street meetings. A suggested reason is that early street parade cases generally involved the Salvation Army, whereas the cases dealing with meetings often involved socialists, communists, and other radicals.[79] An additional explanation may be that, since municipal authorities grant permits freely to lodges, veterans' associations, and fraternal societies to hold street parades, discriminating against others in denying permits is easily spotted; the fact of discrimination is likely to be obvious. Thus some ordinances aimed at the Salvation Army were held unconstitutional by the courts because of the exemptions extended to other groups.[80]

There has never been any doubt of the propriety of an ordinance that requires a permit for street meetings. But there has been lively debate on the nature and scope of the discretion that the ordinance vests in the licensing authority. In the leading case of *Commonwealth v. Davis*,[81] the Massachusetts court sustained the conviction of a man who, contrary to a local ordinance, made a public address on the Boston Common without a permit from the mayor. Speaking for the Supreme Judicial Court, Justice Holmes said flatly: "For the legislature absolutely or conditionally to forbid public speaking in a highway or public park is no more an infringement of the rights of a member of the public than for the owner of a

---

78 *Id.* at 178.

79 See Comment, 47 YALE L.J. 404, 430 (1938).

80 Anderson v. Wellington, 40 Kan. 173 (1888); State *ex rel.* Garrabad v. Dering, 84 Wis. 585, 591 (1893): The Salvation Army "in law . . . has the same right, and is subject to the same restrictions, in its public demonstrations, as any secular body or society which uses similar means for drawing attention or creating interest. . . ."

81 162 Mass. 510 (1895).

private house to forbid it in his house."[82] In affirming, the Supreme Court of the United States could see nothing wrong in the fact that under Massachusetts law there is no right to use the Common except in such manner and subject to such regulations as the legislative body may prescribe.[83] The Fourteenth Amendment, the Court said in *Davis*, did not destroy the power of the states to enact police regulations as to subjects within their control. On the strength of this opinion, a number of state courts upheld ordinances that gave an undefined discretion to grant or deny permits; their theory was that if an official acted unfairly or arbitrarily, his action could be corrected by the courts.[84] According to this view, even though the ordinance does not say as much, the administrative official must exercise his discretion in a fair and impartial manner. Similarly, ordinances controlling the holding of street processions in order to avoid public annoyance,[85] riot, or other public disorder,[86] have been sustained over objections directed at the scope of discretionary power involved.

The more recent position of the Supreme Court, however, is that a statute or ordinance that vests uncontrolled or insufficiently defined discretion to grant or withhold permits is unconstitutional on its face. This principle was established in *Hague v. C.I.O.*[87] Five of seven participating Justices joined in holding invalid an ordinance of Jersey City, though they differed as to which provision of the Fourteenth Amendment controlled the judgment. The ordinance provided that no public parades or meetings could be conducted on the streets of the city without a prior permit from the Director of Public Safety; he could refuse a permit in order to prevent "riots, disturbances or disorderly assemblage." A permit

---

82 Id. at 511

83 Davis v. Massachusetts, 167 U.S. 43 (1897).

84 Duquesne v. Fincke, 269 Pa. 112 (1920); People *ex rel.* Doyle v. Atwell, 197 App. Div. 225 (2d Dept. 1921), *aff'd*, 232 N.Y. 96 (1921), *writ of error dismissed*, 261 U.S. 590 (1923). See also Bloomington v. Richardson, 38 Ill. App. 60 (3d Dist. 1890).

85 Chariton v. Simmons, 87 Iowa 226 (1893).

86 Thomas v. Casey, 121 N.J.L. 185 (1938), *aff'd*, 123 N.J.L. 447 (1939).

87 307 U.S. 496 (1939).

had repeatedly been denied to a labor organization to hold street meetings for the purpose of discussing the newly enacted National Labor Relations Act. Justices Roberts and Black thought that the ordinance denied one of the privileges and immunities of United States citizenship, secured by Section 1 of the Fourteenth Amendment; Justices Stone and Reed preferred to base their decision on the Due Process Clause. While Mr. Chief Justice Hughes agreed that the right of citizens to meet in order to discuss a national statute was a federal right or privilege, he also felt that the record did not adequately support a holding on this theory. Accordingly, he joined with those who invoked the Due Process Clause. Mr. Justice McReynolds dissented on the ground that it exceeded the competence of federal courts to interfere by injunction "with the essential rights of the municipality to control its own parks and streets," which are "intimate local affairs."[88] Mr. Justice Butler also dissented, arguing that *Davis v. Massachusetts* was controlling.

Whether the ordinance violated the Privileges and Immunities Clause or the Due Process Clause of the Fourteenth Amendment, the majority agreed that it was constitutionally defective. Mr. Justice Roberts argued that the use of the streets for purposes of assembly, "communicating thoughts between citizens, and discussing public questions," is an immemorial one. While he agreed that this use of the streets is not absolute, and "must be exercised in subordination to the general comfort and convenience, and in consonance with peace and good order," nevertheless the right must not be abridged or denied under the guise of regulation. Mr. Justice Roberts agreed with the holding of the trial court that the ordinance was void upon its face:[89]

> It does not make comfort or convenience in the use of streets or parks the standard of official action. It enables the Director of Safety to refuse a permit on his mere opinion that such refusal will prevent "riots, disturbances or disorderly assemblage." It can thus, as the record discloses, be made the instrument of arbitrary suppression of free expression of views. . . . Uncontrolled official suppression of the privilege cannot be made a substitute for the duty to maintain order. . . .

---

[88] *Id.* at 532.

[89] *Id.* at 516.

The basic premise of *Hague v. C.I.O.* was reaffirmed and restated in *Kunz v. New York*.[90] Kunz, a Baptist minister, was convicted and fined $10 for holding a religious meeting on the streets of New York without a permit. He had requested and been refused a permit several times without receiving any reason for the refusals. A city ordinance made it unlawful to meet for public worship on the streets without first obtaining a permit from the police commissioner. The Supreme Court pointed out that the ordinance made no mention of particular reasons for which a permit application could be refused, and that, under the interpretation of the state courts, the police commissioner was thereby allowed to exercise an absolute discretion in denying applications, using his own interpretation of what conduct the ordinance prohibits. Thus, said Mr. Chief Justice Vinson, the ordinance gave an administrative officer discretionary power to control in advance the right of citizens to speak on religious matters on the streets of New York. Such a prior restraint was clearly invalid. While the Court had recognized in *Cox v. New Hampshire*[91] that a statute may be enacted that prevents serious interference with the normal usage of streets and parks, the Chief Justice noted that "we have consistently condemned licensing systems which vest in an administrative official discretion to grant or withhold a permit upon broad criteria unrelated to proper regulation of public places."[92] If, as argued by the state, Kunz's previous meetings had caused disorder, appropriate public remedies to protect the peace and order of the community were available. But the issue was suppression, not punishment. "It is sufficient to say," the Chief Justice concluded, "that New York cannot vest restraining control over the right to speak on religious sub-

[90] 340 U.S. 290 (1951). For a discussion of this and other cases referred to in this section and the next one, in the context of the problem of religious freedom, see Kurland, *Of Church and State and the Supreme Court,* 29 U. Chi. L. Rev. 1 (1961).

[91] 312 U.S. 569 (1941). *Cox* upheld a statute that required persons using the public streets for a parade or procession to receive a special license from the local authorities. "The authority of a municipality to impose regulations in order to assure the safety and convenience of the people in the use of public highways has never been regarded as inconsistent with civil liberties but rather as one of the means of safeguarding the good order upon which they ultimately depend." *Id.* at 574. It was emphasized that the state court had construed the statute as not vesting an arbitrary or an unfettered discretion in the licensing board.

[92] 340 U.S. at 294.

jects in an administrative official where there are no appropriate standards to guide his action."[93]

Mr. Justice Jackson alone dissented in this case, at considerable length and with great vigor. He emphasized the fact that Kunz had specialized in scurrilous attacks upon Catholics and Jews and weighed the value of insulting speech against its potentiality for harm. "[To] blanket hateful and hate-stirring attacks on races and faiths under the protections for freedom of speech may be a noble innovation. On the other hand, it may be a quixotic tilt at windmills which belittles great principles of liberty."[94] He insisted that it made "a world of difference" that Kunz had been speaking in street meetings, since that posed the question whether New York was obliged to place its streets at his service "to hurl insults at the passerby." He thought that this case fell within the "fighting words" doctrine of the *Chaplinsky* case.[95] The Constitution, he argued, does not prohibit a city from controlling its streets by means of a permit system that takes into account damage to public peace and order. He insisted that established doctrine dealing with prior restraints upon speech does not apply to street meetings that have a different impact upon public order. It seemed hypocritical to him for the Court to strike down the ordinance because it lacked standards for administrative action when the Justices themselves did not agree upon First Amendment standards.

A number of state courts have taken the view, some even before these recent Supreme Court decisions, that it is unconstitutional to give officials an undefined discretion to grant or withhold permits to hold meetings or processions in the streets.[96] The highest court of Connecticut once said that it is improper to make the constitutional liberties of the citizen depend upon "the good impulses of a subordinate official entrusted with unlimited discretion"; that "there can be no reasonable presumption that an unlimited discretion will

---

93 *Id.* at 295.

94 *Ibid.*

95 Chaplinsky v. New Hampshire, 315 U.S. 568 (1942).

96 See Matter of Frazee, 63 Mich. 396 (1886); Chicago v. Trotter, 136 Ill. 430 (1891); Rich v. Naperville, 42 Ill. App. 222 (2d Dist. 1891); *In re* Gribben, 5 Okla. 379 (1897); Anderson v. Tedford, 80 Fla. 376 (1920); State v. Coleman, 96 Conn. 190 (1921); A.C.L.U. v. Cortlandt, 109 N.Y.S.2d 165 (Sup. Ct. Westchester Co. 1951).

not be exercised when the ordinance itself reposes an unlimited discretion."[97]

Generally, the rules that apply to meetings in the streets apply to meetings in public parks.[98] The controlling Supreme Court decision on this subject, *Niemotko v. Maryland*,[99] was decided by a unanimous Court. The case grew out of the refusal of the park commissioner and city council of Havre de Grace, Maryland, to permit a group of Jehovah's Witnesses to hold Bible-talk meetings in the town park. Though no ordinance spelled out the requirement for a permit, established local custom required a permit from the commissioner, subject to appeal to the council. After the Witnesses were refused a permit, they proceeded with the meeting and were arrested by the police. They appealed their convictions under the Maryland disorderly conduct statute. There was no evidence of disorder, threats of violence, riot, or any sort of conduct which could be considered detrimental to the public peace or order; the evidence of the police showed that each defendant had conducted himself "in a manner beyond reproach." The Court stressed its commitment to the proposition that requirement for a permit is invalid as a prior restraint "in the absence of narrowly drawn, reasonable and definite standards for the officials to follow."[100] In this instance, all the officials' power depended on an "amorphous 'practice' " that vested all authority to grant or withhold permits in the commissioner and council. The Court could find no standards at all, no narrowly drawn limitations, "no circumscribing of this absolute power," but only a "limitless discretion." A search of the record failed to discover any valid basis for the denial of the permit. It was apparent that the city council just didn't like Jehovah's Witnesses. The right to the equal protection of the laws, Mr. Chief

97 State v. Coleman, 96 Conn. 190, 195–96 (1921).

98 The New York Court of Appeals recently sustained a statute requiring permits for speaking in public parks by limiting the authority to refuse a permit to avoid conflicts among meetings and to preserve the parks. People v. Hass, 299 N.Y. 190 (1949), *appeal dismissed*, 338 U.S. 803 (1949). The Wisconsin high court held that a city ordinance forbidding all religious meetings in parks was unconstitutional because of its prohibition of the right to meet and speak. Milwaukee County v. Carter, 258 Wis. 139 (1950).

99 340 U.S. 268 (1951).

100 *Id.* at 271.

Justice Vinson declared, in the exercise of First and Fourteenth Amendment freedoms, "has a firmer foundation than the whims or personal opinions of a local governing body."[101]

Two years later, however, in *Poulos v. New Hampshire*,[102] the Court made it clear that it is constitutional for a city to require a license before one may conduct religious services in a park, where, as interpreted by the state courts, there is "uniform, nondiscriminatory and consistent administration" of the law. Said Mr. Justice Reed: "There is no basis for saying that freedom and order are not compatible. That would be a decision of desperation. Regulation and suppression are not the same, either in purpose or result, and courts of justice can tell the difference."[103] Furthermore, where, under state law, the remedy for a wrongful denial of the permit is appropriate judicial review, although this procedure may be slow and costly, an aggrieved party must follow it and is not free to go ahead with the meeting without a permit. "Delay is unfortunate, but the expense and annoyance of litigation is a price citizens must pay for life in an orderly society where the rights of the First Amendment have a real and abiding meaning."[104] Justices Douglas and Black, however, took the position that any licensing of free speech is an unconstitutional prior restraint. They declared that "there is no free speech in the sense of the Constitution when permission must be obtained from an official before a speech can be made."[105]

IV. The Problem of the Hostile Audience

A thorny problem that the exercise of the right of assembly poses is that of disorder or threatened disorder arising from hostility of the audience. In some states to disturb a meeting is a statutory crime,[106] and there have been a few cases of conviction for disturbing public meetings.[107] But in most jurisdictions, if a public meet-

---

101 *Id.* at 272. 102 345 U.S. 395 (1953). 103 *Id.* at 408.

104 *Id.* at 409. 105 *Id.* at 426.

106 See, *e.g.*, N. Y. Penal Code § 1470: "A person who without authority of law, wilfully disturbs any assembly or meeting, not unlawful in its character, is guilty of a misdemeanor." *Cf.* Wash. Rev. Code § 9.27.010 (1956).

107 Commonwealth v. Porter, 1 Gray 476 (Mass. 1854); People v. Malone, 156 App. Div. 10 (2d Dept. 1913); Literell v. Commonwealth, 266 Ky. 235 (1936); *cf.* Pope v. State, 192 Misc. 587 (Ct. Cl. 1948), *aff'd*, 277 App. Div. 1015 (4th Dept. 1950).

ing is held in a private hall and no permit is required, the police have no right to be present unless there is reasonable ground to believe that a breach of the peace is being committed.[108]

While a disturber of a meeting may be prosecuted for disorderly conduct, the more difficult and basic problem of audience hostility arises when the police interfere with the speaker or with those who are managing the meeting.[109] Clearly an assembly may be halted when a riotous situation has developed and the police are otherwise unable to control the mob.[110] This is a limitation obviously based on necessity. On the other hand, it is unthinkable that the right of assembly should be limited by the possibility that hostile members of the crowd may threaten to create disorder. There is certainly no constitutional right to disturb a meeting, but there is a constitutional right to hold one. Judge Sanborn once stated this point emphatically in a case involving Jehovah's Witnesses:[111]

> The theory that a group of individuals may be deprived of their constitutional rights of assembly, speech and worship if they have become so unpopular with, or offensive to, the people of a community that their presence in a public park to deliver a Bible lecture is likely to result in riot and bloodshed, is interesting but somewhat difficult to accept. Under such a doctrine, unpopular political, racial, and religious groups might find themselves virtually inarticulate. Certainly the fundamental rights to assemble, to speak, and to worship cannot be abridged merely because persons threaten to stage a riot or because peace officers believe or are afraid that breaches of the peace will occur if the rights are exercised.

And Judge Sanborn concluded with the observation that "the only sound way to enforce the law is to arrest and prosecute" those who unlawfully prevent or interfere with the holding of a lawful meeting. Nevertheless, Judge Sanborn was unwilling to say that the danger of riot would never justify an interference with such rights

---

108 See Note, *Right of the Police To Attend Political Meetings*, 4 INT'L JUR. ASS'N BULL. 6–9 (January, 1936).

109 See Quillian, *Soapbox Oratorical Privileges versus Municipal Tranquility*, 14 GA. B.J. 191 (1951); Note, *Free Speech and the Hostile Audience*, 26 N.Y.U. L. REV. 489 (1951).

110 See Star Opera Co., Inc. v. Hylan, 109 Misc. 132 (Sup. Ct. N.Y. Co. 1919).

111 Sellers v. Johnson, 163 F.2d 877, 881 (8th Cir. 1947), *cert. denied,* 332 U.S. 851 (1948).

as that of assembly. But the evidence on which the police may find a danger to the peace of the community must be something more solid than "unconfirmed rumors, talk and fears."

The nature of this particular problem was thoroughly explored by the Supreme Court in *Feiner v. New York*.[112] In this case the police had broken up an open-air meeting at a street corner in Syracuse when an onlooker threatened violence if the police did not interfere with the speaker. Feiner had stirred up some excitement in a crowd of about eighty people by making derogatory remarks about the President, the American Legion, the Mayor of Syracuse, and other local officials. When he refused to obey a police order to stop talking, he was arrested and convicted of disorderly conduct. Speaking for the six Justices who voted to affirm the conviction, Mr. Chief Justice Vinson insisted that this was not a case of "blind condonation by a state court of arbitrary police action."[113] Feiner had had a full, fair trial at which the judge, after hearing testimony on both sides, decided that the police had been justified in acting to prevent a breach of the peace. Furthermore, this exercise of discretionary power by the police officers was later approved by two appellate courts. All three state courts recognized Feiner's right to hold a street meeting where he did and to make derogatory remarks about public officials and the American Legion. But they also found that in making the arrest the officers had been motivated solely by a proper concern for the preservation of order and protection of the general welfare. This Court must respect, Mr. Chief Justice Vinson declared, "the interest of the community in maintaining peace and order on its streets."[114] He agreed that ordinary murmurings and objections from a hostile audience cannot be sufficient to warrant silencing a speaker, and he declared that he was not unmindful of the danger of giving zealous police officials complete discretion to break up an otherwise lawful public meeting. "It is one thing to say that the police cannot be used as an instrument for the suppression of unpopular views, and another

---

112 340 U.S. 315 (1951). For an interesting debate on this decision see Dembitz, *Free Speech v. Free-for-All*, 173 THE NATION 29–31 (1951); Countryman, *Freedom for Insulting Speech—A Reply*, 173 THE NATION 50–52 (1951).

113 340 U.S. at 319.

114 *Id.* at 320.

to say that, when as here the speaker passes the bounds of argument or persuasion and undertakes incitement to riot, they are powerless to prevent a breach of the peace."[115]

Of course, one of the leading issues of this case was whether Feiner had actually incited to riot. The majority came close to saying that this is a question of fact to be determined by the police officers in the first instance, subject to review by the courts. They seemed to be impressed with the fact that no fewer than three New York courts—the trial court and two appellate courts—had agreed on the factual issue of the existence of a crisis justifying the drastic police action to preserve peace and order. Mr. Justice Douglas, however, could find nothing except an unsympathetic audience and the threat of one man to oust the speaker from his box. He insisted that in the face of this type of threat, it is the duty of the police to protect the speakers, not to silence them. "If . . . the police throw their weight on the side of those who would break up the meetings, the police become the new censors of speech."[116] Mr. Justice Black declared that the Court was taking "a long step toward totalitarian authority." He did not believe that the facts indicated any imminent threat of riot or uncontrollable disorder, and he did not agree that one isolated threat to assault the speaker was evidence of impending disorder. But what concerned Mr. Justice Black above all was the implication of the majority opinion that the police were not obliged to protect Feiner's right to talk. Of course they have the power to prevent breaches of the peace, but they should first make every reasonable effort to protect the speaker before interfering with him for the sake of preserving order, even to the extent of arresting the man who threatened to intervene. It is true that Feiner continued to talk after he was ordered to desist, but, said Mr. Justice Black, "a man making a lawful address is certainly not required to be silent merely because an officer directs it."[117]

There is no ready and easy solution to the problem of the hostile audience. The state has an incontestable duty to preserve order by controlling mobs; but it is unthinkable that the right to hold a public meeting should be determined by the least tolerant people

---

115 *Id.* at 321.

116 *Id.* at 331.

117 *Id.* at 327–28.

in the community. It has been suggested that various subjective criteria as to both the speaker and the audience should be evaluated in each particular case.[118] There is a great deal of difference between a speaker whose purpose is to communicate ideas and one who intends to promote disorder and breaches of the peace. The former is entitled to protection; the latter is not. Similarly, there are two types of audiences, those honestly if unjustifiably enraged by the speech and those with a preconceived design to create disturbances. Various combinations of circumstances are possible, and "the clearest case for prohibition of the meeting is made out when both the audience and the speaker are motivated by a desire for civil strife."[119] On the other hand, if the speaker's desire is to communicate ideas and the audience is genuinely aroused, the speech should be permitted when the speaker is not responsible for the intolerance of his audience. Finally, the point is worth making that since the right to hold public meetings is both important and constitutionally guaranteed, all factual doubts had best be resolved in favor of the right rather than against it. Since in concrete cases the outcome depends upon the facts, great weight must be given to the judgment of those who bear the initial responsibility for ascertaining the facts. But if police officers are not well selected and properly trained to understand the nature of the citizen's constitutional rights, these rights may be crushed under the weight of the presumption in favor of the regularity of official actions.

V. The Freedom of Association

The right of Americans freely to associate with whom they choose is universally recognized as fundamental in a democratic society.[120] But like all rights, this one does not and cannot function in a social and political vacuum: under some circumstances it is legitimate for government to regulate in order to protect other rights. Nonetheless, governmental measures bearing upon freedom of association must ultimately pass the judicial test of reasonableness. To take a simple example, when one of the supreme officers

---

118 Note, *Freedom of Speech and Assembly: The Problem of the Hostile Audience*, 49 Colum. L. Rev. 1118–24 (1949).

119 *Id.* at 1123.

120 See Laski, *Freedom of Association*, 6 Encyc. Soc. Sci. 447–50 (1931).

of the Order of Owls undertook to solicit new members to form a new nest, he was prosecuted for violating a statute which provided that all officers of secret fraternal organizations who solicit dues-paying members must have been elected by chapter delegates. The New York court ruled that this statute was an arbitrary and unreasonable regulation because, since the society was neither illegal nor immoral, no issue of public health, safety, morals, or protection against fraud was involved.[121]

Of course the government may forbid criminal, immoral, or seditious associations, but the power to regulate may also be exercised under less obvious circumstances. There are regulations—corrupt-practices acts—which apply to political organizations, statutes requiring the registration of lobbyists, and legislation dealing with the distribution of anonymous political circulars. In order to prevent fraud, states are free to require some form of local registration of those who solicit contributions or members. Associations may be required to accomplish some sort of registration with a designated public official in order to permit service of process and to ensure some measure of financial responsibility. Furthermore, if the public interest is served thereby, government may go pretty far in forbidding certain types of association that are generally regarded, in the absence of prohibitory legislation, to be quite lawful.

A familiar example is found in the right of the state to abolish or forbid student membership in fraternities or other secret societies, now well established in American constitutional law. Most of the state cases deal with orders of school boards forbidding high school students to belong to fraternities or other secret organizations. The courts have invariably sustained such regulations as being reasonable.[122] This question reached the Supreme Court only once, some years ago, in a case that held valid a Mississippi statute prohibiting Greek-letter fraternities, sororities, or other secret societies in all of the state's educational institutions, including the University of

[121] People *ex rel.* Niger v. Van Dell, 85 Misc. 92 (Sup. Ct. Erie Co. 1914).

[122] Isgrig v. Srygley, 210 Ark. 580 (1946); Wilson v. Abilene Independent School District, 190 S.W.2d 406 (Tex. Civ. App. 1945); Coggins v. Board of Education of Durham, 223 N.C. 763 (1944); Satan Fraternity v. Board of Public Instruction for Dade County, 156 Fla. 222 (1945); Wayland v. Hughes, 43 Wash. 441 (1906); Antell v. Stokes, 287 Mass. 103 (1934).

Mississippi.[123] The Court was unanimous in concluding that the statute violated neither the Due Process Clause nor the Equal Protection Clause of the Fourteenth Amendment: the statute was a reasonable disciplinary regulation. Mr. Justice McKenna said that whether fraternities were, as the appellants contended, a moral and disciplinary force, was for the state itself to determine; the state may have thought that membership in the prohibited societies divided the attention of the students, distracting them from that singleness of purpose that the state desired to exist in its public educational institutions. It was not the province of the Supreme Court, he observed, to annul state statutes by choosing between disputable considerations regarding their wisdom or necessity.

Ever since Queen's Bench took jurisdiction in 1844 over a case involving expulsion from the Caledonian Society,[124] Anglo-American courts have been willing to take jurisdiction over cases involving suspension or expulsion from a private club. The legal basis for a court's granting relief in such cases is not on any theory of property or contract, but because of the member's relation to the association.[125] A few courts have allowed damages, but this is an awkward procedure, and the usual remedy sought is reinstatement or a declaration that the member had been wrongfully expelled. The customary and preferred remedy is mandamus.[126]

In general, American courts follow reasoning in the landmark case of *Dawkins v. Antrobus*.[127] That case involved the expulsion of a member from the Travellers' Club, according to the rules and procedures of the club, for writing a pamphlet reflecting upon the conduct of another member. It was ruled that a court will not interfere with the decision of a club to expel a member under its rules unless (1) the rules themselves are contrary to natural justice,

---

123 Waugh v. Board of Trustees, 237 U.S. 589 (1915).

124 Innes v. Wylie, 1 Car. & K. 257, 174 Eng. Rep. 800 (Q.B. 1844).

125 Chafee, *The Internal Affairs of Associations Not for Profit*, 43 Harv. L. Rev. 993 (1930).

126 Lahiff v. St. Joseph's Total Abstinence & Benev. Soc., 76 Conn. 648 (1904); Mitchell v. Jewish Progressive Club, 253 Ala. 195 (1949).

127 17 Ch.D. 615 (1881). For a lively account of this famous case, see Chafee, *supra* note 125, at 993–99.

or (2) the act of expulsion was accomplished in violation of the rules, or (3) there was malice or lack of good faith in the expulsion.

Actually, within the ambit of these three propositions, courts have been willing to intervene for a variety of reasons:[128] where basic principles of justice were violated; where a fair hearing or trial was denied; where expulsion was in bad faith, or in violation of law, or in violation of the regulations of the association; where there were serious irregularities in the expulsion proceedings; where the expulsory tribunal was not duly constituted; or where a regulation concerned with expulsion was invalid. Courts have been especially reluctant to interfere where an expulsion from a church was due to factional trouble or involved purely doctrinal questions, unless property rights were involved,[129] or the expulsion was due to fraud, since "fraud vitiates all transactions."[130] Courts will inquire whether the expulsion was ordered by an authority having the power to take such action.[131] This reluctance of civil courts to become involved in theological disputes is wholly understandable in a country committed to the separation of church and state. Courts are also slow to intervene in cases involving schools and colleges, since a high value is attached there to autonomy, or in cases involving secret societies, where it is too much trouble to learn their ritual. On the other hand, where expulsion may result in very serious consequences, such as the loss of a job or the weakening of a person's professional standing, courts are more willing to take jurisdiction. Such situations arise where a skilled worker has been expelled from his trade union, a doctor from a medical society, or a broker from his stock exchange.

VI. The Right To Belong to a Political Party

Since the political party is an indispensable instrumentality of democratic government, the right to associate freely with a party

---

[128] See the analyses in Blenko v. Schmeltz, 362 Pa. 365 (1949); Mitchell v. Jewish Progressive Club, 253 Ala. 195 (1949); Richards v. Morison, 229 Mass. 458 (1918).

[129] See Mt. Olive Primitive Baptist Church v. Patrick, 252 Ala. 672 (1949); Bouldin v. Alexander, 15 Wall. 131 (1872).

[130] Hendryx v. People's United Church, 42 Wash. 336 (1906).

[131] See Watson v. Jones, 13 Wall. 679 (1871).

of one's choice is equally fundamental. Mr. Chief Justice Warren stated this point with great clarity in 1957:[132]

> Our form of government is built on the premise that every citizen shall have the right to engage in political expression and association. This right was enshrined in the First Amendment of the Bill of Rights. Exercise of these basic freedoms in America has traditionally been through the media of political associations. Any interference with the freedom of a party is simultaneously an interference with the freedom of its adherents.

It is interesting to note that there is no direct authorization of political parties in our federal and state constitutions, though parties are mentioned in one way or another in many state constitutions.[133] Actually, the right to form and belong to political parties is a byproduct of many constitutional guaranties, such as the right of petition and assembly, the rights of free speech and free press, and the right to vote. Courts also take the view that the inherent right of the people to form political parties is a necessary incident of free government. The highest court of California said many years ago:[134]

> No one can be so ignorant as not to appreciate the value, indeed, the necessity, of opposing political parties in a government such as ours. No one, it would seem, can be so thoughtless as not to realize that government by the people is a progressive institution which seeks to give expression and effect to the wisest and best ideas of its members. No statement is needed in the declaration of rights to the effect that electors holding certain political principles in common may freely assemble, organize themselves into a political party, and use all legitimate means to carry their principles of government into active operation through the suffrages of their

---

[132] Sweezy v. New Hampshire, 354 U.S. 234, 250 (1957). For an eloquent appreciation of the indispensable role of political parties in American democracy, see ROOT, THE CITIZEN'S PART IN GOVERNMENT (1907), especially ch. 2.

[133] See Starr, *The Legal Status of American Political Parties*, 34 AM. POL. SCI. REV. 439, 685 (1940).

[134] Britton v. Board of Election Commissioners, 129 Cal. 337, 344 (1900). See also *Ex parte* Wilson, 7 Okla. Cr. 610 (1912); Davidson v. Hanson, 87 Minn. 211, 219 (1902): "The right to agitate and organize political parties is inherent, and secured by the constitution. . . ."; Sarlls v. State *ex rel.* Trimble, 201 Ind. 88, 106 (1929); "The people have an inalienable right to organize and operate political parties. . . ."

> fellows. Such a right is fundamental. It is inherent in the very form and substance of our government, and needs no expression in its constitution.

It follows that the courts generally hold to the view that political parties are not the creatures of government[135] and therefore have the right to govern themselves. In the absence of statutory regulation, they have an inherent right to manage their own affairs.[136] They may organize themselves by electing officers and committees. Party committees have the right to judge the qualifications of their own members, fix the site for conventions, and fill the vacancies in the slate of candidates caused by death or withdrawal. A party has the right to adopt and amend its constitution and by-laws.[137] Nevertheless, it is equally incontestible that political parties are subject to reasonable regulation by government, and almost all states have fairly substantial bodies of legislation on the subject. Thus, most states define parties in terms of numerical strength, and their authority to do so has often been affirmed by the courts.[138] Furthermore, the nomination of candidates is now controlled by detailed legislation. Nevertheless, the courts will hold legislation regulatory of political parties unconstitutional if arbitrary, discriminatory, or unreasonable, just as they have the power so to rule with regard to most types of regulatory enactments.[139]

Many states have in recent years taken to barring "un-American"

---

135 See Bell v. Hill, 123 Tex. 531 (1934): A political party is "a *voluntary association,* an association formed of the free will and unrestrained choice of those who compose it. No man is compelled by law to become a member of a political party; or, after having become such, to remain a member. He may join such a party for whatever reason seems good to him, and may quit the party for any cause, good, bad, or indifferent, or without cause. A political party is the creation of free men, acting according to their own wisdom, and in no sense whatever the creation of any department of the government."

136 *Cf.* Brown v. Costen, 176 N.C. 63 (1918), holding that, in the absence of statute, a court of equity has no power to interfere with political parties in the choice of candidates, or to regulate the methods and agencies by which they are selected. See Mitau, *Judicial Determination of Political Party Organizational Autonomy,* 42 MINN. L. REV. 245 (1957).

137 See Starr, *supra* note 133, at 448–52.

138 See State *ex rel.* McGrael v. Phelps 144 Wis. 1 (1910); Progressive Party v. Flynn, 400 Ill. 102 (1948).

139 See Morrow v. Wipf, 22 S.D. 146 (1908).

parties from the ballot.[140] One type of statute requires each party to file an affidavit with some state official affirming that it does not advocate seditious doctrines and is not affiliated with an organization that does.[141] Another excludes the Communist Party by name from the ballot.[142] A few state appellate courts have upheld the constitutionality of this legislation.[143] But the Ohio court has stressed that if the state bars a party that advocates violent overthrow of government from a place on the ballot, the legislative finding to this effect must be supported by substantial evidence.[144] A number of rulings, however, have gone the other way. The California statute that in effect denied recognition to the Communist Party was held unconstitutional in 1942 by the state supreme court as a legislative infringement on the constitutional right to vote.[145] The court also ruled that, while the legislature may deny any party advocating the forceful overthrow of the government a place on the ballot, it is not within the legislative power to determine that a particular party advocates the doctrine in question. The Supreme Court of Washington refused to permit the Washington secretary of state to bar the Communist Party from the ballot without statutory authorization to do so.[146] In 1950 the New

---

140 See Ward, *The Communist Party and the Ballot,* 1 BILL OF RIGHTS REV. 286 (1941); GELLHORN, THE STATES AND SUBVERSION 404–405 (1952); Jaynes, *The Washington Subversive Activities Act: Its Restriction on Access to the Election Process,* 29 WASH. L. REV. 63 (1954); Hill, *A Critique of Recent Ohio Anti-Subversive Legislation,* 14 OHIO ST. L. J. 439 (1953).

141 See DEL. CODE ANN. tit. 15, § 4101 (1953); IND. STAT. ANN. § 29-3812 (Burns 1949); OHIO REV. CODE ANN. § 3517.07 (Page 1954); PA. STAT. ANN. tit. 25, §§ 2831, 2936 (Supp. 1958); TENN. CODE ANN. § 2-1203 (1955); TEX. ELECTION CODE art. 6.02 (Vernon 1952); WASH. REV. CODE § 9-81-100 (1956).

142 See ARK. STAT. ANN. §§ 3-1604.5 (1956); CAL. ELECTION CODE § 2540.9 (1953); WYO. STAT. ANN. § 31-1404 (1945); OKLA. STAT. tit. 26, §§ 6.1–2 (1951); ILL. STÄT. ANN. § 29.3812 (Burns 1949); TEX. ELECTION CODE art. 6.03 (Vernon 1952); WIS. STAT. § 685 (1955).

143 Field v. Hall, 201 Ark. 77 (1940); State *ex rel.* Berry v. Hummel, 42 Ohio L. Abs. 40 (1944); Huntamer v. Coe, 40 Wash.2d 767 (1952).

144 State *ex rel.* Beck v. Hummel, 150 Ohio St. 127 (1948).

145 Communist Party v. Peek, 20 Cal.2d 536 (1942). See Note, *May the States, by Statute, Bar Subversive Groups from the Ballot?* 25 NOTRE DAME LAW. 319 (1950); see also Feinglass v. Reinecke, 48 F. Supp. 438 (N.D. Ill. 1942).

146 Washington *ex rel.* Huff v. Reeves, 5 Wash.2d 637 (1940).

Jersey courts held unconstitutional a statute that required all candidates for state office to take a special oath swearing to non-belief and non-membership in subversive organizations, on the ground that the legislature could not alter the requirements for public office spelled out in the state constitution.[147] On the other hand, in 1951 the Supreme Court sustained the validity of a Maryland law that denied a place on the ballot for a municipal election to a candidate who refused to sign an oath that he was not *knowingly* a member of an organization that has engaged in any attempt to overthrow the government by force or violence.[148] The Court stressed the requirement of "knowing" membership in a subversive organization.

VII. The Right To Join a Trade Union

It is well known that the common law treated trade unions as illegal combinations or conspiracies in restraint of trade and contrary to the public interest. Such was the decision of the Mayor's Court of Philadelphia in the first American labor case, the *Philadelphia Cordwainers' Case* of 1806.[149] Of course, the *Cordwainers' Case* did not stand alone in this period of our history.[150] Beginning with the landmark decision in 1842 of Chief Justice Shaw in *Commonwealth v. Hunt*,[151] however, American courts gradually abandoned the common-law doctrine of criminal conspiracy as a weapon for the suppression of labor unions, and statutes were adopted by legislative bodies to protect the right of workers to organize. Thus Congress declared in 1935, in the National Labor Relations

---

[147] Imbrie v. Marsh, 5 N.J. Super. 239 (1949), *aff'd*, 3 N.J. 578 (1950); *contra:* Huntamer v. Coe, 40 Wash.2d 767 (1952).

[148] Gerende v. Board of Supervisors, 341 U.S. 56 (1951).

[149] For the text, see 3 Commons & Gilmore, A Documentary History of American Industrial Society 61 (1910). For an excellent analysis of the *Cordwainers' Case*, see Nelles, *The First American Labor Case*, 41 Yale L.J. 165 (1931); see also Dulles, Labor in America 30 (1949); Gregory, Labor and the Law ch. 1 (2d ed. 1958).

[150] See People v. Melvin, 2 Wheller Cr. Cas. 262 (N.Y. 1810); Pittsburg Cordwainers' Case (1815), 4 Commons & Gilmore, *op. cit. supra* note 149, at 15–87; People v. Fisher, 14 Wend. 10 (N.Y. 1835). State v. Donaldsòn, 32 N.J.L. 151 (1867), was one of the last of these cases.

[151] 4 Met. 111 (Mass. 1842).

Act,[152] that it was the policy of the United States to encourage "the practice and procedure of collective bargaining" and to protect "the exercise by workers of full freedom of association, self-organization, and designation of representatives of their own choosing. . . ." In sustaining the statute over constitutional objections, Mr. Chief Justice Hughes declared that the right of workers to self-organization, to bargain collectively through representatives of their own choosing, was a "fundamental right. Employees have as clear a right to organize and select their representatives for lawful purposes as the respondent has to organize its business and select its own officers and agents."[153] He went on to say that long ago the Court had explained the underlying reasons for labor organizations:[154]

> We said that they were organized out of the necessities of the situation; that a single employee was helpless in dealing with an employer; that he was dependent ordinarily on his daily wage for the maintenance of himself and family; that if the employer refused to pay him the wages that he thought fair, he was nevertheless unable to leave the employ and resist arbitrary and unfair treatment; that union was essential to give laborers opportunity to deal on an equality with their employer.

Some years ago a town in Florida adopted an ordinance that in effect made it unlawful to organize or attempt to organize any labor union within the town, and prohibited the solicitation of union

---

[152] Act of July 5, 1935, ch. 372, § 1, 49 Stat. 449. For the forerunner of this concept, see National Industrial Recovery Act, 48 Stat. 198, ch. 90, § 7(a) (1933). The Labor-Management Relations (Taft-Hartley) Act, § 101, 61 Stat. 136 (1947), 29 U.S.C. § 145 (1952), opens with a reaffirmation of the declaration of the Wagner Act that workers are entitled to "full freedom of association, self-organization, and designation of representatives of their own choosing. . . ."

[153] N.L.R.B. v. Jones & Laughlin Steel Corp., 301 U.S. 1, 33 (1937).

[154] *Ibid.* This is a paraphrase of a classic statement of the right of workers to organize trade unions written by Mr. Chief Justice Taft in American Steel Foundries v. Tri-City Central Trades Council, 257 U.S. 184, 209 (1921). See also Brown v. Stoerkel, 74 Mich. 269, 276 (1889), where, speaking of an unincorporated local of the old Knights of Labor, the court said: "It was purely a benevolent and social organization, having also in view the protection, benefit, and welfare of its members in their various employments. It must now be considered as well settled that persons have a right to enter into such associations, and to bind themselves as to their membership and rights in such societies. . . ."

memberships on the streets or in any public place. The Supreme Court of Florida held this ordinance unconstitutional as an abridgement of a fundamental right.[155] The court said it was not permissible to impair "the well settled legal right of employed workers to organize labor unions and to use their powers of persuasion to induce others to join them, so long as no fraud or coercion is resorted to."[156]

Trade unions have generally had the status of unincorporated associations, although under the laws of many states incorporation is available to them. Before the adoption of the Labor-Management Relations Act of 1947, there was some pressure to compel unions to incorporate because of a desire to hold them more effectively liable for wrongful acts. Apprehensions on this score were eliminated by Sections 301 and 303 of the 1947 statute, which make it perfectly clear that unincorporated unions may be used. On the other hand, it is clear that a union may, in many circumstances, sue on behalf of its members since "there is a direct community of interest between it and its members. . . ."[157] The Colorado legislature adopted a Labor Peace Act in 1943 that required all unions to incorporate, but the following year the Colorado Supreme Court held this provision unconstitutional as going beyond the limits of permissible regulation.[158] It held that the statute unconstitutionally denied unincorporated unions the right to assemble and function, and that the guaranty of the right of assembly was not restricted to the literal right of meeting together to petition the government for a redress of grievances.

No one has ever pretended, however, that trade unions are altogether immune from proper statutory regulation, although the Supreme Court will go far in construing an act of Congress to avoid imputing to that body any intention of interfering with a

155 Pittman v. Nix, 152 Fla. 378 (1943). The court relied heavily upon Paramount Enterprises, Inc. v. Mitchell, 104 Fla. 407 (1932), which affirmed a denial of an injunction to restrain union picketing.

156 152 Fla. at 384–85.

157 Brotherhood of Stationary Engineers v. St. Louis, 212 S.W.2d 454 (Mo. App. 1948). An association has no standing to sue in court to enjoin the enforcement of a statute if it is not itself subject to the challenged enactment. Northwestern Pennsylvania Phonograph Ass'n v. Meadville, 359 Pa. 549 (1948); Georgia Music Operators Ass'n v. Atlanta, 183 Ga. 794 (1937).

158 American Federation of Labor v. Reilly, 113 Colo. 90 (1944).

union's exercise of such constitutional rights as that of publishing its views on political matters.[159] Similarly, since union meetings are entitled to privacy, a federal court once enjoined members of the state police from attending union meetings, because it was found that their presence had the effect of active interference.[160] The court asserted that the right to speak freely and to assemble peaceably for any lawful purpose without the interference of officials is not limited to assembling and speaking in a public forum. Equally protected by the Constitution is "the freedom and liberty to express ourselves privately and to hold private assemblies for lawful purposes and in a lawful manner without governmental interference or hindrance. . . ."[161] Similarly, the Supreme Court ruled in 1945 that a state may not require labor organizers to register, since this is an improper restraint upon the rights of free speech and peaceable assembly.[162]

Unions are, however, subject to a variety of limitations. While peaceful persuasion and picketing by union members are lawful,[163] picketing in a context of violence,[164] or for unlawful objectives,[165] as well as unlawful or riotous assembly,[166] are not constitutionally protected. Since there is no constitutional right to injure someone who is not a party to the labor dispute, statutes making secondary

---

159 United States v. C.I.O., 335 U.S. 106 (1948). Coming directly to the point in a concurring opinion, Mr. Justice Rutledge said: "The expression of bloc sentiment is and always has been an integral part of our democratic electoral and legislative processes. They could hardly go on without it." *Id.* at 143. But see Wellington, *supra*, p. 49.

160 Local 309, United Furniture Workers v. Gates, 75 F. Supp. 620 (N.D. Ind. 1948).

161 *Id.* at 624.

162 Thomas v. Collins, 323 U.S. 516 (1945).

163 Thornhill v. Alabama, 310 U.S. 88 (1940); Carlson v. California, 310 U.S. 106 (1940).

164 Milk Wagon Drivers Union v. Meadowmoor Dairies, Inc., 312 U.S. 287 (1941).

165 Giboney v. Empire Storage & Ice Co., 336 U.S. 490 (1949); Building Service Union v. Gazzam, 339 U.S. 532 (1950); Hughes v. Superior Court, 339 U.S. 460 (1950); Teamsters Union v. Hanke, 339 U.S. 470 (1950).

166 Lair v. State, 316 P.2d 225 (Okla. Cr. 1957); State v. Johnson, 89 Iowa 594 (1894).

boycotts illegal have been sustained by the courts.[167] States are at liberty to forbid trade unions to deny membership or otherwise discriminate by reason of race, creed, or color.[168] State legislation outlawing the closed shop has also been sustained on the theory that the state is as free to safeguard the opportunity of non-union workers to get and hold jobs as it is to legislate in favor of union membership.[169] State policy must give way, however, in such areas of federal interest as the railroad field, which is covered by a federal statute[170] permitting union shop agreements.[171] Congress has great latitude in regulating the labor relations of interstate industries, and the choice of the union shop as a stabilizing force is an allowable one. Speaking for a unanimous Court, Mr. Justice Douglas observed that "one would have to be blind to history to assert that trade unionism did not enhance and strengthen the right to work."[172] But the Taft-Hartley Act of 1947 validly forbids the unions to do a great many things that it describes as unfair labor practices.

Membership in a trade union is normally a valuable right, the denial of which is subject to judicial review.[173] To be sure, unions are free to expel members or officers for a variety of reasons, such as publicly criticizing the officers or the board of the union contrary to the union constitution or without permission,[174] or refusing

---

167 See Carpenters & Joiners Union v. Ritter's Cafe, 315 U.S. 722 (1942); State v. Casselman 69 Idaho 237 (1949), *cert. denied*, 338 U.S. 900 (1949). The state may also forbid a union "slow-down" as an unfair labor practice. United Auto Workers v. Wisconsin Employment Relations Board, 336 U.S. 245 (1949).

168 Railway Mail Ass'n v. Corsi, 326 U.S. 88 (1945).

169 Lincoln Union v. Northwestern Iron & Metal Co., 335 U.S. 525 (1949); American Federation of Labor v. American Sash & Door Co., 335 U.S. 538 1949).

170 Railway Labor Act. § 2, Eleventh, 64 Stat. 1238 (1958), 45 U.S.C. § 152, Eleventh (1958).

171 Railway Employes' Dept. v. Hanson, 351 U.S. 225 (1956).

172 *Id.* at 235.

173 See Williams, *The Political Liberties of Labor Union Members*, 32 TEX. L. REV. 826 (1954); Note, *Constitutional Right to Membership in a Labor Union*, 8 J. PUB. L. 580 (1959).

174 Dame v. LeFevre, 251 Wis. 146 (1947); Elfer v. Marine Engineers Beneficial Ass'n, 179 La. 383 (1934); Love v. Grand International Division, B.L.E., 139 Ark. 375 (1919). In Pfoh v. Whitney, 62 N.E.2d 744 (Ohio App. 1945), a member was expelled for circulating a political campaign letter to a number of lodges, without the approval of the president as required by the union constitution. In Hall v.

to pay a special political assessment levied to finance a fight against a state anti-union security law.[175] But courts are quite competent to annul expulsions from unions, and have often done so on various grounds, such as lack of hearing,[176] faulty charge,[177] procedural failures,[178] or invasion of free speech.[179] It has been pointed out that "numerous cases hold that where the expulsion or suspension of a member of the Union affects the individual's property rights, a court of equity will award relief to a member wrongfully expelled or suspended from the Union by decreeing his re-instatement, at least where a resort to the internal remedies within the union would be futile, illusory or useless, or would not accord to the members in question substantial or practical justice."[180]

There has been a great deal of public concern in recent years with issues regarding the uses of trade union power, as the labor movement becomes more and more institutionalized and bureaucratized. In particular, questions have been raised about the rights of rank-and-file members within the unions.[181] Following prolonged hearings by its committees, especially the McClellan Committee, Congress adopted the Labor-Management Reporting and Disclosure Act of 1959,[182] which has not yet been tested in the courts on constitutional grounds. Whether justified or not, its provisions add up to an extraordinary amount of governmental intervention into the affairs of voluntary associations.[183]

Morrin, 293 S.W. 435 (Mo. App. 1927), the member was suspended for five years for bringing a law suit claiming that an international officer had wantonly declared a local election void.

175 DeMille v. American Federation of Radio Artists, 175 P.2d 851 (Cal. App. 1946), *aff'd*, 31 Cal.2d 139 (1947), *cert. denied*, 333 U.S. 876 (1948). But see Wellington, *supra*, p. 49.

176 O'Brien v. Papas, 49 N.Y.S.2d 521 (Sup. Ct. Kings Co. 1944).

177 Johnson v. International of United Brotherhood, 52 Nev. 400 (1930).

178 Polin v. Kaplan, 257 N.Y. 277 (1931).

179 Crossen v. Duffy, 90 Ohio App. 252 (1951). In this case members had been fined for pamphleteering in a union election in opposition to the incumbents.

180 *Id.* at 273–74.

181 See COLEMAN, LIPSET & TROW, UNION DEMOCRACY (1956); Baldwin, *Union Administration and Civil Liberties*, 248 ANNALS 54 (1946).

182 73 Stat. 519 (1959), 29 U.S.C. § 401 *et seq.* (1960). See the symposium on this statute, 48 GEO. L. J. 205 (1959).

183 Title I of this comprehensive statute is entitled: "Bill of Rights of Members of Labor Organizations." The statute declares that "every member of a labor organ-

It remains to be noted that if, as a general proposition, workers in this country have a right to join trade unions, limitations on this right have been recognized in the field of public employment. In the absence of a statute forbidding it, the general rule is that public employees may organize. A notable exception is that policemen are usually forbidden to belong to unions, and courts have invariably upheld such a prohibition.[184] The rationale behind this rule is that policemen have very special functions to perform that require undivided allegiance to the public. These men are paid by all and must act without any favoritism in the discharge of their important duties. It is also stressed that the police force is a semi-military organization, in which order, discipline, and authority are absolutely essential. The fear is expressed that membership in a union might cause friction and dissension, to the prejudice of law enforcement. For about the same reasons American courts regard firemen as constituting a class apart who may be denied the privilege of belonging to trade unions.[185]

---

ization shall have equal rights and privileges within such organization, to attend membership meetings and to participate in the deliberations and voting upon the business of such meetings, subject to reasonable rules and regulations in such organization's constitution and bylaws." § 101(a)(1), 29 U.S.C. § 411(a)(1) (1960). It also provided that "every member of any labor organization shall have the right to meet and assemble freely with other members; and to express any views, arguments, or opinions; and to express at meetings of the labor organization his views, upon candidates in an election of the labor organization or upon any business properly before the meeting, subject to the organization's established and reasonable rules. . . ." § 101(a)(2), 29 U.S.C. § 411(a)(2). The statute then spells out certain safeguards in the levying of dues, initiation fees, and assessments, § 101(a)(3), 29 U.S.C. § 411(a)(3), and protects the members' rights to sue in court or in a proceeding before administrative agencies, § 101(a)(4), 29 U.S.C. § 411(a)(4). Finally, it is stipulated that no member may be fined, suspended, expelled, or otherwise disciplined, except for non-payment of dues, "unless such member has been (A) served with written specific charges; (B) given a reasonable time to prepare his defense; (C) afforded a full and fair hearing." § 101(a)(5), 29 U.S.C. §411(a)(5).

184 Jackson v. McLeod, 199 Miss. 676 (1946), *cert. denied*, 328 U.S. 863 (1946); King v. Priest, 357 Mo. 68 (1947), *appeal dismissed*, 333 U.S. 852 (1948); State Lodge of Michigan v. Detroit, 318 Mich. 182 (1947), *cert. denied*, 332 U.S. 818 (1947); Fraternal Order of Police v. Lansing Board of Comm'rs, 306 Mich. 68 (1943), *cert. denied*, 321 U.S. 784 (1944); Perez v. Board of Police Comm'rs, 78 Cal. App.2d 638 (1947); Goodwin v. Oklahoma City, 199 Okla. 26 (1947).

185 Carter v. Thompson, 164 Va. 312 (1935); Hutchinson v. Magee, 278 Pa. 119 (1923); McNatt v. Lawther, 223 S.W. 503 (Tex. Civ. App. 1920); San Antonio Fire Fighters' Local Union No. 84 v. Bell, 223 S.W. 506 (Tex. Civ. App. 1920).

Except for such special classes as policemen and firemen, city and state employees are generally conceded the right to join unions,[186] though a city does not act unlawfully if it prohibits any of its employees from becoming a member of a labor union.[187] Ever since the Lloyd-La Follette Act of 1912[188] confirmed the right of postal workers to organize unions, the Civil Service Act has recognized that federal employees may organize.[189] But while most governmental employees in the United States are free to join unions, they are not permitted to strike or picket.[190] As Governor Calvin Coolidge of Massachusetts declared so succinctly in connection with the famous Boston police strike: "There is no right to strike against the public safety by anybody, anytime, anywhere."[191] Thus, the Taft-Hartley Act of 1947 provides that "it shall be unlawful for any individual employed by the United States or any agency thereof including wholly owned Government corporations to participate in any strike."[192] The penalty for striking is immediate discharge, forfeiture of civil service status, and ineligibility for reemployment for three years. In addition, Congress has stipulated that no money shall be payable to anyone who strikes against the United States or who belongs to an organization of government workers that asserts that right.[193] Many states now have no-strike statutes of this sort,[194] and it is well established in state decisional law that state governmental employees may not engage in strikes.[195]

---

186 See Hagan v. Picard, 171 Misc. 475 (Sup. Ct. Albany Co. 1939), *aff'd*, 258 App. Div. 771 (3d Dept. 1939).

187 C.I.O. v. Dallas 198 S.W.2d 143 (Tex. Civ. App. 1946).

188 37 Stat. 539 (1912), 5 U.S.C. § 652(c)(d) (1958).

189 37 Stat. 555 1912), as amended, 62 Stat. 354 (1948), 5 U.S.C. § 652(c) (1952).

190 Strikes against government have occurred. See ZISKIND, ONE THOUSAND STRIKES OF GOVERNMENT EMPLOYEES (1940); SPERO, GOVERNMENT AS EMPLOYER (1948); LEEK, GOVERNMENT AND LABOR IN THE UNITED STATES ch. 15 (1952).

191 See WHITE, PURITAN IN BABYLON 166 (1938).

192 61 Stat. 136, § 305 (1947), 29 U.S.C. § 145 (1952).

193 60 Stat. 910, 918 (1946), as amended, 69 Stat. 624 (1955), 5 U.S.C. §§ 118p–118r (1958).

194 See, *e.g.*, NEW YORK CIVIL SERVICE LAW § 108.

195 See Los Angeles v. Los Angeles Bldg. & Constr. Trades Council, 94 Cal. App.2d 36 (1949); Broadwater v. Otto, 370 Pa. 611 (1952); Goodfellow v. Detroit Civil Service Commission, 312 Mich. 226 (1945).

In addition, governments in the United States, with a few exceptions, do not and may not enter into collective bargaining agreements with unions of public employees for reasons of public policy.[196] Thus, federal labor relations statutes, such as the Labor-Management Relations Act of 1947,[197] the Fair Labor Standards Act of 1938,[198] and the War Labor Disputes Act of 1943,[199] exclude public employment from their operations. Accordingly, the National War Labor Board held in 1942 that it had no jurisdiction over unions of public employees in several large cities. Dean Wayne Morse, the public member of the Board, declared that "the well established doctrines in American law pertaining to the sovereign rights of state and local governments, clearly exclude such disputes from the jurisdiction and powers of the Board."[200] It follows that while most public employees may organize, their organizations have limited powers and are not conceded to have normal collective bargaining rights.[201] As the Missouri Supreme Court explained a few years ago, collective bargaining is inappropriate because the wages and hours of public employees are fixed by statute or ordinance and cannot be the subject of bargaining.[202] It noted that "legislative discretion cannot be lawfully bargained away and no citizen or group of citizens have any right to a contract for any legislation or to prevent legislation."[203] It is wholly improper to have government by private agreement. "Under our form of government," it de-

---

196 See Vogel, *What about the Rights of the Public Employees?* 1 Lab. L.J. 604 (1950). The controlling statute, 48 Stat. 58, § 3 (1933), 16 U.S.C. § 831(b) (1952), permits TVA to bargain with employee unions and there is real bargaining in TVA.

197 61 Stat. 137, § 101 (1947), 29 U.S.C. § 152(2) (1952).

198 52 Stat. 1060, § 3 (1938), 29 U.S.C. § 203(d) (1952).

199 57 Stat. 163, § 2 (1943), 50 U.S.C. §§ 1501, 1502(d) (1952).

200 Teller, Labor Disputes and Collective Bargaining 116 (1947 Supp.).

201 See National Council of Railway Patrolmen's Union v. Sealy, 56 F. Supp. 720 (S.D. Tex. 1944); State v. Brotherhood of R. Trainmen, 37 Cal.2d 412 (1951), *cert. denied*, 342 U.S. 876 (1951); Nutter v. Santa Monica, 74 Cal. App.2d 292 (1946); Miami Water Works, Local 654 v. Miami, 157 Fla. 445 (1946); Mugford v. Mayor and City Council of Baltimore, 185 Md. 266 (1945); Cleveland v. Division 268, 30 Ohio Ops. 395 (Com. Pl. Cuyahoga Co. 1945). Most of these cases held that state labor relations acts or federal labor statutes do not apply to city or state employees.

202 Springfield v. Clouse, 356 Mo. 1239 (1947).

203 *Id.* at 1248–49.

clared, "public office or employment never has been and cannot become a matter of bargaining and contract."[204] The questions at issue involve the exercise of legislative powers, and they cannot be delegated away by those to whom the Constitution gives such powers. It should be added that governmental appropriations are not made out of any profit motive, but in furtherance of over-all fiscal policies that often involve important political considerations.[205] Thus, the courts hold that a municipality may not enter into an agreement with a union or group of unions under which it commits itself to employ only union labor.[206] This is regarded as a discrimination against non-union labor. The courts of Maryland and New York, however, have taken the position that if the worker so requests, a city may deduct union dues from wages.[207] The Ohio Supreme Court has ruled against the check-off on the ground that a municipal corporation is not an "employer" and a civil service appointee is not an "employee" within the meaning of the check-off statute.[208]

In a much-quoted letter to the National Federation of Federal Employees, dated August 16, 1937, President Franklin D. Roosevelt wrote:[209]

> All government employees should realize that the process of collective bargaining, as usually understood, cannot be trans-

---

204 *Id.* at 1251.

205 See Railway Mail Ass'n v. Murphy, 180 Misc. 868 (Sup. Ct. Albany Co. 1943): "Much as we all recognize the value and necessity of collective bargaining in industrial and social life, nonetheless, such bargaining is impossible between the Government and its employees, by reason of the very nature of Government itself. . . . Collective bargaining has no place in government service. The employer is the whole people."

206 The leading case is Adams v. Brenen, 177 Ill. 194 (1898). See Note, *Right of Municipality To Enter into Collective Bargaining Agreement on Behalf of Civil Service Employees*, 18 N.Y.U. L.Q. Rev. 247 (1941); Rhyne, *Power of Municipalities To Enter into Labor Union Contracts—A Survey of Law and Experience*, National Institute of Municipal Law Officers, Report No. 76 (1941).

207 Mugford v. Mayor and City Council of Baltimore, 185 Md. 266 (1945), noted 94 U. Pa. L. Rev. 427 (1946); Kirkpatrick v. Reid, 193 Misc. 702 (Sup. Ct. N.Y. Co. 1948).

208 Hagerman v. Dayton, 147 Ohio St. 313 (1947).

209 See The Public Papers and Addresses of Franklin D. Roosevelt 325 (Rosenman ed. 1937).

> planted into the public service. It has its distinct and insurmountable limitations when applied to public personnel management. The very nature and purpose of government make it impossible for administrative officials to represent fully or to bind the employer in mutual discussions with government employee organizations. The employer is the whole people, who speak by means of laws enacted by their representatives in Congress. Accordingly, administrative employees and officials alike are governed and guided, and in many instances restricted, by laws which establish policies, procedures, or rules in personnel matters.

This position is amply reflected in the decisions of American courts.[210]

VIII. The Right of Association and Exposure by Government

It is usually not difficult for business corporations to secure charters from the states, since all states seek to encourage business activity. But many states have special laws dealing with the incorporation of nonprofit associations that give administrative officials some discretion to refuse charters under certain circumstances. There seem to be two vaguely defined criteria for such refusal, both of dubious constitutionality: the association must be in accord with public policy,[211] and the association must not conduct activities already adequately performed by existing organizations.[212] In any event, it is clear that corporations, whether for profit or not, are entitled to the enjoyment of some of our basic constitutional guaranties. While the "liberty" guaranties of the Due Process Clauses of the Constitution are construed as applying only to natural persons,[213] corporations are regarded as persons within the meaning of

---

210 See United States v. United Mine Workers, 330 U.S. 258 (1947).

211 See, *e.g.*, *In re* Mazzini Cultural Center, 185 Misc. 1031 (Sup. Ct. Kings Co. 1945); *In re* Patriotic Citizenship Ass'n, 53 N.Y.S.2d 595 (Sup. Ct. Kings Co. 1945).

212 See, *e.g.*, *In re* Marine Corps Veterans Foundation, 79 N.Y.S.2d 18 (Sup. Ct. Kings Co. 1948); *In re* Voters Alliance for Americans of German Ancestry, 64 N.Y.S.2d 298 (Sup. Ct. N.Y. Co. 1946); Comment, *State Control over Political Organizations: First Amendment Checks on Powers of Regulation*, 66 Yale L.J. 545 (1957).

213 See, *e.g.*, Pierce v. Society of Sisters, 268 U.S. 510, 535 (1925); Western Turf Ass'n v. Greenberg, 204 U.S. 359, 363 (1907); Northwestern National Life Ins. Co. v. Riggs, 203 U.S. 243, 255 (1906).

the "property" part of these guaranties,[214] and by extending the meaning of "property" the Supreme Court has protected the "liberty" of corporations,[215] and relief has also been given to the agents of unincorporated associations.[216]

On the other hand, ever since the end of World War II, and as a consequence largely of "cold war" pressures, questions have arisen regarding the right of government to inquire into the facts of membership in certain types of associations. It is now established that it is constitutionally permissible for the state and national governments to ask individuals whether they are or have ever been members of the Communist Party,[217] and to determine whether public employees are members of subversive associations.[218] The rights of speech and assembly, the Pennsylvania court recently asserted, "do not extend to freedom to meet with others, knowingly and deliberately, for the discussion of plans to overthrow the government by force or violence," and it ruled accordingly that a nurse in a city hospital could be required to state whether she was, knowingly, a member of an organization advocating overthrow of the government by unlawful means.[219] In fact, the federal government now

---

214 See, *e.g.*, Liggett Co. v. Baldridge, 278 U.S. 105 (1928); Smyth v. Ames, 169 U.S. 466, 522 (1898).

215 See, *e.g.*, Pierce v. Society of Sisters, 268 U.S. 510, 535 (1925); Grosjean v. American Press Co., 297 U.S. 233, 244 (1936); Joseph Burstyn, Inc. v. Wilson, 343 U.S. 495 (1952); Pennekamp v. Florida, 328 U.S. 331 (1946).

216 See, *e.g.*, Hague v. C.I.O., 307 U.S. 496 (1939); Thomas v. Collins, 323 U.S. 516 (1945); Thornhill v Alabama, 310 U.S. 88 (1940).

217 Barenblatt v. United States, 360 U.S. 109 (1959); Barsky v. United States, 167 F.2d 241 (D.C. Cir. 1948), *cert denied*, 334 U.S. 843 (1941); United States v. Josephson, 165 F.2d 82 (2d Cir. 1947), *cert. denied*, 333 U.S. 838 (1948), Lawson v. United States, 176 F.2d 49 (D.C. Cir. 1949), *cert. denied*, 339 U.S. 934 (1950); State v. James, 36 Wash.2d 882 (1950).

218 See Bailey v. Richardson, 182 F.2d 46 (D.C. Cir. 1950), *aff'd by equally divided court*, 341 U.S. 918 (1951); Garner v. Board of Public Works of Los Angeles, 341 U.S. 716 (1951) (municipal employees); Lerner v. Casey, 357 U.S. 468 (1958) (city subway conductor); Beilan v. Board of Education, 357 U.S. 399 (1958) (schoolteacher); Thorp v. Board of Trustees of Newark, 6 N.J. 498 (1951), *judgment vacated for mootness*, 342 U.S. 803 (1951) (schoolteacher); *In re* Coon, 44 Cal. App.2d 531 (1941) (employee of state relief administration); see also BROWN, LOYALTY AND SECURITY (1958).

219 Fitzgerald v. Philadelphia, 376 Pa. 379, 386 (1954). See Cramton, *The Supreme Court and State Power To Deal with Subversion and Loyalty*, 43 MINN. L. REV. 1025 (1959).

has a considerable body of legislation that requires individuals to disclose certain facts of association about themselves. Thus, the Taft-Hartley Act required the officers of trade unions, as a condition of enjoying access to the facilities of the National Labor Relations Board, to sign affidavits of non-Communist membership, and the requirement was upheld by the Supreme Court.[220] The McCarran Internal Security Act of 1950[221] requires registration with the Attorney General of "Communist-action" organizations, together with the names and addresses of all officers and members, and of "Communist-front" organizations, with identification of their officers. This statute was amended by the Communist Control Act of 1954[222] to include "Communist-infiltrated organizations." All foreign agents, whether employed by their governments or by organizations subsidized by foreign governments, must register under the Foreign Agents Registration Act of 1938.[223] The Voorhis Anti-Propaganda Act of 1940[224] provides for the registration with the Attorney General of all organizations under foreign control that participate in civilian, military, or political activity. Federal laws require many other classes of people to register, including aliens,[225] lobbyists with Congress,[226] and persons who own publications that use second-class mailing privileges.[227]

---

220 American Communications Ass'n v. Douds, 339 U.S. 382 (1950). This requirement was dropped by the Labor-Management Reporting and Disclosure Act of 1959, 73 Stat. 519, 29 U.S.C. § 401 *et seq.* (1960).

221 64 Stat. 987, §§ 7, 8, 50 U.S.C. §§ 781 *et seq.* See Communist Party v. Subversive Activities Control Board, 351 U.S. 115 (1956). Membership in subversive organizations is made an offense in the Smith Act of 1940, 54 Stat. 670, § 2(3). See Communist Party v. Subversive Activities Control Board, 367 U.S. 1 (1961).

222 68 Stat. 775, 50 U.S.C. §§ 841–44 (1958). For a construction of the California Subversive Organization Registration Act of 1941, see People v. Noble, 68 Cal. App.2d 853 (1945).

223 52 Stat. 631 (1938), as amended, 53 Stat. 1244 (1939), 56 Stat. 248 (1942), 64 Stat. 399 (1950), 22 U.S.C. §§ 601, 611–16 (1958).

224 53 Stat. 1201 (1940), 18 U.S.C. § 2386 (1958).

225 66 Stat. 224 (1952), 8 U.S.C. §§ 1302, 1303 (1958).

226 60 Stat. 839 (1946), 2 U.S.C. §§ 261–70 (1958), upheld in United States v. Harriss, 347 U.S. 612 (1954). See Note, *Registration of Groups Tending To Influence Public Opinion*, 48 COLUM. L. REV. 589 (1948).

227 37 Stat. 553 (1923), 39 U.S.C. § 233 (1958), upheld in Lewis Publishing Co. v. Morgan, 229 U.S. 288 (1913).

The Supreme Court is willing to permit the states to go a long way in prying into the membership of associations alleged to be subversive. Thus in *Uphaus v. Wyman*,[228] the Court upheld a conviction for civil contempt where a witness testifying before a New Hampshire legislative investigating committee refused to name certain persons whose identity the investigation was seeking to establish. Uphaus had been Executive Director of World Fellowship, Inc., a voluntary corporation organized under the laws of New Hampshire which maintained a summer camp in the state. In defiance of a subpoena, Uphaus, who testified as to his own activities, declined to supply the names of all persons who had attended the camp during two previous summers. By a vote of five to four, the Supreme Court overruled several objections, including the argument that the state's action violated the rights of free speech and association. Speaking for the Court, Mr. Justice Clark maintained that the public interests involved outweighed the private interests in associational privacy. The state, he said, is legitimately concerned with the presence of subversives in the state, and the Attorney General of New Hampshire, who conducted the investigation, was found to have reason to believe that the guests might have been subversive persons. It was noted, for example, that at least nineteen speakers at the camp had Communist affiliations. Thus it was thought that the state had established the existence of a nexus between World Fellowship, Inc., and subversive activities. Since the state regarded the Communist Party as posing a serious threat to the security of the state, the Court majority concluded that the investigation had been undertaken in the interest of self-preservation, the ultimate value in any society. "This governmental interest," said Mr. Justice Clark, "outweighs individual rights in an associational privacy which, however real in other circumstances, . . . were here tenuous at best."[229] For it was noted that the camp, as a public one, was required by New Hampshire law to maintain a register open to police inspection. It was thus concluded that the disclosure of the names of the guests would be an inescapable incident of an investigation into the presence of subversive persons within the state.[230]

---

[228] 360 U.S. 72 (1959).

[229] *Id.* at 80.

[230] The four dissenting Justices could find no rational connection with a discernible legislative purpose. They thought that what was involved was over-

The Court is not willing to sanction such prying into associational membership, however, where the association is not subversive and is not engaged in unlawful activities. Here the interest in privacy and the right to associate take priority over asserted public interests. This point has been driven home in recent years in the campaign of some Southern states against the National Association for the Advancement of Colored People, which has spearheaded the drive of the Negroes of the country for the enjoyment of equal rights. Far from being subversive, the overriding purpose of the NAACP is to translate into actuality for all people, regardless of race or color, their basic constitutional rights. Those who seek to deny them their rights are subversive. American Negroes have not been seduced by Communism,[231] and Mr. J. Edgar Hoover recently pointed out that the NAACP has always vigorously denounced and fought Communist attempts at infiltration.[232]

Since the *School Segregation Cases* of 1954[233] many Southern states have carried on sustained and varied legislative and administrative harassment of the NAACP.[234] The attack has proceeded on many fronts. Since one of the principal functions of the NAACP is to manage and finance law suits in behalf of individual Negro complainants,[235] Southern states have adopted new and more stringent laws dealing with the offences of champerty, maintenance, and barratry,[236] or have intensified the enforcement of existing laws of this

---

whelmingly "a roving self-contained investigation of individual and group behavior, and behavior in a constitutionally protected area." *Id.* at 100. They insisted that there was no showing that this simple, wide-ranging exposure campaign was designed to implement a valid legislative purpose, but was merely exposure purely for the sake of exposure.

231 See RECORD, THE NEGRO AND THE COMMUNIST PARTY (1951).

232 MASTERS OF DECEIT 246–47, 252 (1958).

233 Brown v. Board of Education, 347 U.S. 483 (1954).

234 See Murphy, *The South Counterattacks: The Anti-NAACP Laws*, 12 WEST'N POL. Q. 371 (1959); McKay, *The Repression of Civil Rights as an Aftermath of the School Segregation Cases*, 4 HOW. L.J. 9 (1958); *Freedom of Association*, 4 RACE REL. L. REP. 207 (1959).

235 See Vose, *NAACP Strategy in the Covenant Cases*, 6 WEST'N RES. L. REV. 101 (1955).

236 Radin, *Maintenance by Champerty*, 24 CALIF. L. REV. 48 (1935). See Gammons v. Johnson, 76 Minn, 76, 81 (1899): "The general purpose of the law against champerty and maintenance and barratry was to prevent officious intermeddlers

type.[237] In addition, these states have expanded the enforcement of the criminal law, especially on grounds of breach of the peace and disorderly conduct, denied public employment to members of the NAACP, and embarked upon fresh regulation of the local aspects of foreign corporations under general corporation laws. The principal weapon has been to seek to identify publicly the members of the various NAACP chapters and thus expose them to severe community reprisals, such as the loss of employment, the calling or denial of bank loans, foreclosure of mortgages, and assorted types of violence.

The effort to disclose the identity of the members of the NAACP has taken many forms: exploitation of the traditional power of state legislatures to conduct investigations,[238] enactment of new registration statutes requiring submission of the names of contributors and members,[239] and other stratagems designed to bring into the open the names of members of the Association.[240]

In addition to the *Gremillion*[241] case in the 1960 Term, the Supreme Court has disposed of two major cases involving the issue of disclosure of membership lists, one in 1958 and one in 1960. In both

---

from stirring up strife and contention by vexatious or speculative litigation, which would disturb the peace of society, lead to corrupt practices, and prevent the remedial process of the law."

237 See *Inciting Litigation*, 3 RACE REL. L. REP. 1257 (1958).

238 See Gibson v. Florida Legislative Investigation Com. 108 So.2d 729 (Fla. 1958), *cert. denied*, 360 U.S. 919 (1959). While this case upheld a wide legislative power to investigate on this score, it involved only an investigation of Communism, and the court cautioned that it should not be used to conduct witch-hunts, or "merely for the sake of disclosure." For recent legislation authorizing investigations see S.C. Acts 1956, act 920; La. H. Con. Res. No. 27, 1954, and No. 9, 1956; Va. Laws 1956, Extra Sess., chs. 34, 37; Ga. Res. Act 18, 1958; Ga. House Res. Nos. 8, 11, 1957; Fla. Laws 1956, ch. 31498; Fla. Laws 1957, ch. 57–125; Miss. H.B. 1956, ch. 880, Miss. S.B. 1958, ch. 1973 (State Sovereignty Commission); Ark. Acts 1957, No. 83; Ark. Acts 1958, No. 13 (State Sovereignty Commission).

239 See Ark. Acts 1957, No. 85, Ark. Acts 1958, Nos. 10, 12 (Extraordinary Sess.); Ark. Acts 1959, No. 225; S.C. Acts 1957, No. 223; TENN. CODE ANN. § 39-5001–7, § 39-827–34 (Supp. 1958); Tex. H.B. 1957, No. 239 (not enacted following opinion of Attorney General of Texas, May 21, 1957); VA. CODE §§ 18-349.9–17 (Supp. 1959); Ga. Acts 1958, No. 321; LA. REV. STAT. tit. 12, §§ 401 *et seq.* (1950).

240 Robison, *Protection of Associations from Compulsory Disclosure of Membership*, 58 COLUM. L. REV. 614 (1958).

241 See text at note 1 *supra*.

cases the Justices were also unanimously on the side of the NAACP membership.[242] In the first case, *NAACP v. Alabama*,[243] the Court had before it a judgment of civil contempt which Alabama courts had entered against the Association when the Association refused to comply with a court order requiring the production of its membership lists. The issue had arisen when the state's attorney general brought an equity suit, under the Alabama foreign corporations act, to enjoin any further activity of the NAACP, a nonprofit New York corporation, in the state. The NAACP, in the belief that it was exempt, did not comply with the statute. The Alabama court granted an immediate restraining order, and the state then moved for the production of many records and papers, including the names of all agents and members. When the Association refused to comply with the production order regarding its membership lists, it was held in civil contempt and fined $100,000.

All the Justices of the Supreme Court agreed that the state judgment must be reversed on the ground that the production order violated due process. They took the position that group association undeniably enhances effective advocacy of both public and private points of view, and that there is therefore a "close nexus" between the freedoms of speech and assembly. "It is beyond debate," said Mr. Justice Harlan, "that freedom to engage in association for the advancement of beliefs and ideas is an inseparable aspect of the 'liberty' assured by the Due Process Clause of the Fourteenth Amendment."[244] It is important to note that this was the first time that the Supreme Court used the phrase "the right of association" in a forthright constitutional holding. Mr. Justice Harlan added that, "of course, it is immaterial whether the beliefs sought to be advanced by association pertain to political, economic, religious or cul-

---

[242] One case reached the Court testing the validity of the new Virginia laws on registration and barratry, which were designed to discourage litigation on school integration, Harrison v. NAACP, 360 U.S. 167 (1959), but it was held that the federal district court should have abstained from deciding the merits of the issues until the state courts had a reasonable opportunity to construe the statutes. Three Justices, dissenting, protested that where there had been state defiance of the citizen's constitutional rights, the customary reasons for showing this sort of deference to state institutions vanish.

[243] 357 U.S. 449 (1958).

[244] *Id.* at 460.

tural matters, and state action which may have the effect of curtailing the freedom to associate is subject to the closest scrutiny."[245] The Court held, further, that the fact that Alabama had taken no direct action to restrict the right of NAACP members to associate freely was not decisive, since, in the area of indispensable liberties, abridgement may follow from various forms of governmental action. "It is hardly a novel perception," said Mr. Justice Harlan, "that compelled disclosure of affiliation with groups engaged in advocacy may constitute as effective a restraint on freedom of association," as other forms of action previously held to be interferences with freedom of speech.[246] "This Court has recognized," he noted, "the vital relationship between freedom to associate and privacy in one's associations. . . . Inviolability of privacy in group association may in many circumstances be indispensable to preservation of freedom of association, particularly where a group espouses dissident beliefs."[247] Thus the Court concluded that the production order entailed the likelihood of a substantial restraint upon the exercise by the members of the NAACP of their right to freedom of association. It was noted that the NAACP had incontrovertibly shown that on past occasions revealing the identity of rank-and-file members had exposed them to economic reprisal, loss of employment, threats of physical coercion, and other manifestations of public hostility. It followed that compelled disclosure of membership is likely to affect adversely the ability of the NAACP and its members to pursue their collective effort to foster beliefs that they have an admitted right to advocate. And the Court declared that it was not a sufficient answer to say that repression would be due to private community pressures and not to state action, since an exercise of state power would have invoked the pressure.

The Court took the position that Alabama had not demonstrated an interest in obtaining the disclosures that sufficiently justified the deterrent effect that the disclosures would have on the free exercise of the constitutionally protected right of association. Alabama declared that its interest was to determine whether the NAACP was conducting an intrastate business in violation of its foreign corporation registration statute. The Court ruled that the disclosure of the names of the members of the NAACP had no substantial bearing on

---

[245] *Id.* at 460–61. [246] *Id.* at 462. [247] *Ibid.*

this issue. Finally the Court distinguished its 1928 decision in the *Zimmerman* case[248] on the ground that it was based on the nature of the Klan, which engaged in acts of unlawful intimidation and violence, made no effort to comply with any provisions of the New York statute, and declined to give the state any information at all. In contrast, it was pointed out that the NAACP had not refused to comply with Alabama law, but only declined to give the names of its members. It had even been willing to give the names of its officers.

The issue of compulsory disclosure of NAACP membership lists reached the Supreme Court again in 1960, in *Bates v. City of Little Rock*,[249] and again by unanimous vote the position taken in the *Alabama* case was reaffirmed. Whereas in the earlier case the local effort was tied to a purported attempt to enforce the foreign corporation law, in the case of Little Rock an attempt was made to tie it to the local taxing power. Pursuant to statute, Little Rock had for some years, by ordinance, imposed annual license taxes on a broad variety of businesses, occupations, and professions. An amendment adopted in 1957 required any organization operating within the city to give the city clerk, on request, certain information, including the names of all who paid dues, assessments, or contributions, and provided as well that all such information should be public. The custodian of the local branch of the NAACP supplied all the information demanded by the ordinance except the names of members and contributors, on the stated grounds of fear of harassment, economic reprisals, bodily harm, and violation of the Constitution. Evidence at the trial showed that many members had declined to renew their membership because of the ordinance.

Reversing the conviction, the Supreme Court pointed out that the framers of the Constitution regarded the right of peaceable assembly, like freedom of speech and press, "to lie at the foundation of a government based upon the consent of an informed citizenry . . . ," and that "it is now beyond dispute that freedom of association for the purpose of advancing ideas and airing grievances is pro-

---

[248] New York *ex rel.* Bryant v. Zimmerman, 278 U.S. 63 (1928); see section IX, *infra.*

[249] 361 U.S. 516. See Karst, *Legislative Facts in Constitutional Litigation*, 1960 Sup. Ct. Rev. 75, 89.

tected by the Due Process Clause of the Fourteenth Amendment from invasion by the States."[250] Furthermore, this freedom is protected "not only against heavy-handed frontal attack, but also from being stifled by more subtle governmental interference."[251] The Court was satisfied that the record showed that the compulsory disclosure of membership lists in this instance "would work a significant interference with the freedom of association of their members,"[252] since there was substantial uncontroverted evidence that public identification of memberships would be followed by harassment, threats of bodily harm, fear of community hostility, and economic reprisals, and that former members had been induced to withdraw and potential ones not to join. The Court concluded, therefore, that the threat of "substantial government encroachment upon important and traditional aspects of individual freedom is neither speculative nor remote."[253]

To be sure, the City of Little Rock asserted its interest in the taxing power, conceded by all to be a basic function of government. But the Court could find no relevant correlation between the city's power to impose occupation license taxes and the compulsory disclosure and publication of membership lists. For the city had never asserted a tax claim against the NAACP, and the Association had never claimed an exemption. Thus the city had failed to show "a controlling justification for the deterrence of free association. . . ."[254]

In December, 1960, the Supreme Court once again came to the defense of associational freedom in *Shelton v. Tucker*,[255] this time by the close margin of one vote. The Court held unconstitutional an Arkansas statute adopted in 1958 which provided that, as a condition of employment in any state-supported school or college, every teacher must file annually an affidavit listing every organization to which he has belonged or regularly contributed money within the preceding five years. The Court majority agreed with the minority that there is no doubt about the right of a state to investigate the competence and fitness of those it hires to teach in its schools, and that there is no constitutional requirement that a teacher's classroom conduct should be the sole criterion of his fit-

250 361 U.S. at 522–23.
251 *Id.* at 523.
252 *Ibid.*
253 *Id.* at 524.
254 *Id.* at 527.
255 364 U.S. 479.

ness.[256] On the other hand, the majority thought it indisputable that "to compel a teacher to disclose his every associational tie is to impair the teacher's right of free association, a right closely allied to freedom of speech and a right which, like free speech, lies at the foundation of a free society."[257] Furthermore, said Mr. Justice Stewart, this interference with personal freedom "is conspicuously accented when the teacher serves at the absolute will of those to whom the disclosure must be made. . . ."[258] As a matter of fact, he observed that even without disclosure, the pressure on a teacher to avoid any ties that might displease those who control his professional destiny would be constant and heavy. The issue was not whether Arkansas may ask its teachers about certain specified associational ties that are relevant to the issue of their professional fitness, but whether it may ask every teacher to disclose every single organization with which he has been associated over a five-year period. Since the scope of the inquiry is completely unlimited, applying to all sorts of memberships, religious, political, professional, avocational, etc., it will include many that can have no possible bearing upon the teacher's fitness. Thus the Court concluded that "the statute's comprehensive interference with associational freedom goes far beyond what might be justified in the exercise of the State's legitimate inquiry into the fitness and competency of its teachers."[259]

The dissenting Justices argued that the statute was valid on its face, since they saw a relation between the required disclosure and a governmental interest justifying it. But they agreed that should the information be used to further a scheme of terminating the employment of teachers solely because of their membership in unpopular organizations, such a use would violate due process. A record of discriminatory administration would make a difference, but the case went up without a record of administration. It follows that while the Justices were divided in ruling on the validity of the statute on its face, they shared a wide area of agreement as to its possible effects.

---

256 See Beilan v. Board of Education, 357 U.S. 399 (1958).

257 364 U.S. at 485–86.

258 *Id.* at 486.

259 *Id.* at 490.

IX. THE ANTI-KLAN LAWS

The revival of the Ku Klux Klan, particularly in the South, in the years immediately following World War I,[260] quickly led to a situation that tested the limits of the right of association. The Klan created a serious problem for a number of reasons: it operated in secret; it functioned through a membership bound by oaths; it regularly resorted to the use of masks to conceal members' identity; and, above all, it depended upon stirring up fear and prejudice through intimidation and the disregard of law. In short, terrorism was its standard weapon, and under the cloak of its operations, murders, lynchings, bombings, arsons, and whippings occurred. As a result, some state legislatures began to adopt anti-Klan laws.[261]

The earliest of these laws, and the best known, was that of the State of New York, adopted in 1923.[262] Known as the Walker Law, it provides—it is still on the books—that with the exception of labor unions, student fraternities and sororities, and benevolent orders, all oath-bound organizations having more than twenty members must submit annual registration statements to the secretary of state, including a list of officers and roster of membership. The statute was definitely aimed at the Klan. When a Klan officer named George W. Bryant refused to file the necessary registration statement, he was arrested for violating the law. Bryant sued for habeas corpus in the state courts on the ground that the law was unconstitutional. The New York Supreme Court dismissed the petition,[263] the Appellate Division affirmed by a 4–1 vote,[264] and the

---

260 See MECKLIN, THE KU KLUX KLAN (1924); FROST, THE CHALLENGE OF THE KLAN (1924); MYERS, HISTORY OF BIGOTRY IN THE UNITED STATES chs. 14–16 (1943).

261 See Comment, *Anti-Mask and Anti-Klan Laws*, 1 J. PUB. L. 182 (1952).

262 N.Y. Sess. Laws 1923, ch. 664. The statute was amended by N.Y. Sess. Laws 1925, ch. 251, and is now N.Y. CIVIL RIGHTS LAW § 53. Louisiana adopted an anti-Klan law in 1924, La. Acts 1924, No. 2, now LA. REV. STAT. §§ 12:401–409 (1950). The Louisiana law is much broader than that of New York, applying to all "fraternal, patriotic, charitable, benevolent, literary, scientific, athletic, military, or social" organizations, exempting only "regularly organized churches, or National Guard organizations." While this law was not used effectively against the Klan, it has been revived recently for action against the NAACP.

263 People *ex rel.* Bryant v. Sheriff of Erie County, 123 Misc. 859 (Sup. Ct. Erie Co. 1924). The court said: "It is a matter of common knowledge that this organiza-

New York Court of Appeals affirmed unanimously, Judge Pound declaring that "the Legislature may take notice of the potentialities of evil in secret societies and may regulate them reasonably. . . ."[265]

In *New York* ex rel. *Bryant v. Zimmerman*,[266] the Supreme Court sustained the constitutionality of the statute.[267] Speaking for the Court, Mr. Justice Van Devanter declared that the liberty of association, "like most other personal rights, must yield to the rightful exertion of the police power. There can be no doubt that under that power the State may prescribe and apply to associations having an oath-bound membership any reasonable regulation calculated to confine their purposes and activities within limits which are consistent with the rights of others and the public welfare."[268] He thought that the registration requirement was reasonable, "on the two-fold theory that the State within whose territory and under whose protection the association exists is entitled to be informed of its nature and purpose, of whom it is composed and by whom its activities are conducted, and that requiring this information to be supplied for the public files will operate as an effective or substantial deterrent from the violations of public and private right to which the association might be tempted if such a disclosure were not required. The requirement is not arbitrary or oppressive, but reasonable and likely to be of real effect."[269] Finally the Court rejected the main contention advanced by Bryant, that by making the exceptions it did, the statute violated the Equal Protection Clause. It concluded that the legislative classification was reasonable and not arbitrary because the legislature could reasonably conclude

---

tion functions largely at night, its members disguised by hoods and gowns, and doing things calculated to strike terror into the minds of the people."

264 People *ex rel.* Bryant v. Zimmerman, 213 App. Div. 414 (4th Dept. 1925). The court concluded that the statute was a valid "police regulation for the general welfare and safety of the people of the state."

265 People *ex rel.* Bryant v. Zimmerman, 241 N.Y. 405, 410 (1926).

266 278 U.S. 63 (1928).

267 All the Justices agreed on the merits, but Mr. Justice McReynolds voted to dismiss the writ of error on the jurisdictional ground that Bryant had not properly raised any federal question and the real controversy between the parties involved no substantial federal question.

268 278 U.S. at 72.

269 *Ibid.*

that for the Klan (and associations like it) there was a "manifest tendency . . . to make the secrecy surrounding its purposes and membership a cloak for acts and conduct inimical to personal rights and public welfare. . . ."[270]

The Court referred to extensive testimony regarding the Klan, particularly to a recent Congressional hearing,[271] and noted that the legislature had before it uncontroverted evidence:[272]

> that the order was a revival of the Ku Klux Klan of an earlier time with additional features borrowed from the Know Nothing and the A.P.A. orders of other periods; that its membership was limited to native born, gentile, protestant whites; that in part of its constitution and printed creed it proclaimed the widest freedom for all and full adherence to the Constitution of the United States, in another exacted of its members an oath to shield and preserve "white supremacy," and in still another declared any person actively opposing its principles to be "a dangerous ingredient in the body politic of our country and an enemy to the weal of our national commonwealth"; that it was conducting a crusade against Catholics, Jews and Negroes and stimulating hurtful religious and race prejudices; that it was striving for political power and assuming a sort of guardianship over the administration of local, state and national affairs; and that at times it was taking into its own hands the punishment of what some of its members conceived to be crimes.

Mr. Justice Van Devanter concluded that the state courts were right in holding that there was "a real and substantial basis" for the distinction that the statute made between the regulated and the unregulated associations.[273] But it is also worth noting that the Court did not discuss the argument that to repress through exposure was the purpose of the statute.

When Klan activity, again largely in the South, was revived following World War II, the state legislatures again began to write

---

270 *Id.* at 75.

271 Hearings on "The Ku Klux Klan" before the House Committee on Rules, 57th Cong., 1st Sess. (1921).

272 278 U.S. at 76–77.

273 The New York courts have ruled that an organization that exacts only a pledge of its members is not within the coverage of this statute. People v. Mueller, 255 App. Div. 316 (2d Dept. 1938), *appeal dismissed,* 280 N.Y. 669 (1939).

new anti-Klan statutes, of which a 1951 South Carolina act is a good example.[274] Following the example of about a dozen other states,[275] this statute prohibits the wearing of masks in public places and forbids entering the premises of another while wearing a mask, without the permission of the owner of the property. The statute also forbids cross-burning in any public place or on any person's property without his prior permission. Several states now have provisions regarding the burning of crosses that are similar to the South Carolina act. States with a "strong" anti-mask law make it a crime to wear a mask in public; the "weak" laws on the subject require proof of intent to commit a breach of the peace. Thus the Tennessee statute forbids people to prowl or ride or walk about masked or in disguise "to the disturbance of the peace, or to the alarming of the citizens. . . ."[276]

The Supreme Court of Wisconsin ruled in 1925 that a KKK parade on the city streets conducted in an orderly and peaceful manner was not an unlawful assembly, on the theory that experience in the state did not indicate that resentment against the Klan would lead to acts of violence or a tumultuous breach of the peace.[277] On the other hand, the Alabama court ruled in 1949 that when a grand jury is investigating such unlawful acts as terrorism and flogging, it has a lawful right to require an officer of the Federated Ku Klux Klan, an Alabama corporation, to produce certain records in his custody and the membership roster.[278] Refusal to obey a subpoena *duces tecum* was held properly punishable as contempt. The court ruled that the identity of the membership of a

---

[274] S.C. CODE § 16-114–17 (1952). See also ALA. CODE ANN. tit. 14, § 358 (1) (Supp. 1953); FLA. STAT. ch. 876.11–21 (1957); GA. CODE ANN. tit. 26, §§ 5301a–11a (1953). See Geyer, *The "New" Ku Klux Klan,* 63 THE CRISIS 139 (March, 1956).

[275] See THE STATES AND SUBVERSION 403 (Gellhorn ed. 1952). Calif. Gen. Laws 1947, act 4707, § 1.

[276] TENN. CODE ANN. § 39-2801 (1955). An anti-mask city ordinance was upheld over constitutional objections in City of Pineville v. Marshall, 222 Ky. 4, 9 (1927): "Clearly a disguise is a shield and protection to the criminal. . . ."

[277] Shields v. State, 187 Wis. 448 (1925). One justice dissented, arguing that "it is a matter of common knowledge that the KKK is an organization having for its creed certain religious and racial antipathies which have led to disorders, riots, and bloodshed." *Id.* at 457.

[278] *Ex parte* Morris, 252 Ala. 551 (1949).

private fraternal corporation was not privileged. It rejected the argument that the grand jury was engaged in a mere fishing expedition, pointing out that "one of the major functions of a grand jury is to embark upon inquisitorial expeditions to ferret out crime." The central point of this decision was, of course, that the grand jury was looking into criminal activities, which is the original classic purpose of the grand jury.

There has been a federal statute on the books directed against Klan activities ever since Congress adopted the Ku Klux Klan Act, or the Anti-Lynching Act, in April, 1871.[279] The key paragraph, now Section 241 of the Federal Criminal Code, reads as follows:[280]

> If two or more persons conspire to injure, oppress, threaten, or intimidate any citizen in the free exercise or enjoyment of any right or privilege secured to him by the Constitution or laws of the United States, or because of his having so exercised the same; or
>
> If two or more persons go in disguise on the highway, or on the premises of another, with intent to prevent or hinder his free exercise or enjoyment of any right or privilege so secured—
>
> They shall be fined not more than $5,000 or imprisoned not more than ten years, or both.

While this statute has never been held invalid, the Supreme Court has always taken a narrow view of the acts that fall within its scope.[281]

X. Conclusion

The rights of association are central to any serious conception of constitutional democracy. In the big states of modern times the individual cannot function politically with any measure of effectiveness unless he is free to associate with others without hindrance. In fact, most people find much of their identity, whether economic, social, political, professional, or confessional, in some form of group activity. It follows that government has an obliga-

---

279 Act of April 20, 1871.

280 18 U.S.C. § 241 (1958).

281 See Gressman, *The Unhappy History of Civil Rights Legislation*, 50 Mich. L. Rev. 1323 (1952); Fraenkel, *The Federal Civil Rights Laws*, 31 Minn. L. Rev. 301 (1947); Carr, Federal Protection of Civil Rights (1947).

tion to protect the rights of association from invasion and to refrain from making inroads into them through its own activities. While American courts have been dealing with significant problems relating to these rights only in the past few years, such cognate rights as those of peaceable assembly and public meeting have deep roots in the American experience and a well recognized place in our public law. The modern rights of association have therefore developed in a friendly environment.

As the courts devote more and more time to the emerging problems which touch upon the rights of association, it is becoming increasingly evident that the basic problem of defining their scope is very much like the problem of spelling out the metes and bounds of any similar right. It is clear now that the rights of association, however valuable they may be, are no more absolute in character than are such hallowed rights as freedom of religion or freedom of speech. We do not, and cannot, in the nature of things, live in a world of absolute private rights, partly because private rights themselves may conflict with each other and thus necessitate choices of accommodation, and partly because public interests often overshadow private interests in specific situations. While some Justices on the Supreme Court persist in arguing the impropriety of balancing private rights against public interests, a majority of the Court is clearly committed to that process. Just as free speech, for example, ends where libel or sedition begins, so the Court recognizes that the right of association ends where the law of criminal conspiracy begins.

But the importance of the rights of association demands that the law should regard with great suspicions any attempt to denigrate them. Doubts should be resolved in their favor, never against them; the rights of association are the rule; restraints are only exceptions at best, each of them requiring specific and convincing justification. Nevertheless, there are vital public interests in the maintenance of law and order and in restraining criminal conspiracies, and where such interests exist the rights of association must yield. Since the situations posing the problem of drawing the lines are numerous and complex, our courts—and especially the Supreme Court—have a job of obviously formidable proportions on their hands.

HARRY KALVEN, JR.

THE NEW YORK TIMES CASE: A NOTE ON "THE CENTRAL MEANING OF THE FIRST AMENDMENT"

I. Theme

On occasion the Supreme Court hands down a decision in which past doctrine intersects present events in so complex a way as to be the despair of the commentator, not only because its portent is almost beyond prediction, but also because it opens so many avenues for inquiry. Just such a decision was *New York Times Co. v. Sullivan*[1] in which the Court unanimously[2] held that a libel judgment rendered under Alabama law was violative of First Amendment principles and, therefore, of the Fourteenth Amendment.

Since the case involved a rare instance of measuring the common law of defamation by constitutional standards,[3] it clamors for a

Harry Kalven is Professor of Law, The University of Chicago.

1 376 U.S. 254 (1964).

2 There were, however, three opinions. Mr. Justice Brennan wrote the opinion for the Court. Justices Black and Goldberg each wrote a concurring opinion in which Mr. Justice Douglas joined.

3 The question has arisen before primarily in connection with the absolute privilege of high-ranking government executives. See Barr v. Matteo, 360 U.S. 564 (1959); Spaulding v. Vilas, 161 U.S. 483 (1896); see also Schenectady Union Pub. Co. v. Sweeney, 316 U.S. 642 (1942), where the Court was evenly divided on a question of libel to a public official. *Cf.* Beauharnais v. Illinois, 343 U.S. 250 (1952)

careful determination of how much of that traditional body of tort law is affected by it. And for the torts teacher, it has the dizzying consequence of transmuting a part of his domain—one that he traditionally does not reach until the last day of the semester—into constitutional law,[4] the Valhalla of the law school curriculum. Moreover, even a cursory examination of the case reveals that the decision was responsive to the pressures of the day created by the Negro protest movement and thus raises the question so frequently mooted whether the Supreme Court has adhered to neutral principles in reaching its conclusion.[5] And, in this instance, the issue is made particularly attractive by the fact that Herbert Wechsler was counsel to the *Times*, and brilliantly persuasive counsel at that.[6] It is tempting to ask whether Wechsler the advocate secured a result that Wechsler the critic would condone.[7] Again, the case is a major instance of the important consequences of the civil rights issue and the apparatus of protest that accompanies it. The Negro movement is making significant constitutional law not only in the area of the Fourteenth Amendment's Equal Protection Clause but in unexpected sectors of First Amendment theory.[8] Whatever

---

(group libel and criminal sanctions); Near v. Minnesota, 283 U.S. 697 (1931) (defamation of public officials and injunctive remedy).

[4] The question of the constitutionality of the law of defamation has occasioned comparatively little commentary. See Kalven, *The Law of Defamation and the First Amendment*, in THE UNIVERSITY OF CHICAGO LAW SCHOOL, CONFERENCE ON THE ARTS, PUBLISHING, AND THE LAW 3 (1952); Cahn, *Justice Black and First Amendment "Absolutes": A Public Interview*, 37 N.Y.U. L. REV. 549 (1962).

[5] The basic article is Wechsler, *Toward Neutral Principles of Constitutional Law*, 73 HARV. L. REV. 1 (1959).

[6] Professor Wechsler was not alone on the brief. Herbert Brownell, Thomas F. Daly, and seven other distinguished lawyers and law firms were also of counsel.

A careful comparison of the brief and the opinion of the Court would itself be a profitable enterprise. At various critical points, the opinion echoes the carefully precise language of the brief and the structure of the Court's argument reflects the structure of argument in the brief.

[7] However tempting it would be to approach the case in this manner, I think it clear that the opinion satisfies the demand for "neutral principles."

[8] I attempted to develop this theme in a series of lectures at the Ohio State Law School in February 1964. These lectures are scheduled to appear early in 1965 as a book entitled *The Negro and the First Amendment*.

It is worth noting that Mr. Justice Douglas, in a prescient dissent in *Beauharnais*, note 3 *supra*, observed: "Today a white man stands convicted for protesting in

the irritations and crises of "the long hot summer," the protest has maintained the dignity of political action, of an elaborate petition for redress of grievances. And no one has been more sensitive to this sociological reality than the Supreme Court itself.

Beyond these points, the case raises sharply the question of the relevance of history for constitutional interpretation. In the course of the opinions, the Justices directly confronted the question of the constitutional status of the Sedition Act of 1798. The opinions bypassed what historians like W. W. Crosskey and Leonard Levy have said on the subject[9] in order to reach the conclusion that, whatever history might suggest, the Sedition Act is now unconstitutional. It is unconstitutional because the reaction after the passage of the Sedition Act precipitated a national consensus to that effect. "[T]he attack upon its validity has," Mr. Justice Brennan stated, "carried the day in the court of history."[10] This is heady doctrine. The Court has never before been quite so candid about its use of history. A major issue in constitutional doctrine thus beckons.

This article will not, however, be concerned with the attractions of these four siren songs. Instead it will pursue the significance of the case in yet another dimension, that of First Amendment theory and doctrine. In brief compass, my thesis is that the Court, compelled by the political realities of the case to decide it in favor of the *Times*, yet equally compelled to seek high ground in justifying

---

unseemly language against our decisions invalidating restrictive covenants. Tomorrow a Negro will be haled before a court for denouncing lynch law in heated terms." 343 U.S. at 286.

9 See Crosskey, Politics and the Constitution 767 (1953); Levy, The Legacy of Suppression (1960). The very purpose of Dean Levy's book was to ascertain whether the First Amendment was aimed at the abolition of seditious libel. He concluded: "If, however, a choice must be made between two propositions, first, that the clause substantially embodied the Blackstonian definition and left the law of seditious libel in force, or second, that it repudiated Blackstone and superseded the common law, the known evidence points strongly in favor of the former proposition. Contrary to Justice Holmes, history favors the notion." *Op. cit. supra,* at 247–48.

The Court did not ignore the Levy book but cited it, correctly, for the view that the meaning of the First Amendment emerged only after the uproar created by the passage of the Sedition Act. *Id.* at ch. 6. Dean Levy himself did not find the history of the Amendment binding, because the Constitution, at least in the area of civil liberties, "need not be anchored in the past." *Id.* at 4. For a critical review of the Levy thesis, see Anastplo, *Book Reviews,* 39 N.Y.U.L. Rev. 735 (1964).

10 376 U.S. at 276.

its result, wrote an opinion that may prove to be the best and most important it has ever produced in the realm of freedom of speech. I would make it clear, however, that I am not so much predicting what the Court will do with the case as a precedent as I am suggesting that the opinion makes a notable shift in constitutional idiom and could provide a new start for consideration of free-speech problems. Implicit in this approach is a distinction between the history of legal ideas and precedent, at least at the constitutional level. Certainly the Court's ideas about freedom of speech have commanded as much attention and interest as its rulings.

II. The Facts: A First View

I propose to view the facts first in brief compass and then elaborate on them in light of the political demands. The libel action was brought by Sullivan, the police commissioner of Montgomery, Alabama, against four Alabama clergymen, including Reverend Fred L. Shuttlesworth, and the *New York Times*. The allegedly defamatory publication was a full-page advertisement soliciting contributions for "The Committee To Defend Martin Luther King and the Struggle for Freedom in the South." It consisted largely of editorial comment about the mistreatment by the police and the community of Dr. King and Negro students active in protesting the deprivation of civil rights.[11] It spoke eloquently of the growing momentum of the protest movement. Its title: "Heed Their Rising Voices," was taken from a *New York Times* editorial.

The *Times* was sued as the publisher of the advertisement[12] and the four clergymen were sued as sponsors and publishers[13] whose names had appeared prominently in the advertisement along with

[11] The third and sixth paragraphs of the advertisement that form the basis for the suit are set out in the text at note 30, *infra*.

[12] The Court found no significance in the fact that the alleged defamation was contained in a paid advertisement. It sharply distinguished Valentine v. Chrestensen, 316 U.S. 52 (1942), where a commercial advertisement was found unprotected by the First Amendment. "The publication here was not a 'commercial' advertisement in the sense in which the word was used in *Chrestensen*." 376 U.S. at 266.

[13] The Court never reached the question whether these defendants were sufficiently connected with the publication to be treated as publishers. Each of the individual defendants claimed that he had not authorized the advertisement and, in fact, had not seen it prior to the request for a retraction.

those of some eighty others, none of whom seem to have been amenable to suit in Alabama. The case was tried to a jury which brought in a verdict for $500,000 in favor of the plaintiff. A judgment on the verdict was affirmed by the Supreme Court of Alabama.[14]

The Alabama law of defamation appears to have been the same as that of the vast majority of American jurisdictions. It left to the jury the question whether the text of the ad, which did not identify the plaintiff by name or office, referred to the plaintiff.[15] No specific damages were shown by the plaintiff, but, as is customary under Anglo-American libel law, he was held entitled to a presumption of general damages[16] and the Alabama Supreme Court declined to find the damages excessive.[17] The rule of fair comment in Alabama, like that in the majority of jurisdictions in this country, limits the privilege to the expression of defamatory opinions based on facts that are established as true.[18] In the instant case, the defendants were unable to establish the truth of several of the particulars alleged. The trial court, therefore, withdrew from the jury the question whether the text was defamatory; it held it libelous as a matter of law.[19] Since the text charged brutality and harassment in the

---

14 273 Ala. 656 (1963). The Alabama court disposed of the constitutional issues in a single paragraph of a lengthy opinion.

15 See, e.g., GREGORY & KALVEN, CASES AND MATERIALS IN TORTS 968–73 (1959) (hereafter GREGORY & KALVEN).

16 *Id.* at 910–26, 930–38.

17 *Id.* at 926 *et seq.;* Note, 35 A.L.R. 2d 218–63 (1954).

18 GREGORY & KALVEN 1042–58. The basic article on the subject is Noel, *Defamation of Public Officers and Candidates,* 49 COLUM. L. REV. 875 (1949); see also Riesman, *Democracy and Defamation: Fair Game and Fair Comment,* 42 COLUM. L. REV. 1085, 1282 (1942); Veeder, *Freedom of Public Discussion,* 23 HARV. L. REV. 413 (1910).

It is arguable that the fair-comment concept has been awkwardly put in the common-law decisions and that what is really involved is the degree to which the underlying facts are disclosed when the opinion is expressed and the inference drawn. *Cf., e.g.,* Eickhoff v. Gilbert, 124 Mich. 353 (1900); Kellems v. California C.I.O., 68 F. Supp 277 (N.D. Calif. 1946); Veeder, *supra,* at 419–20.

19 The Alabama court spoke of "libel per se" in this connection, apparently meaning no more than the matter was libelous as a matter of law. The phrase has otherwise had a complex and checkered history. See GREGORY & KALVEN 974–81.

In view of the political importance of the *Times* case, there is historical irony in the fact that the court took the question of defamation away from the jury. The

execution of police duties, this step also seems unexceptionable under general tort law. Again, the trial court followed the general rule that there is strict liability in defamation and that no actual malice need be proved.[20] It followed that the misstatement of facts could not be defended on the ground that they were not known to the defendants to be untrue.

The jury was also instructed that it could find punitive damages; that punitive damages need not have any relation to compensatory damages; but that punitive damages required a showing of actual malice. These are all familiar points of the law of defamation.[21] The $500,000 verdict was not separated by the jury into compensatory and punitive portions. Under Alabama law, punitive damages could not be claimed unless a retraction had been requested and refused.[22] The plaintiff did request a retraction and the *Times* did refuse to tender it. In the facts showing the failure to offer a retraction, the Court saw a basis for a finding of malice. Finally, the Alabama court found that the *Times* was sufficiently engaged in business within the state to subject it to personal jurisdiction and that, in any event, it had, by a general appearance, waived any objection to jurisdiction over its person.

The first point established by the facts is that Alabama did not create any special rules of law for these defendants. It simply applied the existing principles of the law of libel. On the surface, the case does not seem essentially different from such standard precedents as *Youssoupof v. Metro-Goldwyn-Mayer Pictures, Ltd.*,[23] *Jones v. E. Hulton & Co.*[24] *Peck v. Tribune Co.*,[25] or *Marr v. Putnam.*[26] It has long been noted that the law of defamation, with its three "galloping presumptions" of damage, falsity, and malice,

great fight over seditious libel in England which culminated in 1792 in the passage of Fox's Libel Act was concerned with right of the jury to define the standard of libel.

20 Gregory & Kalven 982–96.

21 *Id.* at 926–30.

22 See Morris, *Inadvertent Newspaper Libel and Retraction*, 32 Ill. L. Rev. 36 (1934).

23 50 T.L.R. 581 (C.A. 1934).

24 [1909] 2 K.B. 444, *aff'd*, [1910] A.C. 20.

25 214 U.S. 185 (1909).

26 196 Ore. 1 (1952).

can produce strangely artificial results.[27] It is important to stress that the Alabama decision was not simply a sham.

III. The Facts: A Second View

The case cannot, of course, be cut off so completely from the turbulent reality that produced it as the statement of facts set out above would do. Certain additional facts must be deemed relevant to the disposition of the issues.

First, the connection of the *Times* with Alabama could scarcely be more marginal: of the 650,000 published copies of the issues containing the advertisement, only 394 were distributed in Alabama, of which 35 were circulated in Montgomery County.[28] The publication, addressed primarily to a national audience, was all but invisible in the community in which plaintiff was claiming harm to his reputation.

The defamatory import presented an inverse instance of what has become known in the law of defamation as the "wrong-thinking minority problem."[29] The problem usually arises when an assertion about the plaintiff would not be considered defamatory by right-thinking people, *e.g.*, that the plaintiff has Jewish or Negro blood. The rule has been that the court will run the risk of ratifying the prejudice rather than pass on the issue whether the statement ought to have damaged the plaintiff. The plaintiff is entitled to have his reputation protected even among people who do not have "proper" values. The irony in the *Times* case is that the statements of police brutality and harassment would offend those with the "right" values. What is doubtful is that such allegations did, in fact, offend an Alabama audience, in light of the current exacerbations of the civil rights controversy.

This quirk to one side, there was the difficulty of connecting the statements made by the defendant with the plaintiff, an issue that loomed large in the Supreme Court's handling of the case. Quota-

---

27 Courtney, *Absurdities of the Law of Libel and Slander*, 36 Am. L. Rev. 552 (1902); Dean, Hatred, Ridicule or Contempt (1954).

28 376 U.S. at 260 n.3.

29 The leading case is Peck v. Tribune Co., 214 U.S. 185 (1909). See also Riesman, *supra* note 18, at 1300 *et seq.;* Note, *Developments in the Law: Defamation*, 69 Harv. L. Rev. 875, 886–87 (1956); Gregory & Kalven 961–64.

tion of the two offending paragraphs in the advertisement can spotlight this difficulty:[30]

> In Montgomery, Alabama, after students sang "My Country, 'Tis of Thee" on the State Capitol steps, their leaders were expelled from the school, and truckloads of police armed with shotguns and tear-gas ringed the Alabama State College Campus. When the entire student body protested to state authorities by refusing to re-register, their dining hall was padlocked in an attempt to starve them into submission.
>
> . . . .
>
> Again and again the Southern violators have answered Dr. King's peaceful protests with intimidation and violence. They have bombed his home almost killing his wife and child. They have assaulted his person. They have arrested him seven times—for "speeding," "loitering" and similar "offenses." And now they have charged him with "perjury"—a *felony* under which they could imprison him for *ten years*. . . .

The plaintiff argued that as head of the police and responsible for their activities, he was, by inference, charged with: (1) ringing the campus with armed police; (2) arresting Dr. King for spurious offenses. This step, if not compelling, is at least not utterly artificial. Plaintiff claimed further, however, that because these two items referred to him, he would also be understood as one of the persons responsible for: (3) padlocking the dining room and starving the students; (4) bombing the King home; (5) assaulting King; and (6) charging him with perjury. It would seem more reasonable to assume that the "they" referred to in the second quoted paragraph was intended to suggest no specific persons but rather the "Establishment" in which the plaintiff's role would be only incidental. Indeed, both paragraphs would seem to be concerned with such an amorphous group rather than individuals such as the plaintiff.

On a second reading then, there are statements invisibly published in plaintiff's community, which refer to him only by a strained construction of their language, and which, given the mood of the day, would not likely be considered defamatory by a southern audience. It is this marginal harm that the jury added up to $500,000 damages. One further element needs to be added to give the whole picture.

---

30 376 U.S. at 257–58. (Emphasis in original.)

The gossamer thread on which defendant's liability depended was made thinner by the fact that in order to show that the statements of fact were untrue, plaintiff had to reverse the logic by which he showed that the statements referred to him. On this aspect of the case, he argued that the arrests of Dr. King, for example, occurred before his tenure as commissioner and that as commissioner he had nothing to do with the perjury indictment. Therefore, he asserted, the statements were false as to him. There is revealed here a new technique by which defamation might be endlessly manufactured. First, it is argued that, contrary to all appearances, a statement referred to the plaintiff; then, that it falsely ascribed to the plaintiff something that he did not do, which should be rather easy to prove about a statement that did not refer to plaintiff in the first place. As it turned out, the Court did not have to confront this logic, which remains temporarily buried for resurrection at some later time.

The plaintiff did, however, have more traditional allegations of falsity of the statements. And here their relevance to the opinion is of significance. In several nagging particulars, the statements are not absolutely accurate; they reveal an inaccuracy characteristic of hastily drawn newspaper advertisements of this nature. The roster of inaccuracies is something like this: (1) The dining hall was never padlocked. (2) The students did not refuse to reregister. (3) Less than the entire student body protested. (4) The student leaders were not expelled for the protest on the capitol steps. (5) The police at no time literally ringed the campus. (6) Although the police did appear near the campus on three occasions, it was never in connection with the protest at the capitol. (7) Dr. King had not been arrested seven times. (8) The charge that Dr. King was assaulted was flimsy and was based on a single controverted instance of some years before. Nonetheless, almost every allegation had a core of truth. Dr. King had been arrested four times. Police had been deployed near the campus in large numbers. Student leaders had been expelled for taking part in sit-in demonstrations. Most of the student body had protested. The protest had taken the form of boycotting classes.

It is tempting to say that the falsity reduces itself to a charge that Dr. King was arrested seven times rather than four. And that the students sang "My Country 'Tis of Thee," when in fact they sang the national anthem. But the other points are not so trivial. And it would prove a disturbing exercise to see what would be left of the first quoted paragraph if all the facts were stated with absolute precision. Since it is characteristic of the common law of defamation to measure the defense of truth against very stringent standards, the conclusion that the falsity of the statements was harmless would not comport with established legal tests.[31]

Perhaps an additional fact has to be taken into consideration. That is that other Montgomery County officials and the Governor of Alabama had also decided that the advertisement defamed them and four additional libel suits were pending seeking judgments against the *Times* for an additional 2.5 million dollars.

On the second reading of the facts, the inescapable impression is that, although the Alabama law had not been distorted to achieve the result, Alabama somehow pounced on this opportunity to punish the *Times* for its role in supporting the civil rights movement in the South. The judgment, along with the others that were bound to follow, represented a powerful blow in the South's counterattack. In the civil war that is being waged in the courts as well as elsewhere, the political importance of the case could not be ignored.

One problem among the many that the Court faces in cases of this kind is attributable to the fact that it cannot, like the man in the street, simply state the result that it likes. There may be compelling reasons for decision that it cannot offer publicly without jeopardizing its role and image as a court. The "hard" cases of constitutional law demand high judicial statesmanship. In the *Times* case, the Court was prepared to pay the high price of destroying a considerable part of the common law of defamation. Whether the price was too high must be determined by the adequacy of the contribution it has made to First Amendment doctrine.

---

[31] See, *e.g.*, Kilian v. Doubleday & Co., 367 Pa. 117 (1951); Sharpe v. Stevenson, 34 N.C. 239 (1851). The headnote in the *Sharpe* case reads: "In an action of slander (under our statute) for charging that the plaintiff had criminal intercourse with one A, at a particular time and place, the defendant cannot justify by showing that she had such intercourse with A, at another time and place." The common law would seem to have been changed in England by the Defamation Act of 1952, § 5. 15 & 16 Geo. VI & 1 Eliz. II, c. 66.

IV. The Opinion: A First Reading

There are two readings that may be given the Court's opinion by Mr. Justice Brennan which are, perhaps, only subtly different. But in that small margin of difference is to be found the possibility of a major shift in First Amendment theory.

I start with the narrower reading. The Court began by rejecting the view of the Alabama Supreme Court that libel is beneath constitutional protection. This position was lent credence by dicta in cases like *Chaplinsky*,[32] *Near*,[33] *Pennekamp*,[34] and, especially, *Beauharnais*[35] and *Roth*,[36] none of which was directly concerned with libel. The theme was that the mere labels of state law could not effectively foreclose constitutional scrutiny by the Supreme Court. A year or two ago, the Court had used this thesis brilliantly in penetrating the attempt by the State of Virginia to impose sanctions on the NAACP because it improperly engaged in solicitation of legal business.[37] Following this line, the Court at the outset refused to permit the door to be slammed against its scrutiny of the judgment on the simple ground that Alabama had called this libel. This sector of the Court's argument concluded with a sentence that echoes the high literacy of the Wechsler brief:[38] "... libel can claim no talismanic immunity from constitutional limitations. It must be measured by standards that satisfy the First Amendment."

Several issues are intertwined here. At the simplest level, it is, of course, correct that the Court cannot permit the concepts of state law to control constitutional scrutiny. If the constitutional principle, for example, is that the state may regulate X, the principle can become illusory if the state is left free to define X as it will. What is muted in the opinion are two propositions of a less general and less abstract nature. First there is the fact that Alabama was not creating doctrine for this case in order to call it libel. Second is the existence

---

32 Chaplinsky v. New Hampshire, 315 U.S. 568 (1942).

33 Near v. Minnesota, 283 U.S. 697 (1931).

34 Pennekamp v. Florida, 328 U.S. 331 (1946).

35 Beauharnais v. Illinois, 343 U.S. 250 (1952).

36 Roth v. United States, 354 U.S. 476 (1957).

37 N.A.A.C.P. v. Button, 371 U.S. 415 (1963).

38 376 U.S. at 269.

of the two-level theory of the First Amendment used by the Court in *Beauharnais* to justify regulation of group libel and in *Roth* to justify regulation of obscenity.[39]

This screen pushed aside, the Court proceeded to its main argument. "The general proposition [is] that freedom of expression upon public questions is secured by the First Amendment."[40] There followed a brief exposition of the "general proposition" supported, among other authorities, by the Brandeis opinion in *Whitney*.[41] It was felicitously summed up in these words:[42] "Thus we consider this case against the background of a profound national commitment to the principle that debate on public issues should be uninhibited, robust, and wide open." The Court thus appeared to command a strong major premise about freedom of discussion of public issues. In a quick stroke, the Court then asserted that the advertisement in the case was "an expression of grievance and protest on one of the major public issues of our time."[43] It would seem, therefore "clearly to qualify for the constitutional protection."[44]

The Court then turned to the major task of its lengthy opinion, an exploration of the bases for impeaching the prima facie case made in defense of the advertisement. "The question," said Mr. Justice Brennan of the advertisement, "is whether it forfeits that protection by the falsity of some of its factual statements and by its alleged defamation of respondent."[45] The answer to this pivotal question is presented in three instalments. First, the Court rejected "any test of truth" as a First Amendment requirement; "factual error affords no warrant for repressing speech that would otherwise be free."[46] Second, the Court rejected injury to official reputation as grounds for "repressing speech that would otherwise be free."[47] And, finally, the Court rejected the conjunction of factual error and injury to official reputation as providing any more adequate basis for overcoming the prima facie case. "This is the lesson to be

---

39 The effect of the *Times* case on this line of analysis is considered in the text at notes 111 *et seq. infra.*

40 376 U.S. at 269.

41 Whitney v. California, 274 U.S. 357, 375–76 (1927).

42 376 U.S. at 270.

43 *Id.* at 271.

44 *Ibid.*

45 *Ibid.*

46 *Id.* at 272.

47 *Id.* at 272–73.

drawn from the great controversy over the Sedition Act of 1798. . . ."[48]

It is at this point that the opinion departed from the impressive clarity and structure with which it had begun. Having disposed of the grounds for impeaching the prima facie case for constitutional protection of the advertisement, the Court could be expected to conclude immediately that the advertisement was entitled to that protection. Instead, however, the opinion moved on to new grounds concerned with the "inhibiting" effect of damage awards.[49] Apparently it took this position to meet an argument never explicitly made that no restriction on free speech existed in this factual situation because only tort damages and not criminal sanctions are involved. The Court made short shrift of this feeble point:[50] "The judgment awarded in this case—without the need for any proof of actual pecuniary loss—was one thousand times greater than the maximum fine provided by the Alabama criminal statute, and one hundred times greater than that provided by the Sedition Act."

Then the Court returned to an issue that had already been treated: "[T]he state rule of law is not saved by its allowance of the defense of truth."[51] It is difficult to appreciate why that matter had not already been disposed of when the Court so eloquently stated that there is no test of truth in these matters. Originally the point was made that falsity could not be penalized because it was a necessary concomitant of "robust" discussion of public issues. The second time around, the point made was that allowance of truth as a defense could not represent a sufficient policy for protecting freedom of speech because it will impose a kind of "self-censorship" on speakers in the public forum.

In any event, once more the Court had reached the place for ending its opinion. In fact, however, the Court had then just started on its specific grounds for decision. What it required was a rule that would permit good faith error in public discussion. The constitutional rule for fair comment about public officials requires that the plaintiff demonstrate that the falsity was uttered with actual malice. This was, as the Court noted, the minority rule among the American jurisdictions. And its conclusion was buttressed somehow

---

48 *Id.* at 273.

49 *Id.* at 277.

50 *Ibid.*

51 *Id.* at 278.

by analogy to *Barr v. Matteo*,[52] in which the Court had recently stated the government official privilege in the same terms. It would be anomalous, the Court proposed, if the citizen in his official role as critic were to be treated differently from other officials.

The Court then assured that its newly stated rule would not authorize another verdict in the same case on retrial by itself assessing the evidence and determining that it was not adequate to submit the case to the jury. The Court has hitherto rarely displayed such a taste for common sense in deciding a question not directly before it. And then to make assurance doubly sure, it ruled that the evidence was inadequate to connect the plaintiff with the assertions made in the advertisement. This is a powerful point[53] and causes wonder why the Court did not choose to rest on this issue alone, avoiding the embarrassment of upsetting the rule adopted by a majority of the states on the question of fair comment. Conversely, it is equally puzzling why the Court, having found a fatal defect by reason of the fair comment rule applied, felt compelled to add this second basis for disposition. It is this conundrum that brings me to the second reading of the opinion, the one that contains the seed of important new doctrine.

V. The Opinion: A Second Reading

The exciting possibilities in the Court's opinion derive from its emphasis on seditious libel and the Sedition Act of 1798 as the key to the meaning of the First Amendment. My thesis is dependent on four propositions. First, that the importance of the free-speech provision of the Constitution rests on the rejection of seditious libel as an offense. Second, that constitutional history and the traditional analysis had relegated the concept of seditious libel to a curiously unimportant place, although the nagging question of the constitutionality of the Sedition Act of 1798 had never properly been put to rest. Third, that the special virtue of the *Times* opinion is its restoration of seditious libel to its essential role, thus suddenly and dramatically changing the idiom of free-speech analysis and resolving the question of the constitutionality of the Sedition Act. Finally, that the effect of the *Times* opinion is necessarily to discard or

---

52 360 U.S. 564 (1959).

53 *Cf.* Rossman, J., dissenting, in Marr v. Putnam, 196 Ore. 1, 40 (1952).

diminish in importance the clear-and-present danger test, the balancing formula, the two-level speech theory of *Beauharnais* and *Roth*, and the two-tier theory of different effects of the First Amendment on federal and state action. If I am right, the *Times* case represents a happy revolution of free-speech doctrine. Or, to put the matter differently, analysis of free-speech issues should hereafter begin with the significant issue of seditious libel and defamation of government by its critics rather than with the sterile example of a man falsely yelling fire in a crowded theater.

My first proposition need not detain us long. The concept of seditious libel strikes at the very heart of democracy.[54] Political freedom ends when government can use its powers and its courts to silence its critics. My point is not the tepid one that there should be leeway for criticism of the government. It is rather that defamation of the government is an impossible notion for a democracy. In brief, I suggest, that the presence or absence in the law of the concept of seditious libel defines the society. A society may or may not treat obscenity or contempt by publication as legal offenses without altering its basic nature. If, however, it makes seditious libel an offense, it is not a free society no matter what its other characteristics.

My second proposition, the denigration of the importance of seditious libel in establishing First Amendment principles, is more difficult to establish. Perhaps it is only the accident of the sequence in which the speech cases have come to the Court,[55] combined with the fact that the Court never had the sedition laws before it, that leaves the impression of its disregard of seditious libel and its fascination with the clear-and-present danger formula and balancing. Perhaps it is because we have not used functional categories in working out the theory of free speech. In any event, we do not

---

54 See generally on the subject of seditious libel, CHAFEE, FREE SPEECH IN THE UNITED STATES 19 *et seq.*, 497–516 (1948); 2 STEPHEN, HISTORY OF THE CRIMINAL LAW 299, 353 (1883); LEVY, *op. cit. supra* note 9, at 1–17; Cahn, note 4 *supra;* Cahn, *Defamation Control v. Press Freedom: A Current Chapter in Israel,* 13 J. PUB. LAW 3 (1964).

55 Although Near v. Minnesota, note 33 *supra,* presented the same problem of seditious libel, the Court, able to dispose of the case on grounds of prior restraint, had no need to confront the more essential issue.

start with the notion that seditious libel is clearly beyond the power of government and develop our ideas from that proposition.[56]

Certainly, the logic of the clear-and-present danger test does not foreclose the matter. It leaves the status of seditious libel in doubt. It does not suggest that severe criticism of government policy could never be sufficiently dangerous. Indeed, one might cite *Schenck*,[57] *Debs*,[58] and *Abrams*[59] as three cases in which the Court itself reached the opposite conclusion.

Moreover, until its disposition by the *Times* case, the status of the Sedition Act of 1798 remained an open question. It has been a term of infamy in American usage, but sober judgments about its constitutionality have been few indeed. Many distinguished commentators—Corwin,[60] Hall,[61] and Carroll,[62] for example—regarded the Sedition Act as constitutional, and Story might also be numbered among them.[63] Even Chafee, who makes a strong case for the unconstitutionality of the Act in the opening chapter of his classic, seems willing to leave the question unresolved.[64] More recent re-

---

56 For example, Professor Emerson, in his careful and thorough inventory of legal analyses of free speech issues, does not give a prominent part to seditious libel. See Emerson, *Toward a General Theory of the First Amendment*, 72 YALE L. J. 877 (1963).

57 Schenck v. United States, 249 U.S. 47 (1919).

58 Debs v. United States, 249 U.S. 211 (1919).

59 Abrams v. United States, 250 U.S. 616 (1919).

60 Corwin, *Freedom of Speech and Press under the First Amendment: A Resumé*, 30 YALE L. J. 48 (1920).

61 Hall, *Free Speech in War Time*, 21 COLUM. L. REV. 526 (1921).

62 Carroll, *Freedom of Speech and of the Press in the Federalist Period: The Sedition Act*, 18 MICH. L. REV. 615 (1920).

63 STORY, 3 COMMENTARIES ON THE CONSTITUTION OF THE UNITED STATES 743–44 (1833).

64 CHAFEE, *op. cit. supra* note 54, at 28. It is difficult to assess Chafee's position on this point properly. He has deservedly been considered the most influential American writer on free-speech issues and is an important contributor to "the broad consensus" the Court relies on to find that the Sedition Act is unconstitutional. 376 U.S. at 276. And it would seem that Dean Levy regards Chafee as the principal opponent of his thesis that the Framers of the Constitution probably intended to leave the English law of seditious libel unaffected. See LEVY, *op. cit. supra* note 9, at 2 *et seq.* My point is not that Chafee was insensitive to the tension between seditious libel and democracy, but rather that in his desire to make Holmes the chief

searches by Crosskey and Levy[65] have demonstrated how awkward a problem the Sedition Act presents. My point, for the moment, is not to choose the better view of the history of the First Amendment and the Sedition Act, but rather to call attention to the fact that for over 150 years it was not thought necessary to establish the status of the Act as a first step in getting to the meaning of the First Amendment. It was thus possible for the Espionage Act of 1917, as amended in 1918, to contain sections that oddly echoed the idiom of seditious libel:[66] "language intended to bring the form of government of the United States . . . or the Constitution . . . or the flag . . . or the uniform of the Army or Navy into contempt, scorn, contumely, or disrepute." And it was possible for the Government solemnly to urge that the Sedition Act was constitutional in its argument in the *Abrams* case in 1919.[67]

Then there was the performance of the Court in 1952 in *Beauharnais v. Illinois*,[68] where the majority, in an opinion by Mr. Justice Frankfurter, upheld the constitutionality of a group-libel statute. One might have expected that, in dealing with a question of the application of defamation to comments about a public issue—the alleged activities of Negroes moving into white neighborhoods, the principal task of the Court would be to distinguish group libel from seditious libel. Yet the majority opinion is virtually silent on the point.[69]

I turn, then, to the third proposition concerned with the meaning

---

architect of American theory he was led to emphasize clear and present danger as the chief analytical tool and to contrast it, not to seditious libel, but to what he called the "bad tendency test."

65 *Op. cit. supra* note 9.

66 40 Stat. 553 (1918); see CHAFEE, *op. cit. supra* note 54, at 40–41.

67 It was in response to this argument that Holmes, in dissent, made his prestigious and cavalier dismissal of the Sedition Act: "I wholly disagree with the argument of the Government that the First Amendment left the common law as to seditious libel in force. History seems to me against the notion. I had conceived that the United States through many years has shown its repentance for the Sedition Act of 1798, by repaying the fines that it imposed." 250 U.S. at 630.

68 343 U.S. 250 (1952).

69 Mr. Justice Frankfurter did add a faint cautionary note that libels on political parties would raise "quite different problems" from those before the Court in *Beauharnais*. *Id.* at 263 n.18.

of the Court's opinion in the *Times* case. I suggest that the critical statement in Mr. Justice Brennan's opinion is:[70] "If neither factual error nor defamatory content suffices to remove the constitutional shield from criticism of official conduct, the combination of the two elements is no less inadequate. This is the lesson to be drawn from the great controversy over the Sedition Act of 1798, 1 Stat. 586, which first crystallized a national awareness of the central meaning of the First Amendment. See Levy, Legacy of Suppression (1960), at 258 *et seq*. . . ." There follows an extended discussion of the "great controversy," with appropriate quotations from Madison whose views the Court summarizes thus:[71] "The right of free public discussion of the stewardship of public officials was thus, in Madison's view, a fundamental principle of the American form of government."

The Court then, for the first time in its history and some 166 years after the enactment of the Sedition Act, turned squarely to the issue of its constitutionality. The answer was that "the attack upon its validity has carried the day in the court of history."[72] The opinion cited Jefferson, Calhoun, Holmes, Brandeis, Jackson, Douglas, Cooley, and Chafee and concluded:[73] "These views reflect a broad concensus that the Act, because of the restraint it imposed upon criticism of government and public officials, was inconsistent with the First Amendment."

The Court did not simply, in the face of an awkward history, definitively put to rest the status of the Sedition Act. More important, it found in the controversy over seditious libel the clue to "the central meaning of the First Amendment." The choice of language was unusually apt. The Amendment has a "central meaning"—a core of protection of speech without which democracy cannot function, without which, in Madison's phrase, "the censorial power" would be in the Government over the people and not "in the people over the Government." This is not the whole meaning of the Amendment. There are other freedoms protected by it. But at the center there is no doubt what speech is being protected and no doubt why it is being protected. The theory of the freedom of speech clause was put right side up for the first time.

---

[70] 376 U.S. at 273. *Cf*. Brief for the Petitioner, The New York Times, 45–46.

[71] 376 U.S. at 275. [72] *Id*. at 276. [73] *Ibid*.

Although the total structure of the opinion is not without its difficulties, it seems to me to convey, however imperfectly, the following crucial syllogism: The central meaning of the Amendment is that seditious libel cannot be made the subject of government sanction. The Alabama rule on fair comment is closely akin to making seditious libel an offense. The Alabama rule therefore violated the central meaning of the Amendment.

If the opinion can be read in this way, what emerges as of large importance is the generous sweep of the major premise and not the application of it to the point of defamation law involved in the *Times* case. The touchstone of the First Amendment has become the abolition of seditious libel and what that implies about the function of free speech on public issues in American democracy. The drama of the *Times* case then is that the Court, forced to extricate itself from the political impasse that was presented to it, did so by returning to the essence of the First Amendment to be found in its limitations on seditious libel. It gets to very high ground indeed.

There are two other portions of the opinion, already noted, that confirm the proposition that the Court is carried along by a momentum of insight about the democratic necessities for free speech. There is the analogy to *Barr v. Matteo*[74] and the privilege of the high-ranking government executive. The rationale in *Barr* was that the threat of damage suits would dampen the ardor of the official for the performance of his duties. "Analogous considerations support the privilege for the citizen-critic of government. It is as much his duty to criticize as it is the official's duty to administer."[75] It is now not only the citizen's privilege to criticize his government, it is his duty. At this point in its rhetoric and sweep, the opinion almost literally incorporated Alexander Meiklejohn's thesis that in a democracy the citizen as ruler is our most important public official.[76]

Then there is the alternative ground for judgment concerned with the inadequate linking of the plaintiff to the language of the advertisement. If such connection is too easily made, all criticism of government policy, however impersonal, will carry implicit

---

74 360 U.S. 564 (1959).

75 376 U.S. at 282.

76 MEIKLEJOHN, POLITICAL FREEDOM: THE CONSTITUTIONAL POWERS OF THE PEOPLE 34–36 (1948).

defamation of whatever officials were in charge of the policy attacked. Such a rule of construction, said Mr. Justice Brennan, "would sidestep this [constitutional] obstacle by transmuting criticism of government, however impersonal it may seem on its face, into personal criticism, and hence potential libel, of the officials of whom the government is composed. There is no legal alchemy by which a State may thus create the cause of action that would otherwise be denied. . . ."[77] And then, to underscore the centrality of seditious libel for the First Amendment, Mr. Justice Brennan added:[78] "Raising as it does the possibility that a good faith critic of government will be penalized for his criticism, the proposition relied on by the Alabama courts strikes at the very center of the constitutionally protected area of free expression."

When these three passages are taken together, it becomes evident that the Court was not simply uttering, as the Court is wont to do, the occasional sentence that reads felicitously even out of context. It was clearly being driven by a concern for the central meaning of the First Amendment.

VI. Truth, Falsity, and Freedom of Speech

The Court's confrontation of the relevance of truth to a constitutional doctrine of free speech, closely related as it is to the idea of seditious libel, requires further consideration. Here again Mr. Justice Brennan's observations are refreshing because they far transcend in importance the resolution of the specific issue before the Court.

The question may be asked: Does the constitutional protection of freedom of speech simply establish the right to utter the truth? History makes clear that this would be no inconsiderable freedom.[79] Certainly there are various interesting limitations in contemporary law on the immunity of truth tellers.[80] The critical question, however, is whether falsity must not also be protected. The classic de-

---

[77] 376 U.S. at 292. [78] *Ibid.*

[79] It must be acknowledged that a good part of the historic controversy over seditious libel centered on the defense of truth. See note 54 *supra.*

[80] Franklin, *A Constitutional Problem in Privacy Protection: Legal Inhibitions on Reporting of Fact,* 16 Stan. L. Rev. 107 (1963); *The Origins and Constitutionality of Limitations on Truth as a Defense in Tort Law, id.* at 789 (1964).

fenses of freedom of speech have all suggested that the truth should not be used to discriminate between permissible and impermissible speech, at least at the level of ideas. More recently the point has been effectively put by Alexander Meiklejohn:[81] "The vital point . . . is that no suggestion of policy shall be denied a hearing because it is on one side of the issue rather than another. . . . These conflicting views may be expressed, must be expressed, not because they are valid, but because they are relevant."

For at least a generation it has been the prevailing notion that at the level of doctrine and ideas the Constitution did not distinguish between the true and the false.[82] A short time ago, the proposition was admirably summed up by Mr. Justice Stewart in the *Kingsley Pictures* case which was concerned with a state ban on the movie based on *Lady Chatterley's Lover*:[83]

> It is contended that the State's action was justified because the motion picture attractively portrays a relationship which is contrary to the moral standards, the religious precepts, and the legal code of its citizenry. This argument misconceives what it is that the Constitution protects. Its guarantee is not confined to the expression of ideas that are conventional or shared by a majority. It protects advocacy of the opinion that adultery may sometimes be proper, no less than advocacy of socialism or the single tax. And in the realm of ideas it protects expression which is eloquent no less than that which is unconvincing.

What has been less clear was the vulnerability to legal discipline of false statements of fact. And it was to this issue that Mr. Justice Brennan spoke with such force in the opinion in the *Times* case. False statements of fact, at least on public issues, are apparently to be afforded constitutional protection. Two different rationales were tendered in support of this proposition. There was stress on the likelihood that errors of fact will be made. The Court, thus, approvingly quoted from *Cantwell*'s behavioral dictum:[84] "To persuade

---

81 MEIKLEJOHN, POLITICAL FREEDOM 26–28 (1948).

82 Indeed it was a principal puzzle of the *Scopes* case, for example, that the situation seemed to require the court to make a choice between truth and falsity. See Kalven, Emerson, Haber, & Sharp, *The Scopes Case: A 1960 View*, 27 U. CHI. L. REV. 505 (1960).

83 Kingsley Pictures Corp. v. Regents, 360 U.S. 684, 688–89 (1959).

84 Cantwell v. Connecticut, 310 U.S. 296, 310 (1940), quoted 376 U.S. at 271.

others of his own point of view, the pleader, as we know, at times resorts to exaggeration, to vilification of men who have been or are prominent in church or state, and even to false statement." The Court went on to state:[85] ". . . erroneous statement is inevitable in free debate, and . . . must be protected if the freedoms of expression are to have the 'breathing space' that they 'need . . . to survive.' " Once again we are reminded that the national commitment is to debate on public issues that is "uninhibited, robust, and wide open."

The Court is also moved, however, by the difficulty of proving truth in these matters, and of putting the speaker to the risk of proof before fallible judges, juries, or administrative officials. In dealing with this proposition, the Court, put together *Smith v. California*[86] and *Speiser v. Randall*[87] to suggest a new category of invalid regulations: laws that tend to inhibit freedom of speech by generating a kind of "self-censorship." Thus, the bookseller in *Smith*, if left under so loose a requirement of scienter of obscenity, would tend to restrict the books he sells to those he has inspected. The law would then set off a chain reaction of self-censorship "affecting the whole public, hardly less virulent for being privately administered."[88] And the citizen seeking tax exemption in *Speiser*, confronted with the loyalty test there involved which left the burden of proof on the applicant, would become comparably reticent. "The man who knows that he must bring forth proof and persuade another of the lawfulness of his conduct necessarily must steer far wider of the unlawful zone than if the State must bear these burdens."[89] So too in the *Times* case, the "critic of official conduct" would be deterred from uttering what was in fact true "because of doubt whether it can be proved in court or fear of the expense of having to do so."[90] Thus the special vice of such a law is that it introduces a self-censorship that invades the zone of permissible and

---

[85] 376 U.S. at 271–72.

[86] 361 U.S. 147 (1949). See Kalven, *Metaphysics of the Law of Obscenity*, [1960] SUPREME COURT REVIEW 1, 35 *et seq*.

[87] 357 U.S. 513 (1958). See Kalven & Steffen, *The Bar Admission Cases: An Unfinished Debate between Justice Harlan and Justice Black*, 21 LAW IN TRANS. 155, 179 *et seq*. (1961).

[88] 361 U.S. at 153–54.

[89] 357 U.S. at 526.

[90] 376 U.S. at 279.

lawful speech. From these three cases, all written by Mr. Justice Brennan, emerges a fascinating and promising judicial utilization of psychology.

It must be recognized, of course, that a reason implicit in the breadth of the protection afforded speech is due to the judicial recognition of its own incapacity to make nice discriminations. It reflects a strategy that requires that speech be overprotected in order to assure that it is not underprotected. In any event, the *Times* opinion is as great a contribution to the issue of the relevance of truth to protected speech as it is to the issue of the relevance of the doctrine of seditious libel.

VII. "Where Are They Now?"

A not unfamiliar bit of Americana is a series of *New Yorker* articles that ran some years ago under the rubric "Where are they now?" The articles concerned with once familiar personages who seemed to have disappeared from the scene.[91] In the world of constitutional ideas and formulas, it becomes pertinent, after the *Times* case, to ask the same question about once familiar legal doctrines totally ignored by the opinion. Where are they now?

A. THE CLEAR-AND-PRESENT DANGER TEST

It has become a commonplace for commentators on constitutional law to note that the clear-and-present danger test is not flourishing these days. Thus, so careful a student as Professor Thomas I. Emerson recently concluded that the test may have been abandoned by the majority of the Court.[92] Whether the rewriting of it by Judge Learned Hand in the *Dennis* case[93] or the persistent attack on it as a constitutional formula by Mr. Justice Frankfurter[94] or the perplexities of the newer speech issues or the sheer inadequacy of the formula itself caused its decline may be unclear. But it is clear

[91] The leading right-to-privacy case arose out of one of the articles in this series. See Sidis v. F-R Publishing Corp., 113 F.2d 806 (2d Cir. 1940). *Newsweek* now runs a weekly feature under the same title.

[92] Emerson, *supra* note 56, at 912.

[93] United States v. Dennis, 183 F.2d 201 (2d Cir. 1950).

[94] See, *e.g.*, his concurring opinion in Dennis v. United States, 341 U.S. 494, 517 (1951).

that, as of the judgment in the *Times* case, it has disappeared. It did not occur to the Court to test the Alabama law before it in terms of clear and present danger,[95] although barely a decade before, in *Beauharnais,* appeal to that test was the principal argument of the defendant.[96] (It was one of the astute and successful gambles of the Wechsler brief that it did not argue the case in terms of clear and present danger.) The measure of the conceptual revolution promulgated by the *Times* case is that the Alabama law is found unconstitutional, not because there is no clear and present danger of a substantive evil in defendants' speech, but because the law looks too much like punishment for seditious libel.

There was one mention of the clear-and-present danger test in the majority opinion. It occurred in a reference to *Pennekamp v. Florida*[97] when the Court analogized the problem of defamation with that of contempt of court by publication. It would seem that the contempt problem is at least a sibling if not a twin to the one presented in the *Times* case. The former involves defamation of a specific public official, a judge. It might have been expected, therefore, that the same solution would fit both problems. But the modern Supreme Court decisions on the contempt problem—*Bridges,*[98] *Craig,*[99] and *Pennekamp*—all rely for their disposition on the clear-and-present danger test. And as recently as 1962, in *Wood v. Georgia,*[100] the Court adhered to this approach in disposing of a contempt case. The contempt cases make the Court's silence in the *Times* case on the viability of the clear-and-present danger test all the more deafening.

B. BALANCING

Immediately prior to the *Times* decision, the fashionable First Amendment test was what Professor Emerson called "ad hoc bal-

---

95 It is certainly not easy to apply the test to a defamation case. A try at it was made, but with what success? See Kalven, *supra* note 4, at 12–13.

96 The expectation that the Court would have to confront the clear-and-present danger test in an obscenity case survived until 1957. See Kalven, note 86 *supra.*

97 328 U.S. 331 (1946).

98 Bridges v. California, 314 U.S. 252 (1941).

99 Craig v. Harney, 331 U.S. 367 (1947).

100 370 U.S. 375 (1962).

ancing." This formula, which he dates from the *Douds*[101] case in 1950, has been the subject of several celebrated debates within the Court, especially between Justices Black and Harlan. The controversy has centered on large issues about absolutes and the proper role of judicial review.[102] Professor Emerson, a critic of the balancing formula, has defined it:[103] "The formula is that the court must, in each case, balance the individual and social interest in freedom of expression against the social interest sought by the regulation which restricts expression."

It is scarcely a novel suggestion that the law of defamation with its strict liability on the one hand and its complex of offsetting privileges on the other is a prime example of balancing the interest in freedom against the social interest sought by inhibiting communication.[104] It is this balancing that in fact generates the bulk of the law in this area and the special fascination that it has derives from the precision and detail with which the common law has struck the balance in different situations. The issue before the Court in the *Times* case, therefore, would have been peculiarly meet for the application of the balancing formula. Again the failure to speak to the issue, either in the Court's opinion or Mr. Justice Black's concurrence, suggests the necessity for its re-evaluation.

The point, however, is even stronger. In substance, the Court adopted as its constitutional principle the so-called minority view of *Coleman v. MacLennan*,[105] an old Kansas case that Mr. Justice Brennan quoted with approval. *Coleman* contains a stunning, extensive opinion by Justice Burch of the Kansas Supreme Court. The Burch opinion may well be the most elaborate, careful, extended act of balancing in the history of American law. It is one long, able dialogue on the problem. If ever a case was appropriate for the

---

101 American Communications Association, C.I.O. v. Douds, 339 U.S. 382 (1950).

102 See Black, *The Bill of Rights*, 35 N.Y.U. L. Rev. 865 (1960); Meiklejohn, *The First Amendment Is an Absolute*, [1961] Supreme Court Review 245; *The Balancing of Self-Preservation against Political Freedom*, 49 Calif. L. Rev. 4 (1961); Frantz, *The First Amendment in the Balance*, 71 Yale L. J. 1424 (1962).

103 Emerson, *supra* note 56, at 912.

104 Any good torts casebook makes this apparent. See, *e.g.*, Gregory & Kalven 996–1064.

105 78 Kan. 711 (1908).

application of the balancing test, the *Times* case was. But, from the Court, only silence.

The silence here, however, does not suggest the same result as the silence accorded the clear-and-present danger test. It means only that the balancing cases have been treated as having too wide an application. The philosophic debate over balancing has overshot the actual area of controversy. Whatever the Court may have said, it has never used the balancing formula except in a limited type of speech case,[106] a category in which the *Times* case did not fall.

A distinction must be drawn between cases in which legal sanctions are imposed for the specific purpose of restricting speech and those in which the control of speech is a by-product of government action that is otherwise permissible. *Douds*,[107] *Bates*,[108] and *Konigsberg*,[109] for example, did not involve the direct application of a sanction intended to deter speech. It is in these cases that the Court has sought to solve the problems before it by some effort to balance the state's acknowledged interest against the resulting interference with speech. It seems to me that in this regard Mr. Justice Harlan has been clearer than Mr. Justice Black as to the precise scope of the issue. Mr. Justice Harlan would not balance in the ordinary case, but only in these curiously oblique speech cases where he sees no way to avoid it.[110] Mr. Justice Black, on the other hand, often appears to treat the issue as if it involved a reappraisal of all First Amendment cases. And he insists that if there is any governmentally initiated interference with speech, however unintended and however slight, the action is unconstitutional.

I do not mean here to pass judgment on which of the Justices has the better of the argument, but only to stress that the speech issue involved in the *Times* case is different in kind from those in which the Court has utilized its balancing formula. The intended function of the tort law was to discipline certain kinds of speech. The importance of the silence of the *Times* case on the balancing test is that it cuts it down to its appropriate size.

---

106 See Kalven & Steffen, *supra* note 87.

107 Note 101 *supra*.

108 Bates v. Little Rock, 361 U.S. 516 (1960).

109 Konigsberg v. State Bar of California, 366 U.S. 36 (1961).

110 *Id.* at 51.

There is, of course, a sense in which the Court did indulge in balancing. It did not go the whole way and give an absolute privilege to the "citizen-critic." It left open the possibility of liability where the defendant's actions were the result of actual malice. Like Justice Burch, therefore, it has balanced the two obvious conflicting interests. Nonetheless, the idiom of balancing was eschewed in the *Times* case not only by the majority but by the concurring opinions as well.

C. THE TWO-LEVEL THEORY[111]

Beginning with *Chaplinsky*,[112] in 1942, and emerging as the central point of *Beauharnais*[113] in 1952 and *Roth*[114] in 1957, the Court developed a special technique for fitting certain kinds of free-speech problems into the constitutional framework. The technique consisted of dividing speech into two categories: that which is worthy enough to require the application of First Amendment protection and that which is beneath First Amendment concerns. The litany of lower-level speech, so often quoted from *Chaplinsky*, runs as follows:[115] "There are certain well-defined and narrowly limited classes of speech, the prevention and punishment of which has never been thought to raise any Constitutional problem. These include the lewd and obscene, the profane, the libelous, and the insulting or fighting words." This passage had served the Court well in disposing of the problem of group libel in *Beauharnais* and of obscenity in *Roth*. It is not quoted in the *Times* case.

In this instance, however, the point is not passed over in silence. The plaintiffs had urged as a principal argument in defense of the judgment that libel was not constitutionally protected. The Court confronted the issue directly and disposed of it firmly:[116] ". . . 'mere labels' of state law" cannot control constitutional judgment; "libel can claim no talismanic immunity from constitutional limitations. It must be measured by standards that satisfy the First Amendment." No matter how speech is classified, there must still be First Amendment consideration and review. No category of speech is any

---

111 This awkward phrase is my own. See Kalven, note 86 *supra*.

112 Note 32 *supra*.

113 Note 35 *supra*.

114 Note 36 *supra*.

115 315 U.S. at 571–72.

116 367 U.S. at 269.

longer beneath the protection of the First Amendment. Had the *Times* case preceded *Roth*, for example, *Roth* could not have been written the way it was, although the decision might have been the same. Obscenity, too, it would seem, "can claim no talismanic immunity from constitutional limitations."

The special logic of *Chaplinsky*, *Beauharnais*, and *Roth* may well disappear now that the *Times* opinion is on the books. The two-level theory may, in any event, have been the consequence of an attempt to avoid the clear-and-present danger test. Now that that test has been obliterated, there may no longer be a need for the special technique developed to deal with it.

D. THE TWO-TIER THEORY OF THE FIRST AND FOURTEENTH AMENDMENTS

The final pocket of Supreme Court ideology affected by the *Times* case is a special view of federalism. The view was expressed primarily by Mr. Justice Jackson in *Beauharnais* and by Mr. Justice Harlan in *Roth*. It has never received the sanction of a majority of the Court.[117] The point of the argument is that the First Amendment as applied to the federal government has a different and more stringent meaning than the Fourteenth Amendment when it incorporates the standards of the First in application to the states.

In the *Times* case, the Court upset a common-law rule followed in the great majority of the states. The situation seemed ripe for the utilization of the two-tier suggestion. The states might well have been given some leeway in experimenting with what *Coleman v. MacLennan*[118] treated as a close policy question. Once again the arresting fact is that Mr. Justice Harlan let his pet theory go by default. Apparently we need a single national policy on the privilege of fair comment. We are, after all, talking about seditious libel and the core of the First Amendment.

In one brief passage, Mr. Justice Brennan spoke directly to the two-tier thesis and rejected it. The plaintiffs had apparently argued

---

117 See Kalven, *supra* note 86, at 21–23. A thoughtful theoretical argument for federalism in the free speech area has recently been put forward. See Anastaplo, Notes on the First Amendment (unpublished Ph.D. thesis University of Chicago 1964).

118 Note 105 *supra*.

that "the constitutional limitations implicit in the history of the Sedition Act apply only to Congress and not to the States."[119] It did not unnerve the Court that this seemed to have been the view of Thomas Jefferson.[120] The thesis was that the furor over the Sedition Act was the expression of a view about federalism rather than about freedom of speech. The Court, in a grand but illogical gesture, disposed of the challenge summarily:[121] ". . . this distinction was eliminated with the adoption of the Fourteenth Amendment and the application to the States of the First Amendment's restrictions." The argument presumably is that limitations on federal power that have their origin in a deference to state power become by the alchemy of the Fourteenth Amendment limitations on state power.

VIII. The Concurring Opinions

In separate concurring opinions, in each of which Mr. Justice Douglas joined, Justices Black and Goldberg argued essentially the same objection,[122] that the majority did not go far enough to provide adequate protection to critics of official conduct. The minority would make an absolute privilege where the majority created only a qualified one that was defeasible on proof of actual malice. It is possible to speculate on the reasons why the Court stopped short of absolute privilege. The more important question, however, is whether the failure to go all the way impeached the majority's major premise. Has it spoiled the sweep of its powerful new reading of the First Amendment?

Certainly if the "citizen-critic" is now to be viewed as a public official and if strength is to be borrowed from the analogy of the privilege given public officials by *Barr v. Matteo*, it is difficult to see why the citizen is given a lesser privilege than the official. Perhaps a distinction might be based on the difference in numbers between officials and citizens. Arguably the official is a more vulnerable tar-

---

119 376 U.S. at 276.

120 See Levy, Jefferson and Civil Liberties: The Darker Side (1963).

121 376 U.S. at 277.

122 The one difference between the opinions would seem to be that Mr. Justice Goldberg would retain an area of private life in which a public official would have the benefits of the ordinary rules of defamation. He is not dismayed by the difficulty of drawing this distinction. 376 U.S. at 302 n.4.

get for harassment, because there are so few of him and so many of the public. Equally troublesome may be the Court's premise about "self-censorship." If the citizen cannot be put to the hazards of proving truth without deterring him from risking certain useful criticism, is not the same censorship generated by a rule that leaves on him the risk of proof of malice? Here the answer would seem to be that the risks are different because the burden of proving both falsity and malice are now on the plaintiff.

If the majority opinion does seem to have the worst of the debate on these two points, there remain three important countervailing considerations in support of its view. First, the Court's concern has been with the kind of inevitable factual error and exaggeration that are not extraordinary accompaniments of robust criticism. It is willing to forgive this kind of error. Its affirmative policy need not extend to deliberate falsehoods. Second, the Court was showing considerable daring in upsetting so long-standing a rule of common law that prevailed in so large a majority of the states. To hold in favor of absolute privilege would upset the common-law rule in all the states. Finally, it should be remembered that the Court was not dealing simply with Negro defamation of southern public officials. It was dealing with a general rule for limitation of criticism of public officials. The Court makes actual malice a "constitutional fact" that it will review de novo and indeed did review de novo in the case itself. There is thus some protection afforded against a too facile or disingenuous finding of the existence of malice.

I would conclude that the majority opinion survives the concurring opinions in good shape. There can be something demeaning in carping too much about the illiberality of so distinctively liberal an opinion.[123]

IX. Conclusion

We get a sense of difference between a legal theory of freedom of speech and a philosophic theory as we trace the career of

---

[123] Mr. Justice Goldberg does try for a neat debater's point about the constitutionality of the Sedition Act under the standard of the Court's opinion. The Sedition Act, too, provided for prosecutions for malicious statements. But the point was long ago disposed of by establishing the difference in meaning between "actual malice" as used in the Court's opinion and constructive malice that would satisfy the Sedition Act. See Bromage v. Prosser, 4 B. & C. 247 (1825); Smith, *Jones v. Hulton: Three Conflicting Judicial Views as to a Question of Defamation*, 60 U. Pa. L. Rev. 365 (1912).

seditious libel from seventeenth-century England through Fox's Libel Act through the Sedition Act to the *Times* case. It is one thing to assert that a vigorous criticism of the government must be permitted. It is another to choose among the calibrations of freedom that legal institutions and procedures can provide. Initially the great issue about seditious libel was whether judge or jury would have the final say as to what was defamatory of the government. The effect of Fox's Libel Act was simply to shift control from the judges to the juries, from the government and its judges to the people themselves. Then it became important to establish truth as a defense.[124] And, finally, in the *Times* case the critical area involves the degree of privilege to be afforded statements that are not true. We are reminded not only of how much more complex the legal debate over freedom of speech or over seditious libel can be, but again of the arresting problem how much freedom of speech in a legal system must depend on law's conscious distrust of its own processes to make needed discriminations.

The closing question, of course, is whether the treatment of seditious libel as the key concept for development of appropriate constitutional doctrine will prove germinal. It is not easy to predict what the Court will see in the *Times* opinion as the years roll by. It may regard the opinion as covering simply one pocket of cases, those dealing with libel of public officials, and not destructive of the earlier notions that are inconsistent only with the larger reading of the Court's action. But the invitation to follow a dialectic progression from public official to government policy to public policy to matters in the public domain, like art, seems to me to be overwhelming. If the Court accepts the invitation, it will slowly work out for itself the theory of free speech that Alexander Meiklejohn has been offering us for some fifteen years now.[125]

---

124 It is an instructive quirk of history that the Sedition Act of 1798 has come down to us as odious legislation while Fox's Libel Act of 1792 is seen as a milestone on the march to liberty. Yet the Sedition Act followed Fox's Libel Act in providing jury trial and went further by affording the defendant the defense of truth. The fact that this liberalizing of the law of seditious libel was viewed so dimly in the United States suggests, to my mind, some doubts about the validity of Dean Levy's thesis as to the common understanding prior to the Sedition Act crisis.

125 It is perhaps a fitting postscript to say that I had occasion this summer to discuss the *Times* case with Mr. Meiklejohn. Before I had disclosed my own views, I asked him for his judgment of the *Times* case. "It is," he said, "an occasion for dancing in the streets." As always, I am inclined to think he is right.

HARRY KALVEN, JR.

THE CONCEPT OF THE PUBLIC FORUM: COX v. LOUISIANA

"How come you're not saying *we* any more?"

From cartoon of prizefighter who has just been knocked out and is being carried toward the dressing room. He is addressing his manager walking beside him.

I. Theme

It is familiar knowledge that, during the decades of the thirties and forties, the Jehovah's Witnesses, a sect "distinguished by great religious zeal and astonishing powers of annoyance,"[1] brought to the Supreme Court of the United States a large and varied number of issues about the exercise of freedom of speech and religion in public places.[2] Indeed, in their robust evangelism, they appear to have stimulated the expression by the Court of a full chapter of constitutional law. Perhaps in no other corner of First Amendment theory have we had so ready a supply of relevant precedents.[3]

Harry Kalven, Jr., is Professor of Law, The University of Chicago.

[1] Chafee, Free Speech in the United States 399 (1948). A vivid description of their tactics is given in Mr. Justice Jackson's opinion in Douglas v. Jeannette, 319 U.S. 157, 166–74 (1943).

[2] There are more than 30 cases in all beginning with Lovell v. Griffin, 303 U.S. 444 (1938), the large majority of which involve Witnesses.

[3] The cases are conveniently collected and discussed in Mr. Justice Frankfurter's concurring opinion in Niemotko v. Maryland, 340 U.S. 268, 273–89 (1951); see also Emerson, *Toward a General Theory of the First Amendment,* 72 Yale L.J. 877, 926–28, 946–47 (1963).

Despite an occasional celebrated overnight shift in doctrine, as between *Jones v. Opelika*[4] and *Murdock v. Pennsylvania*[5] or, again, between *Saia v. New York*[6] and *Kovacs v. Cooper*,[7] and a frequently brilliant angry dissent from Mr. Justice Jackson,[8] the Court seemed to have the matter well in hand and to have an agreed framework for handling it. As the Communist issues came to the fore in the fifties, the problem receded and the story of the streets became a bit quaint. We were likely to regard the law that had been developed as one that concerned a luxury civil liberty. It was a sign of how tolerant toward a sharply dissident minority our society could be, if the minority was small and eccentric.

It appears now that the story is not over. A year or two ago, the guess would have been that the Negro protest would raise its most interesting legal issue over the use of private property.[9] But the civil rights legislation has largely put to rest the problem of the sit-in,[10] and there is every indication that the civil rights movement is going back onto the streets. While prediction in these matters is always imprudent,[11] it appears that the Court's formidable business in the immediate future will require it to confront the issues raised by today's Negro "evangelism."

The Court has had two major encounters with problems raised by Negro protest in public places. In 1963 it decided *Edwards v. South Carolina*[12] and last Term it added *Cox v. Louisiana.*[13] The

---

4 316 U.S. 584 (1942), *judgment vacated,* 319 U.S. 103 (1943).

5 319 U.S. 105 (1943). 6 334 U.S. 558 (1948). 7 336 U.S. 77 (1949).

8 See, *e.g.*, Murdock v. Pennsylvania, 319 U.S. 105, 166 (1943); Saia v. New York, 334 U.S. 558, 566 (1948); Terminiello v. Chicago, 337 U.S. 1, 13 (1949); Kunz v. New York, 340 U.S. 290, 295 (1951).

9 See Harlan, J., concurring in Garner v. Louisiana, 368 U.S. 157, 185 (1961); KALVEN, THE NEGRO AND THE FIRST AMENDMENT 123–72 (1965).

10 See Hamm v. City of Rock Hill, 379 U.S. 306 (1964).

11 *Cf.* David Riesman's brilliant but erroneous prediction about the coming problem of a Fascist exploitation of the American law of defamation. Riesman, *Democracy and Defamation,* 42 COLUM. L. REV. 727, 1085, 1282 (1942).

12 372 U.S. 229 (1963). In the interval between *Edwards* and *Cox* the Court decided two other Negro protest cases, albeit in a cryptic form. Fields v. South Carolina, 375 U.S. 44 (1963); Henry v. City of Rock Hill, 376 U.S. 776 (1964).

The *Fields* litigation was first reviewed by the Supreme Court of South Carolina in 1962 when, in State v. Brown, 240 S.C. 357, it affirmed a series of convictions for breach of peace. It appears that some 1,000 Negro students in three groups paraded two abreast along the sidewalks in the business section of a town

frustrating variety of opinions within the Court in *Cox*, and the sharp contrast in tone between the opinions in *Edwards* and those in *Cox*, make of *Cox* an appropriate occasion for venturing some reflections about the problems of speech in public places, an occasion for re-examining the concept of the public forum implicit in the earlier cases. The Court having just a year ago, in the *New York Times* case,[14] underwritten the policy that speech on public issues be "uninhibited, robust and wide open" may find its exuberant formula put to hard tests when the speech is in public places.[15]

---

of 20,000, ostensibly on their way to the city square. They refused to disband at request of police and were arrested. The state court held that the background of "high tension between the races in the community" justified a breach-of-peace conviction. The Supreme Court of the United States vacated the state court judgment and remanded for consideration in light of *Edwards*. 372 U.S. 522 (1963). The state court on remand reaffirmed in a per curiam opinion. 242 S.C. 357 (1963). Finally, the Supreme Court, in a per curiam order citing *Edwards*, reversed. 375 U.S. 44 (1963).

Henry had much the same career: the state court again relied on community tension to support convictions for breach of peace. 241 S.C. 427 (1962). It, too, was remanded for consideration in light of *Edwards*. 375 U.S. 6 (1963). In a full opinion expressing bewilderment that the Court in *Edwards* could have meant "to hold that one has an absolute right to commit a breach of peace, provided one is engaged at the time in the exercise of a right protected by the First Amendment to the United States Constitution," the South Carolina court reaffirmed its earlier judgment. 244 S.C. 74, 78 (1963). The Supreme Court reversed in a two-page per curiam opinion. 376 U.S. 776 (1964).

Finally, at the end of last Term, the Court vacated the judgment in Cameron v. Johnson, 381 U.S. 741 (1965), and remanded it to the District Court for reconsideration in light of Dombrowski v. Pfister, 380 U.S. 479 (1965). The case involved a suit by civil rights demonstrators to enjoin enforcement of a Mississippi anti-picketing statute. The Supreme Court did not pass on the merits but only on the procedural question whether there was a basis for federal jurisdiction. There is a sharp and interesting dissent by Mr. Justice Black. See note 89 *infra*.

[13] 379 U.S. 536, 559 (1965).

[14] Sullivan v. New York Times, 376 U.S. 254 (1964); see Kalven, *The New York Times Case: A Note on "the Central Meaning of the First Amendment,"* [1964] SUPREME COURT REVIEW 191.

[15] I am, perhaps somewhat cavalierly, putting the complex story of the labor picketing cases to one side. What is involved in the cases I am discussing is what might be called "public issue" picketing, there is no picket line, there is no specific target, there need be no evoking of economic pressures. I go with Mr. Justice Frankfurter's judgment in *Niemotko* that the picketing cases, although "logically relevant" are set apart by the different "economic and social interests" they involve. 340 U.S. 268, 276 (1951). Further, since there is no argument here that speech in public places is beyond the reach of any regulation, it is not clear what the picketing cases would add. In brief the thesis does not, as I see it, rise or fall with the vicissitudes of Thornhill v. Alabama, 310 U.S. 88 (1940).

II. Preface: Edwards and Cox

The flavor of these cases depends so much on nuances in the facts that there is no tidy way to compare them. Each involved mass parade, picketing, and protest in a public place by Negro students. In each a sizable crowd of white onlookers gathered and there was some suggestion that the crowd was restive. In each the performance was closely watched by police, who were out in force. In each the legal crisis arose when the police, after many minutes of surveillance, finally decided to move in and order the groups to disband.

There are, to be sure, important differences in the location and nature of the public place selected for the demonstrations, in the legal grounds urged against them, and possibly in the fact that in *Edwards* all 179 of the demonstrators were arrested whereas in *Cox* only the leader was subjected to legal proceedings.[16] But before turning to the relevance of such points of difference, it will be helpful to establish the style of the two protests, a style it seems to me they shared.

Mr. Justice Stewart, writing for the majority, set the stage in *Edwards*:[17]

> Late in the morning of March 2, 1961, the petitioners, high school and college students of the Negro race, met at the Zion Baptist Church in Columbia. From there at about noon they walked in separate groups of about 15 to the South Carolina State House grounds, an area of two city blocks open to the general public. Their purpose was to "submit a protest to the citizens of South Carolina, along with the Legislative Bodies of South Carolina, our feelings and our dissatisfaction with present conditions of discriminatory actions against Negroes, in general, and to let them know we were dissatisfied and that we would like for the laws which prohibited Negro privileges in this State to be removed."
>
> Already on the State House grounds when petitioners arrived, were some 30 or more law enforcement officers who had advance knowledge that petitioners were coming. Each group of petitioners entered the grounds through a driveway and parking area known in the record as the "horseshoe."

---

16 Cox was sentenced to four months in jail and a $200 fine for disturbing the peace; to five months in jail and a $500 fine for obstructing public passages; and to $5,000 fine and one year in jail for picketing the courthouse. The sentences were cumulative.

17 372 U.S. at 230–31.

> As they entered they were told by the law enforcement officials that they had a right as a citizen to go through the State House grounds as any other citizen has, as long as they were peaceful. During the next half hour or 45 minutes, the petitioners in the same small groups walked single file or two abreast in an orderly way through the grounds, each group carrying placards bearing such messages as "I am proud to be a Negro" and "Down with segregation."

And here is Mr. Justice Goldberg describing the scene for the majority in *Cox:*[18]

> On December 14, 1961, 23 students from Southern University, a Negro college, were arrested in downtown Baton Rouge, Louisiana, for picketing stores that maintained segregated lunch counters. . . . [After a mass meeting on campus that night,] the students resolved to demonstrate the next day in front of the courthouse in protest of segregation and the arrest and imprisonment of the picketers who were being held in the parish jail located on the upper floor of the courthouse building.
>
> [Next day the students left the campus in mass and marched five miles to Baton Rouge. The student leader having been arrested for violation of an anti-noise statute while using a sound truck, the defendant Cox, a Congregational minister, field secretary of CORE, and adviser to the student movement, came to "pick up this leadership and keep things orderly."] When Cox arrived 1,500 of the 2,000 students were assembling at the site of the old State Capitol building two and one half blocks from the courthouse. Cox walked up and down cautioning the students to keep to one side of the sidewalk while getting ready for their march to the courthouse. The students circled the block in a file two or three abreast occupying about one-half the sidewalk. . . . They walked in an orderly and peaceful file, two or three abreast, one block east, stopping on the way for a red traffic light. . . .
>
> [The students were joined by another group and came to a halt in the next block opposite the courthouse. A colloquy with police officials followed.[19]] The students were then directed by Cox to the west sidewalk across from the courthouse, 101 feet from its steps. They were lined up on this sidewalk about five deep and spread almost the entire length of the block. The group did not obstruct the street. [Several

---

18 379 U.S. at 538–43.

19 It is this colloquy that turns out to be decisive for Mr. Justice Goldberg's disposition of the convictions for picketing near the courthouse. See note 33 *infra*.

hundred onlookers gathered on the sidewalk near the courthouse and some 75 to 80 police and members of the fire department also turned out.]

Several of the students took from beneath their coats picket signs similar to those which had been used the day before. The signs bore legends such as "Don't buy discrimination for Christmas," "Sacrifice for Christ, don't buy," and named stores which were proclaimed "unfair." They then sang "God Bless America," pledged allegiance to the flag, prayed briefly, and sang one or two hymns, including "We Shall Overcome." The 23 students who were locked in jail cells in the courthouse building out of the sight of the demonstrators responded by themselves singing; this, in turn, was greeted with cheers and applause by the demonstrators.

[Cox then made a speech uging them to sit in at the downtown lunch counters that had refused to serve Negroes but admonished them against violence.[20] At this juncture the police moved in and the protest group was disbanded.]

The style of the protest, as I said, seems to me essentially the same in both cases, and the style is worth noting. These are structured ceremonials of protest; they are not riots. The demonstrators were not, as the majority recited the record,[21] trying to bring government to a halt; rather they were expressing the concern of the young Negro about his situation. What was symbolized was a deep grievance, a break with the society. They prayed, they pledged allegiance to the flag, they sang "God Bless America," and—in *Cox*—they even stopped for a red traffic light. Whatever the power, pressure, and anxiety generated by such huge numbers, the demonstrations showed a tact, a grace, a patience, and a distinctive rhetoric of their own.

The tone of the two opinions, on the other hand, is very different. The memorable thing about *Edwards* was that Mr. Justice Stewart,

---

20 For the chief of police this speech was the critical, unlawful act and moved him to intervene and disband the meeting. The issue raised by this advocacy of sit-in demonstrations dropped out of the case, however, thus eliminating a difficult free-speech issue. On what would the legality of advocating sit-ins depend? Clear and present danger of sit-ins? Legality of the sit-ins? *Cf.* Hall, *Free Speech in War Times,* 21 COLUM. L. REV. 526, 531 (1921).

21 Mr. Justice Clark in dissent read the record less sympathetically: "The appellant in an effort to influence and intimidate the courts and legal officials of Baton Rouge . . . agitated and led a mob of over 2,000 students in the staging of a modern Donnybrook Fair across from the courthouse. . . ." 379 U.S. at 585. Mr. Justice Goldberg reviewed the record in some detail in notes 9, 10, and 12 of his opinion. *Id.* at 546–48.

speaking for everyone but Mr. Justice Clark, said of the defendants and of their "rights of free speech, free assembly, and freedom to petition for redress of their grievances":[22] "*The circumstances of this case reflect an exercise of these basic constitutional rights in their most pristine and classic form.*"

At one point in *Cox*, Mr. Justice Goldberg spoke of the "influence or domination by either a hostile or friendly mob"[23] and again "mob law is the very antithesis of due process."[24] Further, in a curious echo of the idiom of *Edwards*, he wrote that the Court was not dealing here with speech "in its pristine form but with conduct of a totally different character."[25] And Mr. Justice Black found it relevant to say:[26] "Those who encourage minority groups to believe that the United States Constitution and federal laws give them a right to patrol and picket in the streets whenever they choose, in order to advance what they think to be a just and noble end, do no service to those minority groups, their cause, or their country."

As a logical matter the decisions in *Cox* and *Edwards* are fully consistent. In *Edwards* the single charge was for breach of the peace, and the Court upset the convictions, emphasizing among other things the absence of a precisely drawn statutory offense. In *Cox* one of the charges was for breach of the peace, and again the convictions were upset, with the Court relying heavily on *Edwards* as precedent. Further, although the Court in *Cox* split on other issues, all nine Justices agreed that the convictions for breach of the peace could not stand.[27]

There was more to *Cox* than a generalized breach-of-peace charge, however, and the additional charges suggest obvious differences between it and *Edwards*. There were two specific statutory violations, one for obstructing a public passageway[28] and the other

---

22 372 U.S. at 235. (Emphasis added.)

23 379 U.S. at 562.

24 *Id.* at 562.

25 *Id.* at 566.

26 *Id.* at 584.

27 Mr. Justice Clark, however, would invalidate the breach of peace convictions only on equal protection grounds. *Id.* at 591.

28 "No person shall wilfully obstruct the free, convenient and normal use of any public sidewalk, street, highway, bridge, alley, road, or other passageway, or the entrance, corridor or passage of any public building, structure, watercraft or ferry, by impeding, hindering, stifling, retarding or restraining traffic or passage thereon or therein.

"Providing however nothing herein contained shall apply to a bona fide legiti-

for picketing near a courthouse.[29] Although in the end the Court also upset the convictions under these two heads, the opinions, as I have said, bristled with cautions and with a lack of sympathy for such forms of protest.

The obstruction charge, which might have forced a fruitful clarification of the law on the public forum, was handled so as to satisfy no one. The Justices split 7 to 2, with Justices White and Harlan voting to uphold the convictions. Further, the seven-man majority in turn split 5 to 2, with Justices Black and Clark finding the statute bad only because it exempted labor picketing and thus, on their view, ran afoul of the Equal Protection Clause. Justices Black and Clark, however, were insistent on making clear their view that a flat nondiscriminatory prohibition of all such activity would be constitutional. The remaining Justices, in an opinion by Mr. Justice Goldberg, faced neither the equal protection issue nor the issue of flat prohibition. Instead they found some evidence that in practice the obstruction-of-public-way statute was administered by an informal permit or licensing arrangement.[30] Because this informal dis-

---

mate labor organization or to any of its legal activities such as picketing, lawful assembly or concerted activity in the interest of its members for the purpose of accomplishing or securing more favorable wage standards, hours of employment and working conditions. . . ." LA. REV. STAT. § 14:100.1 (Cum. Supp. 1962).

29 "Whoever, with the intent of interfering with, obstructing, or impeding the administration of justice, or with the intent of influencing any judge, juror, witness, or court officer, in the discharge of his duty pickets or parades in or near a building housing a court of the State of Louisiana, or in or near a building or residence occupied or used by such judge, juror, witness, or court officer, or with such intent uses any sound-truck or similar device or resorts to any other demonstration in or near any such building or residence, shall be fined not more than five thousand dollars or imprisoned not more than one year, or both. . . ." LA. REV. STAT. § 14:101 (Cum. Supp. 1962).

30 The step was made rapidly. Mr. Justice Goldberg asserted, without citation to the record, that "city officials . . . clearly indicated that meetings and parades . . . obstructing traffic 'are permitted' provided prior approval is obtained." He then simply added that counsel for the state confirmed this in oral argument before the Court. 379 U.S. at 555–56. The record on this point was reviewed more explicitly by Mr. Justice White's dissent: "The sole indication in the record from the state court that such has occurred was contained in the testimony of the Chief of Police who, in the process of pointing out that Cox and his group had not announced the fact or purpose of their meeting, said 'most organizations that want to hold a parade or a meeting of any kind . . . have no reluctance to evidence their desires at the start.'

". . . At the oral argument in response to Mr. Justice Goldberg's question as to whether parades and demonstrations are allowed in Baton Rouge, counsel said, 'ar-

cretion of the licensing official was not properly delineated and bounded, the statute was found bad. The use of this stratagem suggests that there may have been more than four Justices who would have found a flat prohibition valid. But the issue is deliberately left muddied.

The Justices divided 5 to 4 on the issue of courthouse picketing, with Justices Black, Clark, Harlan, and White dissenting. This time the majority, again speaking through Mr. Justice Goldberg,[31] used a different stratagem[32] to upset the convictions. In a colloquy between Cox and the police chief at the time of the demonstration, Cox was allegedly told by the chief that it was all right for the demonstrators to stay on the side of the street opposite the courthouse. To the exasperation of the dissent this was elevated into an official construction of the word "near" in the statute so as to estop the state from prosecuting.[33] This time, however, the majority too was explicit that the statute is constitutional.

Two relevant factors emerge then from *Cox*, read against the background of *Edwards*. First, there is the extraordinary ambivalence of the Court's reaction. As the parade leaves the State House grounds and moves down toward the courthouse, it changes from an attractive group of concerned citizens using democratic avenues of protest on public issues to a mob, heavy with the promise of anarchy, seeking to dominate. Second, despite the awkward split of opinions in *Cox*, a certain scheme of legal results can be discerned: (1) At one extreme, it is clear that this kind of use of public streets

---

rangements are usually made depending on the size of the demonstration, of course, arrangements are made with the officials and their cooperation is not only required it is needed where you have such a large crowd.' " *Id.* at 591–92.

Mr. Justice White also complained that this was an issue of the Court's "own invention" and consequently one on which the parties had no chance to "develop or refute the factual basis underlying the Court's rationale."

[31] There were two separate appeals: No. 24, involving breach of peace and obstructing, reported at 379 U.S. 536 (1965); and No. 49 involving picketing the courthouse, reported at 379 U.S. 559 (1965).

[32] It is true that the case is complicated by the difference between the police image of what was illegal in Cox's conduct and the issues on which he was finally convicted. See note 20 *supra.*

[33] Mr. Justice Clark was moved to an unusually acid dissent: "However, if the Chief's action be consent, I never knew until today that a law enforcement official —city, state or national—could forgive a breach of the criminal laws. I missed that in my law school, in my practice and for the two years I was head of the Criminal Division of the Department of Justice." 379 U.S. at 588–89.

and places cannot be summarily suppressed as a breach of the peace, even though there is some expectation of violence.[34] (2) At the other extreme is the unequivocal clarity of the point that no matter who you are or what your grievance, you cannot picket the courthouse. (3) In the middle, so to speak, is the question of obstructing public passageways, a question that the full Court colored with dicta but studiously avoided deciding, although it is the question on which future use of public places by protest groups will in all probability turn.

To bring matters to a focus as sharply as possible, I would note that there are references in the stated facts in *Edwards* to some blocking of traffic, at least in the sense of forcing other pedestrians off the sidewalks and into the streets, although the majority and the dissent read the record somewhat differently on this point.[35] In *Cox* the statute made it an offense to block traffic, even when that was not the intention. What is left in doubt after *Cox* is whether the exercise of rights "in their pristine and classic form," as in *Edwards*, would nevertheless have been punishable as a crime had the state proceeded under an obstruction statute like that of Louisiana.

I turn now to some reflections about this category of speech problem, reflections that claim no more than to invoke a slightly different way of looking at familiar issues.

III. Toward a Theory of the Public Forum

It may prove helpful to risk the pretentiousness of distinguishing among three closely related gestures of protest often lumped together in popular discussions of the civil rights movement: revolution, civil disobedience, and protest. A revolutionary gesture

---

[34] Like *Edwards*, the *Cox* case touches on the perplexing speech issue of "the heckler's veto." To what extent is the violent reaction expected from the audience a basis for suppressing the speaker? See Kalven, *op. cit. supra* note 9, at 140–41, 145; Note, *Freedom of Speech and Assembly: The Problem of the Hostile Audience*, 49 Colum. L. Rev. 1118 (1949); Note, *Free Speech and the Hostile Audience*, 26 N.Y.U. L. Rev. 489 (1951).

The Louisiana Supreme Court had held that the bringing of the 1,500 Negroes into the "predominantly white business district" was so explosive a move that it "had to be an inherent breach of the peace." The Court, however, found that in fact the police had the situation under control and thus did not find it necessary to confront the full dilemma. See also the *Fields* and *Henry* cases, note 12 *supra*.

[35] *Compare* Mr. Justice Stewart's opinion, 372 U.S. at 232 nn. 5, 6, *with* Mr. Justice Clark's opinion, *id.* at 240 n. 3.

is intended as direct defiance of law and order; it is a declaration of open war; it is coercive and obstructive. It may well be morally justifiable, but only under the stringent conditions by which Western tradition has measured a right of revolution. The suggestion, for example, that Negroes let their water taps run in New York to aggravate the water shortage is just such a revolutionary gesture.

Civil disobedience is deliberate violation of law for the sake of protest and as a matter of individual conscience. It is a gesture we associate with Socrates, Thoreau, and conscientious objectors. In the famous formula of Plato's *Apology* and *Crito* this gesture requires that the actor accept the punishment.[36] It is a refusal to obey the law coupled with a willingness to accept the legal consequences. Insofar as it is symbolic, it is also an intense form of protest. To an uncertain extent, especially in the sit-in demonstrations, the Negro movement has in this sense courted arrest.[37] The important point is that civil disobedience claims exemption from the obligation to obey particular laws on moral grounds but not immunity from punishment.

Finally, there are the various forms of mass protest in public places using parades, picketing, and so on. Here the essential feature is appeal to public opinion.[38] The intention is not to violate the law, and the claim is one of privilege in the exercise of basic rights. Most of the civil rights demonstrations to date, as I see it, fall in this category. This has been one of the extraordinary achievements of the movement. It is this gesture of protest that I am concerned with in this essay. These distinctions are undoubtedly difficult to draw from the facts, and the Negro movement has not itself always been clear about which strategy it was pursuing. The Negro movement shares with the rest of us the task of working out the appropriate forms for its protest.

It is simplistic, if tempting, to reduce the issue to a choice between order and anarchy. I suggest three interrelated propositions for examination. First, that in an open democratic society the streets, the

---

36 The tension between the two dialogues is lucidly explored in MEIKLEJOHN, POLITICAL FREEDOM 21–24 (1960).

37 In Bouie v. City of Columbia, 378 U.S. 347 (1964), for example, the dissent argued that the defendants in their sit-in could not have been misled by any ambiguity in the trespass statute because they "intended" to be arrested. *Id.* at 367 n. 4.

38 Thus, in his opinion in Garner v. Louisiana, 368 U.S. 157, 201–02 (1961), Mr. Justice Harlan eloquently recognized this aspect of the sit-in. See KALVEN, *op. cit. supra* note 9, at 129–33.

parks, and other public places are an important facility for public discussion and political process. They are in brief a public forum that the citizen can commandeer; the generosity and empathy with which such facilities are made available is an index of freedom. Second, that only confusion can result from distinguishing sharply between "speech pure" and "speech plus." And, third, that what is required is in effect a set of Robert's Rules of Order for the new uses of the public forum, albeit the designing of such rules poses a problem of formidable practical difficulty. As will be apparent, there is much in *Cox* that bears on these three points. The Court in strong dicta seems to becloud the first; to rely heavily on the distinction that is denied by the second; and to avoid examining the problem in quite the manner suggested by the third.

I shall pursue my inquiry by recalling two famous dicta, and then revisiting a familiar series of precedents.

A. THE PRINCIPLE AND TWO DICTA

The initial questions are whether the citizen using the street as a forum and not as a passageway is making an anomalous use of it, and whether he is, in a sense, always out of place and out of order when he chooses the streets for his meeting place. Certainly it is easy to think of public places, swimming pools, for example, so clearly dedicated to recreational use that talk of their use as a public forum would in general be totally unpersuasive. Is the street, however, a kind of public hall, a public communication facility?

One would have thought the theoretical issue had been put to rest a generation ago by the collision of dicta in *Davis v. Massachusetts*[39] and *Hague v. C.I.O.*[40] *Davis*, it will be recalled, was one of the less admired efforts of Justice Holmes, then still on the Massachusetts Supreme Judicial Court.[41] In reviewing a conviction for speaking on the Boston Common without a permit, in violation of an ordinance inhibiting many varieties of uses of the Common including "the discharge of cannon" thereon, Justice Holmes observed:[42] "For the Legislature absolutely or conditionally to forbid public speaking in a highway or public park is no more an infringement of rights of a member of the public than for the owner of a private house to forbid it in the house."

---

[39] 167 U.S. 43 (1897).

[40] 307 U.S. 496 (1939).

[41] 162 Mass. 510 (1895).

[42] *Id.* at 511.

When the case reached the United States Supreme Court, the Court endorsed the Holmes decision and its rationale. Said Chief Justice White:[43] "The right to absolutely exclude all right to use, necessarily includes the authority to determine under what circumstances such use may be availed of, as the greater power contains the lesser." This position has at least the virtue of clarity. The citizen uses the streets for political purposes at the sufferance of the state; his use is anomalous and marginal and can be terminated whenever and for whatever reason the state decides.

This view survived until 1937 when Mayor Hague of Jersey City got into an argument, not with Jehovah's Witnesses, but with the CIO, then seeking energetically to organize New Jersey labor.[44] In a complicated lawsuit, the Court passed on the city's claim that its ordinance requiring a permit for an open air meeting was justified by the plenary power rationale of the *Davis* case. In rejecting the point, Mr. Justice Roberts uttered the counter dictum:[45]

> Wherever the title of street and parks may rest, they have immemorially been held in trust for the use of the public and time out of mind, have been used for purposes of assembly, communicating thoughts between citizens, and discussing public questions. Such use of the streets and public places has from ancient times, been a part of the privileges, immunities, rights, and liberties of citizens.

On this view the matter is perhaps not quite so clear, but there is the aura of a large democratic principle. When the citizen goes to the street, he is exercising an immemorial right of a free man, a kind of First-Amendment easement. If so generous a statement of principle does not tell us exactly when his privileges may be curtailed in the interest of other speech or other uses of the street, it does give us a good starting point for the argument.

Perhaps two details about the *Hague* dictum deserve notice. First, it is not altogether clear for whom Mr. Justice Roberts was speaking, as the Court was reminded in 1947 in Mr. Justice Jackson's dissent in *Saia*.[46] On one view of the case he was speaking only for himself and Mr. Justice Black, who joined his opinion, and inferentially

---

[43] 167 U.S. at 48.

[44] The background of the case is sketched in CHAFEE, *op. cit. supra* note 1, at 409 *et seq.*

[45] 307 U.S. at 515.

[46] 334 U.S. at 568 n. 1.

for Chief Justice Hughes, who concurred in part.[47] This is probably too stringent a reading, but it is true that the Roberts dictum, despite its eloquence, is launched with a shaky endorsement from his fellow Justices.

The second detail is that the Court was aided, and obviously made use of a major amicus curiae brief filed by the Bill of Rights Committee of the American Bar Association, among whose members were Zechariah Chafee and Grenville Clark.[48] The brief said in part:[49] "There are many different kinds of benefits to be derived from parks, and one of the most important is the constitutional right of assembly therein. The parks are held by the city subject to this right."

It is not so easy as it should be to tell how the Roberts dictum fares today. It is not enshrined as the starting point for judicial analysis in cases of speech in public places, although it is true that in *Kunz*[50] Chief Justice Vinson did announce: "In considering the right of a municipality to control the use of public streets for the expression of religious views, we start with the words of Mr. Justice Roberts. . . ."

There are subtle but definite transformations of it in two prestigeful opinions, that of Mr. Justice Black in *Jamison v. Texas*[51] in 1943, and that of Mr. Justice Frankfurter in his opinion in *Niemotko*[52] in 1951. In *Jamison,* a leaflet distribution case, Mr. Justice Black said:[53] "But one who is rightfully on a street . . . carries with him there as elsewhere the constitutional right to express his views in an orderly fashion. This right extends to the communication of ideas by handbills and literature as well as by spoken word." Somehow this strikes my ear as a good deal less enthusiastic about the immemorial right of the free man than does the text of Mr. Justice Roberts.[54]

---

47 Justices Frankfurter and Douglas did not participate; Justices McReynolds and Butler dissented; Mr. Justice Stone filed a concurring opinion objecting to Mr. Justice Roberts' reliance on the Privileges and Immunities Clause as the basis for federal injunctive relief against enforcement of state law. For a rundown of the various positions, see CHAFEE, *op. cit. supra* note 1, at 413 n. 77.

48 Parts of the brief are reprinted in 307 U.S. at 678–82. And see the extended discussion of it in CHAFEE, *op. cit. supra* note 1, at 413–35.

49 307 U.S. at 682.

50 340 U.S. at 293.

51 318 U.S. 413 (1943).

52 340 U.S. at 273–89.

53 318 U.S. at 416.

54 Mr. Justice Black continued to phrase the principle this way in *Cox:* "The First and Fourteenth Amendments, I think, take away from government, state and

In *Niemotko*, Mr. Justice Frankfurter made an elaborate summary of all the public-place cases up to that time and a major effort to bring order to them. He was careful to state the issue as one of "how to reconcile the interest in allowing free expression in public places with the protection of . . . the primary uses of streets and parks."[55] If this is the correct phrasing of the issue,[56] it is difficult to see why the primary uses of the streets and parks should not always and easily outweigh the subordinate uses as public forums, again a result not easy to square with the Roberts dictum. Moreover, in summarizing the *Hague* case itself, Mr. Justice Frankfurter carefully abstained from referring to the Roberts formula and asserted the holding to be simply that the state cannot claim totally arbitrary control over its public places.[57]

It is probably not profitable to brood further over the verbal differences among Roberts' immemorial claim of the free man, Black's notion that he does not lose any rights of free speech simply by going out on the street, and Frankfurter's formula that the state cannot be arbitrary in its control of the streets. Since Mr. Justice Roberts was quick to say in *Hague* that these immemorial rights were subject to reasonable regulation in view of other demands for the streets and public places,[58] it is arguable that all three formulations, however different in emotional tone and color, will lead to the same operative results in any actual case.

B. THE TEST QUESTION AND FOUR DECISIONS

The test question is whether the state can bar the use of public places for speech altogether, not on a claim of plenary power as in *Davis*, but in the interest of other uses of the facility. This may well prove to be tomorrow's issue, since municipalities burdened with the perplexities of regulating the current protests may be greatly tempted to opt for flat nondiscriminatory prohibition on the use of streets and parks for anything but transportation and recreation.

---

federal, all power to restrict freedom of speech, press, and assembly *where people have a right to be for such purposes*." 379 U.S. at 578. (Emphasis added.) Thus, in an important sense, for him the questions of speech are subordinate to questions of property. See his dissent in Bell v. Maryland, 378 U.S. 226, 318 (1964); KALVEN, *op. cit. supra* note 9, at 170–72.

55 340 U.S. at 276; see also his rephrasing *id.* at 279.

56 It is true that this is very close to some of the language of Mr. Justice Roberts in *Schneider*. See Schneider v. State, 308 U.S. 147, 160 (1939).

57 340 U.S. at 279.

58 See note 56 *supra*.

In four cases, all involving leaflet distribution, *Schneider*, *Jamison*, *Valentine*, and *Talley*, the Court has given impressive content to the Roberts dictum.

In *Schneider*, Mr. Justice Roberts got the first chance to put his own dictum into operation.[59] The case combined four separate controversies over municipal ordinances, three of which are relevant for our immediate purposes.[60] Each invoked a flat prohibition against the distribution of handbills, circulars, dodgers, etc., in public places. The defendants, Jehovah's Witnesses, were convicted for violation of the ordinances, and in an 8 to 1 decision, Mr. Justice McReynolds dissenting, the Court upset the convictions. What is important here is that the state did not argue its plenary power but argued rather that the purpose of the restraint was to prevent littering the streets. There was, therefore, no need to go back to *Davis*.

At the outset Mr. Justice Roberts made clear that although "pamphlets had become historic weapons in the defense of liberty," the right to distribute leaflets was subject to certain obvious regulations:[61] "For example, a person could not exercise this liberty by taking his stand in the middle of a crowded street contrary to traffic regulations and maintain his position to the stoppage of all traffic."

What was called for was a balancing of the conflicting interests, but with a weight of enthusiasm for the personal rights involved. "This court," Mr. Justice Roberts paused to note,[62] "has characterized the freedom of speech and that of the press as fundamental personal rights and liberties. The phrase is not an empty one and was not lightly used." He continued:[63]

> In every case, therefore, where legislative abridgement of the rights is asserted, the courts should be astute to examine the effect of the challenged legislation. Mere legislative

---

[59] Schneider v. State, 308 U.S. 147 (1939). He did not get to use it directly in *Hague* itself because that case turned on the invalidity of a prior licensing ordinance.

[60] The fourth ordinance involved prior licensing of solicitations.

[61] 308 U.S. at 160.

[62] *Id*. at 161.

[63] The phrasing of how the balance is to be struck is in the idiom of "preferred position"; hence it might be argued that the case is no longer fashionable. But whatever the vicissitudes of the preferred position controversy or its relevance for other speech issues, it seems quite clear that *Schneider* is a live precedent for the Court today and is frequently cited with respect.

It is evident, however, that Mr. Justice Frankfurter would have erased this emphasis from the *Schneider* formula; witness his concurring opinions in *Niemotko*, 340 U.S. at 273, and *Kovacs*, 336 U.S. at 89. See note 76 *infra*.

> preference or beliefs respecting matters of public convenience may well support regulation directed at other personal activities but be insufficient to justify such as diminishes the exercise of rights so vital to the maintenance of democratic institutions. And so, as the cases arise, the delicate and difficult task falls upon the courts to weigh the circumstances and to appraise the substantiality of the reasons advanced in support of the regulation of the free enjoyment of the rights.

He then moved swiftly and surely to the evaluation of the contested ordinances:[64]

> We are of the opinion that the purpose to keep the streets clean and of good appearance is insufficient to justify an ordinance which prohibits a person rightfully on a public street from handing literature to one willing to receive it. Any burden imposed upon the city authorities in cleaning and caring for the streets as an indirect consequence of such distribution results from the constitutional protection of the freedom of speech and press.

The Milwaukee ordinance could not be saved by the argument that in actual practice prosecutions under it were limited to cases where the recipients throw it into the streets. The answer was still that "public convenience in respect to cleanliness of the streets" did not justify an interference with free communication. Nor could the Los Angeles and Worcester ordinances be saved by the circumstance that they were limited to streets and alleys, leaving other public places open. Here the point was met in language with echoes from the *Hague* dictum:[65] "[A]s we have said, the streets are natural and proper places for the dissemination of information and opinion;

---

[64] 308 U.S. at 162. Mr. Justice Roberts went on to suggest that the city had alternative ways of achieving its objective such as arresting the recipient who tossed the leaflets on the street. The case thus might be read as simply upsetting a gratuitously broad regulation. *Cf., e.g.,* Shelton v. Tucker, 364 U.S. 479 (1960). It is difficult to take seriously so impractical an alternative. Moreover, at most this ground points to what is in Mr. Justice Roberts' eyes an additional vice in the regulation and not its decisive flaw. *Cf., e.g.,* Mr. Justice Frankfurter's reading of *Schneider* in his *Niemotko* summary, 340 U.S. at 276.

[65] *Id.* at 163. Does this mean that a city could not solve its problems by setting aside special areas for protests and demonstrations and closing its streets and parks to them otherwise? The American Bar Association committee in its brief in *Hague* considered explicitly the setting-up of "Hyde Parks." See CHAFEE, *op. cit. supra* note 1, at 418–19. Ironically, one difficulty with the Hyde Park solution may be that it does not afford an adequate opportunity to secure an audience, see note 88 *infra.*

and one is not to have the exercise of his liberty of expression in appropriate places abridged on the plea that it may be exercised in some other place."

The result, whether or not one likes it as a policy, had an impressive bite.[66] Leaflet distribution in public places in a city is a method of communication that carries as an inextricable and expected consequence substantial littering of the streets, which the city has an obligation to keep clean. It is also a method of communication of some annoyance to a majority of people so addressed; that its impact on its audience is very high is doubtful. Yet the constitutional balance in *Schneider* was struck emphatically in favor of keeping the public forum open for this mode of communication.

Two years later Mr. Justice Roberts etched in his point still more firmly in *Valentine v. Chrestensen*.[67] Once again there was an ordinance prohibiting discrimination of handbills and circulars. The one distinguishing feature of this ordinance was its limitation to commercial and advertising matter. The defendant was the owner of a former United States submarine that he sought to exhibit for profit. Accordingly he prepared handbills advertising the ship and soliciting visitors for a stated admission fee. Advised by the police that only handbills on public issues would be lawful, the defendant resourcefully attempted to alchemize his leaflet into a message of social significance by printing a protest against the police and the ordinance on one side and his advertisement on the other. He then proceeded to distribute his double-edged leaflet. Threatened further by police displeasure, he brought suit to enjoin the police from interfering with his distribution. He won in the lower courts, but the Supreme Court reversed in a unanimous decision, and in so doing added meaurably to the point made by *Schneider* and the *Hague* dictum.

Mr. Justice Roberts began with a sturdy reaffirmation of the dictum:[68]

> This court has unequivocally held that the streets are proper places for the exercise of the freedom of communicating in-

---

66 "And yet, much as I like this broad language, there is something about the handbill and phonograph cases that makes me uncomfortable. The limitations they impose on governmental control of street distributions and solicitations look a bit fragile in a rough and tumble world. I wonder whether they can last." CHAFEE, *op. cit. supra* note 1, at 405.

67 316 U.S. 52 (1942).

68 *Id.* at 54.

> formation and disseminating opinion and that though the states and municipalities may appropriately regulate the privilege in the public interest, they may not unduly burden or proscribe its employment in these public thoroughfares.

He then made short shrift of the distributor's claim. The stratagem was transparent; this was still advertising matter. The issue is a different one where distribution of commercial advertising is at stake. Here the judgment of the legislature concerning the appropriate accommodation of interests is final.[69] There was clear recognition of the principle of public use that was urged in *Schneider:*[70] "The question is not whether the legislative body may interfere with the harmless pursuit of a lawful business, but whether it must permit such pursuit by what it deems an undesirable invasion of, or interference with, the full and free use of the highways by the people in fulfillment of the public use to which streets are dedicated."

It is now apparent that what was involved in *Schneider* was imperfectly characterized as freedom from arbitrariness in the state's control of public places, for that, after all, was the measure of the commercial distributor's claim. What was involved was reasonable regulation of the immemorial claim of the free man to use the streets as a forum. The regulation in order to be deemed reasonable, the Court was telling us, must recognize the special nature and value of that claim to be on the street.

The pattern was developed slightly by *Jamison v. Texas*[71] in the following year. Again we had a Jehovah's Witness charged with violation of a municipal ordinance forbidding the distribution of leaflets on the streets. In a unanimous decision the Court reversed the conviction. For the most part the issues were repetitions of those already decided. The city once again argued for plenary power, citing *Davis,* and was told by Mr. Justice Black that the argument had been "directly rejected by this Court."[72] The one

---

69 *Cf.* Breard v. Alexandria, 341 U.S. 622 (1951), drawing again the sharp distinction between commercial and political or religious use of the streets. For discussion of the underlying principle involved, see Meiklejohn, *The Priority of the Market Place of Ideas;* Director, *The Parity of the Economic Market Place;* and Freund, *Competing Freedoms in American Constitutional Law,* UNIVERSITY OF CHICAGO LAW SCHOOL, CONFERENCE ON FREEDOM AND THE LAW 3, 16, 26 (1953).

70 316 U.S. at 54–55.

71 318 U.S. 413 (1943).

72 *Id.* at 416.

new point was that the city was unsuccessful in its effort to bring the case within *Valentine* on the ground that the activity was commercial, because the Witnesses solicited contributions in the course of their distribution. The Court thus indicated that it had a realistic functional distinction in mind when it so sharply separated commercial from noncommercial speech.

The handbill sequence may be brought to a close for my purposes with consideration of *Talley v. California*,[73] a 1960 decision related only obliquely to the previous cases. It represents, however, the high-water mark of the Court's protection of speech by handbill. The case is set apart by the fact that the ordinance banned, not all handbills, but only those that did not carry the name and address of the author, printer, and sponsor. It is a key precedent, therefore, for problems of compulsory disclosure.[74] The defendants were arrested for distributing handbills, without the required identification, urging boycotts of certain merchants for discriminating in employment against "Negroes, Mexicans, and Orientals."

The Court upset the convictions, but this time there was disagreement within the ranks. Mr. Justice Harlan filed a separate concurrence[75] and there were dissents from Justices Clark, Whittaker, and Frankfurter. The majority opinion of Mr. Justice Black framed the issue in a curious manner. The ban on leaflet distribution, we were told, fell under the rulings in *Schneider* and *Jamison*, "unless the ordinance is saved by the qualification that handbills can be distributed 'if they carry the appropriate identification.'" In an interesting and important passage, the Court then analyzed the virtues of anonymity in the fight for freedom, and concluded that the qualification did not save the ordinance. Nor was the state's interest in preventing fraud sufficiently related to the identification requirement to justify the ordinance.

At the very least the decision can be read as saying that leaflet distribution cannot be barred except for very good reasons and that anonymity of the leaflets is not a good enough reason, whatever its connection with preventing fraud. More generously, the case can

---

73 362 U.S. 60 (1960).

74 See KALVEN, *op. cit. supra* note 9, at 120–21.

75 Mr. Justice Harlan placed his decision squarely on the state's failure to show a rational connection between the objective of preventing fraud and the means used. 362 U.S. at 66.

be read as treating the distribution of leaflets in the public forum as so basic a right that it cannot be burdened with even the modest sanction of compulsory disclosure of sponsorship.

Although there are some differences between a lone distributor of leaflets on a city street and two thousand pickets at a courthouse, the leaflet cases furnish the relevant model for analysis of the complex speech issues involved.[76] The operative theory of the Court, at least for the leaflet situation, is that, although it is a method of communication that interferes with the public use of the streets, the right to the streets as a public forum is such that leaflet distribution cannot be prohibited and can be regulated only for weighty reasons. And the distinctive First Amendment underpinning for this protection is reflected in the fact that the privilege does not apply to commercial leaflets.

IV. Cox Revisited

The above theory is clearly not that with which the Court approached its problem in *Cox.* Mr. Justice Goldberg, after citing

---

[76] The sound-truck cases deserve a special word since the sound truck rather than the leaflet might be thought to provide the relevant analogy for protest speech. The analogy is spoiled, however, by the peculiar history of the issue in the Court.

The initial case, Saia v. New York, 334 U.S. 558 (1948), although it speaks of "loud speakers as today indispensable instruments of effective public speech," *id.* at 561, decides no more than that the prior licensing scheme involved was bad because of the unfettered discretion of the public official, a familiar point not involving any distinctive evaluation of the sound truck.

The second sound-truck case, Kovacs v. Cooper, 336 U.S. 77 (1949), has at times been loosely read as a reversal of the protection given in *Saia.* The 5 to 4 decision is difficult to scan for several reasons. The five-man majority produced three separate and different opinions. Mr. Justice Frankfurter, in his concurring opinion, elected this as the occasion for a major opinion attacking any "preferred position" principle. Mr. Justice Jackson in his concurring opinion read the result as "a repudiation" of *Saia.* Further, the ordinance in question was ambiguous on whether it banned all sound trucks or only "loud and raucous" ones. The angry dissenters read the decision as sweepingly as possible to intensify their dissents. Mr. Justice Rutledge appropriately complained of "such a hashing of different views of the thing forbidden." *Id.* at 105. But if the four dissenters in *Kovacs* (Black, Douglas, Rutledge, and Murphy) are taken with the majority other than Frankfurter and Jackson (Burton, Reed, Vinson), we have seven Justices who certainly did not decide that all sound trucks could be banned.

The sound truck may invite the question whether a form of speech, a sound truck or a parade, might not be so collaterally disruptive as to make total barring of it appropriate, regardless of time, place, or circumstance. I think the answer is no, so long as we are talking of behavior intended as communication. *Cf.* Martin v. Struthers, 319 U.S. 141 (1943); see note 88 *infra* on the captive-audience aspects of protest speech.

all the relevant cases, concluded:[77] "The rights of free speech and assembly, while fundamental in democratic society, still do not mean that everyone with opinions or beliefs to express may address a group at any public place and at any time." The "falling off," to use Hamlet's phrase, between this dictum and that of Mr. Justice Roberts in *Hague* is not to be explained on the ground that the Court had forgotten, or even that it would like to forget, the Roberts theory, but rather that it sees great differences between leaflets, which are "speech pure," and parades, pickets, and protest, which are "speech plus."

Mr. Justice Goldberg made this point explicit:[78] "We emphatically reject the notion urged by appellant that the First and Fourteenth Amendments afford the same kind of freedom to those who would communicate ideas by conduct such as patrolling, marching, and picketing on streets and highways as these amendments afford to those who communicate by pure speech." Mr. Justice Black was equally emphatic:[79] "The First and Fourteenth Amendments, I think, take away from government, state and federal, all power to restrict freedom of speech, press, and assembly *where people have a right to be for such purposes*. This does not mean, however, that these amendments also grant a constitutional right to engage in conduct of picketing or patrolling whether on publicly owned streets or privately owned property." And at an earlier point in his opinion Black spoke of the state regulating patrolling and marching as distinguished from "*speech*." (The emphasis was his.)

It is now clear how the Court wished to conceptualize its problem. There are two kinds of communication activity—"speech pure" and "speech plus." Out of respect for precedent, the Court will be generous to "speech pure" in public places, but this does not apply to the cases at hand involving "speech plus." Hence, if there were a concept of the streets as a public forum, it does not protect "speech plus." Mr. Justice Black was willing to say outright that there is no constitutional bar to the flat prohibition of "speech plus"

---

77 379 U.S. at 554.

78 *Id.* at 555. See also *id.* at 563: "The examples are many of the applications by this court of the principle that certain forms of conduct mixed with speech may be regulated or prohibited."

79 *Id.* at 578. (Emphasis in original.) See also *id.* at 581: "Standing, patrolling, or marching back and forth on streets is conduct not speech, and as conduct can be regulated and prohibited."

in the streets. Mr. Justice Goldberg was unwilling to decide that issue, although he was quite willing to raise it gratuitously.

A. SPEECH PURE AND SPEECH PLUS

The Court's neat dichotomy of "speech pure" and "speech plus" will not work. For it leaves us without an intelligible rationale. For one thing the exercise of constitutional rights in their "most pristine and classic form" in *Edwards* has become an exercise in "speech plus." For another the Court seems to have forgotten *Valentine*. What in this scheme is commercial speech? Or is there now a three-level theory of speech[80] in public places: "speech pure," "speech plus," and "speech commercial," each with its appropriate degree of regulation?

To begin with, I would suggest that all speech is necessarily "speech plus." If it is oral, it is noise and may interrupt someone else; if it is written, it may be litter. Indeed this is why the leaflet cases were an appropriate model: they involved speech with collateral consequences that invited regulation. But the leaflets were not simply litter; they were litter with ideas.

Perhaps this is the time to bring into the discussion a classic distinction in speech theory. It is the distinction between regulations like Robert's Rules of Order and regulation of content. No one has ever argued that speech should be free of the restraints of reasonable parliamentary rules, and any concessions on this front should not be taken as relevant to the questions most central to speech theory—questions of control of content. The point then is that, in any theory, speech has always been dependent on some commitment to order and etiquette. There is, therefore, nothing novel in the vulnerability of protest speech to regulation on this score. This is not, as the Court was willing to assume in *Cox*, a characteristic setting it apart from traditional speech and hence summarily subject to regulation.

Listen for a moment to Alexander Meiklejohn describing a town meeting:[81]

> In the town meeting the people of a community assemble to discuss and to act upon matters of public interest—roads,

---

80 Some commentators have discovered a two-level theory at work in the obscenity cases. See Kalven, *The Metaphysics of the Law of Obscenity*, [1960] SUPREME COURT REVIEW 1.

81 MEIKLEJOHN, *op. cit. supra* note 36, at 24–28.

schools, poorhouses, health, external defense, and the like. Every man is free to come. They meet as political equals. Each has a right and a duty to think his own thoughts, to express them, and to listen to the arguments of others. The basic principle is that the freedom of speech shall be unabridged. And yet the meeting cannot even be opened unless, by common consent, speech is abridged. A chairman or moderator is, or has been, chosen. He "calls the meeting to order." And the hush which follows that call is a clear indication that restrictions upon speech have been set up. The moderator assumes, or arranges, that in the conduct of the business, certain rules of order will be observed. Except as he is overruled by the meeting as a whole, he will enforce those rules. His business on its negative side is to abridge speech. For example, it is usually agreed that no one shall speak unless "recognized by the chair." Also, debaters must confine their remarks to "the question before the house." If one man "has the floor," no one else may interrupt him except as provided by the rules. The meeting has assembled, not primarily to talk, but primarily by means of talking to get business done. And the talking must be regulated and abridged as the doing of the business under actual conditions may require. If a speaker wanders from the point at issue, if he is abusive or in other ways threatens to defeat the purpose of the meeting, he may be and should be declared "out of order." He must then stop speaking, at least in that way. And if he persists in breaking the rules, he may be "denied the floor" or, in the last resort, "thrown out" of the meeting. The town meeting, as it seeks for freedom of public discussion of public problems, would be wholly ineffectual unless speech were thus abridged. . . .

These speech-abridging activities of the town meeting indicate what the First Amendment to the Constitution does not forbid. When self-governing men demand freedom of speech they are not saying that every individual has an inalienable right to speak whenever, wherever, however he chooses. They do not declare that any man may talk as he pleases, when he pleases, about what he pleases, about whom he pleases, to whom he pleases. The common sense of any reasonable society would deny the existence of that unqualified right. No one, for example, may, without consent of nurse, or doctor, rise up in a sickroom to argue for his principles or his candidate. In the sickroom, that question is not "before the house." The discussion is, therefore, "out of order." To you who now listen to my words, it is allowable to differ with me, but it is not allowable for you to state that difference in words until I have finished my reading.

> Anyone who would thus irresponsibly interrupt the activities of a lecture, a hospital, a concert hall, a church, a machine shop, a classroom, a football field, or a home, does not thereby exhibit his freedom. Rather, he shows himself to be a boor, a public nuisance, who must be abated, by force if necessary.

The Meiklejohn passage demonstrates that there is something askew in the distinction between "speech pure" and "speech plus." Certainly his recalcitrant participant at the town meeting is engaged in "speech plus"; but if he is, who is not? And surely it is sobering to note that the call for regulation of such activity on behalf of the rational use of speech resources comes from the champion of the position that the First Amendment is an abolute.[82]

B. COX V. NEW HAMPSHIRE

The Supreme Court has one great precedent on the issue, *Cox v. New Hampshire*,[83] another Jehovah's Witness legacy. The city of Manchester had an ordinance requiring a permit for any "theatrical or dramatic representation . . . parade or procession upon any public street or way." The defendants were convicted of parading without a permit. The case come to the same Court that had just decided *Hague* and *Schneider*, with the exception that Justice Murphy had replaced Justice Butler. In a unanimous decision, the Court affirmed the convictions. As in the distinction between *Schneider* and *Valentine*, the Court once again had a firm principle in hand. The case had come to it with the great advantage of a strong construction of the ordinance by the New Hampshire Supreme Court.[84] It was, therefore, established that discretion in granting permits was limited exclusively to considerations of time, place, and manner, and in effect to the unbeatable proposition that you cannot have two parades on the same corner at the same time.

Chief Justice Hughes began by restating the *Hague-Schneider* formula:[85] "As regulation of the use of the streets for parades and

---

[82] Meiklejohn, *The First Amendment Is an Absolute*, [1961] SUPREME COURT REVIEW 245.

[83] 312 U.S. 569 (1941).

[84] 91 N.H. 137, 148 (1940): "A license to permit its enjoyment may not be required as a form of censorship, but a license to permit its enjoyment in fair adjustment with the enjoyment of other relations and conditions is not understood to be under the ban of the federal constitution."

[85] 312 U.S. at 574.

processions is a traditional exercise of control by local government, the question in a particular case is whether that control is exerted so as not to deny or unwarrantedly abridge the right of assembly and the opportunities for the communication of thought and the discussion of public questions immemorially associated with resort to public places." The Court noted that the New Hampshire arrangement had the "obvious advantage," not merely of avoiding overlapping parades, but also of giving the public authorities notice in advance so "as to afford opportunity for proper policing."[86] And the state court was pellucidly clear that the licensing officials had only the most limited authority under the ordinance. "The defendants, said the court, 'had a right under the Act to a license to march when, where, and as they did, if after a required investigation it was found that the convenience of the public in the use of the streets would not thereby be unduly disturbed, upon such changes in conditions or changes in time, place, and manner as would avoid disturbance.' "[87] All that the ordinance required was that the parade not be, in Mr. Meiklejohn's phrase, "out of order."

Of course, *Cox v. New Hampshire* did no more than to give a general standard for accommodation of the conflicting interests. It did not tell whether certain congested areas or certain times of the day might not always be held unavailable for parading, nor whether the size of some crowds might always be too large. But it seems to me to symbolize the ideal of Robert's Rules of Order for use of the public forum of the streets.

Admittedly there is a difference between the town meeting and the street. In the former the only problems of order and competing use relate to speakers, and the problem can be solved under a formula seeking to provide the maximum opportunity for speech at the meeting. The streets on the other hand, although a meeting place for free men from time out of mind, are also dedicated to other uses, such as travel. Hence, the speech interests compete in this instance with non-speech interests and the appropriate accommodation is more difficult.[88] Despite this difference it strikes me that

---

86 *Id.* at 576.

87 *Ibid.*

88 On Mr. Justice Black's view there is an additional complication. "Were the law otherwise, people on the streets, in their homes, and anywhere else could be compelled to listen against their wish to speakers they did not want to hear." 379 U.S. at 578. The implications for free-speech theory of the concept of the captive audience are profound. See KALVEN, *op. cit. supra* note 9, at 156–60. It is not easy to

Robert's Rules are a happy analogy because they make it so clear that the concern ought not to be with censorship, or with the content of what is said; what is needed is a phasing or timing of the activity, not a ban on it. It remains to be seen, of course, whether even under this generous view, the protest movement may not generate sharp controversies by asking for "prime time." But so long as the intention is not obstruction or harassment, as in general it has not been in the past demonstrations, it should be possible, if difficult, to work out mutually satisfactory arrangements.

Thus, Mr. Justice Roberts really had it all worked out in *Schneider*. Since all speech was "speech plus," it was subject to regulation of time, place, manner, and circumstance, but to be acceptable the regulation had to weigh heavily the fact that communication was involved. It is not clear to me why that formula was not the appropriate one for evaluating the protest conduct in *Edwards*. And, finally, to take the last step, why it was not also a good formula to be applied to the conduct in *Cox*.[89]

C. ECCE! TWO HOBGOBLINS: BALANCING AND PRIOR RESTRAINTS

The *Schneider* rationale may, however, seem to have unwanted overtones for free-speech enthusiasts. Does it not embrace two hobgoblins, a balancing test of First-Amendment interests, and a commitment to prior restraints by licensing?

It is, of course, clear that a formula calling for the weighing of speech interests in the public forum against interests in the other uses of public places requires that the Court engage in balancing.

---

see, however, why they bother Mr. Justice Black so much more here than did the leaflets in *Schneider*, the street-corner speech in Feiner v. New York, 340 U.S. 315 (1951), the sound truck in *Saia* or *Kovacs*, or the door-bell ringing in Martin v. Struthers, 319 U.S. 141 (1943).

89 Arguably, the anti-picketing statute involved in Cameron v. Johnson, *supra* note 12, will ultimately provide the test of the thesis. The statute prohibited picketing which interfered with ingress or egress into public buildings or obstructed the free use of public streets and ways "contiguous thereto." It was thus substantially more limited than the obstruction statute in *Cox*. The Court did not pass on the merits but remanded the case on procedural grounds and is almost certain to have to confront it again. Mr. Justice Black, in dissent, made even sharper his position that there was no constitutional bar to banning such activity from the streets altogether and that, a fortiori, the Mississippi statute was not unconstitutional on its face. He said, among other things, "Every person who has the slightest information about what is going on in this country can understand the importance of these issues." 381 U.S. at 742.

Perhaps it is but another indication of how fruitless the controversy over balancing has been and of how awkward for many speech problems the clear-and-present-danger test has proved.[90] Here the balancing test comes down to us with the *Schneider* mandate that the thumb of the Court be on the speech side of the scales, and there is the further reminder, if one is needed, from *Valentine* that this is not pure, or "mere," substantive due process with full deference to legislative judgment. Finally, the matter should be put to rest by the fact, never more conspicuous than in his opinion in *Cox*,[91] that this is the one kind of speech case in which Mr. Justice Black has always been willing to balance.

The judgments of time, place, and manner required must be so linked to the factual situation as to make detailed legislative regulation a clumsy, inflexible device. The result is that the citizen may need a license to use the public forum. It is true that prior licensing has come down to us bearing some historical stigma. And, as we all know, it was once thought with Blackstone that the chief meaning of freedom of speech was simply absence of prior restraints.[92] Indeed, the first of the series of public forum cases, *Lovell v. Griffin*[93] in 1937, invalidated an ordinance requiring a permit for the distribution of circulars of any kind, because it was construed to apply to all kinds of literature and all methods of distribution anywhere in the city, without any limiting criteria for licensor discretion. The Court, after calling on John Milton, said:[94] "Legislation of the type of this ordinance in question would restore the system of license and censorship in its baldest form."

But there is little, if anything, left today to the idea that prior licensing is bad per se, regardless of the criteria used.[95] It now appears that the historical reaction was against general licensing with

---

[90] See Kalven & Steffen, *The Bar Admission Cases: An Unfinished Debate between Justice Harlan and Justice Black*, 21 LAW IN TRANS. 155, 173–79 (1961); KALVEN, *op. cit. supra* note 9, at 120–21.

[91] "This Court does, and I agree that it should, 'weigh the circumstances' in order to protect, not to destroy, freedom of speech, press, and religion." 379 U.S. at 578.

[92] The relevant history of ideas is traced in Chief Justice Hughes's opinion in Near v. Minnesota, 283 U.S. 697, 713–16 (1931).

[93] 303 U.S. 444 (1938).

[94] *Id.* at 452.

[95] Emerson, *The Doctrine of Prior Restraint*, 20 LAW & CONT. PROB. 648 (1955); Freund, *The Supreme Court and Civil Liberties*, 4 VAND. L. REV. 533 (1951).

unlimited or unspecified grounds for exercise of discretion.[96] The recent *Times Film* case[97] has definitively put to rest any question whether all prior restraints are necessarily bad.[98] And, in any event, *Cox v. New Hampshire* stands as a strong and healthy precedent for use of a prior restraint, at least in regulating the public forum.

D. EQUAL PROTECTION AND CENSORSHIP

The rise of the Equal Protection Clause as a major weapon for the current Court has been the subject of comment.[99] It will be recalled that Justices Clark and Black made use of it in *Cox* as their ground for upsetting the convictions for obstructing public passageways. It is likely to provide a second line of defense for vigorous users of the public forum. If some groups are exempted from a prohibition on parades and pickets, the rationale for regulation is fatally impeached. The objection can then no longer be keyed to interferences with other uses of the public places, but would appear to implicate the kind of message that the groups were transmitting. The regulation would thus slip from the neutrality of time, place, and circumstance into a concern about content. The result is that equal-protection analysis in the area of speech issues would merge with considerations of censorship. And this is precisely what Mr. Justice Black argued in *Cox*:[100]

> But by specifically permitting picketing for the publication of labor union views, Louisiana is attempting to pick and choose among the views it is willing to have discussed on its streets. It is thus trying to prescribe by law what matters of public interest people it allows to assemble on its streets may and may not discuss. This seems to me to be censorship in a most odious form. . . .

---

96 The definitive discussion is found in Kunz v. New York, 340 U.S. 290 (1951), and Niemotko v. Maryland, 340 U.S. 268 (1951). See also A Quantity of Books v. Kansas, 378 U.S. 205 (1964).

97 Times Film Corp. v. City of Chicago, 365 U.S. 43 (1961).

98 There has not been time as yet to digest all the implications of Freedman v. Maryland, 380 U.S. 51 (1965), upsetting a Maryland movie censorship scheme because of the absence of procedural safeguards insuring prompt final determination. The opinion revives talk of the "heavy presumption" against prior restraints. *Id.* at 57.

99 Kurland, "*Equal in Origin and Equal in Title to the Legislative and Executive Branches of the Government*," 78 HARV. L. REV. 143 (1964).

100 379 U.S. at 581.

The point should have considerable practical significance. Everyone at some time or other loves a parade whatever its effect on traffic and other uses of public streets. Municipalities pressed by concern with the protest movement may be inhibited in any rush to flat nondiscriminatory prohibitions by the difficulty of distinguishing between the parades we like and others. Equal protection may, therefore, require freedom for the parades we hate.

In the Jehovah's Witness cases, the Court has been outspokenly sensitive "to the poor man's printing press"[101] theme. Labor picketing apart, perhaps, the parade, the picket, the leaflet, the sound truck, have been the media of communication exploited by those with little access to the more genteel means of communication. We would do well to avoid the occasion for any new epigrams about the majestic equality of the law prohibiting the rich man, too, from distributing leaflets or picketing.

What this consideration implies, I suggest, is not that the Negro, because he lacks control of television, radio, newspapers, and national magazines, be allowed compensating privileges to irritate on the streets, but rather that his unusual means of communication be recognized as robust and amateur means of communication and not be too quickly read as tactics of obstruction and harassment.

V. The Picket, the Courthouse, and the Narrow Statute

The one clear point that emerges with the force of precedent from the mixture of views in *Cox* is that you cannot picket the courthouse. I have no particular enthusiasm for picketing courthouses as a form of protest nor do I think the issue is likely to be one of practical importance. But it is worth pausing for a moment to see, by way of conclusion, what the rule that you cannot picket the courthouse adds to the notions of the public forum we have been pursuing.

The *Cox* ruling bristles with perplexities, noted but not fully resolved in the opinions. Would this same protest, the obstruction issue aside, have been permissible if moved a few blocks away? Could one, for example, distribute leaflets highly critical of the court near the courthouse? Is there pressure and intimidation in the protest in front of the courthouse that ceases to be present when it is in front of the state house? Or is the principle that it is all right

[101] *E.g.*, Mr. Justice Black, in Martin v. Struthers, 319 U.S. at 146: "Door to door distribution of circulars is essential to the poorly financed causes of little people."

to intimidate legislatures but not courts?[102] Is the vice in the picketing not so much in the time, place, and manner as in the message addressed to the court, and, if this is the vice, how can the result be squared with the insistent line of precedents on contempt by publication?[103] And, is it that in the courthouse situation the Court finally perceives the reality behind the gesture, so that *Cox* is a harbinger of increasingly stringent restrictions on protests? Or is the point the precise opposite, that only the special sensitivity of the law to the decorum of court proceedings makes the conduct bad? Few if any other places can claim such special protection. Hence, *Cox* may be the exception that will prove the rule of freedom.

Mr. Justice Goldberg made a most elaborate effort to deal with these points, but the unpersuasiveness of several of his reasons, given the other commitments the Court appears to have, is striking. "Mob law," we are told, "is the very antithesis of due process."[104] And so it is, but again there is the shadow of *Edwards*. What about "mob law" and the legislature? Again we are told that a state may protect "its judicial process from being misjudged in the minds of the public."[105] If the judge, however staunch and independent, happens to decide in favor of the protest side, is there not a risk that the public will misunderstand and think he yielded to pressure? But if this is a valid point, does it not apply equally to editorials and telegrams from labor leaders?[106] And, again, when confronted with the clear-and-present-danger formula, which still thrives in the contempt by publication cases, Mr. Justice Goldberg manfully said that if the formula is to be the test for such speech then "crowds, such as this, demonstrating before a courthouse . . . inherently threaten the judicial process,"[107] although the editorial and the telegram do not.

---

102 Perhaps this is just one more sign of the conventional view of the permissible non-rationality of the legislative as contrasted to the judicial process. Mr. Justice Goldberg is careful to say that different considerations would apply if the demonstrators were "picketing to protest the actions of a mayor or other official of a city completely unrelated to any judicial proceedings, who just happened to have an office located in the courthouse building." 379 U.S. at 567.

103 Bridges v. California, 314 U.S. 252 (1941); Pennekamp v. Florida, 328 U.S. 331 (1946); Craig v. Harney, 331 U.S. 367 (1947); Wood v. Georgia, 370 U.S. 375 (1962).

104 See note 24 *supra*.

105 379 U.S. at 565.

106 See note 103 *supra*.

107 379 U.S. at 566.

One cannot entirely escape a feeling that Mr. Justice Goldberg had forgotten the facts about the demonstration he himself had summarized. Although the group was enormous in size and did very pointedly march up to the sidewalk opposite the courthouse, the demonstration meeting appears to have paid little attention thereafter to the judicial process. The picket signs protested discrimination in the stores, the group sang anthems and hymns, while the jailed students joined in responsive singing. The defendant, in his speech to the group, simply said that the arrests were illegal because other people were allowed to picket and then urged them to go forth and sit in at lunch counters.

These are genuine difficulties in the *Cox* opinions, but the rationality and circumspection of the result is saved by one further circumstance on which the Court explicitly placed some stress. The circumstance is that the Court had the benefit of a narrow, precise state statute representing a legislative judgment that in this one limited area picketing is improper. The result would have been different had the state courts in the absence of the statute proceeded to treat the picketing as contempt. The point is not simply that a precise statute avoids vagueness[108] or reduces the chances of unequal administration or even that by leaving other places and times available it presents the Court with only a modest restriction. It is rather that, in the difficult balancing process these cases force upon the Court, it has the benefit of the counsel of a deliberate, specific, and relevant legislative judgment.[109] This is all, in the end, that the flaming commandment against picketing the courthouse in *Cox* should forebode for regulation in other cases.

VI. Conclusion

Cox v. Louisiana is not one of the Court's more impressive performances. The Court has among its precedents a fine tradition about the public forum on which it did not sufficiently rely. Rather is displayed irritation and anxiety in confronting one of the most difficult practical issues of the moment. Among the many hallmarks of an open society, surely one must be that not every group of people on the streets is "a mob," and another that "its streets time out of mind have been used for purposes of assembly, communicating thoughts between citizens, and discussing public questions."

[108] This seems to be Mr. Justice Black's view of the point.

[109] *Cf.* Mr. Justice Roberts' opinion in Cantwell v. Connecticut, 310 U.S. 296, 311 (1940).

JEROLD H. ISRAEL

ELFBRANDT V. RUSSELL: THE DEMISE OF THE OATH?

In *Elfbrandt v. Russell*,[1] the Supreme Court, in a 5-to-4 decision, declared unconstitutional Arizona's requirement of a loyalty oath from state employees. At first glance, *Elfbrandt* appears to be just another decision voiding a state loyalty oath on limited grounds relating to the specific language of the particular oath.[2] Yet, several aspects of Mr. Justice Douglas' opinion for the majority suggest that *Elfbrandt* is really of far greater significance:[3] it may sharply

---

Jerold H. Israel is Professor of Law, University of Michigan.

[1] 384 U.S. 11 (1966).

[2] Immediate reaction generally placed the case in this category. The *New York Times*, for example, made the following comments in describing *Elfbrandt:* "The decision avoided sweeping terms that might also have invalidated loyalty oaths of other states. But it continued the high court's recent tendency to resolve all constitutional doubts against loyalty oath laws. . . .

"In the early nineteen-fifties the Supreme Court upheld loyalty oaths relating to Los Angeles city employees, teachers in New York State, and candidates for public office in Maryland. But in recent years without overruling the principle that public employees can be required to sign such oaths, it has struck down several, finding that they were improperly drafted." N.Y. Times, April 19, 1966, p. 1, col. 6; p. 1, col. 4. See also Chicago Tribune, April 19, 1966, p. 3, cols. 1–3; NEWSWEEK 21 (May 2, 1966).

[3] Even if the *Elfbrandt* ruling were limited to the particular language of the Arizona statute, it would still have a significant impact on the laws of several states since the Arizona provision is based on Maryland's widely copied "Ober Act." See MD. ANN. CODE, art. 85a, §§ 1, 10, 11 (1965 Supp.); FLA. REV. STAT., tit. 44, ch. 876, §§ 22, 24, 25 (1965 Supp.); MISS. CODE ANN., tit. 17, ch. 10, §§ 4064-01, 4064-02, 4064-03 (1964 Supp.); N.H. REV. STAT. ANN., ch. 588, §§ 1, 9 (1965 Supp.); OKLA. STAT.

limit the scope and coverage of loyalty oaths generally and, indeed, may presage a ruling invalidating all such oaths. Of course, only the Supreme Court can determine this. In the meantime, some evaluation by others seems appropriate, particularly in light of the numerous attacks against loyalty oaths currently being mounted in various state courts and legislatures.[4]

I. The Elfbrandt Opinions

A. The Background

In form, if not in substance, the Arizona loyalty oath considered in *Elfbrandt* was unusual. For its language contained none of the negative disclaimers of affiliation or advocacy that mark the test oath.[5] The employee merely swore to "support and defend the constitution of the United States against all enemies, foreign and domestic"; that he would "bear true faith and allegiance to the same"; and that he would "well and faithfully discharge the duties of [his] office."[6] An oath in this form had been required of Arizona's public employees since 1901.[7] In 1961, however, the legislature, in adopting Arizona's version of the Communist Control Act,[8] put a gloss on the 1901 oath that, in effect, turned it into a more typical loyalty oath. Section 5 of the Arizona Communist Control Act made it a crime "subject to all the penalties for perjury" for any employee, having taken the positive oath of allegiance, thereafter "knowingly and willfully" (1) to "commit or aid in the commission of any act to overthrow [the state government] by force or violence," (2) to advocate the overthrow of the state government by such means, or (3) to "become or remain a member of the Communist party, its subordinate organizations, or any

Ann., tit. 21, ch. 52, §§ 1266.4, 1266.6 (1965 Supp.); Pa. Stat. Ann., tit. 65, ch. 11, §§ 212, 213, 214 (1965 Supp.); see also Ind. Stat. Ann., tit. 10, ch. 52, §§ 10-5203, 10-5207 (1965 Supp.).

4 See ACLU, Feature Press Service Bulletin, § 2266, May 16, 1966.

5 See Brown, Loyalty and Security 92–95 (1958); Koenigsberg & Stavis, *Test Oaths: Henry VIII to the American Bar Association*, 11 Law. Guild Rev. 111 (1951). See generally Hyman, To Try Men's Souls (1960).

6 Ariz. Stat. § 38-231 (1965 Supp.).

7 Ariz. Rev. Stat. § 222 (1901). The oath was originally adopted while Arizona was still a territory, and consequently was amended in several respects when Arizona was admitted to statehood.

8 Ariz. Laws 1961, c. 108, § 1-9.

other organization having for one of its purposes the overthrow by force or violence of the [state] government" where the employee "had knowledge of said unlawful purpose of said organization or organizations."[9] To supplement § 5, the Arizona act also required all government employees to resubscribe to the oath of allegiance as interpreted in the light of the new section.[10]

Petitioner Elfbrandt, a teacher in the Tucson public schools, refused to take the oath and brought suit in the Arizona state courts to have the state oath requirement declared unconstitutional.[11] That litigation lasted five years and was twice taken to the United States Supreme Court before the Arizona statute was finally held unconstitutional.[12]

---

[9] That section amended § 38-231 to read as follows: "E. Any officer or employee as defined in this section having taken the form of oath or affirmation prescribed by this section, and knowingly or wilfully at the time of subscribing the oath or affirmation, or at any time thereafter during his term of office or employment, does commit or aid in the commission of any act to overthrow by force or violence the government of this state or of any of its political subdivisions, or advocates the overthrow by force or violence of the government of this state or of any of its political subdivisions, or during such term of office or employment knowingly and wilfully becomes or remains a member of the communist party of the United States or its successors or any of its subordinate organizations or any other organization having for one of its purposes the overthrow by force or violence of the government of the state of Arizona or any of its political subdivisions, and said officer or employee as defined in this section prior to becoming or remaining a member of such organization or organizations had knowledge of said unlawful purpose of said organization or organizations, shall be guilty of a felony and upon conviction thereof shall be subject to all the penalties for perjury; in addition, upon conviction under this section, the officer or employee shall be deemed discharged from said office or employment and shall not be entitled to any additional compensation or any other emoluments or benefits which may have been incident or appurtenant to said office or employment."

All references to § 5 in the text of this article refer to this provision, now ARIZ. REV. STAT. § 38-231E (1965 Supp.).

[10] ARIZ. REV. STAT. § 8-231(c) (1965 Supp.).

[11] Although the Arizona act requires all employees to take the oath, the only sanction provided for failure to do so is denial of compensation. Consequently, the petitioner retained her job and simply continued to teach without pay. This aspect of the case attracted at least as much attention from the press as did the Court's opinion. See, *e.g.*, NEWSWEEK, *supra* note 2. The back pay accumulated by petitioner and her husband, a fellow teacher who also refused to take the oath, amounted to over $60,000, but apparently the school boards involved were not entirely sure of the Elfbrandts' right to the money even after the Supreme Court decision. Ann Arbor News, June 23, 1966, p. 7, cols. 2–5.

[12] The Arizona Supreme Court later found in an opinion as yet unreported that the petitioner still was required to take the oath, although the special gloss of

On the first appeal to the Supreme Court, an Arizona Supreme Court decision upholding the oath was vacated,[13] and the case was remanded for reconsideration in the light of *Baggett v. Bullitt*.[14] In *Baggett* the Supreme Court had found unconstitutionally vague a Washington oath that contained language very much like that found in the first clause of § 5.[15] On remand, however, a majority of the Arizona court found that *Baggett* was inapplicable since the reference in § 5 to activity aiding an act designed to overthrow the government had a much narrower and more traditional scope than did a similar reference in the Washington oath.[16] One member of the Arizona court, Justice Bernstein, dissented on the ground that *Baggett* was controlling.[17] The dissent was not based on the first clause of § 5, however, but was tied entirely to the third clause of that section, which prohibits an employee from knowingly becoming a member of any organization "having for one of its purposes the overthrow by force or violence of the government."[18] Justice Bernstein found that this clause failed adequately to identify the nature of the organization in which membership was barred, and, therefore, that it was unconstitutionally vague. As an illustration, he pointed to the university scientist, who, he said, "could not know whether membership is prohibited in an international scientific organization which includes members from neutralist nations and Communist bloc nations—the latter admittedly dedicated to the overthrow of our government and which control the organization. . . . Though all might agree that the principal purpose of such organization is scientific, the statute makes [the scientist's] membership a crime if any subordinate purpose is the overthrow

§ 38-231E was no longer applicable. See Ann Arbor News, June 23, 1966, p. 7, cols. 2–5.

13 378 U.S. 127 (1964), *vacating* 94 Ariz. 1 (1963).

14 377 U.S. 360 (1964).

15 Washington required public employees to swear that they were not subversive persons as defined by statute: " 'Subversive person' means any person who commits, attempts to commit, or aids in the commission, or advocates, abets, advises or teaches by any means any person to commit, attempt to commit, or aid in the commission of any act intended to overthrow, destroy or alter, or to assist in the overthrow, destruction or alteration of the constitutional form of the government of the United States, or of the state of Washington or any political subdivision of either of them by revolution, force, or violence. . . ." Wash. Laws 1955, c. 377.

16 97 Ariz. 140 (1965).

17 *Id.* at 147.

18 See note 9 *supra*.

of the state government." "The vice of vagueness here," he concluded, "is that the scientist cannot know whether membership in the organization would result in a prosecution for violation of [§ 5] or in honors from his university for the encyclopedic knowledge acquired . . . in part through his membership."[19]

B. THE MAJORITY OPINION

On review of the Arizona decision, Mr. Justice Douglas, speaking for himself, the Chief Justice, and Justices Black, Brennan, and Fortas, agreed with Justice Bernstein that the invalidity of the third or so-called membership clause of § 5 rendered Arizona's oath requirement unconstitutional. In reaching this conclusion, however, the majority opinion, though quoting extensively from Justice Bernstein's dissent, did not rely upon the "void for vagueness" rationale that he had used.[20] Rather, Mr. Justice Douglas' opinion was based squarely on the ground that the membership clause of § 5 violated a basic principle restricting the scope of statutes affecting First Amendment rights. Quoting from *Cantwell v. Connecticut* and *Shelton v. Tucker*, Mr. Justice Douglas described that principle as follows:[21]

> "[A] statute touching . . . protected rights must be narrowly drawn to define and punish specific conduct as constituting a clear and present danger to a substantial interest of the state." . . . Legitimate legislative goals "cannot be pursued by means that broadly stifle fundamental personal liberties when the end can be more narrowly achieved."

Mr. Justice Douglas found that the Arizona statute failed to meet this standard because it applied to employees who might knowingly join organizations favoring violent overthrow of the government but who themselves might not subscribe to that goal. In including such persons, § 5 necessarily relied, said Mr. Justice Douglas, on an improper theory of "guilt by association" and the section therefore had "infringe[d] unnecessarily" on protected First Amendment rights.[22]

The crux of the reasoning that led Mr. Justice Douglas to this

---

19 97 Ariz. at 147–48.

20 384 U.S. at 14–15.

21 *Id.* at 18, quoting from Cantwell v. Connecticut, 310 U.S. 296, 311 (1940), and Shelton v. Tucker, 364 U.S. 479, 488 (1960).

22 384 U.S. at 19.

conclusion is found in several paragraphs toward the end of his opinion.[23] First, he noted that in *Scales v. United States*,[24] the Court had recognized that " 'a blanket prohibition of association with a group having both legal and illegal aims' would pose 'a real danger that legitimate political expression or association would be impaired.' "[25] Accordingly, the Court in *Scales* had carefully limited the application of the membership clause of the Smith Act to those members of organizations advocating overthrow who were both "active" in their membership and had the "specific intent of assisting in achieving the unlawful ends of the organization."[26] The constitutional significance of the "specific intent" requirement imposed by *Scales* had been clearly established in *Aptheker v. Secretary of State*[27] when the Court voided a statute prohibiting the issuance of passports to members of "Communist organizations" precisely because that statute "covered membership which was not accompanied by a specific intent to further the unlawful aims of the organization."[28] The Arizona "oath and accompanying statutory gloss suffer from an identical constitutional infirmity" as the statute in *Aptheker*[29] Under § 5 a state employee who knowingly joins an organization "which has as 'one of its purposes' the violent overthrow of the government is subject to immediate discharge and criminal penalties" even though he "does not subscribe to the organization's unlawful ends."[30] As a result, here, as in *Baggett v. Bullitt*, persons risk prosecution by engaging in "knowing but guiltless" activity. Illustrative might be the teacher who attends the Pugwash Conference or "joins a seminar group predominantly Communist and therefore subject to control by those who are said to believe in the overthrow of the government."[31] Surely, Mr. Justice Douglas continued:[32] "Those who join an organization but do not share its unlawful purposes and who do not participate in its unlawful activities pose no threat, either as citizens or public employees." A law which encompasses such persons "impose[s], in effect, a conclusive presumption that the member shares the unlawful aims of the organizations," and for that reason alone is clearly unconstitutional.[33] Summarizing the Court's position at the conclusion of the opinion, Mr. Justice Douglas wrote:[34]

---

23 *Id.* at 15–18.
24 367 U.S. 203 (1961).
25 384 U.S. at 15.
26 *Ibid.*
27 378 U.S. 500 (1964).
28 384 U.S. at 16.
29 *Ibid.*
30 *Ibid.*
31 *Id.* at 17.
32 *Ibid.*
33 *Ibid.*
34 *Id.* at 19.

> A law which applies to membership without "the specific intent" to further the illegal aims of the organization infringes unnecessarily on protected freedoms. It rests on the doctrine of "guilt by association" which has no place here. . . . Such a law cannot stand.

C. THE DISSENTING OPINION

Mr. Justice White's dissenting opinion, joined by Justices Clark, Harlan, and Stewart, noted at the outset that "[a]ccording to unequivocal prior holdings of this Court, a state is entitled to condition public employment upon its employees abstaining from knowing membership in . . . organizations advocating the violent overthrow of the government which employs them," and "the state is [also] constitutionally authorized to inquire into such affiliations and . . . discharge those who refuse to affirm or deny them."[35] The dissent cited eight previous decisions in support of this proposition, and noted that Mr. Justice Douglas' opinion "does not mention or purport to overrule these cases."[36] Neither does the majority opinion, as Mr. Justice White read it, "expressly hold" that a state "must retain" as employees those who knowingly hold membership in organizations aiming at violent overthrow. "It would seem, therefore," he concluded, "that the Court's judgment is only aimed at the criminal provisions of the Arizona law which exposes an employee to a perjury prosecution if he swears falsely about membership when he signs the oath or if he later becomes a knowing member while remaining in public employment."[37]

Mr. Justice White then argued that the distinction the Court appears to have drawn between criminal and civil sanctions is invalid. The right to punish for intentional falsification is clear from prior cases. As for the punishment of employees who later join an organization of the proscribed type:[38] "If a State may disqualify for knowing membership . . . , it is likewise within its

[35] *Ibid.*

[36] *Id.* at 20. Six cases were cited directly: Gerende v. Board of Supervisors, 341 U.S. 56 (1951); Garner v. Board of Public Works, 341 U.S. 716 (1951); Adler v. Board of Education, 342 U.S. 485 (1952); Beilan v. Board of Education, 357 U.S. 399 (1958); Lerner v. Casey, 357 U.S. 468 (1958); Nelson v. County of Los Angeles, 362 U.S. 1 (1960). The dissent cited as "see also" two other cases: Wieman v. Updegraff, 344 U.S. 183 (1952); Slochower v. Board of Education, 350 U.S. 551 (1956).

[37] 384 U.S. at 20.

[38] *Id.* at 21.

powers to move criminally against the employee who knowingly engages in disqualifying acts during his employment." "The crime provided by the Arizona law," Mr. Justice White emphasized, "is not just the act of becoming a member of an organization but it is that membership plus concurrent public employment."[39]

The dissent also argued that "there is nothing in *Scales* . . . or *Aptheker* . . . dictating the result reached by the Court."[40] *Scales* involved the general criminal provisions of the Smith Act and therefore was not in point. Neither was *Aptheker*, since the statutory provision involved there applied to members who actually lacked knowledge of the organization's illicit purpose. In fact, *Speiser v. Randall*,[41] another case cited by the majority, had "carefully preserved" *Gerende v. Board of Supervisors*[42] and *Garner v. Board of Public Works*,[43] two cases upholding test oaths for employees that were based on the same principles as the Arizona oath. Finally, Mr. Justice White suggested that even if one were to accept the majority's position and were to hold that Arizona may not take criminal action against employees who are knowing members of organizations aiming at violent overthrow of the government, the appropriate remedy would not be to invalidate the Arizona oath requirement as the majority had done, but to remand the case to the state court to determine the severability of the criminal provisions of the Arizona statute.

D. THE IMPLICATIONS OF SILENCE

When viewed in light of the dissent, two aspects of Mr. Justice Douglas' opinion immediately stand out. Both deal, not unsurprisingly, more with what the opinion left unsaid than with what it said. The first is the complete absence of any reply to the dissent, either with respect to its narrow characterization of the majority ruling or with respect to the cases Mr. Justice White cited as clearly controlling if the majority had sought to rely on a broader ground. The second is the absence in both opinions, but particularly in the majority opinion, of any meaningful discussion of the nature of the state's interests in the loyalty oath requirement. These omissions are significant for more than the light they may shed

---

39 *Ibid.*

40 *Id.* at 22.

41 357 U.S. 513 (1958).

42 341 U.S. 56 (1951).

43 *Id.* at 716.

on the professional quality of the Court's opinion. The inferences to be drawn from the opinion's silence on these matters probably will determine what impact *Elfbrandt* will have upon the permissible scope and coverage of loyalty oaths.

II. The Significance of the Criminal Sanction

Dissenting opinions are hardly the best source for determining the breadth of a majority ruling. This is particularly true when a case is decided by a close vote as *Elfbrandt* was, and when the dissent is concerned with the next case and the possibility of accomplishing a shift in the Court's position not inconsistent with the immediate decision. Nevertheless, Mr. Justice White's characterization of the Court's ruling as grounded solely on Arizona's use of criminal sanctions finds just enough support in the majority opinion that it cannot be dismissed out of hand as simply a dissenter's tactic.

First, there is the fact that the majority made no effort to reply to Mr. Justice White's statement of its ruling. Admittedly Mr. Justice Douglas' opinion does not place primary emphasis on the criminal sanctions imposed by § 5, although it does make frequent mention of these sanctions.[44] It is also true, as will be seen later, that the cases cited by Mr. Justice White as otherwise controlling are distinguishable on grounds other than Arizona's reliance on criminal sanctions in § 5.[45] Still, since it would have taken so little flatly to reject Mr. Justice White's interpretation, it is difficult to understand why this was not done. Perhaps Mr. Justice Douglas, who had dissented in several of the cases cited by Mr. Justice White, felt that any attempt to distinguish those cases would give them undue recognition.[46] Perhaps the majority's failure to reply to the dissent reflects no more than the often criticized tendency of members of the present Court to engage "in separate monologues rather than a dialogue."[47] Yet the absence of any reply to an obvious attempt to limit a majority opinion is unusual, and a

---

[44] See 384 U.S. at 16–17.

[45] See text *infra*, at section III.

[46] Mr. Justice Douglas dissented in five of the eight cases cited by Mr. Justice White: *Garner*, *Adler*, *Beilan*, *Lerner*, and *Nelson*. See note 36 *supra*.

[47] Shapiro, *The Supreme Court and Constitutional Adjudication: Of Politics and Neutral Principles*, 31 Geo. Wash. L. Rev. 587, 591 (1963).

possible inference therefrom is that at least one member of the majority accepted Mr. Justice White's interpretation of its ruling.

Another element that may be cited in support of Mr. Justice White's interpretation is the fact that the two cases on which Mr. Justice Douglas relied most heavily, *Scales* and *Aptheker*, both involved criminal statutes.[48] Moreover, insofar as *Scales* was concerned, it was commonly recognized that the Court there had employed a standard of review far different from that used in previous loyalty oath cases, such as *Garner* and *Gerende*.[49]

Nevertheless, Mr. Justice White's interpretation of the majority's ruling is most difficult to accept because such a decision would be unsupportable in either precedent or logic. Admittedly, the Court has generally distinguished statutes imposing criminal sanctions on speech or association, such as the Smith Act, from statutes imposing more "limited" sanctions, such as disqualification from employment under a state loyalty program. No matter whether the standard has been described in terms of balancing, overbroadness, or defining protected speech, the Court has always given considerably more leeway to a legislature's non-criminal sanctions.[50] Thus, in the Hatch Act case, *United Public Workers v.*

---

48 *Scales* involved a criminal prosecution under the Smith Act. 18 U.S.C. § 2385. *Aptheker* involved a suit for a declaratory judgment in which the Court was asked to declare unconstitutional a criminal provision of the Subversive Activities Control Act, 50 U.S.C. § 785 (1964).

49 Although the Court had not actually discussed *Scales* as it related to the loyalty oath cases, the First Amendment issues in *Scales* were resolved largely on the basis of Dennis v. United States, 341 U.S. 494 (1951). *Dennis* involved a considerably more restrictive standard of review than the loyalty oath cases. See, *e.g.*, Konigsberg v. State Bar, 366 U.S. 36, 49–51 (1961); Speiser v. Randall, 357 U.S. 513, 527–28 (1958).

50 In Konigsberg v. State Bar, 366 U.S. 36 (1961), Mr. Justice Harlan described this distinction—actually based on the function of the restriction on speech—in terms of the difference between those cases in which the Court determines whether "the speech . . . [is] outside the scope of constitutional protection" and those in which the Court applies what is commonly referred to as the "balancing" test. *Id.* at 49–51. Unfortunately, the wide-ranging debate over use of "balancing" in First Amendment cases has tended to obscure the distinction drawn by Mr. Justice Harlan. Certainly, all decisions in this area, whether phrased in terms of balancing or defining the scope of "protected" speech necessarily involve an evaluation of competing interests. See Nutting, *Is the First Amendment Obsolete?* 30 GEO. WASH. L. REV. 167 (1961); Karst, *Legislative Fact in Constitutional Litigation*, [1960] SUPREME COURT REVIEW 75, 95. It is also true that the Court may sometimes speak in terms of balancing even in dealing with restrictions upon borderline classes of speech. See,

Mitchell,[51] the Court sustained the power of the federal government to discharge employees who engaged in certain political activities, although a criminal statute inhibiting such action by the general public clearly would be unconstitutional.[52] The distinction drawn in *Mitchell* and similar cases has not, however, rested on the nature of the sanction employed by the legislature, but on the purpose of the legislation.[53] Criminal sanctions gener-

---

e.g., Dennis v. United States, 341 U.S. 494, 510 (1951), dealing with speech advocating illegal activity. But the type of balancing referred to by Mr. Justice Harlan in *Konigsberg* rests upon an entirely different approach, if not a different process, than that balancing involved without recognition in the obscenity cases and with recognition in *Dennis*. See generally Kalven, *The New York Times Case: A Note on "The Central Meaning of the First Amendment,"* [1964] SUPREME COURT REVIEW 191, 213–17. But see Frantz, *The First Amendment in the Balance*, 71 YALE L. J. 1424, 1429–32 (1962).

Unlike *Dennis* and other cases involving direct restraints, the Court in *Elfbrandt* does not proceed from the premise that there is a central core area of clearly protected speech and the relation of the legislatively proscribed speech to that core will, in large measure, determine the constitutionality of the proscription. See Kalven, *supra*, at 204–11. See also Dennis v. United States, 183 F.2d 201, 207 (2d Cir. 1950). Since the legislative restriction on speech in Mr. Justice Harlan's second category of cases is an incidental aspect of a general regulation, the nature of the speech involved obviously becomes less significant, and the basic assumption is that "compelling" state interest will justify an incidental restriction imposed even on speech within the central core area. See generally Bates v. Little Rock, 361 U.S. 516, 524 (1960). Accordingly, the Court's approach to "weighing" competing interests in this class of cases is much more akin to the normal standard of substantive due process than is the evaluation of the nature of the speech and the legislative interest in cases of direct restraints on speech, such as *Dennis*, or New York Times v. Sullivan, 376 U.S. 254 (1964).

[51] 330 U.S. 75 (1947).

[52] *Id.* at 101–04. The political activity involved in the case before the Court was participation "as [an] executive committeeman and a worker at the polls." *Id.* at 103.

[53] Although the Court in *Mitchell* did not attempt to distinguish cases involving restrictions aimed directly at the content of speech, it did emphasize that the congressional purpose in the Hatch Act was to preserve the efficiency of the federal service and not to restrict political activities. See 330 U.S. at 101–04. The distinction between cases like *Mitchell* and those involving direct restraints on speech was clearly stated in later cases. In Konigsberg v. State Bar, 366 U.S. 36, 49–51 (1961), the Court described that distinction as follows: "Throughout its history this Court has consistently recognized at least two ways in which constitutionally protected freedom of speech is narrower than an unlimited license to talk. On the one hand certain forms of speech, or speech in certain contexts, have been considered outside the scope of constitutional protection. See, *e.g.*, *Schenck* v. *United States*, 249 U.S. 47; *Chaplinsky* v. *New Hampshire*, 315 U.S. 568; *Dennis* v. *United States*, 341 U.S. 494; *Beauharnais* v. *Illinois*, 343 U.S. 250; *Yates* v. *United States*, 354 U.S. 298; *Roth* v. *United States*, 354 U.S. 476. On the other hand, general regulatory

ally have been used in legislation aimed directly at suppressing a particular class of speech, either because of disagreement with its content or concern for its impact upon an audience.[54] The more limited sanctions, such as disqualification from public office or the denial of permission to use public streets for political rallies, are usually found in legislation aimed at the prevention of certain conduct other than that produced by the speech.[55] The regulation of speech in these circumstances imposes what the Court describes as an "indirect" restriction on speech, an "incidental" by-product of the prohibition of undesirable conduct.[56] Thus, the purpose of the Hatch Act was not to suppress political activities, but to prevent a situation conducive to the administrative evils of a spoils system.[57] Similarly, prohibitions against the employment of persons who advocate the overthrow of the government have traditionally been looked upon as an "indirect" restriction on speech because the legislation is aimed not at the content of the speech,

---

statutes, not intended to control the content of speech but incidentally limiting its unfettered exercise, have not been regarded as the type of law the First or Fourteenth Amendments forbade Congress or the state to pass, when they have been found justified by subordinating valid governmental interests, a prerequisite to constitutionality which has necessarily involved a weighing of the governmental interest involved. See *e.g.*, *Schneider* v. *State*, 308 U.S. 147, 161; *Cox* v. *New Hampshire*, 312 U.S. 569; *Prince* v. *Massachusetts*, 321 U.S. 158; *Kovacs* v. *Cooper*, 336 U.S. 77; *American Communications Ass'n* v. *Douds*, 339 U.S. 382; *Breard* v. *Alexandria*, 341 U.S. 622." See also American Communications Ass'n v. Douds, 339 U.S. 382, 396, 399 (1950). But *cf.* United States v. Brown, 381 U.S. 437, 456–60 (1965).

[54] See, *e.g.*, the first group of cases cited by Mr. Justice Harlan in the excerpt from *Konigsberg* quoted in note 53 *supra.*

[55] See, *e.g.*, American Communications Ass'n v. Douds, 339 U.S. 382, 396 (1950): "But the question with which we are here faced is not the same one that Justices Holmes and Brandeis found convenient to consider in terms of clear and present danger. Government's interest here is not in preventing the dissemination of Communist doctrine or the holding of particular beliefs because it is feared that unlawful action will result therefrom if free speech is practiced. Its interest is in protecting the free flow of commerce from what Congress considers to be substantial evils of conduct that are not the products of speech at all. Section 9(h), in other words, does not interfere with speech because Congress fears the consequences of speech; it regulates harmful conduct which Congress has determined is carried on by persons who may be identified by their political affiliations and beliefs." See also Speiser v. Randall, quoted *infra* note 58.

[56] See Konigsberg v. State Bar, 366 U.S. 36, 49–51 (1961); Speiser v. Randall, 357 U.S. 513, 527 (1958); American Communications Ass'n v. Douds, 339 U.S. 382, 396, 399 (1950).

[57] 330 U.S. at 102–03.

but at the potential performance of the speaker in public office. The reference to the speech of a particular content is viewed, in effect, merely as a means of identifying a person who is more likely to engage in undesirable conduct as an employee.[58]

While not all the members of the Court have agreed that statutes restricting government employment on the basis of speech or association should be characterized as indirect restraints on speech, generally they all do recognize that the key to such characterization must be the purpose of the legislation, not the nature of the sanction used to implement that purpose.[59] The Court has

[58] See note 56 *supra*. See also Speiser v. Randall, 357 U.S. 513, 527 (1958): "The appellees, in controverting this position, rely on cases in which this Court has sustained the validity of loyalty oaths required of public employees, *Garner* v. *Board of Public Works*, 341 U.S. 716; candidates for public office, *Gerende* v. *Board of Supervisors*, 341 U.S. 56, and officers of labor unions, *American Communications Assn.* v. *Douds, supra*. In these cases, however, there was no attempt directly to control speech but rather to protect, from an evil shown to be grave, some interest clearly within the sphere of governmental concern. The purpose of the legislation sustained in the *Douds* case, the Court found, was to minimize the danger of political strikes disruptive of interstate commerce by discouraging labor unions from electing Communist Party members to union office. While the Court recognized that the necessary effect of the legislation was to discourage the exercise of rights protected by the First Amendment, this consequence was said to be only indirect. The congressional purpose was to achieve an objective other than restraint on speech. Only the method of achieving this end touched on protected rights and that only tangentially. The evil at which Congress had attempted to strike in that case was thought sufficiently grave to justify limited infringement of political rights. Similar considerations governed the other cases. Each case concerned a limited class of persons in or aspiring to public positions by virtue of which they could, if evilly motivated, create serious danger to the public safety. The principal aim of those statutes was not to penalize political beliefs but to deny positions to persons supposed to be dangerous because the position might be misused to the detriment of the public."

But *cf.* United States v. Brown, 381 U.S. 437, 456–60 (1965). *Brown* possibly could be extended further to undermine this line of analysis. The Court there suggested that the legislative purpose to prohibit misuses of office could constitute "punishment" for the purposes of the bill of attainder prohibition. Whether the Court would then use the clause to invalidate a restriction stated in terms of a class larger than the membership of a particular organization remains to be seen. Certainly the opinion in *Brown* and certain aspects of *Elfbrandt* indicate it would not. 381 U.S. at 461–62; see text *infra*, at note 111–14.

[59] Of the present Justices who were then sitting, only Justices Black and Douglas did not join in the characterization of the loyalty oath cases as indirect restraints in *Konigsberg* or *Speiser*, *supra* note 56. Both Justices have rejected the application of the "balancing" test in these cases, but this stems from their belief that loyalty oaths are not really aimed at preventing misuse of conduct, but are "direct" restrictions designed primarily to punish speech. See Konigsberg v. State Bar, 366

recognized that indirect restraints *e.g.*, a limitation on the use of sound amplifiers, may be enforced by criminal sanctions.[60] The Court has also recognized that direct restraints need not always take the form of criminal prohibitions, as is illustrated by the restriction on the receipt of mail recently invalidated in *Lamont v. Postmaster*,[61] and the denial of a veterans' tax exemption voided in *Speiser v. Randall.*[62] To be sure, the purpose of the legislation has not always been clearly identified as the important factor in distinguishing between direct and indirect restraints.[63] As a result, there has been occasional confusion in the lower courts,[64] as indeed was exhibited by the Arizona Supreme Court in its first consideration of the *Elfbrandt* case.[65] But the Supreme Court itself has consistently recognized the basis of the distinction, although there has often been disagreement over its application.[66] Accordingly, whatever limitation *Elfbrandt* imposes upon the use of political association as a basis for restricting employment should, according to precedent, be applicable irrespective of whether the state implements its policy by discharging the employee or by imposing penal sanctions. Moreover, precedents aside, a different result would make little sense in terms of any theory of First Amendment

---

U.S. 36, 56, 68–70 (1960); Barenblatt v. United States, 360 U.S. 109, 134, 141–53 (1959); Beilan v. Board of Education, 357 U.S. 399, 412, 414–15 (1958); Wieman v. Updegraff, 344 U.S. 183, 192 (1952). It is not entirely clear whether their view is based primarily on the history of loyalty oaths or on a general suspicion of any standard that operates with reference to the content of speech. Compare *Wieman* and *Barenblatt, supra,* with *Konigsberg.* In any event, it is clear that both Justices recognize the special nature of incidental restrictions on speech where it is clear that the restriction is not "aimed at speech" and does not "depend for its application upon the content of speech." Konigsberg v. State Bar, *supra,* at 70. See also Barenblatt v. United States, *supra;* Viereck v. United States, 318 U.S. 237, 249, 250–51 (1942).

60 See Kovacs v. Cooper, 336 U.S. 77 (1949). See also Cox v. New Hampshire, 312 U.S. 569 (1941); Prince v. Massachusetts, 321 U.S. 158 (1944).

61 381 U.S. 301 (1965), especially at 307–08 (Brennan, J.).

62 357 U.S. 513 (1958).

63 See, *e.g.*, Adler v. Board of Education, 342 U.S. 485, 492 (1952); Brotherhood of Railroad Trainmen v. Virginia Bar, 377 U.S. 1, 7–8 (1964).

64 See, *e.g.*, Brown v. United States, 334 F.2d 488, 492–96 (9th Cir. 1964), *affirmed on other grounds,* 381 U.S. 437 (1965); Weaver v. Jordan, 49 Cal. Rptr. 537, 543 (1966); In re Schlessinger, 404 Pa. 584 (1961).

65 94 Ariz. at 9–10.

66 See Kalven, *supra* note 50, at 216.

protection, especially in view of the fact that, as the Court itself often has recognized, non-criminal sanctions may often pose more of a danger to the preservation of protected rights than criminal sanctions.[67]

In the light of this background, Mr. Justice White's interpretation of the majority ruling may be nothing more than an artfully employed "straw man." The failure of the majority opinion to reply to the dissent on this point probably can be attributed to Mr. Justice Douglas' views on the art of opinion writing.[68] The citation of *Scales* without mention of the difference in the nature of the statute there involved can probably be similarly explained. Mr. Justice Douglas has never been willing to accept the premise that loyalty oath cases should be treated as indirect restrictions on speech,[69] and, in large degree, he has been unwilling even to acknowledge that previous decisions have drawn a distinction between statutes like the Smith Act and employment disqualification provisions.[70] Also, since *Aptheker*, a case involving an indirect restraint under the traditional view, had already drawn upon reasoning similar to that employed in *Scales*, the distinction between the Smith Act and the Arizona legislation may well have been viewed as without importance for the purpose of applying *Scales* to this case.[71]

III. The Scope of Elfbrandt: Sub Silentio Overruling

The rejection of Mr. Justice White's interpretation of the Court's ruling does not eliminate all the problems presented by the majority's failure to respond to the argument of the dissent. There remains in particular the several cases cited by Mr. Justice White as generally controlling if the majority opinion were not

---

67 See *e.g.*, New York Times Co. v. Sullivan, 376 U.S. 254, 277–78 (1964); Garrison v. Louisiana, 379 U.S. 64 (1964); see also *In re* Sawyer, 360 U.S. 622 (1959).

68 See generally Rogat, *Mr. Justice Pangloss*, N.Y. Rev. of Books, Oct. 22, 1964, pp. 5–7; see also Kurland, *Foreword*, "*Equal in Origin and Equal in Title to the Legislative and Executive Branches of the Government*," 78 Harv. L. Rev. 143, 167–68 (1964).

69 See note 60 *supra*.

70 See, *e.g.*, Killian v. United States, 368 U.S. 231, 261 (1961) (dissenting opinion) (relying on *Scales* and *Yates* in a loyalty test case).

71 Aptheker v. Secretary of State, 378 U.S. 500, 511–12 (1964); *cf.* United States v. Brown, 381 U.S. 437, 456 (1965).

narrowly based on Arizona's use of criminal sanctions to implement its loyalty oath.

Six of the eight cases cited by the dissent can be distinguished without serious difficulty. Four, *Lerner v. Casey*,[72] *Beilan v. Board of Education*,[73] *Nelson v. County of Los Angeles*,[74] and *Slochower v. Board of Education*,[75] deal solely with the right of federal or state officials to require an employee to reveal any past or present membership in organizations advocating violent overthrow of the government.[76] The determination that state and federal authorities had this power in no way established that such membership alone is an adequate basis for denying employment. The Court's rulings only indicated that the subject of the state's inquiry could be relevant to some valid standard for disqualification.[77] Since a question is relevant if it relates to any aspect of the state's standard, inquiry about membership in an organization advocating overthrow clearly would be relevant even under a standard that, consistent with *Elfbrandt*, was limited to exclusion only of those members who had a specific intent to further the illegal aims of the organization.

Both *Wieman v. Updegraff*[78] and *Adler v. Board of Education*[79] deal directly with use of speech and association as a basis for denying government employment, but they too can be distinguished. In *Wieman*, the Court voided an Oklahoma loyalty oath on the ground that it indiscriminately barred from employment all members of organizations advocating violent overthrow regardless of whether the members were aware of the organization's illegal

---

[72] 357 U.S. 468 (1958).

[73] 357 U.S. 399 (1958).

[74] 362 U.S. 1 (1960).

[75] 350 U.S. 551 (1956).

[76] In *Slochower* the Court found that the state acted arbitrarily in discharging the petitioner solely because he relied upon the Fifth Amendment privilege against self-incrimination to refuse to answer an inquiry concerning past membership in the Communist party. *Beilan*, *Lerner*, and *Nelson* all upheld discharges under somewhat similar circumstances when the state based the discharge upon the employee's general lack of co-operativeness in failing to answer the inquiries, rather than upon his use of the privilege. See, *e.g.*, Nelson v. County of Los Angeles, 362 U.S. 1, 6–8 (1960).

[77] See, *e.g.*, Lerner v. Casey, 357 U.S. 468, 474, 477 (1958), where the Court specifically noted that it need not determine whether the particular standard employed by the state in that case was valid. See also Beilan v. Board of Education, 357 U.S. 399, 405 (1958); Nelson v. County of Los Angeles, 362 U.S. 1, 8 (1960).

[78] 344 U.S. 183 (1952).

[79] 342 U.S. 485 (1952).

purpose. While the opinion did not mention that the oath also failed to except the member who knew of, but did not share, that purpose, little significance can be attached to that omission, since the Court had no reason to consider the need for a "specific intent" requirement once the statute was found unconstitutional on other grounds.[80] In *Adler*, the Court sustained the New York loyalty program for teachers under the Feinberg Law. The Court's opinion dealt primarily with a provision making knowing membership in an organization advocating violent overthrow "prima facie evidence" of disqualification for employment.[81] Although the Feinberg Law was supposedly designed to implement a statute that denied employment to all knowing members of such organizations,[82] the Court's opinion indicates that it assumed, probably on the basis of a lower court opinion,[83] that an employee could successfully rebut the prima facie case by showing that he did not share the illegal aims of the organization.[84]

Gerende v. Board of Supervisors[85] and *Garner v. Board of*

---

80 The arguments advanced by the Court in rejecting the Oklahoma oath related solely to the member who was unaware of the organization's illegal objectives and were not readily applicable to the knowing member who did not subscribe to the organization's illegal goals. See 344 U.S. at 190–91.

81 N.Y. EDUC. LAW § 3022.

82 The Feinberg Law does require the removal of all "subversive persons from the public school system," but it does not define "subversive persons." The Act defines subversive organizations, however, as those that advocate, advise, embrace, or teach the doctrine of violent overthrow. The N.Y. CIVIL SERVICE LAW § 12(a), the Act that the Feinberg Law was designed to implement, see 342 U.S. at 487–89, provides for the disqualification from public employment of any person who "becomes a member of any . . . group . . . which teaches or advocates that the government of the United States or of any state . . . shall be overthrown by force or violence. . . ." Accordingly the significance of the provision making membership in such organizations constitute only prima facie evidence of disqualification is not entirely clear from the face of the statute.

83 See L'Hommedieu v. Board of Regents, 97 N.Y.S.2d 443, 452–53 (App. Div. 3d Dept. 1950), *aff'd*, 301 N.Y. 476 (1950). *L'Hommedieu* was a companion case to *Adler*.

84 See 342 U.S. at 495–96, emphasizing the individual's opportunity to rebut the prima facie presumption arising from knowing membership. See also *id.* at 492, noting that only "unexplained" knowing membership in an organization advocating overthrow constituted a basis for removal under the New York statute.

The decision in Nostrand v. Little, 368 U.S. 436 (1962), apparently was based on the same assumption as *Adler*. See 362 U.S. 474 (1960); 58 Wash.2d 111 (1961).

85 341 U.S. 56 (1951).

Public Works[86] also deal directly with the state's power to deny employment to individuals solely on the basis of their associations, but these cases are difficult to distinguish from *Elfbrandt.* In *Gerende*, a unanimous Court, including Justices Black and Douglas, upheld a Maryland requirement that every candidate for political office "make oath that he is not a person who is engaged 'in one way or another in the attempt to overthrow the government by *force or violence*,' and that he is not knowingly a member of an organization engaged in such an attempt."[87] Although the Maryland oath made no exception for knowing members who lacked the specific intent to support the organization's illegal goals,[88] the Court sustained the state oath requirement in a one-paragraph per curiam opinion that made no mention of the specific intent question. *Gerende* can nevertheless be distinguished from *Elfbrandt* on two grounds. First—and this ground will be discussed more fully—the oath in *Gerende* was limited to officials with policy-making functions.[89] Second, the Maryland oath might be interpreted as applying only to membership in organizations engaged in a present attempt to overthrow the government. Knowing membership in such a group could be distinguished from membership in a group that had merely advocated violent overthrow sometime in the future, on the ground that the immediate danger presented by the first type of organization so clearly established the individual's support for the organization's illegal objective that inquiry into his "specific intent" was unnecessary. Such a narrow interpretation of the Maryland oath, however, is subject to question. The oath applies to attempts "in one way or another" to overthrow the government, and this might well require no more than advocacy itself, especially when it is remembered that

---

[86] 341 U.S. 716 (1951).

[87] *Id.* at 56–57. (Emphasis in original.)

[88] Moreover, there was nothing in the opinion of the Maryland Court of Appeals to suggest that a requirement of "specific intent" had been read into the state statute. See Shub v. Simpson, 196 Md. 177 (1950).

[89] See *infra,* at section VI. Although it is possible that not all elected officials would possess the type of discretionary authority that might be manipulated to serve an organization seeking violent overthrow, certainly the group as a whole can be classified as having such authority. Perhaps, a separate ground of distinction might be found in the very fact that these officials are elected. See DOUGLAS, THE RIGHT OF THE PEOPLE 130 (1958). But there is nothing in the subsequent treatment of *Gerende* that indicates the Court considered this an important factor.

the concept of advocacy used in this area is that of urging future action in language "reasonably and ordinarily calculated to incite persons to such action."[90] If this broad interpretation of the Maryland oath is accepted, then *Gerende* presents, aside from the first ground of distinction, the same difficulty in reconciliation with *Elfbrandt* as *Garner.*

In *Garner,* the Court upheld a statute denying employment to any person who within five years had been a knowing member of any organization that "advised, advocated, or taught the overthrow by force or violence" of the state or federal government.[91] Although no mention of the point was made in either the majority or dissenting opinions (including those of Justices Black and Douglas),[92] the statute in *Garner* clearly would exclude from employment knowing members who lacked the specific intent to further the organization's unlawful aims.[93] *Garner* therefore seems, at least on the surface, to be in direct conflict with *Elfbrandt.* Yet, cases are not ordinarily overruled sub silentio,[94] and Mr. Justice

---

90 See Yates v. United States, 354 U.S. 298, 316 (1957); Dennis v. United States, 341 U.S. 494, 511–12 (1951). The same standard is ordinarily applied to loyalty oaths. See, *e.g.,* 94 Ariz. at 8. Of course, *Gerende* was decided before *Dennis* and *Yates,* but this would not have prevented the Court from viewing "*Yates*-style" advocacy as constituting an attempt "in one way or another to overthrow the government by force and violence."

91 341 U.S. at 717–18.

92 The dissenting opinion of Mr. Justice Douglas, joined by Mr. Justice Black, concentrated entirely on the contention that the Los Angeles ordinance was a bill of attainder. See 341 U.S. at 731–33. Mr. Justice Black's short dissenting opinion briefly mentioned the First Amendment issue, but discussed it in general terms. *Id.* at 730–31. Both Mr. Justice Frankfurter's separate opinion and Mr. Justice Clark's opinion for the Court did discuss that issue, however, in connection with the possible application of the ordinance to members who were unaware of an organization's illegal activity, the majority assuming that the statute incorporated a requirement of scienter, and Mr. Justice Frankfurter finding the statute unconstitutional because that assumption reasonably could not be made. *Id.* at 720–21, 723–24, 724.

93 But see Horowitz, *Report on the Los Angeles City and County Loyalty Programs,* 5 STANFORD L. REV. 233, 244 (1953), possibly suggesting that the element of scienter read into the ordinance in *Garner* might make the ordinance inapplicable to the "employee [who] was a member of the organization but continually fought against policies of overthrow." The language of *Garner,* however, quite clearly discussed scienter strictly in terms of knowledge rather than intent. 341 U.S. at 723–24. This was reaffirmed in Wieman v. Updegraff, 344 U.S. 183 (1952).

94 See Israel, *Gideon v. Wainwright: The "Art" of Overruling,* [1963] SUPREME COURT REVIEW 211, 214 n. 15, 215–26.

Douglas' opinion failed to mention the *Garner* case. It could reasonably be assumed that there was a basis for reconciling the two cases, and that *Garner* remains controlling precedent until explicitly overruled.[95]

A ground for reconciling *Garner* and *Elfbrandt* in fact can be found, if not without difficulty. The *Garner* statute applied to membership in organizations that were actively engaged in the advocacy of violent overthrow, and the Court obviously treated it as aimed at the Communist party or similar organizations that made the overthrow of the government a dominant organizational goal.[96] *Elfbrandt*, on the other hand, involves a statute prohibiting employee membership in an organization that has the violent overthrow of the government merely as "one of its purposes."[97] As Justice Bernstein noted in the Arizona court, the Arizona statute would encompass an organization for which overthrow was merely a "subordinate purpose."[98] Both Justice Bernstein and Mr. Justice Douglas mentioned the possible application of the Arizona statute to a teacher's membership in a seminar group dominated by Communist scientists. Certainly, a member of such a group cannot be compared to a member of an organization like the Communist party, either in terms of his contribution to the potential violent overthrow of the government or his lack of dedication to the present form of government.[99] The Court could have adopted the position that membership in such an organization does not justify employment disqualification without a showing of the individual's support for the policy of violent overthrow, although knowing membership in an organization like the Communist party would be sufficient justification for disqualification. In any event, the argument might continue, since *Elfbrandt*

---

95 *Cf.* United States *ex rel.* Vajtauer v. Commissioner of Immigration, 273 U.S. 103, 112 (1927), noting the need for caution in drawing "inferences from silence."

96 See 341 U.S. at 719–20. The oath was combined with a requirement that every employee execute an affidavit stating whether he had ever been a member of the Communist party. *Ibid.*

97 See note 9 *supra.*

98 97 Ariz. at 148; see text *supra,* at note 19.

99 It might also be argued that a restriction extending to any organization that might have violent overthrow as "one of its purposes" would impose a greater deterrent to free association because the employee would have greater concern about not being able to recognize all the subordinate organizational purposes. The statute in *Elfbrandt* was limited to members with knowledge, but the impact of that safeguard upon the individual's willingness freely to join various organizations is questionable.

went no further than to declare invalid a law covering the first situation, *Garner* still remains a valid precedent until the Court faces a statute dealing solely with membership in groups actively advocating overthrow.

Support for this view of the limited scope of the *Elfbrandt* opinion can be found in various portions of Mr. Justice Douglas' opinion. Justice Bernstein's dissent, which was based entirely on the "subordinate purpose" theme, is quoted at length in the majority opinion.[100] Mr. Justice Douglas also added his own discussion of the same point, including his hypotheticals concerning teacher participation in such events as the Pugwash Conference. Finally, throughout the majority opinion, Mr. Justice Douglas spoke solely in terms of organizations with an illegal "purpose" or "aim." No reference is made to membership in an organization presently advocating overthrow.[101] Nevertheless, although these elements of the majority opinion give this reading of the Court's ruling far more support than that suggested by Mr. Justice White, it too should be rejected.

If *Elfbrandt* is viewed as going no further than to invalidate a statute so broad as to encompass membership in a scientific seminar dominated by Communists, it becomes very difficult indeed to understand why the case was not clearly controlled by *Baggett v. Bullitt*,[102] and, if so, why (1) two members of the *Baggett* majority dissented in *Elfbrandt*[103] and (2) the majority relied primarily on *Scales*, and *Aptheker* rather than *Baggett*. In *Baggett*, the Court, with only Justices Clark and Harlan dissenting, held unconstitutional a Washington statute that barred from public employment all persons, *inter alia*, who "aid[ed] in the commission of any act intended to overthrow, destroy, or alter or assist in the overthrow, destruction, or alteration" of the state or federal government.[104] While Mr. Justice White's opinion for the Court was based on the ground that the statute was unduly vague, this rationale was keyed to the impact of the statute on First Amendment rights. The vagueness in the Washington statute entered the picture primarily because a

---

100 384 U.S. at 14–15. The quotation included the entire discussion by Justice Bernstein of the "scientist" hypothetical.

101 See, *e.g.*, 384 U.S. at 16, 17.

102 377 U.S. 360 (1964).

103 The majority in *Baggett* included Justices White and Stewart, both of whom dissented in *Elfbrandt*.

104 377 U.S. at 362.

literal interpretation of the statute so clearly imposed on protected speech that the Court assumed that a somewhat narrower, but less well defined, compass was intended.[105] In listing the obviously impermissible bases for denial of employment that could fall within the state statute if literally interpreted, Mr. Justice White offered an illustration almost identical to that cited by Mr. Justice Douglas in *Elfbrandt*—the denial of employment to a scholar who "attends and participates in an international convention of mathematicians and exchanges views with scholars from Communist countries."[106] Mr. Justice White's discussion of this and other illustrations clearly indicated that the state could not deny employment to an individual simply because he unintentionally lent indirect aid to the "cause" of violent overthrow by engaging in lawful activities that he knew might add to the power of persons supporting illegal overthrow.[107] Thus, although the Washington statute, when read literally, was much broader in scope than the statute in *Elfbrandt*, the basic principle expressed in the *Baggett* opinion clearly would control *Elfbrandt* if that case were viewed as concerned primarily with the application of the Arizona statute to such matters as membership in a Communist-dominated scientific seminar.

While the Court's opinion in *Elfbrandt* does cite *Baggett v.*

---

105 *Id.* at 366–68. The opinion of the Court does not clearly express the interrelationship of the vagueness doctrine and the overbreadth of the statute when it is read literally. This point is given more explicit recognition, however, in a subsequent opinion that relied primarily on *Baggett*. See Dombrowski v. Pfister, 380 U.S. 479, 486–87, 490–92, 493–94 (1965); see also Aptheker v. Secretary of State, 378 U.S. 500, 515–16 (1964); United States v. National Dairy Corp., 372 U.S. 29, 36 (1963); N.A.A.C.P. v. Button, 371 U.S. 415, 432–33 (1963); Shelton v. Tucker, 364 U.S. 479, 491–92 (1960) (dissenting opinion); Amsterdam, *The Void for Vagueness Doctrine,* 109 U. PA. L. REV. 67 (1960).

106 377 U.S. at 369.

107 Although the Court's opinion in *Baggett* raises some question concerning the nature of the individual's awareness that his acts would aid those seeking overthrow, the opinion also indicates that the activity discussed would be protected even if the individual knew "that his aid or teaching would be used by another and that the person aided has the requisite guilty intent." The discussion relating to the possible ambiguity in the oath's scienter requirement was discussed as a supplementary point. See 377 U.S. at 368–69. See also Dombrowski v. Pfister, 380 U.S. 479, 492–93. *Dombrowski* also indicates that the protection afforded by *Baggett* would be equally applicable to the person who is a member of an organization that itself lends indirect and unintended aid to those supporting overthrow by participating for other purposes in legal activities that will strengthen the position of such groups. *Ibid.*

Bullitt in connection with the discussion of the hypotheticals concerning scientific conferences, it does not rely heavily on that decision.[108] Both the citation and the hypotheticals seem to serve merely to supplement the argument for requiring an element of "specific intent" by presenting an extreme example of what could happen when a loyalty oath contained no exemption of members who lacked such intent. The primary emphasis in *Elfbrandt* is on *Scales* and *Aptheker,* both of which involved membership in the Communist party.[109] Reliance on these decisions, when *Baggett* was otherwise sufficient precedent, indicates that the Court's rejection of employment disqualification based solely on knowing membership in an organization supporting the violent overthrow of the government extends to all such organizations, including those in which violent overthrow is a matter of primary emphasis. *Garner v. Board of Public Works* must, therefore, be viewed as overruled. Admittedly, the assumption that the Court overruled an earlier precedent sub silentio is not to be lightly indulged. But two recent opinions by Mr. Justice Douglas seem to overrule several other cases in this manner.[110] And certainly the thrust of the majority opinion, as well as the cases cited therein, indicates that *Garner* was intended to share the same fate.

Actually, there are a few statements in *Elfbrandt* suggesting that a statute like that in *Garner* would be deficient on not one but two grounds. While Mr. Justice Douglas' several statements of the Court's ruling in the majority opinion consistently refer only to the improper disqualification of the knowing member who lacks "a 'specific intent' to further the illegal aims of the organization," a few comments in the opinion suggest that even a statutory restriction on employment limited to members with "specific intent" would not be valid. For example, in citing the *Scales* case, Mr. Justice Douglas noted that the majority there read the Smith Act "membership clause" to require not only that the member have the requisite intent but also that he be an "active" member.[111] At another point, the opinion might be taken to suggest that even "active" participation in the group's activities would not be enough

---

108 384 U.S. at 16–17.

109 See 367 U.S. at 205–06, 378 U.S. at 504–05

110 See Kurland, *supra* note 68, at 150, 167–68, discussing Gray v. Sanders, 372 U.S. 368 (1963), and Schneider v. Rusk, 377 U.S. 163 (1964).

111 384 U.S. at 15; see 367 U.S. at 222–24, 255 n. 29.

if the activities involved were all legal. Mr. Justice Douglas stated that those "who join an organization but do not share its unlawful purposes and who do not participate in its unlawful activities surely pose no threat to society."[112] While this could be viewed as suggesting alternative requirements, it may indicate that the Court will not allow employment disqualification to be based on political association absent a showing of specific intent to promote the violent overthrow of the government plus previous participation in illegal activities serving that end. Some support for this second requirement might also be found in Mr. Justice Douglas' statement that a statute denying employment on the basis of speech-related activities must be "narrowly drawn to define and punish specific conduct as constituting a clear and present danger to a substantial interest of the state." The clear-and-present-danger standard, especially as viewed by Mr. Justice Douglas, could easily be taken to require prior participation in illegal activity.[113]

If these statements do not in themselves impose any additional requirements, they lay the foundation for a future decision to that effect.[114] Whether the Court's ruling will be expanded to require active membership or even actual participation in illegal activities will depend in large part on the precise nature of the considerations that led the Court to reject Arizona's reliance upon knowing membership as an appropriate basis for denying government employment. The nature of those considerations will also have considerable bearing on whether *Elfbrandt* will be applied to a statute requiring loyalty oaths of only a limited group of employees, such as those in sensitive positions. Unfortunately, however, the identification of these relevant considerations is hidden to a large degree

---

112 384 U.S. at 17.

113 See, *e.g.*, Dennis v. United States, 341 U.S. 494, 581 (1951) (dissenting opinion).

114 The dissent at one point suggested that the majority did impose a requirement of active membership. See 384 U.S. at 22–23: "[T]he Court errs in holding that the act is overbroad because it includes state employees who are knowing members but who may not be active and who may lack the specific intent to further the illegal aims of the Party."

The majority opinion, however, refers to an "active" membership requirement only in connection with its general description of the *Scales* case. *Id.* at 15. The discussion of *Aptheker*, the reference to the possible scope of the statute, and the summary of the Court's ruling at the end of the opinion speak only of the element of "specific intent." *Id.* at 16–19.

by the manner in which the *Elfbrandt* opinion utilized the rule against overbroadness as the basis for its ruling.

IV. Overbroadness and the Nature of the State's Interests

The rule against overbreadth in legislation affecting First Amendment rights is a doctrine very much favored by the present Court.[115] In large part, this is probably due to the fact that it represents one of the few common meeting grounds for the variant views of the meaning of the First Amendment.[116] But, as one might expect of a doctrine serving this function, the rule is frequently used in different ways by different Justices in writing opinions for the Court. Thus, in some cases, the Court would seem to have rejected legislation as overbroad primarily because the means employed by the state bore little or no relationship to the interests it sought to implement.[117] In other cases, the Court has acknowledged the presence of a substantial relationship, but has still found the legislation invalid because the state interest could be attained by an alternative means that would impose less severe restrictions on the individual's personal liberty.[118] In still other cases, the Court seemed to reject legislation because, whatever the possible alternative

---

115 See, *e.g.*, Aptheker v. Secretary of State, 378 U.S. 500 (1964); N.A.A.C.P. v. Alabama, 377 U.S. 288, 307–08 (1964); N.A.A.C.P. v. Button, 371 U.S. 415, 432–44 (1963); Louisiana v. N.A.A.C.P., 366 U.S. 293 (1961); Shelton v. Tucker, 364 U.S. 479 (1960); Talley v. California, 362 U.S. 60, 62–64 (1960).

116 Shapiro, Freedom of Speech: The Supreme Court and Judicial Review 140–41 (1966). *Compare* Justices Douglas' and Black's joining opinion for the Court in Shelton v. Tucker, *supra* note 115, *with* their use of a separate concurring opinion in Bates v. Little Rock, 361 U.S. 516, 527 (1960).

117 See, *e.g.*, N.A.A.C.P. v. Button, *supra* note 115; Talley v. California, *supra* note 115; Lovell v. Griffin, 303 U.S. 444 (1938). Frequently, as in *Lovell* and, perhaps, *Talley*, there is the further suggestion that the restriction upon speech was so significant that the statute would not be sustained even if it did bear a relationship to some state interest. In fact, the decisions probably rested on this ground, since the state's use of an absolute prohibition against the distribution of all literature, as in *Lovell*, or all anonymous handbills, as in *Talley*, does serve the state's interest in eliminating obscene or libelous publications in the sense that the flat prohibition against distribution obviously is considerably easier to administer than one that attempted to specify what literature might fall in the obscene or libelous category. *Cf.* Note, *The Supreme Court, 1959 Term*, 74 Harv. L. Rev. 97, 130 (1960).

118 See, *e.g.*, Aptheker v. Secretary of State, *supra* note 115; Shelton v. Tucker, *supra* note 115; Saia v. New York, 334 U.S. 558, 562 (1942).

means, the state interest served by the legislation was deemed insufficient to justify the extensive restriction it imposed upon protected speech or association.[119] While these varying uses of the "overbroadness" doctrine all rest on the same basic process of evaluating competing interests, the differences in underlying rationale may be relevant in determining the degree to which the rejection of legislation as "overbroad" might preclude an attempt to satisfy the same state interest through different means. Yet, opinions relying upon the "overbroadness" rule often provide no more indication of the Court's analysis than a conclusionary statement that a particular aspect of the statutory infringement on speech was overly broad as it applied to the particular interest that the state advanced in that case.[120] The majority opinion in *Elfbrandt* fits this pattern and, indeed, is more delinquent, since the Court failed in large part even to identify the state interest against which the legislation was balanced.

Mr. Justice Douglas' opinion starts with a description and evaluation of the interest of the individual in joining organizations having both legal and illegal objectives, and, except for one or two sentences, it never leaves that aspect of the case. Although the opinion states in conclusion that the Arizona statute "infringes unnecessarily on protected freedoms," it never clearly defines the state interests in relation to which the infringement was deemed "unnecessary."[121] The lack of any extended discussion of the state's interest is not surprising in an opinion by Mr. Justice Douglas, who generally seeks to avoid creating any impression that the Court might be engaged in "balancing" individual rights against a state's interests.[122] In the area of the legislation involved in *Elfbrandt*,

---

119 See, *e.g.*, N.A.A.C.P. v. Alabama, *supra* note 115; Louisiana v. N.A.A.C.P., *supra* note 115. See also Shelton v. Tucker, *supra* note 115, at 493 n. 3 (dissenting opinion).

120 See, *e.g.*, Louisiana v. N.A.A.C.P., *supra* note 115; Talley v. California, *supra* note 115.

121 384 U.S. at 19. Although relying upon *Aptheker* for other purposes, the opinion ignores the statement in *Aptheker* that application of the rule against overbroadness requires examination of the state's interest. See Aptheker v. Secretary of State, *supra* note 115, at 508.

122 Consider, for example, his treatment of the state's interest in the following description of *N.A.A.C.P. v. Alabama* and *Bates v. Little Rock*, as they relate to the power to compel disclosure of membership lists: "We deal with a constitutional right, since freedom of association is included in the bundle of First Amendment rights made applicable to the states by the Due Process Clause of the Four-

however, this omission takes on special significance, since at least three different state interests are commonly advanced to justify disqualification of individuals from public employment on the basis of membership in organizations advocating the violent overthrow of the government: (1) The elimination of persons who present a potential for sabotage, espionage, or other activities directly injurious to national security. (2) The elimination of persons who are likely to be either incompetent or untrustworthy in the performance of their duties. (3) The elimination of persons who, aside from any question of danger or fitness, simply are not considered deserving of a government position because they oppose the basic principles on which the government is founded. The *Elfbrandt* opinion contains no reference to any of these interests aside from a single ambiguous sentence. In that sentence, Mr. Justice Douglas emphasized that members who do not share an organization's unlawful purposes and never participate in its unlawful activities "surely pose no threat, either as citizens or as public employees."[123] The nature of the "threat" to which Mr. Justice Douglas is referring is not entirely clear, but the context of the sentence indicates that he was probably making reference only to the possibility of sabotage or similar activities. Since all three state interests were advanced in justification of the Arizona legislation, however, either in the briefs or in the opinions below,[124] it must be assumed that the Court found the statute unnecessarily broad as applied to all of them. And, as previously noted, the considerations that led the Court to reject these interests will determine the possibilities for the extension of the *Elfbrandt* ruling to loyalty oaths more limited than Arizona's.[125]

---

teenth Amendment . . . [citations omitted]. And where it is shown, as it was in *N.A.A.C.P.* v. *Alabama, supra,* 462–463, that disclosure of membership lists results in reprisals against and hostility to the members, disclosure is not required. And see *Bates* v. *Little Rock, supra,* 523–524." Louisiana v. N.A.A.C.P., *supra* note 115, at 296.

123 384 U.S. at 17.

124 Although the respondent's brief placed emphasis upon the first of the state interests mentioned above, the opinion of the lower court made reference to the other two. See Brief for Respondent, pp. 8, 13; 94 Ariz. at 6, 10–11. See also the *Report of the Arizona Judiciary Committee in Support of the Committee Amendment to H.B. 115,* reproduced as Appendix B in Respondent's brief.

125 Of course, even if the opinion had clearly identified the state's interest and explained why the statute was overbroad in relation to those interests, the Court

V. The Denial of Support to Disloyal Groups

It has frequently been argued that persons who lack "fidelity to the very presuppositions of our scheme of government" should be denied public employment simply because the government need not support those who oppose it.[126] Taxpayers' funds," so the argument goes, "should not be spent to support . . . a person of doubtful loyalty to the very governmental system for which he wants to work."[127] Or, to look at it from the other side, the state should be allowed to promote loyalty to our basic institutions by employing only those who accept those institutions.[128]

Although this argument probably serves as the primary basis for much of our "loyalty" legislation,[129] the state interest it advances has not always been recognized as separate from that of excluding

---

need not have committed itself on the weight of those interests in the case of a modified statute. See Karst, *The First Amendment and Harry Kalven: An Appreciative Comment on the Advantages of Thinking Small*, 13 U.C.L.A. L. Rev. 1, 15–17 (1965). Yet that would be the inevitable result of reliance upon several of the possible grounds for judgment that are discussed in the next three sections of this article.

126 Garner v. Board of Public Works, 341 U.S. 716, 725 (1951) (concurring opinion). See Brown, *op. cit. supra* note 5, at 205, 333, 335, 337; Linde, *Justice Douglas on Freedom in the Welfare State*, 39 Wash. L. Rev. 39 (1964) (both noting the argument, but not supporting it).

127 Linde, *supra* note 126, at 39. As used in this argument, "disloyalty" means only the denial of the basic premises on which the government is founded. In the case of persons believing in violent overthrow, it is the denial of the premise that change in government can take place only through the democratic means provided by the Constitution. See Brown, *op. cit. supra* note 5, at 6–7, 389.

Another concept of loyalty sometimes advanced in connection with this argument rests on the individual's alleged subservience to a foreign nation. See, *e.g.*, Ariz. Rev. Stat., tit. 16, ch. 2, § 16-205 (1965 Supp.) (Arizona Communist Control Act). This concept, however, does not relate to all groups advocating overthrow of the government, and it has been employed primarily in connection with Communist Control Acts. It could provide an entirely separate basis for denial of support through employment disqualification. See People v. Crane, 124 N.Y. 154, 161, 164 (1915), *aff'd*, 239 U.S. 195 (1915). But it would present essentially the same difficulties as *Elfbrandt* with respect to the need for a showing that the individual member owed his allegiance to a foreign country.

128 *Cf.* First Unitarian Church v. County of Los Angeles, 48 Cal.2d 419, 438–39 (1957), *rev'd*, 357 U.S. 545 (1958).

129 See Willcox, *Invasions of the First Amendment through Conditioned Public Spending*, 41 Cornell L.Q. 12, 48 (1955); Linde, *supra* note 126, at 39; Brown, ***op.*** *cit supra* note 5, at 337, 340.

potentially unreliable and incompetent employees. The two interests do often overlap, but they are distinct in one important respect.[130] The state's interest in obtaining fit employees relates to the individual's potential performance in public employment, while its interest in denying support to "disloyal" persons may relate only to the individual's attitude toward basic principles of constitutional government.[131] Thus, associational ties that might not be adequate to establish the likelihood that a person will act improperly in office may nevertheless be sufficient to show a lack of "loyalty," for example, in the individual's acceptance of a general theory that the violent overthrow of government is preferable to the constitutional processes for change provided in the Constitution.

The Court in *Elfbrandt* obviously found that the state interest in denying support to "disloyal" persons could not justify the Arizona loyalty oath. That conclusion may have been based on at least two distinct approaches, each furnishing somewhat different implications of the future effect of the decision. On the more limited approach, the Court may have agreed that the state has an interest in denying support to "disloyal" persons but still have found that the Arizona statute was not sufficiently related to that interest. Since, under the state's theory, the basis for denial of employment turns on the individual's rejection of the basic principles of constitutional government, the loyalty oath, to implement that theory, logically should exclude only those members who themselves subscribe to the illegal objective of violent overthrow.[132] The Arizona statute, as related to this state interest, could very properly be described as unnecessarily broad. A ruling based on this analysis would go no further than to require that the element of "specific intent" be added to the "membership clause" of § 5. The addition of an element of active participation in the organization's affairs would not be needed, since, as noted, "disloyalty" for the purpose of this theory need not be related to action.

---

130 See BROWN, *supra* note 5, at 205. See also 94 Ariz. at 6, 10–11.

131 See note 127 *supra*. See also Sacks, *Federal Civilian Employees Security Program: An Analysis of the Wright Commission Report,* 52 NW. U. L. REV. 715, 719 (1958).

132 The Court adopted a similar view in interpreting the requirement of "attachment to the principles of the constitution" under the Nationality Act of 1906. See Nowak v. United States, 356 U.S. 660 (1958); Maisenberg v. United States, 356 U.S. 670 (1958).

This analysis would not in itself answer the argument, suggested by the dissent, that the individual by lending "his name and influence" to the organization automatically aided its illegal objectives, whatever his intent, and that the state could, therefore, exclude him from employment as a means of denying support to a "disloyal" organization.[133] On this point, the Court would be required to answer that the state's justification for a loyalty oath must relate directly to the denial of support to the individual, rather than to the organization, since it is the individual who suffers the brunt of the restriction. Some support for this position may be found in *Wieman v. Updegraff*,[134] where the Court held that the state could not deny employment to members of organizations advocating overthrow who were not aware that the organization had this objective. Certainly, a member in that category could give the organization as much aid by lending it "his name and influence" as the knowing member who did not share the organization's purpose.[135] While there is a significant difference in the fact that the member in the second case has knowledge of the organization's illegal goals, *Baggett v. Bullitt* indicates that, at least in the case of somewhat more indirect assistance such as united activity in support of a joint political objective, it matters not that the individual realizes that his assistance will indirectly further the organization's illegal objectives.[136] Membership in an organization actually advocating overthrow may, of course, constitute a much more direct contribution to its illegal objectives. But when the importance *Wieman* attached to freedom of association is also considered, the Court might well conclude that the state's interest in shutting off this additional element of organizational support was insufficient to outweigh the restriction on individual freedom. In sum then, under this first approach, the Arizona oath would be rejected because (1) the state's interest in denying support to "disloyal" persons is not sufficient so long as the individual does not himself subscribe

---

133 384 U.S. at 20. This argument was also suggested in the Arizona Supreme Court. See 94 Ariz. at 10–11.

134 344 U.S. 183 (1952).

135 The Court has recognized that an individual can be an active member of an organization and still not be aware of its illegal objective. See Nowak v. United States, *supra* note 132; Maisenberg v. United States, *supra* note 132; *cf.* Rowoldt v. Perfetto, 355 U.S. 115 (1957).

136 See text at note 107 *supra*.

to an organization's illegal goals, and (2) the state's interest in denying the organization whatever support comes from the membership of a person who does not favor its illegal ends is not sufficient to justify restricting that individual's right to join that organization in order to work for a legal objective he does favor.

A second and more far-reaching approach to both aspects of this problem would hold that the state's interest in denying support to "disloyal" persons or organizations is never a proper basis for employment disqualification, except possibly where the grounds of disqualification are limited to speech or association that could be directly proscribed under the Constitution. At the outset, it should be noted that the Court never has had occasion directly to accept or reject the principle that a state can base a loyalty test on its desire to deny employment to those persons who reject the basic principles of constitutional government. Scattered statements in one or two opinions might be taken as recognizing the state's interest in this regard, but these opinions dealt primarily with other state goals.[137] Moreover, these opinions were written before *Speiser v. Randall*.[138]

---

[137] See Garner v. Board of Public Works, 341 U.S. 716, 725 (1951) (concurring opinion); Adler v. Board of Education, 342 U.S. 485, 492–93 (1952). The statements in *Adler* are ambiguous because the Court never defines the term "loyalty" when it speaks of determining "fitness and loyalty." Moreover, the various statements in *Adler* emphasizing the so-called privilege rationale were sharply limited only a year later in Wieman v. Updegraff, 344 U.S. 183 (1953).

[138] 357 U.S. 513 (1958). One post-*Speiser* statement that could be bracketed with the cases cited in note 137 is found in Flemming v. Nestor, 363 U.S. 603 (1960). The Court there sustained a statutory provision disqualifying from social security benefits persons who "had been deported on several grounds, including membership in the Communist Party." The Court noted that a rational justification for the statute might rest on the deportee's inability to aid the domestic economy by spending the benefits locally. The opinion then went on to make the following statements: "For these purposes, it is, of course, constitutionally irrelevant whether this reasoning in fact underlay the legislative decision, as it is irrelevant that the section does not extend to all to whom the postulated rationale might in logic apply. . . . Nor, apart from this, can it be deemed irrational for Congress to have concluded that the public purse should not be utilized to contribute to the support of those deported on the grounds specified in the statute."

It is not entirely clear whether the last sentence refers to the fact that the deportee would be residing abroad or whether it establishes a right to deny support simply because alien Communists are not "deserving" of benefits. See Linde, *supra* note 126, at 17, suggesting the latter interpretation. In any event, subsequent cases, apparently viewing *Flemming* as based entirely on the first rationale, have treated *Speiser* and *Flemming* as consistent in the general principle each applied. See, *e.g.*, Sherbert v. Verner, 374 U.S. 398, 404–05, 409 n. 9 (1963).

In *Speiser* the Court held unconstitutional a California statute requiring every applicant for a veteran's tax exemption to swear that he was not presently advocating the violent overthrow of the federal or state government. The California statute was based on essentially the same state interest as is advanced to deny employment to "disloyal" persons. It was designed to "encourage . . . loyalty to our institutions" by denying support of persons who advocated the violent overthrow of those institutions.[139] Unlike the Arizona loyalty oath, however, the standard for denial of benefits was limited to speech that had been held to be outside the protection of the First Amendment.[140] The Court, therefore, did not have to deal directly with the question whether the denial of tax benefits could have been based on speech that could not be directly prohibited under the Constitution. Nevertheless, the Court's opinion indicated quite clearly that if such exemptions can be denied on the basis of speech at all, it must be on the basis of "proscribed speech for which [the individual] might be fined or imprisoned."[141] In particular, the opinion emphasized that legislation serving the function of the California statute constituted a direct restraint on speech, since it was "frankly aimed at the suppression of dangerous ideas," rather than the control of particular conduct relating to the benefit granted.[142] The Court carefully distinguished prior loyalty oath cases, such as *Gerende*, on the ground that the "principal aim of those statutes was not to penalize political beliefs but to deny positions to persons supposed to be dangerous because the position might be misused to the detriment of the public."[143] Finally, the Court, relying in part on *Wieman v. Updegraff*, rejected the argument that tax exemptions constituted a privilege and therefore were not subject to constitutional limitations upon the infringement of speech.[144]

In light of *Speiser*, a loyalty oath justified solely in terms of the state's interest in denying support to "disloyal" persons, as opposed to an interest in insuring employee reliability, must be viewed as a

---

139 357 U.S. at 527. See also statement of Clark, J., dissenting: "The interest of the State . . . is dual in nature, but its primary thrust is summed up in an understandable desire to insure that those who benefit by tax exemption do not bite the hand that gives it." *Id.* at 543.

140 *Id.* at 519–20.

141 *Id.* at 520.

142 *Id.* at 519.

143 *Id.* at 527.

144 *Id.* at 518–19.

direct restraint on speech. It follows that the only permissible standard for an oath serving that interest would be one tied, as in *Speiser*, to speech or association that might generally be made criminal under such legislation as the Smith Act.[145] Moreover, even if the standard employed were to meet the requirements of the *Scales* case, for example, there still might be some question about its validity when used in the context of a loyalty oath. *Speiser* only assumed *arguendo* that a state could deny benefits solely on "disloyalty" grounds where the speech involved was directly punishable.[146] The opinion then went on to reject the California statute because, in any event, it improperly shifted the burden of proof. In reaching this result, *Speiser* compared the California provision to a statute imposing a penalty for a crime.[147] Extending this reasoning, the Court might well rule, if forced to meet the issue, that a loyalty requirement "frankly aimed at suppressing speech," even if limited to constitutionally prohibitible speech, would still be invalid because it fails to afford the safeguards of the Sixth Amendment.[148] This would, in effect, reject any state employment test designed as a means of denying support to "disloyal" persons or organizations unless the standards under that test were relevant also to the quality of the employee's performance on the job.

Even if *Speiser* is not extended to its logical extreme, its application to the area of government employment still presents the problem of distinguishing (or rejecting) two "practical" precedents that are often cited to justify loyalty qualifications for government employees. The first is the traditional practice of hiring and firing under the spoils system that was so prevalent in this country before the advent of civil service (and is still not unheard of today).[149] If Republicans can deny employment to Democrats simply because they are Democrats, why not, it is asked, permit both parties to exclude persons who believe in the overthrow of the government?

---

145 See Thompson v. Gleason, 317 F.2d 901, 906 (D.C. Cir. 1952); *cf.* Danskin v. School Board, 28 Cal.2d 536 (1946); United States v. Schneider, 45 F. Supp. 848 (E.D. Wisc. 1942).

146 357 U.S. at 519–20.

147 *Id.* at 525, citing Lipke v. Lederer, 259 U.S. 557 (1922).

148 Cf. Kennedy v. Mendoza-Martinez, 372 U.S. 144, 184 n. 39 (1963) (relying on Lipke v. Lederer, *supra* note 147).

149 See Bailey v. Richardson, 182 F.2d 46, 59–60, 62–63 (D.C. Cir. 1950), *aff'd by equally divided court,* 341 U.S. 918 (1951) (collecting sources).

A possible answer could be that the spoils system was basically a product of a different era in which the characterization of employment as a privilege carried far more weight than it does today.[150] But the better answer is that the patronage system of employment has operated behind the Court's general refusal to examine the basis of the government's employment decisions unless the grounds for those decisions are clearly announced.[151] If the basic premise of the spoils system, insofar as it is not related to fitness, were clearly stated in statute or regulation, it would be rejected as arbitrary. This point seems clear from *United Public Workers v. Mitchell*, where the Court noted that "none would deny" that "Congress may not enact a regulation providing that no Republican, Jew, or Negro shall be appointed to federal office."[152]

The second precedent relied upon is the general requirement that government employees take an oath swearing to "bear true faith and allegiance" to the government, to "support and defend the Constitution against all enemies, foreign and domestic," and to "faithfully discharge the duties of [public] office."[153] An "affirmative" oath of this nature has been required of federal employees in the executive branch since 1884,[154] and a somewhat similar oath is required of the President by Article II of the Constitution. The contents of the oath, particularly the general requirement of defense of the Constitution, seems to indicate that it extends to matters beyond the individual's performance in office. Accordingly, it is argued that a requirement that employees believe in democratic processes for change, as opposed to violent overthrow, merely restates in a more specific fashion the employee's affirmative duty to defend the Constitution and to bear true allegiance to the government formed under the Constitution.[155] The short answer here

150 See generally Willcox, *supra* note 129, at 12–15, 37–44. *Compare* Heim v. McCall, 239 U.S. 175, 191 (1915), *with* Wieman v. Updegraff, 344 U.S. 183, 192 (1952). See also Powell, *The Right To Work for the State*, 16 Colum. L. Rev. 99 (1916).

151 See, *e.g.*, Cafeteria and Restaurant Workers Union v. McElroy, 367 U.S. 886 (1961).

152 330 U.S. at 100.

153 5 U.S.C. § 16 (1964). See Constanzo, *Loyalty Oath Affidavit*, 37 U. Det. L. J. 718, 728 (1960); Willcox, *supra* note 129, at 49.

154 See 5 U.S.C. § 16 (1964); 23 Stat. 22 (1884).

155 The fact that the affirmative oaths refer to future conduct and therefore would not likely be enforced by a perjury prosecution would not in itself serve as an

is that the affirmative oath of allegiance refers only to positive acts in violation of a constitutionally imposed legal duty. In *In re Summers*,[156] for example, the Court, in finding that a person unwilling to bear arms could not conscientiously take the oath to "support the Constitution," specifically rested its conclusion on the assumption that the draft exemption for conscientious objectors was not constitutionally required and that the failure of a conscientious objector to bear arms could validly be made a crime. Similarly, the affirmative oath, if it applies to speech at all, creates a duty to abstain only from such seditious speech or association as could be directly prohibited consistent with the Constitution. This would be entirely consistent with at least the more limited view of *Speiser v. Randall* as restricting the basis for the denial of benefits "to proscribed speech for which [the individual] might be imprisoned or fined."[157]

As previously noted, the Court's opinion in *Elfbrandt* does not clearly indicate why it found the state's interest in denying support to "disloyal" persons insufficient to justify the Arizona loyalty oath. The Court probably did not advance beyond the first approach suggested above, that membership without specific intent to further illegal objectives bore an insufficient relationship to the state interest. The more broadly based ground would have required a discussion of *Speiser*, and that case was cited only once and for a different point.[158] On the other hand, four members of the *Elfbrandt* majority had previously urged a very broad interpretation

---

adequate basis for distinguishing the loyalty oath. See Baggett v. Bullitt, 377 U.S. 360, 374 (1964): "Without the criminal sanctions, it is said, one need not fear taking this oath. . . . This contention ignores not only the effect of the oath on those who will not solemnly swear unless they can do so honestly and without prevarication and reservation, but also its effect on those who believe the written law means what it says."

[156] 325 U.S. 561, 569–73 (1945). *Summers* involved the duty to support the state constitution (Illinois), but, at that time, a similar construction had been placed upon the requirement of support of the federal constitution in the oath of allegiance required by the Naturalization Act of 1906. See United States v. Schwimmer, 279 U.S. 644 (1929); United States v. MacIntosh, 283 U.S. 605 (1931), *overruled* by Girouard v. United States, 328 U.S. 61 (1945). The *Girouard* case found that Congress had not intended to make willingness to bear arms an absolute prerequisite to citizenship.

[157] See note 141 *supra*.

[158] 384 U.S. at 17–18.

of *Speiser* in another context.[159] Perhaps they viewed *Speiser* as so clearly rejecting this interest that no discussion was necessary. If this is true, *Elfbrandt* will have bearing beyond the employment situation and may, along with *Speiser*, provide the basis for rejecting such loyalty restrictions as that imposed under the recent Medicare legislation.[160]

VI. The State's Interest in Insuring the Fitness of Its Employees

The ruling in *Elfbrandt* indicates also that the Arizona oath requirement could not be sustained by the state's interest in insuring the fitness of its employees. Here again the significance of the decision will depend in large degree on which of two somewhat different rationales led the Court to this conclusion.

The first rationale would be based primarily on the total coverage of the Arizona statute. Although petitioner in *Elfbrandt* happened to be a teacher, the Arizona oath was required of all state and local employees, including janitors, street cleaners, and others with purely ministerial functions.[161] As applied to persons in these positions, the case for determining the prospective employee's potential performance on the basis of his membership in an organization advocating overthrow is very weak. The traditional argument for denying state employment to members of such organizations has rested on the likelihood that they would use their positions to strengthen the organization's ability eventually to attempt violent overthrow by (1) promoting the organization's influence through favoritism in the distribution of governmental benefits to those groups sympa-

---

159 See Konigsberg v. State Bar, 366 U.S. 36, 75–80, 80–81 (1961) (dissenting opinions). See also the concurring opinion of Mr. Justice Douglas, joined by Mr. Justice Black, in *Speiser*. 357 U.S. at 532, 535–38.

160 See 79 Stat. 333 (1965), 42 U.S.C. § 427 (note) (Supp. 1965). This section generally extends hospital benefits to persons not insured under Social Security or Railroad Retirement, but makes an exception for a member of any organization ordered by the Subversive Activities Control Board to register as a Communist organization under the Internal Security Act of 1950. See also the various provisions cited in Note, *Unconstitutional Conditions*, 73 Harv. L. Rev. 1595, 1601–02 (1960).

161 Ariz. Rev. Stat. § 38-231 (B), (C) (1965). The Arizona oath was required of "any person elected, appointed or employed, either on a part-time or full-time basis by the state or any of its political subdivisions or any county, city, town, municipal corporation, school district, public educational institution, or any board, commission or agency of any of the foregoing." *Ibid.*

thetic to the organization's goals and (2) using government power to achieve social and economic conditions that are prerequisites to a successful attempt at revolution.[162] Typical examples offered in support of this position are the employees of legislative committees who attempted "to manipulate hearings so as to favor the friends of the party and depreciate its enemies,"[163] and the public school teachers who used their position to indoctrinate students through the teaching of "a prescribed party line."[164] While the Court has previously accepted the state's interest in preventing such misuse of office as an appropriate basis for imposing loyalty restrictions on teachers[165] and lawyers,[166] it would seriously strain this reasoning to sustain restrictions upon numerous positions that do not allow the employee sufficient discretion to permit any significant manipulation to benefit the organization. Nevertheless, the strained reasoning has been offered in several arguments supporting the application of loyalty tests to all government positions.

One such argument defends total coverage on the ground that it

---

162 See SELZNICK, THE ORGANIZATIONAL WEAPON 215–24 (1960); BROWN, *op. cit. supra* note 5, at 215–18, 336–38. A special danger frequently mentioned in connection with employment of Communist party members is their tendency "to influence specific [policy] decisions, especially on matters of less than central interest to the target government which may help a communist faction abroad or may increase vulnerability to Soviet diplomacy." SELZNICK, at 220. This possibility presents basically the same type of problems in devising an appropriate scope for loyalty oath requirements as the two types of misuse of position mentioned in the text.

163 SELZNICK, *op. cit. supra* note 162, at 222, citing statements by former Senator R. M. La Follette, Jr., concerning the activities of "pro-communist elements" on the staffs of congressional committees.

164 N.Y. Laws 1949, c. 360 (legislative findings supporting the Feinberg Law). See also HOOK, HERESY YES—CONSPIRACY NO 184–87 (1953); THOMAS, THE TEST OF FREEDOM 90–93 (1954).

165 Adler v. Board of Education, 342 U.S. 485, 489–93 (1951). See also Beilan v. Board of Education, 357 U.S. 399 (1958).

166 Konigsberg v. State Bar, 366 U.S. 36 (1961). Although the primary issue before the Court in the second *Konigsberg* case concerned the state's power to compel a bar applicant to answer an inquiry concerning membership in the Communist party, the Court did indicate that the standard for disqualification to which the inquiry related—advocacy of violent overthrow—was constitutionally valid. See *id.* at 51–52: "It would indeed be difficult to argue that a belief firm enough to be carried into advocacy, in the use of illegal means to change the form of the State or Federal government is an unimportant consideration in determining the fitness of applicants for membership in a profession in whose hands so largely lies the safekeeping of this country's legal and political institutions."

is not administratively feasible to identify those positions in which the opportunity for misuse of office in favor of organizational objectives is either nonexistent or negligible.[167] This is a difficult position to sustain in the light of the ability of the federal government, for example, to distinguish between sensitive and non-sensitive positions under the employee security program and between discretionary and ministerial functions under the Federal Torts Claims Act.[168] Also, it seems particularly unlikely to appeal to a Court that itself has undertaken the task of distinguishing between different state positions in order to determine which persons are "public officials" for the purpose of the *New York Times Co. v. Sullivan* rule.[169]

Another argument favoring total coverage rests on the thesis that the employment of members of groups advocating overthrow, no matter what the individual's position, will give the government service a bad public image and therefore impair its general effectiveness. Assuming that such public reaction is a reality,[170] decisions like *Wieman v. Updegraff*[171] would seem to foreclose its use for imposing a restriction upon constitutionally protected association. Although *Wieman* deals with the member of an organization who is unaware of its illegal objectives and *Elfbrandt* with the knowing member who merely does not support those objectives, the difference in the two is unlikely to be significant insofar as public reaction to employment of such persons is concerned. Except in unusual cases, the member's lack of awareness of the organization's objectives is unlikely to be a matter of public knowledge, and where it is, it will often be disbelieved.[172] Similarly, although *Wieman*, unlike

---

167 *Cf.* Brief for Respondent, pp. 36–43, 56–60; Garner v. Board of Public Works, 341 U.S. 716 (1951).

168 See Cole v. Young, 351 U.S. 536 (1956); Dalehite v. United States, 346 U.S. 15 (1953). This is not to say that either of these distinctions is satisfactory for determining which positions might easily be misused to support organizational objectives, but only to suggest that the process of classifying government jobs for this purpose is no more difficult than drawing the distinctions required under the Federal Security program or the Federal Torts Claim Act.

169 See Rosenblatt v. Baer, 383 U.S. 75 (1966).

170 See STOUFFER, COMMUNISM, CONFORMITY AND CIVIL LIBERTIES 39–45 (1955).

171 344 U.S. 183 (1952).

172 See generally Mowitz, *Michigan—State and Local Attack on Subversion,* in THE STATES AND SUBVERSION 184, 206–15, 228–30 (1952) (Gellhorn ed.); STOUFFER, *op. cit. supra* note 170, at 39.

Elfbrandt, concerned membership in "front" organizations as well as those directly advocating overthrow, the Court has clearly indicated that the ruling there is applicable to members of either type of organization.[173] The negative impact upon free association is, of course, presumably less in *Elfbrandt* than in *Wieman* because the Arizona statute does include the element of "scienter." Yet this difference hardly seems likely to alter what might well be viewed in *Wieman* as a total rejection of public reaction as a factor that may be used in determining employment qualifications.[174] Adverse public reaction may justify otherwise irrational government action in other areas,[175] but the Court is not willing to give such reaction any weight where it would affect the exercise of a constitutionally protected right. As Mr. Justice Frankfurter stated in his separate opinion in *Garner*:[176] "[S]urely a government could not exclude from public employment members of a minority group merely because they are odious to the majority." This seems equally true whether the minority is defined in terms of race, religion, or politics.

Finally, the Court in *Garner* sustained the total coverage of a loyalty oath requirement on the ground that membership in a group such as the Communist party might be viewed as likely to affect the individual's performance in all government positions, "both high and low."[177] Unfortunately, the Court's opinion concentrated primarily on other issues and offered little explanation of its conclusion on this point.[178] The opinion does suggest that the Court viewed

---

173 See Aptheker v. Secretary of State, 378 U.S. 500, 510 (1964); Schware v. Board of Bar Examiners, 353 U.S. 232, 239 (1957); see also Sweezy v. New Hampshire, 354 U.S. 234, 247–48 (1957).

174 344 U.S. at 190–91; see also *id.* at 194–97 (concurring opinion). Although the Court did not specifically mention the possible impact upon the public image of government service, the opinion clearly recognized the community attitude about persons discharged on loyalty grounds and emphasized that there was no state interest that justified imposing that burden on the "innocent" member. *Id.* at 191.

175 *Cf.* NEWSWEEK, *supra* note 2 (improper sexual activities); Scott v. Macy, 349 F.2d 182 (D.C. Cir. 1965).

176 341 U.S. at 724.

177 *Id.* at 720.

178 The Court devoted only two paragraphs to this issue, the first dealing primarily with the state's power to require that employees disclose by affidavit any past membership in the Communist party: "We think that a municipal employer is not disabled because it is an agency of the State from inquiring of its employees as to matters that may prove relevant to their fitness and suitability for the public service. Past conduct may well relate to present fitness; past loyalty may have a reasonable relationship to present and future trust. Both are commonly inquired into

the individual's willingness to support illegal overthrow of the government as a reasonable indication of a general lack of "integrity." It also has been suggested that members of such organizations tend to be inefficient and easily disgruntled employees because of their strong opposition to the government for which they work.[179] Additionally, their intense psychological involvement in the organization's "cause" allegedly makes them less able to devote their full efforts to their work.[180] All these points have relevance, however, only to the person who is deeply involved with the organization's purpose. Although there are obviously some hard core members ("cadres") of whom it may be true,[181] certainly membership with knowledge of the organization's illegal purpose would hardly indicate in itself that the individual falls in that category.[182] Accordingly, even if the Court gave full recognition to this argument, it could still reject a loyalty requirement applicable to all knowing members of an organization advocating overthrow irrespective of their purpose in joining the organization or their degree of participation in the organization's activities.[183]

---

in determining fitness for both high and low positions in private industry and are not less relevant in public employment. The affidavit requirement is valid.

"2. In our view the validity of the oath turns upon the nature of the Charter amendment (1941) and the relation of the ordinance (1948) to this amendment. . . . We assume that under the Federal Constitution the Charter amendment is valid to the extent that it bars from the city's public service persons who, subsequent to its adoption in 1941, advise, advocate, or teach the violent overthrow of the Government or who are or become affiliated with any group doing so. The provisions operating thus prospectively were a reasonable regulation to protect the municipal service by establishing an employment qualification of loyalty to the State and the United States. Cf. *Gerende* v. *Board of Supervisors of Elections,* 341 U.S. 56 (1951). Likewise, as a regulation of political activity of municipal employees, the amendment was reasonably designed to protect the integrity and competency of the service. This Court has held that Congress may reasonably restrict the political activity of federal civil service employees for such a purpose, *United Public Workers* v. *Mitchell,* 330 U.S. 75, 102–103 (1947), and a State is not without power to do as much." 341 U.S. at 720–21.

179 Brown, *op. cit. supra* note 5, at 336–37; Almond, The Appeals of Communism 103, 260–62 (1954).

180 Brown, *op. cit. supra* note 5, at 337; Almond, *op. cit. supra* note 179, at 258–59.

181 Meyer, The Moulding of Communists 132–52, 161–65 (1961); Almond, *op. cit. supra* note 179, at 232–33.

182 Selznick, *op. cit. supra* note 162, at 83–85; Meyer, *op. cit. supra* note 181, at 105–31.

183 In *Garner*, the total coverage of the Los Angeles oath was emphasized only in the ACLU brief as amicus curiae, p. 8. Respondent's reply simply brushed over

The Court's rejection of the state's interest in insuring employee fitness thus could have been based, in large part, upon the total coverage of the Arizona oath. Yet, although Mr. Justice Douglas does not in any sense reject this as the ground for decision, it seems likely that the *Elfbrandt* decision was intended to have a much greater reach. While the opinion does note that the Arizona statute applies to all employees, it places no emphasis on this factor.[184] On the other hand, the point on which Mr. Justice Douglas placed the greatest stress, the denial of employment to members lacking "specific intent," would seem to have significance no matter what the coverage of the statute. Thus, although it is far from clear, the opinion indicates that the Court would have reached the same conclusion had the Arizona oath been limited to employees, such as teachers, whose jobs were clearly capable of being manipulated to serve the interests of an organization advocating violent overthrow. If that is true, the Court's ruling is of considerably more significance, from a doctrinal as well as a practical viewpoint.

On a test oath limited to employees with discretionary authority, the state's argument for the exclusion of all knowing members of an organization advocating violent overthrow would rest essentially on the recognized tendency of these organizations to "promote" the "misuse" of such authority. As the Court at one time recognized in a related context, even members of such organizations who have no interest in promoting the overthrow of the government may be induced to misuse public power to achieve organizational objectives.[185] Thus, it has been suggested that teachers belonging to the Communist party will use their classes to advance the party line, not because they necessarily believe in overthrow, but because they be-

---

this objection as an administrative matter on which the state's judgment must be respected. Respondent's brief, p. 66. Other than this the briefs concentrated almost entirely on the bill of attainder argument. Very little attention was given to the membership clause, and there was no mention of the absence of a requirement of specific intent to support the organization's illegal objective.

184 384 U.S. at 12. The Court mentioned the total coverage only in the general description of the facts of the case.

185 See American Communications Ass'n v. Douds, 339 U.S. 382, 387–89 (1950). The Taft-Hartley provision sustained in *Douds* extended to all members of the Communist party, irrespective of the individual's attitude toward its illegal objectives. Of course, *Douds* has been undercut to a great extent by United States v. Brown, 381 U.S. 437 (1965), and though *Brown* rejects the *Douds* analysis primarily on other points, the opinion there suggests that the Court also would reject this aspect of the *Douds* reasoning. See *id.* at 455–56.

lieve in the legal objectives of the party and because the party strongly urges its members to engage in this activity as a means of achieving those objectives.[186] The statute in *Elfbrandt* was not, of course, limited in application to the Communist party, but the manipulation of public offices in the manner previously described would be an essential ingredient of the program of any organization that hoped to overthrow the government. In sum, the argument would be that even members who do not subscribe to the organization's illegal ends pose a danger because (1) the organization imposes great pressure on its members to build group strength through the employee's manipulation of discretionary authority, and (2) the nature of the manipulation is sufficiently related to the group's legal objectives to encourage participation by members who favor only those objectives. The first factor, the constant stress on manipulation, also serves to distinguish the state's regulation here from the possibly unconstitutional denial of employment to members of other groups that might profit by manipulation of public power. Thus, it provides the answer to the argument that the exclusion of Communist teachers logically would also permit the exclusion of Catholic clergy teaching in public schools because they too engaged in classroom indoctrination.[187] Although members of some other groups may occasionally misuse their public position to aid the group, only organizations advocating overthrow have actively promoted such activity, as logically they must if they are to achieve their basic goal.[188]

The opinion in *Elfbrandt* does not clearly indicate whether the Court considered this argument or, if so, on what grounds it rejected it. Certainly, the majority's reliance on the prohibition against "guilt by association" would not be an adequate ground. The denial of employment to all knowing members does not rest on a "conclusive presumption that the member shares the unlawful aims of the organization,"[189] but rather on the potential danger presented

---

[186] See generally Hook, *op. cit. supra* note 164, at 181–86; Brown, *op. cit. supra* note 5, at 340–41.

[187] See Zeller v. Huff, 236 P.2d 949 (N.M. 1951); see also Hook, *op. cit. supra* note 164, at 219–20.

[188] Hook, *op. cit. supra* note 164, at 219–20; see also Selznick, *op. cit. supra* note 162, at 221–24.

[189] 384 U.S. at 17.

by the member even when he does not share these aims. In fact, the Court's reliance on this argument might well indicate that it did not appreciate the state's position in this regard.

On the other hand, the Court relied heavily on *Aptheker v. Secretary of State*,[190] which does provide an adequate basis for rejecting the state's argument. In *Aptheker* the Court held unconstitutional a section of the Securities Activities Control Act that made it a crime for any member of an organization found to be a "communist organization" to seek a United States passport.[191] The congressional purpose in enacting this provision had been to prevent travel abroad that could further the organization's relationship with the "world Communist movement" through the exchange of secret communiqués, the training of local leaders, and similar activities.[192] The Court majority there, including four members of the *Elfbrandt* majority,[193] held the statute unconstitutional because, as in *Elfbrandt*, the legislature had sought to achieve its objective "by means that sweep unnecessarily broadly and thereby invade the area of protected freedom."[194] The unnecessary breadth came from Congress' failure to take into consideration several factors that were considered relevant to "the likelihood that travel by such a person would be attended by the type of activity which Congress sought to control."[195] The Court particularly emphasized that the statute automatically denied the member's right to travel without regard to his knowledge of the organization's improper purpose, "his commitment to its purpose," "his degree of activity in the organization," his "purposes" for wishing to travel, and "the security-sensitivity of the areas in which he wishes to travel."[196]

Despite certain differences, a strong analogy can be drawn between *Aptheker* and *Elfbrandt*. Although the holding in *Aptheker* was framed in terms of the Fifth Amendment right to travel,[197] various references in the opinion indicate that the decision was

190 378 U.S. 500 (1964).

191 64 Stat. 993, 50 U.S.C. § 785 (1964).

192 378 U.S. at 526–27 (dissenting opinion).

193 The Chief Justice and Justices Black, Douglas, and Brennan. Mr. Justice Fortas, the fifth member of the *Elfbrandt* majority, was not then a member of the Court.

194 378 U.S. at 508, quoting from N.A.A.C.P. v. Alabama, 377 U.S. 288, 307 (1964).

195 378 U.S. at 510.

196 *Id.* at 510, 512.

197 *Id.* at 505–07, 514, 517.

grounded on the restriction upon free association. The Court relied in large part on First Amendment cases,[198] and specifically analogized the restrictions on the issuance of passports to loyalty restrictions on government employment.[199] Also, although the legislation extended to "Communist front" organizations and therefore included groups in which a large majority of members were unlikely to be aligned with the "world Communist movement,"[200] the Court's opinion did not refer to this fact, and it made no effort to distinguish between members of "Communist front" and "Communist action" organizations. Thus, despite Mr. Justice White's objection that "*Aptheker* did not deal with the government employee,"[201] the ruling in *Aptheker* clearly was entitled to significant consideration in determining the validity of an employment test imposing a similar type of restriction upon the individual's right of association.

Mr. Justice White also distinguished *Aptheker* on the ground that the statute involved there applied to members who were unaware of the organization's ties to the "world Communist movement."[202] The *Aptheker* opinion indicates, however, that the addition of this element of knowledge would not have altered the result in that case. The opinion placed great stress on the legislature's failure to consider the individual's "activity, commitment, and purpose in the places for travel."[203] Perhaps, the Court's reliance upon one of these factors, the member's commitment to the organization's purposes, could be distinguished in the situation presented by *Elfbrandt*. Unlike the prospect of manipulation of public office, the activities that Congress sought to inhibit in the passport legislation

---

198 See, *e.g., id.* at 517, 525; see also Note, 78 HARV. L. REV. 143, 195–99 (1964).

199 378 U.S. at 508, 510, 513–14.

200 Communist front organizations are those (1) "substantially directed, dominated, or controlled by a Communist action organization," and (2) "primarily operated for the purpose of giving aid and support to a Communist-action organization . . . or the world Communist movement." 64 Stat. 989, 50 U.S.C. § 785 (1964). See American Committee for the Protection of the Foreign Born v. S.A.C.B., 331 F.2d 63 (D.C. Cir. 1962), *vacated,* 380 U.S. 503, 505 (1965).

201 384 U.S. at 22.

202 *Ibid.*

203 *Id.* at 514. "In addition to the absence of criteria linking the bare fact of membership to the individual's knowledge, activity or commitment, § 6 also excludes other considerations which might more closely relate the denial of passports to the stated purpose of the legislation." *Id.* at 511.

would be undertaken only by members who shared the organization's goal of promoting the "world Communist movement." But the stress that *Aptheker* places on the other factors of activity and purpose of travel, especially when viewed in the light of the administrative burdens involved in considering those factors,[204] suggests a general policy, equally applicable to *Elfbrandt*, against the use of knowing membership as an indicator of an individual's tendency to act improperly on behalf of an organization. Surely, if this policy required legislative consideration of so many factors beyond the element of scienter in *Aptheker*, it could easily make similar demands of Arizona.

Reliance upon *Aptheker* becomes more difficult, however, if *Elfbrandt* is viewed as establishing a standard that would be applicable to a loyalty oath requirement limited to employees with discretionary authority. Although the *Aptheker* Court stated that several factors were relevant to the congressional purpose in restricting travel, it did not state that a legislative standard necessarily must include every one of these factors. In fact, it clearly avoided this conclusion when it stated that there was no need to consider the constitutionality of the passport regulation as applied to the petitioners—both very active high officials of the party—because the petitioners could, in any event, attack the legislation on its face.[205] Certainly the opinion left open the possibility that Congress might condition the issuance of passports on most of the factors mentioned, yet exclude others as not equally significant. Thus,

---

[204] The Court did not mention the obvious administrative difficulties involved in considering all of these factors. The reference to the federal employees loyalty program, however, apparently constituted its answer to this problem. Whether the problems could be handled by an administrative program is uncertain. Could an administrative hearing determine, for example, whether Aptheker's purpose was *merely* to travel and lecture abroad, to visit the Bodleian library, etc.? In any event, the increase in administrative burden would obviously be great. But this factor was not considered worthy of discussion.

[205] See, *e.g.*, 378 U.S. at 514–17. One of the major questions presented in *Aptheker* was whether the Court should consider the lack of statutory recognition of such elements as scienter and active membership when the petitioners themselves clearly met those requirements. This question would have been irrelevant if, for example, the "purposes and places of travel" were factors that the legislature had to take into consideration. If that were the case, the statute would clearly be unconstitutional even as it related to the petitioners. The Court, however, did not rule on the statute as it applied to the active member, but held that the petitioners had standing to attack the validity of the statute "on its face." *Id.* at 515.

it might provide that all knowing members of "communist organizations," would be denied passports to visit the U.S.S.R. or the "satellite" countries except in connnection with very limited purposes. Whether the Court would reject this provision because it was not also limited to active members committed to the organization's illicit purposes is not settled by *Aptheker*. The validity of a loyalty oath based on knowing membership, but limited in application to a specific group, such as teachers, would present a roughly similar question. If *Elfbrandt* was intended to control in this situation, then it clearly has proceeded, albeit without discussion, beyond the position taken in *Aptheker*. This is not to suggest that the general tenor of the opinion in *Aptheker* might not furnish some support for such an extension. Certainly the basic thrust of Mr. Justice Goldberg's opinion in *Aptheker* might be viewed as indicating that legislation characterizing individuals according to membership will be accepted only when the class of members is so sharply limited by consideration of all relevant facts that the tendency ascribed to the group is shown to be an almost uniform characteristic of each member.[206] Under this premise, of course, *Elfbrandt's* requirement of "specific intent" is easily sustainable without regard to the limited nature of the positions covered by the oath requirement.

This view of *Aptheker* would also lend support to the suggestion in *Elfbrandt* that an appropriate loyalty oath would require that the excluded individual be an "active" member of the organization. Requiring this additional element would mean, in effect, that the constitutional limits imposed upon an indirect restraint aimed at preventing improper manipulation of public office would be identical, in the end, with the constitutional limits presently imposed under *Scales* on direct restraints on association.[207] Actually, as previously noted, the *Elfbrandt* opinion at one point suggests that the constitutional restrictions on the loyalty oath standard might be taken one step further to require membership with "specific intent"

---

206 Acceptance of this view of *Aptheker* might place the legislature on the horns of a dilemma, since legislation limited to such a specific class could present difficulties under the newly expanded concept of "bills of attainder" as presented in United States v. Brown, 381 U.S. 437 (1965). See also note 58 *supra*.

207 See Scales v. United States, 367 U.S. 203 (1961); Noto v. United States, 267 U.S. 290 (1961).

plus past participation in the organization's unlawful activities. This proposal reflects the views of Justices Black and Douglas that "government can concern itself only with the actions of men, not with their opinions or beliefs."[208] If this position were applied literally to government employment, the Court would probably be forced to overrule all the cases cited in the *Elfbrandt* dissent, including the *Gerende* decision in which Justices Black and Douglas joined.[209] Moreover, the standard suggested would obviously extend beyond the security area and raise a serious question of the validity of common employment criteria, *e.g.*, personality profiles that are based in large part upon the individual's general attitudes and viewpoints.[210] It seems unlikely that the single reference in *Elfbrandt* to the individual's past participation in illegal action reflected the willingness of the majority as a whole to take this step. Chief Justice Warren and Mr. Justice Brennan, in particular, have carefully avoided joining those Black and Douglas dissents that suggest such a position.[211] The reference in *Elfbrandt* may reflect a possible change of heart on their part, but similar language found in Mr. Justice Black's opinion in *Schware* turned out to have little consequence.[212]

---

208 Beilan v. Board of Education, 357 U.S. 399, 412, 415 (1958) (Black and Douglas, JJ., dissenting); see also Speiser v. Randall, 357 U.S. 513, 535–36 (1958) (same). But *cf.* DOUGLAS, *op. cit. supra* note 89, at 118–19.

Justices Douglas and Black have on several occasions argued that participation in the organization's illegal activities should be a prerequisite for employment disqualification. See, *e.g.*, Killian v. United States, 368 U.S. 231, 258 (1961); Beilan v. Board of Education, 357 U.S. at 412–16; Adler v. Board of Education, 342 U.S. at 511. Mr. Justice Douglas also has suggested that such activity is a constitutional prerequisite for the deportation of aliens. See Carlson v. Landon, 342 U.S. 524, 568–69 (1952) (dissenting opinion).

209 But see DOUGLAS, *op. cit. supra* note 89, at 130.

210 See generally, Mirel, *The Limits of Governmental Inquiry into the Private Lives of Government Employees*, 46 B.U. L. REV. 1 (1966); Creech, *Psychological Testing and Constitutional Rights*, [1966] DUKE L.J. 332.

211 See, *e.g.*, Beilan v. Board of Education, 357 U.S. 399, 411, 417 (1958) (dissenting opinions); Speiser v. Randall, 357 U.S. 513 (1958). Mr. Justice Brennan has been particularly consistent in this regard. See, *e.g.*, Konigsberg v. State Bar, 366 U.S. 36, 80 (1961); Wilkinson v. United States, 365 U.S. 399, 429 (1961); Braden v. United States, 365 U.S. 431, 446 (1961); Barenblatt v. United States, 360 U.S. 109, 166 (1959).

212 Schware v. Board of Bar Examiners, 353 U.S. 232, 245–46 (1957); Konigsberg v. State Bar, 353 U.S. 252, 267 (1957).

VII. The State's Interest in Protecting Internal Security

The Court's ruling in *Elfbrandt* also constituted a rejection of the state's interest in preserving internal security as a justification for the Arizona oath. The problems presented by this aspect of the Court's decision are basically the same as those discussed in connection with the rejection of the state interest in insuring employee reliability. Here also, the significance of the decision depends in large part on how the Court viewed the state's interest as presented in *Elfbrandt*.

The Court has asserted that the state's interest in guarding against acts injurious to internal security, such as sabotage, espionage, or the unintentional release of confidential information, will be given substantial weight in justifying indirect restrictions upon speech.[213] The difficulty in *Elfbrandt*, once again, was that Arizona's oath requirement applied to all state employees. The decision in *Cole v. Young*,[214] although not based on constitutional grounds, certainly indicates that little, if any, weight will be given to the state's alleged interest in preserving internal security where no effort has been made to separate the sensitive from the non-sensitive position. The Court in *Cole* held that a federal statute authorizing summary discharge of employees "in the interest of national security"[215] could not properly be applied to all government positions. The dissent had argued that total coverage was necessary because "one never knows just which job is sensitive."[216] The majority concluded, however, that the task of distinguishing between jobs on the basis of task, access to information, and similar factors was not so difficult as to suppose that Congress meant to include all federal positions under an extraordinary procedure that denied the employee the normal safeguards of civil service procedures. Certainly, with First Amendment rights involved, the Court would expect the states to be equally capable of distinguishing between positions. Accordingly, insofar as the state's interest in protecting against subversion is concerned, a loyalty restriction encompassing all state employees might easily be characterized as using "means that broadly stifle

---

213 See, *e.g.*, Communist Party v. S.A.C.B., 367 U.S. 1, 93–96 (1961); Barenblatt v. United States, 360 U.S. 109, 127–29 (1959).

214 351 U.S. 536 (1956).

215 64 Stat. 476, 5 U.S.C. § 22 (1964).

216 351 U.S. at 569.

fundamental personal liberties when the end can be more narrowly achieved."

As previously noted, however, there is little to indicate that the Court in fact based its decision on the total coverage of the Arizona oath requirement. On the other hand, as Mr. Justice White emphasized in his dissent, the majority opinion nowhere "expressly holds that a state must retain, even in its most sensitive positions, those who lend such support as knowing membership entails to those organizations, such as the Communist party, whose purposes include the violent destruction of democratic government."[217] The nature of the test oath is such, however, that it is unlikely to be used as a primary security device for the "most sensitive position," nor, for that matter, is the state government likely to have many such positions.[218] Nevertheless, a loyalty requirement of the type employed in *Elfbrandt* might well be imposed for a limited group of persons, such as state civil defense workers, police officers, and others who would occupy particularly important positions in time of emergency.[219] As limited to such positions, a state could defend a standard excluding all knowing members of organizations urging violent overthrow on at least two grounds that have considerable support in practice under state and federal security programs.

First, the state might argue that the importance of its interest in safeguarding against potential subversion justifies exclusion of all knowing members as the most effective administrative means of insuring complete exclusion of these knowing members who do

---

217 384 U.S. at 20.

218 Loyalty oaths are usually required of general classes of employees, *e.g.*, all teachers and civil defense workers. Those state employees who have access to classified information will usually constitute only a small group of upper-level officials within a department, *e.g.*, senior officers within the state militia. These people will often be subject to federal clearance, and the state is unlikely to single them out as the subjects for a special loyalty oath.

219 See generally Brown, *op. cit. supra* note 5, at 92–109, 235–53, 470–71. Various states presently require civil defense workers to take an oath patterned after the federal civil defense oath. 64 Stat. 1256, 50 U.S.C. § 2255 (1964). See, *e.g.*, Conn. Rev. Stat. § 28-12 (1965 Supp.); Ill. Ann. St., ch. 127, § 286 (1966 Supp.); Miss Rev. Stat. 38610-18 (1964). A 1965 compilation of state statutes listed thirty states with special civil defense oaths. Fund for the Republic, Digest of the Public Record of Communism 347–82 (1955). Although these oaths vary in context, they all require a denial of membership in any group that advocates the overthrow of the government.

share the organization's illegal objectives.[220] The effectiveness of a provision like § 5 of the Arizona statute depends upon the deterrence potential of possible criminal prosecution for improperly subscribing to the state loyalty oath. Yet, while most knowing members arguably do support the organization's illegal objectives, proof of "specific intent" as it relates to a particular individual may often be very difficult.[221] Accordingly, to make the loyalty requirement an effective device, the state must be given administrative leeway to encompass an area of membership somewhat larger than that which is the direct source of the supposed evil. Admittedly, administrative leeway of this sort is not ordinarily accorded in areas affecting free association, but here, where the statute is appropriately limited to sensitive positions, the impact of the restriction on association is also limited and the state's need is greater. Any indication in previous cases that only knowing members may be automatically excluded even from sensitive positions in no way constitutes a rejection of this position.[222] Failure to require that the member at least be aware of the organization's illegal goals would vastly increase the area of associational freedom that would be subject to restraint. Moreover, the element of knowledge, so the argument goes, is not nearly so difficult to prove as that of specific intent to further the organization's illegal purposes.[223]

The state may also argue that the exclusion of all knowing members is justified because even the knowing member who does not share the organization's objective of violent overthrow may present a threat to internal security. As the Court has recognized on several occasions, security requirements for sensitive positions extend far beyond the individual's loyalty to his government.[224] A person who does not favor violent overthrow of the government but nevertheless joins an organization supporting that objective, either does not

[220] See Brown, *op. cit. supra* note 5, at 235–43, 265.

[221] See Noto v. United States, 367 U.S. 290 (1961).

[222] *E.g.*, Wieman v. Updegraff, 344 U.S. 183 (1952). *Wieman*, of course, involved an oath required of all state employees and could be distinguished on that ground. See Willcox, *supra* note 129, at 12, 50 n. 158.

[223] See Killian v. United States, 368 U.S. 231, 244–58 (1961). See also Hook, *op. cit. supra* note 164, at 89; Gellhorn, Individual Freedom and Government Restraints 135 (1956).

[224] See, *e.g.*, Cafeteria and Restaurant Workers v. McElroy, 367 U.S. 886, 898–99 (1961); Lerner v. Casey, 357 U.S. 468, 478 (1958); Cole v. Young, 351 U.S. 536 (1956).

consider that organization a serious threat or considers the achievement of other values more important than possibly increasing the risk of overthrow. In either case, the individual indicates a lack of appropriate concern for security measures.[225] Similarly, it might also be argued that anyone who associates with potential subversives necessarily puts himself in a position where he becomes a more likely subject of coercive pressure to join a subversive activity.[226] While both these arguments have an Orwellian air about them, the state could cite experience under the federal loyal security program to support their use in the case of employees who occupy sensitive jobs.[227]

Assuming the Court in *Elfbrandt* meant to reject all arguments of this type, the basis for its conclusion, at least as indicated by the majority opinion, again would rest primarily on *Aptheker*. The *Aptheker* decision seems to be relevant here in much the same sense as it would be in the situation where the state seeks to insure against possible misuse of public office by excluding knowing members from positions carrying considerable discretionary authority.[228] The difference in the nature of the interest in safeguarding against subversion is not likely to be controlling. *Aptheker*, after all, was itself presented to the Court as a case involving national security.[229] An argument could be made that the state's security interest is so greatly sharpened when only sensitive positions are involved that a policy announced in connection with the general restriction on travel voided in *Aptheker*, even if equally applicable to more limited restrictions concerning other state interests, would not be applicable here. Both past decisions and *Elfbrandt* itself suggest, however, that the *Elfbrandt* majority would not be receptive to such an argument, if for no other reason than that they would refuse to attach any special significance to the state interest in safeguarding against subversion by such groups as the police or civil defense workers.

The Chief Justice, and Justices Black, Douglas, and Brennan

---

225 *Cf.* Atomic Energy Commission, In the Matter of J. Robert Oppenheimer (1954). See Hook, *op. cit. supra* note 164, at 225.

226 See Brown, *op. cit. supra* note 5, at 254–61, 272; Selznick, *op. cit. supra* note 162, at 70–72.

227 See Brown, *op. cit. supra* note 5, at 37, 254–79.

228 See text at notes 204–07 *supra*.

229 378 U.S. at 509.

all have indicated that they draw an important distinction between government positions classified as "sensitive" because of special access to confidential information and those placed in that category simply because of their potential significance during a period of national emergency. In fact, for Justices Black and Douglas, the state's interest in protecting against subversion by employees in the latter situation will rank no higher than its interest generally in preventing other types of misuse of position. Thus, in *Lerner v. Casey*,[230] Mr. Justice Douglas' dissent, joined by Mr. Justice Black, clearly gave no special weight to the fact that the employee, a New York subway conductor, was classified as working in a "sensitive" position under the New York Risk Law. Mr. Justice Douglas treated the question of the state's power to discharge the conductor on the basis of his speech or association as no different from its power to discharge the teacher involved in a companion case from Pennsylvania.[231] In response to the state's argument that the conductor's access to an important transportation facility placed him in an especially sensitive position, Mr. Justice Douglas quoted a lower court opinion noting that vast numbers of persons throughout the economy had access to prime sites for sabotage, that the imposition of restrictive security regulations on all such persons would be constitutionally impermissible, and therefore "in the event of war" we may just have to take our chances with the possibility of "Black Tom explosions on every waterfront, poison in our water systems, and sand in all important industrial machines."[232] Mr. Justice Douglas has recognized, on the other hand, that special considerations may require more flexibility in permitting the discharge of persons who have access to classified information or restricted locations.[233] Mr. Justice Brennan, along with the Chief Justice, also

---

[230] 357 U.S. 468 (1958).

[231] 357 U.S. at 415–16.

[232] *Id.* at 416–17, quoting Judge Pope in Parker v. Lester, 227 F.2d 708, 721 (9th Cir. 1955). See also Black v. Cutter Laboratories, 351 U.S. 292, 300, 303–04 (1956) (dissenting opinion).

[233] See DOUGLAS, THE RIGHT TO BE LET ALONE 118, 121 (1958). Although recognizing the importance of the security interest in this situation, Mr. Justice Douglas still opposes any type of administrative program that might involve "labeling." He would prefer that the executive in charge have absolute discretion to discharge men and women in "sensitive jobs for good reasons or for no reasons at all." *Id.* at 121. Exactly what would happen to the normal civil service protection of employees in this category is not stated, but the loss of that safeguard is apparently deemed to be the lesser of two evils.

has recognized this distinction, although it is not clear that they would go quite so far as Mr. Justice Douglas in their treatment of the fact that a particular government position provides the potential to cause substantial harm in an emergency situation.[234] While the remainder of the Court has not spoken to this point, it seems likely that at least Mr. Justice Fortas, who was in the majority in *Elfbrandt*, would also be reluctant to attach any substantial weight to the state's interest in preventing subversion as it related to jobs with particular security significance only under the "remote risk of a mass breakdown."[235]

VIII. The Practical Significance of Elfbrandt and the Future of Loyalty Oaths

In terms of the legal limits upon loyalty oaths, the ultimate significance of *Elfbrandt* will depend upon how the Court answers various questions left unanswered by Mr. Justice Douglas' opinion: whether the *Garner* case has been overruled; whether the Court has rejected the state's interest in denying support to "disloyal" persons as an appropriate basis for a test oath; whether the addition of an element of "specific intent to further the illegal aims of the organization" would be required in an oath limited in application to employees in positions that could easily be manipulated to serve organizational ends; whether the same would be true of an oath applicable only to employees in positions classified as "sensitive" from the standpoint of protecting internal security; and, finally, whether, wherever the specific intent element must be added, the Court will also insist upon a requirement of active participation in the organization's affairs, or even participation in illegal activities. On the other hand, in terms of its practical significance, the impact of *Elfbrandt* will be much the same whether these questions are answered in one way or in another.

Obviously, many oaths, no matter what view of *Elfbrandt* is taken, will survive litigation, at least temporarily. State courts, taking a page from the *Scales* case,[236] may "read into" the mem-

---

234 Lerner v. Casey, 357 U.S. 468, 417, 421–22 (1958).

235 Brown, *op. cit. supra* note 5, at 248.

236 367 U.S. 203 (1961). The Court there interpreted the Smith Act membership clause to require both "active" membership and "specific intent" to support violent overthrow, although neither element was mentioned in the statute. State courts have followed this pattern in the past with respect to the element of scienter. See Adler v. Board of Education, 342 U.S. 485, 494 n. 8 (1952).

bership clause of state oaths the requirements of specific intent and perhaps even active membership. In other instances, while the membership clause may be held unconstitutional, the state court will retain as properly severable that clause dealing with the individual's own advocacy of overthrow.[237] Even where the entire oath is voided, the likelihood is that the legislature will swiftly re-enact it in appropriately modified form. For the combination of cold war exasperation, fear, and chauvinism that produces community support for loyalty tests apparently is still present in most parts of the country. While Congress was repealing the loyalty affidavit requirements of the Defense Education Act and Economic Opportunity Act,[238] it was adopting a new loyalty requirement in the Medicare Act,[239] and the Office of Economic Opportunity was adding still another loyalty requirement for antipoverty workers.[240] Similarly, on the state level, organized efforts to gain legislative repeal of oaths have been noticeably unsuccessful.[241]

It is equally clear that the ardent opposition to the oaths will be only slightly mollified, if at all, by the addition to the oaths of such requirements as the member's "specific intent" to support the organization's illegal objectives. In the past that opposition has gone primarily to the basic concept of the loyalty oath, rather than to the specific standards employed in the oaths.[242] Resentment of individuals at being singled out as government employees or teachers to swear to such oaths will remain.[243] As for those employees whose associations might have been determined in part by the fear of a possible prosecution or loss of job, the addition of the elements of "specific intent" and "active membership" is unlikely to provide great comfort—especially when the Court itself warns that both prosecutors and juries are only "human" and may therefore have a

---

237 *Cf.* Cramp v. Board of Public Instruction, 137 So. 2d 828 (Fla. 1962).

238 76 Stat. 1070 (1962); 79 Stat. 973 (1961). See N.Y. Times, Oct. 12, 1962, p. 13, col. 3; N.Y. Times, Oct. 18, 1962, p. 1, col. 2.

239 79 Stat. 333, 42 U.S.C. § 427 (note). See note 160 *supra*. This requirement has been implemented by the use of an oath.

240 ACLU, Feature Press Service Bulletin, § 2265, May 9, 1966.

241 See note 4 *supra*.

242 See Byse, *A Report on the Pennsylvania Loyalty Act,* 101 U. PA. L. REV. 480, 486 (1953).

243 See N.Y. Times, March 11, 1966, p. 9, cols. 3, 4.

tendency to "label as Communist [any] ideas which they oppose."[244]

In light of these facts, it is not surprising that current legal attacks against loyalty oaths frequently are concentrated not on standards used in the oaths, but on the alleged invalidity of any and all loyalty oaths, no matter what standards they employ.[245] The main argument being advanced is that, assuming the state may utilize some form of loyalty test based upon certain classes of speech and association to serve the legitimate interests of protecting internal security and insuring employee reliability, the loyalty oath is invalid because it is a totally inappropriate means of serving those interests. Thus, the petitioner in *Elfbrandt* based his argument in part on the alleged ineffectiveness of loyalty oaths in keeping undesirable persons out of government employment.[246] In support of this position, petitioner cited several commentators who have noted that oaths have been most ineffective in disclosing potential subversives.[247] The only employees who have objected to newly imposed oaths have been those with conscientious objections to the oath. On the other hand, "the really dangerous 'Reds,' the unidentified plotters, are unlikely to stickle at taking the oaths."[248] Mr. Justice Douglas took a similar extrajudicial view of the loyalty oath.[249] And the *Elfbrandt* opinion quotes an Arizona legislative report that notes the ineffectiveness of oaths against "the Communist trained in fraud and perjury."[250] The report appears to have been used to make another point,[251] however, and it seems unlikely that the Court as a whole would be willing to base its judgment in any large degree upon the alleged ineffectiveness of the

---

244 384 U.S. at 16–17. See also Adler v. Board of Education, 342 U.S. 485, 509 (1952).

245 See note 4 *supra*.

246 Brief for Petitioner, 6, 27–28.

247 *Id.* at 28, citing Horowitz, *supra* note 93; Byse, *supra* note 242; Elson, *People, Government and Security*, 51 Nw. U. L. Rev. 83 (1956); O'Brian, *New Encroachments on Individual Freedom*, 66 Harv. L. Rev. 1 (1952).

248 Gellhorn, *op. cit. supra* note 223, at 367–68, quoted in Byse, *supra* note 242, at 485.

249 Douglas, *op. cit., supra* note 89, at 135–36.

250 384 U.S. at 18, quoting from the report of the Arizona Judiciary Committee, Journal of the Senate, 1st Reg. Sess., 25th Legislature of Arizona 424 (1961).

251 The remainder of the quotation dealt with the impact of the oath upon public employees generally, and the report was cited to emphasize Mr. Justice Douglas' argument on that point. See 384 U.S. at 17–18.

oaths. Since the effectiveness of the oaths depends in large degree upon the fear of a possible prosecution for false swearing,[252] any attempt to evaluate its operation is necessarily speculative. Individuals who openly refuse to take the oath afford no basis for judgment.[253] The active member of an organization who might potentially misuse his office or even engage in subversion to assist the organization is not likely to announce that he is leaving government employment because he fears a possible criminal prosecution for false swearing. In the end, the effectiveness of the loyalty oath in forcing such persons out of government remains in large part a matter of conjecture.[254]

A more substantial argument supporting the rejection of all oaths could be based on the rationale of *Aptheker* and *Elfbrandt*, that the oath constitutes an unnecessarily restrictive means of accomplishing the state's objectives. First, it might be argued that the only legitimate objective of a loyalty oath is the exclusion of persons who might engage in undesirable conduct as an employee. This would require that the Court expand upon the theme of *Speiser* and find that the denial of employment for reasons unrelated to the employee's prospective performance in office constitutes punishment and cannot be imposed without the procedural guarantees afforded by the Sixth Amendment.[255] With this point established, it could be argued that the loyalty oath constituted an unnecessarily broad and rigid means of judging the employee's potential performance. The determination that an individual is likely to misuse his public position in order to aid a subversive organization or to engage in subversion cannot rest on the automatic application of any set criterion. Several factors, it could be argued, must be considered, and each is a variable that must be viewed in the light of the others. Even, for example, the individual's commitment to

---

252 A substantial number of prosecutions for false swearing were brought on the basis of the Taft-Hartley loyalty oath sustained in American Communications Ass'n v. Douds, 339 U.S. 382 (1950). See 1 EMERSON & HABER, POLITICAL AND CIVIL RIGHTS IN THE UNITED STATES 472 (1954). At least one criminal prosecution relating back to the Taft-Hartley oath is still pending. See Dennis v. United States, 384 U.S. 855 (1966).

253 On the other hand, it is relevant in determining the impact of the restriction on the free exercise of the right of association. See Byse, *supra* note 242, at 484–85.

254 See BROWN, *op. cit. supra* note 5, at 94–95.

255 See text at notes 138–52 *supra*.

the illegal goals of an organization and his active membership in the organization cannot be treated as sufficient. The state must also examine the nature of the position involved, the employee's past attitude toward his work, and the nature of the "subversive" organization to which he belongs. All of these are factors that must be considered and weighed on an individual basis. The oath is not sufficiently flexible to permit this and, as a result, may easily exclude a person who, upon consideration of all the relevant factors, would be found not to present a potential for either direct subversion or misuse of office. Accordingly, the argument would conclude, the loyalty oath constitutes a means of achieving a legitimate state end that "broadly stifle[s] fundamental personal rights when the end can be more narrowly achieved."[256]

Support for this argument could come from both *Aptheker* and *Elfbrandt* in so far as both cases suggest that multiple factors must be considered in administrating an employment standard related to speech or association. *Aptheker* also lends some support for the position that these factors cannot be weighted automatically by a loyalty oath. In striking down a statutory prohibition against the issuance of passports to members of "communist organizations," the Court in *Aptheker* specifically pointed to the Federal Employee Loyalty program as an analogous illustration of a "less drastic" means of achieving the congressional purpose of safeguarding national security.[257] The same federal program illustrates that here also the state's interests "can be adequately protected by means which, when compared with [the loyalty oath] are more discriminately tailored to the constitutional liberties of the individual."[258]

Although this position may indeed find a fair degree of support in *Aptheker* and *Elfbrandt*, its acceptance by the Court would be most unfortunate. It would ignore the fact that the rule prohibiting a state from using means that "broadly stifle fundamental rights when the end can be more narrowly achieved" represents a judicial, not a legislative, standard, and it is to be applied within the limits of the judicial function in reviewing legislation. As noted by Mr. Justice Frankfurter:[259]

---

256 Shelton v. Tucker, 362 U.S. 479, 488 (1961).

257 358 U.S. at 512–14.

258 *Id.* at 514.

259 364 U.S. at 493–94.

> The consideration of feasible alternative modes of regulation . . . [does] not imply that the Court might substitute its own choice among alternatives for that of a state legislature or that the states . . . [are] to be restricted to the narrowest workable means of accomplishing an end. . . . The issue remains whether, in light of the particular kind of restriction upon individual liberty which a regulation entails, it is reasonable for a legislature to choose that form of regulation rather than others less restrictive. To that determination, the range of judgments easily open to a legislature in considering the relative degrees of efficiency of alternative means in achieving the end it seeks is pertinent.

The argument for total rejection of loyalty oaths simply fails to give weight to these pertinent factors. To suggest that the loyalty oath is unconstitutional because a loyalty program will provide less rigid standards and, therefore, will reach more appropriate results in an individual case is to ignore all considerations of cost, of administrative ease,[260] and perhaps even of the over-all impact on society in its exercise of associational rights. For one can easily argue that a loyalty program has a far greater restrictive impact on speech than does the loyalty oath. Admittedly, the program offers the individual a chance to explain his position, and therefore should produce a decision in which the individual would have more confidence. But loyalty programs also permit broad-ranging investigations of an individual's beliefs and background, involve considerably more delay and expense to the individual, and offer far greater opportunity for serious injury to his reputation.[261] In any event, irrespective of which type of regulation in fact constitutes a more serious deterrent to the exercise of individual rights, this hardly seems to be the type of judgment that the Court can adequately or appropriately make.

The relative merits or demerits of the loyalty oath and loyalty program point up the practical limits of a decision that would go so far as to find all loyalty oaths invalid. As noted, the public concern over security and loyalty matters still runs strong. The rejec-

---

260 The costs of administration here are obviously far more substantial than in *Shelton*. See KALVEN, THE NEGRO AND THE FIRST AMENDMENT 103–05 (1965). See also Karst, *supra* note 125, at 15–18; BICKEL, THE LEAST DANGEROUS BRANCH 113–17 (1962).

261 See Adler v. Board of Education, 342 U.S. 485, 508 (1952) (dissenting opinion); Vitarelli v. Seaton, 359 U.S. 535, 540–45 (1959); BROWN, *op. cit. supra* note 5, at 21–61, 183–201, 235–83. But see Green, *Q-Clearance: The Development of a Personnel Security Program,* 20 BULL. ATOMIC SCIENTISTS 9 (1964).

tion of loyalty oaths might only produce a new series of loyalty programs. The Court has directly considered the constitutionality of a loyalty program only in *Adler*,[262] and even then it scrutinized only a part of the program. Nevertheless, the nature of the response by both majority and dissent to earlier cases involving the federal program indicates that with appropriate procedure and labels an administrative loyalty program limited in application to special groups of employees will be sustained.[263] Admittedly, administrative programs cost more to administer than loyalty oaths and consequently will not be used as extensively.[264] Yet it seems likely also that loyalty programs will be used in connection with those positions, such as public school teachers, where the programs can do the greatest damage to the spirit of free inquiry. In the end, looking to the impact on free association throughout the society, one must wonder which is the lesser evil. It must be recognized, however, that the loyalty oath and loyalty program can be, and sometimes are, cumulative and not alternative devices. In this light, a prohibition against oaths might well appeal to the Court as affording some diminution of the total restriction that may be imposed upon speech by loyalty measures.

IX. Conclusion: The Elfbrandt Opinion

At last, a few comments should be made concerning the *Elfbrandt* opinion, not as it reflects upon the future of loyalty oaths, but simply as it reflects on the art of opinion writing as practiced in the Supreme Court. If one were asked to pick that opinion in the 1966 Term that best lends support to the recent criticism of the Court's opinions,[265] there is no doubt that *Elfbrandt* would

---

262 Adler v. Board of Education, 342 U.S. 485 (1952).

263 See Greene v. McElroy, 360 U.S. 474 (1959); Vitarelli v. Seaton, 359 U.S. 539 (1959); Peters v. Hobby, 349 U.S. 331 (1955). While Justices Black and Douglas have not hesitated in other cases to go beyond the procedural issue presented and find the entire state or federal program invalid, see, *e.g.*, Carlson v. Landon, 342 U.S. 524, 568 (1952); Lerner v. Casey, 357 U.S. 468, 512 (1958), they have not suggested here that the entire federal program is invalid. Mr. Justice Brennan and the Chief Justice clearly have been willing to assume that a program would be valid provided the proper procedures were followed and employees were not categorized as disloyal. See Beilan v. Board of Education, 357 U.S. 399, 417, 422 (1958).

264 The New York experience shows, however, that they are hardly so expensive as to be out of the state's reach. See also Horowitz, *supra* note 93.

265 See Shapiro, *supra* note 47, at 591 (collecting sources); Kurland, *supra* note 68, at 144–45.

rank at least among the quarter finalists. Certainly this is an opinion that ignores past precedent, that fails to define carefully the interests involved in the case, and that fails even to attempt to rebut the arguments of its opponents. Perhaps these features are a product of compromise among five Justices who could not agree, for example, on just how *Garner* should be handled and therefore decided that the best treatment was silence. Yet it seems likely from comparison with other opinions that *Elfbrandt* was less the product of compromise than the product of Mr. Justice Douglas' general approach to the writing of opinions. That approach, a reflection of what has been described as Mr. Justice "Douglas's relentless effort to simplify our understanding of the world,"[266] is rather nicely analyzed by Yosal Rogat as follows:[267]

> As presented by Justice Douglas, not a single case is hard enough to perplex a right thinking man; a case does not present a tangle of competing principles, but a single transcendent principle—for instance, free speech or religious freedom—which need only be identified for the solution to be plain. In this way, he avoids the task, so basic to legal analysis, of reconciling competing principles. Instead, he substitutes simple labels and lines. . . .

Obviously opinions of this type will hardly qualify Mr. Justice Douglas for membership in Holmes's Society of Jobbists,[268] a position to which Mr. Justice Douglas undoubtedly does not aspire.[269] Still, opinions like *Elfbrandt* seemingly also would leave a good deal to be desired for those who, like Mr. Justice Douglas, are interested in "results," not craftsmanship. Opinions that fail to resolve the competing issues, that ignore precedent and speak in generalities, are also opinions that are easy to distinguish. They provide stepping stones for moving backward or sideward as well as forward. Such opinions constitute "the law" for only so long as their author has the ready votes. To some degree this is always true, but Mr. Justice Douglas to the contrary notwithstanding, the weight of precedent does have a significant effect even in the area of constitutional law. To have such effect, however, an opinion should at least explore fully the issues before the Court and clearly and carefully resolve them.

---

266 Rogat, *supra* note 68, at p. 5, col. 1.

267 *Id.* at p. 6, col. 2.

268 Kurland, *supra* note 68, at 144–45.

269 *Cf.* Brennan, *Charles Fahy*, 54 Geo. L. J. 1, 2 (1965).

HARRY KALVEN, JR.

THE REASONABLE MAN AND THE FIRST AMENDMENT: HILL, BUTTS, AND WALKER

> While I agree with the results announced by Mr. Justice Harlan in both of these cases, I find myself in disagreement with his stated reasons for reaching those results. Our difference stems from his departure from the teaching of *New York Times* v. *Sullivan*, 376 U.S. 254 (1964), to which we both subscribed only three years ago.[1]

I. Theme

Since March, 1964, when the United States Supreme Court handed down its decision in *New York Times v. Sullivan*,[2] there has been much speculation about what would happen next. Would the Court take seriously the new idiom and work a general revolution in the thinking about the First Amendment? Or would it limit the new principles and rhetoric to cases involving libel of public officials and simply add one more special cluster of precedents to the many it had already created in the free speech area?[3] Whatever their view

---

Harry Kalven, Jr., is Professor of Law, The University of Chicago.

[1] Chief Justice Warren, concurring, in Curtis Publishing Co. v. Butts, 388 U.S. 130 (1967).

[2] 376 U.S. 254 (1964).

[3] This, for example, was the question on which I ended in Kalven, *The New York Times Case: A Note on "The Central Meaning of the First Amendment,"* 1964 Supreme Court Review 191, 221.

See also Brennan, *The Supreme Court and the Meiklejohn Interpretation of the*

of the *New York Times* case, students of the Court were all deeply curious to see if, and how, it would grow. In the three intervening years, the law reports, state and federal,[4] have been rich in what Mr. Justice Harlan has called "*New York Times* . . . and its progeny."[5] After a few skirmishes with the *Times* rule,[6] in the 1966 Term, the

---

First Amendment, 79 HARV. L. REV. 1 (1965); Pedrick, *Freedom of the Press and the Law of Libel; The Modern Revised Translation*, 49 CORNELL L.Q. 581 (1964); Pierce, *The Anatomy of an Historic Decision: New York Times v. Sullivan*, 43 N.C. L. REV. 315 (1965); Berney, *Libel and the First Amendment—a New Constitutional Privilege*, 51 VA. L. REV. 1 (1965); Meiklejohn, *Public Speech and the First Amendment*, 55 GEO. L. J. 234 (1966); Karst, *The First Amendment and Harry Kalven: An Appreciative Comment on the Advantages of Thinking Small*, 13 U.C.L.A. L. REV. 1 (1965); and *cf*. Franklin, *The Origins and Constitutionality of Limitations on Truth as a Defense in Tort Law*, 16 STAN. L. REV. 789 (1964).

4 The cases are collected in Afro-American Publishing Co. v. Jaffe, 366 F.2d 649 (D.C. Cir. 1966); Pauling v. Globe-Democrat Publishing Co., 362 F.2d 188 (8th Cir. 1966); and in the Court's footnote in *Butts*, 388 U.S. at 134 n. 1.

5 Time, Inc. v. Hill, 385 U.S. 374, 407 (1967).

6 Garrison v. Louisiana, 379 U.S. 64 (1964); Henry v. Collins, 380 U.S. 356 (1965); Rosenblatt v. Baer, 383 U.S. 75 (1966); and see also Linn v. Plant Guard Workers, 383 U.S. 53 (1966). The cases appear more interesting in retrospect now that *Hill*, *Butts*, and *Walker* have come down than they did at the time.

For present purposes it is sufficient to note that *Garrison* involved criminal libel of judges who were unquestionably public officials, although the attack could be said to have concerned their private lives, and that the conviction was upset. The Court held that the *New York Times* principle applied to the crime of libel and reiterated that something more than "mere negligence" was required to convict, namely, knowing falsehood or reckless disregard for the truth.

In *Rosenblatt*, the statement in question was an oblique comment in a local newspaper column allegedly referring to and defaming the plaintiff, the former supervisor of a municipal ski resort. The case had been tried prior to the decision in *New York Times* and the Court reversed and remanded plaintiff's libel judgment for a new trial. The Court indicated that if the plaintiff were a public official, it was an error not to have applied the *New York Times* standard to the defendant. There was a strong implication that *New York Times* would not be relevant and the matter no longer of constitutional concern, if plaintiff were not a public official. It was this implication that is the most interesting point in *Rosenblatt* in view of the development in *Butts* and *Walker* of the concept of the "public figure."

The opinions in both cases were by Mr. Justice Brennan who wrote the opinion in *New York Times*. Justices Black and Douglas voiced their unhappiness in both cases about the *New York Times* formula, "so pale and tame." Mr. Justice Fortas made the point he later elaborated in *Hill*, that because the cases were tried prior to *New York Times* the granting of certiorari was improvident, and the verdicts should be allowed to stand. Mr. Justice Harlan did not foreshadow the major attack he was to make on the scope of the *Times* rule but confined himself to dissenting on the impersonal libel point in *Rosenblatt*. Mr. Justice Stewart, who was silent in the latter cases but whose voting pattern is arresting (see note 28 *infra*), wrote

Court had two major confrontations with it and produced three new precedents: *Time, Inc. v. Hill*,[7] *Curtis Publishing Company v. Butts*, *Associated Press v. Walker*.[8]

The three new cases have yielded roughly 100 new pages of judicial writing on freedom of speech. But even with so substantial a gloss, it appears that the story has not yet run its course. *New York Times* has not yet become the dominant precedent in the law of free speech and has been applied only in cases not far removed from the issue of libel of public officials. On the other hand, it is showing vitality and is stirring formidable controversy within the Court. It may yet live up to its earlier billing.[9]

I said, in another context, that "the greatest fascination of law study is to watch some great event from the real world intersect with existing legal doctrine."[10] But there is also fascination in watching the centuries-old rigidities, complexities, and elegances of the Anglo-American law of defamation collide with a rapidly developing corner of American constitutional law. The one certain prediction I can make is that judicial review of the common law of defamation, launched by the *New York Times* case, is to be with us for a while to come.[11]

---

a vigorous concurrence in *Rosenblatt*, stressing the large social values performed by the law of defamation.

Henry was a brief per curiam opinion in a civil action for libel of a county attorney and a chief of police. The sole issue went to the wording of the jury instructions concerning defendant's state of mind. The Court reversed judgments for the plaintiffs on the ground that the instructions might "have been understood to allow recovery on a showing of intent to inflict harm, rather than intent to inflict harm through falsehood."

Linn is tangential, since it involved libel in the course of a labor dispute, and the issue was one of federal preemption. Finally, it might be noted that *Times* was cited in Keyishian v. Bd. of Regents, 385 U.S. 589, 598 (1967), on "the dangers [inherent] in the word 'seditious,'" and in *Bond v. Floyd*, 385 U.S. 116 (1966), on whether the public official was to have as much protection as the citizen critic.

7 385 U.S. 374 (1967).

8 *Butts* and *Walker* are reported together at 388 U.S. 130 (1967).

9 "In brief compass, my thesis is that the Court, compelled by political realities of the case to decide it in favor of the *Times*, yet equally compelled to seek high ground in justifying its result, wrote an opinion that may prove to be the best and most important it has ever produced in the realm of freedom of speech." Kalven, *supra* note 3, at 193–94.

10 KALVEN, THE NEGRO AND THE FIRST AMENDMENT 3 (Phoenix ed. 1965).

11 One can only marvel at the law's capacity for growth here, and for growth in surprising directions. A decade or so ago I had occasion to look at the constitution

There is one other point of special interest in the new sequence of cases. It centers on the role of Mr. Justice Harlan. A silent partner in the opinion of the Court in *New York Times*, he is the major voice in the current cases. Indeed, much of the intellectual interest in the new opinions is due to his writing. In *Hill* and in *Butts*, he made a major effort to limit the *New York Times* rule to the special problems of libel of public officials. He warned against attributing to *New York Times* "an unintended inexorability at the threshold of this new constitutional development."[12] Once again, he essayed his familiar role as the Justice who, in the aftermath of a fresh burst of energy by the Court, comes forward to tidy things up.[13]

II. The Facts in Hill, Butts, and Walker

Hill proves to be a somewhat complicated case to capture. It involved not libel but a new species of invasion of privacy, undreamed of by Warren and Brandeis: the so-called "false light"

ality of the law of defamation and was hard put to get enough material together to round out a brief talk. Kalven, *Defamation and the First Amendment*, in Conference on Art, Publishing, and the Law (University of Chicago Conference Series, 1952).

The courts may soon get the problem in a new form. In April, 1967, the Federal Communications Commission issued a notice of a proposed rule to codify two phases of the "fairness" doctrine. 10 Pike & Fisher, Radio Reg. 2d 1911 (1967). The phase relevant here would provide in effect for a right of reply whenever a "personal attack" upon a group or individual had occurred during a broadcast relating to a controversial public issue. Various broadcasting groups have filed suit challenging the proposal as a violation of the *New York Times* rule. And see Red Lion Broadcasting Co. v. F.C.C., 10 Pike & Fisher, Radio Reg. 2001 (D.C. Cir. 1967).

It might be noted that of the six Supreme Court cases since *Times*, only *Henry* and *Walker* have any connection with issues generated by Negro protest. Whatever the ad hoc stimulus that was the occasion for *New York Times v. Sullivan*, it is apparent that it is now following a logic of its own.

12 388 U.S. at 148.

13 *Compare, e.g.*, Watkins v. United States, 354 U.S. 178 (1957), *with* Barenblatt v. United States, 360 U.S. 108 (1959); and *compare* Lerner v. Casey, 357 U.S. 468 (1958), and Beilan v. Board of Education, 357 U.S. 399 (1958), *with* Slochower v. Board of Higher Education, 350 U.S. 551 (1956); and *compare* Konigsberg v. State Bar of California, 353 U.S. 252 (1957), *with* Konigsberg v. State Bar of California, 366 U.S. 36 (1961), and *In re* Anastaplo, 366 U.S. 82 (1961).

The movement, however, is by no means always in the same direction. See also Yates v. United States, 354 U.S. 298 (1957); Manual Enterprises Inc. v. Day, 370 U.S. 478 (1962).

case,[14] which has emerged in recent years as a rival to the traditional remedies in defamation.[15]

In September, 1952, James Hill and his wife and five children became the subjects of a national news story when they were held hostage for nineteen hours by three escaped convicts in their suburban home in Pennsylvania. It appears that the convicts in fact treated them courteously and departed leaving them unharmed. The Hills subsequently moved to Connecticut and made efforts to avoid the public spotlight.

In the spring of 1953 James Hayes published *Desperate Hours*, a novel that concerned the adventures of a family of four held hostage by three escaped convicts in their suburban home. In the Hayes story the convicts are not so polite; there is some violence against the father and son and "a verbal sexual insult" against the daughter. It appears that Hayes had collected news stories of comparable incidents and based his novel on a composite impression. The Hill news story had, however, "triggered" the writing of the novel. The Hills appear never to have taken exception to the novel.

In February, 1955, *Life* magazine ran a picture story about the fact that the novel was to be made first into a play and later into a movie. The very brief text[16] that accompanied the photos an-

---

[14] This special category of privacy was christened by Dean Prosser in *Privacy*, 48 CALIF. L. REV. 383 (1960).

[15] It is examined in careful detail in Wade, *Defamation and the Right of Privacy*, 15 VAND. L. REV. 1093 (1962), and criticized in Kalven, *Privacy in Tort Law: Were Warren and Brandeis Wrong?* 31 LAW & CONTEMP. PROB. 326, 339–41 (1966). It seems that one consequence of the *Hill* case will be to retard substantially, if not altogether block, the tendencies of false light privacy to take over the field of defamation.

[16] The full text of the *Life* story as quoted by the Court, 385 U.S. at 377, read as follows:

"Three years ago Americans all over the country read about the desperate ordeal of the James Hill family, who were held prisoners in their homes outside Philadelphia by three escaped convicts. Later they read about it in Joseph Hayes' novel, *The Desperate Hours*, inspired by the family's experience. Now they can see the story re-enacted in Hayes' Broadway play based on the book, and next year will see it in his movie, which has been filmed but is being held up until the play has a chance to pay off.

"The play, directed by Robert Montgomery and expertly acted, is a heartstopping account of how a family rose to heroism in a crisis. LIFE photographed the play during its Philadelphia tryout, transported some of the actors to the actual house where the Hills were besieged. On the next page scenes from the play are re-enacted on the site of the crime."

nounced that the play was based on the novel that had "been inspired by the family's experience." It heralded the play as "a heart-stopping account of how a family rose to heroism in a crisis." The thrust of the story, however, was in the photos showing the play's cast re-enacting "scenes from the play" in the house that the Hills had occupied at the time of the incident.

The Hills' lawsuit was based on the *Life* article. The grievance was that it had given the false impression that the play "mirrored the Hill family's experience," and that it had sensationalized the story by adding the note of violence. Perhaps crucial was the disclosure at the trial that the text had originally stated the play was a "somewhat fictionalized" account of the incident and that in final editing these words had been dropped.

The plaintiff won a verdict for $50,000 compensatory damages and $25,000 punitive damages from a jury that had not been instructed on the issue of the defendant's state of mind. On appeal, a new trial was ordered solely on damages. At the retrial without a jury, plaintiff was awarded $30,000 compensatory damages. It was that award that was appealed.[17] In the Supreme Court, after the case had been argued twice,[18] the judgment for the plaintiff was reversed and the case remanded for a new trial under proper instructions.

The key facts about *Hill* were that it involved privacy and not libel; that the Hills were private citizens who involuntarily became subjects of public interest; that the magazine story was held actionable solely because under New York law the inaccuracies in *Life*'s reporting defeated the privilege *Life* otherwise would have had to report newsworthy events. It is perhaps also important to note that the case had been in litigation since 1955; that it was originally tried years before *New York Times* was decided; and that there is evidence in the record that *Life*'s handling of the story was sloppy. And finally, it may also be important that the Hills' grievance is not easy to perceive. The *Life* story did not show the Hills in an unfavorable light. Indeed, part of the inaccuracy was that it stressed their "heroism in a crisis." Whatever harm the story inflicted was not because of the falsity but because it once again exposed the Hills

---

17 It appears that in the initial trial the wife also won a substantial verdict ($75,000 compensatory and $25,000 punitive), but the case "was apparently dismissed by stipulation." See 385 U.S. at 379 n. 2.

18 It is perhaps of some interest to note that counsel for the Hills was Richard M. Nixon.

to the gaze of a national public. This is harm, however, for which New York law would have left the Hills without redress had the story been accurate.[19]

In contrast to *Hill*, in *Butts* the grievance is easy to grasp. The *Saturday Evening Post*, following a change of editorial policy designed to jack up sagging sales, decided to emphasize "sophisticated muckraking" articles. In keeping with the new policy it ran the article in question under the title "The Story of a Football Fix." A prefatory note from the editors set the tone and gave the gist of the piece:[20]

> "Not since the Chicago White Sox threw the 1919 World Series has there been a sports story as shocking as this one. . . . Before the University of Georgia played the University of Alabama . . . Wally Butts . . . gave (to its coach) . . . Georgia's plays, defense patterns, all the significant secrets Georgia s football team possessed."

The text revealed that one George Burnett, an insurance salesman, had accidentally through an electronic error, overheard a telephone conversation between Butts and Paul Bryant, the Alabama coach, in which Butts disclosed the plays. Burnett had made notes and supplied specific instances of the plays for the article. The article went on to describe the dismayed reaction of the beleaguered Georgia players to the game and the presentation by Burnett of his notes to the Georgia coach which led to Butts's resignation as athletic director. The story ended on a note as unequivocal as the one on which it began:[21]

> The chances are that Wally Butts will never help any football team again. . . . The investigation by university and Southeastern Conference officials is continuing; motion pictures of other games are being scrutinized; where it will end no one so far can say. But careers will be ruined, that is sure.

Butts brought a libel action against the *Post*. The principal defense at the trial was truth, but the jury found against the defendants on this point and awarded $60,000 compensatory damages and $3 million in punitive damages. On appeal the punitive damages were cut to $400,000. It was this judgment for Butts for $460,000 that was taken to the United States Supreme Court and affirmed.

---

[19] See the discussion of newsworthy truthful reporting under New York law, text *infra*, at notes 32–34.

[20] 388 U.S. at 136.

[21] *Id.* at 137.

The jury had been instructed that punitive damages could be awarded on a finding of "actual malice," defined in part as "a wanton or reckless indifference or culpable negligence with regard to the rights of others."[22] The record showed little effort by the *Post* editors to check up on the story despite the gravity of the charges contained in it. As in *Hill*, the *Butts* trial had taken place before *New York Times* had come down.

Walker on its facts is somewhat similar to *Butts*. The communication in question was an AP dispatch reporting the activities of General Walker on the University of Mississippi campus on the night of September 30, 1962, when a riot erupted following the efforts of federal marshals to enroll James Meredith at the University pursuant to court order. The dispatch, an eyewitness account, stated that Walker had "assumed command" of the crowd and that "he had led a charge against the marshals." Walker brought a libel action against the Associated Press.[23] As in *Butts*, the defense of truth failed. This time the jury awarded $500,000 compensatory damages and $300,000 punitive damages. The trial judge, who could find no evidence of malice, struck the punitive damage award. He also found that *New York Times* would have required a verdict for the defendant but ruled that there were "no compelling reasons of public policy requiring additional defenses to libel" and that *New York Times* was not applicable. On appeal he was sustained on both rulings by the Texas courts. The United States Supreme Court reversed, directing a judgment for the defendant. It appeared that the Associated Press had assigned a young reporter to the Mississippi riot who had pretty much done the best he could to observe and note what had happened in the high excitement of the moment.

---

22 *Id.* at 173.

23 Gen. Walker also brought a series of other libel actions against various newspapers which had printed the AP dispatch. See, for example, Walker v. Courier-Journal and Louisville Times Co., 246 F. Supp. 231 (W.D. Ky. 1965); Walker v. Associated Press, 417 P.2d 486 (Colo. 1966); Walker v. Kansas City Star, 406 S.W.2d 44 (Mo. 1966).

The opinion below in the instant case was reported in 393 S.W.2d 671 (Tex. App. 1965). The Texas court, in affirming Walker's judgment, found it unnecessary to mention *New York Times v. Sullivan*. In the other *Walker* cases, however, the courts agreed that *Times* controlled. Accordingly the *Courier-Journal* suit was dismissed, but the other two suits survived against a motion to dismiss on the view that General Walker had sufficiently pleaded malice to satisfy the *Times* standard.

III. You Can't Tell the Players without a Score Card

It has become a commonplace for the Supreme Court to resort to multiple opinions suggesting unseemly disagreement among the brethren. The combinations and permutations of positions in the three new cases, however, when combined with *New York Times*, are so spectacular as to justify a brief summary.

Only one of the four judgments survived constitutional scrutiny. In *Butts*, the plaintiff walked away from the Supreme Court with his judgment for $460,000 intact. In *Hill*, after eleven years of litigation and two arguments in the Supreme Court, the judgment was reversed and the case remanded for a new trial. In *Walker*, as in *New York Times*, the Court not only upset the judgment but directed a judgment for the defendant. The decisions in *New York Times* and *Walker* were unanimous. In *Hill*, the vote was 6 to 3 and in *Butts* it was 5 to 4. But the positions of the Justices are far more intricate than this pattern of votes would suggest, for the votes disclose little of the real pattern of disagreement.

In all four cases the Justices agreed that, to a considerable extent, state tort law is limited by First Amendment considerations. The disagreements arose over two other issues.[24] (1) There was disagreement about the level of privilege that a defendant is to be accorded.

---

[24] There are at least four other subissues in the cases: (1) Whether some concessions should be made in the requirements for precision in the wording of the jury instructions in light of the fact that the litigation was begun before *New York Times* was decided and its rule had become manifest. (2) Whether, in *Butts*, the defendants had waived the constitutional issue by not raising it prior to trial. (3) When will an appellate court, making a *de novo* finding on the constitutional facts about defendant publisher's state of mind, accept a jury verdict? In *Butts* Mr. Justice Brennan, although finding enough in the record to support a verdict against the defendant, favored remand for a new trial so that a properly instructed jury could exercise its own judgment. (4) Whether in *Hill*, the Court could avoid holding the New York statute invalid on its face. By holding the statute valid but unconstitutionally applied, the Supreme Court seems to have ordered the New York court to change its construction of its own statute.

The waiver issue led Mr. Justice Harlan to the rueful public acknowledgment in *Butts* that the decision in *New York Times* may have come as something of a surprise to the bar. "Although our decision in *New York Times* did draw upon earlier precedents in state law, e.g., Coleman v. MacLennan, 78 Kan. 711, 98 Pac. 281 . . . and there were intimations in a prior opinion and the extra-judicial comments of one Justice, that some applications of libel law might be in conflict with the guarantees of free speech and press, there was strong precedent indicating that civil libel actions were immune from general constitutional scrutiny." 388 U.S. at 143–44. See *supra* note 11.

(2) There was disagreement about the adequacy of the jury instructions sufficiently to safeguard the defendant's privilege.

Essentially it was the varied positions on jury instructions that account for the dissents.[25] In *New York Times* and *Walker*, all the Justices agreed that the instructions were inadequate. In these cases, they reversed the judgments and directed verdicts for the defendants. In *Hill*, the three dissenters, Justices Fortas and Clark and the Chief Justice, felt that the instructions were roughly satisfactory whatever the appropriate rule of law and that a remand for a new trial would be too harsh on the plaintiff. In *Butts*, Justices Brennan and White favored a remand for a new trial so that a properly instructed jury might pass on the matter.[26]

If the positions on the adequacy of jury instructions explain the votes, the positions on the level of privilege serve to account for most of the content of the opinions. Three basic views emerge. In the center there is Mr. Justice Brennan, who, in all three of the new cases, would apply the standard of privilege adopted in *New York Times*. The Chief Justice and Mr. Justice White joined him in this position, although, as noted, the Chief Justice disagreed with Justices Brennan and White in *Butts* about whether the jury instructions given at the trial adequately met this standard. To the left of the Brennan position, so to speak, were Justices Black and Douglas repeating the arguments they had made in *New York Times*[27] that the defendant's privilege in these cases should be absolute, a view they would apply equally in all three of the new cases. And to the other side of the Brennan position was Mr. Justice Harlan, who would give a lesser privilege to the defendant in *Butts* than in *New York Times*, and even a lesser privilege to the defendant in *Hill* than to the defendant in *Butts*. He appeared to be alone in *Hill*, but was joined by Justices Fortas, Clark, and Stewart in *Butts*.

---

[25] Although no inconsiderable part of the opinions was concerned with the jury instruction issue, discussion of the merits of the instructions is beyond the scope of this essay. I reluctantly put to one side the lively debate between Mr. Justice Fortas and Justices Brennan and Harlan in *Hill* and thus forgo examining the hypothesis that the special sensitivity of the law to the protection of freedom of speech may include not only a distinctive emphasis regarding prior licensing, ambiguity, challenge to statutes on their face, and inappropriate choice of means to an end, but also an exceptional regard for precision in the wording of instructions to the jury.

[26] There were four dissenting votes in *Butts*. The other two votes were those of Justices Black and Douglas, who would have directed a verdict for the defendant on the ground that he had an absolute privilege.

[27] And in *Garrison v. Louisiana* and again in *Rosenblatt v. Baer*. See note 6 *supra*.

The complexities thus derive from the combinations of the two sources of disagreement. For example, no one explicitly joined Mr. Justice Harlan in *Hill,* because Justices Fortas and Clark and the Chief Justice committed themselves only on the adequacy of the instructions and not on the issue of the privilege.

The sense of complexity is heightened when the positions of Justices Stewart and Harlan in *Hill* and *Butts* are compared. It will be remembered Mr. Justice Harlan would distinguish both cases from *New York Times,* and further would distinguish them from each other. So that although in neither case would the defendant be accorded as strong a privilege as in *New York Times,* the defendant would get a stronger privilege in *Butts* than in *Hill.* On the other hand, Mr. Justice Stewart joined with Mr. Justice Brennan to equate *Hill,* Harlan's least favored category of case, with *New York Times;* but he then agreed with Mr. Justice Harlan in distinguishing *Butts* from *New York Times.*[28]

Perhaps two other points are worth noting. First what might be called membership in the Harlan faction, that is, the Justices who are conservative on the scope of *New York Times,* can be viewed as going from zero to one to four, as we move from *Times* itself, to *Hill,* to *Butts.* The final oddity is the relation of *Butts* to *Walker,* decisions that came down on the same day. The opinion of the Court in *Butts* was written by Mr. Justice Harlan and adopted his refusal to extend the *New York Times* privilege. Chief Justice Warren concurred in the results in order to save the plaintiff's verdict, but he emphatically disagreed with Mr. Justice Harlan and would extend the *New York Times* privilege to the case. Chief Justice Warren was joined in his position on the privilege by Justices White and Brennan, thus making three Justices who were explicitly in favor of the *Times* privilege. Justices Black and Douglas, however, elected in *Butts* to file unqualified dissents. The upshot, therefore, was a 5 to 4 decision in *Butts,* but a 4 to 3 to 2 alignment on the privilege issue, although it is clear that Justices Black and Douglas must, as the lesser evil, prefer the *New York Times* rule to

---

[28] Mr. Justice Stewart may well see privacy and defamation as presenting different First Amendment issues, with, however, publishers deserving more protection against suits alleging invasions of privacy than in suits alleging defamation. He did not write a separate opinion in any of the three more recent cases, but his concurring opinion in *Rosenblatt* stressed that "the preventive effect of liability for defamation serves an important public purpose." 383 U.S. 75, 83 (1966).

the Harlan rule. Moreover, the 5 to 4 decision for the plaintiff in *Butts* was, in the end, simply a result of the desire of Chief Justice Warren, a strong supporter of an across-the-board application of *New York Times*, to avoid upsetting the verdict, because he thought in the particular circumstances the instruction under which the case had been tried had come close enough to the *New York Times* standard.

In *Walker*, however, Justices Black and Douglas elected to be more statesmanlike, since the judgment was to be reversed in any event. This time, therefore, they joined the Warren opinion, which thereby became the opinion of a bare majority of the Court.

After the dust has settled on this Balkan diplomacy, it becomes evident that, despite resistance, the *New York Times* rule *has won across the board.* This is not an impression that any quick or conventional reading of the decisions would leave!

It is apparent that behind all this judicial maneuvering lie substantial issues about how to reason by analogy from the *New York Times* case, and more important, some fresh theorizing, especially by Mr. Justice Harlan, about freedom of speech. Throwing away our score card, it is to such matters that I now turn.

It may be convenient to distinguish two closely related issues in applying *New York Times* to new situations. First, there is the question of the *ambit* of constitutional protection. To what situations, other than libel of public officials, does the bonus of constitutional scrutiny and protection extend? Second, there is the question already noted concerning the *level* of the protection. What kind of privilege does the Constitution require that the defendant be given? These seem to me quite distinct questions, although it is perhaps a prime strategy of Mr. Justice Harlan to link them together.

One would have thought that the first issue would be the focus of excitement in the debate and the second would reduce to a technical detail. Exactly the opposite proved to be the case. There was easy and almost casual consensus on the ambit of constitutional protection; there was intense controversy over the level of that protection.

IV. The Ambit of Constitutional Protection

The ambit question might be restated thus: At what point does the First Amendment no longer permit the states to afford tort remedies for harms caused by speech?

In *New York Times* the Court had fully confronted the fact that critical discussion of government actions would often involve not only impersonal criticisms of general policy but also, as an inextricable by-product, criticisms of individual persons who were the executors of that policy.[29] Since freedom to criticize government "robustly" was taken to be the crucial, the central freedom in the First Amendment,[30] it was necessary to subject to the closest scrutiny claims of any aggrieved individual officials. It was thought necessary to do so lest it should turn out that tort law would give to the official the power to censor or silence the citizen-critic of government.

Public discussion and debate other than criticisms of government action appear to have the same tendencies to implicate individuals. One question *New York Times* left for the future was whether First Amendment theory and rationale would require a comparable constitutional scrutiny of the censorial power of aggrieved individuals.

Conceivably, *New York Times* could be read as generating a narrow technical rule limited to government officials and analogous to the specific constitutional rule immunizing members of Congress from being "questioned in any other place" for their "speech or debate" on the floor of Congress. On this approach the question in each new case would be simply one of the classification of the plaintiff. Or it might be argued that the analogy fails here since the congressional immunity has its source in the specific provisions of Article 1, § 6, whereas the immunity rule of *New York Times* has its source in "the central meaning" of the First Amendment.

On their facts, the three new cases offered nice gradations, if a narrow approach were to be taken. In *Hill* the plaintiff was a private citizen who had involuntarily become newsworthy. In *Walker* the

29 The matter was especially obvious in *New York Times,* since the statement in question appeared on its face to refer only to general governmental policy and not to particular officials. Indeed it took considerable ingenuity on the part of the plaintiff to connect the statements to himself. The alternative grounds of the decision in *New York Times* provided an important new constitutional limitation on the state law of defamation regarding when defamation was sufficiently "of and concerning" the plaintiff. This is also a principal point in *Rosenblatt v. Baer, supra* note 6; see Kalven, *supra* note 3, at 209; GREGORY & KALVEN, CASES AND MATERIALS IN TORTS 968–73 (1959).

30 That such avoidance of seditious libel as an offense was seen as the central freedom was the point of the special excitement displayed in Kalven, *supra* note 3.

plaintiff was a retired United States general of considerable national prominence and a potential leader of a third force in national politics. In *Butts* the plaintiff was a nationally known football coach, now athletic director at a state university, who was being paid not by the state but by the Athletic Alumni Association, a separate and private group.

There were five opinions in *Hill,* by Justices Brennan, Black, Douglas, Harlan, and Fortas. Yet there was no debate and remarkably little discussion of the ambit of constitutional scrutiny of state tort law.[31]

The *Hill* case, it will be remembered, involved invasion of privacy and not libel, and it is in this circumstance, I suspect, that we find the key to the structure of Mr. Justice Brennan's opinion. Traditionally, invasions of privacy have involved statements that are true, in distinction to defamation where the statement is presumed to be false. It was a special complication of the *Hill* case that it concerned a "false light" privacy claim. Since the tort law of privacy deals primarily with true statements, there has grown up under the common-law rules a defendant's privilege quite different from anything found in the common law of defamation.[32] The general rule is that if defendant's statement deals with newsworthy events and people, it is privileged, that is, it cannot be made the predicate for tort liability.[33]

The first step in Mr. Justice Brennan's opinion was to establish that under the New York privacy statute "truth is a complete defense in actions under the statute based upon reports of newsworthy people or events."[34] Indeed this was one of the two points on which the Court had requested reargument in the *Hill* case. Mr. Justice Brennan, however, worded the point so as to jar the ear of a teacher of torts. The point really is not so much that truth is a defense as that newsworthiness is a defense.

---

31 There had been some discussion of the ambit issue in *Rosenblatt,* turning on whether the plaintiff, supervisor at a ski resort, could be regarded as a "public official" in the sense of the *New York Times* rule; see note 6 *supra;* and see especially the Court's footnote, 383 U.S. at 86 n. 12.

32 Kalven, *supra* note 15, at 336–38.

33 In defamation there has been no analogous concept. Rather there are a series of specific privileges for "public" discussion, such as record libel and fair comment. See generally Gregory & Kalven, *supra* note 29, at 1022–64; Franklin, *supra* note 3; and discussion in the text *infra* at notes 62–70.

34 385 U.S. at 383.

The apparently elliptical quality in the Brennan opinion, then, arises because circumstances have made it unnecessary to make explicit the key premise. That premise is that the First Amendment requires that the truthful reporting of newsworthy events and people not be subjected to liability.[35] The premise did not call for argument because there was the ready consensus on all sides that the New York privacy statute protects newsworthy reporting when there is no issue of falsity. What this quick consensus has concealed from view is that the ambit of "constitutionally scrutinizable" speech is measured by newsworthiness. Or to put this in McLuhanese, newsworthiness measures the ambit. The newsworthy is a kind of speech which is public enough so that its protection cannot be left entirely to state policy. Presumably, had this point been challenged in *Hill*, we would have been given the explicit statement of why this category of speech requires constitutional protection.

Having established the newsworthiness privilege under New York law, the Brennan opinion traced with care via the *Spahn* case[36] the New York law about reports that were newsworthy but

---

[35] "There is a possibility that the newsworthiness privilege in privacy will acquire constitutional status and thus become independent of state policy." Kalven, *supra* note 15, at 336 n. 57. The Court in quoting from this article in *Hill*, 385 U.S. at 383 n. 7, omits the observation that "today since *New York Times v. Sullivan* the privilege may arguably have some constitutional status."

[36] Spahn v. Messner, 18 N.Y.2d 324 (1966). The Supreme Court granted certiorari in *Spahn* and remanded it for a new trial in light of *Hill*. 387 U.S. 239 (1967).

The difficulties with the New York rule go not only to the point that concerned the United States Supreme Court, namely, that it imposes strict liability for "false light" privacy invasions, but also to the fact that the New York courts have been so preoccupied with the role of "falsity" in erasing the newsworthy privilege that they have not looked to see if there was a prima facie invasion of privacy in the first place that required the protection of a privilege to avoid liability. That is, the falsity, although not defamatory (and in *Hill*, arguably laudatory), has somehow magnified what would otherwise appear to be a trivial grievance.

The triviality of the grievance in *Hill* was of course not a proper consideration for the United States Supreme Court, but rather for the New York Court of Appeals. (Fuld, J., dissented in the *Hill* case in the New York Court of Appeals, 15 N.Y.2d 986 [1965].) The reactions of the Justices to the facts in *Hill*, however, are curious. Mr. Justice Black saw it as "at most a mere understandable and incidental error," 385 U.S. at 400; Mr. Justice Harlan spoke of the "severe risk of irremediable harm," *id.* at 410; Mr. Justice Fortas wrote of "reckless and irresponsible assault upon himself and his family," *id.* at 411.

Possibly, the case does involve a very subtle form of defamation in the circumstance that one item of "falsity" was the portrayal of the father making a "brave try" to save his family.

not totally accurate. The opinion then announced the relevant principle:[37]

> If this [the view of the New York Court of Appeals in *Spahn* that "fictionalized" biography is not within constitutional protection] is meant to imply that the proof of knowing or reckless falsity is not essential to a constitutional application of the statute in these cases, we disagree with the Court of Appeals. We hold that the constitutional protections for speech and press preclude the application of the New York statute to redress false reports of matters of public interest in the absence of proof that the defendant published the report with knowledge of its falsity or in reckless disregard of the truth.

The argument offered in support of this conclusion was notably brief. First, we were told that the "guarantees for speech and press are not the preserve of political expression or comment on public affairs, essential as those are to healthy government."[38] The point left implicit, presumably, is that while the avoidance of seditious libel may be the central purpose of the First Amendment, it is not its only purpose. *New York Times v. Sullivan* gave an invaluable perspective to free speech analysis; it did not, however, attempt to set the outermost boundaries of First Amendment protection.

Second, Mr. Justice Brennan took judicial notice of "the vast range of published matter which exposes persons to public view, both private citizens and public officials. Exposure of the self to others in varying degrees is a concomitant of life in a civilized community. The risk of this exposure is an essential incident of life in a society which places a primary value on freedom of speech and press."[39] We were being reminded, as I see it, that newsworthiness defines the ambit of constitutional concern and that this is so even though the public aspects of such communications are interlaced inextricably with comments on individuals. Names make news, but they do not thereby take it out of the public domain. For the moment, as the argument moved, it did not crucially matter whether the statements in question were true or false. What mattered was that they were in some sense public and that the domain of "mixed utterance,"[40] speech that has both public and individual aspects, is vast and of high importance to civilized life.[41]

---

37 385 U.S. at 387–88. 38 *Id.* at 388. 39 *Ibid.*

40 *Cf.* United States v. Dennis, 183 F.2d 201, 207 (2d Cir. 1959), where Judge Learned Hand spoke of utterances which have a "double aspect; *i.e.*, when persua-

It remained for the Brennan opinion to take only one further step—to add the minor premise—and the argument about ambit would be completed. "We have no doubt," the opinion reads, "that the subject of the *Life* article, the opening of a new play linked to an actual incident is a matter of public interest."[42]

This then is the Brennan thesis: Newsworthiness defines the ambit of constitutional concern. The *Life* report in the instant case was newsworthy. It is therefore within the sphere in which state-law remedies for aggrieved individuals are subject to judicial review under the First Amendment. All that remained was to determine what level of privilege the Constitution required state law to afford the defendant publisher.

The most striking thing about Mr. Justice Brennan's opinion is that he apparently reached his result without reasoning by analogy from *New York Times*. In fact he found it unnecessary to mention *Times* in this part of his argument. Yet *Times* would seem to be a silent partner in the decision. What it did was to illuminate for the Court the possibilities for censorship, by individual libel actions, of criticism of government operation and policy. It thus set the perspective the Court took toward the events in *Hill*. The individual tort action, albeit in privacy, carries a comparable threat of censorship over valued, albeit less urgently valued, public speech. Thus although *Hill* with its mild entertainment news value was on its facts a world removed from *New York Times* on its grim facts about Negro protests, the two cases were seen to fall within a common sphere—speech affecting individuals that is of public interest.

One other point clamors for attention before I turn to the other four opinions. Although it was not necessary in *Hill* to delineate the outer boundaries of the newsworthy, the Court may be surprised by the extent of its commitment. The tort law of privacy has wrestled with the matter for some years now; and it is a rough generalization that the courts will not, and indeed cannot, be arbiters of what is

---

sion and instigation were inseparably confused." The inextricable linking of "bad" speech with "good" is a charateristic also of the obscenity problem. See Kalven, *The Metaphysics of the Law of Obscenity*, 1960 SUPREME COURT REVIEW 1, 11–12.

41 The Court quotes the following from Thornhill v. Alabama, 310 U.S. 88, 102 (1940): "Freedom of discussion, if it would fulfill its historic function in this nation, must embrace all issues about which information is needed or appropriate to enable the members of society to cope with the exigencies of their period."

42 385 U.S. 374, 388 (1967).

newsworthy. Newsworthiness will almost certainly become a descriptive and not a normative term.[43] In brief, the press will be the arbiters of it and the Court will be forced to yield to the argument that whatever the press prints is by virtue of that fact newsworthy. This has been pretty much the experience with the common-law policy. It is not clear that the matter will prove more tractable if we try it as constitutional policy. The upshot, and it is an important one, is that the logic of *New York Times* and *Hill* taken together grants the press some measure of constitutional protection for anything the press thinks is a matter of public interest.

There is little to discuss in the other four opinions as they bear on the ambit issue. The Justices were saving their fire for other issues.

Mr. Justice Black, as would be expected, had no quarrel with the newsworthiness criterion. He devoted his opinion to repeating his complaint that the protection given the press was not absolute. In the final sentences of his opinion, however, one can detect his full agreement that the press *qua* press be given constitutional protection for whatever it sees fit to print:[44]

> One does not have to be a prophet to foresee that judgments like the one we here reverse can frighten and punish the press so much that publishers will cease trying to report news in a lively and readable fashion as long as there is—and there always will be—doubt as to the complete accuracy of the newsworthy facts. Such a consummation hardly seems consistent with the clearly expressed purposes of the Founders to guarantee the press a favored spot in our free society.

Mr. Justice Douglas was equally happy with the ambit of protection and equally unhappy with its level. He stated explicitly that the First and Fourteenth Amendments protect the press "where the discussion concerns matters in the public domain."[45] And he went on to draw flatly the analogy to the *New York Times* case. "Here a private person is catapulted into the news by events over which he had no control. He and his activities are then in the public domain as fully as the matters at issue in *New York Times* v. *Sullivan*."[46]

Mr. Justice Harlan in his interesting and complex opinion took issue only with the level of protection that the Court gave. Indeed he was more explicit than was Mr. Justice Brennan that if the story

[43] See Kalven, *supra* note 15; *cf.* Franklin, *A Constitutional Problem in Privacy Protection: Legal Inhibitions on Reporting of Fact*, 16 STAN. L. REV. 107 (1963).

[44] 385 U.S. at 400–01.

[45] *Id.* at 401.

[46] *Ibid.*

had been true it would require protection.[47] He agreed, too, that some degree of protection was constitutionally required for the falsity involved in the *Hill* case. And he joined in reversing the judgment for the failure of the state law to provide the requisite degree of protection. It might, however, be closer to the spirit of his opinion to read him as taking issue with the possibility of separating ambit from level as sharply as I have done. His whole approach is to vary the level of protection as the speech in question moves away from matters of central public concern—and he is willing to calibrate exceedingly fine to work out his design.

Mr. Justice Fortas in a spirited opinion came closest to open quarrel on the ambit issue. His principal point, however, as I have noted, was that the instructions given at the *Hill* trial were close enough to the Court's standards to make it wasteful and indecent to remand the eleven-year-old case for another trial. But before he turned to his analysis of the instructions, he spoke out vigorously for privacy as "a basic right" and suggested that it belonged in the top drawer of "great and important values in our society" along with those "reflected in the First Amendment."[48] Although he did not quite join issue on the point, it is apparent that for him newsworthiness would not invariably and inflexibly outweigh privacy. Then in a telling passage he observed:[49]

> I have no hesitancy to say, for example, that where political personalities or issues are involved or where the event as to which the alleged invasion of privacy occurred is in itself a matter of current public interest, First Amendment values are supreme and entitled to at least the types of protection that this Court extended in *New York Times* v. *Sullivan.*

Yet, in the end, his opinion remains unclear. I cannot tell whether he was complaining that the *Life* story was not a matter of public interest or about the degree of falsity he found in it. I suspect that had the *Life* story been fully accurate Mr. Justice Fortas, too, would have yielded the claims of the Hills for privacy to the public interest in news.

It may be worth risking some repetition to underscore once again what seems to have happened in *Hill.* Although a bare five of the nine Justices were amenable to upsetting Mr. Hill's hard-won verdict, the four who disagreed with the Court's handling of the case

---

[47] *Id.* at 404. [48] *Id.* at 412. [49] *Id.* at 415.

somehow dissipated their attack and failed to provide any effective or central criticism of the key fact that the Court had now extended constitutional scrutiny of state tort law to whatever is newsworthy. Moreover the Court had taken this giant step without being forced to an explicit justification for it and without openly invoking *New York Times.*

In retrospect it appears that the Court may have been handicapped by the sequence in which the cases came to it. *Hill* was a curiously difficult case to handle so soon after *New York Times.* The Court's task might have been easier had the more obvious problems of *Butts* and *Walker* been disposed of first. In any event, I turn now to those two cases and to the Court's response to the ambit issue.

Butts and *Walker* were decided just six months after *Hill,* and this time there were four opinions: those of the Chief Justice and Justices Harlan, Black, and Brennan. In the opinions of Warren and Harlan there was full recognition of the ambit issue.

If it was a puzzle why in *Hill* the Court did not draw openly on *New York Times,* it is equally a puzzle in *Butts* and *Walker* why the Court did not see the relevance of *Hill,* which had arguably foreclosed the ambit issue. Instead it now went back to *New York Times* for guidance on the extent of constitutional protection.

The Harlan opinion in *Butts* opens with a sketch of the contentions of opposing counsel. On the one hand, it was argued that because Butts was in a sense a minor public official in his role as athletic director at a state university and because General Walker had "thrust himself into the vortex"[50] of public controversy, the two cases were literally within the *Times* holding. On the other hand, it was stressed that these cases were far removed from "seditious libel prosecutions." Quoting *Buckley v. New York Post,*[51]

50 The "vortex" metaphor originated in Mr. Justice Brennan's opinion in *Rosenblatt v. Baer,* 383 U.S. at 86 n. 12; see also Pauling v. Globe-Democrat Publishing Co., 362 F.2d 188, 195 (2d Cir. 1966).

51 373 F.2d 175, 182 (2d Cir. 1967). The quotation is from the opinion of Judge Friendly. Judge Friendly was discussing whether the First Amendment offered an obstacle to the claim of Connecticut to jurisdiction in a libel action over the defendant newspaper, a Delaware corporation with its principal place of business in New York. He was not discussing what risks of tort liability are to be placed on publishers. The rest of the sentence reads: ". . . and injured persons should not be relegated to forums so distant as to make collection of their claims difficult or impossible unless strong policy considerations demand." *Cf.* 388 U.S. at 147. On the precise issue of how far *New York Times* extends, see Judge Friendly's opinion in

plaintiffs urged that "Like other enterprises that inflict damage in the course of performing services highly useful to the public" the press "must pay the freight."

The force of these competing considerations requires, we were told, "an accommodation between them . . . not only in these cases but in all libel actions arising from a publication concerning public issues."[52] Then Mr. Justice Harlan squarely confronted the ambit issue:[53]

> From the point of view of deciding whether a constitutional interest of free speech and press is properly involved in the resolution of a libel question, a rational distinction "cannot be founded on the assumption that criticism of private citizens who seek to lead in the determination of . . . policy will be less important to the public interest than will criticism of public officials."

It was thus *New York Times* and not *Hill* that provided the touchstone for Mr. Justice Harlan. The ambit of constitutional concern was to be measured not by a concept of newsworthiness but less sweepingly by step-by-step analogies to public officials. The ambit of protection had been extended, to use the Justice's idiom, from public officials to "public figures." The conclusion was "that libel actions of the present kind cannot be left entirely to state libel laws, unlimited by any overriding constitutional safeguards."[54]

This summary does not do justice, however, to Mr. Justice Harlan's complex and fresh theorizing in *Butts* and *Walker* about free speech because his expressed interest was not so much in the extent to which state law is "overridden" by constitutional considerations as in the precise level of safeguard the Constitution will require for the speech. In brief his thesis is that *New York Times* may set the ambit of protection, but it emphatically does not set the level of protection. It does not incorporate "the only appropriate accommodation of the conflicting interests at stake."[55]

The other explicit discussion of ambit in *Butts* is found in the

---

Pauling v. News Syndicate Co., 335 F.2d 659 (2d Cir. 1964), readily extending it to Dr. Linus Pauling, a private citizen engaged in public controversy.

52 388 U.S. at 147.

53 *Id.* at 147–48. Mr. Justice Harlan was quoting from Judge Blackmun, in Pauling v. Globe-Democrat Pub. Co., 362 F.2d 188, 196 (8th Cir. 1966)

54 388 U.S. at 155.

55 *Ibid.*

opinion of Chief Justice Warren. "All of us agree," he stated, "that the basic considerations underlying the First Amendment require that some limitations be placed on the application of state libel laws to 'public figures' as well as 'public officials.' "[56]

Then in a passage with arresting overtones of contemporary sociology he argued that there is no longer a sharp difference in modern life between the governmental and the private:[57]

> To me, differentiation between "public figures" and "public officials" and adoption of separate standards of proof for each has no basis in law, logic, or First Amendment policy. Increasingly in this country, the distinctions between governmental and private sectors are blurred. Since the depression of the 1930's and World War II there has been a rapid fusion of economic and political power, a merging of science, industry, and government, and a high degree of interaction between the intellectual, governmental, and business worlds. Depression, war, international tensions, national and international markets, and the surging growth of science and technology have precipitated national and international problems that demand national and international solutions. While these trends and events have occasioned a consolidation of governmental power, power has also become much more organized in what we have commonly considered to be the private sector. In many situations, policy determinations which traditionally were channeled through formal political institutions are now originated and implemented through a complex array of boards, committees, commissions, corporations, and associations, some only loosely connected with the Government. This blending of positions and power has also occurred in the case of individuals so that many who do not hold public office at the moment are nevertheless intimately involved in the resolution of important public questions or, by reason of their fame, shape events in areas of concern to society at large.

The minor premise—the application of the "public figure" formula to the facts in *Butts* and *Walker*—did not detain the Justices for long. And, for this purpose at least, the Court saw no difference between Wally Butts and General Walker. Mr. Justice Harlan stated:[58]

> We note that the public interest in the circulation of the materials here involved, and the publisher's interest in circulating them, is not less than that involved in *New York Times*. And both Butts and Walker commanded a substantial amount of

[56] *Id.* at 162.

[57] *Id.* at 163–64.

[58] *Id.* at 154–55.

> public interest at the time of the publications; both in our opinion would have been labeled "public figures" under ordinary tort rules. . . . Butts may have attained that status by position alone and Walker by his purposeful activity amounting to a thrusting of his personality into the "vortex" of an important public controversy.

Chief Justice Warren, after noting that both cases involved "public figures," was explicit only with respect to General Walker: "Under any reasoning, General Walker was a public man in whose public conduct society and the press had a legitimate and substantial interest."[59]

There is little basis for complaint about the logic by which the Court has expanded the range of protected speech in *Butts* and *Walker*. It has done exactly what would have been predicted from *New York Times*, radiating outward gradually by analogy[60] from the core protection in *Times*. What is difficult to fit in is the response to the *Hill* precedent. We ask again why did *Hill* not make an a fortiori case for some constitutional protection in *Butts* and *Walker?* Why was it necessary in *Butts* and *Walker* to make a fresh argument on the ambit issue? Are we to conclude that, for the moment, there are two ambits of constitutionally protected speech, one appropriate only for false statements about individuals treated as privacy actions, the other reserved for false statements about individuals treated as libel actions? If Mr. Hill had been defamed, would he have met no constitutional obstacles to his recovery? Or is he too a "public figure"?[61]

If the cases had come to the Court in the opposite order, I suspect the Court would have "worried" the issue whether Mr. Hill was sufficiently a public figure, and very likely would have decided he

---

[59] *Id.* at 165.

[60] And what was easily done by the courts of appeals in the *Pauling* cases. Pauling v. Globe-Democrat Publishing Co., 362 F.2d 188 (8th Cir. 1966); Pauling v. News Syndicate Co., 335 F.2d 659 (2d Cir. 1964); and foreshadowed in *Rosenblatt v. Baer*, 383 U.S. at 86 n. 12.

[61] Despite all this, it is difficult to down the impression that the Court's silence about *Hill* was deliberate and that it has seen the two cases as presenting problems it wishes to keep separate. Perhaps its point is that it does not wish to inhibit libel actions as much as it does privacy actions, since the former reflect a more serious and more traditional form of harm. But this can scarcely be the thesis of Justices Harlan, Fortas, and Clark, since their proposal was to give the plaintiff more protection in *Hill* than in *Butts* by giving the defendant publisher a less generous privilege; see note 28 *supra.*

was not. Since it seems to me that the *Hill* case was rightly decided and that the Court now has in hand a single coherent doctrine for handling the problem of false statements about individuals that interlace public discourse, perhaps the sequence of the cases was a benign accident.

V. The Level of Constitutional Protection

We come at last to the issue on which the Justices fall out among themselves in lively and sharp debate: granted that, because of the public interest in his communication, the defendant cannot be left to the mercy of state policy, just how much protection does the First Amendment require that he be given?

The common law of defamation, yielding slowly to the policies favoring a free press, worked out an elaborate series of accommodations for the competing interests, and as a complement thereto an elaborate gradation of privileges for false statements about individuals. There is the absolute privilege of judge, legislator, and executive when at work, a privilege indefeasible whatever the state of mind of the defendant.[62] There is the qualified privilege for the useful, private communication, such as the employee character reference.[63] And here there is a split of authority, some states holding the privilege defeasible only by proof of malice, recklessness, or knowing falsity, other states holding that ordinary negligence is enough.[64] To complicate matters further, there are the two sets of privileges for "public" communications: fair comment and record libel. The record libel privilege covers the repeating of defamation contained in a public record and is probably not defeasible at all so long as the statement accurately reports what the public record contains.[65] Fair comment, as the Court discovered in *New York Times*, is mysterious doctrine relying heavily on distinctions between fact and opinion and the degree of disclosure of underlying fact.[66] And there may be still further differences between com-

---

[62] Barr v. Matteo, 360 U.S. 564 (1959).

[63] See, *e.g.*, Watt v. Longsdon, [1930] 1 K.B. 130.

[64] See the note in Gregory & Kalven, *supra* note 29, at 1018–21

[65] See, *e.g.*, Cresson v. Louisville Courier-Journal, 299 Fed. 487 (6th Cir. 1924); and see Gregory & Kalven, *supra* note 29, at 1023–32.

[66] See, *e.g.*, Eickhoff v. Gilbert, 124 Mich. 353 (1900); and see Noel, *Defamation of Public Officers and Candidates*, 49 Colum. L. Rev. 875 (1949); Gregory & Kalven, *supra* note 29, at 1032–58; Veeder, *Freedom of Public Discussion*, 23 Harv. L. Rev. 413 (1910).

ment by way of literary criticism and comment on public officials, candidates for office, or other public figures. And as to public officials or figures there have been at least two rules of fair comment. One imposes strict liability for accuracy in statements of fact but affords a privilege to the expressions of opinion, as did the Alabama law in *New York Times*. The other broadens the privilege so as also to protect error in the underlying statements of fact if made in good faith. And arguably "good faith" in this formula might mean either the absence of negligence or something more. It was into this bramble bush of distinctions that the Court jumped in *New York Times*.

There is one other principle of the common law of defamation that needs to be noted. The normal basis of liability in defamation, in sharp and puzzling contrast to most of the rest of the law of torts, is strict liability. In the ordinary case it does not matter how innocent the defendant is if his communication can be read as defaming the plaintiff.[67] The great role of the common-law privileges in defamation has been, therefore, to abate the harshness of the strict liability principle rather than to give exceptional protection to a particular category of communication. Arguably, if defamation had been assimilated in nineteenth-century tort theory and keyed to liability limited to negligence, no doctrines of privilege would have ever developed. And finally as a footnote to *Hill*, I would note that under the New York statute, "false light" privacy is also a matter of strict liability.[68]

As Mr. Justice Harlan acutely notes in *Butts*, the common law of defamation "originated in soil entirely different from that which nurtured these constitutional values."[69] It began with a perception of the harms to individuals and only very gradually yielded to any competing perception of the public interest in speech. We need only remember that it was not until *Wason v. Walter*[70] in 1868

---

67 The classic analysis is Smith, *Jones v. Hulton: Three Conflicting Judicial Views as to a Question in Defamation*, 60 U. PA. L. REV. 365 (1912).

68 In sharp contrast to defamation, there has been little discussion of the basis of liability in privacy; see Kalven, *supra* note 15, at 334–35.

69 388 U.S. at 151.

70 L.R. 4 Q.B. 73 (1868). Lord Cockburn observed: "It seems to us impossible to doubt that it is of paramount public and national importance that the proceedings of the houses of parliament shall be communicated to the public, who have the deepest interest in knowing what passes within their walls, seeing that on what is there said and done, the welfare of the community depends. Where would be our con-

that English law recognized a privilege in the press voluntarily to republish proceedings in Parliament. If, however, one begins in the opposite corner with the First Amendment and with a perception of the public interest in free public discourse, the question is whether such a common-law calculus of interests is the appropriate model.

Against this common-law backdrop the question in the three new cases is whether there is any middle ground on which Mr. Justice Brennan and his allies can stand. The Black and Douglas position, that any risk of liability whatsoever must somewhat inhibit speech on matters of public interest and hence be a violation of the First Amendment, and the Harlan position, that more than a public interest in speech and press is involved and that no single formula can accommodate sensibly the competing interests, appear on the surface to occupy the two possible intellectual positions. Is the Brennan position, then, simply a matter of political expediency, a compromise impeachable by both the right and the left as lacking in principle? Can Mr. Justice Brennan resist the Black and Douglas absolutism without finding he has embraced Harlan; and conversely can he argue against Harlan's elaborate calculus without finding he has embraced Black and Douglas?

This time the three cases can conveniently be read together. Mr. Justice Brennan made the argument in *Hill* and it was restated by Chief Justice Warren in *Butts*. Justices Black and Douglas each stated their argument in *Hill* and Mr. Justice Black stated it once again for their side in *Butts*. Finally, Mr. Justice Harlan made an

---

fidence in the government of the country or in the legislature by which our laws are framed, and to whose charge the great interests of the country are committed,—where would be our attachment to the constitution under which we live,—if the proceedings of the great council of the realm were shrouded in secrecy and concealed from the knowledge of the nation? How could the communications between the representatives of the people and their constituents, which are so essential to the working of the representative system, be usefully carried on, if the constituencies were kept in ignorance of what their representatives are doing? What would become of the right of petitioning on all measures pending in parliament, the undoubted right of the subject, if the people are to be kept in ignorance of what is passing in either house? Can any man bring himself to doubt that the publicity given in modern times to what passes in parliament is essential to the maintenance of the relations subsisting between the government, the legislature, and the country at large?" *Id.* at 89. See also Stockdale v. Hansard, 9 Ad. & E. 1 (1839), and the delightful account of this historic conflict between court and Parliament, in DEAN, HATRED, RIDICULE AND CONTEMPT 202–11 (1953).

elaborate and careful argument for his position in *Hill*, and again in *Butts*.

The Black and Douglas opinions in *Hill* understandably have a somewhat tired sound. The Justices had made their point originally in *New York Times* and repeated it in *Rosenblatt v. Baer*.[71] A variety of points were put forward this time: "[R]eckless disregard of the truth" will prove, Mr. Justice Black argued, little protection for defendants in the world of real trials. The "*New York Times*' dilution of First Amendment rights,"[72] they prophesied, will be shown by experience to be as inadequate as the rule of *Betts v. Brady*. The defeasible privilege of the majority would not be arrived at "without using the recently popularized weighing and balancing formula."[73]

Turning to the case itself, Mr. Justice Black noted: "*Life*'s conduct here was at most a mere understandable and incidental error of fact in reporting a newsworthy event."[74] Since the majority reversed only to remand for a new trial and did not on this record direct for the defendant, we get, he implied, a clue to what a slender reed the majority's criterion of "malice" will prove to be.

The point is sharpened by Mr. Justice Douglas in *Hill*. Speaking of the "knowing or reckless falsity" test, he said:[75]

> Such an elusive exception gives the jury, the finder of the facts, broad scope and almost unfettered discretion. A trial is a chancy thing, no matter what safeguards are provided. To let a jury on this record return a verdict or not as it chooses is to let First Amendment rights ride on capricious or whimsical circumstances, for emotions and prejudices often do carry the day.

The acerbity increased in Mr. Justice Black's restatement of the theme in *Butts*. He saw the reversal in *Walker* and the affirmance in *Butts* as "quite contradictory action"[76] depending on the Court's subjective judgments about the offensiveness of the libel and the quality of the reporting, and went on to argue solemnly that the Court's involvement with questions of fact under the *New York Times* test is "in flat violation of the Seventh Amendment."[77] He then delivered what must be the unkindest cut of all—he stated that

---

71 383 U.S. 75 (1966).

72 385 U.S. at 399.

73 *Ibid.*

74 *Id.* at 400.

75 *Id.* at 402.

76 388 U.S. at 171.

77 *Ibid.*

the Court was getting itself into the same "quagmire" in libel as it had in obscenity.[78] He once again predicted that *New York Times* will go the way of *Betts v. Brady* and concluded with the point-blank challenge: "I think it is time for this Court to abandon *New York Times* v. *Sullivan* and adopt the rule to the effect that the First Amendment was intended to leave the press free from the harassment of libel judgments."[79]

The Black-Douglas argument does not seem to me to deepen in repetition. We are not told whether it is only the press who are to be the beneficiaries of an immunity from libel. Are other communicators to be left to its rules? We are not told whether the only reason for making the protection absolute is a distrust of the capacity of the legal system to discriminate or whether there is some value in the circulation of knowing falsehood.[80] There seems to be no sense of surprise at finding out after all these years that all or most of the law of defamation has been wholly unconstitutional. There is no recognition that counterspeech cannot be the remedy for this evil.[81] Again there is no recognition that the countervalue to the speech this time is the risk of harm to individuals. What, for example, would the Black and Douglas position say about a libel judgment such as that in *Faulk v. Aware, Inc.*?[82] The special weakness of the legal system in libel, its use of the jury, is a point that certainly would have ironic overtones as a matter of history. Finally, in calling for the abandonment of the *New York Times* rule, there is a sense of not knowing who one's friends are.

Nevertheless there is a point to their thesis. One might develop a free-speech theory on the premise that we must overprotect speech in order to protect the speech that matters. At least then it would be clear what the argument was and was not about. Moreover, once it has been conceded, as all Justices do in *Hill* and *Butts*, that the speech in question is within the ambit of some constitutional protection, there is admittedly bite in the Black-Douglas challenge

---

78 *Ibid.*

79 *Id.* at 172.

80 As, so notably, John Stuart Mill had argued in *On Liberty*.

81 See, however, discussion of Mr. Justice Harlan's reliance on counterspeech in these cases, text *infra*, at notes 99–100.

82 244 N.Y. S.2d 259 (1963). The dramatic history of the case is recounted in FAULK, FEAR ON TRIAL (1964), and again in NIZER, THE JURY RETURNS 225–438 (1966).

of how we can permit constitutionally significant speech to be inhibited—a challenge, it hardly needs stating, that will be felt most acutely by Mr. Justice Brennan and his allies.

The argument that the Court has not given enough protection to speech was aired in *New York Times.* New ground was broken, however, by the challenge from Mr. Justice Harlan and his colleagues that the Court is now giving too much protection to speech, a position no one had argued for in *New York Times.*

Mr. Justice Harlan announced at the outset of his opinion in *Hill* that he expressed disagreement only "after finding much with which I agree in the opinion of the Court."[83] He then proceeded to restate the areas of agreement: the instructions under which the case was tried cannot, as Mr. Justice Fortas valiantly argued, be read as providing any privilege for unintentional falsity; the *Life* story was within the ambit of constitutional concern—"an article of this type could have been prepared without liability."[84] He was then ready for his principal point: "Having come this far with the Court's opinion, I must part company with its sweeping extension of the principles of *New York Times* v. *Sullivan.*[85]

The problem, as he lucidly stated it, is what impact falsity is to have on otherwise constitutionally protected speech. *New York Times,* he recognized, said in effect that "mere falsity" would not remove the constitutional protection. But the protection of falsity, he ably argued, is strategic; the Court "has never found independent value in false publications nor any reason for their protection except to add to the protection of truthful communication."[86] But the strategy must vary, depending on the exact need for the "overprotection" in a given context and on the countervalue the state is seeking to protect.

In the special circumstances of *New York Times,* as he saw it, there were two factors that made it appropriate to afford the privilege to make false statements about individuals. First, there was, because of public interest in the official's behavior, some chance for counterspeech to challenge and correct false impression. Second, the aggrieved individuals had, as public officials, to some extent

83 385 U.S. at 402.   84 *Id.* at 404.   85 *Id.* at 405.

86 This understated Mill's point on behalf of falsity; but Mill was concerned with the utility of false doctrine, not false fact about individuals. See text *infra,* at notes 99–100.

assumed the risk of false publicity, thus reducing the state's interest in protecting them.

In the *Hill* case, however, neither of these factors was present. Mr. Hill was involuntarily a newsworthy figure; he was not hardened to the vicissitudes of publicity; and he could not be said to have assumed its risks. There was, therefore, "a vast difference in the state interest in protecting individuals like Mr. Hill from irresponsibly prepared publicity and the state interest in similar protection for a public official."[87]

Mr. Justice Harlan also saw significant differences in the opportunities for counterspeech in the two cases. In cases of public officials there could be "a competition among ideas" that would reduce the harm from the falsity left uncorrected by legal means. But in *Hill* "such a competition is extremely unlikely." "It would be unreasonable to assume," we are told in a remarkable sentence, "that Mr. Hill could find a forum for making a successful refutation of the *Life* material or that the public's interest in it would be sufficient for the truth to win out by comparison as it might in that area of discussion central to a free society."[88]

These two distinctions drawn, the argument moved quickly to its conclusion. The "knowing or reckless disregard" standard of *New York Times* strikes the wrong balance here where private persons, involuntarily newsworthy, are involved. In this context it is a poor strategy and it leaves an undue risk of harm from falsehood. Therefore the Constitution should be satisfied if the state grants the press a qualified privilege defeasible upon a showing of negligence. This difference in state of mind between negligence[89] and reckless disregard, then, is for Mr. Justice Harlan the appropriate measure of the relevant differences in the two contexts of communications, albeit each involves a matter of public interest.

There are three interesting addenda to the Harlan argument. If it is argued that this rule will unduly inhibit the press in dealing with what are avowedly matters of public interest, the Harlan

87 385 U.S. at 408.

88 *Id.* at 407–08.

89 It must be acknowledged that Mr. Justice Harlan did not state explicitly at any one place in his opinion the precise formula for the standard. On page 409, he talked of holding the press "to a duty of making a reasonable investigation of the underlying facts." On page 410 the phrasing shifted to creating "a severe risk of irremediable harm," and again on page 410 he referred to the duty he would impose as "this minimal responsibility."

answer "from a pragmatic standpoint" is that the New York press has been operating under the more inhibiting rules of the New York privacy statute and "has certainly remained robust."[90] We are also admonished, in a sentence that matches Mr. Justice Black in tone, that if even this minimal responsibility cannot under *New York Times* constitutionally be imposed on the press, that case "will prove in its long range impact to have done a disservice to the true values encompassed in the freedoms of speech and press."[91] (It is hard not to say, borrowing from W. C. Fields, that a case that is so vigorously condemned from both left and right cannot be altogether bad.) And finally, in an arresting aside, we are reminded that "other professional activity of great social value is carried on under a duty of reasonable care and there is no reason to suspect the press would be less hardy than medical practitioners or attorneys for example."[92]

Mr. Justice Harlan returned to this argument in *Butts*. This time it was somehow less elegant and less concise. After acknowledging that the communications about Butts and Walker as public figures were within the ambit of constitutional protection, he went back to his principal interest—showing that *New York Times* does not represent the only accommodation between the conflicting interests. But, as on the ambit issue, there was again a curious reluctance to utilize directly what was said in *Hill*. Instead we are given a somewhat lengthy essay on the history of free speech and then a shorter essay on the quite different soil from which the law of defamation sprang, underscoring the consequent tension between these two legal traditions.

After this preface, Mr. Justice Harlan took up the cases at hand. One might have thought, he said, that truth would mark the boundary between protected and unprotected speech, but the Court was committed to giving some protection to inadvertent falsity. This was the lesson of *New York Times*.[93] *Times*, however, is to be sharply distinguished. It lay close to seditious libel and nothing of that was present in the instant cases. Plaintiffs were not public officials. There was, however, one similarity: both Butts and Walker

---

90 *Id.* at 409–10. 91 *Id.* at 410–11. 92 *Id.* at 410.

93 "In any event, the *Times* opinion is as great a contribution to the issue of the relevance of truth to protected speech as it is to the issue of the relevance of the doctrine of seditious libel." Kalven, *supra* note 3, at 213.

"commanded sufficient continuing public interest and had sufficient access to the means of counterargument to be able 'to expose through discussion the falsehoods and fallacies' of the defamatory statements."[94] The cases were, therefore, like *Times* in some respects and unlike it in others. There was no mention of their relationship to *Hill.* In any event the appropriate balance of competing interests this time would be struck if defendant publishers were accorded a privilege defeasible on a showing not of mere negligence but of "highly unreasonable conduct constituting an extreme departure from the standards of investigation and reporting ordinarily adhered to by responsible publishers,"[95] in brief, gross negligence.

The full scheme is indeed elaborate. We have first public officials, public figures, and the involuntarily newsworthy. The cases are now being scaled by three factors: (1) proximity to seditious libel; (2) assumption of risk of publicity by plaintiff; and (3) possibility of counterargument to correct falsity. *New York Times* scores a plus in all three categories. *Butts* and *Walker* score only in the last two categories, and *Hill* scores in none of the categories. Accordingly maximum legal protection is given the speech in *Times*, minimum protection in *Hill*, and medium-range protection in *Butts* and *Walker*. And this is done by moving the condition of the privilege down from malice to gross negligence to negligence. And if we add to the roster *Barr v. Matteo*[96] on the absolute privilege of high-level public officials as defendants, we get still a fourth level of protection.

This was not quite all, however. In the course of the argument Mr. Justice Harlan turned again to the comparison of communication to other worthwhile activities in the society. *New York Times* being inapposite, "we are prompted, therefore, to seek guidance from the rules of liability which prevail in our society with respect to compensation of persons injured by the improper performance of a legitimate activity by another. Under these rules a departure from the kind of care society may expect from a reasonable man performing such activity leaves the actor open to judicial shifting of loss."[97]

This, then, was the Harlan position. In contrast to the stark sim-

94 388 U.S. at 155.

95 *Ibid.*

96 360 U.S. 564 (1959).

97 388 U.S. at 154.

plicity of the Black and Douglas absolute privilege, it offers momentarily a refreshingly elaborate edifice of privileges. In the end the thesis was built on two lines of analysis. First, an insistence that the *Times* privilege should be restricted to the quite special facts of *Times* and that a reliance on a close calculus of competing interests and risks was needed to work out privileges for other situations. Second, a simple but forceful challenge to the proposition that the press needs to be distinguished from other useful services in terms of criteria for liability. Why, he demanded, could not publishers, too, be required to act like reasonable men?

For a moment, but only for a moment, the scheme carries the promise of an original rethinking of the problems of free speech. The cardinal difficulty is that it appears to lack constitutional dimensions. It makes at a constitutional level more discriminations than two centuries of tort law has worked out at the common-law level! If policies are to be weighed on scales this exquisite, surely it is the function of the legislature to do the weighing. Is the difference between "reckless disregard" of *Times* and the gross negligence of *Butts* and *Walker* a constitutional difference? Moreover there is perhaps a special embarrassment in this for Mr. Justice Harlan. In the obscenity cases he opted for a time for a "two tier" view of the First Amendment, arguing that it applied less stringently to the states through the Fourteenth Amendment than it did to the federal government in its own right.[98] But if the states are to be left any discretion in these matters, must they not be left the very judgments Mr. Justice Harlan would here take away from them?

There is a kindred difficulty. The scheme rests to a surprising degree on sociological guesses lightly made. How free and robust is the New York press? How hardened are public officials to irresponsible publicity? Do they knowingly assume these risks? What are the relative possibilities for counterargument in the various situations? If we are to deal in conjectures and rough guesses of this sort about human behavior, is it not again the task of the legislature and not the Court to do the guessing? Or, at least, the business of the states?

The more one contemplates the scheme the less secure it seems. It is a doubtful reading of *New York Times* to see it resting so

---

[98] See Kalven, *supra* note 40, at 21–23.

heavily on a concern with counterargument. Indeed the whole discussion of competition of ideas and counterargument seems to me misplaced in this context. These are, to be sure, key principles when we are talking about doctrines and ideas. Here, with Mr. Justice Brandeis,[99] we look to counterargument as the correct remedy for the mischief of false and pernicious ideas and doctrine. And we grant an absolute privilege to false doctrine. All this is well understood, widely shared, and invaluable.[100]

But these notions sound only the faintest echo when we turn to false statements of fact about individuals. For centuries it has been the experience of Anglo-American law that the truth never catches up with the lie, and it is because it does not that there has been a law of defamation. I simply do not see how the constitutional protection in this area can be rested on the assurance that counterargument will take the sting out of the falsehoods the law is thereby permitting. And if this premise is not persuasive, the whole Harlan edifice tumbles.

Again, there is a special puzzle about the discrimination between *Butts* and *Walker*, and *Times*. In *Butts* and *Walker* the two factors that set *Times* apart in *Hill* are present: there is said to be chance for counterargument and plaintiffs as public figures could be said to have assumed the risks of publicity. Yet *Times* is thought inapposite because there are no overtones of seditious libel, a point Mr. Justice Harlan did not bother to make in *Hill*. This is of course a real difference between the cases, but it is not easy to see what relevance it has for the level of the privilege, unless the implication is that we are to scale the value of the speech too. But Mr. Justice Harlan is quite firm that the public interest in this speech "is not less than that involved in *New York Times*."[101]

And still again, if one is to use golden scales, why not consider the gravity of the comment about the aggrieved individual? Might we not ask for more care from a man risking the remark that Wally Butts had been a dishonest athletic director than from a man risking the apparently innocuous remark that Mr. Hill had heroically come to the aid of his beleaguered family? Or might we not change the

[99] Concurring in Whitney v. California, 274 U.S. 357 (1927).

[100] The classic statement is by Mr. Justice Stewart in Kingsley Pictures v. Regents, 360 U.S. 684, 688–89 (1959).

[101] 388 U.S. at 154.

rank by weighing the fact that the *Hill* story was merely entertainment whereas the other stories were "serious" news? Not the least of the troubles with the scaling game is that there are so many ways to play it. At least this time in his long debate with Mr. Justice Harlan, Mr. Justice Black seems to be correct: balancing has run riot.

In many ways the most arresting part of the Harlan argument is the effort to bring the reasonable man into free speech. It poses a fresh version of the preferred-position problem. If a service as useful to society as medicine can be subjected to liability for professional malpractice, why cannot the press be held to a comparable standard?[102] If the risk of jury judgments under a negligence standard is not too inhibiting for other useful activity, why is it so undue a burden on communication? The question is a good one and the answer is not that we think communication will be inhibited more than the other activity, but simply that we are less willing to have it inhibited. It is a special kind of activity in our society. That, in brief, is what the traditions of the First Amendment are all about—a special sensitivity to the risks of inhibiting communications activity and services.

Moreover, Mr. Justice Harlan has not, fortunately, had the courage of his conviction. Although he appeals most fully to the reasonable man standard in *Butts*, he is unwilling to use it there and exacts a privilege defeasible only by gross negligence. Also, in *Times* itself he concurred in exacting an even stronger privilege. Why, to repeat his question, cannot the communication activities in both those cases survive under the standard we apply to the useful services of doctors?

Further, the premise that the rules of tort liability that have been found appropriate for other activity are presumptively appropriate too for communication activities could lead to some unanticipated results. It is no longer true, if it ever was, that negligence represents the single consensus of society regarding the point at which losses are to be shifted. There is the doctrine of strict liability for extra hazardous activities enshrined in § 519 of the *Restatement of Torts*.

---

102 The press might not oppose the malpractice standard if they could be assured that, like the doctors, they would be presumed to have met professional standards *unless* there was explicit *expert* testimony that they had not. Given the famous conspiracy of silence by the press in reporting libel actions against fellow newspapers, it would be interesting indeed to hear them testify about each other's professionalism.

Perhaps more important there is today the explosion of strict liability in the field of products liability. In these cases, to put it as Mr. Justice Harlan has, the society has judged that these useful activities[103]—excavating for foundations, operating oil wells, exterminating pests, and the manufacturing and distributing of food, automobiles, knit wear, power tools—would not be unduly burdened by shifting all losses to them. Would he then follow the tort law and impose strict liability on communications for the risk of falsity?

It is tempting, although perhaps unfair, to push the logic one step further. Since communication activity is equated with other useful activity for purposes of selecting an appropriate rule of liability; and since in *Hill* Mr. Justice Harlan finds strict liability an unconstitutional burden on communications, we would appear to get to the delightful conclusion that the rule of § 519 of the *Restatement of Torts* itself is unconstitutional!

The Harlan observations raise, however, a question of genuine depth not only for the theory of free speech but also for the theory of tort liability. When we juxtapose communication as a risk-creating activity alongside all other risk-creating activity, it may look as though we have selected communication from other useful activity in the society in order to overprotect it. Or the analogy may move us in the other direction and it may look as though we elsewhere have underestimated the inhibiting impact of tort liability, have seen it clearly only for speech, and therefore have been underprotecting other activity.[104]

---

[103] Ironically, the special rationale of the *Restatement* would emphasize how valuable the extrahazardous activity is to society. Thus, the defendant is not said to be negligent in engaging in it, and we do not aim to inhibit him by imposing liability. See Keeton, *Conditional Fault in the Law of Torts,* 72 HARV. L. REV. 401 (1959).

[104] What is specially arresting, given this moment in the debate about tort theory, is the evaluation of the impact of liability insurance in the two contexts. It has become a commonplace of tort talk to argue that insurance eliminates any deterrent impact of tort liability. See CONARD, MORGAN, *et al.*, AUTOMOBILE ACCIDENT COSTS AND PAYMENTS (1964). There is, however, no intimation in any of the Justices' opinions that there is such a thing as libel insurance.

For a sample of current tort debate see KEETON & O'CONNELL, BASIC PROTECTION FOR THE TRAFFIC VICTIM (1965); Calabresi, *Fault, Accidents and the Wonderful World of Blum and Kalven,* 75 YALE L.J. 216 (1965); Blum & Kalven, *The Empty Cabinet of Dr. Calabresi—Auto Accidents and General Deterrence,* 34 U. CHI. L. REV. 239 (1967).

The possibilities are rich indeed. One might build a Calabresi argument for strict

My appetite for generalization is not up to an effort to unify tort theory and speech theory. The two traditions are too different. My preference, in this novel context at least, is to accord to speech and press "a preferred position" among useful activities or services. In a profound sense the commitment to free speech is quixotic and gallant; it is not a matter for prudence. Mr. Justice Brennan captured the flavor exactly in *New York Times* when he mentioned "the principle that debate on public issues should be uninhibited, robust, and wide-open."[105] I suspect that, properly viewed, there is in the world of the First Amendment no place for "the reasonable prudent man."

So much then for the extremes. It remains to observe what Justices Brennan and Warren make of the middle position. The logic of Mr. Justice Brennan in *Hill* combines a favorite thesis of his about the dangers of stimulating self-censorship with a thesis suggestive of his two-level approach to obscenity in *Roth*. In contrast to the approach of Mr. Justice Harlan, the principal question for him is the risk of inhibiting what is admittedly speech on matters of public interest. He is very clear about the gravity of this risk, under the special facts of the *Hill* case:[106]

> We create grave risk of serious impairment of the indispensable service of a free press in a free society, if we saddle the press with the impossible burden of verifying to a certainty the facts associated in news articles with a person's name, picture, or portrait, particularly as related to non-defamatory matter. Even negligence would be a most elusive standard, especially when the content of the speech itself affords no warning of prospective harm to another through falsity.

---

liability in communications in order to capitalize on general deterrence of communications "accidents," or build a James argument in order to spread the losses of communications accidents, or, with Mr. Justice Harlan, stick to nineteenth-century liability for fault theory, or, with Mr. Justice Brennan, limit liability in effect to intentional torts only, or finally, with Justices Black and Douglas, eliminate liability altogether.

It should be noted, however, that the proponents of strict liability in tort have generally been eager to eliminate liability for pain and suffering and to leave such losses on the victim. Arguably, that is the most relevant tort analogy here. See Keeton & O'Connell, *supra;* Green, Traffic Victims: Tort Law and Insurance (1958); and Blum & Kalven, Public Law Perspectives on a Private Law Problem 34–36 (1965).

105 376 U.S. at 270.

106 385 U.S. at 389.

He then goes on to point up the uncertainty of jury performance in such cases under a negligence standard, and then to stress the invitation to the press to censor themselves, and thus not to exercise their "constitutional guarantees" fully: "Fear of large verdicts in damage suits for innocent or mere negligent misstatement, even fear of the expense involved in their defense, must inevitably cause publishers to 'steer far wider of the unlawful zone.' "[107]

This then was the answer to the Harlan position. It has the special virtue of paying some attention to the peculiarity of the grievance in *Hill.* And it left the door open just a little for a different response in *Butts* and *Walker*, where the statement carried notice of its risk on its face.

But having stressed so much in reply to Harlan the dangers of inhibiting public speech, Brennan still had to answer to Justices Black and Douglas. The answer, it appears, had already been given in *Garrison v. Louisiana*[108] from which he quoted heavily. It turned on the special disutility of "calculated falsehood" and on the ease of avoiding it. A publisher does not have to "steer far wider" to avoid calculated falsehood; hence liability keyed to it does not risk triggering a chain of self-censorship. Moreover, the calculated falsehood falls into that bottom drawer of speech which, in the formula of *Chaplinsky,* is "no essential part of any exposition of ideas."[109] We are back once again in the family of *Chaplinsky, Beauharnais,*[110] and *Roth.*[111] We have a form of speech which is beneath contempt, or at least beneath constitutional concern. Calculated falsehood is, after all, a kind of pornography. And whatever the difficulties of the two-level theory as applied to alleged obscenity, it does have a considerable appeal here.[112]

There emerged then a coherent statement of position nicely keyed to the concerns of free speech: Speech on matters of public interest is within the ambit of First Amendment scrutiny. Such speech remains of public interest and serves a public purpose even though it will from time to time deal with individuals. There is danger in exposing such speech to tort actions by aggrieved individ-

---

107 *Ibid.*

108 379 U.S. 64 (1964).

109 Chaplinsky v. New Hampshire, 315 U.S. 568 (1942).

110 Beauharnais v. Illinois, 343 U.S. 250 (1952).

111 Roth v. United States, 354 U.S. 476 (1957).

112 See Kalven, *supra* note 40.

uals because the chance of inadvertent falsity cannot be avoided in active "robust" communication, and because fear of liability will engender self-censorship and cause publishers to "steer far wider of the unlawful zone." To key liability to calculated falsehood, however, will not engender self-censorship and in any event it is singularly worthless speech.[113]

The clarity and coherence of the position as theory are dimmed somewhat by two circumstances. First the test does not stick to the narrow and unambiguous criterion of calculated falsehood, as does the rationale. It expands to embrace "reckless disregard of the truth," a concept which belongs to the negligence family. Second, on the record in *Hill*, Mr. Justice Brennan was willing to remand for a new trial, meaning that if a jury, properly instructed, were to find against the defendant publishers, he would have no objection. There was a point, therefore, to Mr. Justice Black's complaint that the action of remanding on this record gives a clue to what the test is to mean in actual operation.

Mr. Justice Brennan had two final observations to add which are of high interest. Although *New York Times* had apparently been applied to reach the decision in *Hill*, we are expressly told that the Court got there "not through blind application of *New York Times Co. v. Sullivan*, relating solely to libel actions by public officials,"[114] but only upon consideration of the specific problem of the New York privacy statute and private individuals. "Therefore, although the First Amendment principles pronounced in *New York Times* guide our conclusion, we reach that conclusion only by applying these principles in this discrete context."[115] I would happily read this as meaning that *New York Times* is a seminal case in that it gave a reading to the First Amendment that can properly guide the Court in cases not involving libel or public officials. The point pre-

---

[113] In a recent panel discussion Professor Martin Shapiro observed that the final result of this extension of the *Times* rule might be a net loss of robust critical speech. His point was that critics of government or public policy might now be inhibited from entering public controversy by the risks that as "public figures" they would forfeit the protection the laws of libel had hitherto given them. Interestingly enough, this is precisely the counterargument that was unsuccessfully made in Coleman v. MacLennan, 78 Kan. 711 (1908), against broadening the fair comment privilege, *viz.*, that good men would be inhibited thereby from seeking public office. The Supreme Court does not deal with this counterrisk to speech, but I am fairly sure it would see the balance falling on the other side. In any event, I would.

[114] 385 U.S. at 390.

[115] *Id.* at 390–91.

sumably is that we are reasoning by analogy not for the purposes of tort law but for the purposes of constitutional law.

Mr. Justice Brennan then turned directly to the Harlan position. He met it not on the merits, but on the grounds that "this is [not] a libel action."[116] If it were, some of the Harlan distinctions as "between the relative opportunities of the public official and private individual to refute defamatory charge might be germane. And the additional state interest in the protection of the individual against damage to his reputation would be involved."[117] Once again, Mr. Justice Brennan appeared to be leaving the door open for a different result when libel of a newsworthy person is the issue, as was to be the case six months later in *Butts* and *Walker*.

When it finally was a question of libel, Mr. Justice Brennan found the *Times* standard appropriate after all. He devoted his opinion in *Butts* and *Walker* exclusively to arguing that the instructions in *Butts* were not close enough to the standard and that the case should be sent back for a new trial. It was left, therefore, to the Chief Justice to carry on the argument for the *Times* standard.

Chief Justice Warren tackled the job with gusto. First he labeled the Harlan standard of reportorial malpractice ("extreme departure from the standards of the investigation and reporting ordinarily adhered to by responsible publishers") as "an unusual and uncertain formulation."[118] He doubted that it could guide a jury of laymen.

Next, in a passage already quoted,[119] Chief Justice Warren argued that under the conditions of modern life there are no relevant differences between public officials and public figures. Hence he would have applied the same standard to both. And picking up Mr. Justice Harlan's emphasis in *Hill* on the possibilities of counterargument, he stated: "surely as a class these 'public figures' have as ready acccess as 'public officials' to mass media of communication, both to influence policy and to counter criticism of their views and activities."[120] If, then, the possibility of counterargument were the test, as Mr. Justice Harlan contended, public figures and public officials are fungible. And, reflecting Mr. Justice Harlan's taste for nuance, Chief Justice Warren found a subtle difference between public officials and public figures which moves in the direction of

---

116 *Id.* at 390.

117 *Ibid.*

118 388 U.S. at 163.

119 Text *supra*, at note 57.

120 388 U.S. at 164.

giving more protection, if distinctions are to be drawn, to the critic of the public figure! Unlike officials, public figures are not subject "to the restraints of the political process."[121] This means that society may have to rely on public opinion as "the only instrument by which society can attempt to influence their conduct."[122] This again shows that one trouble with "balancing" is that there are too many ways to do it.

The Chief Justice then concluded with some words of praise for the *Times* standard. It is manageable, "readily stated and understood,"[123] and moreover reflects a proper balancing of the interests involved. He stressed that the standard is not so restrictive as to limit recovery to cases where there is "knowing falsehood"; it included, after all, "reckless disregard for the truth."

This is perhaps the fitting moment to pause to marvel at the pattern of the Court's argument on this issue. The Court was divided 5 to 4 on whether the constitutional standard for the conditional privilege of those who libel public figures is that it be defeasible only upon a showing of "reckless disregard for truth" or merely on a showing of an "extreme departure" from professional newspaper standards! Further it was understood that the chief significance of the standard relates simply to how jury instructions will be worded. Yet this nuance triggered a major debate in the courts on the theory of free speech. Nor was this quite all. Perhaps there is poetic justice in the fact that each side can make a claim to victory. The Harlan standard, as we noted at the outset, has its *Butts;* the Brennan-Warren standard has its *Walker!*

When, however, we remember that the appearance of victory for Harlan in *Butts* is a fluke, occasioned by Warren's vote to save the verdict for the plaintiff, it is apparent that the Court stands 5 to 4 in favor of the Brennan-Warren standard and hence in favor of an across-the-board application of *New York Times.* The decisive precedent on the issue of the standard is therefore *Walker*—and behind it *New York Times.*

What are we to make, in the end, of the Court's disposition to argue so fiercely over so tiny a difference in jury instructions? Was Mr. Justice Fortas perhaps the one who really had the matter properly in focus when he admonished the Court in *Hill:*[124]

---

121 *Ibid.*

122 *Ibid.*

123 *Ibid.*

124 385 U.S. at 418.

> But a jury instruction is not abracadabra. It is not a magical incantation, the slightest deviation from which will break the spell. Only its poorer examples are formalistic codes recited by a trial judge to please appellate masters. At its best, it is simple, rugged communication from trial judge to jury of ordinary people, entitled to be appraised in terms of its net effect.

Was he disdaining to join the Court in debate on the merits?[125]

I have no inside information on why these issues held such extraordinary power to move the Supreme Court. I have no socio-psychological theories about small group process in the current Court or about its incapacity to reach consensus. I do have a few final hunches about what it all might mean, and they are benign.

First, it shows that the free speech issue etched in the sequence from *Times* to *Butts* and *Walker* of public speech interlaced with comment on individuals is a new issue never really confronted before in legal theory about freedom of speech and press. And it is a surprisingly troublesome issue. Second, it shows once again—and it is a splendid thing—that all members of this Court care deeply about free speech values and about their proper handling by law. Only a concerned Court would have worked so hard on such a problem. And finally, I think it shows a special respect for the potential of *New York Times* as a precedent on the First Amendment. In a sense the quarrel is over preserving the trademark of the *New York Times* case. If it is applied across the board in these cases, it retains its salience as a key precedent and it gives the Court a touchstone for the future; if the standard is nibbled away, a promising starting point for analysis of future problems is wasted.[126]

---

125 Yet in *Butts* he joined Mr. Justice Harlan in the gross negligence standard against the "reckless disregard" formula" of Warren and *New York Times!*

126 This is not the place seriously to inventory the intriguing questions left in the future of *New York Times v. Sullivan,* but the following at least come quickly to mind: (1) Whether *Beauharnais v. Illinois,* 343 U.S. 250 (1952), upholding the constitutionality of group libel laws is still "good law." (2) Whether the Court will ever re-examine, in light of *Times,* the rationale it gave in *Roth v. United States,* 354 U.S. 476 (1957), for the constitutionality of obscenity regulation. (3) Whether the fact-opinion distinction, on which so much of the common law on fair comment is based, is to be operative at the constitutional level. That is, is there an absolute privilege to express opinions, no matter how deliberately unfair, on public officials and public figures? (4) Will the libel per se controversy (which relates to whether special damages need be shown where the statement is not libelous on its face but requires extrinsic facts to spell out the full implication) have a constitutional dimension? It would indeed be a remarkable step in the growth of

However we may feel about the almost endless complexity of the arguments among the individual Justices, it seems to me the Court in *Hill*, *Butts*, and *Walker* has, as an institution, played its proper role very well indeed.

---

the law if the libel per quod rule, which has seemed to many to be simply a technical error in handling doctrine in the law of defamation, were to acquire status under the First Amendment as a safeguard for speech. See Prosser, *Libel Per Quod*, 46 VA. L. REV. 839 (1960); Eldridge, *The Spurious Rule of Libel Per Quod*, 79 HARV. L. REV. 733 (1966); Prosser, *More Libel Per Quod*, 79 HARV. L. REV. 1629 (1966); and see Afro-American Publishing Co. v. Jaffe, 366 F.2d 649, 660 (D.C. Cir. 1966). (5) In recent years it has become apparent that the right of privacy encompasses not only a dignitary tort but also a tort of unfair appropriation, a right of publicity. Prosser, *Privacy*, 48 CALIF. L. REV. 383 (1960). Does *Hill* carry implications for such claims when made by public figures? Or will it be compatible with the First Amendment that public figures be paid the market price for their photos, their stories, their biographies, as well as for their endorsements? (6) Will there be further development of the constitutional law on the connection between the plaintiff and the statement, the so-called "of and concerning" issue of the law of defamation?

DEAN ALFANGE, JR.

FREE SPEECH AND SYMBOLIC CONDUCT: THE DRAFT-CARD BURNING CASE

The Warren Court earned much of its libertarian reputation by its concern for First Amendment guarantees of freedom of expression. The constitutional defenses available to the radical political dissenter are far greater at the close of Warren's tenure than they were when the Chief Justice took office in the midst of Smith Act prosecutions and contempt convictions of witnesses before the Un-American Activities Committee. Wholesale prosecutions under the Smith Act have been judicially discouraged.[1] Congressional committees investigating allegedly subversive activities are now required to cut square procedural corners.[2] Meaningful First Amendment barriers have been established that place substantial limitations on state inquiries into these matters.[3] Two sections of the Subversive Activities Con-

Dean Alfange, Jr., is Assistant Professor of Government, University of Massachusetts.

[1] Yates v. United States, 354 U.S. 298 (1957); Noto v. United States, 367 U.S. 290 (1961). But *cf.* Scales v. United States, 367 U.S. 230 (1961). See also the loyalty oath cases, note 6 *infra,* which raise doubts about the constitutionality of the Smith Act on grounds of vagueness. In *Baggett v. Bullitt,* for example, where the Court struck down the Washington loyalty oath, Justice Clark in dissent said: "It appears to me from the statutory language that Washington's 1955 Act is much more clear than the Smith Act. Still the Court strikes it down. Where does this leave the constitutionality of the Smith Act?" 377 U.S. 360, 384 (1964).

[2] See Gojack v. United States, 384 U.S. 702 (1966).

[3] See DeGregory v. Attorney General of New Hampshire, 383 U.S. 825 (1966); Gibson v. Florida Legislative Investigation Committee, 372 U.S. 539 (1963).

trol Act have been struck down on the ground that they impose unnecessarily broad restrictions on the constitutional liberties of members of the Communist Party.[4] One of these invalidations marked the second time (both in the Warren era) that the Court has struck down a federal statute on First Amendment grounds.[5] Moreover, a succession of state loyalty oaths have fallen, on grounds of overbreadth or vagueness.[6] The efforts of southern states to thwart organized Negro demands for the equal protection of the laws provided the Court with the opportunity to establish landmark constitutional doctrines in the areas of freedom of association and libel,[7] of which the former, at least, is of crucial importance in the protection of the right to dissent.

It is ironic, therefore, that in the last freedom of expression decision handed down in the 1967 Term—in an opinion written by the Chief Justice himself—the Court not only rejected a First Amendment claim of a political dissenter that was by no means frivolous but dismissed it in an astonishingly cavalier manner. The case, *United States v. O'Brien*,[8] involved a conviction under the recently enacted amendment to the Universal Military Training and Service Act, making it a felony knowingly to destroy or to mutilate a Selective Service certificate.[9] O'Brien had been found guilty of burning his draft card in front of a Boston courthouse. A very persuasive argument can be made that the conviction of a war protester under this law is an abridgment of the First Amendment guarantee of freedom of speech.[10] On the other hand, the

---

4 Aptheker v. Secretary of State, 378 U.S. 500 (1964); United States v. Robel, 389 U.S. 258 (1967).

5 United States v Robel, *supra* note 4. The other case was Lamont v. Postmaster General, 381 U.S. 301 (1965).

6 Whitehill v. Elkins, 389 U.S. 54 (1967); Keyishian v. Board of Regents, 385 U.S. 589 (1967); Elfbrandt v. Russell, 384 U.S. 11 (1966); Baggett v. Bullitt, 377 U.S. 360 (1964); Cramp v. Board of Public Instruction, 368 U.S 278 (1961).

7 See KALVEN, THE NEGRO AND THE FIRST AMENDMENT (Phoenix ed. 1965). The leading case on freedom of association is NAACP v. Alabama, 357 U.S. 449 (1958). On libel: New York Times v. Sullivan, 376 U.S. 254 (1964); see Kalven, *The New York Times Case: A Note on "The Central Meaning of the First Amendment,"* 1964 SUPREME COURT REVIEW 191.

8 391 U.S. 367 (1968).

9 50 U.S.C. App. § 462(b)(3).

10 See Rachlin, *Draft Cards and Burning the Constitution*, 32 BROOKLYN L. REV. 334 (1966); Velvel, *Freedom of Speech and the Draft Card Burning Cases*, 16 U. KANS. L. REV. 149 (1968).

case for the constitutionality of the law as a valid regulation of conduct unrelated to speech is even easier to construct.

Only when one attempts to determine the extent to which either side of the argument may need to be modified in order to take cognizance of the valid points in the other position does the case become complex. Unfortunately, the Court chose not to deal with the complexities of the matter. In upholding the constitutionality of the amendment, it made no attempt to discuss, let alone to answer, the difficult and disturbing constitutional questions presented. Instead, it trivialized the issues and handed down an opinion that has all the deceptive simplicity and superficial force that can usually be achieved by begging the question.

I. The Passage of H.R. 10306

On May 5, 1965, several hundred University of California students, protesting American intervention in the rebellion in the Dominican Republic, staged a rally on the campus, at the culmination of which they marched to the office of the draft board in Berkeley, presented the official on duty with a black coffin, and some forty of them publicly set fire to their draft cards. The card burning did not at that time cause a great deal of consternation, nor did it appear to reflect violent opposition to the concept of conscription. It was, instead, a demonstration of opposition to one particular use of American troops. One of the students declared: "It's purely a symbolic protest. We have been told we can get new cards if we apply for them."[11]

As American involvement in Vietnam deepened in 1965, however, opposition to the draft became increasingly intransigent. Moral criticism of the war was converted into moral criticism of the system which forced individuals to give up their civilian pursuits and take part in what was, to the protesters, unbridled military aggression. Protest meetings became more frequent, and the focal point was often an army induction center. Commonly, at such meetings, draftees were vainly urged not to submit to induction, and, on occasion, one or more of the protesters would demonstrate his contempt for and defiance of the draft laws by putting a match to his draft card. But Selective Service officials did not seem perturbed. After five persons burned draft cards in a tin pot in front of the army induction center in New York City on July 29, 1965,

[11] N.Y. Times, May 6, 1965, p. 13.

Colonel Paul W. Akst, director of Selective Service for the city, remarked: "It's just a nuisance. They'll just come in to their local boards in a few days and get a duplicate card."[12] He added that burning draft cards was not illegal and that, while possession of a draft card was legally required, there was no penalty for non-compliance.

On the latter point, Colonel Akst was wrong. Section 12(b)(6) of the Universal Military Training and Service Act of 1948 provides that any person "who knowingly violates or evades any of the provisions of this title or rules and regulations promulgated pursuant thereto relating to the issuance, transfer, or possession of such [registration or other authorized] certificate, shall, upon conviction, be fined not to exceed $10,000 or be imprisoned for not more than five years, or both."[13] Regulations promulgated to implement the act provide that every person registered with and classified by the Selective Service System must "have in his personal possession at all times" his Registration Certificate (SSS Form No. 2)[14] and his Notice of Classification (SSS Form No. 110).[15] Presumably, therefore, anyone publicly burning his draft card would reveal himself as a violator of the regulations requiring possession and would become subject to the heavy penalties provided by § 12(b)(6).[16]

Despite the relative unconcern of Selective Service officials such as Colonel Akst and Selective Service director Lieutenant General Lewis B. Hershey[17] with draft-card burnings, and despite the fact

[12] N.Y. Times, July 30, 1965, p. 2.

[13] 50 U.S.C. App. § 462(b)(6).

[14] 32 CFR § 1617.1 (1962).

[15] 32 CFR § 1623.5 (1967). Hereafter, both the Registration Certificate and the Notice of Classification will be referred to interchangeably as "draft cards."

[16] Convictions for nonpossession of Selective Service certificates have been obtained and upheld. See United States v. Kime, 188 F.2d 677 (7th Cir. 1951), *cert. den.*, 342 U.S. 823 (1951); United States v. Hertlein, 143 F. Supp. 742 (E.D. Wis. 1956).

[17] General Hershey, on June 23, 1965, in response to a letter from Representative John P. Saylor of Pennsylvania inquiring whether revision of the Selective Service laws was needed to deal with those who burned draft cards, wrote that "adequate authority exists to enforce compliance with the law either through accelerated induction or by criminal prosecution." 111 *Cong. Rec.* 16040 (1965). On the validity of accelerated induction of those who destroy their draft cards, and thus fail to possess them, see Wills v. United States, 384 F.2d 943 (9th Cir. 1967), *cert. den.*, 392 U.S. 908 (1968) (Douglas, Brennan, and Stewart, JJ., dissenting).

that those who engaged in this practice thereby instantly exposed themselves to prosecution, Congress proceeded to make the destruction of a draft card an express federal offense. On August 5, 1965, Representative L. Mendel Rivers of South Carolina introduced H.R. 10306, a prohibition against knowing destruction or knowing mutilation of a draft card.[18] The bill passed both Houses of Congress and was signed by the President, all in less than a month.

The legislative history of this bill is skimpy and not particularly distinguished. Neither House held hearings on its merits. The favorable reports of the Armed Services Committees of both Houses were very brief and uninstructive.[19] The floor debates were all but nonexistent, consisting entirely of statements by two members of the House and one senator angrily denouncing those who would engage in such unpatriotic action.[20] Nowhere in the legislative

---

[18] For purposes of speed, a parallel bill, S. 2381, was introduced in the Senate by Senator Thurmond. After it was reported favorably by the Senate Armed Services Committee, it was bypassed in favor of the Rivers bill. 111 *Cong. Rec.* at 19746, 20433–34.

[19] H.R. Rep. No. 747, 89th Cong., 1st Sess. (1965); S. Rep. No. 589, 89th Cong., 1st Sess. (1965). The report of the Senate Armed Services Committee contains only two sentences that in any way serve to provide a reason for its passage: "The committee has taken notice of the defiant destruction and mutilation of draft cards by dissident persons who disapprove of national policy. If allowed to continue unchecked this contumacious conduct represents a potential threat to the exercise of the power to raise and support armies." Quoted 391 U.S. at 387. The committee did not undertake to explain how the destruction of draft cards threatened the exercise of this power except as an expression of opposition to its exercise and did not explain why existing law relating to the nonpossession of draft cards and the hindering or interfering with the administration of the draft was not adequate to meet any potential threat posed by the burnings. The report of the House Armed Services Committee, after expressing "deep concern" with the defiance of authority represented by the destruction of draft cards and noting that "the present provisions of the Criminal Code with respect to the destruction of Government property may appear broad enough to cover all acts having to do with the mistreatment of draft cards," stated that it was the belief of the committee "that in the present critical situation of the country, the acts of destroying or mutilating these cards are offenses which pose such a grave threat to the security of the Nation that no question whatsoever should be left as to the intention of the Congress that such wanton and irresponsible acts should be punished." Quoted *id.* at 387–88. The report contained no explanation of why the destruction of draft cards threatened national security except as an expression of dissent and defiance of authority.

[20] In the House, the speakers were Representative Rivers and Representative William G. Bray of Indiana. In the Senate, there was only a very brief statement by Senator Thurmond. Rivers declared that his bill was "a straightforward clear answer to those who would make a mockery of our efforts in South Vietnam by

history is there any specific indication that the bill was needed for the implementation or execution of the Selective Service laws, nor was any purpose suggested for it except the desire to obtain a measure of retribution against those who would so openly and defiantly attack the military effort of the United States. Yet nearly unanimous support was obtained for its enactment. It passed the House by a recorded vote of 393 to 1,[21] and passed the Senate by a voice vote without any expression of opposition.[22]

II. Draft-Card Burning and the Courts

A. THE COURTS OF APPEALS

With the passage of the Rivers amendment, Congress had thrown down the gauntlet and provided an invitation to martyrdom certain to be irresistible to those who felt the need to make a personal sacrifice for the cause of conscience. Predictably, it was not long before a number of young men came forward to flout the new law. On October 15, 1965, a day in which antiwar rallies were held in various American cities, David J. Miller, a 22-year-old pacifist and member of the Catholic Worker movement, took center stage at the rally in New York City and climaxed it by setting fire to his draft card in the presence of agents of the FBI and members of the New York Police Department. On October 20, Stephen L. Smith, a student at the University of Iowa, burned his

---

engaging in the mass destruction of draft cards." 111 *Cong. Rec.* at 19871. Bray, in a much longer and more emotional statement, argued: "The need of this legislation is clear. Beatniks and so-called 'campus cults' have been publicly burning their draft cards to demonstrate their contempt for the United States and our resistance to Communist takeovers." He argued for the imposition of "some legal control over those who would destroy American freedom," and concluded: "If these 'revolutionaries' are permitted to deface and destroy their draft cards, our entire Selective Service System is dealt a serious blow." *Id.* at 19871–72. Senator Thurmond declared that the draft-card burnings "constitute open defiance of the warmaking powers of the Government and have demonstrated an urgent need for this legislation." He went on: "Such conduct as public burnings of draft cards and public pleas for persons to refuse to register for their draft should not and must not be tolerated by a society whose sons, brothers, and husbands are giving their lives in defense of freedom and countrymen against Communist aggression." *Id.* at 20433.

21 *Id.* at 19872. The lone opposing vote was cast by Representative Henry P. Smith of New York, who had served as a member of a draft board for nearly fifteen years. Representative Smith explained that while he was in sympathy with the aims of the bill, he believed that the punishment provided "is far too excessive for this type of misdemeanor." N.Y. Times, Aug. 11, 1965, p. 14.

22 111 *Cong. Rec.* at 20433–34.

draft card before a crowd gathered at the Iowa Memorial Union on the campus. On November 6, at a rally in Union Square in New York, five men burned their draft cards simultaneously.

Miller, Smith, and four of the five who burned cards at the Union Square rally were indicted and convicted of violating the amended draft law. Of the convictions which were appealed, all were upheld at the Court of Appeals level.[23] The fullest discussion of the issues in any of these cases is to be found in the opinion of the Second Circuit in the *Miller* case.[24] The Eighth Circuit in *Smith* and the Second Circuit in a later ruling[25] were content to follow the reasoning in *Miller* without significant elaboration. But these early convictions did not have much visible effect in deterring the practice of burning draft cards.

In early 1966, a number of protest demonstrations were held at which cards were burned. One of these took place in front of a courthouse in Boston where four men who were to appear in court to answer charges stemming from an earlier rally set fire to their draft cards as an ultimate expression of their feelings. One of the four who participated in this demonstration was David P. O'Brien, whose case was ultimately to reach the Supreme Court. O'Brien was quickly arrested, indicted, and convicted of having knowingly destroyed his draft card; he was sentenced under the Youth Corrections Act[26] to a period of up to six years in the custody of the Attorney General, up to four of which could be spent at the Federal Youth Correctional Center in Chillicothe, Ohio. He appealed his conviction to the Court of Appeals for the First Circuit, which declared the amendment to the draft law unconstitutional as an abridgment of freedom of expression but sustained the conviction on other grounds.[27]

Although the decisions of the First and Second Circuits were in direct conflict, the opinions of both panels were unanimous. The basis of their disagreement concerned the purpose of Congress in amending the draft law. Judge Feinberg, writing for the Second

---

23 United States v. Miller, 367 F.2d 72 (2d Cir. 1966), *cert. den.*, 386 U.S. 911 (1967); Smith v. United States, 368 F.2d 529 (8th Cir. 1966); United States v. Edelman, 384 F.2d 115 (2d Cir. 1967). See also United States v. Miller, 249 F. Supp. 59 (S.D. N.Y. 1965); United States v. Smith, 249 F. Supp. 515 (S.D. Iowa 1966).

24 Note 23 *supra*.

25 Note 23 *supra*.

26 18 U.S.C. § 5010(b).

27 O'Brien v. United States, 376 F.2d 538 (1st Cir. 1967).

Circuit in *Miller*, did not seriously attempt to deny that the amendment was aimed at putting a stop to draft-card burning as a form of protest. But, he stated, since the law was essentially a supplement to the nonpossession regulation that long predated the controversy over card burning, it could not be deemed unrelated to a rational legislative objective, and thus could not be declared unconstitutional, whatever the factors that prompted its passage.[28] Chief Judge Aldrich, writing for the First Circuit, on the other hand, could find no proper legislative purpose for the amendment precisely because it appeared to add nothing to the nonpossession regulations. A person destroying his draft card obviously could no longer possess it. If the amendment, therefore, is not entirely superfluous, it can only be because "the destruction itself is an act of some consequence." Inasmuch as the simple act of destruction is consequential only if it is done publicly, the amendment must be "precisely directed at public as distinguished from private destruction." And, since the purpose of public destruction is symbolic speech, "the amendment strikes at the very core of what the First Amendment protects."[29]

The First Circuit, however, did not direct O'Brien's acquittal, for the court held that, on the evidence, he had been proved to be in violation of the nonpossession regulation, which, in its view, was a lesser included offense of the crime of knowing destruction or mutilation.[30] While the maximum punishment provided by § 12(b)(6) for violation of a regulation was the same as that for knowing destruction, the court found it appropriate to remand the case to the District Court for resentencing because that court may have considered destruction a more serious offense than nonpossession. If the trial court had shared the widely held view that draft-card burning was a hateful act because of the attitude it

---

[28] 367 F.2d at 76–77. The Second Circuit relied in part on People v. Stover, 12 N.Y.2d 462 (1963), *appeal dism.*, 375 U.S. 42 (1963). See text *infra*, at notes 143–44.

[29] 376 F.2d at 541. In two footnotes, Judge Aldrich disclaimed any intention to examine the motives of individual members of Congress who supported the bill. The court, he declared, was not concluding from the legislative history that Congress was motivated by an improper purpose but was merely taking cognizance of the fact that the legislative history failed to suggest a proper purpose. He did note, however, that "we regard it as significant that the impact on certain expressions of dissent is no mere random accident, but quite obviously the product of design." *Id.* at 541 n. 7.

[30] *Id.* at 541.

represented and had taken this into consideration in imposing sentence, that, Judge Aldrich stated, "would be to punish defendant, pro tanto, for exactly what the First Amendment protects. The only punishable conduct was the intentional failure to carry his card."[31]

Because the First Circuit found the amendment void on its face, it had no occasion to discuss whether the law, if valid, could be constitutionally applied to one whose knowing destruction of his draft card was done for purposes of expression. It was the opinion of the Second Circuit that, on a balancing of interests,[32] the amendment could be so applied. Prohibitable actions, Judge Feinberg noted, do not automatically become protected because they are undertaken as a means of expression.[33] Draft cards, he observed, were useful in the administration of the Selective Service, and thus there was a legitimate governmental interest in preventing their

---

[31] *Id.* at 542.

[32] It was argued on behalf of Miller that the "clear and present danger" test should be employed rather than a balancing of interests. Judge Feinberg, however, declined to apply "clear and present danger" standards because, he maintained, the Supreme Court had adopted the balancing approach to determine the validity of legislation which indirectly affects speech. 367 F.2d at 80. On this point, he was on shaky ground. He was able to cite no case in support of this contention more recent than Communist Party v. Subversive Activities Control Board, 367 U.S. 1 (1961). Since 1961, the Court has appeared to avoid clear reliance on the balancing of interests in all types of First Amendment cases. In United States v. Robel, 389 U.S. 258, 268 n. 20 (1967), for example, a case arguably involving an indirect abridgment of speech, the Court employed a lengthy footnote to make clear that its holding was not based on balancing. On the other hand, the rejection of "clear and present danger," although not supported by any citations in the Second Circuit's opinion, is perhaps justified by Cox v. Louisiana, 379 U.S. 559, 565–66 (1965), in which the Court held that "clear and present danger" was not the test for determining the validity of an individual application of a law forbidding picketing near a courthouse. Where the state's interest was real and important, the Court stated, the legislature was itself entitled to conclude that conduct involving speech presented a "clear and present danger" of interfering with the attainment of that interest, and to forbid that conduct by means of a narrowly drawn statute. See text *infra,* at notes 69–76.

[33] 367 F.2d at 79. Judge Feinberg cited examples of activities that might be engaged in as symbolic expression—ranging from political assassination to hanging clothes lines in front yards, dumping garbage on streets, and turning on water faucets during a water shortage—to demonstrate that otherwise illegal acts cannot be given constitutional immunity merely because the act was intended to dramatize an idea. *Cf.* Reynolds v. United States, 98 U.S. 145 (1878), in which it was held that the constitutional guarantee of freedom of religion did not allow illegal acts to be committed with impunity in the name of religion. For a criticism of the relevance of treating draft-card burning on the same constitutional level as garbage dumping, see Velvel, note 10 *supra,* at 156–62.

destruction. In support of this contention, he offered a brief inventory of the uses which draft cards serve.[34] On the other hand, the restriction imposed by the amendment on freedom of speech was extremely small—freedom to dissent and to oppose the war in Vietnam by means other than the destruction of draft cards was left unimpaired.[35]

B. THE SUPREME COURT

The Supreme Court granted certiorari in *O'Brien* to reconcile the conflict in the decisions of the two circuits.[36] It upheld the constitutionality of the amendment both on its face and as applied.[37]

The seven members of the Court who addressed themselves to the First Amendment questions in the case (Mr. Justice Marshall did not participate and Mr. Justice Douglas dissented on other grounds) were unanimous in rejecting O'Brien's claims. The Court was far less frank than the Second Circuit in conceding that congressional outrage at draft-card burning as a form of antiwar protest was at least a primary factor underlying the passage of the amendment. Instead, the opinion of the Chief Justice treated the amendment essentially without reference to the context in which it was enacted, and thereby discussed the principal constitutional question in sterile isolation from the reality that gave it its substance. The amendment was considered nothing more than an innocuous and unexceptionable regulation related to the more efficient administration of Selective Service, and, by so viewing it, the Court had no difficulty in affirming its constitutionality.

The Court was barely willing to concede that the case presented any First Amendment questions at all. "We cannot accept the view," the Chief Justice wrote, "that an apparently limitless variety of conduct can be labelled 'speech' whenever the person engaging in the conduct intends thereby to express an idea."[38] But even on

---

[34] 367 F.2d at 80–81. See also Forkosch, *Draft Card Burning—Effectuation and Constitutionality of the 1965 Amendment*, 32 BROOKLYN L. REV. 303, 324–25 (1966).

[35] 367 F.2d at 81.

[36] 389 U.S. 814 (1967). At the same time, it granted the cross-petition filed by O'Brien to obtain review of the First Circuit's holding that nonpossession was a lesser included offense of knowing destruction or mutilation and that O'Brien could be held to have been convicted of that offense. The Court's disposition of the case rendered moot the questions raised in the cross-petition.

[37] United States v. O'Brien, 391 U.S. 367 (1968).

[38] *Id.* at 376.

the theory that conduct undertaken for purposes of expression may be said to fall within the scope of the First Amendment, a proposition to which the Court avoided giving approval, the conduct may still be constitutionally regulated if the governmental interest in so doing may be described by an adjective such as "compelling," "substantial," "subordinating," "paramount," "cogent," or "strong."[39] And, in a passage that Mr. Justice Harlan described in his brief concurring statement as the "crux of the Court's opinion,"[40] Chief Justice Warren explained how it may be determined if any of these adjectives apply:[41]

> Whatever imprecision inheres in these terms, we think it clear that a government regulation is sufficiently justified [1] if it is within the constitutional power of the government; [2] if it furthers an important or substantial governmental interest; [3] if the governmental interest is unrelated to the suppression of free expression; and [4] if the incidental restriction on alleged First Amendment freedom is no greater than is essential to the furtherance of that interest.

Applying the four segments of this test to the draft law amendment on its face, the Court found that the amendment satisfied the requirements of each of them in turn. First, the power to protect Selective Service certificates from knowing destruction is, like the power to create and maintain the Selective Service System itself, an appropriate adjunct of Congress' constitutional power to "raise and support Armies."[42] Second, "legislation to insure the continuing availability of issued certificates serves a legitimate and substantial purpose in the system's administration."[43] In support of this assertion, the Court provided an inventory, similar to that of the Second Circuit, indicating the potential uses to which draft cards might be put and possible justifications for the law forbidding their destruction.[44]

---

[39] *Id.* at 376–77. The Court found that these adjectives had been used in the following cases involving conflicts between guarantees of the First Amendment and other societal interests: NAACP v. Button, 371 U.S. 415 (1963); NAACP v. Alabama, 357 U.S. 449 (1958); Bates v. Little Rock, 361 U.S. 516 (1960); Thomas v. Collins, 323 U.S. 516 (1945); Sherbert v. Verner, 374 U.S. 398 (1963).

[40] 391 U.S. at 388.

[41] *Id.* at 377. (Numbers in brackets are added.)

[42] *Ibid.*

[43] *Id.* at 377–78.

[44] *Id.* at 378–80. The items in the inventory included: (1) It "serves as proof that the individual described thereon has registered for the draft," can help to rectify a

The Court also sought to answer the contention basic to the First Circuit's decision, that the amendment served no purpose not already served by the existing regulations requiring possession.[45] Nonpossession and knowing destruction are not the same thing, the Chief Justice pointed out. To be sure, the First Circuit did not argue that they were, but, rather, that neither the legislative history nor any other source had suggested any purpose for prohibiting destruction except to require possession. The amendment adds to the regulation by prohibiting the destruction of someone else's certificate. And, in any event, except where multiple punishment is thereby imposed, Congress is perfectly free to protect the same interest through separate statutes and can certainly give statutory protection to an interest previously protected only by an administrative regulation.[46] Finally, since the interest in efficient operation of the draft bears no relation whatever to the suppression of free speech, and since the interest in insuring the preservation of draft cards cannot be more narrowly attained than by a law prohibiting their destruction, the Court held that all aspects of the test were satisfied and that the law must be deemed constitutional as applied to one who burned his draft card as an expression of protest.[47]

To the contention that the amendment was void on its face because the purpose of Congress in enacting it was to punish

---

"mix-up in the registrant's file," and "assures a rapid and uncomplicated means for determining his fitness for immediate induction, no matter how distant . . . he may be from his local board." (2) The cards provide information that makes it easier for the registrant to communicate with and provide information for his local board, and makes it easier for the board to respond to his communications. (3) They serve as "continual reminders that the registrant must notify his local board of any change of address, and other specified changes in his status." (4) If not destroyed or mutilated, they can provide evidence that may help in detecting abuses of the certificates, such as forgery or alteration. *Cf.* United States v. Miller, 367 F.2d, at 80–81; Forkosch, note 34 *supra*, at 324–25. For a disparagement of the values of these uses, see Velvel, note 10 *supra*, at 163–66. It should be noted, however, that insofar as draft cards may be thought to have utility because evidence of nonregistration or of forgery or alteration may be obtained if individuals are required to present these certificates upon demand, as is suggested by uses (1) and (4) in the Court's inventory, interesting questions of compulsory self-incrimination would be raised by any attempt to put draft cards to such use. See Rachlin, note 10 *supra*, at 349; Mansfield, *The Albertson Case: Conflict between the Privilege against Self-Incrimination and the Government's Need for Information,* 1966 SUPREME COURT REVIEW 103, 125–27; United States v. Olson, 253 Fed. 233 (W.D. Wash. 1917).

[45] 391 U.S. at 380–81.

[46] *Id.* at 380.

[47] *Id.* at 382.

expressions of dissent, the Court scarcely bothered to respond. Legislative history may be used to ascertain congressional purpose when the question is one of statutory construction, but, the Chief Justice remarked: "It is a familiar principle of constitutional law that this Court will not strike down an otherwise constitutional statute on the basis of an alleged illicit legislative motive."[48] In a footnote, the Chief Justice admitted that where the constitutionality of a statute depended on whether or not the intention of the legislature was to impose punishment, as in bill of attainder cases, judicial inquiry into legislative motives might be required.[49] But the basic rule in constitutional adjudication was that if the legislation would be valid if the legislative motivation were proper, it is not to be invalidated on the basis of judicial "guesswork" as to motivation based on the statements of a small number of legislators.[50]

There were two brief separate opinions. Mr. Justice Harlan, in a one-paragraph concurrence, declared simply that the Court's four-part test ought not to "foreclose consideration of First Amendment claims in those rare instances . . . [when a statute meeting the requirements of the test] has the effect of entirely preventing a 'speaker' from reaching a significant audience with whom he could not otherwise lawfully communicate." But, he added, this caveat had no applicability to this case because forbidding O'Brien to destroy his draft card did not prevent him from expressing his views in many other ways.[51]

The dissent of Mr. Justice Douglas did not raise the First Amendment issue. The fundamental question presented by this case was,

---

[48] *Id.* at 383. The Court found it necessary to single out and explain away two decisions which appear to turn on judicial evaluation of legislative motivation. Grosjean v. American Press Co., 297 U.S. 233 (1936), and Gomillion v. Lightfoot, 364 U.S. 339 (1960). Neither case was based, the Court insisted, on judicial disapproval of legislative purposes. Instead, the Court declared enigmatically, the statutes were considered unconstitutional because their "inevitable effect" was to abridge constitutional rights. 391 U.S. at 384–85. See text *infra*, at notes 119–29.

[49] 391 U.S. at 383 n. 30.

[50] *Id.* at 384. The Court noted that only three members of Congress had spoken on this bill, and reproduced in an Appendix to its opinion the brief remarks in the committee reports explaining the need for its passage, *id.* at 386–88, apparently for the purpose of disproving the nonexistence of proper congressional motivation, although neither report contained anything other than the most general and unsubstantiated statements regarding need. See note 19 *supra.*

[51] *Id.* at 388–89.

for him, whether Congress had the power to carry on a military draft at all "in the absence of a declaration of war."[52] Presumably, if it could not, there would be no power to issue draft cards, and no power to prohibit their destruction. He conceded that this question had been neither briefed nor argued, but, he maintained, the case should nevertheless have been returned to the calendar for reargument on this issue,[53] a course of action that, to say the least, would have been spectacular.

III. Draft-Card Burning as Protected Speech

A. The Merits of O'Brien's Case: Some Pros and Cons

When, in the course of the litigation that was to lead to the enrollment of James Meredith at the University of Mississippi, the federal district court accepted the contention of the university that it was not a racially segregated institution, the Fifth Circuit commented that the case had been tried in "the eerie atmosphere of never-never land."[54] When, in *O'Brien*, the Supreme Court declared that the defendant was being punished for the "noncommunicative impact of his conduct, and for nothing else,"[55] it generated a never-never land atmosphere equally eerie. For the profoundly disturbing aspect of this case was that, as a matter of ascertainable fact, the essential contentions raised on behalf of

---

[52] *Id.* at 389. The Court, in its opinion, had stated that Congress' power "to classify and conscript manpower for military service is 'beyond question.'" *Id.* at 377. Mr. Justice Douglas insisted, however, that this power was "beyond question" only in wartime. The validity of conscription in peacetime, he pointed out, had never been specifically decided. *Id.* at 389 n. 1.

[53] *Id.* at 391. In two cases in which the Court denied certiorari on the same day that *O'Brien* was decided, Holmes v. United States, 391 U.S. 936 (1968), and Hart v. United States, 391 U.S. 956 (1968), Mr. Justice Douglas dissented on the ground that these cases, like *O'Brien*, raised the question of the validity of peacetime conscription, which the Court should answer. Mr. Justice Stewart, who had joined Mr. Justice Douglas in dissent from the denial of certiorari in Mora v. McNamara, 389 U.S. 934 (1967), which had raised the issue of the validity of the presidential action sending troops into an international conflict without a declaration of war, did not dissent in *Holmes* and *Hart*, explaining that had these cases presented the question of the commitment of troops in the war, and had not merely concerned peacetime conscription, he would have favored granting certiorari. *Cf.* Mitchell v. United States, 386 U.S. 972 (1967) (*cert. den.*) (Douglas, J., dissenting). *O'Brien*, of course, in no way raised the issue of the constitutionality of American military involvement in Vietnam.

[54] Meredith v. Fair, 298 F.2d 696, 701 (5th Cir. 1962).

[55] 391 U.S. at 382.

O'Brien with regard to the symbolism of the burning and the suppressive intent of Congress, which the Court passed off apparently as farfetched, were manifestly sound, if not necessarily controlling.

When a war protester burns his draft card, he does so entirely because of the value of the act as expression. The burning has never been intended as a means of interfering with the draft, not because the protesters have no desire to interfere with the draft, but because it has seemed obvious that the destruction of an individual's draft card could have no tangible obstructive effect. Moreover, the symbolic meaning of the burnings was not lost on members of Congress. What emerges with indisputable clarity from an examination of the legislative history of the amendment is that the intent of its framers was purely and simply to put a stop to this particular form of antiwar protest, which they deemed extraordinarily contemptible and vicious—even treasonous—at a time when American troops were engaged in combat. Selective Service officials had not expressed a need for the legislation. There is no evidence to be found in the legislative history that destruction of draft cards had created, or appeared likely to create, a problem in the administration of the draft laws. The ability of draft boards to perform their functions was, so far as Congress knew, entirely unimpaired. The three speakers in favor of passage all emphasized a single objective, to stop so brazen a display of lack of patriotism.[56]

While the proponents of the amendment on the floor and the reports of the committees recommending enactment occasionally used phrases indicating that destruction of draft cards could deal Selective Service a "serious blow," or that it "represents a potential threat to the exercise of the power to raise and support armies," or poses "a grave threat to the security of the Nation," no explanation was ever given of how card destruction, per se, presented such a threat.[57] Although the Court found the suggestion of proper legislative purpose contained in the committee reports to be so significant that it reproduced the few relevant sentences from these reports in an appendix to its opinion, the complete absence from both reports of any specific statement explaining the need for this legislation is striking.

On the basis of this legislative history, it is not open to doubt that the attitude of defiance manifested in the draft-card burnings was

---

[56] See note 20 *supra*.

[57] See notes 19 and 20 *supra*.

what represented the threat seen by Congress, and that the infuriating offensiveness of this mode of dissent was what drove Congress to prohibit it. Which is to say that Congress was engaged in the abridgment of speech when it enacted the amendment, that O'Brien's First Amendment claims were not frivolous, and that these claims were entitled to more serious consideration than they were given by the Court, despite the hatefulness of the ideas expressed or the infuriating offensiveness of the manner of their expression.[58] It is one thing for the Court to recognize manifest facts and to reject them as lacking legal or constitutional significance. It is quite another for it to blink the facts or to suggest that they do not exist. It is because the Court deliberately chose the latter course that its opinion is unpersuasive. Chief Justice Taft once suggested that it was poor policy for the Court to profess ignorance of matters which "[a]ll others can see and understand,"[59] and, while the decision in which this observation was made is no longer greatly revered, the wisdom of the observation has not diminished.[60]

On the other hand, it is far less clear that the result arrived at by the Court was wrong. For while O'Brien's First Amendment claims were not lacking in substance, other factors were also

58 "[A] function of free speech under our system of government is to invite dispute. It may indeed best serve its high purpose when it induces a condition of unrest, creates dissatisfaction with conditions as they are, or even stirs people to anger. Speech is often provocative and challenging. It may strike at prejudices and preconceptions and have profound unsettling effects as it presses for acceptance of an idea. That is why freedom of speech, though not absolute, . . . is nevertheless protected against censorship or punishment, unless shown likely to produce a clear and present danger of a serious substantive evil that rises far above public inconvenience, annoyance, or unrest. . . . There is no room under our Constitution for a more restrictive view. For the alternative would lead to standardization of ideas either by legislatures, courts, or dominant political or community groups." Terminiello v. Chicago, 337 U.S. 1, 4–5 (1949).

59 Bailey v. Drexel Furniture Co. (Child Labor Tax Case), 259 U.S. 20, 37 (1922). See text *infra*, at notes 108–09.

60 Even an advocate of judicial self-restraint as resolute as Justice Frankfurter was moved to refer approvingly to Chief Justice Taft's admonition. In United States v. Rumely, 345 U.S. 41, 44 (1953), writing the majority opinion in a decision reversing a conviction for contempt of Congress of a witness who refused to answer questions asked by a congressional committee, Frankfurter declared: "And so, we would have to be that 'blind' Court, against which Mr. Chief Justice Taft admonished in a famous passage . . . that does not see what '[a]ll others can see and understand' not to know that there is wide concern, both in and out of Congress, over some aspects of the exercise of the congressional power of investigation." *Cf.* Jacobson v. Massachusetts, 197 U.S. 11, 30 (1905) (per Harlan, J.): "What everybody knows the court must know. . . ."

present that served to lessen their force. In the first place, the extent of the abridgment of speech imposed by the draft law amendment is small. The amendment does not forbid the expression of opposition to the war or contempt for military conscription. It forbids only dramatizing dissent by destroying or mutilating a draft card, and, as Mr. Justice Harlan pointed out in his concurrence, "O'Brien manifestly could have conveyed his message in many ways other than by burning his draft card."[61] Second, the law is a limitation of conduct, and conduct that may legitimately be prohibited normally may not be engaged in with impunity just because it also serves as a form of expression. The destruction of draft cards would appear to be legitimately prohibitable conduct. The inventory of potential uses of draft cards provided in the opinion of the Court[62] does not suggest that the cards are vital, but it does suggest that there are advantages of convenience in having them readily available, and Congress may properly legislate to forbid acts that are administratively inconvenient. Finally, in one important sense, the amendment is not an abridgment of speech at all. It does no more than prohibit action that was already effectively prohibited under existing federal law and does not even increase the maximum permissible punishment. Burning one's draft card, whether or not for purposes of expression, necessarily entails, in most circumstances, a concomitant violation of the nonpossession regulations. Those regulations were promulgated long before, were clearly not the product of improper motivation, and attest the existence of a legitimate interest in the preservation of draft cards.

B. FREE SPEECH AND NARROW STATUTES

The Court, however, made no use of its opportunity to contribute to the development of meaningful First Amendment doctrine. It skirted the First Amendment issues almost completely, even though the case plainly invited judicial examination of the question of the extent to which expression by conduct rather than utterance is protected by the First Amendment, or, conversely, the extent to which governments are free from the limitations of

---

[61] 391 U.S. at 389. For a vigorous argument that since draft-card burning receives much more publicity than mere verbal statements of opposition to the war, its suppression prevents dissenters from making their views known to a wider audience and is thus much more than a minimal abridgment of speech, see Velvel, note 10 *supra*, at 152–53, 166 n. 74.

[62] 391 U.S. at 378–80. See note 44 *supra*, and text *infra*, at note 147.

the First Amendment in suppressing expression that takes the form of symbolic conduct. The Court's discussion of this issue was brief and, at best, superficial. Speech that takes the form of conduct, it declared, may be suppressed if the legislation prohibiting the conduct meets a four-part test.[63] The most remarkable feature of the test is that, although its purported use was to determine the constitutionality of a statute as applied, all four of its parts relate solely to the face of the law that is to be tested and not to its application.

It seems clear that First Amendment cases involving statutes that regulate conduct and are not invalid on their face can hardly be satisfactorily decided by means of a formula that makes it unnecessary to evaluate the impact upon speech of a particular application of the challenged statute, the importance of the public interest that the statute protects, or the danger to that interest presented by the conduct that is being suppressed.[64] The Court's test requires a consideration of none of these factors. Simply stated, the test is this: If the governmental interest is real, apparently unrelated to the suppression of speech, and related to a proper subject of legislative concern, all applications of a statute that protects this interest are constitutional if the statute itself is sufficiently narrowly drawn so that "the incidental restriction on alleged First Amendment freedom is no greater than is essential to the furtherance of that interest."[65]

The crucial factor in the Court's test is plainly the narrowness of the statute. If the statute is narrowly drawn, and is not on its face concerned with speech, courts are excused from the task of examining the degree of abridgment of expression that may be brought about by a particular application. In a sense, such a rule is the other side of the coin from the Court's repeated insistence that statutes having the effect of restricting speech in order to secure other social interests must not be vague or overbroad. "Be-

---

[63] See text *supra*, at note 41.

[64] With regard to the question of the applicability of the First Amendment as a protection of the conduct of civil rights demonstrators, Ira Michael Heyman has written: "Simplistic analyses supporting either the protestants or law and order are insufficient. Hard questions in a variety of factual situations must be answered. Sweeping statements avoid the hard questions and only exacerbate already emotion-laden issues." Heyman, *Civil Rights 1964 Term: Responses to Direct Action*, 1965 SUPREME COURT REVIEW 159, 186.

[65] 391 U.S. at 377.

cause First Amendment freedoms need breathing space to survive," the Court has said, "government may regulate in the area only with narrow specificity,"[66] and the constitutional requirement of narrowness has become the Court's most potent weapon in protecting freedom of expression against governmental incursion.[67] But simply because overbroad statutes affecting speech are unconstitutional, it does not follow that narrow and specific statutes that limit speech only indirectly are valid as applied in all cases. It is certainly true that a narrow statute specifically aimed at protecting a recognizable social interest and reflecting a precise legislative judgment that certain clearly defined conduct would endanger that interest is entitled to a considerable degree of judicial deference. As Justice Roberts stated in *Cantwell v. Connecticut* in 1940: "Violation of an Act exhibiting such a legislative judgment and narrowly drawn to prevent the supposed evil, would pose a question differing from that we must here answer. Such a declaration of the State's policy would weigh heavily in any challenge of the law as infringing constitutional limitations."[68] But while this factor properly "would weigh heavily" on the judicial scales, it need not foreclose all other considerations, and it is noteworthy that Justice Roberts was careful not to indicate that it would.

Cox v. Louisiana[69] had made clear the doctrine of the Court. The narrowness of a statute proscribing conduct would insulate it from constitutional challenge on the ground that its application in an individual instance would abridge freedom of expression. In *Cox* the Court, ironically, reversed a conviction under a state law specifically forbidding picketing near a courthouse because it found this demonstration to have been authorized by the police despite the law.[70] The "clear and present danger" approach,

[66] NAACP v. Button, 371 U.S. 415, 433 (1963).

[67] For a discussion of the Court's use of this technique, see Amsterdam, *The Void-for-Vagueness Doctrine in the Supreme Court*, 109 U. PA. L. REV. 67, 75–85, 98–115 (1960). Recently, the doctrine has been most significantly employed in cases involving loyalty oaths, see cases cited note 6 *supra;* freedom of association, see United States v. Robel, 389 U.S. 258 (1967); NAACP v. Button, 371 U.S. 415 (1963); Shelton v. Tucker, 364 U.S. 479 (1960); and the rights of civil rights demonstrators, see Cox v. Louisiana, 379 U.S. 536 (1965); Edwards v. South Carolina, 372 U.S. 229 (1963).

[68] 310 U.S. 296, 307–08 (1940).

[69] 379 U.S. 559 (1965).

[70] This led the dissenters to inquire how it was that police officers could authorize a violation of a valid criminal statute and thereby protect the violator from prosecu-

which would have allowed the Court to invalidate applications of this law where it appeared that barring the picketing would represent an abridgment of freedom of expression greater than the threat to the administration of justice posed by picketing in a particular instance, was held by the Court to have no applicability even though it was the test generally applied in instances where courts have punished, as contempt, utterances believed to endanger the fairness of judicial proceedings.[71] Speaking for the majority, Justice Goldberg wrote:[72]

> Here we deal not with the contempt power but with a narrowly drafted statute and not with speech in its pristine form but with conduct of a totally different character. Even assuming the applicability of a general clear and present danger test, it is one thing to conclude that the mere publication of a newspaper editorial or a telegram to a Secretary of Labor, however critical of a court, presents no clear and present danger to the administration of justice and quite another thing to conclude that crowds, such as this, demonstrating before a courthouse may not be prohibited by a legislative determination based on experience that such conduct inherently threatens the judicial process.

Of course, the Court's position in *Cox* is not entirely clear. Justice Goldberg rejected the "clear and present danger" test because the legislature had embodied in a narrow statute its rational judgment that a crowd demonstrating in front of a courthouse was inherently dangerous. But would this judgment be considered equally rational, and the "clear and present danger" test equally inapplicable, if, instead of a demonstrating crowd of Negroes protesting racial discrimination in law enforcement, a single picket had been assigned to stand across the street from the courthouse in a silent vigil of symbolic protest against the alleged deprivation of the civil rights of defendants awaiting trial? The single picket, like the demonstrators in the crowd, would have violated the

---

tion. In Mr. Justice Black's words: "I fail to understand how the Court can justify the reversal of this conviction because of a permission . . . which could not have been authoritatively given. . . ." *Id.* at 582–83. See also the dissent of Mr. Justice Clark. *Id.* at 588–89.

71 See Wood v. Georgia, 370 U.S. 375 (1962); Craig v. Harney, 331 U.S. 367 (1947); Pennekamp v. Florida, 328 U.S. 331 (1946); Bridges v. California, 314 U.S. 252 (1941).

72 379 U.S. at 566.

narrow Louisiana law.[73] But it is not at all certain that the First Amendment objections he might raise in challenging his conviction under this law could be satisfactorily disposed of by simple reference to the fact that the statute was narrowly drawn and prohibits only specifically defined conduct.[74] Moreover, even with regard to crowds, it must be recognized, as Professor Harry Kalven has noted, that "not every group of people on the streets is 'a mob,' "[75] and that the right to demonstrate peacefully may be an important aspect of freedom of expression[76]—perhaps too im-

[73] "Whoever, with the intent of interfering with, obstructing, or impeding the administration of justice, or with the intent of influencing any judge, juror, witness, or court officer, in the discharge of his duty pickets or parades in or near a building housing a court of the State of Louisiana . . . shall be fined not more than five thousand dollars or imprisoned not more than one year, or both." LA. REV. STAT. § 14:101 (Cum. Supp. 1962).

[74] This, of course, points up one of the principal difficulties in the Court's insistence upon narrowness in statutes touching on First Amendment rights. Narrowness, like vagueness, is a vague concept, and the doctrine is, therefore, almost infinitely manipulatable. If the Court finds the general aims of a challenged statute to be worthy or important, it can ignore a certain amount of carelessness in drafting. If, on the other hand, it is less sympathetic, it can demand extreme specificity. Thus, in *Cox*, the Court could have held that the state law (note 73 *supra*) was overbroad because it did not narrowly prohibit only that type of picketing that presented a danger to the administration of justice because of its loudness, disorderliness, or the number of picketers participating, but, instead, unnecessarily abridged freedom of expression by prohibiting all picketing near a courthouse. But that would have been a churlish way to treat a state law that was an exact copy of a federal statute (18 U.S.C. § 1507), drafted and enacted at the behest of the Judicial Conference of the United States. See 379 U.S. at 561. An example of a demand for specificity carried to the point of ludicrousness is Talley v. California, 362 U.S. 60 (1960). Even the amendment to the draft law that was before the Court in *O'Brien* could, had the Court desired, have been treated as overbroad, despite its apparent specificity. It is not limited to draft-card destruction which might impair the efficiency of the Selective Service System but forbids all draft-card destruction, even that which is intended to be expressive and which can in no way adversely affect the administration of the draft. For example, in 1966, a number of new enlistees, who are required by regulation to surrender their draft cards upon entry into active duty, burned them in the presence of their enlisting officer as an expression of patriotism. N.Y. Times, Feb. 5, 1966, p. 31. Although both the regulation pertaining to the Registration Certificate (32 CFR § 1617.1) and the regulation pertaining to the Notice of Classification (32 CFR § 1623.5) expressly authorize destruction of these cards by enlisting officers when they are turned in, the literal language of the amendment clearly forbids such action. If this type of destruction is not punishable under the amendment, the amendment is patently vague.

[75] Kalven, *The Concept of the Public Forum: Cox v. Louisiana*, 1965 SUPREME COURT REVIEW 1, 32.

[76] *Id.* at 30.

portant to allow it to be sacrificed in all cases to a narrow statute.[77] It is likely that the warning offered by Justice Jackson a quarter of a century ago—that the Court was making too much of the distinction between broad and narrow laws in civil liberties cases—still retains its relevance:[78]

> I had supposed that our question, except in respect to ordinances invalid on their face, is always whether the ordinance as applied denies constitutional rights. Nothing in the Constitution says or implies that real rights are more vulnerable to a narrow ordinance than to a broad one.

C. SYMBOLIC CONDUCT AND THE FIRST AMENDMENT

One of the ingredients of constitutionality in the Court's test is that the governmental interest protected by the statute must be "unrelated to the suppression of free expression."[79] If the government's interest is related to curbing expression, as in a law such as the Smith Act prohibiting the advocacy of particular ideas,[80] or curbing the distribution of particular publications,[81] or forbidding certain types of meetings,[82] the narrowness of the statute would presumably not be enough to insure its constitutionality as applied. If the government's interest is related, however, not to speech but to conduct that is within the reach of its regulatory power, the Court's test would not, given a narrowly drawn statute, leave room for a comparison of the importance of the conduct as a means of expression with the danger to be apprehended from the conduct in an individual instance.

---

77 In Edwards v. South Carolina, 372 U.S. 229 (1963), as Professor Kalven has pointed out note 75 *supra,* at 7, the Court described a peaceful demonstration in front of a legislative hall as "an exercise of these basic constitutional right [of speech, assembly, and petition] in their most pristine and classic form." 372 U.S. at 235. Yet demonstrations in front of a legislature may endanger the integrity of the legislative process to as great an extent as demonstrations in front of a courthouse endanger the integrity of the judicial process. Could these also be prohibited by a narrowly drawn statute aimed at the conduct determined by the legislature to be dangerous, and, if so, would all applications of this statute be constitutional even though it restricts the classic form of exercise of basic constitutional rights?

78 Douglas v. Jeannette, 319 U.S. 157, 175–76 (1943).

79 391 U.S. at 377.

80 See Dennis v. United States, 341 U.S. 494 (1951); Gitlow v. New York, 268 U.S. 652 (1925).

81 See Near v. Minnesota, 283 U.S. 697 (1931); Roth v. United States, 354 U.S. 476 (1957).

82 See Hague v. CIO, 307 U.S. 496 (1939).

Expressive conduct, the Court pointed out, has long been held to be subject to regulation where there is a sufficient public interest in limiting the conduct. The Court's test was put forward as a means of determining whether the government's interest could properly be described by one of the terms found in the relevant precedents, where, it was held, such interest had to be "compelling," "substantial," "subordinating," "paramount," "cogent," or "strong."[83] These are emphatic adjectives, and manifestly the only reason for requiring the interest to be of sufficient magnitude to warrant its description in such terms is that it must be great enough to override a competing interest—in this case the value of the conduct as a means of exercising a First Amendment freedom. If there were no competing interest against which it was to be measured, surely a slight government interest would be enough to justify regulation or prohibition of the conduct. Yet the absence of any attempt at comparison in the Court's opinion is striking. The Court was content to demonstrate that the government's interest in preventing the destruction of draft cards is real, that is, not imaginary or nonexistent. But an interest may well be real without being important enough to sustain an abridgment of speech. It is true that the Court used the adjective "substantial" (or the adverb "substantially") to describe the government's interest no less than seven times in this part of its opinion.[84] (The modifier appears essentially every time reference is made to the existence of a governmental interest that would support the draft law amendment.) But the Court's own inventory of possible draft-card uses[85] indicates that both the Registration Certificate and the Notice of Classification serve functions of dispensable convenience rather than urgent necessity. The Court's use of "substantial," therefore, is more appropriate if the term is understood in its sense of "having substance" or "not imaginary," rather than the sense of "considerable" or "large."

The conclusion of the Court that "a sufficient governmental interest has been shown to justify O'Brien's conviction"[86] is explicitly based on the ground that since the draft law amendment forbids a particular type of conduct that is not necessarily expressive, and since O'Brien engaged in that conduct, all First Amendment con-

83 See text *supra*, at note 39.

84 391 U.S. at 376–82.

85 *Id.* at 378–80. *Cf.* Velvel, note 10 *supra*, at 163–66.

86 391 U.S. at 382.

siderations may be set aside as irrelevant, and the magnitude of the government's interest in the amendment need not be measured against any countervailing interest. Conduct and speech are thus treated as discrete and entirely separable entities. Such a conceptual division may facilitate reasoning, but it fails altogether to correspond with reality. Moreover, it fails to square with several decisions of the Court that have conceded the expressive quality of certain forms of symbolic conduct, such as picketing,[87] saluting (or not saluting) flags,[88] and "sit-ins."[89] It has been noted that symbolic conduct is "speech plus" and thus is not entitled to the same degree of constitutional protection as "pure speech,"[90] but to quote once more from Harry Kalven, "all speech is necessarily 'speech plus.' If it is oral, it is noise and may interrupt someone else; if it is written, it may be litter."[91] Perhaps the most persuasive statement of the possible interrelationship of speech and conduct was that of Mr. Justice Harlan, pointing out in his concurring opinion in *Garner v. Louisiana* why "sit-in" demonstrations merited the protection of the First Amendment:[92]

> There was more to the conduct of those petitioners than a bare desire to remain at the "white" lunch counter and their refusal of a police request to move from the counter. We would surely have to be blind not to recognize that petitioners were sitting at these counters, where they knew they would not be served, in order to demonstrate that their race was being segregated in dining facilities in this part of the country.
>
> Such a demonstration, in the circumstances of these two cases, is as much a part of the "free trade in ideas" . . . as is

[87] Thornhill v. Alabama, 310 U.S. 88 (1940).

[88] West Virginia State Board of Education v. Barnette, 319 U.S. 624 (1943); Stromberg v. California, 283 U.S. 359 (1931).

[89] Brown v. Louisiana, 383 U.S. 131 (1966). In *Brown*, Mr. Justice Fortas stated that First Amendment rights "are not confined to verbal expression. They embrace appropriate types of action which certainly include the right in a peaceable and orderly manner to protest by silent and reproachful presence, in a place where the protestant has every right to be, the unconstitutional segregation of public facilities." *Id.* at 141–42.

[90] See, *e.g.*, with regard to picketing, Giboney v. Empire Storage & Ice Co., 336 U.S. 490 (1949); Carpenters & Joiners Union v. Ritter's Cafe, 315 U.S. 722 (1942); Milk Wagon Drivers Union v. Meadowmoor Dairies, 312 U.S. 287 (1941); with regard to "sit-ins" or other demonstrations, Cox v. Louisiana, note 69 *supra;* Adderley v. Florida, 385 U.S. 39 (1966).

[91] Kalven, note 75 *supra,* at 23.

[92] 368 U.S. 157, 201–02 (1961) (concurring opinion).

> verbal expression, more commonly thought of as "speech." It, like speech, appeals to good sense and to "the power of reason as applied through public discussion" . . . just as much as, if not more than, a public oration delivered from a soapbox at a street corner. This Court has never limited the right to speak, a protected "liberty" under the Fourteenth Amendment, . . . to mere verbal expression. . . . If the act of displaying a red flag as a symbol of opposition to organized government is a liberty encompassed within free speech as protected by the Fourteenth Amendment, . . . the act of sitting at a privately owned lunch counter with the consent of the owner, as a demonstration of opposition to enforced segregation, is surely within the same range of protections.

To paraphrase Mr. Justice Harlan, the Court would surely have had to be blind not to recognize that there was more to O'Brien's conduct than a bare desire to destroy a Selective Service certificate. He was burning his draft card to demonstrate that the war in Vietnam was, in his view, immoral, and this conduct was undertaken as a part of the "free trade in ideas"[93] and as an appeal to good sense and to "the power of reason as applied through public discussion."[94] His conduct, therefore, was within the range of the First Amendment's protections.

Manifestly, however, the expression of ideas through symbolic conduct must be subject to regulation or prohibition. Just as the First Amendment guarantee of the free exercise of religion does not allow freedom for the commission of socially harmful acts on the ground that commission of these acts is a religious duty,[95] the commission of socially harmful acts in the name of freedom of expression is also not to be tolerated. The effect of the First Amendment in this area, therefore, could only be to limit the capacity of government to prohibit symbolic conduct wherever it would appear that the conduct in question is not likely to cause a harm greater than the abridgment of freedom of expression that would result from its prohibition.[96] Again, resolution of the question must turn

---

[93] The phrase is from Abrams v. United States, 250 U.S. 616, 630 (1919) (Holmes, J., dissenting).

[94] The phrase is from Whitney v. California, 274 U.S. 357, 375 (1927) (Brandeis, J., concurring).

[95] See FELLMAN, RELIGION IN AMERICAN PUBLIC LAW 13–42 (1965). The leading case is Reynolds v. United States, 98 U.S. 145 (1878).

[96] The decision that probably demonstrates most clearly the requirements of this approach is a case that involved conduct as a religious duty rather than conduct as

on a comparison, or balancing, of the competing interests—and this is precisely what the Supreme Court avoided.

In this respect, the Court's approach differs sharply from that of both the First and the Second Circuit, for, while the courts of appeals reached conflicting conclusions, both sought to weigh the importance of the government's interest against the impact of the draft law amendment on freedom of speech. The Second Circuit, in affirming Miller's conviction, concluded simply that both certificates issued to draft registrants serve legitimate purposes in furthering the administration of Selective Service. Although the court did not attempt to describe the importance of the cards as "substantial," it did hold that the interest was adequate to sustain the constitutionality of the amendment because the degree of abridgment of freedom of speech represented by a ban on the destruction of draft cards was so slight, given the fact that the ordinary means of expressing dissent were unaffected.[97] The First Circuit, on the other hand, did not argue that the amendment constituted a major abridgment of speech. Instead, it struck down the amendment because it could find no legitimate purpose it could serve that was not already fulfilled by the nonpossession regulations and, therefore, concluded that its only purpose was the unconstitutional suppression of symbolic dissent.[98]

---

a symbol of expression: Prince v. Massachusetts, 321 U.S. 158 (1944). There the Court upheld, by the narrow margin of 5 to 4, provisions of the state child labor laws prohibiting children from selling newspapers, periodicals, or other items on the streets, and prohibiting also the employment of children for such purposes, as applied to the selling of religious literature by a nine-year-old girl who was accompanied by her aunt and guardian, and who, as a member of the Jehovah's Witnesses, believed it to be her religious duty to attempt to sell the publications of the sect. Over a vigorous dissent by Mr. Justice Murphy, who argued that the harm that was realistically to be apprehended as a result of this type of street selling was not great enough to justify the limitation on freedom of religion, the Court, through Mr. Justice Rutledge, concluded that the child labor laws served such a vital function, and the potential harms to the children from failure to observe them were so great, that the slight abridgment of freedom of religion caused by the enforcement of these laws in this case was constitutionally warranted.

[97] 367 F.2d at 81. To the argument that the real limiting effect of the amendment was its denial to the antiwar protester of the most efficacious means of communicating his ideas, the Second Circuit responded by reference to Kovacs v. Cooper, 336 U.S. 77, 88–89 (1949), where the Supreme Court held that even though sound trucks represented one of the easiest and cheapest ways of communicating with the public, the valid interest in curbing the noise of these devices was sufficiently great that a limitation on this means of expression was not unconstitutional as long as other means were so easily available.

[98] 376 F.2d at 540–41.

In view of the fact that the amendment does not punish dissent per se, but merely forbids one very specific means of conveying the expression of dissent, it cannot seriously be contended that the amendment's effect upon speech is anything but minor. Certainly draft-card burning is dramatic and very effective in attracting public attention. Nevertheless, as long as there remain undisturbed the traditional modes of voicing opposition to the war, including such attention-gathering techniques as rallies and parades, the mere prohibition of the destruction or mutilation of draft cards would not appear to make significant inroads on freedom of speech. The amendment, therefore, would be constitutionally justifiable if it served a governmental purpose of measurable utility. But, because the amendment does unquestionably impose some limitation on expression, the importance of the government's interest must be more than barely minimal. The factor in the equation which needs to be determined is the magnitude of the government's interest.

If one accepts at face value, as did both the Court and the Second Circuit, the reasons suggested by the government why the prohibition of draft-card burning would assist the administration of the Selective Service System, and if, at the same time, one suspends awareness that this is a rationalization conceived after the fact of enactment rather than a statement of the considerations underlying the amendment's passage, the judgment that the law is constitutional follows almost automatically. If, however, the legislative history is examined and the all but inescapable conclusion drawn therefrom that the motivating purpose of the congressional action was suppression, the case becomes much more difficult. Resolution of the case, consequently, requires reconsideration of one of the oldest of the traditional judicial taboos—that courts must never attempt to adjudge the motives of the legislature in assessing the constitutionality of a statute.

D. LEGISLATIVE MOTIVES AND THE CONSTITUTIONALITY OF STATUTES

As early as 1810, in *Fletcher v. Peck*,[99] John Marshall declined to examine legislative motives, even in the face of the grave allegation that the legislators who voted in favor of an act were induced to do so by outright bribery. "[I]f the act be clothed with all the requisite forms of a law," he declared, "a court, sitting as a court of law, cannot sustain a suit brought by one individual against

[99] 6 Cranch 87 (1810).

another founded on the allegation that the act is a nullity, in consequence of the impure motives which influenced certain members of the legislature which passed the law."[100] The issue became significant in American constitutional law, however, in the period of "dual federalism"[101] when the Tenth Amendment was looked upon as a limitation on congressional power, and when it was frequently urged that congressional action purportedly taken under one of the delegated powers was unconstitutional because the real purpose of Congress was the indirect exercise of a power not delegated to it and thus reserved to the states. The issue could be skirted, of course, as the Court generally did in commerce cases. For example, in *Hammer v. Dagenhart*,[102] although the Court held the child labor act of 1916 unconstitutional as an invasion of an area of state responsibility rather than a valid exercise of the commerce power, it based its holding on the "necessary effect"[103] of the statute and specifically disclaimed any power to scrutinize the motives of the legislature.[104] But the use of the federal taxing power to regulate intrastate activities brought the issue to the fore.

In 1904, in *McCray v. United States*,[105] the Court upheld a federal tax of 10 cents a pound on oleomargarine artificially colored to

---

100 *Id.* at 131. It may be noted that Marshall did not state that legislative motives may never be inquired into, but merely that it could not be done collaterally in the course of a suit between private individuals. Earlier in his opinion, he pointed out that whether legislative motivation was at all a proper subject for judicial scrutiny was a matter that needed to be approached "with much circumspection," for it would involve a myriad of difficult questions including how many members of the legislature would have to be shown to have acted improperly, and what degree of impropriety would be necessary to nullify the act. *Id.* at 130.

101 See Corwin, *The Passing of Dual Federalism*, 36 VA. L. REV. 1 (1950).

102 247 U.S. 251 (1918).

103 *Cf.* the Court's insistence in *O'Brien* that Grosjean v. American Press Co., 297 U.S. 233 (1936), and Gomillion v. Lightfoot, 364 U.S. 339 (1960), were both based on an assessment of the "inevitable effect" of the challenged statute rather than the legislative purpose. 391 U.S. at 384. See text *infra* at note 121.

104 247 U.S. at 276. The Court could fall back on the doctrine that legislative motives were not to be examined if it ruled that a particular exercise of the commerce power was valid. In Weber v. Freed, 239 U.S. 325 (1915), for example, the Court declared "frivolous" a challenge on Tenth Amendment grounds to an act of Congress forbidding the importation into the United States of prizefight films. It was argued that the real purpose of the law was to forbid local exhibition of these films, but the Court declared that "the proposition plainly is wanting in merit, since it rests upon the erroneous assumption that the motive of Congress in exerting its plenary power may be taken into view for the purpose of refusing to give effect to such power when exercised." *Id.* at 330.

105 195 U.S. 27 (1904).

look like butter. (If not so colored, the tax was to be one-quarter of a cent per pound.) Although the manifest purpose of the act was to discourage the manufacture of colored oleomargarine, the Court held the tax to be, on its face, a valid revenue measure and expressly and emphatically denied that "the motives or purposes of Congress are open to judicial inquiry in considering the power of that body to enact the laws in question."[106] In *United States v. Doremus*, in 1919, the Court, on the same grounds, upheld federal regulations on the sale of narcotics that were effectuated by means of a one-dollar annual tax imposed on persons dealing in narcotics, and by a requirement that all sales (except as prescribed by a physician) be accomplished through a written order on a form to be provided by the Commissioner of Internal Revenue."[107] When Congress attempted to use the taxing power to control conditions of child labor by placing a heavy excise on goods produced without compliance with standards specified in the act for the employment of children, however, the Court, through Chief Justice Taft, balked.[108] The *McCray* and *Doremus* precedents made it difficult for the Court to take the course adopted in *Hammer v. Dagenhart*, and to declare the law invalid because its "necessary effect" was to invade the area reserved to the states. A more direct approach was required, and, in a memorable passage, the Chief Justice took it:[109]

> In the light of these features of the act, a court must be blind not to see that the so-called tax is imposed to stop the employment of children within the age limits prescribed. Its prohibitory and regulatory effect and purpose are palpable. All others can see and understand this. How can we properly shut our minds to it?

The Child Labor Tax Act was invalid, in Taft's view, because Congress had enacted it not for the purpose of raising revenue, but for the purpose of regulating labor standards, a matter which, under the Tenth Amendment, was "an exclusively state function." The soundness of the conclusion regarding congressional intent is not open to question. The soundness of the decision, on the other

106 *Id.* at 53.

107 249 U.S. 86 (1919). Interestingly, Chief Justice White, who wrote the Court's opinion in *McCray*, was one of four Justices who dissented. He stated laconically that the narcotics law was "beyond the constitutional power of Congress to enact because to such extent the statute was a mere attempt by Congress to exert a power not delegated, that is, the reserved police power of the states." *Id.* at 95.

108 Bailey v. Drexel Furniture Co., 259 U.S. 20 (1922).

109 *Id.* at 37.

hand, is indeed questionable, because the Tenth Amendment is not now looked upon as in any sense a limitation on the powers of Congress.[110] It is not because the Court misread the motives of Congress that its opinion is no longer persuasive, or because legislative motives are necessarily irrelevant to questions of constitutionality, but because the particular motive ascribed to Congress, although accurate, could not be a basis for invalidating the law.[111] The simple fact is that Congress is no longer constitutionally forbidden to use its powers to accomplish ends that are normally within the range of state concern.[112]

Insofar as the *Child Labor Tax Case* retained any precedential value at all, it did so only during the period that the Tenth Amendment was used as a basis for invalidating acts of Congress.[113] When, in 1953, in *United States v. Kahriger*, the Court was faced with a challenge to the constitutionality of the federal occupational tax on bookmakers, it sustained the tax, pointing out that "it was hard to understand why" the taxing power should be any more limited than the other powers of Congress by the fact that its exercise might indirectly affect matters which are normally of state concern.[114]

---

110 United States v. Darby Lumber Co., 312 U.S. 100 (1941).

111 But *cf.* the somewhat different analysis in the dissenting opinion of Justice Frankfurter in United States v. Kahriger, 345 U.S. 22, 37–38 (1953).

112 See Heart of Atlanta Motel v. United States, 379 U.S. 241 (1964); Katzenbach v. McClung, 379 U.S. 294 (1964).

113 See Hill v. Wallace, 259 U.S. 44 (1922), decided the same day as *Bailey*, which relied on that case in invalidating, as a regulatory rather than a revenue measure, a heavy tax on sales of grain futures not made through boards of trade approved by the Secretary of Agriculture. In United States v. Constantine, 296 U.S. 287 (1935), a federal excise tax of $1,000 on retail liquor dealers whose business was being carried on in violation of state law was struck down on the ground that it was not a revenue measure but a penalty for violating state law and that the latter purpose could not constitutionally be achieved by Congress in light of the Tenth Amendment. *Cf.* Sonzinsky v. United States, 300 U.S. 506 (1937), upholding a federal excise tax on sawed-off shotguns, machine guns, mufflers, and silencers, in which Justice Stone stated: "Inquiry into the hidden motives which may move Congress to exercise a power constitutionally conferred upon it is beyond the competency of courts." *Id.* at 513–14.

114 345 U.S. 22, 29–31 (1953). The *Kahriger* decision was overruled in Marchetti v. United States, 390 U.S. 39 (1968), which held that the requirement to register and to pay the occupational tax violated the Fifth Amendment privilege against compulsory self-incrimination. The Court specifically noted in *Marchetti* that its decision was not intended to affect the vitality of the precedents that held that such taxes were, in the absence of questions concerning self-incrimination, within the reach of the federal taxing power.

Nevertheless, the *Child Labor Tax Case* remains a good example that legislative motives may sometimes be so clear that courts cannot mistake them. Given a situation in which the motive of the legislature is to attain a plainly unconstitutional end, the precedential value of that case as an approach to constitutional adjudication might profitably be restored.

If Congress is not forbidden to attain a particular end, the fact that it intends to attain it indirectly through the use of one of its delegated powers seems irrelevant, but where constitutional prohibitions are concerned, entirely different considerations prevail. It would be an unfortunate doctrine that a constitutionally forbidden purpose could be achieved without fear of judicial invalidation so long as it was accomplished by means of a statute that, on its face, was innocuous and appeared to be related to a matter of proper governmental concern. As a matter of fact, this is not a rule of constitutional law, for the United States Reports are rife with judicial declarations that legislatures cannot attain an invalid end in the guise of exercising a valid power. Such statements are not lacking in First Amendment cases. Most commonly they may be found in cases involving indirect restrictions upon the freedom of expression or association of unpopular groups.[115] The cases that provide the most frequent occasions for judicial assessment of legislative motivation, however, are those involving state restrictions on interstate commerce or claims of denial of the equal protection of the laws. In commerce cases, the Supreme Court openly examines legislative facts to insure that state laws assertedly necessary for the protection of health, safety, or welfare are not disguised attempts to obtain commercial advantages for local businesses.[116] In equal protection

[115] *E.g.*, Hague v. CIO, 307 U.S. 496, 515–16 (1939): "The privilege of a citizen of the United States to use the streets and parks for communication of views on national questions may be regulated in the interest of all; . . . but it must not, in the guise of regulation, be abridged or denied." Louisiana v. NAACP, 366 U.S. 293, 297 (1961): "[R]egulatory measures . . . , no matter how sophisticated, cannot be employed in purpose or in effect to stifle, penalize, or curb the exercise of First Amendment rights." NAACP v. Button, 371 U.S. at 438–39: "[I]t is no answer to the constitutional claims asserted by petitioner to say . . . that the purpose of these regulations was merely to insure high professional standards and not to curtail free expression. For a State may not, under the guise of prohibiting professional misconduct, ignore constitutional rights."

[116] See Alfange, *The Relevance of Legislative Facts in Constitutional Law*, 114 U. Pa. L. Rev. 637, 667–78 (1966), and the cases cited therein.

cases, since legislative classifications are invalid only if they do not relate to a proper public purpose, courts may be faced with the task of deciding, through evaluation of legislative motivation, whether a particular classification is supported by its relation to a valid public interest or whether it is unconstitutionally discriminatory.[117]

The Court has not, in any of these cases, announced that it has examined the motives of the legislature, discerned a nefarious intent, and is striking the law down to frustrate the evil scheme. Doctrines of overbreadth, balancing of interests, or of the "necessary effect" of the statute serve the purpose far more discreetly. What the cases do show, however, is that where the Court perceives a legislative interest in attaining a forbidden end, it may be more critical in its evaluation of a legislative declaration that the statute is needed to protect a valid public interest and less likely to permit the asserted interest to be used to sustain the constitutionality of the law.[118]

In *O'Brien*, it was urged on behalf of the defense that at least

---

[117] See Tussman & tenBroek, *The Equal Protection of the Laws*, 37 CALIF. L. REV. 341 (1949). While the authors express their disfavor of judicial attempts to search for legislative motives as a "hopeless" task requiring "the analysis or psychoanalysis of legislative behavior," *id.* at 359, they concede that in a very real sense "the prohibition against discriminatory legislation is a demand for purity of motive. It erects a constitutional barrier against legislative motives of hate, prejudice, vengeance, hostility, or alternatively, of favoritism, and partiality. The imposition of special burdens, the granting of special benefits, must always be justified. They can only be justified as being directed at the elimination of some social evil, the achievement of some public good. When and if the proscribed motives replace a concern for the public good as the 'purpose' of the law, there is a violation of the equal protection prohibition against discriminatory legislation." *Id.* at 358–59.

[118] Perhaps the clearest example of this approach in a First Amendment case is Bates v. Little Rock, 361 U.S. 516 (1960). There the Court struck down an amendment to a municipal tax ordinance requiring all organizations operating in the city to supply, among other items of information, a statement that would disclose the names of all its members and contributors. The ostensible purpose of this requirement was to prevent tax evasion, but it also gravely threatened the associational freedom of members of the NAACP in Little Rock, for public disclosure of the membership lists would have made possible economic and social reprisals against them. The Court conceded: "It cannot be questioned that the governmental purpose upon which the municipalities rely is a fundamental one." *Id.* at 524. But it quickly added: "But governmental action does not automatically become reasonably related to the achievement of a legitimate and substantial governmental purpose by mere assertion in the preamble of an ordinance." *Id.* at 525. Because the membership lists had not been shown to have particular relevance for the prevention of tax evasion, the asserted governmental purpose was held to be inadequate to justify the limitation of freedom of association that would result from the required disclosure.

two Supreme Court decisions—*Grosjean v. American Press Co.*[119] and *Gomillion v. Lightfoot*[120]—served as outstanding examples of cases in which exertions of unquestioned legislative powers in the form of statutes innocuous on their face had been struck down because improper legislative motivation had been recognized. The Court summarily rejected this contention, adopting as the explanation of both cases the reasoning employed in *Hammer v. Dagenhart* that the ground of invalidation was the "necessary effect" of the statute rather than the motives of the legislature.[121] This explanation, however, does not suffice in either case.

In *Grosjean*, the Court struck down as an abridgment of freedom of the press a Louisiana law imposing a gross receipts tax of 2 percent on the sale of advertising for newspapers with a circulation greater than 20,000 copies per week. The law was, the Court stated, "a deliberate and calculated device in the form of a tax to limit the circulation of information."[122] In *O'Brien* it was argued that this was nothing more than a holding affirming "the right of publications to be free from certain kinds of taxes."[123] But, in light of the fact that the same Court that had decided *Grosjean* dismissed, in the following year, for want of a substantial federal question, an appeal from a judgment of the Supreme Court of Arizona upholding the application to newspapers of a nondiscriminatory privilege tax of 1 percent on the gross income of businesses,[124] it is apparent that the Court did not consider newspapers constitutionally exempt from taxes on their gross income. What shines through the language of the *Grosjean* opinion, although never specifically mentioned, is the Court's awareness of a point that was common knowledge to those familiar with Louisiana politics and that was stressed in the argument for the publishers—that because the tax applied only to

---

119 297 U.S. 233 (1936).

120 364 U.S. 339 (1960).

121 See text *supra*, at note 103.

122 297 U.S. at 250.

123 391 U.S. at 384.

124 Giragi v. Moore, 301 U.S. 670 (1937). The state court decision was Giragi v. Moore, 49 Ariz. 74 (1937). For the Arizona Supreme Court there was no question but that *Grosjean* had been based on an evaluation of the motives of the Louisiana legislature. In its opinion it specifically distinguished *Grosjean* on the ground that the palpable purpose of the tax invalidated there was to penalize or drive out of business those newspapers opposed to the regime in power, whereas the Arizona tax was a simple revenue measure that was not intended to, and that did not, abridge the freedom of the press and that, therefore, was not violative of the federal constitution. The Supreme Court, without opinion, allowed this judgment to stand.

two Supreme Court decisions—*Grosjean v. American Press Co.*[119] and *Gomillion v. Lightfoot*[120]—served as outstanding examples of cases in which exertions of unquestioned legislative powers in the form of statutes innocuous on their face had been struck down because improper legislative motivation had been recognized. The Court summarily rejected this contention, adopting as the explanation of both cases the reasoning employed in *Hammer v. Dagenhart* that the ground of invalidation was the "necessary effect" of the statute rather than the motives of the legislature.[121] This explanation, however, does not suffice in either case.

In *Grosjean*, the Court struck down as an abridgment of freedom of the press a Louisiana law imposing a gross receipts tax of 2 percent on the sale of advertising for newspapers with a circulation greater than 20,000 copies per week. The law was, the Court stated, "a deliberate and calculated device in the form of a tax to limit the circulation of information."[122] In *O'Brien* it was argued that this was nothing more than a holding affirming "the right of publications to be free from certain kinds of taxes."[123] But, in light of the fact that the same Court that had decided *Grosjean* dismissed, in the following year, for want of a substantial federal question, an appeal from a judgment of the Supreme Court of Arizona upholding the application to newspapers of a nondiscriminatory privilege tax of 1 percent on the gross income of businesses,[124] it is apparent that the Court did not consider newspapers constitutionally exempt from taxes on their gross income. What shines through the language of the *Grosjean* opinion, although never specifically mentioned, is the Court's awareness of a point that was common knowledge to those familiar with Louisiana politics and that was stressed in the argument for the publishers—that because the tax applied only to

---

119 297 U.S. 233 (1936).

120 364 U.S. 339 (1960).

121 See text *supra*, at note 103.

122 297 U.S. at 250.

123 391 U.S. at 384.

124 Giragi v. Moore, 301 U.S. 670 (1937). The state court decision was Giragi v. Moore, 49 Ariz. 74 (1937). For the Arizona Supreme Court there was no question but that *Grosjean* had been based on an evaluation of the motives of the Louisiana legislature. In its opinion it specifically distinguished *Grosjean* on the ground that the palpable purpose of the tax invalidated there was to penalize or drive out of business those newspapers opposed to the regime in power, whereas the Arizona tax was a simple revenue measure that was not intended to, and that did not, abridge the freedom of the press and that, therefore, was not violative of the federal constitution. The Supreme Court, without opinion, allowed this judgment to stand.

by a state of a power that had been recognized as plenary,[129] and despite the fact that on its face this exercise of that power was no different from any other, the Court insisted that because it could be seen that the effect of this act was to abridge the right to vote on racial grounds, a judicial examination could be undertaken to determine whether the legislature had had any valid reasons for the realignment of the boundaries that would adequately explain its action and that would demonstrate that its motives were not improper. What the Court was being asked to do in *O'Brien* was essentially no different from what it had agreed to do in *Gomillion.*

"Motives" is, nevertheless, a harsh word. In a sense, it connotes more than "purpose," for it involves, in the case of free speech, for example, not only the question whether the legislature was concerned with suppressing the freedom of speech of an unpopular group but also the question why the legislature desired to suppress the speech of that group. It is when it is taken in this broad sense that the practice of judicial examination of motives has been most effectively criticized. Thus, in dissenting from a decision applying the *Child Labor Tax Case* to strike down as a regulatory rather than a proper revenue measure a federal tax on liquor dealers operating in violation of state law, Justice Cardozo declared:[130]

> The judgment of the court, if I interpret the reasoning aright, does not rest upon a ruling that Congress would have gone beyond its power if the purpose that it professed was the purpose truly cherished. The judgment of the court rests upon the ruling that another purpose, not professed, may be read beneath the surface, and by the purpose so imputed the statute is destroyed. Thus the process of psychoanalysis has spread to unaccustomed fields.

In the same vein, it has been vigorously argued that "[t]o become involved in the search for motives, in the analysis or psychoanalysis of legislative behavior, is a task any sensible mortal might shun in the easiest of circumstances."[131] And that "[l]egislative motive is at best a fictional concept, since the term implies that on a given issue dealt with statutorily, the legislature was possessed of some unanimous, collective, composite reason for action."[132]

---

129 See, *e.g.*, Hunter v. Pittsburgh, 207 U.S. 161 (1907).

130 United States v. Constantine, 296 U.S. at 298–99 (dissenting opinion).

131 Tussman & tenBroek, note 117 *supra*, at 359.

132 Howell, *Legislative Motive and Legislative Purpose in the Invalidation of a Civil Rights Statute*, 47 Va. L. Rev. 439, 449–50 (1961).

But in a more realistic sense, and the sense intended here, to speak of legislative motives is essentially nothing more than to speak of legislative purpose. Psychoanalytical considerations may be set aside.[133] The question that is to be answered by an examination of legislative motives is not why did the members of the legislature desire to accomplish those ends that the law will serve, but simply what end did they desire to accomplish–what need did they perceive that caused them to fashion a law to meet it? One would suppose that any lingering belief that the aim or policy or purpose of the legislature is never judicially discernible through the examination of legislative history could not have survived the critical analysis of James Landis.[134] As Justice Frankfurter has written: "Such hesitations and restraints are in limbo."[135] They are in limbo because, as he stated:[136]

> Legislation has an aim; it seeks to obviate some mischief, to supply an inadequacy, to effect a change of policy, to formulate a plan of government. That aim, that policy is not drawn, like nitrogen, out of the air; it is evinced in the language of the statute, as read in the light of other external manifestations of purpose.

Legislative purpose may be examined in order to assist in determining the constitutionality of a statute, as well as to aid in statutory construction. The basic problem that must be answered, however, by courts deciding the constitutionality of an enactment, such as the draft law amendment, which on its face is explainable in terms of a proper governmental interest but which may have the incidental effect of burdening expression, is whether the asserted interest is sufficiently great or sufficiently endangered to warrant the accompanying limitation on freedom of speech. Thus, the factor of crucial importance when legislative purpose is examined for constitutional reasons is the quantity of evidence available to the

---

133 See Frankfurter, *Some Reflections on the Reading of Statutes,* 47 COLUM. L. REV. 527, 538–39 (1947), where the phrase "legislative intent" is categorically rejected because of its "overtones of subjective design." In its stead, Mr. Justice Frankfurter employed "a less beclouding characterization," such as "purpose" or "policy."

134 Landis, *Statutes and the Sources of Law,* in HARVARD LEGAL ESSAYS 213 (1934); Landis, *A Note on "Statutory Interpretation,"* 43 HARV. L. REV. 886 (1930).

135 Frankfurter, note 133 *supra,* at 543.

136 *Id.* at 538–39.

legislature that the governmental interest to be served by the statute was actually in jeopardy and in need of legislative protection. Legislative history can serve this function admirably. If the need is great, the evidence of it should appear in the historical materials. The greater the evidence, the more justified the conclusion that the legislative motive, or purpose, was in fact the satisfaction of that need. The weaker the evidence, particularly in the face of legislative awareness that the law would impose a burden on an unpopular group, the more irresistible the conclusion that satisfaction of the asserted need was not the consideration that prompted the passage of the law. Surely the courts should be permitted to take either conclusion into account in arriving at a judgment on whether the government has demonstrated "a subordinating interest which is compelling."[137]

Courts are naturally and properly loath to ascribe unjust, discriminatory, or unconstitutional motives to a coordinate branch of government. But such ascription would not be necessary. It would be adequate to state that, where the application of the challenged statute would have a repressive effect upon the exercise of constitutional freedoms, and sufficient evidence does not appear that it is of such importance to the vindication of a valid public interest, its limitations of these freedoms is not justified.

The reasons for outright judicial refusal to consider legislative motivation as a factor in determining the constitutionality of a statute are not solidly grounded either on considerations of policy or of judicial capability. Especially in a situation in which "[a]ll others can see and understand" that the legislative motive was directed toward the achievement of an invalid goal, it would seem inadvisable for the Court to maintain a pretense of unawareness. Conscious refusal to admit cognizance of reality is no better a policy for courts than for any other agency of government. At the very least, heed should be given to the admonition of Justice Frankfurter, who, in *United States v. Kahriger*, declared, with regard to tax laws such as the federal occupational tax on gamblers there involved:[138]

> The motive of congressional legislation is not for our scrutiny, provided only that the ulterior purpose is not expressed in ways

[137] Bates v. Little Rock, 361 U.S. at 524.

[138] 345 U.S. at 40 (dissenting opinion).

> which negative what the revenue words on their face express and which do not seek enforcement of the formal revenue purpose through means that offend those standards of decency in our civilization against which due process is a barrier.

The soundness of this advice is not limited to cases involving revenue measures. It is particularly applicable in cases in which the "ulterior purpose" of Congress to penalize the expression of a hated idea appears in the legislative history with such clarity as to "negative what the . . . words [of the statute] on their face express." In *O'Brien*, as in *Kahriger*, to use another phrase from Justice Frankfurter's opinion, the "history of this legislation as it went through Congress . . . give[s] one the libretto to the song, the context of the circumstances which brought forth this enactment."[139] These factors indicate beyond cavil that the congressional purpose behind the draft law amendment was not the purpose expressed on the face of the law. There appears to be no reason why it should have been necessary for the Court to feign obliviousness of this fact.

IV. The Result in O'Brien

The constitutional problem presented in the *O'Brien* case would be far simpler and less perplexing if the mere ascertainment of congressional purpose were enough to provide a solution. But it is not. For it has been correctly noted that "it is altogether possible for a law which is the expression of a forbidden motive to be a good law."[140] And, as Chief Justice Warren noted in *O'Brien*, it would hardly seem advisable for the Court to strike down a law "which could be reenacted in its exact form if the same or another legislator made a 'wiser' speech about it."[141] Constitutionality must depend upon an assessment of the actual governmental interest protected by the law, not merely the interest seen by the legislators who enacted it. The nature and importance of the governmental interest seen by the legislators is, of course, a significant criterion in evaluating the amount of credence to be given to the govern-

---

139 *Id.* at 38–39.

140 Tussman & tenBroek, note 117, *supra*, at 360. *Cf.* Watkins v. United States, 354 U.S. 178, 200 (1957), where it was noted that members of a congressional investigating committee might be improperly motivated, but that "motives alone would not vitiate an investigation which had been instituted by a House of Congress if that assembly's legislative purpose is being served."

141 391 U.S. at 384.

ment's claims that the law serves a necessary function, but that in itself is not the controlling factor. If it were, what of the law that served no significant interest when enacted but that later came to serve a vital function because of a drastic change in existing circumstances? Presumably such a law should not have to be repassed to provide a convincing legislative history that would sustain its constitutionality. The measure of the government's interest, therefore, must be taken at the time of the application, not the time of the passage, of the law.[142] And it must be measured by more than the wisdom of the speeches made on the floor of the legislature in its support. Such a determination necessarily involves consideration of several factors.

The first of these factors must be the legislative history, which, of course, in this case, militates very strongly against constitutionality. If there was any interest to be attained by the passage of the amendment other than the suppression of an offensive manner of dissent, it was not made clear by any official means to any of the members of Congress who voted for it. The only statements that in any way made reference to a valid need were those in the committee reports that destruction of draft cards might endanger the power to raise armies or threaten the security of the nation. But these were left entirely unexplained and unsubstantiated, and provided no specific evidence of need whatever. If a need for the legislation existed, it existed unbeknown to Congress.

The second factor, which also militates against constitutionality, is that it was known to the members of Congress that the law would repress a form of dissent that had gained considerable notoriety. The repressive effect was not an unpredictable by-product of legislation on another subject. It was the deliberate purpose of the amendment. Considered as acts of defiance of the regulations requiring possession of the certificates, the draft-card burnings were examples of civil disobedience, and an integral part of the theory of civil disobedience is that those who violate the law on moral

[142] One may find examples of laws which are constitutional when enacted but which may become unconstitutional because of changing circumstances. Among these would be legislative apportionment statutes, see, *e.g.*, Reynolds v. Sims, 377 U.S. 533 (1964), or acts of Congress enacted under the war power to meet an emergency situation, see Chastleton Corp. v. Sinclair, 264 U.S. 543 (1924). There are even examples of statutes which were unconstitutional when enacted but which have gained constitutionality with the passage of time, such as Sunday closing laws. See McGowan v. Maryland, 366 U.S. 420 (1961).

grounds must accept the consequences that the law provides. Considering the burnings as acts of defiance of the draft law amendment, however, the categorization is not quite so clear. It is true that the burnings which took place after the passage of the amendment were deliberate violations of existing law, and, in that sense, they are readily categorizable as civil disobedience, but the fact that the amendment was enacted after numerous instances of card burning had taken place gives the law, in a practical if not a constitutional sense, an *ex post facto* quality. Punishing someone for an act of symbolic conduct in knowing violation of previously existing law is at least arguably different from enacting a law to punish that conduct after its practice has become a popular means of expressing dissent. The impact on expression of the law in the latter situation may be no greater, but the law should certainly be more suspect.

The *ex post facto* quality of such a law, however, is also not a decisive determinant of constitutionality. Legislatures are not sufficiently prescient to be able to identify and forbid all harmful acts in advance of their initial occurrence. It is a normal sequence of events for an unforbidden act to be committed, for it to be called to the attention of the legislature that such acts are offensive or dangerous, and for the legislature to enact a prohibitory statute. There is no reason why this may not be a perfectly adequate explanation of the legislature's conduct even when the forbidden acts are recognized as symbolic representations of an idea. The case of *People v. Stover,*[143] which was rather heavily relied on by the Second Circuit in *Miller,* is in point. There, the city of Rye, New York, adopted an ordinance prohibiting the erection of clothes lines in front yards after a couple, in a well-publicized protest against high municipal taxes, had hung a clothes line draped with unsightly objects in their front yard and, each year thereafter until the passage of the ordinance, proceeded to hang an additional and equally unsightly line. The New York court ruled that while it was "a fair inference that adoption of the ordinance before us was prompted by the conduct and action of the defendants" (which had no purpose other than as an expression of protest), the ordinance was on its face nondiscriminatory and constitutional, and thus could not be struck down "because of its motivation."[144]

143 12 N.Y.2d 462 (1963), *appeal dism.,* 375 U.S. 42 (1963).

144 12 N.Y.2d at 466.

The Rye ordinance is clearly constitutional if one concedes that the city has a legitimate interest in preserving aesthetic values. The limitation on expression was small, and the ugliness of the clothes line undoubtedly great. The fact that it had not occurred to the city council that individuals would be so unmindful of aesthetic considerations as deliberately to clutter their front yards with clothes lines until it was done as a form of expressive conduct does not deprive the council of the power to cope with the situation once it arose. There is, however, one major distinction between the clothes-line ordinance and the draft law amendment that renders the *Stover* case not entirely apposite. In *Stover*, there was no question but that it was the conduct that the city objected to, not the idea represented by the conduct. No one is likely to find a protest against high taxes so odious as to desire to suppress a symbolic expression of that point of view. But the legislative history makes clear that, in the case of the draft law amendment, it was the nature of the idea expressed, not the nature of the conduct, that led to the demand for congressional action.

Examination of the factors relating to legislative purpose thus provides no evidence that would aid in sustaining the constitutionality of the amendment. Nevertheless, the critical element remains the utility of the prohibition contained in the amendment for the purpose of administering the draft. Are draft cards sufficiently important that a ban on their destruction, enacted after destruction by burning had become a publicized means of dissent and, as far as can be discerned from the legislative history, enacted solely for the purpose of suppressing that means of dissent, would be constitutional despite its effect of imposing a limited restriction on freedom of expression?

The contention of the defense was that the government's interest in preventing the destruction of draft cards was trivial. As characterized by the Chief Justice, O'Brien "essentially adopts the position that such certificates are so many pieces of paper designed to notify registrants of their registration or classification, to be retained or tossed in the wastebasket according to the convenience or taste of the registrant."[145] Certainly the fact that a registrant does not keep either his Registration Certificate or his Notice of Classification in his possession does not affect in any way the ease of his induction. Induction of registrants is accomplished by use of records

[145] 391 U.S. at 378.

maintained in the office of the local board and is not dependent upon the disposition an individual makes of his draft card.[146] The interests that the government suggested would be served by preservation and personal possession of the draft card have nothing to do with protecting the ability of Selective Service boards to carry out their basic functions. The list of possible uses which draft cards might serve that was contained in the opinion of the Court indicates that the cards are of more peripheral utility. The list includes, in addition to the initial notification, proof of an individual's registration, verification of the local board's records in the event of possible administrative error, evidence of availability for induction in the event of emergency, a reminder to the registrant of the address of his local board and his Selective Service number, knowledge of which would facilitate communication with the board, a reminder of the individual's obligation to keep the board aware of changes of address and possible changes of status, and evidence of forgery or other deceptive use of the certificates.[147]

With the exception of the use pertaining to the facilitation of emergency call-up, the list contains no item that rises in importance above the level of administrative convenience. While the fact that a law provides for an administrative convenience is, in ordinary circumstances, more than enough to establish its constitutionality, convenience is not normally an adequate justification for the imposition of restrictions on freedom of expression.[148] And, where a law is enacted with foreknowledge that it would have the effect of suppressing a form of dissent, it would not be unreasonable to demand that its utility be more than merely conjectural.

On the surface, the uses of draft cards suggested by the government appear plausible. The genuineness of the convenience is obvious. In the computer age, it is difficult to deny that an individual's knowledge of his Selective Service number might greatly simplify the processing of any inquiry he might make or the insertion into his records of changes that might affect his classification status. And

146 At Miller's trial, an official of the local board with which he was registered testified that the papers necessary for processing induction were all maintained by the board. Appendix to Brief of Appellant, United States v. Miller, p. 35a.

147 391 U.S. at 378–80. See note 44 *supra.*

148 See, *e.g.*, Schneider v. Irvington, 308 U.S. 147, 163 (1939), where the Court held that "the public convenience in respect of cleanliness of the streets does not justify an exertion of the police power which invades the free communication of information and opinion secured by the Constitution."

the possibility that an emergency might arise that would necessitate the use of the Notice of Classification to determine an individual's availability for on-the-spot induction is not so remote as to be beyond comprehension. Nevertheless, it is striking that, if these considerations are as potentially important as the government contended, so little attention was paid to insuring that the cards would be preserved for these uses until draft-card burning became a means of dissent, and that the one step taken to insure their maintenance, which had not been requested by Selective Service officials, would appear to be totally useless for this purpose in that it would not insure the retention of the cards by those registrants who were not inclined openly to destroy them.

With the sole exception of the adoption of the regulations requiring continuous personal possession of the two draft cards—which appear to have been enforced only in situations involving overt refusal to submit to Selective Service requirements[149]—no attention was paid, prior to the enactment of the amendment, to whether or not registrants actually kept their draft cards. Spot checks were not systematically undertaken (except perhaps by tavern keepers). The trial judge in the *Miller* case admitted that "almost certainly thousands of men in recent decades have unwittingly failed to carry their cards at all times without ever having been called to show or produce them."[150] And the director of Selective Service for New York City, while aware of the existence of the possession regulations, believed that there was no penalty for noncompliance, and yet remained unconcerned.[151] If any Selective Service official had expressed a belief prior to the enactment of the amendment that noncompliance with the possession regulations was threatening, or could potentially threaten, the efficiency of the administration of the draft laws, such a statement does not appear to have come to light. Until the passage of the amendment, that part of the "Offenses and Penalties" section of the draft act that pertains to Selective Service certificates dealt exclusively with the prohibition of misuses or deceptive uses of the certificates, such as forgery, fraudulent alteration, or misrepresentation, and no concern was indicated with their discard or destruction except that the final

---

149 See cases cited note 16 *supra.*

150 United States v. Miller, 249 F. Supp. at 64.

151 See text *supra,* at note 12.

subsection provides generally for punishment for noncompliance with authorized regulations.[152]

A remarkably close analogy is provided in a case recalled a few years ago by Professor Paul Freund.[153] In this case,[154] the Supreme Court upheld a New York law that forbade the shipment into the state of cattle not certified by the chief sanitary officer of the state from which they were shipped as coming from a herd free of Bang's disease. Certainly, in view of facts presented at the trial to show the seriousness and infectiousness of the disease, this seems like a reasonable police regulation, as the Court held, and, therefore, not an invalid restriction of interstate commerce. But, Professor Freund notes, what the Supreme Court was unaware of was that, as later revealed, Bang's disease was prevalent in New York at that time, and the state was doing nothing to insure that cattle from other states certified as being from a clean herd were then placed in clean herds upon their arrival in New York. Professor Freund's incontestable observation was that, had the Court known these facts, the case "would probably have been decided otherwise."[155]

What these facts demonstrate is that the state took one step to achieve a goal that was superficially reasonable. The achievement of that goal, however, would have required additional steps, in the

---

152 50 U.S.C. App. § 462(b), which, before its amendment, provided: "(b) Any person (1) who knowingly transfers or delivers to another, for the purpose of aiding or abetting the making of any false identification or representation, any registration certificate, alien's certificate of nonresidence, or any other certificate issued pursuant to or prescribed by the provisions of this title or rules or regulations promulgated hereunder; or (2) who, with intent that it be used for any purpose of false identification or representation, has in his possession any such certificate not duly issued to him; or (3) who forges, alters, or in any manner changes any such certificate or any notation duly and validly inscribed thereon; or (4) who, with intent that it be used for any purpose of false identification or representation, photographs, prints, or in any manner makes or executes any engraving, photograph, print, or impression in the likeness of any such certificate, or any colorable imitation thereof; or (5) who has in his possession any certificate purporting to be a certificate issued pursuant to this title or rules and regulations promulgated hereunder, which he knows to be falsely made, reproduced, forged, counterfeited, or altered; or (6) who knowingly violates or evades any of the provisions of this title or rules and regulations promulgated pursuant thereto relating to the issuance, transfer, or possession of such certificate, shall, upon conviction, be fined not to exceed $10,000 or be imprisoned for not more than five years, or both. . . ."

153 Freund, *Review and Federalism*, in CAHN, SUPREME COURT AND SUPREME LAW 99 (1954).

154 Mintz v. Baldwin, 289 U.S. 346 (1933).

155 Freund, note 153 *supra*.

absence of which the initial step was manifestly futile. Where, as in this case, the step taken imposes a restriction on interstate commerce, its constitutionality must depend upon an assessment of the actual importance of the restriction for the protection of valid state interests. But, because of the failure of the state to take the other steps obviously necessary for the attainment of its asserted goal, the restriction could not effectively serve in the achievement of the state's interest, and therefore the burden it placed on interstate commerce was unwarranted and consequently unconstitutional.

O'Brien is identical with this pattern. The reasons for which the government might desire to protect against the destruction of draft cards are superficially plausible. The prohibition against knowing destruction or mutilation, however, is manifestly enforceable only against those who destroy their cards in the presence of witnesses or those who confess. Against others, *scienter* could not be proved. The law, in practice, can thus have an effect only upon the handful of dissenters who destroy their cards publicly or who announce that they have destroyed them.[156] But if the reasons asserted by the government as the basis for the law are correct, the government's interest goes far beyond the actions of the dissenters; it pertains to all registrants. The fact that Congress chose to protect this interest by employing a law that has practical application only against draft-card burners, when, at the same time, no meaningful steps were looked upon as necessary to insure preservation of draft cards by the vast majority of individuals, is a persuasive indication that the burden imposed by the amendment upon freedom of expression is not an important step in the protection of the government interest. Since the constitutional validity of a law such as this, which suppresses symbolic conduct, depends in large part upon its importance for the protection of the interest it is said to serve, the fact that it cannot effectively serve that interest is cogent evidence of its unconstitutionality.

If the draft law amendment stood by itself, therefore, its consti-

---

[156] *Compare* the statement of the Court: "The Amendment does not distinguish between public and private destruction, and it does not punish only destruction engaged in for the purpose of expressing views," 391 U.S. at 375, *with* the statement in the opinion of the First Circuit: "We would be closing our eyes . . . if we did not see on the face of the amendment that it was precisely directed at public as distinguished from private destruction." Judge Aldrich went on: "In singling out persons engaging in protest for special treatment the amendment strikes at the very core of what the First Amendment protects." 376 F.2d at 541.

tutionality, given the circumstances of its passage and the effect of its application, would be difficult to sustain. It does not, however, stand by itself. It stands together with the possession regulations, the origins of which are not tainted with evidence that they were promulgated for the purpose of suppressing dissent. They were adopted in times of less divisiveness for the undoubted purpose of serving the functions of convenience that the government argued was also the purpose of the amendment. Although they are extremely difficult to enforce effectively, and no attempt to do so appears ever to have been initiated, their constitutionality is not open to question. They are nondiscriminatory, unrelated to speech, and, even as applied to instances of symbolic conduct, capable of imposing only a minor restriction on expression. In fact, as has been mentioned earlier, in relation to these regulations, the burning of a draft card (which makes further possession impossible) is a perfect example of civil disobedience, for which the perpetrator of the act must expect to be punished.

If the possession regulations are treated as constitutional, as they must be, the invalidation of the draft law amendment would not serve to protect freedom of expression. While the draft-card burner could not be convicted under the amendment, the act of burning would make him liable for violation of the regulations. This was the dilemma which the First Circuit squarely faced when it held the amendment void. It resolved it by ruling that O'Brien had effectively been found guilty of breaking the regulations, and asking that future prosecutions of draft-card burners be brought under § 12(b)(6) of the draft act, which prohibits noncompliance with the regulations, rather than the amended § 12(b)(3).[157] But, since the same punishment is provided in § 12(b) for all offenses, including those actions expressly forbidden in the statute as well as all breaches of regulations, from the most serious to the most trivial, the shifting of the basis of the conviction from one part of § 12(b) to another would not seem to be of great significance.

The draft law amendment is thus sustainable as a reasonable supplement to the possession regulations. If the government may validly require possession of the draft cards, there is no reason why it may not forbid an act which would necessarily preclude continued possession, at least as long as the additional prohibition does not impose an increased burden on freedom of expression. As Chief

157 376 F.2d at 541–42.

Justice Warren declared in *O'Brien:* "In the absence of a question as to multiple punishment, it has never been suggested that there is anything improper in Congress providing alternative statutory avenues of prosecution to assure the effective protection of one and the same interest."[158] There is the possibility, of course, that the question of multiple punishment may arise if the government should attempt to prosecute a draft-card burner both for knowing destruction and for nonpossession. In such a case, the amendment would no longer be simply a supplement to the regulation, or an alternative means of requiring possession, but would be an independent offense, and thus a means of increasing the already severe punishment imposable under § 12(b)(6). Such a use of the amendment would revive the same constitutional considerations discussed above which suggest that, except as an "alternative statutory avenue of prosecution" for nonpossession, the law would be vulnerable to a First Amendment challenge.

It is true that burning involves an additional deliberate act beyond simple nonpossession, and, to that extent, the elements of the two offenses are different, but the only interest that the government has in preventing the burning of a draft card is, in the Court's words, that of "assuring the continuing availability of issued Selective Service certificates,"[159] and that is also the sole governmental interest in requiring possession. Therefore, although the Court argued that the regulations and the amendment "protect overlapping but not identical governmental interests,"[160] it is difficult to see in what respects the interests differ. The burning of a card is not in itself an evil; it is only an evil in that its necessary consequence is nonpossession and its attendant inconveniences.[161] If a card burner is prosecuted for both offenses as a result of a single act, the amendment could not be said to be vindicating the government's interest in insuring possession, for enforcement of the

158 391 U.S. at 380.

159 *Id.* at 381, 382.

160 *Id.* at 381.

161 In the opinion of the Court, it is pointed out that it is possible for an individual not to violate the nonpossession regulations—by destroying someone else's draft card. *Ibid.* This is, of course, true, and presumably, there would be no constitutional objection to prosecution in such a case. But this does not demonstrate the existence of a different governmental interest. The government's interest is still the same, preventing nonpossession. The act of burning the draft card of another is an evil because its necessary consequence is nonpossession on the part of the individual whose card is burned.

regulations accomplishes that purpose. In light of the fact that knowing public destruction of a draft card is an act unlikely to be committed except for purposes of symbolic conduct, a prosecution for knowing destruction in addition to nonpossession would serve only to penalize dissent, and thus ought not to be constitutionally sustainable.[162]

Although the result in *O'Brien* is defensible despite the deficiencies of manifest oversimplification in the Court's opinion, one further point needs to be raised concerning the sentences that may properly be imposed for violation of the draft law amendment. If the courts cannot always protect freedom of expression when the expression takes the form of civil disobedience through symbolic conduct, they should nevertheless be able to assure that the punishment imposed is not measured by the hatefulness of the ideas expressed, but by the gravity of the evil to be apprehended from the conduct. As Professor Morris Forkosch wrote at the conclusion of an article which defended the constitutionality of the amendment: "While it is concluded that the 1965 addition is a constitutional exercise of Congressional power, whether under the power to raise an army, to conduct war, or to prepare for a 'hotter'

---

162 The question of multiple punishment for separate offenses growing out of the commission of a single act is one on which the Court is gravely divided. See Gore v. United States, 357 U.S. 386 (1958). The traditional rule is that of Carter v. McClaughry, 183 U.S. 365 (1902), that the same act may be punished as separate offenses if different evidence is required to prove the commission of each offense. The Court, however, has not always adhered strictly to this rule. See, *e.g.*, Prince v. United States, 352 U.S. 322 (1957), in which the Court ruled, as a matter of statutory interpretation, that bank robbery and entering a bank with intent to commit a felony were not to be treated as separate offenses for which cumulative punishment could be imposed, because commission of the former offense necessarily involved commission of the latter, and the apparent purpose of Congress in making the latter an offense was not to increase the punishment for robbery, but to make possible the imposition of punishment where a person entered a bank intending to commit a robbery but was prevented from consummating the act. The Court held that it was not necessary to treat the two as entirely separate offenses "in order to vindicate the apparent purpose" of Congress. *Id.* at 327. In the case of draft-card burning, it could be argued, even in the absence of First Amendment considerations, that since the amendment and the regulations serve the identical interest, and that (at least in the case of one who burns his own card) violation of the amendment necessarily involves violation of the regulations, the imposition of multiple punishment would not serve to vindicate the legitimate governmental purpose. This argument finds support in the judgment of the First Circuit in *O'Brien*, which held that nonpossession was a lesser included offense of the crime of knowing destruction of a draft card. 376 F.2d at 541.

emergency, the independent judiciary should not be influenced by Congressional emotion or factors other than strictly legal."[163]

Section 12, that part of the Universal Military Training and Service Act dealing with offenses and penalties, does not grade allowable punishments according to the seriousness of the offense committed. All offenses under this section, including draft evasion, interference with the administration of the draft by force or violence, or failure to observe any of the regulations promulgated under the authority of the act, are punishable by imprisonment for up to five years, plus a $10,000 fine.[164] Since the 1965 draft law amendment simply inserted a prohibition against knowing destruction or knowing mutilation of a draft certificate into the existing language of the act, the allowable punishment for that offense, like the offense of nonpossession of a draft card, is the same. But surely an offense such as draft evasion or interference with the administration of the draft by force or violence is a more serious crime than nonpossession of a draft card, which is undoubtedly being committed by large numbers of persons daily without causing any apparent alarm. In the absence of aggravating circumstances, such as the theft and destruction of a considerable number of cards for the purpose of hindering the draft, the only valid interest that the government has in forbidding the destruction of a draft card (which, in itself, is an innocuous act) is to prevent nonpossession,[165] and sentences should be measured accordingly.[166]

If imprisonment for a term of years is altogether too harsh for the offense of nonpossession of a draft card, it is also too harsh for the knowing destruction of such a card. It is not too harsh, however, if one considers the public burning of a draft card to be an expression of treason. But then the offense is being punished, not because of its intrinsic gravity, but for the abhorrent nature of the view

---

[163] Forkosch, note 34 *supra*, at 332.

[164] Note 13 *supra*.

[165] See the statement of the First Circuit in *O'Brien:* "We see no possible interest, or reason, for passing a statute distinguishing between a registrant obligated to carry a card who mails it back to his draft board . . . and one who puts it in his wastebasket. The significant fact in both of these instances is that he is not carrying it." 376 F.2d at 541.

[166] It should be recalled that the only recorded vote against the amendment in Congress was by a member of the House who had had long service as a member of a draft board. He voted against the bill only because he considered the possible punishment "far too excessive." See note 21 *supra*.

which the conduct is intended to symbolize. This was recognized by the First Circuit, which, prior to reversal by the Supreme Court, had ordered the trial court to resentence O'Brien. In explaining its decision to remand, it observed:[167]

> Very possibly, in imposing sentence, the court took into consideration what the statute, by virtue of the amendment, indicated to be aggravating circumstances. Clearly it was an aggravated offense in the eyes of the proponents of the legislation. . . . Doubtless, too, the defendant chose his particular conduct precisely because of its "speaking" aspect. For the court to conclude, as was suggested in the legislative report, . . . that the impact of such conduct would impede the war effort, and measure the sentence by the nature of his communication, would be to punish defendant, pro tanto, for exactly what the First Amendment protects. The only punishable conduct was the intentional failure to carry his card.

While federal appellate courts have consistently declined to review the validity of a sentence authorized by the terms of a statute,[168] it may not unreasonably be maintained that if the First Amendment forbids legislatures from punishing expression, it should also forbid courts from punishing expression by maximizing sentences for relatively trivial offenses when the offense is committed for the purpose of symbolically expressing a hated idea. The adoption of such a doctrine seems to be especially suitable in dealing with statutes such as the draft act, which do not specify a particular level of punishment for each described offense, but simply provide a maximum allowable punishment for all violations of the act from the most serious to the most minor. It can hardly be contended that Congress consciously concluded, for example, that nonpossession of a draft card might warrant imprisonment for up to five years. Since there is no legislative judgment to which to defer, appellate court refusal to grant automatic deference to the judgment of a trial court appears justified as a means of avoiding unnecessary limitations on constitutional rights.[169]

---

167 376 F.2d at 542.

168 *E.g.*, the First Circuit, immediately after making the remarks quoted in the text at note 167 *supra*, was at pains to point out that "we do not have, and do not purport to exercise, jurisdiction to review a lawful sentence." *Ibid*. See also Gore v. United States, 357 U.S. 386, 393 (1958); Zaffarano v. Blackwell, 383 F.2d 719, 721 (5th Cir. 1967); Jones v. United States, 327 F.2d 867, 869 (D.C. Cir. 1963).

169 In Kawakita v. United States, 343 U.S. 717, 745 (1952), the Supreme Court left open the question "[w]hether a sentence may be so severe and the offense so trivial

Considered entirely apart from its significance as expression, and entirely apart from other acts, often committed by the same persons, that might represent a greater degree of refusal of cooperation with Selective Service, it is hardly conceivable that draft-card burning could constitute such a serious threat to the legitimate government interest in raising armies as to merit long imprisonment. The net result of *O'Brien*, however, is that the government, in dealing with a dissenter, is allowed to eat its cake and have it, too. It can obtain a conviction on the theory that it is conduct, not expression, that is being punished, and then obtain a sentence that reflects the objection to the expression, not the conduct.[170]

---

that an appellate court should set it aside." Because of the First Amendment considerations involved in the draft-card destruction cases, the reopening of this question seems not unwarranted.

170 For example, O'Brien was sentenced under the Youth Corrections Act (18 U.S.C. § 5010(b)) to up to six years in the custody of the Attorney General. Under the provisions of this act, he need spend no time in confinement, but if conditional release is not granted by the Youth Correction Division, he may be confined in the Youth Correctional Center for as long as four years. Other long sentences include a one-year term imposed upon Terry John Sullivan for ripping his 4-F draft card and refusing to carry another, N.Y. Times, July 30, 1966, p. 54; a two-year term imposed upon Gary G. Hicks for burning his draft card at the same demonstration at which O'Brien burned his, *id.* Feb. 7, 1967, p. 2; and a 2½-year sentence imposed upon David Miller, who had originally been given a suspended sentence, but who had violated the terms of his probation by refusing to apply for another card, *id.* Apr. 7, 1967, p. 6.

An argument raised at the trial court level in the draft-card burning cases, see, *e.g.*, United States v. Miller, 249 F. Supp. at 64–65; United States v. Smith, 249 F. Supp. at 519, but which does not appear to have been pressed on appeal, is that severe punishment for a minor offense might constitute a cruel and unusual punishment in violation of the Eighth Amendment. Such an argument is not patently frivolous, although a great deal of constitutional doctrine has not been built around the Eighth Amendment. The phrase "cruel and unusual punishments" has usually been taken to refer to punishment by torture or manifestly bizarre means. See, *e.g.*, Louisiana *ex rel.* Francis v. Resweber, 329 U.S. 459 (1947); *Ex parte* Kemmler, 136 U.S. 436 (1890); Wilkerson v. Utah, 99 U.S. 130 (1879).

In view of the fact, however, that the amendment prohibits "excessive bail" and "excessive fines," it would be surprising if it did not impose any limitation on excessive, but not unusual, punishment. Since very little light has been thrown on the origins of the amendment, however, no authoritative assertion can be made on this point. See the extended discussion of this question in Weems v. United States, 217 U.S. 349, 368–73 (1910). There the Court used language that seems to imply that the length of imprisonment alone, given the nature of the offense, was unconstitutionally severe. *Id.* at 380–81.

Other judicial statements may be found to the effect that punishments which are excessively severe in proportion to the offense charged are violative of the "cruel and unusual punishments" clause. The most prominent of these is the vigorous dissent of Justice Field in O'Neil v. Vermont, 144 U.S. 323 (1892). See also the remark

V. Conclusion

The saga of the draft-card burning cases is not a happy chapter in American civil liberties. Neither Congress nor the Court performed well, and the outcome was the enactment and upholding of a law which transparently has no real purpose except to offer the determined antiwar protester a choice between refraining from expressing contempt for the military effort in Vietnam through an extremely dramatic and, for his purposes, wonderfully irritating form of symbolic conduct, or going to jail. Despite Congress' ostensible responsibility to observe the guarantees of the Constitution,[171] the draft law amendment was enacted with extraordinary speed, little meaningful consideration, and no expressed opposition. Despite the Warren Court's record of defending the civil liberties of the political dissenter against legislative attack, it coyly chose in this case to accept the law uncritically on its face and to avoid recognition of the manifest congressional purpose. Perhaps the episode serves largely as another reminder of Justice Holmes's observation that "many things that might be said in time of peace . . . will not be endured so long as men fight."[172]

---

of Justice Frankfurter, in Lambert v. California, 355 U.S. 225, 231 (1957), that "a cruelly disproportionate relation between what the law requires and the sanction for its disobedience may constitute a violation of the Eighth Amendment as a cruel and unusual punishment." In 1963, Justice Goldberg, joined by Justices Douglas and Brennan, dissented from the Court's denial of certiorari in a case in which the death penalty had been imposed for the crime of rape even though the crime had not involved the endangering of the life of the victim. Rudolph v. Alabama, 375 U.S. 889 (1963). Among other questions which he argued should have been answered was whether such a punishment was so disproportionate to the offense as to violate the Eighth Amendment. *Id.* at 891. In view of the fact that courts in draft-card burning cases sometimes impose sentences of one or more years' imprisonment for an offense that is arguably no more serious than simple failure to have a draft card in one's personal possession, the Eighth Amendment contention in these cases merits attention.

171 See Morgan, Congress and the Constitution (1966).

172 Schenck v. United States, 249 U.S. 47, 52 (1919).

FRANK R. STRONG

FIFTY YEARS OF "CLEAR AND PRESENT DANGER": FROM SCHENCK TO BRANDENBURG—AND BEYOND

The fiftieth anniversary of the "clear and present danger" test is not a happy one for it. Commentators no less than Justices have been undertaking to inter the test for some little time. Hailed at the outset as the interpretational device for effective realization of First Amendment liberties, the danger test has lost favor to the point where the Court only irregularly admits to its employment,[1] and there are few who would grieve at its total demise.[2]

Frank R. Strong is Professor of Law, University of North Carolina; Dean and Professor of Law Emeritus, The Ohio State University.

1 See BERNS, FREEDOM, VIRTUE AND THE FIRST AMENDMENT 72 (1967); Krislov, *From Ginzburg to Ginsberg: The Unhurried Children's Hour in Obscenity Litigation*, 1968 SUPREME COURT REVIEW 153, 178–79. *Cf.* Karst, *The First Amendment and Harry Kalven: An Appreciative Comment on the Advantages of Thinking Small*, 13 U.C.L.A. L. REV. 1, 8–9 (1965); Van Alstyne, *First Amendment and the Suppression of War Mongering Propaganda in the United States*, 31 LAW & CONTEMP. PROB. 530, 546–47 n. 56 (1966).

2 Among those on the non-mourners bench would be Corwin, *Bowing Out "Clear and Present Danger,"* 27 NOTRE DAME LAWY. 325 (1952); Emerson, *Toward a General Theory of the First Amendment*, 72 YALE L.J. 877, 910–12 (1963); FREUND, THE SUPREME COURT OF THE UNITED STATES 42–44 (1961); Kalven, *The New York Times Case: A Note on "The Central Meaning of the First Amendment,"* 1964 SUPREME COURT REVIEW 191; KRISLOV, THE SUPREME COURT AND POLITICAL FREEDOM 89–90, 122 (1968).

Brandenburg v. Ohio,[3] decided at the end of the last Term of the Warren era, is significant on the doctrine's current status among sitting Justices. The decision was announced in a per curiam opinion of a length and importance that in normal practice would be written for the Court and attributed to an individual Justice. In this opinion there is assiduous avoidance of any reference to, let alone admitted employment of, the "clear and present danger" test. Yet invalidation of the Ohio Criminal Syndicalism Act stems from the overruling of *Whitney v. California*.[4] Brandeis and Holmes, although technically concurring in *Whitney*, took strong exception to its thesis in the name of a virile formulation of the danger test. But *Whitney* was overruled because "thoroughly discredited by later decisions. See *Dennis v. United States*, 341 U.S. 494, at 507," the very decision in which a majority of the Court adopted Learned Hand's diluted reformulation of the test. The page citation provides the clue to reconciliation. The "clear and present danger" test, whatever its degree of potency, applies to all legislation, whether directly prohibitive of designated speech or indirectly restrictive of utterances through prohibition of acts capable of effectuation by speech. Nevertheless, "[t]hese later decisions have fashioned the principle that the constitutional guarantees of free speech and free press do not permit a State to forbid or proscribe advocacy of the use of force or of law violation except where such advocacy is directed to inciting or producing imminent lawless action and is likely to incite or produce such action."[5]

While this language appears to install as current doctrine the Holmes-Brandeis conception of the danger formula, a footnote assertion of its consistency with the holding in *Dennis* leaves open the interpretation that the test remains, but sapped of its earlier potency. We are left by *Brandenburg* with something seemingly akin to a definitional approach to constitutional determination:[6]

> As we said in *Noto* v. *United States*, 367 U.S. 290, 297–298, "the mere abstract teaching . . . of the moral propriety or even moral necessity for a resort to force and violence, is not the same as preparing a group for violent action and steeling it to such action." See also *Herndon* v. *Lowry*, 301 U.S. 242, 259–261 (1937); *Bond* v. *Floyd*, 385 U.S. 116, 134 (1966). A statute which fails to draw this distinction imper-

---

[3] 395 U.S. 444 (1969).

[4] 274 U.S. 357 (1927), see text *infra*, at notes 21–25.

[5] 395 U.S. at 447.

[6] *Id.* at 447–48.

> missibly intrudes upon the freedoms guaranteed by the First and Fourteenth Amendments. It sweeps within its condemnation speech which our Constitution has immunized from governmental control.

Although concurring in reversal, Justices Black and Douglas wanted it clear that in their opinion the doctrine of "clear and present danger" "should have no place in the interpretation of the First Amendment." Mr. Justice Black was largely content to join in the views of Mr. Justice Douglas, who entered an extended caveat on this point. The Douglas position was stated this way:[7]

> Though I doubt if the "clear and present danger" test is congenial to the First Amendment in time of a declared war, I am certain it is not reconcilable with the First Amendment in days of peace. . . .
>
> In *Bridges* v. *California*, 314 U.S. 252, 261–263, we approved the "clear and present danger" test in an elaborate dictum that tightened it and confined it to a narrow category. But in *Dennis* v. *United States*, 341 U.S. 494, we opened wide the door, distorting the "clear and present danger" test beyond recognition. . . .
>
> When one reads the opinions closely and sees when and how the "clear and present danger" test has been applied, great misgivings are aroused. First, the threats were often loud but always puny and made serious only by judges so wedded to the *status quo* that critical analysis made them nervous. Second, the test was so twisted and perverted in *Dennis* as to make the trial of those teachers of Marxism an all-out political trial which was part and parcel of the cold war that has eroded substantial parts of the First Amendment. . . .
>
> The line between what is permissible and not subject to control and what may be made impermissible and subject to regulation is the line between ideas and overt acts.

The attitude of commentators has been equally unfriendly. "Today almost no one seems to believe that this formula can be very helpful in deciding concrete cases" is Professor McCloskey's verdict.[8] Kalven's is more extreme. In a tribute to the Warren Court he asserted that[9]

---

7 *Id.* at 452–54, 456.

8 McCloskey, *Reflections on the Warren Court*, 51 Va. L. Rev. 1229, 1236 (1965).

9 Kalven, *"Uninhibited, Robust, and Wide-Open"—A Note on Free Speech and the Warren Court*, 67 Mich. L. Rev. 289, 297 (1968).

> the most significant step [in] the abrogation of outmoded ideas . . . has been the great reduction in the status and prestige of the clear-and-present danger test. Immediately prior to the advent of the Warren Court, this test had a considerable claim as *the* criterion of the constitutionality of an exercise of governmental authority over communication. In limited areas the test may still be alive, but it has been conspicuous by its absence from opinions in the last decade. Since the test—whatever sense it may have made in the limited context in which it originated—is clumsy and artificial when expanded into a general criterion of permissible speech, the decline in its fortunes under the Warren Court seems to be an intellectual gain.

The weakness of the danger test is shown by attempted reliance upon it as a complete constitutional solvent. No such role was originally conceived for it. In its beginning it scarcely purported to rise to a constitutional level at all. For a unanimous Court in *Schenck v. United States*,[10] Mr. Justice Holmes employed it essentially as a rule of evidence. Under a statute prohibiting interference with war effort, speech could be punished only on evidence of clear and present danger that that speech would lead to the evil which Congress had sought to forbid by the Espionage Act.

This technical usage of the test was turned against Holmes by the majority in *Gitlow v. New York*,[11] involving the New York statutory prohibition of advocacy of criminal anarchy:[12]

> It is clear that the question in such cases [as this] is entirely different from that involved in those cases where the statute merely prohibits certain acts involving the danger of substantive evil, without any reference to language itself, and it is sought to apply its provisions to language used by the defendant for the purpose of bringing about the prohibited results. . . . In such cases it has been held that the general provisions of the statute may be constitutionally applied to the specific utterance of the defendant if its natural tendency and probable effect was to bring about the substantive evil which the legislative body might prevent. . . . [T]he general statement in the *Schenck Case* . . . was manifestly intended, as shown by the context, to apply only in cases of this class, and has no application to those like the present, where the legislative body itself has previously determined the danger of substantive evil arising from utterances of a specified character.

---

[10] 249 U.S. 47 (1919).

[11] 268 U.S. 652 (1926).

[12] *Id.* at 670–71.

It is familiar knowledge that the distinction was washed out by *Dennis*:[13] the opinion for the Court elected the "Holmes-Brandeis rationale" despite *Gitlow*. Yet the distinction continued long enough into the period during which the danger test was used in an attempt to resolve issues of validity to produce the conflict, manifest in *Dennis* and later, between those insisting on jury determination of clear and present danger and those declaring that the making of that judgment was a question of law for the court. That the origin of the danger test was basically a rule of evidence must account for this conflict. For, as one acute commentator has observed: "Juries are not supposed to declare statutes unconstitutional. Such a practice (and it might have come about in the Dennis case if Douglas had had his way) would be consistent neither with practical wisdom nor with American judicial tradition."[14] It can be added that juries are not supposed to rule statutes (or other forms of governmental action) constitutional. This is the essential teaching of the Court's continued insistence upon the doctrine of constitutional fact.[15]

Professor Kalven recently observed that Holmes's attitude in *Debs*[16] "makes it evident that the clear-and-present-danger dictum did not in his mind become a constitutional test until sometime after *Schenck*," referring to Chafee's suggestion that Holmes "was waiting for *Abrams*."[17] Holmes's dissent in *Abrams v. United States*,[18] in which he was joined by Brandeis, contained the following familiar and substantiating language:[19]

> I wholly disagree with the argument of the Government that the First Amendment left the common law as to seditious libel in force. History seems to me against the notion. I had conceived that the United States through many years had shown its repentance for the Sedition Act of 1798, by repaying fines that it imposed. Only the emergency that makes it completely dangerous to leave the correction of evil counsels to time warrants making any exception to the sweeping command, "Congress shall make no law . . .

---

13 341 U.S. 494 (1951).

14 BERNS, note 1 *supra*, at 63.

15 See Brennan, *The Supreme Court and the Meiklejohn Interpretation of the First Amendment*, 79 HARV. L. REV. 1, 7–8 (1965); Strong, *The Persistent Doctrine of "Constitutional Fact,"* 46 N.C. L. REV. 223, 279–80 (1968).

16 Debs v. United States, 249 U.S. 211 (1919).

17 Kalven, note 9 *supra*, at 291 n. 18.

18 250 U.S. 616, 624–31 (1919).

19 *Id*. at 630–31.

> abridging the freedom of speech." Of course I am speaking only of expressions of opinion and exhortations, which were all that were uttered here, but I regret that I cannot put into more impressive words my belief that in their conviction upon this indictment the defendants were deprived of their rights under the Constitution of the United States.

Elevated to constitutional level, the danger test, retaining much of its original evidentiary flavor, became a device whereby, for legislation to pass constitutional muster, it must be demonstrated that a permissible objective of government is imminently and substantially threatened. Permissible objectives were identified without analysis as "certain substantive evils" with respect to which government possessed some authority. Yet by the new test government was empowered to take action only on proof of the immediacy of serious peril to one or more of those substantive evils. The following paragraph from the *Abrams*' dissent specifies the reach of the test as a potent yet not total constriction on governmental power with respect to utterances:[20]

> I never have seen any reason to doubt that the questions of law that alone were before this Court in the cases of *Schenck*, *Frohwerk*, and *Debs*, 249 U.S. 47, 204, 211, were rightly decided. I do not doubt for a moment that by the same reasoning that would justify punishing persuasion to murder, the United States constitutionally may punish speech that produces or is intended to produce a clear and imminent danger that it will bring about forthwith certain substantive evils that the United States constitutionally may seek to prevent. The power undoubtedly is greater in time of war than in time of peace because war opens dangers that do not exist at other times.

The Brandeis concurrence in *Whitney v. California*,[21] in which Mr. Justice Holmes joined, is properly viewed as an invigorated articulation of their conception of the danger test as a measure of First Amendment freedom of speech. Early in this opinion this categorical assertion was made:[22]

> That the necessity which is essential to a valid restriction does not exist unless speech would produce, or is intended to produce, a clear and imminent danger of some substantive evil which the State constitutionally may seek to prevent has been settled. See *Schenck* v. *United States*, 249 U.S. 47, 52.

---

[20] *Id.* at 627–28.

[21] 274 U.S. at 372–80.

[22] *Id.* at 373.

At the same time:[23]

> This Court has not yet fixed the standard by which to determine when a danger shall be deemed clear; how remote the danger may be and yet be deemed present; and what degree of evil shall be deemed sufficiently substantial to justify resort to abridgement of free speech and assembly as the means of protection.

There followed the stirring Brandeis statement of the nature of the nation sought to be created by "[t]hose who won our independence." "Believing in the power of reason as applied through public discussion, they eschewed silence coerced by law—the argument of force in its worst form."[24] As a consequence:[25]

> [N]o danger flowing from speech can be deemed clear and present, unless the incidence of the evil apprehended is so imminent that it may befall before there is opportunity for full discussion. . . .
>
> Moreover, even imminent danger cannot justify resort to prohibition of these functions essential to effective democracy, unless the evil apprehended is relatively serious.

This potent formulation of the danger test received its most clear-cut and continuing application in the line of cases involving interference with the administration of justice. There was in these cases such complete agreement on the legitimacy of protecting the adjudicative function from disruptive forces that the permissibility of this objective went unquestioned:

> We start with the premise that the right of courts to conduct their business in an untrammeled way lies at the foundation of our system of government and that courts necessarily must possess the means of punishing for contempt when conduct tends directly to prevent the discharge of their functions.[26]
>
> . . . Among the "substantive evils with which legislation may deal" is the hampering of a court in pending controversy, because the fair administration of justice is one of the chief tests of a true democracy.[27]

The issue for the majority in this series of cases has been solely whether a contempt citation can stand because of a clear and pres-

[23] *Id.* at 374. [24] *Id.* at 375–76. [25] *Id.* at 377.

[26] Wood v. Georgia, 370 U.S. 375, 383 (1962) (Warren, C. J.).

[27] Pennekamp v. Florida, 328 U.S. 331, 353 (1946) (Frankfurter, J., concurring).

ent danger that adverse comment on judicial behavior in pending cases or other judicial business imperils impartial administration of justice.

In the initial case involving Harry Bridges and the *Los Angeles Times*, Mr. Justice Black, after an interesting employment of the technical distinction taken in *Gitlow* to buttress support for the use of the danger test,[28] asserted: "What finally emerges from the 'clear and present danger' cases is a working principle that the substantive evil must be extremely serious and the degree of imminence extremely high before utterances can be punished."[29] By this test every one of the four challenges to state contempt citations has been sustained.

Yet in three of these four cases[30] vigorous dissents were registered, and the decision in the first was by a bare majority of one. Justice Frankfurter's powerful dissent in *Bridges* carried a paragraph that in retrospect presaged what was to happen to this formulation of the danger test a decade later in *Dennis*.[31]

> Comment however forthright is one thing. Intimidation with respect to specific matters still in judicial suspense, quite another. . . . A publication intended to teach the judge a lesson, or to vent spleen, or to discredit him, or to influence him in his future conduct, would not justify exercise of the contempt power. Compare Judge Learned Hand in *Ex parte Craig*, 282 F. 138, 160–161. It must refer to a matter under consideration and constitute in effect a threat to its impartial disposition. It must be calculated to create an atmospheric pressure incompatible with rational, impartial adjudication. But to interfere with justice it need not succeed. As with other offenses, the state should be able to proscribe attempts

---

28 "For here the legislature of California has not appraised a particular kind of situation and found a specific danger sufficiently imminent to justify a restriction on a particular kind of utterance. The judgments below, therefore, do not come to us encased in the armor wrought by prior legislative deliberation. Under such circumstances, this Court has said that 'it must necessarily be found, as an original question,' that the specified publications involved created 'such likelihood of bringing about the substantive evil as to deprive [them] of the constitutional protection.' *Gitlow* v. *New York,* 268 U.S. 652, 671." Bridges v. California, 314 U.S. 252, 260–61 (1941).

29 *Id.* at 263.

30 The fourth case in the line, third in time of disposition, was Craig v. Harney, 331 U.S. 367 (1947).

31 314 U.S. at 291–92.

> that fail because of the danger that attempts may succeed. The purpose, it will do no harm to repeat, is not to protect the court as a mystical entity or the judges as individuals or as anointed priests set apart from the community and spared the criticism to which in a democracy other public servants are exposed. The purpose is to protect immediate litigants and the public from the mischievous danger of an unfree or coerced tribunal. The power should be invoked only where the adjudicatory process may be hampered or hindered in its calm, detached and fearless discharge of its duty on the basis of what has been submitted in court. The belief that decisions are so reached is the source of the confidence on which law ultimately rests.

Terminiello v. Chicago,[32] decided at the close of the 1940's, marked the apogee in the employment of the danger test under the *Abrams-Whitney* formulation. There all the Justices who addressed themselves to the merits agreed on the applicability of the test to the validity of conviction of a Chicago priest for a virulent address, before eight hundred persons, protested by an "angry and turbulent" crowd of "about one thousand persons" gathered immediately outside the auditorium. Reversing the conviction, Mr. Justice Douglas for the Court, explained that "a function of free speech under our system of government is to invite dispute," and declared:[33]

> That is why freedom of speech, though not absolute, *Chaplinsky* v. *New Hampshire* . . . is nevertheless protected against censorship or punishment, unless shown likely to produce a clear and present danger of a serious substantive evil that rises far above public inconvenience, annoyance, or unrest. See *Bridges* v. *California* . . . ; *Craig* v. *Harney*. . . . There is no room under our Constitution for a more restrictive view. For the alternative would lead to standardization of ideas either by legislatures, courts, or dominant political or community groups.

With this Mr. Justice Jackson took issue in a dissent (joined by Justice Burton and the views of which Justice Frankfurter declared he shared):[34]

> Rioting is a substantive evil, which I take it no one will deny that the State and the City have the right and the duty to prevent and punish. Where an offense is induced by speech, the Court has laid down and often reiterated a test of the

---

[32] 337 U.S. 1 (1949). [33] *Id.* at 4–5. [34] *Id.* at 25–26.

> power of the authorities to deal with the speaking as also an offense. "The question in every case is whether the words *used are used in such circumstances* and are of *such a nature* as to create a *clear and present danger* that they will bring about the substantive evils that Congress [or the state or city] has a right to prevent." (Emphasis supplied.) Mr. Justice Holmes in *Schenck* v. *United States*, 249 U.S. 47, 52. No one ventures to contend that the State on the basis of this test, for whatever it may be worth, was not justified in punishing Terminiello. In this case the evidence proves beyond dispute that danger of rioting and violence in response to the speech was clear, present and immediate. If this Court has not silently abandoned this longstanding test and substituted for the purposes of this case an unexpressed but more stringent test, the action of the State would have to be sustained.

Familiar, yet sufficiently important for requotation, are the three paragraphs in Part III of the Vinson opinion for the Court in *Dennis* that embraced the Frankfurter-Jackson viewpoint. These rejected, at least in the context of international communism, the danger test as evolved by Holmes and Brandeis and applied in the contempt cases, all but the last of which were decided in the 1940's:[35]

> In this case we are squarely presented with the application of the "clear and present danger" test, and must decide what that phrase imports. We first note that many of the cases in which this Court has reversed convictions by use of this or similar tests have been based on the fact that the interest which the State was attempting to protect was itself too insubstantial to warrant restriction of speech. In this category we may put such cases as *Schneider* v. *State*, 308 U.S. 147 (1939); *Cantwell* v. *Connecticut*, 310 U.S. 296 (1940); *Martin* v. *Struthers*, 319 U.S. 141 (1943); *West Virginia Board of Education* v. *Barnette*, 319 U.S. 624 (1943); *Thomas* v. *Collins*, 323 U.S. 516 (1945); *Marsh* v. *Alabama*, 326 U.S. 501 (1946); but cf. *Prince* v. *Massachusetts*, 321 U.S. 158 (1944); *Cox* v. *New Hampshire*, 312 U.S. 569 (1941). Overthrow of the Government by force and violence is certainly a substantial enough interest for the Government to limit speech. Indeed, this is the ultimate value of any society, for if a society cannot protect its very structure from armed internal attack, it must follow that no subordinate value can be protected. If, then, this interest may be

---

[35] 341 U.S. at 508–10.

> protected the literal problem which is presented is what has been meant by the use of the phrase "clear and present danger" of the utterances bringing about the evil within the power of Congress to punish.
>
> Obviously, the words cannot mean that before the Government may act, it must wait until the *putsch* is about to be executed, the plans have been laid and the signal is awaited. If Government is aware that a group aiming at its overthrow is attempting to indoctrinate its members and to commit them to a course whereby they will strike when the leaders feel the circumstances permit, action by the Government is required. The argument that there is no need for Government to concern itself, for Government is strong, it possesses ample powers to put down a rebellion, it may defeat the revolution with ease needs no answer. For that is not the question. Certainly an attempt to overthrow the Government by force, even though doomed from the outset because of inadequate numbers or power of the revolutionists, is a sufficient evil for Congress to prevent. The damage which such attempts create both physically and politically to a nation makes it impossible to measure the validity in terms of the probability of success, or the immediacy of a successful attempt. In the instant case the trial judge charged the jury that they could not convict unless they found that petitioners intended to overthrow the Government "as speedily as circumstances would permit." This does not mean, and could not properly mean, that they would not strike until there was certainty of success. What was meant was that the revolutionists would strike when they thought the time was ripe. We must therefore reject the contention that success or probability of success is the criterion.
>
> The situation with which Justices Holmes and Brandeis were concerned in *Gitlow* was a comparatively isolated event, bearing little relation in their minds to any substantial threat to the safety of the community. Such also is true of cases like *Fiske* v. *Kansas*, 274 U.S. 380 (1927), and *De Jonge* v. *Oregon*, 299 U.S. 353 (1937); but cf. *Lazar* v. *Pennsylvania*, 286 U.S. 532 (1932). They were not confronted with any situation comparable to the instant one—the development of an apparatus designed and dedicated to the overthrow of the Government, in the context of world crisis after crisis.

Concurring separately, Justice Jackson was even more vigorous in his rejection of the test urged by petitioners. He first reinforced the assertions of the Chief Justice:[36]

[36] *Id.* at 570–71.

> The authors of the clear and present danger test never applied it to a case like this, nor would I. If applied as it is proposed here, it means that the Communist plotting is protected during its period of incubation; its preliminary states of organization and preparation are immune from the law; the Government can move only after imminent action is manifest, when it would, of course, be too late.
>
> The highest degree of constitutional protection is due to the individual acting without conspiracy. But even an individual cannot claim that the Constitution protects him in advocating or teaching overthrow of government by force or violence. I should suppose no one would doubt that Congress has power to make such attempted overthrow a crime. But the contention is that one has the constitutional right to work up a public desire and will to do what it is a crime to attempt. I think direct incitement by speech or writing can be made a crime, and I think there can be a conviction without also proving that the odds favored its success by 99 to 1, or some other extremely high ratio.

But more than this he then declared that Holmes's opinion for a unanimous Court in *Frohwerk*[37] demonstrated that "[t]he names of Mr. Justice Holmes and Mr. Justice Brandeis cannot be associated with such a doctrine of governmental disability."[38]

In the hour of its greatest test, against the tough opponent of national security at mid-twentieth century, the rule of clear and present danger lost its bid for general acceptance as a requirement that for state or federal restriction of speech to be valid it must be shown that a legitimate objective of government is imminently and substantially imperiled. Mr. Justice Black saw this clearly in his dissent. Even on the "radical assumption . . . that petitioners although not indicted for the crime of actual advocacy, may be punished for it . . . the other opinions in this case show that the only way to affirm these convictions is to repudiate directly or indirectly the established 'clear and present danger' rule."[39] In a separate dissent Mr. Justice Douglas made a case for the proposition that communism in this country is only a bogeyman. But the demonstration was unresponsive to the majority's position that the danger test in the formulation brought to the argument by petitioners was inapplicable.

---

37 Frohwerk v. United States, 249 U.S. 204, 206 (1919).

38 341 U.S. at 571.

39 *Id.* at 579–80.

In retrospect, *Dennis* has the dubious distinction of bringing to a head the paradox that the Holmes-Brandeis formulation of the danger test as a constitutional solvent would satisfy but few. To be sure, it is employed occasionally, as is attested by its reappearance in the last of the contempt cases. It will even turn up in surprising contexts, as where Mr. Justice Harlan, concurring in *Garner v. Louisiana*,[40] invoked it after explicit reference back to Holmes in *Abrams* and Brandeis in *Whitney*.[41] But to many it became, after *Dennis*, largely or wholly unsatisfactory because either too virile or overly weak. Extrajudicially, Mr. Justice Brennan not long ago limited it to the contempt cases and those involving subversive action.[42] Professor Freund had earlier thought even this went too far. Although finding the formulation "a useful criterion of illicit speech where the social harm apprehended from the speech would flow from the effect of the ideas conveyed," he regarded it as "not appropriate where the harm is such that a corrective could not be sought through countervailing speech: contempt of court, pornography, and political activities by civil servants are examples."[43]

In his monumental quest for a satisfactory theory of the First Amendment, Professor Emerson suggested that it was in dissent in *Scales v. United States*[44] that Mr. Justice Douglas abandoned the clear and present danger test which he, alone among the Justices, "made a serious attempt to apply" in *Dennis*.[45] The covert rejection clearly represented not delayed adherence to the *Dennis* majority view that the test was too strong, but embrasure of the quite opposite view that its unsatisfactoriness lay in its weakness. In Emerson's words: "To permit the state to cut off expression as soon as it comes close to being effective is essentially to allow only abstract or innocuous expression."[46] This is the absolutist theory in espousal of which Mr. Justice Douglas thus joined Mr. Justice Black, both undoubtedly influenced heavily by the views of Dr.

---

40 368 U.S. 157, 185–207 (1961).

41 *Id.* at 201–03. "The life of the law can be full of surprises. One does not . . . hear much about clear and present danger these days under any circumstances; it is amazing to find the formula so seriously discussed in a case involving a sit-in." KALVEN, THE NEGRO AND THE FIRST AMENDMENT 132 (Phoenix ed. 1966).

42 Brennan, note 15 *supra*, at 8.

43 FREUND, note 2 *supra*, at 44.

44 367 U.S. 203 (1961).

45 Emerson, note 2 *supra*, at 911 n. 35.

46 *Id.* at 911.

Meiklejohn.[47] The judgment passed on the danger test is, however, the same as that of those concerned over its potency:[48]

> There is still some blood remaining in the doctrine, and it has continued to be used in certain types of situations [citing to *Wood v. Georgia,* the latest contempt case]. But, as a general test of the limits of the first amendment, the clear and present danger test must be regarded as unacceptable.

In the second *Konigsberg*[49] classic confrontation between absolutist and balancing theories of First Amendment interpretation, Mr. Justice Harlan for the majority sought to ground the latter partly on the proposition "[t]hat the First Amendment immunity for speech, press and assembly has to be reconciled with valid but conflicting governmental interests was clear to Holmes, J. (*Abrams* v. *United States* . . .); to Brandeis, J. (*Whitney* v. *California* . . .); and to Hughes, C. J. (*Near* v. *Minnesota* . . .)."[50] With the concurrence of Douglas, Mr. Justice Black assailed this bid for good paternity for the balancing test:[51]

> The Court attempts to justify its refusal to apply the plain mandate of the First Amendment in part by reference to the so-called "clear and present danger test" forcefully used by Mr. Justice Holmes and Mr. Justice Brandeis, not to narrow but to broaden the then prevailing interpretation of First Amendment freedoms. I think very little can be found in anything they ever said that would provide support for the "balancing test" presently in use.

Rather it was "the sudden transformation of the 'clear and present danger test' in *Dennis* v. *United States*" that equated it with the balancing test; "diluted and weakened by being recast in terms of this 'balancing' formula, there seems to me to be much room to doubt that Justices Holmes and Brandeis would even have recognized their test."[52]

---

[47] See Meiklejohn, *The First Amendment Is an Absolute,* 1961 SUPREME COURT REVIEW 245.

[48] Emerson, note 2 *supra,* at 912.

[49] Konigsberg v. State Bar of California, 366 U.S. 36 (1961).

[50] *Id.* at 50 n. 11.

[51] *Id.* at 62.

[52] *Id.* at 64. Contrast Mr. Justice Black's statement of the case in Martin v. City of Struthers, 319 U.S. 141, 143 (1943): "We are faced in the instant case with the necessity of weighing the conflicting interests of the appellant in the civil rights she claims, as well as the right of the individual householder to determine whether he

The Frankfurter concurrence in *Dennis* is clearly cast in terms of essential equivalency between "clear and present danger" and "careful weighing of conflicting interests." To be sure, he was dissatisfied with acceptance by others in the majority of Learned Hand's recasting of the danger test:[53]

> In all fairness, the [defendants'] argument cannot be met by reinterpreting the Court's frequent use of "clear" and "present" to mean an entertainable "probability." In giving this meaning to the phrase "clear and present danger," the Court of Appeals was fastidiously confining the rhetoric of opinions to the exact scope of what was decided by them. We have greater responsibility for having given constitutional support, over repeated protests, to uncritical libertarian generalities.

Yet his fulfilment of that "greater responsibility" led him, not into an attack on judicial balancing, but into an exposition and defense of it as "on the whole" the underlying rationale of the cases and the basis for resolving the issue in *Dennis*:[54]

> On the one hand is the interest in security. The Communist Party was not designed by these defendants as an ordinary political party. . . .
>
> On the other hand is the interest in free speech. The right to exert all governmental powers in aid of maintaining our institutions and resisting their physical overthrow does not include intolerance of opinions and speech that cannot do harm although opposed and perhaps alien to dominant, traditional opinion.

A full decade before the fateful decision in *Dennis* one of the ablest of commentators had sensed in the danger test a quality that would not make difficult its assimilation into the concept of balancing. Professor Wechsler observed:[55]

> Speech or assembly may be repressed or limited when it gives rise or is intended to give rise or may reasonably be thought by the legislature to give rise to a genuine danger of some substantive evil which the state has a right to prevent, unless the evil is not great enough to warrant the sup-

---

is willing to receive her message, against the interest of the community which by this ordinance offers to protect the interests of all of its citizens, whether particular citizens want that protection or not."

[53] 341 U.S. at 527.

[54] *Id.* at 546, 548.

[55] Wechsler, *Symposium on Civil Liberties*, 9 A. L. Sch. Rev. 881, 887 (1941).

> pression of speech or assembly as a means to its prevention, or to say the same thing in a different way, unless the speech or assembly is justified by some end which outweighs the evil which it admittedly threatens. But if this is the clear and present danger test for which liberals have fought and bled, it needs no argument to show that the formula which it provides is only a formula; that it does little more than to state the general principle of justice which would be accepted in evaluating any legislation which interferes with individual freedom. The use to which freedom is put must threaten social interests; the danger inherent in the threat must not be outweighed by an affirmative good which the behavior entails. In short, what the clear and present danger test can do, and all it can do, is to require an extended judicial review in the fullest legislative sense of the competing values which the particular situation presents. And the scope of that judicial review may be limited by what is in effect a presumption of validity, or a deference to legislative judgment, at least where the legislation condemns specific doctrine or specifically described types of meetings.

Despite, therefore, employment of the Holmes-Brandeis brand of danger test from *Herndon v. Lowry*[56] through the 1940's to the very year of *Dennis*,[57] there was latent an element about it that would not make difficult its assimilation into the concept of balancing, as balancing came to be practiced and understood by Frankfurter in *Dennis* and by Harlan in *Konigsberg II.* Most commentators now assume a balancing role for the danger test. " 'Clear and present danger' is, to be sure, essentially a balancing formula," one has recently observed.[58] Professor Karst has insisted:[59]

> The clear-and-present-danger test, even with its original emphasis on the immediacy of the threatened harm, was always a "balancing" test. The Justices who used the language of clear-and-present-danger did not shrink from making the legislative judgments which are inescapable in our systems of judicial review.

Professor Kalven is the exception in continuing to distinguish "balancing [from] any form of clear and present danger."[60]

---

56 301 U.S. 242 (1937).

57 In Niemotko v. Maryland, 340 U.S. 268 (1951); Kunz v. New York, 340 U.S. 290 (1951); Feiner v. New York, 340 U.S. 315 (1951).

58 Krislov, note 2 *supra*, at 121.

59 Karst, note 1 *supra*, at 10.

60 Kalven, note 41 *supra*, at 86, 121.

Metamorphosed into a balancing formula, "clear and present danger" fares no better as a test for satisfactory delineation of constitutional boundaries. Clearly unsatisfactory to the absolutists, it has, as well, deficiencies for those to whom balancing is necessary. Commentators are, for one, critical of it as an adequate vehicle for balancing. Paul Freund has often been quoted on this point:[61]

> Even where it is appropriate, the clear-and-present-danger test is an oversimplified judgment unless it takes account also of a number of other factors: the relative seriousness of the danger in comparison with the value of the occasion for speech or political activity; the availability of more moderate controls than those the state has imposed, and perhaps the specific intent with which the speech or activity is launched. No matter how rapidly we utter the phrase "clear and present danger," or how closely we hyphenate the words, they are not a substitute for the weighing of values. They tend to convey a delusion of certitude when what is most certain is the complexity of the strands in the web of freedom which the judge must disentangle.

Citing this passage, another commentator more recently observed that "to sophisticated balancers" clear and present danger as a balancing formula[62]

> suggests a simplification of the problem, an incomplete enumeration of the factors involved in balancing. This distortion is at a minimum in face-to-face situations. Yet, even there, external factors are not typically considered, and little play is given to a relative evaluation of the significance of the speech or the seriousness of the evil. In short, less freedom is given the judge than the balancers prefer.

The hazards of inadequate consideration of factors pertinent to the balancing operation are well illustrated by Mr. Justice Black's dissent in *Barenblatt*,[63] in which he was joined by Chief Justice Warren and Mr. Justice Douglas:[64]

> But even assuming what I cannot assume, that some balancing is proper in this case, I feel that the Court after stating the test ignores it completely. At most it balances

---

[61] FREUND, note 2 *supra*, at 44.

[62] KRISLOV, note 2 *supra*, at 121. To similar effect is McKay, *The Preference for Freedom*, 34 N.Y.U. L. REV. 1182, 1212, 1222 (1959).

[63] Barenblatt v. United States, 360 U.S. 109, 134 (1959).

[64] *Id.* at 144, 145.

> the right of the Government to preserve itself, against Barenblatt's right to refrain from revealing Communist affiliations. Such a balance, however, mistakes the factors to be weighed. In the first place, it completely leaves out the real interest in Barenblatt's silence, the interest of the people as a whole in being able to join organizations, advocate causes and make political "mistakes" without later being subjected to governmental penalties for having dared to think for themselves. . . .
>
> Moreover, I cannot agree with the Court's notion that First Amendment freedoms must be abridged in order to "preserve" our country. That notion rests on the unarticulated premise that this Nation's security hangs upon its power to punish people because of what they think, speak or write about, or because of those with whom they associate for political purposes. The Government, in its brief, virtually admits this position when it speaks of the "communication of unlawful ideas." I challenge this premise, and deny that ideas can be proscribed under our Constitution.

A further deficiency lies in the limitations of the type of balancing with which the diluted danger test has fused, even when that form takes into account all relevant factors of private right and public interest. This type, now known as ad hoc balancing, although ably defended,[65] has in the present decade come under growing criticism.[66] That criticism finds in ad hoc balancing a congenital infirmity. Because of the decisional character of the juristic process by which the weighing is done, no facet of speech, press, or assembly is protected if the intensity of the governmental interest is deemed "on balance" to override the private values in opposition. Mr. Frantz is mordaciously critical:[67]

> If the arguments employed to justify balancing are carried to their logical conclusion, then the Constitution does not contain—and is not even capable of containing—anything what-

[65] Kauper, Book Review of MEIKLEJOHN, POLITICAL FREEDOM, 58 MICH. L. REV. 619 (1960); Karst, *Legislative Facts in Constitutional Litigation,* 1960 SUPREME COURT REVIEW 75; Karst, note 1 *supra;* see Morris & Powe, *Constitutional and Statutory Rights to Open Housing,* 44 WASH. L. REV. 1, 28–46 (1968), for employment of ad hoc balancing in an analysis at one of the cutting edges of constitutional litigation.

[66] Emerson, note 2 *supra,* at 912–14; Frantz, *The First Amendment in Balance,* 71 YALE L. J. 1424, 1441–45 (1962); Nimmer, *The Right to Speak from* Times *to* Time: *First Amendment Theory Applied to Libel and Misapplied to Privacy,* 56 CALIF. L. REV. 935, 935–47 (1968).

[67] Frantz, note 66 *supra,* at 1445.

> ever which is unconditionally obligatory. Defendants in criminal cases can be tried in secret, or held incommunicado without trial, can be denied knowledge of the accusation against them, and the right to counsel, and the right to call witnesses in their own defense, and the right to trial by jury. Ex post facto laws and bills of attainder can be passed. Habeas corpus can be suspended, though there is neither rebellion nor invasion. Private property can be taken for public use without just, or any, compensation. Suffrage qualifications based on sex or race can be reinstituted. Anything which the Constitution says *cannot* be done *can* be done, if Congress thinks and the Court agrees (or is unwilling to set aside the congressional judgment) that the interests thereby served outweighed those which were sacrificed. Thus the whole idea of a government of limited powers, and of a written constitution as a device for attaining that end, is at least potentially at stake.

Unable on the other hand to accept in naked form Mr. Justice Black's absolutist approach to interpretation of the First Amendment,[68] these critics opt for what they describe as definitional balancing, some of them urging that this is actually what Mr. Justice Black is getting at in his rejection of ad hoc balancing.[69] In definitional balancing, weighing takes place, yet the juristic process is said to be significantly different:[70]

> To be sure, a judge who is obliged to formulate a new rule of law must consider what its advantages and disadvantages would be and weigh them against the advantages and disadvantages of the possible alternative rules which might be adopted. For example, if the judge is asked to decide whether the first amendment protects the refusal to state one's political affiliations, he must take into consideration the possible dangers to political freedom and other values of denying such protection. And he must also consider whether protecting that refusal would strip the government of power which may be needed for legitimate, non-repressive purposes. Mr. Justice Black provided an example of this type of "balancing" when, in order to decide whether the first amendment protects a right to anonymous publication, he took into consideration the possible social values of anonymous publication as indicated by the role such publications

[68] See, *e.g.*, Nimmer, note 66 *supra.*

[69] Emerson, note 2 *supra,* at 914–16; Frantz, note 66 *supra,* at 1433–38.

[70] Frantz, note 66 *supra,* at 1434–35.

> have played in the past, and the danger of repressing controversial views if identification of the proponents were required. But, though the mental process by which a judge determines what rule to adopt can be described as "balancing," this does not make it the same as balancing, independently of any rule, to determine what is the best disposition to make of a particular case. Deciding the scope to be accorded a particular constitutional freedom is different from deciding whether the interest of a particular litigant in freely expressing views which the judge may consider loathsome, dangerous, or ridiculous is outweighed by society's interest in "order," "security," or national "self-preservation."

In a concluding footnote Frantz leaves to others the major task of determining "how constitutionally protected speech should be defined," offering only the suggestion that the "starting point" be the Meiklejohn thesis that "freedom of speech is essential to self-government."[71] Professor Emerson laid the groundwork for this task through his excellent formulation of the function of freedom of expression in a democratic society.[72] Professor Nimmer's recent article, following Emerson in embracing definitional balancing as a viable theory of the First Amendment, finds it properly applied by the Court in *Times* but not in *Time*.[73] In the present context it is not necessary to stop to judge the validity of the Nimmer conclusions on either decision, in contrast with those of the Court majority or indeed of the Justices in dissent. The significant feature is the intellectual process employed by both Court and commentator in defining the contours of the First Amendment.

The difference in approach to constitutional interpretation is marked. Professor Kalven, who it will be recalled has not followed others in viewing balancing as equivalent to any form of the danger test, immediately observed of the *Times* opinion: "There is not a word of clear and present danger or of balancing."[74] Expanding on the significance of these omissions, he subsequently said of the danger test:[75]

> Whether the rewriting of [the clear and present danger test] by Judge Hand in the *Dennis* case or the persistent

---

[71] *Id.* at 1449–50 n. 105.

[72] Emerson, note 2 *supra*, at 878–86.

[73] Nimmer, note 66 *supra*, at 948–67; New York Times v. Sullivan, 376 U.S. 254 (1964); Time, Inc. v. Hill, 385 U.S. 374 (1967).

[74] KALVEN, note 41 *supra*, at 57.

[75] Kalven, note 2 *supra*, at 213–15.

attack on it as a constitutional formula by Mr. Justice Frankfurter or the perplexities of the newer speech issues or the sheer inadequacy of the formula itself caused its decline may be unclear. But it is clear that, as of the judgment in the *Times* case, it has disappeared. It did not occur to the Court to test the Alabama law before it in terms of clear and present danger, although barely a decade before, in *Beauharnais*, appeal to the test was the principal argument of the defendant. (It was one of the astute and successful gambles of the Wechsler brief that it did not argue the case in terms of clear and present danger.) The measure of the conceptual revolution promulgated by the *Times* case is that the Alabama law is found unconstitutional, not because there is no clear and present danger of a substantive evil in defendants' speech, but because the law looks too much like punishment for seditious libel.

There was one mention of the clear-and-present-danger test in the majority opinion. It occurred in a reference to *Pennekamp v. Florida* when the Court analogized the problem of defamation with that of contempt of court by publication. It would seem that the contempt problem is at least a sibling if not a twin to the one presented in the *Times* case. The former involves defamation of a specific public official, a judge. It might have been expected, therefore, that the same solution would fit both problems. But the modern Supreme Court decisions on the contempt problem—*Bridges*, *Craig* and *Pennekamp*—all rely for their disposition on the clear-and-present-danger test. And as recently as 1962, in *Wood v. Georgia*, the Court adhered to this approach in disposing of a contempt case. The contempt cases make the Court's silence in the *Times* case on the viability of the clear-and-present-danger test all the more deafening.

Immediately prior to the *Times* decision, the fashionable First Amendment test was what Professor Emerson called "ad hoc balancing." This formula, which he dates from the *Douds* case in 1950, has been the subject of several celebrated debates within the Court, especially between Justices Black and Harlan. The controversy has centered on large issues about absolutes and the proper role of judicial review. Professor Emerson, a critic of the balancing formula, has defined it: "The formula is that the court must, in each case, balance the individual and social interest in freedom of expression against the social interest sought by the regulation which restricts expression."

It is scarcely a novel suggestion that the law of defamation with its strict liability on the one hand and its complex of offsetting privileges on the other is a prime example

> of balancing the interest in freedom against the social interest sought by inhibiting communication. It is this balancing that in fact generates the bulk of the law in this area and the special fascination that it has derives from the precision and detail with which the common law has struck the balance in different situations. The issue before the Court in the *Times* case, therefore, would have been peculiarly meet for the application of the balancing formula. Again the failure to speak to the issue, either in the Court's opinion or Mr. Justice Black's concurrence, suggests the necessity for its re-evaluation.

The Court's contemporaneous opinion in *Garrison v. Louisiana*,[76] extending the *Times* principle to criminal libel of public officials, bears out the Kalven analysis. The judicial balancing is of the definitional, not the ad hoc, type:[77]

> Truth may not be the subject of either civil or criminal sanctions where discussion of public affairs is concerned. . . . [O]nly those false statements made with the high degree of awareness of their probable falsity demanded by *New York Times* may be the subject of either civil or criminal sanctions. For speech concerning public affairs is more than self-expression; it is the essence of self-government.

On the other hand:[78]

> [T]he use of the known lie as a tool is at once at odds with the premises of democratic government and with the orderly manner in which economic, social, or political change is to be effected. Calculated falsehood falls into that class of utterances which "are no essential part of any exposition of ideas, and are of such slight social value as a step to truth that any benefit that may be derived from them is clearly outweighed by the social interest in order and morality. . . ." *Chaplinsky* v. *New Hampshire*, 315 U.S. 568, 572. Hence the knowingly false statement and the false statement made with reckless disregard of the truth, do not enjoy constitutional protection.

Advocates of definitional, as opposed to ad hoc, balancing can find Court support for their views not alone in the line of libel cases but, as well, in the longer line of obscenity decisions. The unsatisfactoriness in results achieved from *Roth-Alberts*[79] to *Stanley*

---

76 379 U.S. 64 (1964).

77 *Id.* at 74–75.

78 *Id.* at 75.

79 Roth v. United States, 354 U.S. 476 (1957).

v. Georgia[80] does not mitigate from the fact that the Court has been at work attempting to define the reach of First Amendment liberties in the morals area. And there is Chief Justice Warren's footnote disclaimer of ad hoc balancing at the close of his opinion for the Court in *United States v. Robel:*[81]

> It has been suggested that this case should be decided by "balancing" the governmental interests expressed in § 5(a)(1)(D) against the First Amendment rights asserted by the appellee. This we decline to do. We recognize that both interests are substantial, but we deem it inappropriate for this Court to label one as being more important or more substantial than the other. Our inquiry is more circumscribed. Faced with a clear conflict between a federal statute enacted in the interests of national security and an individual's exercise of his First Amendment rights, we have confined our analysis to whether Congress has adopted a constitutional means in achieving its concededly legitimate legislative goal. In making this determination we have found it necessary to measure the validity of the means adopted by Congress against both the goal it has sought to achieve and the specific prohibitions of the First Amendment. But we have in no way "balanced" those respective interests. We have ruled only that the Constitution requires that the conflict between congressional power and individual rights be accommodated by legislation drawn more narrowly to avoid the conflict. There is, of course, nothing novel in that analysis. Such a course of adjudication was enunciated by Chief Justice Marshall when he declared: "Let the end be legitimate, let it be within the scope of the constitution, and all means which are appropriate, which are plainly adapted to that end, *which are not prohibited, but consist with the letter and spirit of the constitution* are constitutional." *M'Culloch* v. *Maryland*, 4 Wheat. 316, 421 (1819) (emphasis added). In this case, the means chosen by Congress are contrary to the "letter and spirit" of the First Amendment.

Such trends in Court commitment and commentator critique would appear to spell the end of the line for "clear and present danger" after a half-century of vicissitudes. This, whether or not the weakened danger test was fully fused by *Dennis* into ad hoc balancing. It is therefore not surprising to find a funereal atmosphere permeating the fiftieth anniversary of "clear and present danger." But the current tearless farewells take no account of still another

80 394 U.S. 557 (1969).

81 389 U.S. 258, 268 n. 20 (1967).

facet in the life of "clear and present danger," a facet with a great potential future if definitional balancing is to be the standard approach to resolution of First Amendment boundaries. For, while definitional balancing draws the constitutional line generically, by determining the meaning of constitutional guarantees for different classes of situation (*e.g.*, price regulation, control of obscenity), another step is essential to disposition of any individual case. That step involves a judgment on whether legislation or other governmental action under challenge bears a sufficient nexus to objectives of government determined, through the definitional process, to be consistent with the reach of constitutional restriction. Clearly, the tightness of the nexus that is required will have a direct bearing on the outcome in a given context of validity or invalidity. Thus requirement of but a rational nexus would result in little invalidity. By a metamorphosis no more strained than those earlier experienced, "clear and present danger" could transform into a requirement in First Amendment litigation of a strong demonstration of constitutionality that would force governmental respect for the protected civil interests of the individual.

Although expressed in the conjectural, as a role that "clear and present danger" could play in the future, there is considerable basis in the decided cases for such a development. Origins can be traced back to the 1938 decision in the first *Carolene Products* case.[82] Congressional prohibition of the movement of filled milk in interstate commerce was sustained against Due Process challenge because "regulatory legislation affecting ordinary commercial transactions is not to be pronounced unconstitutional unless in the light of the facts made known or generally assumed it is of such a character as to preclude the assumption that it rests upon some rational basis within the knowledge and experience of the legislators."[83] But to this statement was appended what has become the famous "footnote four," the first two paragraphs of which, with omission of citations, read:[84]

> There may be narrower scope for operation of the presumption of constitutionality when legislation appears on its face to be within a specific prohibition of the Constitution, such as those of the first ten amendments, which are deemed

---

82 United States v. Carolene Products Co., 304 U.S. 144 (1938).

83 *Id.* at 152.

84 *Id.* at 152–53 n. 4.

> equally specific when held to be embraced within the Fourteenth. . . .
>
> It is unnecessary to consider now whether legislation which restricts those political processes which can ordinarily be expected to bring about repeal of undesirable legislation, is to be subjected to more exacting judicial scrutiny under the general prohibitions of the Fourteenth Amendment than are most other types of legislation. . . .

Among numerous citations following the text of this second paragraph are "*Whitney* v. *California*, 274 U.S. 357, 373–378 . . . and see Holmes, J., in *Gitlow* v. *New York*, 268 U.S. 652, 673." Significantly the page references are to the essence of the Holmes-Brandeis dissent in *Gitlow* and of the Brandeis-Holmes concurrence in *Whitney*. The most immediate judicial consequence of footnote four was the Court's probing of the ramifications of the "political process" theory, wherein the two flag-salute decisions figured so prominently.[85] With the vacating of the original judgment in *Opelika*,[86] Stone's reformulation of the footnote thesis in terms of preferred freedom became majority doctrine in *Murdock v. Pennsylvania*.[87] "Freedom of press, freedom of speech, freedom of religion are in a preferred position."[88]

In *Barnette*'s repudiation of *Gobitis*,[89] which followed six weeks after *Murdock*, Mr. Justice Jackson did not employ the new phrase. But its essence pervaded his opinion and the tie with "clear and present danger" was present, when he put the matter this way:[90]

> Much of the vagueness of the due process clause disappears when the specific prohibitions of the First become its standard. The right of a State to regulate, for example, a public utility may well include, so far as the due process test is concerned, power to impose all of the restrictions which a legislature may have a "rational basis" for adopting. But freedoms of speech and press, of assembly, and of worship may not be infringed on such slender grounds. They are susceptible of restriction only to prevent grave and immediate danger to interests which the State may lawfully protect.

---

85 Minersville School District v. Gobitis, 310 U.S. 586 (1940); West Virginia State Board of Education v. Barnette, 319 U.S. 624 (1943).

86 Jones v. Opelika, 319 U.S. 103 (1943), *vacating* 316 U.S. 584 (1942).

87 319 U.S. 105 (1943).

88 *Id.* at 115.

89 Note 85 *supra.*

90 319 U.S. at 639.

Three years later, at the hands of Justice Rutledge, although for a sharply divided Court, this distinction in judicial rule was explained explicitly in terms of the "preferred freedom" theory:[91]

> The case confronts us again with the duty our system places on this Court to say where the individual's freedom ends and the State's power begins. Choice on that border, now as always delicate, is perhaps more so where the usual presumption supporting legislation is balanced by the preferred place given in our scheme to the great, the indispensable democratic freedoms secured by the First Amendment. Cf. *Schneider* v. *State*, 308 U.S. 147; *Cantwell* v. *Connecticut*, 310 U.S. 296, *Prince* v. *Massachusetts*, 321 U.S. 158. That priority gives these liberties a sanctity and a sanction not permitting dubious intrusions. And it is the character of the right, not of the limitation, which determines what standard governs the choice. Compare *United States* v. *Carolene Products Co.*, 304 U.S. 144, 152–153.

The evolutionary relation between "clear and present danger" and the "preferred freedom" theory is thus quite clear. As Dean McKay has observed:[92]

> [I]t appears essential to recognize at least that the original formulation of the clear and present danger test by Justice Holmes in *Schenck v. United States* was a recognition that when first amendment values are involved, the otherwise permissible prohibitions which government might impose are to be examined in a different context and measured by a more critical standard. This, then, is the essence of the preferred position—the exercise of judgment to protect first amendment freedoms in a variety of ways.

On the other hand, it was not clear for a time that the theory of the preferred place of the First Amendment articulated a concept different from the Holmes-Brandeis formulation of the danger test as a full and distinct solvent for constitutional issues involving speech and related guarantees. This is evident from the passage in the Rutledge opinion in *Collins* which immediately follows the paragraph already quoted:[93]

> For these reasons any attempt to restrict those liberties must be justified by clear public interest, threatened not doubtfully

[91] Thomas v. Collins, 323 U.S. 516, 529–30 (1945).

[92] McKay, note 62 *supra*, at 1191.

[93] 323 U.S. at 530.

> or remotely, but by clear and present danger. The rational connection between the remedy provided and the evil to be curbed, which in other contexts might support legislation against attack on due process grounds, will not suffice. These rights rest on firmer foundation. Accordingly, whatever occasion would restrain orderly discussion and persuasion, at appropriate time and place, must have clear support in public danger, actual or impending. Only the gravest abuses, endangering paramount interests, give occasion for permissible limitation.

Of those five sentences, the first, fourth, and fifth sound in terms of the Holmes-Brandeis test. Independently, they might be taken to imply the repudiation for First Amendment matters of the "any tendency" test of the *Gitlow* majority. Yet, linked by the second and third sentences a different meaning could be intended. These sentences place the concept of "clear and present danger" in an entirely new context. That context is an associational one, as is true under the Holmes-Brandeis view. But it is now a matter of essentially qualitative, rather than quantitative, connection.

For a Court again divided, Mr. Justice Black had three weeks earlier, in *Korematsu v. United States*,[94] made a direct linkage between the concepts of "clear and present danger" and nexus:[95]

> In the light of the principles we announced in the *Hirabayashi* case, we are unable to conclude that it was beyond the war power of Congress and the Executive to exclude those of Japanese ancestry from the West Coast war area at the time they did. True, exclusion from the area in which one's home is located is a far greater deprivation than constant confinement to the home from 8 P.M. to 6 A.M. Nothing short of apprehension by the proper military authorities of the gravest imminent danger to the public safety can constitutionally justify either. But exclusion from a threatened area, no less than curfew, has a definite and close relationship to the prevention of espionage and sabotage. The military authorities, charged with the primary responsibility of defending our shores, concluded that curfew provided inadequate protection and ordered exclusion. They did so, as pointed out in our *Hirabayashi* opinion, in accordance with Congressional authority to the military to say who should, and who should not, remain in the threatened areas.

94 323 U.S. 214 (1944).

95 *Id.* at 217–18.

The new function of the test is here clearer than in *Collins*. To withstand constitutional attack, the challenged governmental action must be shown to be closely and intimately connected with a permitted objective of government.

The requirement of an immediate or tight nexus for constitutionality dooms legislative restrictions and prohibitions cast in embracive terms. In this characteristic it contrasts with the rational nexus test, which because of its looseness ensures constitutionality on the meager showing of an iota of possible connection between the governmental action under attack and some permissible objective of government. Adoption of the test of "clear and present danger" nexus for First Amendment issues therefore requires that policy formulations, whether by court, city council, state assembly, or Congress, must be tightly drafted to guarantee that their thrust is confined to objectives that government is free to attain. The closing paragraphs of the Douglas opinion for the Court in *Murdock* bring this point to crystal focus, and relate it to what Edmond Cahn later aptly characterized as "the firstness of the First Amendment."[96] Excerpting from those paragraphs at once saves space and heightens effect:[97]

> Jehovah's Witnesses are not "above the law." But the present ordinance is not directed to the problems with which the police power of the state is free to deal. It does not cover, and petitioners are not charged with, breaches of the peace. . . . Furthermore, the present ordinance is not narrowly drawn to safeguard the people of the community in their homes against the evils of solicitation. See *Cantwell* v. *Connecticut*. . . . As we have said, it is not merely a registration ordinance calling for an identification of the solicitors so as to give the authorities some basis for investigating strangers coming into the community. . . . Nor can the present ordinance survive if we assume that it has been construed to apply only to solicitation from house to house. The ordinance is not narrowly drawn to prevent or control abuses or evils arising from that activity. . . .
>
> The judgment in *Jones* v. *Opelika* has this day been vacated. Freed from that controlling precedent we can restore to their high, constitutional position the liberties of itinerant evangelists who disseminate their religious beliefs and the tenets of their faith through distribution of literature.

---

96 Cahn, *The Firstness of the First Amendment*, 65 YALE L.J. 464 (1956).

97 319 U.S. at 116–17.

Tight drafting as a constitutional necessity traces back to *Thornhill v. Alabama*[98] and *Cantwell v. Connecticut*,[99] decided a month apart in 1940. In each the requirement that the statute be "narrowly drawn" is associated with the danger test. The language used, however, is such that one cannot be sure the danger test had been dissociated from its formulation at the hands of Holmes and Brandeis. This is especially true of the *Cantwell* opinion, to which the Court referred in *Murdock*. With no dissent, Justice Roberts in *Cantwell* declared:[100]

> Although the contents of the [phonographic] record not unnaturally aroused animosity, we think that, in the absence of a statute narrowly drawn to define and punish specific conduct as constituting a clear and present danger to a substantial interest of the State, the petitioner's communication, considered in the light of the constitutional guarantees, raised no such clear and present menace to public peace and order as to render him liable to conviction of the common law offense in question [breach of the peace].

But the Murphy opinion in *Thornhill*, for all save Justice McReynolds, had been suggestive of the conception of "clear and present danger" as requiring a close connection between permitted objective of, and challenged action by, government:[101]

> The power and the duty of the State to take adequate steps to preserve the peace and to protect the privacy, the lives, and the property of its residents cannot be doubted. But no clear and present danger of destruction of life or property, or invasion of the right of privacy, or breach of the peace can be thought to be inherent in the activities of every person who approaches the premises of an employer and publicizes the facts of a labor dispute involving the latter. We are not now concerned with picketing *en masse* or otherwise conducted which might occasion such imminent and aggravated danger to these interests as to justify a statute narrowly drawn to cover the precise situation giving rise to the danger. Compare *American Foundries* v. *Tri-City Council*, 257 U.S. 184, 205. Section 3448 in question here does not aim specifically at serious encroachments on these interests and does not evidence any such care in balancing these interests against the interest of the community and that of the individual in freedom of discussion on matters of public concern.

---

98 310 U.S. 88 (1940).

99 310 U.S. 296 (1940).

100 *Id.* at 311.

101 310 U.S. at 105.

The years following were not propitious ones for further development in the transformation of the danger test into a strong nexus test for application in First Amendment and, as in *Korematsu*, related civil liberties cases. To adapt a favorite Frankfurter phrase, in the disposition of the bulk of litigation involving free speech and associated concepts of personal liberty, the thrust of judicial action was elsewhere—on the scope and application of the Holmes-Brandeis formulation, on the emergence and retirement of ad hoc balancing, and on the post-*Dennis* interrelationships between the danger test and that form of balancing.

The "preferred freedom" theory did not, as such, long survive the strictures leveled at it by Justice Frankfurter in his concurrence in *Kovacs v. Cooper*,[102] although its underlying philosophy of a "preference for freedom" did not abate. Where the Court's approach to constitutional resolution directly employed the nexus rationale, the connection required tended to be reduced to the substantial nexus level generally used by state courts to test the validity of exertions of governmental policy in the areas of both civil and economic liberty. The origin of this trend in *United Public Workers v. Mitchell*[103] may well explain it. Counsel for the Union had great difficulty identifying the constitutional protection allegedly breached by the Hatch Act's call for "political sterilization" of federal employees. In any event, a relaxed nexus test was employed in the earlier "membership list" cases. In *N.A.A.C.P. v. Alabama*,[104] invalidity followed from the absence of a demonstration of substantial connection between disclosure and legitimate objective. The language in *Bates v. Little Rock*[105] suggested an even less stringent test although perhaps unintentionally: "When it is shown that state action threatens significantly to impinge upon constitutionally protected freedom it becomes the duty of this Court to determine whether the action bears a *reasonable* relationship to the achievement of the governmental purpose [here license taxation] asserted as its justification."[106] Meantime in *Uphaus v. Wyman*,[107] involving legislative investigation, it was a dissenting Justice who insisted that "for an investigation in the field of the

102 336 U.S. 77, 95–96 (1949).

103 330 U.S. 75 (1947).

104 357 U.S. 449 (1958).

105 361 U.S. 516 (1960).

106 *Id.* at 525. (Emphasis added.)

107 360 U.S. 72 (1959).

constitutionally protected freedoms of speech and assemblage to be upheld by the broad standards of relevance permissible in a legislative inquiry, some relevance to a valid legislative purpose must be shown."[108]

The requirement that an ordinance or statute be "narrowly drawn," if there is threat of trespass upon First Amendment territory, fared better, thanks largely to its reciprocal. This reciprocal concept, that such legislation to be constitutional must avoid "overbreadth," can be taken to have had its origin in *Winters v. New York*.[109] There a section of the New York Penal Law, construed by the New York Court of Appeals to include within its prohibitions distribution of magazines in which stories of deeds of bloodshed "are massed so as to incite to violent crimes," was invalidated for vagueness and indefiniteness. Significantly, vagueness and indefiniteness arose not alone from uncertainty as to statutory coverage but also from the possibility that the section as officially construed could be restrictive of freedoms of the press guaranteed against abridgment by the First Amendment. The distinction between voidness for vagueness and voidness for overreach is now clear, with the latter concept standing firmly on its own constitutional feet. Thus in *Zwickler v. Koota*[110] there appears the following paragraph:[111]

> But we have here no question of a construction of § 781-b [the New York statutory prohibition on distribution of anonymous political handbills] that would "avoid or modify the constitutional question." Appellant's challenge is not that the statute is void for "vagueness," that is, that it is a statute "which either forbids or requires the doing of an act in terms so vague that men of common intelligence must necessarily guess at its meaning and differ as to its application. . . ." *Connally* v. *General Construction Co.*, 269 U.S. 385, 391. Rather his constitutional attack is that the statute, although lacking neither clarity nor precision, is void for "overbreadth," that is, that it offends the constitutional principle that "a governmental purpose to control or prevent activities constitutionally subject to state regulation may not be achieved by means which sweep unnecessarily broadly and thereby invade the area of protected freedoms." *N.A.A.C.P.* v. *Alabama*, 377 U.S. 288, 307. [Other citations omitted.] Appellee does not con-

108 *Id.* at 100.

109 333 U.S. 507 (1948).

110 389 U.S. 241 (1967).

111 *Id.* at 249–50.

> test appellant's suggestion that § 781-b is both clear and precise; indeed, appellee concedes that state court construction cannot narrow its allegedly indiscriminate cast and render unnecessary a decision of appellant's constitutional challenge. See *Aptheker* v. *Secretary of State*, 378 U.S. 500.

In the 1960's, Court explanation of unconstitutionality in terms of overbreadth has become common. More and more, judicial references to statutory overbreadth and to lack of statutory narrowness are employed interchangeably. From among recent decisions the following are illustrative, both of these and of related developments toward the shaping of "clear and present danger" into a test of immediate nexus. In *Shelton v. Tucker*:[112]

> The scope of the inquiry required by Act 10 is completely unlimited. The statute requires a teacher to reveal the church to which he belongs, or to which he has given financial support. It requires him to disclose his political party, and every political organization to which he may have contributed over a five-year period. It requires him to list, without number, every conceivable kind of associational tie—social, professional, political, avocational or religious. Many such relationships could have no possible bearing upon the teacher's occupational competence or fitness.
>
> In a series of decisions this Court has held that, even though the governmental purpose be legitimate and substantial, that purpose cannot be pursued by means that broadly stifle fundamental personal liberties when the end can be more narrowly achieved. The breadth of legislative abridgment must be viewed in the light of less drastic means for achieving the same basic purpose. . . .
>
> As recently as last Term we held invalid an ordinance prohibiting the distribution of handbills because the breadth of its application went far beyond what was necessary to achieve

---

112 364 U.S. 479, 488–89 (1960). In both *Talley* and *Shelton* the opinions of the Court reach back for doctrinal basis to Lovell v. Griffin, 303 U.S. 444 (1938), the original decision invalidating a handbill ordinance unlimited in its embrasure. This momentous determination, rejecting the Holmesian proposition in Commonwealth v. Davis, 162 Mass. 510, *aff'd*, Davis v. Massachusetts, 167 U.S. 43 (1897), that a city has the same dominion over its streets, parks, and other public areas as does a private landowner over his property, precipitated a situation in which thousands of ordinances and hundreds of statutes from an earlier constitutional period became invalid for overbreadth and under the constitutional necessity of being "more narrowly drawn." During the thirty years since *Lovell*, the implications and ramifications of that revolutionary decision have grown steadily clearer to all involved in this phase of constitutional litigation.

> a legitimate governmental purpose. *Talley* v. *California*, 362 U.S. 60. In that case the Court noted that it had been "urged that this ordinance is aimed at providing a way to identify those responsible for fraud, false advertising and libel. Yet the ordinance is in no manner so limited. . . . Therefore, we do not pass on the validity of an ordinance limited to prevent these or any other supposed evils. This ordinance simply bars all handbills under all circumstances anywhere that do not have the names and addresses printed on them in the place the ordinance requires." 362 U.S., at 64.

The *Button*[113] and *Cox*[114] decisions are especially instructive. The former has in it "something for everybody." For one thing, in a novel context the definitional approach to constitutional resolution is clear-cut in the majority opinion, while the dissent reflects continued adherence to ad hoc balancing. Having found the NAACP activities a protected form of "political expression," Mr. Justice Brennan for the majority went on to observe:[115]

> The objectionable quality of vagueness and overbreadth does not depend upon absence of fair notice to a criminally accused or upon unchanneled delegation of legislative powers, but upon the danger of tolerating, in the area of First Amendment freedoms, the existence of a penal statute susceptible of sweeping and improper application. Cf. *Marcus* v. *Search Warrant*, 367 U.S. 717, 733. These freedoms are delicate and vulnerable, as well as supremely precious in our society. . . . Because First Amendment freedoms need breathing space to survive, government may regulate in the area only with narrow specificity. *Cantwell* v. *Connecticut*, 310 U.S. 296, 311.

Mr. Justice White was forced to concur in part and dissent in part because:[116]

> If we had before us, which we do not, a narrowly drawn statute proscribing only the actual day-to-day management and dictation of the tactics, strategy and conduct of litigation by a lay entity such as the NAACP, the issue would be considerably different, at least for me; for in my opinion neither the practice of law by such an organization nor its management of the litigation of its members or others is constitutionally protected. . . .

---

113 N.A.A.C.P. v. Button, 371 U.S. 415 (1963).

114 Cox v. Louisiana, 379 U.S. 536 and 559 (1965).

115 371 U.S. at 432–33.

116 *Id.* at 447–48.

> It is not at all clear to me, however, that the opinion of the majority would not also strike down such a narrowly drawn statute. To the extent that it would, I am in disagreement.

On the other hand the three dissenters, in an opinion by Mr. Justice Harlan, insisted that to[117]

> declare that litigation is a form of conduct that may be associated with political expression does not resolve this case. Neither the First Amendment nor the Fourteenth constitutes an absolute bar to government regulation in the fields of free expression and association. . . . The problem in each such case is to weigh the legitimate interest of the State against the effect of the regulation on individual rights. . . .
>
> So here, the question is whether the particular regulation of conduct concerning litigation has a reasonable relation to the furtherance of proper state interest, and whether that interest outweighs any foreseeable harm to the furtherance of protected freedoms.

In *Cox I* the Louisiana breach-of-peace statute went down because "unconstitutionally vague in its overly broad scope." But in *Cox II* the Louisiana statute modeled on 18 U.S.C. § 1507 itself passed muster:[118]

> Here we deal not with the contempt power but with a narrowly drafted statute and not with speech in its pristine form but with conduct of a totally different character. Even assuming the applicability of a general clear and present danger test, it is one thing to conclude that the mere publication of a newspaper editorial or a telegram to a Secretary of Labor, however critical of a court, presents no clear and present danger to the administration of justice and quite another thing to conclude that crowds, such as this, demonstrating before a courthouse may not be prohibited by a legislative determination based on experience that such conduct inherently threatens the judicial process. We therefore reject the clear and present danger argument of appellant.

This language of Mr. Justice Goldberg cannot have been intended to reestablish the majority view in *Gitlow.* Yet it does reject the Holmes-Brandeis formulation of the danger test as fully and consistently applied in the contempt cases. What appears in evolutionary process is a reading of the test as requiring that legislation and equivalent forms of articulated governmental policy must, if they

---

117 *Id.* at 453, 455.

118 379 U.S. at 566.

are to withstand constitutional scrutiny, bear such a close and immediate nexus to valid objectives beyond the reach of the First Amendment that there is no danger of jeopardy to the values protected by that amendment. This result is achieved by the Court's insistence that "the statute be narrowly drawn." The requirement is clearly more than one of relative narrowness, and certainly different in kind from the judicial requirement that policy formulation in the public sector satisfy the constitutional demand for reasonable certainty in meaning. It is a requirement that draftsmanship, whether by one or another branch of government, be such as to insure that the full scope of constitutional guarantees as demarcated by the Court is not weakened by laws so inclusively drawn that in administration they reach with civil or criminal sanctions territory determined to be off limits to government in the interest of individual civil liberty.

The two recent "burning" cases demonstrate the growing centrality in the Court's mind of the narrowness doctrine as thus understood. Concluding his sustainment in *United States v. O'Brien*[119] of the hotly disputed amendment of the Universal Military Service and Training Act, Chief Justice Warren for the Court found that[120]

> because of the Government's substantial interest in assuring the continuing availability of issued Selective Service certificates, because amended § 462(b) is an appropriately narrow means of protecting this interest and condemns only the independent noncommunicative impact of conduct within its reach, and because the noncommunicative impact of O'Brien's act of burning his registration certificate frustrated the Government's interest, a sufficient governmental interest has been shown to justify O'Brien's conviction.

Of the decision it has been said in the pages of this *Review*:[121]

---

119 391 U.S. 367 (1968). 120 *Id*. at 382.

121 Alfange, *Free Speech and Symbolic Conduct: The Draft-Card Burning Case*, 1968 SUPREME COURT REVIEW 1, at 18–19. Professor Alfange then continued with the assertion that "simply because overbroad statutes affecting speech are unconstitutional, it does not follow that narrow and specific statutes that limit speech only indirectly are valid as applied in all cases." *Id*. at 19. Later, *id*. at 21 n. 74, he demonstrated from both *Cox II* and *O'Brien* that the statutes there involved could be said to have overreached constitutional bounds. The footnote illustrations make clear, what is not clear in the text of the article, that Professor Alfange understands "narrowness" to be a word of art and not just a way of speaking comparatively with respect to the reach of various statutes.

> The crucial factor in the Court's test is plainly the narrowness of the statute. If the statute is narrowly drawn, and is not on its face concerned with speech, courts are excused from the task of examining the degree of abridgment of expression that may be brought about by a particular application. In a sense, such a rule is the other side from the Court's repeated insistence that statutes having the effect of restricting speech in order to secure other social interests must not be vague or over-broad. "Because First Amendment freedoms need breathing space to survive," the Court has said [in *Button*, quoted earlier], "government may regulate in the area only with narrow specificity," and the constitutional requirement of narrowness has become the Court's most potent weapon in protecting freedom of expression against governmental incursion.

For the Court in *Street v. New York*,[122] Mr. Justice Harlan identified "four governmental interests" that inferentially he postulated to be constitutionally permissible objectives. The second of these was breach of the peace arising from physical retaliation against inflammatory words. Testing against this objective Street's conviction for flag burning under the New York statute, the majority could not[123]

> say that appellant's remarks were so inherently inflammatory as to come within that small class of "fighting words" which "are likely to provoke the average person to retaliation, and thereby cause a breach of the peace." *Chaplinsky* v. *New Hampshire*, 315 U.S. 568, 574 (1942). And even if appellant's words might be found within that category, § 1425, subd. 16, par. d, is not narrowly drawn to punish only words of that character, and there is no indication that it was so interpreted by the state courts. Hence, this case is again distinguishable from *Chaplinsky*, *supra*, in which the Court emphasized that the statute was "carefully drawn so as not unduly to impair liberty of expression. . . ."

Inasmuch as a "narrowly drawn" statute (or narrowly formulated common-law principle) is, in constitutional context, one so drawn (or formulated) as to foreclose attainment of impermissible objectives of government, it is but a different mode of expression to cast the functional concept into terms of close or immediate nexus. As earlier asserted, therefore, "there is considerable grounding in the decided cases" for the development of a new, and meaningful,

122 394 U.S. 576 (1969).

123 *Id.* at 592.

role for the "clear and present danger" test. The major "relic on the waters of the law," to adapt another Frankfurter phrase, is one of that Justice's own creation. This is his assertion in *Beauharnais,*[124] approvingly quoted by Mr. Justice Brennan in *Roth-Alberts:*[125]

> Libelous utterances, not being within the area of constitutionally protected speech, it is unnecessary, either for us or for the State courts, to consider the issues behind the phrase "clear and present danger." Certainly no one would contend that obscene speech, for example, may be punished only upon a showing of such circumstances. Libel, as we have seen, is in the same class.

Frankfurter may be excused for failing to anticipate *New York Times v. Sullivan.*[126] But the difficulty with the passage goes deeper. The assertion is correct only in terms of the Holmes-Brandeis formulation of the danger test. Under that formulation if the nature and circumstances of particular speech bring it under the First Amendment's protective mantle, the test applies. If not, then by definitional limitation the test has no relevancy to the constitutional question. Transformed into a requirement of immediate nexus for constitutionality, however, the danger test is always applicable where First Amendment rights are potentially in jeopardy. The only way to be certain that challenged governmental action will not invade protected freedoms is to ensure that it cannot, by subjecting it to the test of immediate nexus. Any less stringent requirement reduces pro tanto the certainty that that action, whatever its form, will not in its operation reach into areas that the Constitution has blocked off from intrusion by government. Thus reconceived, the test of "clear and present danger" has a vital role to play in future civil-liberty litigation.

Only the opinion, and not the result, would vary in such cases as *Roth, New York Times,* and *Brandenburg.* With *Roth,* reliance upon the *Beauharnais* assertion of the inapplicability of "clear and present danger" would have to be stricken, and the opinion rephrased to articulate the result as the consequence of the Court's satisfaction of the existence of a close nexus between the federal and state statutes as judicially construed and that obscenity which lies

---

124 Beauharnais v. Illinois, 343 U.S. 250, 266 (1952).

125 354 U.S. at 486–87.

126 376 U.S. 254 (1964).

beyond the protection of the First Amendment. In *Times*, the opinion would scarcely require alteration. Once the Alabama common law on libel was stated and the constitutional line drawn, it would be self-evident that no tight nexus could possibly be demonstrated between the applicable state law and a constitutionally permissible objective of the state. In *Brandenburg* it would be a matter of a short addendum to the opinion stating by way of summarization that the reach of the Ohio law, measured against the constitutional line separating the valid from the invalid, was such as to negate any close nexus between it and permissible objectives of government.

Significant as could be the role of "clear and present danger" in civil liberties litigation, there is an even greater place for the revamped danger test if Court orientation is to be one of neutral principle rather than preferred result. The point has been earlier made that the rational nexus test affords no protection whatever against governmental violation of constitutional rights, yet this is the controlling test long employed by the Court where the constitutional challenge is to governmental regulation in the economic sphere. *Carolene I*[127] is a classic illustration. *Collins*[128] is noteworthy as a case situation on the border line between the economic and the civil. Since *Nebbia v. New York*[129] installed as majority doctrine the classic dissent of Justice Holmes in *Lochner v. New York*,[130] American governments are essentially free to choose from among competing economic policies. "A constitution is not intended to embody a particular economic theory, whether of paternalism and the organic relation of the citizen to the State or of *laissez faire*."[131] Despite this fact, however, the Constitution of the United States has never been authoritatively interpreted as being devoid of constitutional protection for economic values. Decisions of Holmes and Brandeis in their time attest to this,[132] as do recent

127 Note 82 *supra*.

128 Note 91 *supra*.

129 291 U.S. 502 (1934).

130 198 U.S. 45, 74–76 (1905).

131 *Id.* at 75.

132 Pennsylvania Coal Co. v. Mahon, 260 U.S. 393 (1922) (Holmes and Brandeis dissenting); Louisville Joint Stock Land Bank v. Radford, 295 U.S. 555 (1935) (Brandeis); Thompson v. Consolidated Gas Utilities Corp., 300 U.S. 55 (1937) (Brandeis).

utterances of a current liberal Justice, Hugo Black.[133] The *Carolene* litigation is instructive on this score. Notwithstanding the ease with which the Court in *Carolene I* sustained the validity of the Filled Milk Act on demurrer to the indictment, the opinion in *Carolene II*[134] is careful to emphasize:[135]

> In the action of Congress on filled milk there is no prohibition of the shipment of an article of commerce merely because it competes with another such article which it resembles. Such would be the prohibition of the shipment of cotton or silk textiles to protect rayon or nylon or of anthracite to aid the consumption of bituminous coal or of cottonseed oil to aid the soybean industry.

Outright governmental product favoritism is constitutionally suspect despite *Powell v. Pennsylvania.*[136] *Carolene II*'s validation of the federal law on review of the conviction under the indictment is justified in terms of the concededly permissible objective of protection of the public from product misrepresentation:[137]

> Here a milk product, skimmed milk, from which a valuable element—butterfat—has been removed is artificially enriched with cheaper fats and vitamins so that it is indistinguishable in the eyes of the average purchaser from whole milk products. The result is that the compound is confused with and passed off as the whole milk product in spite of proper labeling.

So long as property interests enjoy some, although limited, constitutional protection, a strong nexus should be required between challenged governmental exertions and permissible objectives of government. It is a contradiction in terms for the Court to postulate the existence of areas of constitutional immunity while at the same time employing a rational nexus test, as was done in the *Carolene* cases. For the looseness of that test lays open to the government the indirect achievement of that which is directly

---

133 Bell v. Maryland, 378 U.S. 226, 318 (1964) (dissent); Amalgamated Food Employees Union Local v. Logan Valley Plaza, Inc., 391 U.S. 308, 327, 330 (1968) (dissent) ("I believe that, whether this Court likes it or not the Constitution recognizes and supports the concept of private ownership of property.") See also Adderley v. Florida, 385 U.S. 39 (1966).

134 Carolene Products Co. v. United States, 323 U.S. 18 (1944).

135 *Id.* at 31.

136 127 U.S. 678 (1888).

137 323 U.S. at 31.

denied to government. It is significant that the great majority of state supreme courts have never accepted, in interpreting their own constitutions, the Supreme Court's dichotomy. Rather, they have insisted upon demonstration of a substantial nexus regardless of the nature of the rights in litigation. A substantial nexus is one where there exists approximately as much evidence supporting, as disputing, connection between the challenged act of government and a permissible objective of government as determined by definitional balancing in constitutional interpretation. The usual state court approach has the merit of consistency, and the quality of the nexus required is a marked improvement over the mere demand for rationality.[138] Nevertheless, the substantial nexus test cannot guarantee that enclaves of constitutional immunity for the individual will not be invaded. From this it must be concluded that only the danger test as judicially redesigned can provide this assurance in optimum degree for all facets of constitutional litigation. If the first fifty years of "clear and present danger" prove to have brought this much of a contribution to the complexities of constitutional judicial review, the test's trials and tribulations of a half-century will have been worth the long period of gestation.

---

[138] Illustration may be found in STRONG, AMERICAN CONSTITUTIONAL LAW 688–96 (1950).

GEOFFREY R. STONE

FORA AMERICANA: SPEECH IN PUBLIC PLACES

The Supreme Court has consistently adhered to the view that the First Amendment "rests on the assumption that the widest possible dissemination of information from diverse and antagonistic sources is essential to the welfare of the public."[1] For "it is only through free debate and free exchange of ideas that government remains responsive to the will of the people and peaceful change is effected."[2] This attitude presupposes the existence of a "marketplace of ideas" in which advocates of all stripes may argue the merits of their positions and submit their views to public scrutiny and consideration. What, then, are the boundaries and ground rules of this "marketplace of ideas"? How do we determine who gets to speak where, when, how, and to whom? What conditions must prevail before the channels of communication may be closed? The answers we give to these and similar questions reflect the seriousness of our commitment to the First Amendment itself.

The dominant forum for the dissemination of information and ideas today is, of course, the mass media. In recent years, the opera-

---

Geoffrey R. Stone is Assistant Professor of Law, The University of Chicago.

AUTHOR'S NOTE: I should like to express my indebtedness to Harry Kalven, Jr., not only for personal guidance on this article, but also for the inspiration of his scholarship in this field. I should like also to thank Gerhard Casper and Richard Epstein for their helpful comments on an earlier draft of this article. I should like to offer a special word of thanks to *K*.

1 Associated Press v. United States, 326 U.S. 1, 20 (1945).

2 Terminiello v. Chicago, 337 U.S. 1, 4 (1949).

tion of this forum has been the subject of mounting criticism. Considerable controversy has been generated by proposals that, in an effort to encourage debate and stimulate diversity, individuals be granted a right of "access" to radio, television, and newspaper facilities for the purpose of expressing their views on public issues. Whatever the merits,[3] or the future,[4] of the "access" concept, it is important to recognize that the "marketplace of ideas" does not exist solely within the confines of the mass media. On the contrary, effective exercise of freedom of expression requires "access" to a broad range of *non-media* forums. In light of recent developments, the time seems ripe for an examination of the current status of First Amendment jurisprudence concerning the right of individuals to utilize these alternative channels of communication.

I. Lehman v. City of Shaker Heights[5]: A Vehicle for Discussion

The city of Shaker Heights owns and operates the Shaker Heights Rapid Transit System: fifty-five transit vehicles that transport passengers between suburban Shaker Heights and Cleveland. Each vehicle contains twenty interior advertising spaces available for lease through Metromedia, Inc., the transit system's exclusive advertising agent. Under contract with the city, Metromedia accepts advertising from cigarette companies, banks, liquor companies, retail and service establishments, churches, and civic and public service oriented groups, but will not accept advertising bearing political or public issue messages.

In 1970, Harry J. Lehman, a candidate for state representative, attempted to lease transit advertising space in an effort to promote his candidacy. The vast majority of its six to eight thousand adult riders each day are residents of the election district. This was

---

[3] The merits of the "access" concept have been widely debated in the literature. See the authorities cited in Lange, *The Role of the Access Doctrine in the Regulation of the Mass Media: A Critical Review and Assessment*, 52 N. Car. L. Rev. 1, 2 n.5 (1973).

[4] After taking what seemed at the time to be an important first step toward acceptance of the "access" concept, see Red Lion Broadcasting Co. v. F.C.C., 395 U.S. 367 (1969), the Court in two more recent decisions has turned a cold shoulder. See Columbia Broadcasting System v. Democratic National Committee, 412 U.S. 94 (1973); Miami Herald Publishing Co. v. Tornillo, 94 S. Ct. 2831 (1974). As a result of these decisions, the future of the "access" concept seems dim indeed.

[5] 94 S. Ct. 2714 (1974).

therefore a relatively inexpensive, convenient, and effective means of reaching potential voters. Although advertising space was available and Lehman's proposed advertisement[6] met Metromedia's copy standards, rental space was denied solely on the ground that Metromedia's contract with the city forbade acceptance of political advertising. After an unsuccessful attempt to persuade the city to alter its ban on political advertising, Lehman brought suit seeking declaratory and injunctive relief, claiming that the city's policy infringed his right to freedom of speech and denied him equal protection of the laws. The Ohio Supreme Court denied relief[7] and, in a 5-to-4 decision, the United States Supreme Court affirmed.

Mr. Justice Blackmun, in an opinion joined by Chief Justice Burger and Justices White and Rehnquist, concluded that car card space in publicly owned transit vehicles did not constitute a First Amendment forum, and that the selective exclusion of political and public issue advertising did not violate the Equal Protection Clause. In reaching this result, Mr. Justice Blackmun emphasized the commercial nature of the enterprise, the risks of imposing upon an assertedly "captive" audience, and the potential administrative difficulties that might arise if political and public issue advertising were accepted. In a separate concurring opinion, Mr. Justice Douglas reasoned that the display of any car cards in a publicly owned vehicle, regardless of the message conveyed, would infringe the constitutional rights of "captive" commuters. Mr. Justice Brennan, speaking for Justices Stewart, Marshall, and Powell, dissented. The dissenters found it unnecessary to decide the public forum issue, concluding instead that the city's policy violated the Equal Protection Clause. *Lehman* calls for examination of four separate, yet related, aspects of First Amendment jurisprudence: the right to a public forum; the right of individuals to utilize signs, posters, billboards, and similar devices for the exercise of First Amendment rights; the problem of the "captive" audience; the relationship between the Equal Protection Clause and the right to freedom of expression.

---

[6] The text of the proposed advertisement, *id*. at 2715, read as follows:

> Harry J. Lehman Is Old
> Fashioned! About Honesty,
> Integrity, And Good
> Government
> State Representative–District 56

[7] 34 Ohio St.2d 143 (1973) (4-to-3 decision).

II. In Search of Effective Forums

Wherever you begin, you will have to begin again twice over.[8]

In what circumstances, if any, does the First Amendment guarantee the right to utilize publicly owned property for the purpose of exercising freedoms of speech, press, assembly, and petition?[9] Or, in what circumstances, if any, does the First Amendment permit the state to deny an individual access to publicly owned property for the purpose of exercising these fundamental freedoms? The problem is many-faceted, involving an almost limitless variety of situations. It encompasses the religious evangelist seeking to speak in a publicly owned park and the political candidate seeking to place campaign signs in a publicly owned bus; the leaflet distributor in the streets and the one in a welfare office; the solitary picketer standing in silent vigil near a school and the twenty thousand demonstrators gathered on the grounds of the state capitol. The issues are difficult and they are important. What is required is a fair accommodation of the individual's interest in effective self-expression, the public's interest in preserving "the widest possible dissemination of information from diverse and antagonistic sources," and the state's often competing interest in preserving order. The adjustment of these interests poses a central challenge to any society devoted to assuring maximum freedom for all its members.

The Supreme Court has wrestled with this problem for almost eighty years now and, until recently, has been markedly unsuccessful in its efforts to construct a fully satisfactory theory of the public forum. During the past decade, however, the Court has taken important, if halting, steps toward the development of such a theory.

The public forum saga began, and very nearly ended, with Justice Holmes's uncharacteristically forgettable opinion for the Supreme Judicial Court of Massachusetts in *Commonwealth v. Davis*.[10] Davis, a preacher whose congregation apparently consisted of the

---

[8] Erikson, Childhood and Society 45 (1963).

[9] I do not address myself to the question whether, and if so in what circumstances, an individual may commandeer property owned by another private individual for the exercise of these rights. On the problem of "privately owned forums," see Marsh v. Alabama, 326 U.S. 501 (1946); Amalgamated Food Employees Local 590 v. Logan Valley Plaza, 391 U.S. 308 (1968); Lloyd Corp. v. Tanner, 407 U.S. 551 (1972).

[10] 162 Mass. 510 (1895).

crowds on the Boston Common, was convicted under a city ordinance which forbade, among other things, "any public address" upon any publicly owned property "except in accordance with a permit from the mayor." In affirming the conviction, Holmes not only upheld the constitutionality of the permit ordinance but also indicated in dictum that an absolute ban on use of the park for speech purposes would be constitutionally permissible: "For the Legislature absolutely or conditionally to forbid public speaking in a highway or public park is no more an infringement of the rights of a member of the public than for the owner of a private house to forbid it in his house."[11]

On appeal, the United States Supreme Court, speaking through Justice Edward White, unanimously adopted the Holmes position.[12] Noting that the federal Constitution "does not have the effect of creating a particular and personal right in the citizen to use public property in defiance of the constitution and laws of the State,"[13] White concluded: "The right to absolutely exclude all right to use, necessarily includes the authority to determine under what circumstances such use may be availed of, as the greater power contains the lesser."[14] Thus, under the Holmes-White approach, the state possessed the power absolutely to prohibit the exercise of First Amendment rights of speech on public property simply by asserting the prerogatives traditionally associated with the private ownership of land. The complex and difficult problem of the public forum had been "solved" by resort to common law concepts of private property.

Forty-two years later, in *Hague v. C.I.O.*,[15] the Supreme Court reopened the question. The case, which arose out of Mayor Hague's efforts to break up an organizing campaign by the CIO in Jersey City, required the Court to consider the constitutionality of a municipal ordinance forbidding all public meetings in the streets and other public places without a permit. The city argued that the ordinance was justified by the *Davis* dictum. In a plurality opinion,[16]

---

11 *Id.* at 511.

12 Davis v. Massachusetts, 167 U.S. 43 (1897).

13 *Id.* at 47–48.

14 *Id.* at 48.

15 307 U.S. 496 (1939).

16 Justice Black joined the Roberts opinion and Chief Justice Hughes concurred in part; Justice Stone, joined by Justice Reed, concurred in the result on due process grounds; Justices McReynolds and Butler dissented; Justices Frankfurter and Douglas did not participate.

Justice Roberts rejected this contention, answering the *Davis* dictum with dictum of his own:[17]

> Wherever the title of streets and parks may rest, they have immemorially been held in trust for the use of the public and, time out of mind, have been used for purposes of assembly, communicating thought between citizens, and discussing public questions. Such use of the streets and public places has, from ancient times, been a part of the privileges, immunities, rights, and liberties of citizens. The privilege of a citizen of the United States to use the streets and parks for communication of views on national questions may be regulated in the interest of all; it is not absolute, but relative, and must be exercised in subordination to the general comfort and convenience, and in consonance with peace and good order; but it must not, in the guise of regulation, be abridged or denied.

Perhaps the most interesting aspect of the Roberts dictum is its implicit acceptance of the underlying premise of the Holmes-White position—that the public forum issue must be defined in terms of the common law property rights of the state. Rather than challenging that premise head-on, Roberts conveniently adapted it to his own advantage, predicating the public forum right upon established common law notions of adverse possession and public trust. As a result, although Roberts's approach constituted an important step forward, it was a half step at best. For by focusing on the fact that parks and streets had historically been used for speech and assembly, instead of forthrightly recognizing that access to public property for speech purposes is essential to effective exercise of First Amendment rights, the Roberts rationale created by implication two distinct classes of public property respecting public forum theory. On the one hand, the streets, parks, and similar public places are subject to what Professor Kalven has termed "a kind of First-Amendment easement."[18] Since such places have been used, "time out of mind," for purposes of speech and assembly, the Constitution now requires that their continued use for these purposes not "be abridged or denied." On the other hand, all publicly owned property that cannot satisfy the "time out of mind" requirement remained subject to the *Davis* dictum, and access to such places for purposes of

[17] 307 U.S. at 515–16.

[18] Kalven, *The Concept of the Public Forum: Cox v. Louisiana*, 1965 SUPREME COURT REVIEW 1, 13.

speech and assembly could be denied absolutely upon the state's naked assertion of title.

As might be expected in light of this contradiction, the Roberts dictum, which has played a central role in the development of public forum theory, has evolved along two separate but connected paths. Although these paths have tended to converge in recent years, reflecting perhaps the emergence of a new and more vital public forum rationale, they can best be traced separately.

A. A BRIEF JAUNT THROUGH THE STREETS AND PARKS

The evolution of the streets and parks aspect of the Roberts dictum has been discussed at great length elsewhere,[19] and so I will attempt only a brief review here. Although Justice Roberts spoke for only a minority of the Court in *Hague*, his views quickly came to be accepted as the prevailing doctrine. Indeed, within four years of *Hague* the Court, in a series of three decisions, fully endorsed and elaborated upon the Roberts dictum. In essence, these decisions—*Schneider v. State*,[20] *Cox v. New Hampshire*[21] and *Jamison v. Texas*[22]—established four fundamental propositions.

In *Jamison*, the Court reviewed the constitutionality of a Dallas ordinance absolutely forbidding the distribution of any handbill upon any public street or sidewalk. Relying upon the *Davis* dictum, the city argued "that it has the power absolutely to prohibit the use of the streets for the communication of ideas."[23] The Court, speaking through Justice Black, gave this argument short shrift, citing Justice Roberts's opinion in *Hague* as evidence that the argument had previously been "directly rejected by this Court."[24] Thus, *Jamison* made clear that the mere assertion of title by the state could not, standing alone, justify a flat ban on the use of streets and parks for speech purposes.

In *Schneider*, the Court considered three municipal ordinances almost identical to the ordinance involved in *Jamison*.[25] Here, however, the ordinances were arguably justified, not by reference to *Davis*, but on the ground that a flat prohibition on leaflet distribu-

---

19 See EMERSON, THE SYSTEM OF FREEDOM OF EXPRESSION 299–304 (1970); Kalven, note 18 *supra*, at 15–27.

20 308 U.S. 147 (1939).

21 312 U.S. 569 (1941).

22 318 U.S. 413 (1943).

23 *Id*. at 415.

24 *Id*. at 416.

25 A fourth ordinance involved in *Schneider* concerned prior licensing of solicitations.

tion was necessary to prevent littering.[26] Nearly all forms of communication necessarily interfere with some legitimate state interest. Leafleting leads to littering; billboards and posters may be deemed unaesthetic; public speaking, whether or not amplified, may annoy passersby; picketing or marching may obstruct traffic; and so on. As a result, acceptance of the state's contention in *Schneider* might well have led to the complete elimination of the streets and parks as effective forums for communication. Roberts, speaking for eight members of the Court,[27] was not prepared to accept an argument that would so obviously frustrate the position he had staked out only eight months earlier in *Hague*. After noting that the Court had "characterized the freedom of speech and that of the press as fundamental personal rights and liberties,"[28] Roberts reasoned that although "[m]ere legislative preferences or beliefs respecting matters of public convenience may well support regulation directed at other personal activities," they may nevertheless "be insufficient to justify such as diminishes the exercise of rights so vital to the maintenance of democratic institutions."[29] Thus, "as cases arise, the delicate and difficult task falls upon the courts to weigh the circumstances and to appraise the substantiality of the reasons advanced in support of the regulation of the free enjoyment of the rights."[30] Roberts then proceeded to apply the doctrine to the case at hand, concluding that, in the Court's view, the state's interest in keeping "the streets clean and of good appearance is insufficient to justify an ordinance which prohibits a person rightfully on a public street from handing literature to one willing to receive it."[31] By adopting a balancing approach, with the scales tipped markedly in favor of First Amendment rights, *Schneider* preserved the streets and parks as effective forums for communication, thereby giving impressive content to the *Hague* dictum.

The third proposition established in these post-*Hague* cases also derives from *Schneider*. Two of the ordinances at issue were defended on the ground that the ban on leafleting was limited to the streets and alleys, leaving other public places, such as parks, avail-

[26] In Lovell v. Griffin, 303 U.S. 444 (1938), decided one year before *Hague* and *Schneider*, the Court intimated that a ban on leafleting intended to prevent "littering of the streets" might be permissible. *Id.* at 451.

[27] Justice McReynolds dissented without opinion.

[28] 308 U.S. at 161.

[29] *Ibid.*

[30] *Ibid.*

[31] *Id.* at 162.

able for such activities. Roberts, apparently mindful of the potential dangers of limiting speech to specially ordained "Hyde Parks," rejected the argument out-of-hand, stating emphatically that "one is not to have the exercise of his liberty of expression in appropriate places abridged on the plea that it may be exercised in some other place."[32]

Finally, if the state cannot absolutely prohibit use of its streets and parks for speech purposes, the question necessarily arises whether any less restrictive forms of regulation may be employed to protect the state's competing interests. The Court confronted that issue in *Cox v. New Hampshire*, which involved the constitutionality of a Manchester ordinance requiring a permit for any "parade or procession upon any public street or way." The New Hampshire Supreme Court had previously interpreted the ordinance as limiting official discretion exclusively to considerations of time, place, and manner. In an opinion upholding the ordinance as so construed, Chief Justice Hughes, writing for a unanimous Court, began by emphasizing that "[c]ivil liberties, as guaranteed by the Constitution, imply the existence of an organized society maintaining public order without which liberty itself would be lost in the excesses of unrestrained abuses."[33] What was needed, then, was some sort of fair accommodation, preserving "the safety and convenience of the people in the use of public highways," without unwarrantedly abridging "the right of assembly and the opportunities for the communication of thought and the discussion of public questions immemorially associated with resort to public places."[34] The Manchester ordinance, the Court concluded, fit the bill precisely. By focusing the permit process on the time, place, and manner of communicative activity, the ordinance enabled public officials to afford proper policing, avoid overlapping parades, secure convenient use of the streets by others, and minimize the risks of disorder, while at the same time preserving the free and open use of the streets for the exercise of First Amendment rights.

Thus, building upon the Roberts dictum in *Hague*, the *Schneider–Cox v. New Hampshire–Jamison* trilogy established a comprehensive, workable theory of the public forum, at least insofar as use of the streets and parks was concerned. And, indeed, for the next two decades the theory's emphasis on regulation rather than prohi-

---

[32] *Id.* at 163. [33] 312 U.S. at 574. [34] *Ibid.*

bition seemed successfully to withstand the test of time.[35] Nevertheless, in 1965, the Supreme Court's opinion in *Cox v. Louisiana*[36] reopened all the old questions.

In *Cox*, a group of approximately two thousand black students, led by Cox, staged a peaceful civil rights demonstration across the street from the local courthouse. Cox was arrested and subsequently convicted of violating a Louisiana statute providing that "no person shall wilfully obstruct the free, convenient, and normal use of any public sidewalk, street . . . or other passageway, or the entrance, corridor or passage of any public building, . . . by impeding, hindering, stifling, retarding or restraining traffic or passage thereon or therein."[37] In practical effect, then, the statute on its face precluded "all street assemblies and parades."[38] Justice Goldberg, speaking for the Court, began by emphasizing that the "rights of free speech and assembly, while fundamental in our democratic society, still do not mean that everyone with opinions or beliefs to express may address a group at any public place and at any time."[39] This is, of course, a mere truism. Yet as a starting point of analysis it set a tone far different from that adopted in prior cases. After a lengthy

---

[35] See, *e.g.*, Kunz v. New York, 340 U.S. 290 (1951); Talley v. California, 362 U.S. 60 (1960); Edwards v. South Carolina, 372 U.S. 229 (1963). See also the somewhat more problematic sound-truck cases, Saia v. New York, 334 U.S. 558 (1948); Kovacs v. Cooper, 336 U.S. 77 (1949).

[36] 379 U.S. 536 (1965).

[37] Cox was also convicted of violating a Louisiana "disturbing the peace" statute. The Court reversed this conviction on the grounds that Cox's conduct could not constitutionally be defined as breach of the peace and that the statute was unconstitutionally broad in scope. In a companion case, the Court reviewed Cox's conviction under another Louisiana statute prohibiting any person from picketing or parading near a courthouse "with the intent of interfering with, obstructing, or impeding the administration of justice, or with the intent of influencing any judge, juror, witness or court officer, in the discharge of his duty." Cox v. Louisiana, 379 U.S. 559, 560 (1965). The Court was unanimous in the view that the statute was not unconstitutional on its face. The Court's reasoning in support of this conclusion is tenuous, at best. See Emerson, note 19 *supra*, at 354–57; Kalven, note 18 *supra*, at 30–32. It should be emphasized, however, that the courthouse statute is only a form of "place" regulation, justified by the need to protect substantial governmental interests. Thus, the Court's approval of the statute is not necessarily inconsistent with the propositions established in *Hague* and the *Schneider–Cox v. New Hampshire–Jamison* trilogy.

[38] 379 U.S. at 556. The statute exempted labor picketing from its otherwise blanket prohibition.

[39] *Id.* at 554.

discourse on the need for ordered liberty, with the emphasis on "order," Goldberg latched on to the highly problematic speech-conduct distinction, "emphatically" rejecting "the notion . . . that the First and Fourteenth Amendments afford the same kind of freedom to those who would communicate ideas by conduct such as patrolling, marching, and picketing on streets and highways, as these amendments afford to those who communicate ideas by pure speech."[40] Nevertheless, since the case could be disposed of on other grounds,[41] the Court was not required "to consider the constitutionality of the uniform, consistent, and nondiscriminatory application of a statute forbidding all access to streets and other public facilities for parades and meetings."[42] The mere statement of the question, however, necessarily carried the implication that the issue was still open to debate. Moreover, Justices Black, Clark, Harlan, and White left no doubt that, in their view, an absolute ban on the use of streets and parks for purposes of marching, picketing, or patrolling would be constitutionally permissible.[43] Thus, although *Cox* left the issue unresolved, it raised threatening questions as to the continued vitality of *Hague* and its progeny.

The Court's next foray into the field was again somewhat inconclusive. In *Cameron v. Johnson*,[44] the Court unanimously upheld the constitutionality of the Mississippi Anti-Picketing Law, which made it unlawful "to engage in picketing or mass demonstrations in such a manner as to obstruct or unreasonably interfere with free . . . use of public streets, sidewalks, or other public ways adjacent or contiguous thereto." In reaching this result, however, Mr. Justice Brennan specifically highlighted the fact that "this statute does not prohibit picketing . . . unless engaged in in a manner which ob-

[40] *Id.* at 555.

[41] Noting that city officials had in fact permitted some meetings and parades, Goldberg reasoned that the situation was the same as if the statute had permitted "peaceful parades or demonstrations in the unbridled discretion of the local officials." 379 U.S. at 557. Justices Black and Clark voted to reverse the conviction on the ground that the statute's exemption of labor picketing violated the Equal Protection Clause. Justices White and Harlan voted to affirm.

[42] 379 U.S. at 555.

[43] For Justices Black and Clark, however, the view was expressed only as dictum. See note 41 *supra*.

[44] 390 U.S. 611 (1968).

structs or unreasonably interferes with" use of the streets.[45] "Prohibition of conduct which has this effect," he continued, "does not abridge constitutional liberty 'since such activity bears no necessary relationship to the freedom to . . . distribute information or opinion.' "[46] Thus, in the Court's view, the Mississippi statute was a mere regulatory measure rather than an absolute prohibition, forbidding only that picketing that unnecessarily interferes with use of the streets. Although this view of the statute seems questionable, depending upon the meaning of "obstruct" and "unreasonably interfere," the Court's approach in *Cameron* indicated an attitude at least vaguely reminiscent of the pre-*Cox* decisions.

Less than one month later, in *Amalgamated Food Employees Local 590 v. Logan Valley Plaza*,[47] the Court returned unequivocally to the *Hague* doctrine. Justice Marshall, speaking for the Court, recognized that leafleting, such as was involved in *Schneider* and *Jamison*, "like picketing, involves conduct other than speech, namely, the physical presence of the person distributing leaflets on municipal property."[48] Both forms of communication must therefore be governed by the same fundamental principles. And although, in both instances, the state may regulate the "conduct" aspects of these forms of communicative activity, the focus must always be on regulation rather than prohibition. Thus, after citing *Hague*, *Schneider*, and *Jamison*, he went on to declare that, even where picketing is concerned, "streets, sidewalks, parks, and other similar public places are so historically associated with the exercise of First Amendment rights that access to them for the purpose of exercising such rights cannot constitutionally be denied broadly and absolutely."[49] Any lingering doubts that may have remained after *Logan Valley* were quickly erased in the Court's subsequent opinions in *Shuttlesworth v. Birmingham*[50] and *Grayned v. Rockford*,[51] both of which recited the *Hague* dictum in full. As *Grayned* made clear, subject to such reasonable time, place, and manner regulations as "may be necessary to further significant governmen-

---

45 *Id.* at 617.

46 *Ibid.*, quoting Schneider v. State, 308 U.S. at 161.

47 391 U.S. 308 (1968).

48 *Id.* at 315–16.

49 *Id.* at 315.

50 394 U.S. 147, 152 (1969).

51 408 U.S. 104, 105, 117 (1972).

tal interests, . . . peaceful demonstrations in public places are protected by the First Amendment."[52]

The struggle for the streets and parks has been a long and arduous one. Yet, in the end, the Court has once again fully endorsed the four fundamental propositions established in *Hague* and the *Schneider–Cox v. New Hampshire–Jamison* trilogy,[53] thereby preserving the streets, parks, and similar public places as effective forums for the exercise of First Amendment rights.

B. OTHER PUBLICLY OWNED PROPERTY: NEW FORUMS

If there is a basic constitutional right to use the streets, parks, and similar public places for purposes of expression, what about other publicly owned property, ranging from the grounds surrounding a public building, to the inside of a welfare office, publicly run bus, or library, to a legislative gallery? To what extent, if any, does there exist a constitutional right to utilize any of these facilities for the exercise of First Amendment rights?

As noted earlier, by accepting the underlying premise of the *Davis* dictum, and therefore defining the public forum right in terms of the common law property rights of the state, Justice Roberts in *Hague* created by implication two distinct classes of publicly owned property for purposes of the First Amendment. Under this approach, all publicly owned property that, unlike the streets and parks, had not been used "time out of mind" for purposes of speech, was presumably still subject to the *Davis* dictum. The difficulty with this distinction is that it focuses on tradition rather than reality. The right to freedom of speech cannot exist in the abstract. It necessarily presupposes the right to communicate. In the absence of an effective and meaningful opportunity to reach the relevant audience, the theoretical right of expression would be hollow. Yet under the Roberts theory of the public forum, the individual may be denied access to an otherwise effective forum simply because the state chooses to exercise its prerogatives as owner of the property. As a result, the ability to reach the relevant audience may be seriously impaired despite the fact that allowance of the communicative

---

[52] *Id.* at 115–16.

[53] As to the third proposition, that "one is not to have the exercise of his liberty of expression in appropriate places abridged on the plea that it may be exercised in some other place," see 408 U.S. at 118–19 n. 40; Spence v. Washington, 94 S. Ct. 2727, 2731 n. 4 (1974); see also Pell v. Procunier, 94 S. Ct. 2800, 2804–06 (1974).

activity would not significantly interfere with any legitimate state interests. This aspect of the Roberts dictum has not survived.

The Supreme Court first directly confronted this issue in *Brown v. Louisiana*.[54] In *Brown*, five blacks entered the public room of a regional public library operated on a segregated basis. In protest against the library's segregation policy, Brown sat down and the four other blacks stood near him. About ten minutes later they were arrested for, and subsequently convicted of, violating the Louisiana breach-of-the-peace statute. In a 5-to-4 decision, the Court reversed the convictions. In an opinion announcing the judgment of the Court, Justice Fortas, joined by Chief Justice Warren and Mr. Justice Douglas, concluded that the convictions were constitutionally invalid because, in his view, the peaceful sit-in did not fall within the scope of the statutory prohibition. He then went on, however, to provide an alternative, and far more controversial, ground of decision. "We are here dealing," he noted, "with an aspect of a basic constitutional right—the right under the First and Fourteenth Amendments guaranteeing freedom of speech and of assembly, and freedom to petition the Government for a redress of grievances."[55] Moreover, these rights "embrace appropriate types of action which certainly include the right in a peaceable and orderly manner to protest by silent and reproachful presence, in a place where the protestant has every right to be, the unconstitutional segregation of public facilities."[56] Thus, since the sit-in caused no disturbance of others and no disruption of library facilities, Fortas concluded that "even if the accused action were within the scope of the statutory instrument, . . . we would have to hold that the statute cannot constitutionally be applied to punish petitioners' actions in the circumstances of this case."[57] Just as Roberts, with the concurrence of only two other Justices, launched a revolutionary theory of the public forum with respect to the streets and parks in *Hague*, Fortas in *Brown*, also with the concurrence of only two other Justices,

---

[54] 383 U.S. 131 (1966). I exclude Edwards v. South Carolina, 372 U.S. 229 (1963), from this discussion because, under the facts of the case, the state capitol grounds seem sufficiently similar functionally to streets and parks to bring them within the "streets and parks" aspect of *Hague*. This would also seem to be true with respect to airports, bus terminals, train stations, and so on. See Wolin v. Port of New York Authority, 392 F.2d 83 (2d Cir. 1968); *In re* Hoffman, 67 Cal.2d 845 (1967). I am concerned here with publicly owned property that is functionally dissimilar to streets and parks.

[55] 383 U.S. at 141. [56] *Id.* at 142. [57] *Ibid.*

planted the seeds for a revolutionary theory with respect to other publicly owned property. For although four, and perhaps five, other Justices clearly rejected the Fortas approach,[58] the important first step had been taken toward acceptance of the view that the right to a public forum could extend, in at least some instances, even to publicly owned property that manifestly was not historically dedicated to the exercise of First Amendment rights.

Although remaining a minority view, the Fortas position gained an additional adherent in *Adderley v. Florida*,[59] decided nine months after *Brown*. In *Adderley*, a group of students was convicted under a Florida trespass statute for conducting a peaceful demonstration on the grounds of a county jail, which were ordinarily closed to the general public. The demonstration protested both the arrest of several other students the previous day and the existence of racial segregation within the jail facility. In a 5-to-4 decision, the Supreme Court affirmed the convictions. Justice Black, writing for the majority, began by distinguishing the Court's prior decision in *Edwards v. South Carolina*,[60] which had upheld a demonstration on the grounds of the South Carolina State Capitol. "Traditionally, state capitol grounds are open to the public. Jails, built for security purposes, are not."[61] Then, after noting that the demonstrators had at least partially blocked a nonpublic jail driveway, Black moved onto broader ground:[62]

> Nothing in the Constitution of the United States prevents Florida from even-handed enforcement of its general trespass statute against those refusing to obey the sheriff's order to remove themselves from what amounted to the curtilage of the jailhouse. The State, no less than a private owner of property, has power to preserve the property under its control for the

---

[58] Black, in a dissenting opinion joined by Justices Clark, Harlan, and Stewart, angrily declared that the First Amendment "does not guarantee to any person the right to use someone else's property, even that owned by the government and dedicated to other purposes, as a stage to express dissident ideas." 383 U.S. at 166. Mr. Justice White, concurring in the result on other grounds, suggested that he would not "deem the First Amendment to forbid a municipal regulation limiting loafing in library reading rooms." *Id.* at 150. Mr. Justice Brennan, concurring in the result on overbreadth grounds, found it "wholly unnecessary to reach, let alone rest reversal, . . . on the proposition that even a narrowly drawn 'statute cannot constitutionally be applied to punish petitioners' actions in the circumstances of this case.' " *Id.* at 149–50.

[59] 385 U.S. 39 (1966).

[60] 372 U.S. 229 (1963).

[61] 385 U.S. at 42.

[62] *Id.* at 47–48.

> use to which it is lawfully dedicated. For this reason there is no merit to the petitioners' argument that they had a constitutional right to stay on the property, over the jail custodian's objections, because this "area chosen for the peaceful civil rights demonstration was not only 'reasonable' but also particularly appropriate. . . ." . . . The United States Constitution does not forbid a State to control the use of its own property for its own lawful nondiscriminatory purpose.

Thus, Black, accepting the underlying premise of *Davis* and the negative implication of the Roberts dictum in *Hague*, viewed the right to a public forum as subordinate to the common law property rights of the state. Since the nonpublic grounds of the jail facility have not historically been dedicated to the exercise of First Amendment rights, the state can erect an absolute bar to the use of such property for speech purposes simply by asserting ownership. Indeed, in such situations, the state's power is "no less than" that of "a private owner of property."

In a strongly worded dissent, Mr. Justice Douglas, joined by Chief Justice Warren and Justices Fortas and Brennan (the new adherent), began by emphasizing the need for access to the jailhouse grounds in order to assure effective freedom of expression:[63]

> The jailhouse, like an executive mansion, a legislative chamber, a courthouse, or the statehouse itself . . . is one of the seats of government, whether it be the Tower of London, the Bastille, or a small county jail. And when it houses political prisoners or those who many think are unjustly held, it is an obvious center for protest. . . . Those who do not control television and radio, those who cannot afford to advertise in newspapers or circulate elaborate pamphlets may have only a more limited type of access to public officials. Their methods should not be condemned as tactics of obstruction and harassment as long as the assembly and petition are peaceable, as these were.

Then, after noting that, in his view, the disruption of normal jail activities caused by the protest was minimal, Mr. Justice Douglas went on to challenge Black's reliance on the common law property rights of the state: "To say that a private owner could have done the same if the rally had taken place on private property is to speak of a different case, as an assembly and a petition for redress of grievances run to the government, not to private proprietors."[64] Black's

---

63 *Id.* at 49–51.

64 *Id.* at 52.

analogy to private property rights was thus tantamount to mixing apples and oranges. Finally, Mr. Justice Douglas concluded with a statement summarizing his approach to the public forum issue:[65]

> There may be some public places which are so clearly committed to other purposes that their use for the airing of grievances is anomalous. There may be some instances in which assemblies and petitions for redress of grievances are not consistent with other necessary purposes of public property. A noisy meeting may be out of keeping with the serenity of the statehouse or the quiet of the courthouse. No one, for example, would suggest that the Senate gallery is the proper place for a vociferous protest rally. And in other cases it may be necessary to adjust the right to petition for redress of grievances to the other interests inhering in the uses to which the public property is normally put. . . . But this is quite different from saying that all public places are off limits to people with grievances.

Thus, for Justices Douglas, Warren, Brennan, and Fortas, the right of an individual to utilize public property for the exercise of First Amendment rights turns, not on the common law property rights of the state but, rather, on whether, in each instance, the particular form of communication involved seriously interferes with the normal uses to which the property is put.

In *Tinker v. Des Moines Independent Community School District*,[66] three public school pupils were suspended from school for violating a regulation prohibiting the wearing of black armbands as protest against the government's policy in Vietnam. In a 7-to-2 decision, Justices Black and Harlan dissenting, the Court held that the actions of the school officials violated the First Amendment. Justice Fortas, speaking for the majority, noted that students did not "shed their constitutional rights to freedom of speech or expression at the schoolhouse gate,"[67] and that the wearing of the armbands therefore could not be prohibited without a showing that it would materially and substantially interfere with the normal functioning of the school or with the rights of other students. The implications of *Tinker* for public forum theory are somewhat difficult to glean, since the Fortas opinion seems to suggest at least three possible rationales.

At the narrowest level, Fortas pointed out "that the school authorities did not purport to prohibit the wearing of all symbols of

---

[65] *Id.* at 54. [66] 393 U.S. 503 (1969). [67] *Id.* at 506.

political or controversial significance."[68] As a result, the specific prohibition of a particular symbol—black armbands worn to protest our involvement in Vietnam—might be viewed as a violation of the Equal Protection Clause. Second, Fortas noted that among the activities "to which the schools are dedicated . . . is personal intercommunication among the students."[69] With this in mind, *Tinker* might properly be viewed as resting upon the proposition that, although functionally unlike the streets and parks, the schools in their own way have nevertheless historically been dedicated to the exercise of First Amendment rights. On this view of the matter, *Tinker* added little to the debate in *Brown* and *Adderley*. Finally, and at the broadest level, Fortas added a passage directly relevant to that debate:[70]

> Under our Constitution, free speech is not a right that is given only to be so circumscribed that it exists in principle but not in fact. Freedom of expression would not truly exist if the right could be exercised only in an area that a benevolent government has provided as a safe haven for crackpots. The Constitution says that Congress (and the States) may not abridge the right to free speech. This provision means what it says. We properly read it to permit reasonable regulation of speech-connected activities in carefully restricted circumstances. But we do not confine the permissible exercise of First Amendment rights to a telephone booth or the four corners of a pamphlet, or to supervised and ordained discussion in a school classroom.

From this perspective, *Tinker* seems to offer considerable, if ambiguous, support to the minority position staked out previously in *Brown* and *Adderley*. Nevertheless, in light of the Court's emphasis on "the special characteristics of the school environment,"[71] it would probably be incautious to read *Tinker* as fully endorsing an expansive theory of the public forum.

Three years later, however, in *Grayned v. Rockford*,[72] the Court left little doubt as to its acceptance of the Fortas–Douglas position. It should be noted that, between decision in *Brown* and *Adderley*, and decision in *Grayned*, the makeup of the Court had changed radically. During that brief interval, Justices Clark, Fortas, Warren,

68 *Id*. at 510.

69 *Id*. at 512.

70 *Id*. at 513.

71 *Id*. at 506.

72 408 U.S. 104 (1972).

Black, and Harlan were replaced by Justices Marshall, Blackmun, Burger, Powell, and Rehnquist. And, in *Grayned*, the new Court seemed prepared to take a fresh look at the problem.

In *Grayned*, the Court upheld the constitutionality of a municipal ordinance forbidding any person, "while on public or private grounds adjacent to any building in which a school or any class thereof is in session," to make "any noise or diversion which disturbs or tends to disturb the peace or good order" of normal school activities. Although recognizing that "the public sidewalk adjacent to school grounds may not be declared off limits for expressive activity by members of the public,"[73] Mr. Justice Marshall, speaking for seven members of the Court,[74] concluded that the ordinance was a reasonable time, place, and manner regulation, designed to further the state's important interest in avoiding disruption of the educational process. Of particular concern here, however, is not the Court's holding but the overall framework for public forum analysis reflected in the following key passage:[75]

> The nature of a place, "the pattern of its normal activities, dictate the kinds of regulations of time, place, and manner that are reasonable." Although a silent vigil may not unduly interfere with a public library, *Brown* v. *Louisiana*, 383 U.S. 131, (1966), making a speech in the reading room almost certainly would. That same speech should be perfectly appropriate in a park. The crucial question is whether the manner of expression is basically incompatible with the normal activity of a particular place at a particular time. Our cases make clear that in assessing the reasonableness of a regulation, we must weigh heavily the fact that communication is involved; the regulation must be narrowly tailored to further the State's legitimate interest.

In this passage, the right to a public forum came of age. No longer does the right to effective freedom of expression turn on the common law property rights of the state, and no longer does it turn

[73] *Id.* at 118.

[74] The Court was unanimously of the view that the ordinance was not unconstitutionally vague. On the overbreadth issue, Mr. Justice Blackmun concurred in the result without opinion, and Mr. Justice Douglas dissented on the ground that the ordinance had been unconstitutionally applied under the facts of the case. Speaking for the majority, Mr. Justice Marshall concluded that the "as applied" issue was not presented.

[75] 408 U.S. at 116–17.

on whether the particular place at issue has historically been dedicated to the exercise of First Amendment rights. The streets, parks, public libraries, and other publicly owned places are all brought under the same roof. In each case, the "crucial question is whether the manner of expression is basically incompatible with the normal activity of a particular place at a particular time." Moreover, as if to drive the point home, Mr. Justice Marshall, displaying just a hint of revisionism, cited *Brown* as if the Fortas position there had prevailed. And later in the opinion, he stated that "in *Adderley*, the Court held that demonstrators could be barred from jailhouse grounds not ordinarily open to the public, at least where the demonstration obstructed the jail driveway and interfered with the functioning of the jail."[76] In the circumstances, such revisionism might perhaps be forgiven.

This is the background for *Lehman*, which raised the question whether an individual has a public forum right under the First Amendment to display political campaign signs on the inside of a publicly owned transit vehicle. Regrettably, Mr. Justice Blackmun, speaking for four members of the Court, tended to blur the public forum and equal protection issues, making the opinion somewhat difficult to follow. Nevertheless, his approach to the public forum issue seems consistent with that set out in *Grayned*. Quoting Lord Dunedin, he noted initially that " 'open spaces and public places differ very much in their character, and before you could say whether a certain thing could be done in a certain place you would have to know the history of the particular place.' "[77] Although at first glance this statement might seem to reflect a return to the "time out of mind" concept, the plain fact is that the "history of a place" is undoubtedly a relevant consideration in evaluating the degree of disorder that could reasonably be tolerated even under the *Grayned* approach. And, indeed, in the very next sentence, the opinion seems to restate the *Grayned* theory. "Although American constitutional jurisprudence, in the light of the First Amendment, has been jealous to preserve access to public places for purposes of free speech, the nature of the forum and the conflicting interests involved have remained important in determining the degree of

---

[76] *Id.* at 121 n. 49.

[77] 94 S. Ct. at 2717, quoting M'Ara v. Magistrates of Edinburgh, [1913] Sess. Cas. 1059, 1073–74.

protection afforded by the Amendment to the speech in question."[78] Applying this standard, Mr. Justice Blackmun concluded that, in light of the nature of the place, the particular form of communication involved, and the arguably substantial state interests in protecting a "captive audience" and avoiding "sticky administrative problems," there is no public forum right to place public issue posters on the inside of a publicly owned transit vehicle.

In a separate concurring opinion, Mr. Justice Douglas reached the same result, noting that "a streetcar or bus is plainly not a park or sidewalk or other meeting place for discussion."[79] The basis for this distinction, however, is not the fact that such vehicles have not been dedicated "time out of mind" to the exercise of First Amendment rights. Rather, Mr. Justice Douglas concluded that, in the context of this case, a transit vehicle is not an appropriate forum because the allowance of such signs would seriously intrude upon the rights of what, in his view, is a captive audience. Finally, Mr. Justice Brennan, in a dissenting opinion joined by Justices Stewart, Marshall, and Powell, specifically adhered to the *Grayned* formulation,[80] but found it unnecessary to decide the public forum issue in light of his conclusion that the selective exclusion of public issue posters violated the Equal Protection Clause. Thus, whether or not the decision actually reached in *Lehman* was the correct one, the opinions seem clearly to reaffirm the expansive public forum theory adopted in *Grayned*.[81]

As with the streets and parks, development of a theory of the public forum with respect to other publicly owned property has been a long time coming. Yet, after years of focusing on the common law property rights of the state, the Court seems finally to have endorsed a comprehensive, intelligible approach to the problem. In each instance, the "crucial question" must be "whether the manner

---

[78] 94 S. Ct. at 2717.

[79] *Id.* at 2718.

[80] See 94 S. Ct. at 2721–22.

[81] In Pell v. Procunier, 94 S. Ct. 2800 (1974), decided one day before *Lehman*, the Court, in a 6-to-3 decision, held that a prison regulation prohibiting "press and other news media interviews with specific individual inmates" did not violate the inmates' rights under the First Amendment. Although the issue actually presented would seem to be one appropriately governed by general First Amendment principles, rather than by public forum theory, it is noteworthy that the Court, quoting *Grayned*, once again emphasized that the "nature of a place, the pattern of its normal activities, dictate the kinds of regulations of time, place, and manner that are reasonable." *Id.* at 2806.

of expression is basically incompatible with the normal activity of a particular place at a particular time." The point, of course, is not that the individual has the right to speak, petition, or assemble whenever and wherever he chooses. It is, rather, that if we are to give content to the right to freedom of expression, we must seek a fair accommodation of the individual's interest in effective exercise of that right, the public's interest in receiving the communication, and legitimate counterveiling interests of the state. The Court's newly promulgated theory of the public forum embodies precisely that type of fair accommodation.

A recent decision of the United States Court of Appeals for the Second Circuit provides an excellent illustration of the impact of the *Grayned* approach.[82] Each Monday, for approximately six months, members of the Albany Welfare Rights Organization, an organization devoted to informing welfare recipients of their legal rights and seeking legal change on behalf of the poor, went to the waiting room of the county welfare office and distributed leaflets to waiting welfare recipients. The leaflets contained legal information about the rights of welfare recipients and information about the AWRO and the welfare rights movement generally. The AWRO members would also answer questions about the recipients' legal rights, and interested persons were invited to join the organization. During this period, the leafleting caused no disturbance of the normal functioning of the office, and AWRO membership grew markedly. At the end of six months, however, the welfare department instituted a new policy prohibiting the distribution of leaflets in the waiting room. In a unanimous decision, the Court of Appeals for the Second Circuit held the absolute ban on leafleting unconstitutional. Although noting that a welfare office waiting room "is not an appropriate place for a picket line or demonstrations," the court concluded that, subject to reasonable regulations, it is a proper place for leafleting and "for private conversation with those waiting to be served."[83] The court emphasized that the leafleters could be prohibited from badgering the waiting recipients and from making excessive noise or engaging in other disruptive activity. In addition, they could be required to remove all discarded material and to desig-

---

[82] Albany Welfare Rights Organization v. Wyman, 493 F.2d 1319 (2d Cir. 1974).

[83] *Id.* at 1324.

nate themselves as not being employees of the welfare department. They could not, however, be prohibited absolutely from using the waiting room as a forum for the exercise of First Amendment rights. Thus, although a rather healthy dose of sensitivity may at times be required, fair accommodation can be achieved.[84]

A somewhat different, and perhaps even more delicate, aspect of the public forum issue concerns the question whether a group or individual ever has any constitutional right to utilize such publicly owned facilities as civic centers, stadiums, or school auditoriums for the exercise of First Amendment free speech rights.[85] Although the Supreme Court has never addressed this question, most lower courts, at least prior to *Grayned*, have assumed that no such right exists.[86] That assumption no longer seems tenable. There can be no doubt that access to such facilities can, particularly in the absence of reasonably available alternatives, be crucial to effective exercise of the rights of speech and assembly. Moreover, since the state presumably can pass on to the user the expenses actually incurred,[87] its interest in denying access to such facilities seems minimal at best.[88] It might be argued, however, that even if there is a right to use such facilities, the state should be permitted to condition such use upon a showing that no reasonably alternative facilities are available. At first glance, this suggestion might seem to fly in the face of the doctrine, first announced in *Schneider*, that "one is not to have the exercise of his liberty of expression in appropriate places abridged on the plea that it may be exercised in some other place." Unlike most pub-

---

[84] See also Unemployed Workers Union v. Hackett, 332 F. Supp. 1372 (D. R.I. 1971).

[85] I am not concerned here with the question whether the state can make such facilities available to some private groups but not others. That, of course, is essentially an equal protection issue, and almost all courts that have considered the question have held such selective exclusions unconstitutional. See, *e.g.*, Bynum v. Shiro, 219 F. Supp. 204 (E.D. La. 1963); Madole v. Barnes, 20 N.Y.2d 169 (1967); East Meadow Community Concerts Ass'n v. Bd. of Education, 18 N.Y.2d 129 (1966); Buckley v. Meng, 35 Misc.2d 467 (N.Y. Co. 1962); Danskin v. San Diego Unified School Dist., 28 Cal.2d 536 (1946).

[86] See, *e.g.*, cases cited in note 85 *supra*.

[87] See, *e.g.*, Follett v. McCormick, 321 U.S. 573 (1944); Murdock v. Pennsylvania, 319 U.S. 105 (1943); Jones v. Opelika, 319 U.S. 103 (1943); Cox v. New Hampshire, 312 U.S. 569 (1941). See also Blasi, *Prior Restraints on Demonstrations*, 68 MICH. L. REV. 1482, 1527–32 (1970).

[88] Of course, the state can adopt reasonable time, place, and manner regulations to assure that its own use of the facility is fully preserved.

lic forum situations, however, where the speaker seeks access to a pre-existing audience, the speaker here brings his own audience with him. As a result, and again unlike the typical public forum situation, restricting the speaker to a reasonably alternative forum is likely to affect neither the effectiveness of the communication nor the makeup of the audience. This being so, such a condition might well be permissible.

As these two examples indicate, proper application of the *Grayned* doctrine can be as difficult as it is important. Yet it is clearly worth the effort. For it is only through the search for a fair accommodation of these competing interests that the promise of the First Amendment can be made a reality.

III. Billboards, Posters, Signs, Bumper Stickers, etc.

The Supreme Court has consistently recognized that the right to freedom of expression necessarily encompasses, not only the right to exercise that freedom in appropriate places, but also the right to utilize effective means of communication. Indeed, in a long series of decisions the Court has held that the First Amendment protects the right to make speeches,[89] to distribute leaflets,[90] to distribute anonymous leaflets,[91] to canvass door to door,[92] to use sound-trucks,[93] to picket,[94] to march,[95] to "sit-in,"[96] to wear armbands,[97] and so on. Each of these varied modes of communication possesses its own unique characteristics and advantages, and preservation of the widest possible diversity in the means of communication available is essential to the effective and robust exer-

[89] See, *e.g.*, Kunz v. New York, 340 U.S. 290 (1951); Terminiello v. Chicago, 337 U.S. 1 (1949).

[90] See, *e.g.*, Flower v. United States, 407 U.S. 197 (1972); Schneider v. State, 308 U.S. 147 (1939); Lovell v. Griffin, 303 U.S. 444 (1938).

[91] See Talley v. California, 362 U.S. 60 (1960).

[92] See, *e.g.*, Martin v. City of Struthers, 319 U.S. 141 (1943).

[93] See Kovacs v. Cooper, 336 U.S. 77 (1949); Saia v. New York, 334 U.S. 558 (1948); see also Grayned v. Rockford, 408 U.S. 104, 116 (1972).

[94] See, *e.g.*, Grayned v. Rockford, 408 U.S. 104 (1972); Amalgamated Food Employees Local 590 v. Logan Valley Plaza, 391 U.S. 308 (1968).

[95] See, *e.g.*, Shuttlesworth v. City of Birmingham, 394 U.S. 147 (1969); Gregory v. Chicago, 394 U.S. 111 (1969).

[96] See, *e.g.*, Brown v. Louisiana, 383 U.S. 131 (1966).

[97] See, *e.g.*, Tinker v. Des Moines Independent Community School Dist., 393 U.S. 503 (1969).

cise of First Amendment rights. The question I would consider first, then, is whether the display of billboards, signs, posters, and bumper stickers, on privately owned property, for the purpose of expressing views on public issues, constitutes another form of constitutionally protected activity.

Surprisingly, the Supreme Court has never specifically addressed the question. In two closely analogous situations, however, the Court has clearly indicated that this means of expression is indeed protected under the First Amendment. Thus, in *Stromberg* v. *California*,[98] the Court held that the display of a red flag as a symbol of opposition to organized government constituted an appropriate exercise of the right to freedom of speech. More recently, in *Spence* v. *Washington*,[99] the Court held that the display out of an apartment window of a United States flag, to which a large peace symbol had been affixed, constituted "a form of protected expression." Even without those decisions, however, the question hardly seems open to debate. The use of billboards, posters, and signs as a method of disseminating information on public issues has gained widespread acceptance largely because of its unique similarity, in functional terms, to the use of newspaper, radio, and television "advertorials." Like such "advertorials," and unlike most other forms of communication, the use of billboards, signs, posters, and bumper stickers does not require the physical presence of the "speaker," thereby enabling him to "speak" in several places at the same time. It is a relatively inexpensive, highly convenient, and markedly effective outlet for the promulgation of ideas and information by persons who do not themselves have access to more traditional media facilities.

To what extent, in light of the constitutionally protected status of this means of expression, may its employment be regulated or absolutely prohibited by the state?[100] On the one hand, it seems clear that the mere fact that these public issue billboards, posters,

[98] 283 U.S. 359 (1931).

[99] 94 S. Ct. 2727, 2730 (1974).

[100] On several occasions, but always in a commercial context, the Court has held that absolute, or at least highly restrictive, prohibitions on the use of billboards and advertising vehicles do not constitute a deprivation of property in violation of the Due Process Clause. None of those decisions addressed the First Amendment issue, however, and they are therefore inapposite to the question here under consideration. See Railway Express Agency v. New York, 336 U.S. 106 (1949); Packer Corp. v. Utah, 285 U.S. 105 (1932); St. Louis Poster Advertising Co. v. St. Louis, 249 U.S. 269 (1919); Cusak Co. v. Chicago, 242 U.S. 526 (1917); Fifth Avenue Coach Co. v. New York, 221 U.S. 467 (1911).

and signs are located on private property does not insulate them from reasonable state regulation. For although located on private land, these devices may nevertheless interfere with the state's legitimate interests in promoting traffic safety and preserving the overall aesthetic quality of the community. On the other hand, as legitimate as these state concerns may be,[101] it seems equally clear that an absolute ban on the use of such devices would be constitutionally impermissible. Indeed, an absolute ban on all public issue billboards or signs for aesthetic or traffic safety reasons would be no more justifiable than an absolute ban on leafleting to prevent littering,[102] or an absolute ban on door-to-door canvassing to prevent crime.[103] As always, what is needed is fair accommodation. Thus, although the state, taking location into account, may narrowly regulate the size, structure, appearance, and perhaps the quantity of such devices, it may not prohibit them altogether.[104]

This, then, brings me to *Lehman*, which raised the far more complex and intriguing question whether there is ever a public forum right to affix such posters and signs to publicly owned property.[105] There is no simple answer. On the one hand, the suggestion that there can be no such right since, after all, the state must possess some absolute control over the use of publicly owned property, seems reminiscent of the overly simplistic attitude reflected in *Davis*. On the other hand, recognition of such a right might well seem to open a Pandora's box of immense proportions, conjuring up images of all our public buildings plastered from top to bottom with unaesthetic political signs.

The issue can perhaps best be approached by example. Suppose an individual, in an effort to communicate his views to welfare recipients, seeks permission to place a sign expressing those views

---

[101] The "captive audience" aspect of this problem is discussed in text at notes 126–31, *infra*.

[102] See Schneider v. State, 308 U.S. 147 (1939).

[103] See Martin v. City of Struthers, 319 U.S. 141 (1943).

[104] See, *e.g.*, Ross v. Goshi, 351 F. Supp. 949 (D. Hawaii 1972); Farrell v. Township of Teaneck, 126 N.J. Super. 460 (1974); Peltz v. City of South Euclid, 11 Ohio St.2d 128 (1967); see also Howard v. State Dept. of Highways of Colorado, 478 F.2d 581 (10th Cir. 1973); Ghaster Properties, Inc. v. Preston, 176 Ohio St. 425 (1964).

[105] Once again, it is important to distinguish between the public forum right and the equal protection right. The latter, with which I am not here concerned, arises only after the state has chosen to "open up" its facilities by permitting their use by some persons and not others.

on the wall of the waiting room of the local welfare office. In short, he seeks to affix the leaflet to the wall. As noted earlier, this is a cheap, convenient and effective means of communication, enabling the individual to "speak" in several welfare offices at the same time. Moreover, since he need not be physically present, this technique permits the individual to exercise his right to communicate without surrendering his job. In this context, may the state absolutely forbid the posting of such signs?

At the theoretical level, it might be argued that what is involved here is not merely access to a public forum but, rather, an effort to compel the state to provide the means of comunication. In other words, the request is functionally similar to a demand that an individual be permitted to commandeer publicly owned sound-trucks. The point seems unpersuasive to me for at least two reasons. First, even assuming that this place-means distinction is a valid one, it seems doubtful that the wall of a welfare office can properly be characterzed as a "means" of communication. Unlike a sound-truck, a wall is, after all, simply a physical part of the place. One might just as easily argue that, although there may be a right to communicate in a welfare office, there is no right to use the floor since, like the walls, that is a "means" of communication.[106] Second, the means-place distinction itself seems to rest on the fact that the state rarely possesses a monopoly over the means of speech. For example, an individual seeking to communicate by sound-truck can ordinarily obtain the device from private sources. Accordingly, denial of a right to use the state's sound-trucks would not seriously impair that individual's right to effective freedom of expression. Here, however, the individual seeking to affix a sign to the welfare office wall is at the mercy of the state. There are only four walls, and the state owns them all. Thus, even if the wall could properly be viewed as a "means" of communication, that fact should not affect the analysis.[107]

106 It might be argued, however, that unlike use of the walls, use of the floor is a necessary adjunct to the right to speak in a welfare office. The point is, of course, a circular one, since it is predicated upon an unspoken preference for one form of communication over another.

107 The airwaves are a means of communication over which the state possesses essentially monopoly control. In Columbia Broadcasting System v. Democratic National Committee, 412 U.S. 94 (1973), the Court held that there is no constitutional right to purchase airtime for the expression of views on public issues. That decision, however, clearly was not predicated solely on the fact that what was involved was a means, rather than a place, for communication. On the contrary,

There is the further problem, however, that the posting of such signs may mar the beauty of the office and damage the wall. Here we move onto more familar ground. It is difficult to see why the state's aesthetic concerns here should be viewed as qualitatively any different from its interest in preventing littering or its interest in preserving the overall aesthetic quality of the community when such signs or posters are displayed on private property facing the street. Some sacrifice of aesthetics is of course inevitable, and the fact that the communicative activity takes place indoors may well necessitate a greater degree of control. Nevertheless, the principle of fair accommodation requires that the state pursue its aesthetic concerns through reasonable regulation of size, appearance, and quantity, rather than by absolute prohibition. Moreover, any damage to the wall caused by the posting of such signs, the cost of which could in any case be passed on to the users,[108] is likely to be minimal at best. And, of course, the state is free to avoid this problem entirely simply by providing a bulletin board, although it would be under no constitutional duty to do so.[109]

Finally, there is the problem of administration. The attractiveness of this means of communication, when combined with the obviously limited amount of space available, could at least conceivably create a situation where the demand for space outstrips the supply. Should that occur, the state would then be required to determine who gets to use the space, and for how long. The difficulties involved in making such determinations hardly seem insurmountable. In any event, the mere possibility that such a situation might arise, and that the state might then be unable to deal with it effectively, can hardly be viewed as sufficient advance

---

the Court's decision was reached only after careful consideration of all the relevant circumstances. Moreover, it might be noted that at least two of the points emphasized by the Court in support of its decision in *CBS*—the existence of the Fairness Doctrine and preservation of the First Amendment rights of broadcasters—are clearly inapplicable to the question whether there is ever a public forum right to place signs and posters on publicly owned property.

108 See cases cited in note 87 *supra*.

109 If the state has already provided a bulletin board for its own use, the individual's right to use that board, without interfering with the state's use of the facility, would of course be even more compelling. In a similar situation, at least one court has already recognized a public forum right to post notices on a preexisting bulletin board. See Velez v. Amenta, 370 F. Supp. 1250, 1257 (D. Conn. 1974).

justification to support an absolute prohibition. All things considered, then, it seems to me that, in at least some instances, a reasonably persuasive case can be made for the proposition that the First Amendment does indeed guarantee the right to place signs and posters on publicly owned property. Once again, it must be emphasized that the individual clearly does not have a right to place signs of whatever size he chooses wherever he chooses. On the contrary, there may be some places where this particular means of communication is wholly inappropriate and, in those instances where it is appropriate, the state surely must be granted considerable latitude to determine the proper location, size, appearance, and quantity of such devices. But an absolute ban on all signs in all places in all circumstances would seem constitutionally impermissible.

The approach suggested above does not, by itself, resolve the problem in all of its many facets. It does, however, provide a starting point for analysis. If experience is any teacher, one thing we have nothing to fear is that we will be swamped by individuals seeking to express their views on public issues. The danger of our times is not that we as a people have become aroused to fever pitch by the excitement of ideas. When an individual does seek to take advantage of an effective, convenient means of communication, the Constitution cannot permit what are often in reality relatively trifling objections to stand in his way. Because of its emphasis on the assertedly "captive audience" aspects of the case, the Court's decision in *Lehman* does not dispose of this issue in its entirety.[110] The Court, it is hoped, will continue to wrestle with the problem for years to come.

---

[110] In at least one passage, however, Mr. Justice Blackmun goes well beyond the "captive audience" point, noting his fear that a contrary result in the case would mean that "display cases in public hospitals, libraries, office buildings, military compounds, and other public facilities immediately would become Hyde Parks open to every would-be pamphleteer and politician. This," Mr. Justice Blackmun concludes, "the Constitution does not require." 94 S. Ct. at 2718. See also Mr. Justice Rehnquist's expression of a similar view in Spence v. Washington, 94 S. Ct. 2727, 2734 (1974) (dissenting opinion). In his separate concurring opinion in *Lehman*, Mr. Justice Douglas clearly ties his position to the "captive audience" point, and intimates no view on the question whether, in the absence of a "captive audience," there is ever a public forum right to affix signs and posters to publicly owned property. The four dissenters also express no view on this issue. Thus, for at least five of the Justices, it remains an open question.

IV. Audience Captors, Captive Auditors, and the Problem of Audience Captivity

The Supreme Court has consistently adhered to the principle that the First Amendment does not guarantee one individual the right to press his views upon another individual who is unwilling to receive them.[111] Thus where X seeks to communicate with Y, Y seeks to avoid the communication, and no other interests are at stake, the state would be justified in protecting Y's right to be let alone. Ideally, of course, in a democratic system, Y would be willing to receive and consider all available information and ideas, and recognition of Y's absolute right to freedom from speech in this context may be seen as having the ironic effect of "making the closed mind a principal feature of the open society."[112] Nevertheless, if an open society is truly to exist, it must be founded upon respect for freedom of thought, as well as freedom of speech, and must preserve the dignity, independence, and integrity of all of its members. The principle of freedom from speech seems well suited to these ends.[113]

Regrettably, this principle does not take us very far in our efforts to come to grips with the problem of the captive audience. For in almost all instances, X seeks to communicate, not only with Y, but also and at the same time with Z—a willing listener. And although X may have no constitutional right to force his views upon Y, he clearly does have a constitutionally protected right to communicate with Z. Moreover, to complicate matters, Z possesses his own independent right under the First Amendment to receive X's communication.[114] In this context, Y's right to be let alone

111 See, *e.g.*, Schneider v. State, 308 U.S. 147, 162 (1939); Martin v. City of Struthers, 319 U.S. 141, 148 (1943); Rowan v. Post Office, 397 U.S. 728, 736–37 (1970).

112 Kalven, The Negro and the First Amendment 159 (1965).

113 This principle is, of course, inapplicable with respect to public officials acting in their official capacity. The right to petition for redress of grievances necessarily presupposes that such public officials will receive and consider communications from their constituents. Thus, although reasonable restrictions may perhaps be placed on such communications, for example a prohibition on unnecessary late night telephone calls to the homes of public officials, there is no blanket right to reject unwanted communications.

114 See, *e.g.*, Procunier v. Martinez, 94 S. Ct. 1800, 1809 (1974); Stanley v. Georgia, 394 U.S. 557, 564 (1969); Griswold v. Connecticut, 381 U.S. 479, 482 (1965); Lamont v. Postmaster General, 381 U.S. 301, 305 (1965); Martin v. City of Struthers, 319 U.S. 141, 143 (1943).

may come into direct conflict with the rights of X and Z, and it then becomes necessary to determine when, if ever, Y's interest in avoiding unwanted communications provides sufficient justification to close the channels of communication between X and Z.

In *Cohen* v. *California*,[115] Justice Harlan announced the appropriate standard for making this determination:[116]

> The ability of government, consonant with the Constitution, to shut off discourse solely to protect others from hearing it is . . . dependent upon a showing that substantial privacy interests are being invaded in an essentially intolerable manner.

Although the *Cohen* formulation provides a framework for analysis, its operative significance ultimately depends upon the terms "substantial privacy interests" and "essentially intolerable manner." How, then, do we give content to these facially ambiguous concepts? In each case, four factors must be considered.

First, it is necessary to identify the particular "privacy interests" at issue. These exist in essentially two varieties. On the one hand, there is the individual's interest in avoiding unwanted exposure to ideas. Some individuals, at least at the particular time and place involved, may resent their exposure to any ideas, regardless of the message conveyed. They wish simply not to be bothered. For other individuals, the resentment may be more selective, focusing on their unwilling exposure to ideas that they find offensive or distasteful. In either event, the underlying "privacy interest" at stake may be defined as the right to freedom from unwilling exposure to ideas. The second "privacy interest" that may be threatened is the individual's desire not to be disturbed by the means of communication employed. For example, a late-night telephone call may in itself constitute an annoyance, wholly apart from the ideas actually communicated. If the recipient is offended by the caller's ideas, that simply adds insult to injury. In each case, it is necessary to determine whether one, or both, of these "privacy interests" is at issue.

Second, it is necessay to evaluate the "substantiality" of the particular privacy interest or interests actually involved. In large part, this will turn, to borrow a phrase, on the extent to which the unwilling listener can be said to have a "reasonable expectation of privacy" at the time and place of the unwanted communication.

---

115 403 U.S. 15 (1971).

116 *Id.* at 21.

At the extremes, this "reasonable expectation" would obviously be greatest in the home, and least in the streets.

Third, it is necessary to consider the extent to which the unwilling listener is in fact "captive" to the communication. That is, how difficult is it for him to avoid either initial or continued exposure to the speaker's message?

Finally, and often of greatest importance, it is necessary to determine whether any means exist whereby the state can protect the unwilling listener without shutting off communication between the speaker and willing listeners. If such a "less restrictive method" is available, the state cannot constitutionally opt for a broader approach that would unnecessarily restrict First Amendment rights. Moreover, since such a "less restrictive method" individualizes the decision whether to receive the communication, thereby leaving open the channels of communication with willing listeners, it becomes unnecessary to test the constitutionality of the "less restrictive method" against the *Cohen* standard. In examining the application of these four considerations in specific factual contexts, I shall begin with the fourth factor, and then move on to those situations where no "less restrictive method" is available.

Martin v. City of Struthers[117] provides perhaps the best illustration of the "less restrictive method" approach. In *Martin*, the Court reviewed the constitutionality of a municipal ordinance prohibiting any person to "ring the door bell, sound the door knocker, or otherwise summon" the occupants of any residence for the purpose of distributing handbills or circulars. Many men in the town worked night shifts, and the ordinance had as one function the protection of their daytime sleep. Moreover, it seems evident that, once a homeowner answered the door, he would, either out of timidity or courtesy, often be obliged to accept the proffered handbill and even to engage in at least some unwanted conversation with the canvasser. The Court, speaking through Justice Black, held the ordinance violative of the First Amendment. Noting that "[d]oor to door distribution of circulars is essential to the poorly financed causes of little people," Black observed that the Court was faced with the necessity of weighing the conflicting interests of the canvasser, against "the right of the individual householder to determine whether he is willing to receive her

---

117 319 U.S. 141 (1943).

message, [and both] against the interest of the community which . . . offers to protect the interests of all of its citizens, whether particular citizens want that protection or not."[118] In an effort to strike a proper balance, Black emphasized that the city's objectives could be achieved simply by making it "an offense for any person to ring the bell of a householder who has appropriately indicated that he is unwilling to be disturbed."[119] Such an approach "leaves the decision as to whether distributers of literature may lawfully call at a home where it belongs—with the homeowner himself."[120] In light of the availability of this "less restrictive method," the ordinance could not pass constitutional muster.

The problem of unwanted mail is also subject to "less restrictive method" analysis. In *Lamont v. Postmaster General*,[121] the Court reviewed a federal statute requiring the postmaster general to detain all communist political propaganda mailed from abroad unless the addressee, after receiving notice, specifically requested its delivery. The Government sought to justify this provision on the ground that unwilling recipients often found this class of mail particularly offensive. Although the statutory scheme did not absolutely bar receipt of such material, the Court nevertheless held it "unconstitutional because it requires an official act (*viz.*, returning the reply card) as a limitation on the unfettered exercise of the addressee's First Amendment rights."[122] On the other hand, in *Rowan v. Post Office*,[123] the Court upheld a federal statute enabling a householder, acting through the postmaster general, to forbid particularly named mailers to send any future correspondence to his home. The key difference between the two statutes is that, although both provide for individualized decisions whether to receive the communication, the *Rowan* statute, by placing the burden upon unwilling rather than willing recipients, is less restrictive of First Amendment rights.[124]

As these decisions indicate, whenever a state seeks to deal with a potential captive audience situation, it must utilize the "least

---

118 *Id.* at 143.

119 *Id.* at 148.

120 *Ibid.* Black also noted, of course, that reasonable regulations governing the hours of distribution would likewise be constitutionally permissible.

121 381 U.S. 301 (1965).

122 *Id.* at 305.

123 397 U.S. 728 (1970).

124 Similarly, the problem of unwanted telephone calls can be handled simply by enabling the homeowner to obtain an injunction prohibiting future calls, or by making it a criminal offense to call an individual within a fixed time after having been instructed not to call in the future.

restrictive method" available. That is, it must attempt to individualize the recipient's decision so that protection of the unwilling recipient does not block communication with those desirous of receiving the message. Moreover, as noted earlier, since such a scheme does not shut off discourse with willing recipients, its constitutionality need not be tested against the *Cohen* standard. This does not mean, however, that such schemes are invariably immune to constitutional challenge. On the contrary, in at least some instances, even individualized protection of the unwilling listener might impair, albeit indirectly, communication with willing listeners. For example, under the *Rowan* statute, the record-keeping burdens imposed upon mass mailers necessarily affect, to some extent, their ability to reach willing recipients. In such situations, it is necessary to weigh the "privacy interests" of unwilling recipents against the degree of indirect impairment of First Amendment rights.[125]

This, then, brings us to those situations where no "less restrictive method" is available.[126] Here, individualization is impossible, and the state is faced with only two choices. It may protect the unwilling listener and close the channels of communication, or it may leave the channels of communication open at the expense of the unwilling listener. The state's freedom to choose between these two alternatives, however, is limited by the First Amendment. As Justice Harlan made clear in *Cohen*, the "ability of government, consonant with the Constitution, to shut off discourse to protect others from hearing it is . . . dependent upon a showing that substantial privacy interests are being invaded in an essentially intolerable manner." As indicated earlier, to make this determination, it is necessary in each case to consider whether one or both of the possible "privacy interests" are at stake, the extent to which the unwilling listener can be said to have a "reasonable expectation of privacy" at the time and place of the communication, and

125 To take another example, suppose that, in order to "protect" passersby, a city enacted a rule limiting soapbox orators to specifically designated locations. Although such a scheme theoretically individualizes the listener's decision, and is clearly "less restrictive" than an absolute ban on all public speaking, its impairment of First Amendment rights is so extensive that its constitutionality would have to be tested against a standard virtually identical to that enunciated in *Cohen*.

126 In order to be deemed "available," the less restrictive method must itself of course be constitutionally permissible. See note 125 *supra*.

the extent to which the unwilling listener can avoid either initial or continued exposure to the unwanted communication. A few illustrations may prove helpful.

First, suppose a state, in an effort to protect the sensibilities of passersby, enacts a law prohibiting the display of any billboard, sign, or poster facing a public street or highway. Here, only one privacy interest—avoidance of unwanted exposure to ideas—is at issue. The means of communication itself, apart from the message conveyed, does not intrude upon any privacy interests of the unwilling viewer. Moreover, however great one's right to be let alone at home may be, it is necessarily limited when one ventures upon public thoroughfares. The individual's "reasonable expectation of privacy" in these circumstances is clearly minimal.

Finally, there is the "captivity" question itself. It seems evident that, in many instances, initial exposure to the display will be largely unavoidable. In this sense, at least, the individual can be said to be "captive" to the communication. But this sort of "captivity" exists with respect to virtually all forms of comunication. While browsing through a newspaper, the unsuspecting reader might unwittingly come across a headline or photograph he finds offensive. When an individual switches on his television or radio he may suddenly be confronted with views he finds distasteful. And while strolling through a park, the individual may unintentionally overhear a speech or even a conversation he finds indecent. Society cannot, however, spin a protective cocoon around each individual, insulating him absolutely from all unwanted communications. The true measure of an individual's privacy in this context consists, not in his total protection from initial exposure to unwelcome ideas but, rather, in his ability to avoid continued exposure to those ideas once he has rejected them. Viewed in this light, the billboard situation involves a relatively minor form of actual "captivity." For although initial exposure to the display may be largely unavoidable, unwilling viewers can ordinarily avoid continued bombardment of their sensibilities simply by averting their eyes and walking or driving past. Thus, taking all three factors into account, our hypothetical statute would seem to be unconstitutional when tested against the *Cohen* standard.

The majority opinions in *Lehman*, however, cast some doubt upon the validity of this conclusion. In order to explain this development, I must begin with the Court's decision, some forty years ago, in *Packer Corp. v. Utah.*[127] In *Packer Corp.*, the Court held that a Utah statute, prohibiting the advertisement of tobacco products on billboards, streetcar signs, and placards, but permitting such advertisements in newspapers, magazines, and periodicals, did not violate the Equal Protection Clause. The decision was premised, in part, upon the observation that, unlike readers of newspapers, magazines, and periodicals, viewers of billboards, streetcar signs, and placards constitute a captive audience.[128] No First Amendment issue was raised, however, and none was decided. The sole question presented was whether the statutory classification was so "arbitrary" as to constitute a denial of equal protection.[129] The degree of "captivity" necessary to justify a finding of non-arbitrariness in that context is obviously far different from the degree of "captivity" necessary to justify a restriction on the exercise of First Amendment rights under the *Cohen* formulation. Nevertheless, in *Lehman*, where the First Amendment issue was presented, Justices Blackmun and Douglas both quoted *Packer Corp.* with approval,[130] thereby at least implying that viewers of billboards may indeed constitute a captive audience even for First Amendment purposes. Whether the implication was intended remains to be seen.[131]

---

127 285 U.S. 105 (1932).

128 The distinction was justified on the ground that the billboard is "thrust upon" the viewer, whereas "there must be some seeking by the one who is to see and read the advertisement" in a newspaper or magazine. *Id.* at 110. It has been argued, however, and not unpersuasively, that "[g]iven the assumption that one browses through a newspaper or magazine, he is just as subject to an unexpected full-page ad being 'thrust upon' him as when out driving on the highways—which he also makes a choice to do or not to do." Haiman, *Speech v. Privacy: Is There a Right Not To Be Spoken To?*, 67 Nw. U.L. Rev. 153, 178 (1972).

129 The Court also held that the statute did not constitute a deprivation of property without due process of law, and that it did not violate the Commerce Clause. Neither of those aspects of the decision are relevant to the First Amendment issue.

130 94 S. Ct. at 2717 (Blackmun), *id.* at 2719 (Douglas).

131 The issue was further clouded by the Court's decision, handed down the same day as *Lehman*, in Spence v. Washington, 94 S. Ct. 2727 (1974). In *Spence*, the appellant affixed a large peace symbol to a United States flag and displayed it out the window of his apartment. He was convicted for violating a state "flag misuse" statute, and the Court overturned the conviction by a vote of 6 to 3. In a per curiam opinion, joined only by the four *Lehman* dissenters, the unknown author went out of his way to note that "appellant did not impose his ideas upon a captive audience. Anyone who might have been offended could easily have avoided the display." *Id.* at 2731. None of the other Justices mentioned the point.

The second illustration of the *Cohen* principle should prove less troublesome. Suppose an individual, in an effort to communicate with the occupants of an apartment building, broadcasts his views into the building with the aid of a loudspeaker. Although some residents may be more than a little perturbed at this behavior, others might find it a welcome diversion from their regularly scheduled bout with the afternoon game shows and soap operas. Moreover, unlike the situation in *Martin*, there is no means here by which the state can enable the occupants to determine, on an individual basis, whether they wish to receive the communication. Only two alternatives are available—protect the unwilling listeners, or protect the speaker and the willing listeners. If the state chooses the first alternative, and deprives the speaker of his loudspeaker, will its decision be violative of the First Amendment? The answer, applying the *Cohen* standard, would clearly be no.

Here, unlike the billboard situation, both "privacy interests" are at stake. The unwilling listener in his apartment is exposed, not only to ideas he may find distasteful, but also to sound that may itself interfere with his sleep, reading, conversation, television-watching, or whatever pursuit he may be engaged in at the time. Moreover, the individual here is not on the streets; he is in his home, his "castle," where his right to be let alone is at its peak. Finally, the unwilling listener in this situation cannot avoid continued exposure to the unwanted communication simply by "averting his ears and walking past." His ears do not avert, they hear—whether he wants them to or not. He can, of course, leave the building, lock himself in the bathroom, or don a pair of earmuffs. That much, however, the First Amendment cannot require. If ever there was a true captive audience, this is it.[132]

Our third example takes us into the bus, streetcar, or train. Suppose a passenger decides to make a speech to his fellow travelers.

---

[132] When a loudspeaker is used on the streets or in a park, and private dwellings are not involved, two considerations should be paramount. First, at a sufficiently high decibel level, the sound emitted by a loudspeaker can constitute an aural assault no less painful or annoying than a physical assault. Second, as with the natural voice, one seeking to escape a loudspeaker can always do so simply by walking away. The question, however, is how far he must walk. These two factors, plus of course time and location, should govern the extent to which the state may constitutionally "turn down" the sound. In other words, regulation, but not prohibition. For the Court's rather confused treatment of the sound-truck problem, see Saia v. New York, 334 U.S. 558 (1948); Kovacs v. Cooper, 336 U.S. 77 (1949).

Can the state constitutionally prohibit this mode of communication on the ground that it invades the rights of a captive audience? Applying *Cohen*, the answer would seem to be "yes." Passengers in such vehicles may use their time in transit for many purposes. They may read, worry, daydream, converse, sleep, do crossword puzzles, and so on. The time is their own, and they should be free, within limits, to decide for themselves how it will be used. Our speechmaker, however, subjects these individuals not only to possibly unwanted ideas but also to sound that overrides the normal babble of conversation and directly interferes with whatever pursuits they are engaged in. As a result, both "privacy interests" are at stake. On the other hand, the passengers are in a publicly owned vehicle, and although their "reasonable expectation of privacy" in that situation may be greater than when strolling on the streets, it is surely less than in the home. The third factor—the degree of captivity—would therefore seem to be crucial. The unwilling auditor in this context has two alternatives. He can, of course, leave the vehicle entirely. But in light of the realities of contemporary urban transportation, this can hardly be viewed as a reasonable method of avoidance, particularly if commuters adopt the habit of making such speeches regularly. The second alternative—to try not to listen—is obviously even less satisfactory. Thus, in light of the relatively high degree of actual captivity, and the fact that both "privacy interests" are threatened, the state's ban on this form of communicative activity would seem to be constitutionally permissible.

The fourth, and final, illustration of the *Cohen* principle is *Lehman* itself. The question here is whether passengers exposed to car cards displayed on the interior of such vehicles constitute a captive audience under the *Cohen* formulation. This situation falls somewhere between billboards and transit orators. At the outset, it should be noted that, unlike the transit orator situation, only one privacy interest is here at issue. The mode of communication itself does not in any sense directly interfere with the ability of passengers to read, converse, mediate, work or even catch a short nap. The sole interest at stake is freedom from unwanted exposure to ideas. Moreover, although the "reasonable expectation of privacy" here may be slightly greater than in the billboard situation, these vehicles are, after all, public places where privacy interests are necessarily limited. Finally, there is the captivity factor. In the billboard situation, the unwilling viewer can avoid continued exposure to the message simply by averting his eyes and walking or driving past. Here, however, although the passenger can avert his eyes, he cannot reasonably be expected to leave the vehicle entirely. In other words, he cannot "walk or drive past." On the other hand, the passenger is not asked to do the impossible—to sit and try not to listen. The ability to avert one's eyes from an unpleasant message, even for a relatively prolonged period, should not be lightly dismissed. And this is particularly true where, as here, the sign is small and, in at least most instances, the commuter can simply change seats so that the sign is not in his direct line of vision. Taking all these considerations into account, it does not seem that the display of cars cards on the interior of a rapid transit vehicle constitutes an invasion of "substantial privacy interests . . . in an essentially intolerable manner."[133] To the extent that the Court reached a contrary conclusion in *Lehman*, I find it difficult to agree.[134]

One final aspect of the captive audience problem should at least briefly be mentioned. Up to now, I have focused upon the extent to which, consonant with the First Amendment, the state may shut off discourse with willing listeners in an effort to protect the interests of unwilling listeners. The captive audience issue can also arise, however, where the state itself seeks to expose individuals to unwanted communication. Here, the question is not whether the state can prohibit speech but, rather, whether the state's own invasion of the rights of captive auditors is itself unconstitutional. In *Public Utilities Comm'n v. Pollak*,[135] the Court's only direct confrontation with this issue, the Court held that the broadcasting of news, music, and advertising (but not "objectionable propaganda") on publicly regulated streetcars and buses did not violate the First and Fifth Amendment rights of passengers. In *Lehman*, Mr. Justice Douglas, who dissented in *Pollak*, argued that the display of car cards in such vehicles would violate "the constitutional rights of the commuters."[136] Whatever the merits

---

133 Moreover, there may be a "less restrictive method" available, since the state could permit such signs only in some vehicles, in much the same way that it delineates "smoking" and "non-smoking" cars.

134 It is unclear whether Mr. Justice Blackmun viewed *Cohen* as the applicable standard in *Lehman*. See text *infra*, at notes 167–69.

135 343 U.S. 451 (1952).

136 94 S. Ct. at 2719.

of *Pollak*, the reasoning underlying Douglas's facile extension of his *Pollak* dissent to *Lehman* seems doubtful, at best.[137]

V. Equal Protection, Commercial Speech, and Another Look at the Captive Audience

Assuming there is no public forum right to utilize a particular publicly owned facility for the exercise of First Amendment rights, in what circumstances, if any, may the state, consonant with the Equal Protection Clause, permit some individuals to use that facility while at the same time denying its use to others because of the content of the message they seek to express?[138] The problem of such selective exclusions has long troubled the Court and, indeed, provides the primary justification for the Court's long-standing ban on standardless licensing of communicative activities.[139] The Court first specifically addressed the equal protection issue in *Niemotko v. Maryland*.[140] In *Niemotko*, a group of Jehovah's Witnesses was denied a permit to use a municipal park for Bible talks, although other political and religious groups had been allowed to use the park for similar purposes. Putting the public forum issue aside, the Court noted that the permit was denied because of the city's "dislike for or disagreement with the Witnesses or their views."[141] It therefore concluded that this selective exclusion violated the "right to equal protection of the laws, in

---

[137] As previously indicated, unlike *Pollak*, *Lehman* does not appear to involve a "true" captive audience situation within the meaning of *Cohen*. Moreover, since the state possesses no rights under the First Amendment, the degree of captivity necessary to find a constitutional violation where, as in *Pollak*, the state itself speaks to unwilling listeners, would seem to be somewhat less than the degree of captivity necessary to find such a violation where, as in *Lehman*, the state acts as a neutral intermediary providing only the vehicle of communication for "private" speakers. Even where the state itself speaks, however, the right of willing listeners to receive the communication must of course be considered.

[138] The equal protection issue also arises, of course, where the state defines the selective exclusion in terms of the characteristics of the speaker, rather than the content of his speech. For example, a selective exclusion based upon the speaker's race would obviously violate the Equal Protection Clause. In *Davis*, even Holmes conceded this limitation upon the state's power to control its own property. See 162 Mass. at 512.

[139] See, *e.g.*, Lovell v. Griffin, 303 U.S. 444 (1938); Schneider v. State, 308 U.S. 147, 163 (1939); Largent v. Texas, 318 U.S. 418 (1943); Saia v. New York, 334 U.S. 558 (1948); Kuntz v. New York, 340 U.S. 290 (1951).

[140] 340 U.S. 268 (1951).

[141] *Id.* at 272.

the exercise of those freedoms of speech and religion protected by the First and Fourteenth Amendments."[142] The Court reached a similar result in *Fowler v. Rhode Island*,[143] where the Jehovah's Witnesses once again were refused permission to conduct religious services in a park, although other religious groups had been permitted to do so.

In *Police Dept. v. Mosley*,[144] decided in 1972, the Court offered its most comprehensive explication of the selective exclusion issue. *Mosley* concerned the constitutionality of a Chicago ordinance making it unlawful for any person to picket or demonstrate on a public way within 150 feet of a school building while the school is in session. The ordinance specifically exempted "peaceful picketing of any school involved in a labor dispute" from its otherwise absolute prohibition. For seven months prior to the enactment of the ordinance, Mosley frequently picketed a local high school, during school hours, peacefully protesting the school's alleged racial discrimination. After the ordinance was passed, Mosley ceased picketing, and brought suit claiming that the ordinance was overbroad in that it punished activity protected by the First Amendment, and that its exemption of peaceful labor picketing violated the Equal Protection Clause. The Court, in a unanimous decision, found it unnecessary to decide the overbreadth question, holding instead "that the ordinance is unconstitutional because it makes an impermissible distinction between labor picketing and other peaceful picketing."[145]

At the outset, Mr. Justice Marshall, speaking for the Court,[146] observed that the "central problem with Chicago's ordinance is that it describes permissible picketing in terms of its subject matter."[147] After noting that, "above all else, the First Amendment means that government has no power to restrict expression because of its message, its ideas, its subject matter, or its content,"[148] he continued:[149]

> Necessarily, then, under the Equal Protection Clause, not to mention the First Amendment itself, government may not

[142] *Ibid.* [143] 345 U.S. 67 (1953). [144] 408 U.S. 92 (1972).

[145] *Id.* at 94. See also Grayned v. Rockford, 408 U.S. 104, 107 (1972). Justice Black had previously reached a similar conclusion in Cox v. Louisiana, 379 U.S. 536, 581 (1965) (concurring opinion).

[146] Justices Blackmun and Rehnquist concurred in the result without opinion.

[147] 408 U.S. at 95. [148] *Ibid.* [149] *Id.* at 96.

> grant the use of a forum to people whose views it finds acceptable, but deny use to those wishing to express less favored or more controversial views. And it may not select which issues are worth discussing or debating in public facilities. . . . Once a forum is opened up to assembly or speaking by some groups, government may not prohibit others from speaking or assembling on the basis of what they intend to say. Selective exclusions from a public forum may not be based on content alone, and may not be justified by reference to content alone.

This does not mean, however, that whenever a state permits some individuals to use a public facility for speech purposes, it must necessarily permit all individuals to use that facility without regard to time, place, and manner. On the contrary, "there may be sufficient regulatory interests justifying selective exclusions or distinctions among [speakers.]"[150] But these justifications "must be carefully scrutinized," and "must be tailored to serve a substantial governmental interest."[151]

In defense of its ordinance, Chicago argued that it was a necessary device to prevent disruption of school activities. Although conceding that cities may have a substantial interest in prohibiting picketing that disrupts a school, Mr. Justice Marshall pointed out that "Chicago itself has determined that peaceful labor picketing during school hours is not an undue interference with school."[152] This determination, of course, fatally impeached the city's asserted justification for its ban on peaceful nonlabor picketing. For "however the term 'peaceful' is defined," peaceful nonlabor picketing "is obviously no more disruptive than 'peaceful' labor picketing."[153]

Finally, Chicago sought to justify its statutory classification on the ground that, "as a class, nonlabor picketing is more prone to produce violence than labor picketing."[154] The Court had little sympathy for that sort of argument:[155]

> Predictions about imminent disruption from picketing involve judgments appropriately made on an individualized basis, not by means of broad classifications, especially those based on subject matter. Freedom of expression, and its intersection with the guarantee of equal protection, would rest on a soft foundation indeed if government could distinguish among picketers on such a wholesale and categorical basis.

150 *Id.* at 98.
151 *Id.* at 99.
152 *Id.* at 100.
153 *Ibid.*
154 *Ibid.*
155 *Id.* at 100–01.

Thus, Mr. Justice Marshall concluded that whatever excesses may arise out of nonlabor picketing can, as with labor picketing, " 'be controlled by narrowly drawn statutes,' . . . focusing on the abuses and dealing even-handedly with picketing regardless of subject matter."[156]

This, then, brings me back to *Lehman*, where the equal protection issue may be framed as follows: Assuming that, for whatever reason, there is no public forum right to post signs on the inside of a publicly owned rapid transit vehicle, may the state selectively exclude all such signs bearing public issue or political messages, while at the same time permitting the display of such signs carrying commercial or public service messages? The first, and perhaps most important, observation one can make about *Lehman* is that the Blackmun approach to the equal protection issue did not receive the endorsement of a Court majority. On the contrary, although Mr. Justice Douglas concurred in Mr. Justice Blackmun's disposition of the case, he reached that result for his own, quite distinct, reasons. Unlike Mr. Justice Blackmun, Mr. Justice Douglas concluded that the display of any car cards, regardless of content, would violate the constitutional rights of commuters. On this view of the matter, the equal protection issue falls by the wayside, for the Constitution clearly does not require a state that has engaged in one unconstitutional act to adopt another simply for the sake of equality. Moreover, as if to highlight his disagreement with the Blackmun approach, Douglas specifically declared that he did "not view the content of the message as relevant either to petitioner's right to express it or to the commuters' right to be free from it."[157] With this caveat in mind, I turn to the Blackmun opinion.

In *Mosley*, the Court emphasized that selective exclusions "must be carefully scrutinized," and "must be tailored to serve a substantial governmental interest." In *Lehman*, however, Mr. Justice Blackmun declared that the selective exclusion of political and public issue speech would be permissible so long as that exclusion was not "arbitrary, capricious, or invidious."[158] Although Mr. Justice Blackmun never specifically addressed *Mosley*, he offered at least two arguments that might be viewed as explanations for this departure from the *Mosley* standard.

---

[156] *Id.* at 102.

[157] 94 S. Ct. at 2719–20.

[158] *Id.* at 2717.

First, he emphasized that, in its operation of the transit system and its sale of advertising space, "the city is engaged in commerce."[159] The Court has long recognized, however, that whatever significance the proprietary-governmental distinction may have for other purposes, it is utterly irrelevant to the standards imposed under the Constitution.[160] State action is state action, whether characterized as "proprietary" or "governmental," and the commands of the Constitution do not, and cannot, vary simply because "the city is engaged in commerce." Indeed, if the commercial nature of the enterprise dilutes the equal protection standard in this context, does it have the same effect where the city, in a nonarbitrary effort to provide "pleasant" service to the majority of commuters, excludes all blacks, Italians, or Jews from even riding in its buses? The answer seems as obvious as the unpersuasiveness of the reliance upon the proprietary nature of the venture.[161]

Quoting the Ohio Supreme Court, Mr. Justice Blackmun argued further, however, that "the city has decided that 'Purveyors of goods and services saleable in commerce may purchase advertising space on an equal basis, whether they be house builders or butchers.' "[162] The point seems to be that since all those seeking to purchase advertising space for commercial purposes are treated alike, and all those seeking to purchase such space for public issue or political purposes are treated alike, the equal protection problem disappears. The same argument could, of course, be made in *Mosley*. That is, since all labor picketers are treated alike, and all nonlabor picketers are treated alike, the ordinance must be upheld. The difficulty with this approach is its circularity. The crucial question under the Equal Protection Clause is not whether all those within the classes defined by the state are treated equally but, rather, whether the classification itself is permissible. And to

---

159 *Ibid.*

160 See, *e.g.*, City of Trenton v. State of New Jersey, 262 U.S. 182, 191–92 (1923); City of St. Petersburg v. Alsup, 238 F.2d 830, 831–32 (5th Cir. 1956); Lawrence v. Hancock, 76 F. Supp. 1004, 1008 (S.D. W. Va. 1948); see also Gilmore v. City of Montgomery, 94 S. Ct. 2416 (1974); Burton v. Wilmington Parking Authority, 365 U.S. 715 (1961).

161 This is not to say, of course, that the commercial nature of particular governmental action is necessarily irrelevant to the ultimate question of constitutionality. In some circumstances, this may be a relevant consideration. It does not, however, alter the standards employed.

162 94 S. Ct. at 2717.

answer that question in *Lehman*, one must resort to the *Mosley* standard.

It may be, however, that this quotation from the Ohio Supreme Court represented, in reality, an effort to afford quite a different argument. In its brief to the Court, the city vigorously maintained that since commercial speech is unprotected by the First Amendment,[163] its selective exclusion of political and public issue speech should not be tested under the *Mosley* standard. Rather, since there is no discrimination between classes of protected speech, the sole issue should be whether its policy is "arbitrary, capricious, or invidious." Whatever the merits, or indeed continued validity,[164] of the "commercial" speech doctrine, it offers no succor to the city in *Lehman*. By permitting commercial advertising, while banning public issue and political messages, the city's policy stands that doctrine on its head. Although a discrimination against all public issue or political speech may be somewhat less dangerous than a discrimination among different viewpoints on particular issues, it is a form of censorship just the same, reflecting a favoritism toward the status quo. Moreover, since commercial advertisements frequently carry implicit "political" messages, the city's policy opened the door to *sub rosa* discrimination among constitutionally protected ideas.[165] Mr. Justice Blackmun's protestations to the con-

---

[163] See, *e.g.*, Valentine v. Chrestensen, 316 U.S. 52 (1942); Breard v. Alexandria, 341 U.S. 622 (1951); *cf.* Pittsburgh Press Co. v. Pittsburgh Comm'n on Human Relations, 413 U.S. 376 (1973).

[164] In recent years, several Justices have cast doubt upon the doctrine. See, *e.g.*, Pittsburgh Press Co. v. Pittsburgh Comm'n on Human Relations, 413 U.S. 376, 388 (1973); *id.* at 393 (Burger, C.J., dissenting); *id.* at 397–98 (Douglas, J., dissenting); *id.* at 401 (Stewart, J., dissenting); Spence v. Washington, 94 S. Ct. 2727, 2731 n. 7 (1974).

[165] In a virtually identical context, the California Supreme Court offered several examples: "A cigarette company is permitted to advertise the desirability of smoking its brand, but a cancer society is not entitled to caution by advertisements that cigarette smoking is injurious to health. A theater may advertise a motion picture that portrays sex and violence, but the Legion for Decency has no right to post a message calling for clean films. A lumber company may advertise its wood products, but a conservation group cannot implore citizens to write to the President or Governor about protecting our natural resources. An oil refinery may advertise its products, but a citizens organization cannot demand enforcement of existing air pollution statutes. An insurance company may announce its available policies, but a senior citizens' club cannot plead for legislation to improve our social security program." Wirta v. Alameda-Contra Costa Transit District, 68 Cal.2d 51, 57–58 (1967). See also Mr. Justice Brennan's dissent in *Lehman*, 94 S. Ct. at 2724.

trary notwithstanding, the selective exclusion in *Lehman* should properly have been tested against the *Mosley* standard.

The next question, then, is whether the city's exclusion of political and public issue messages was "tailored to serve a substantial government interest." Mr. Justice Blackmun's primary argument on this front was, of course, that the policy was necessary to protect the sensibilities of a captive audience.[166] Before examining the question whether protection of a captive audience should ever constitute sufficient justification for selective exclusions, two preliminary issues must be considered.

First, assuming at least for the moment that this may be a sufficient justification, what degree of captivity is required? Since *Lehman* involved a situation where government was attempting "to shut off discourse to protect others from hearing it," the standard enunciated by Justice Harlan in *Cohen v. California* would seem applicable.[167] Mr. Justice Blackmun, however, never even mentioned *Cohen*. Rather, he premised his captive audience conclusion upon the Court's observations in *Packer Corp. v. Utah*.[168] His reliance upon this decision was clearly misplaced. In *Packer Corp.*, a billboard company was convicted of violating a state statute prohibiting the advertisement of tobacco products on billboards, streetcars, and placards, but permitting such advertisements in newspapers, magazines, and periodicals. The company contended that this distinction between the means of communication violated the Equal Protection Clause. No First Amendment issue was raised, and the company did not argue that the statute constituted an unconstitutional discrimination against certain speech because of the message conveyed. Accordingly, the Court's conclusion in *Packer Corp.* that billboards and streetcar signs involve a greater captive audience problem than newspapers and magazines, can hardly be viewed as dispositive of the selective exclusion issue presented in *Lehman*. The proper standard was set

---

166 Mr. Justice Blackmun also argued that the policy was justified because, if compelled to permit noncommercial speech, the city would confront several "sticky" administrative problems. See 94 S. Ct. at 2718. The argument is effectively and persuasively answered in the Brennan dissent, *id.* at 2726, and need not be repeated.

167 Indeed, since a selective exclusion of particular viewpoints or ideas poses a greater threat to freedom of expression than even an across-the-board prohibition, the proper standard in such circumstances may be even more stringent than that set forth in *Cohen*.

168 285 U.S. 105 (1932).

forth in *Cohen* and, as indicated earlier, the display of car cards on the interior of a publicly owned transit vehicle would not seem to create a situation in which "substantial privacy interests are being invaded in an essentially intolerable manner."

Second, even assuming that *Lehman* did involve a "true" captive audience situation, is the selective exclusion of all political and public issue speech an appropriate device for protecting the sensibilities of captive commuters? The answer clearly is "no." As a majority of the Court recognized, "[c]ommercial advertisements may be as offensive and intrusive to captive audiences as any political message."[169] However "commercial" speech is defined, it surely does not turn exclusively, or even primarily, on the "offensiveness" of the message conveyed. As the Court emphasized in *Mosley*, predictions as to the "offensiveness" of particular advertisements, be they commercial or political, "involve judgments appropriately made on an individualized basis, not by means of broad classifications, especially those based on subject matter."

Finally, there is the question whether the desire to protect captive auditors from unwanted exposure to "offensive" ideas ever constitutes sufficient justification to support even a narrowly drawn selective exclusion. The Supreme Court has consistently adhered to the view "that under our Constitution the public expression of ideas may not be prohibited merely because the ideas are themselves offensive to some of their hearers."[170] Is this principle waived insofar as the captive audience is concerned? To take a rather extreme example, suppose that, after polling its commuters, the city finds that although the vast majority do not object to the ideas of Democratic and Republican candidates, they "deeply resent" the views expressed by Socialist candidates. Based upon this finding, may the city permit Democratic and Republican candidates to purchase car card space to espouse their "inoffensive" ideas, while at the same time excluding the "offensive" Socialist message? Acceptance of such an approach would necessarily constitute endorsement of the "heckler's veto" in its most odious form.

---

[169] 94 S. Ct. at 2720 (Douglas, J., concurring); see *id.* at 2725 (Brennan, J. dissenting).

[170] Street v. New York, 394 U.S. 576, 592 (1969); *accord, e.g.*, Spence v. Washington, 94 S. Ct. 2727, 2731 (1974); Bachellar v. Maryland, 397 U.S. 564, 567 (1970); see also Cox v. Louisiana, 379 U.S. 536, 551 (1965); Watson v. City of Memphis, 373 U.S. 526, 535 (1963); Niemotko v. Maryland, 340 U.S. 268, 284 (1951) (Frankfurter, J., concurring).

Government should never be in the business of facilitating majority censorship of dissident views. Moreover, the discrimination here is twofold. This approach not only permits the suppression of unpopular or controversial ideas, it also fails to provide equal protection to those captives who, because of their unorthodoxy, may find the so-called "inoffensive" ideas even more obnoxious. If a "true" captive audience exists, the state may protect the sensibilities of unwilling listeners by banning all speech, regardless of content. It should never, however, be permitted to use the captive audience as a lever for censorship.[171]

The Court's decision in *Lehman* does not mark a high point in its continuing struggle to give meaning and vitality to the First Amendment. The majority opinions raise more questions than they answer, and the answers that are offered are often unpersuasive, at best. The problems posed by the First Amendment in a constantly changing, ever more complex society are by no means easy ones. But no one ever suggested that preservation of freedom of expression would be easy. The task of accommodating the exercise of our most cherished liberty with competing, often important, state concerns requires a healthy dose of sensitivity. And that, indeed, was sorely lacking in *Lehman*.

---

171 This principle might not apply where the state excludes "unprotected" speech.

HADLEY ARKES

CIVILITY AND THE RESTRICTION OF SPEECH: REDISCOVERING THE DEFAMATION OF GROUPS

A few years ago James Q. Wilson reported a survey of more than one thousand Boston homeowners, who were asked what was the biggest problem facing the city.[1] The "usual" urban problems—housing, transportation, pollution, urban renewal—were a major concern of only 18 percent of those questioned. Only 9 percent mentioned jobs and unemployment, even though many of the persons interviewed had incomes at, or even below, what was often regarded as the poverty level. The issue that more than any other concerned these people was described rather variously in terms of crime, violence, rebellious youth, racial tension, public immorality, delinquency. This was the concern among blacks as well as whites, liberals as well as conservatives. Although it might have looked on the surface like a reaction to "crime in the streets," many of the things that were mentioned were not criminal in any strict legal sense. They involved what one might call forms of incivility or of public indecencies: verbal assaults in the streets; unconstrained, rowdy teenagers; lurid advertisements in front of neighborhood movies; tawdry paperbacks and magazines. As Wilson summed it up, the concern seemed to be for improper behavior in public places[2]

Hadley Arkes is Associate Professor of Political Science, Amherst College.

[1] Wilson, *The Urban Unease: Community vs. City*, 12 Public Interest 25 (1968).

[2] *Id.* at 27.

and the apparent disintegration of any standards that might claim to govern behavior in a public place according to some understanding of civility.

When we speak of civility, however, we speak, really, about the fostering of moral codes and about the kind of life, the manners, even the modes of making a living that we hold up for emulation—about the occupations that are more or less respectable for people suited to live in a civil society. And not the least of the elements of civility, giving some insight into ourselves and our standards, are the things we regard as respectable to say in public.

Madison warned in *Federalist* No. 10 that the greatest threat to civility in a republic found its sources in the character of the regime itself: In a regime of personal liberty, where individuals and groups were free to express their interests in public, the violence and calumnies of faction promised to be an enduring part of the public arena of politics. The demands and interests of groups may provide the raw materials of politics, and the assault and defense of groups may take a dominant share in what passes for our public discourse on politics. As factional conflict reaches the limits of freedom that a republican regime affords, one can expect, too, that the public rhetoric of the day will get less, rather than more, subtle, and that speech may become almost conventionally libelous, routinely hateful. If one adds to that the conditions of a modern urban society, where transitions are abrupt, and differences of race, culture, class, and ethnicity sharply confront one another, the collision of groups may at times reach a level that is truly explosive. In this setting, as Justice Frankfurter observed, the attack on racial and religious groups may not only promote civil strife but "tend powerfully to obstruct the manifold adjustments required for free, ordered life in a metropolitan, polyglot community."[3]

The question of civility might be posed then with the greatest consequence for a society in the defamation of groups, or what has been known more commonly as group libel. But the problem has a special force in relation to those groups defined by race, religion, and nationality, and it is with the libel directed at those kinds of

---

3 Beauharnais v. Illinois, 343 U.S. 250, 259 (1952). The best modern example is the race riots that took place in Chicago in 1919. For the background and analysis of these riots, see Chicago Commission on Race Relations, The Negro in Chicago (1922); Drake & Cayton, Black Metropolis, 8–18, 31–65 (1945); and on a more impressionistic but very evocative level, Farrell, Studs Lonigan (1938).

groups that I will be chiefly concerned. For other groups, the current understanding in the law seems sensible enough and quite adequate to its ends: an action for libel will hold more easily to the extent that the group is smaller and that an individual can be identified more readily as a member of the group.[4] With this variety of libel, the remedy has been, quite properly, a civil suit, in which individuals may seek an award for personal damages. But there are certain kinds of defamation that cannot be dealt with reasonably through civil suits, and the injuries they produce are not always so immediate or direct that they can be weighed instantly in the courts. These injuries are not any less real. But, for them, the criminal law might provide a more suitable instrument. But here there would be an obligation to be most careful and explicit about the grounds on which the criminal law would rest. Not the least of the complications is that, since the speech involved in these cases has moved quite patently beyond the level of individuals to the defamation of whole groups, it has moved beyond the plane of private quarrels to disputes that are more nearly public and "political" in nature. Therefore, the problem raises the question whether speech on matters of public agitation can ever legitimately be restricted out of a regard for civility.

Since the 1930s and 1940s, when fascist organizations were engaged in the systematic defamation of racial and religious groups, the interest in group libel statutes has declined markedly. There are now only four state group defamation statutes on the books in this

---

[4] In one notable case, for example, suits were brought against the authors of *U.S.A. Confidential* for charging in their book that some of the models and salesgirls in the Neiman-Marcus store in Texas had often served as call girls, and that most of the male salesmen were homosexuals. Suits were brought by 9 models, who constituted the entire staff of models at the time the book was published; by 15 salesmen out of a group of 25; and by 30 saleswomen out of a group of 382. The defendants did not contest the suit brought by the models, but they moved to dismiss the claims made by the salesmen and saleswomen. The court rejected the motion to dismiss as to the salesmen, because the group was small and the allegation had been made that "most" of the men were homosexuals. The court did, however, reject the suit brought by the saleswomen. It pointed to the large size of the group, and it argued that "no reasonable man would take the writer seriously and conclude from the publication a reference to any individual saleswoman." Neiman-Marcus v. Lait, 13 F.R.D. 311 (S.D. N.Y. 1952). See also WITTENBERG, DANGEROUS WORDS chs. 11–12 (1947); Lewis, *The Individual Member's Right to Recover for a Defamation Leveled at the Group*, 17 U. MIAMI L. REV. 519 (1963).

country,[5] prosecutions have been rare, and convictions even rarer.[6] Indeed, the concept of group libel itself seems to have fallen into disfavor among legal scholars.[7] To put it mildly, it is not treated any longer with the same plausibility or even esteem that it held in the 1940s.[8] Among "professional" civil libertarians, the concept is treated as an anachronism, and its general disuse in recent years is taken as a sign of its ultimate inaptness in our constitutional law. For spokesmen of the American Civil Liberties Union, it has been a matter both of principle and strategy that group libel be held in disgrace, and they have expressed their alarm on those occasions when the concept has shown even a flickering sign of vitality.[9]

The irony is that there are important parts of our public policy today—including sections of our recent civil rights acts—which would be hard to understand or justify on anything other than group libel grounds. The deeper irony is that both the ACLU and the Justice Department, in their tendency to avoid the group libel argument as a ground of justification, have fallen back on formulas that are far more threatening to free speech and that should be even more suspect to civil libertarians. What is involved here, of course, is the old distinction that has been drawn between political and commercial speech, and the willingness to rest with an unjustified serenity on the "clear and present danger" test in cases where it would tend to work with effects that are decidedly less than libertarian.

Beyond that, the choice in the group libel problem is not between the restraint of free expression and the absence of restraint. It is rather a choice between two forms of restraint: one carried out by private groups operating outside the law, and another, of a more limited nature, carried out by legal authorities under the constraints

---

5 Conn. Gen. Stat. § 53-37 (1958); Burns Ind. Stat. Ann. §§ 10-914 (1956); Mass. Ann. Laws ch. 272, § 98(C) (1956); and West Va. Code § 55-7-14 (1966).

6 On this point, see Tanenhaus, *Group Libel*, 35 CORN. L.Q. 261, 276, 286 (1950).

7 See, *e.g.*, KALVEN, THE NEGRO AND THE FIRST AMENDMENT ch. 1 (1965).

8 There is no better example on the latter point than David Riesman's classic series of articles *Democracy and Defamation*, 42 COLUM. L. REV. 727, 1085, 1282 (1942). Even Joseph Tanenhaus, who was more apprehensive about the effects that group libel laws might have in restricting legitimate forms of expression, could still regard group libel, much in the way Riesman did, as a serious concern of a liberal society and a fit object of legal remedy. See note 6 *supra*.

9 See Pemberton, *Can the Law Provide a Remedy for Race Defamation in the United States?*, 14 N.Y. L. FORUM 33 (1968).

of a formal statute. In the earliest writings on libertarian thought, the host of repressions carried out in society outside the law were no less to be apprehended than a program of censorship imposed by the government, and in some respects they could be vastly worse. As Mill wrote in *On Liberty*:[10]

> Like other tyrannies, the tyranny of the majority was at first, and is still vulgarly, held in dread, chiefly as operating through the acts of the public authorities. But reflecting persons perceived that when society is itself the tyrant—society collectively over the separate individuals who compose it—its means of tyrannizing are not restricted to the acts which it may do by the hands of its political functionaries. Society can and does execute its own mandates; and if it issues wrong mandates instead of right, or any mandates at all in things with which it ought not to meddle, it practices a social tyranny more formidable than many kinds of political oppression, since, though not usually upheld by such extreme penalties, it leaves fewer means of escape, penetrating much more deeply into the details of life. . . . Protection, therefore, against the tyranny of the magistrate is not enough: there needs protection also against the tyranny of the prevailing opinion and feeling; against the tendency of society to impose, by other means than civil penalties, its own ideas and practices as rules of conduct.

In the present period, the consent of the majority is often taken to mean the appeasement of the minority whose interests are more directly engaged in any case, and who are more likely to take action to protect their interests. If one puts in the place of Mill's amorphous "majority" the organized minorities and "veto groups," which may exercise extraordinary leverage in their relations with newspapers and the broadcast media, one may find the forces which constitute the "majority" that Mill suspected and which produce, in combination, that "social tyranny" he anticipated. That these small acts of censorship may be carried on in the name of "responsiveness to the local community" is no warrant for their innocence. That we are more inclined to let them pass unnoticed—out of the mistaken belief, quite often, that there is nothing public policy can do to affect them—says something more about the limits of our sensitivity as libertarians than about the triviality or the harmlessness of these private intimidations.

---

10 MILL, ON LIBERTY 4 (Basil Blackwell ed., 1946).

I. The Problem of Group Libel: Beauharnais v. Illinois

Beauharnais v. Illinois[11] was the first group libel case to come before the Supreme Court, and in the twenty years since it was decided, no similar case has come before it.[12] In an opinion by Justice Frankfurter in which four other Justices joined, the Court upheld an Illinois statute that established criminal penalties for the defamation of "a class of citizens, of any race, color, creed or religion." But a serious question exists whether the decision has survived, particularly in light of *New York Times v. Sullivan*[13] and the cases that followed in its train. In the *Times* case, the Court for the first time explicitly rejected the concept of seditious libel, and it constricted the power of public officials to use libel laws to silence their citizen-critics. The Court argued in that case for a certain "breathing space" for speech, on the understanding that political speech is often heated and exaggerated, that it often takes place in the public streets, under conditions of excitement that make it impossible to verify every assertion that is made as though one were working in a library on a piece of scholarly research. The Court contracted the grounds of libel of public officials to a very narrow test of "malice" (which would subsequently prove very hard indeed to satisfy): the allegedly defamatory statement had to be made with knowledge that it was false, or with "reckless disregard" of whether it was false or not.[14]

With a few short steps over the next three years, the Court went even further in rolling back this coverage of the law of libel. From public officials it moved to "public figures" (*i.e.*, celebrities who may not hold or be a candidate for office),[15] and then finally even to the inadvertent subjects of publicity who just happened to be involved in events that one of the news media considered news-

---

11 343 U.S. 250 (1950).

12 There were earlier cases that were not appealed to the Supreme Court, in which statutes were sustained that allowed criminal prosecutions for the defamation of groups. See People v. Turner, 28 Cal. App. 766 (1915); Crane v. State, 14 Okl. Crim. 30 (1917); Alumbaugh v. State, 39 Ga. App. 559 (1929); People v. Speilman, 318 Ill. 482 (1925).

13 376 U.S. 254 (1964).

14 *Id.* at 280; see also St. Amant v. Thompson, 390 U.S. 727 (1968).

15 Curtis Pub. Co. v. Butts, 388 U.S. 130 (1967); see also Kalven, *The Reasonable Man and the First Amendment: Hill, Butts, and Walker*, 1967 Supreme Court Review 267.

worthy.[16] It has become vastly harder now to win a libel suit.[17] In view of the erosion in the concept of libel, one must wonder whether the ground has been cut out from under the decision in *Beauharnais*. There were some who thought, when the *Times* case was decided, that it marked the end of *Beauharnais*. But in less than a year, in a case that affirmed the emerging lines of the *Times* decision, the Court mentioned *Beauharnais* approvingly, and it seemed to suggest then that *Beauharnais* was not really threatened by the radiations from the *Times* case.[18] That brought a sharp dissent from Mr. Justice Douglas, who had apparently thought that *Beauharnais* had been overruled by the *Times* case. He railed against *Beauharnais* as a "misfit in our constitutional system," a decision that was out of line with "the dictates of the First Amendment," and if it had not been overruled earlier, he thought the Court should waste no time in overruling it now.[19]

Thus, the status of *Beauharnais* is a live question. If *Beauharnais* has not been extinguished sub silentio by the *Times* cases and the precedents built upon it, there is still a chance to look again at the case on its merits, to test again the adequacy of its reasoning, and possibly to reestablish its authority, if we can, by stating the case anew.

Section 224a of the Illinois Criminal Code made it unlawful to:[20]

> manufacture, sell, or offer for sale, advertise or publish, present or exhibit in any public place in this state any lithograph, moving picture, play, drama or sketch, which publication or exhibition portrays depravity, criminality, unchastity, or lack of virtue of a class of citizens, of any race, color, creed or religion which said publication or exhibition exposes the citi-

---

16 Time, Inc. v. Hill, 385 U.S. 374 (1967).

17 See, for example, Ocala Star-Banner Co. v. Damron, 401 U.S. 295, 296 (1971) (candidate for public office); Time, Inc. v. Pape, 401 U.S. 279 (1971) (police officer); and Rosenbloom v. Metromedia, 406 U.S. 29 (1971) (private citizen). The *Rosenbloom* case has been set aside more recently in Gertz v. Welch, 94 S. Ct. 2997 (1974), but the Court made it clear at the same time that it was not disturbing the decision in *Time, Inc. v. Hill.*

18 Garrison v. Louisiana, 379 U.S. 64, 70 (1964).

19 *Id.* at 82.

20 Ill. Crim. Code, § 224a, Ill. Rev. Stat., c. 38, Div. 1, § 471 (1949). The legislation was later repealed, though not, apparently, because of any weakness or lack of precision in the statute itself. It is worth noting that the Illinois law compared rather favorably with other "model" statutes on group libel that were being proposed in the 1940s. See Tanenhaus, note 6 *supra*, at 293 *et seq.*

> zens of any race, color, creed or religion to contempt, derision, or obloquy or which is productive of breach of the peace or riots. . . .

Joseph Beauharnais was the president of the White Circle League, with headquarters in Chicago. In January 1950 he gave out packages of leaflets to volunteers who offered to distribute them on street corners in downtown Chicago. Beauharnais himself organized and directed this effort, and on 7 January 1950 the leaflets were in fact distributed as he had planned. The leaflets, which were cast in the form of a petition to the mayor and City Council of Chicago, called upon the officials of the city "to halt the further encroachment, harassment and invasion of white people, their property, neighborhoods and persons, by the Negro—through the exercise of the Police Power." The leaflet went on to urge "One million self respecting white people in Chicago to unite under the banner of the White Circle League" to support the petition and resist the national campaign carried on by "Truman's infamous civil rights program and many Pro Negro Organizations to amalgamate the black and white races with the object of mongrelizing the white race!"[21] It suggested, further, that "[i]f persuasion and the need to prevent the white race from becoming mongrelized by the negro will not unite us, then the aggressions . . . rapes, robberies, knives, guns and marijuana of the negro, surely will." The statement ended with the declaration that "the first loyalty of every white person is to his race" and that "the hour has struck for all normal white people to stand up and fight.[22] Beauharnais's name appeared at the bottom of the text, along with a coupon that could serve as an application form for membership in the White Circle League.[23]

Beauharnais was arrested under the group libel statute, and in the trial that followed, the judge confined the jury to the narrow factual issues whether Beauharnais was in fact guilty of manufacturing, publishing, or distributing the leaflet, as proscribed by law. The judge found that the leaflet was indeed defamatory within the terms of the statute. He refused either to submit that question to the jury or to follow the request of the defendant and let the conviction hinge upon a finding by the jury "that the article complained of was likely to produce a clear and present danger of a serious substantive evil that rises far above public inconvenience,

21 343 U.S. at 276. 22 *Ibid.* 23 *Ibid.*

annoyance or unrest."[24] Under these holdings, and with the evidence at hand, Beauharnais was convicted rather easily and assessed a fine of $200.

On appeal, Beauharnais argued that the statute abridged his rights of freedom of speech and of the press. Moreover, he contended that the law was too vague, under the requirements of the Due Process Clause, to support a conviction.

Among the dissenting judges, the issue of vagueness was taken up only by Justice Reed,[25] and, for the most part, Justice Frankfurter was able to move through that question without too much resistance. Frankfurter did recall the history of race riots in Illinois, from the violence that erupted in Springfield in 1908 to the Cicero riots of 1951, which also included, along the way, the bloody rioting that took place, first in East St. Louis in 1917 and then in Chicago in 1919. But even without giving prime weight yet to the particular experience in Illinois that made the prospect of racial violence something more than an abstract question, Frankfurter found the statute sufficiently clear, both in its drafting and its application, to survive a constitutional challenge. "The statute before us," he wrote, "is not a catchall enactment left at large by the State court which applied it":[26]

> It is a law specifically directed at a defined evil, its language drawing from history and practice in Illinois and in more than a score of other jurisdictions a meaning confirmed by the Supreme Court of that State in upholding this conviction. We do not, therefore, parse the statute as grammarians or treat it as an abstract exercise in lexicography. We read it in the animating context of well-defined usage . . . and State court construction which determines its meaning for us.

The issue of vagueness was really an offshoot of the more general complaint raised by Beauharnais: that the statute put an unjustifiable burden on the kind of speech and publication that the First Amendment was designed to protect. As one would expect, this issue produced far more division on the Court, because it turned on the question whether the statute presented an unreasonable regulation of speech. The decision was bound up with all the

---

[24] *Id.* at 253. As Frankfurter noted in his opinion for the majority, the action of the trial court here followed the set rule for the prosecution of libels in Illinois and other states. See *id.* at 254 and n.2.

[25] See *id.* at 277–84.

[26] *Id.* at 253.

disputes that divided the Court over the nature of the standards one would need, and the conditions that would have to exist, before one could ever be justified in restricting public speech. One measure of the perplexity encountered in this case is that the differences that were evident among the dissenting judges were often as great as the differences that set them apart, as a group, from their colleagues in the majority.

II. On Libels, Injuries, and Political Speech: The Black Dissent

Justice Frankfurter viewed Beauharnais and his White Circle League and the literature as bristling with charges against a whole racial group and, therefore, as a matter of group libel. Black insisted that what was involved in this case, rather, was a group of citizens out "peacefully [to] petition" the government. And so, according to Justice Black, what the Court was restricting in *Beauharnais* was the freedom "to petition for and publicly discuss proposed legislation."[27] The complaint in Black's opinion was that all the facts that added texture to the case dissolved once the case was assimilated to the law of libel. And if there was a choice as to how one conceived the case, then there were compelling reasons, in Black's estimate, for not treating the case under the general rubric of libel when one was dealing, as here, with a matter of group libel. Black's argument here is in two parts.

First, criminal libel had been restricted in the past, with good reason, to charges that were made against individuals and not against "huge groups." That meant that the punishment of speech and expression had been confined "to the narrowest of areas involving nothing more than purely private feuds." Every expansion, then, of the law of libel threatened to punish "discussions of matters of public concern" and invade the area of speech protected by the First Amendment.[28] The argument here, again, bore some reflections of *Federalist* No. 10, or at the very least it was deepened by an awareness of a regime of public competition. Where the demands of groups became the very stuff of politics, it could be impossible to talk about political things in public without assaulting or defending the interests of identifiable groups—unions, real estate boards, civil rights groups—and if political discourse was often in-

[27] *Id*. at 267–68, 275.

[28] *Id*. at 271–72.

temperate, one could expect that a great deal of it would involve the maligning of groups in public. And so how could one prosecute for the defamation of groups without touching at many points the kind of speech that is constitutionally protected—or, as Black put it, without making it "very dangerous indeed to say something critical of one of the groups."[29]

Justice Black's argument had to rest on more than the assumption that speech directed at individuals was less "public" or "political" than speech directed at groups. That assumption was far too problematic, and it could not explain why Black still regarded an action for libel as acceptable in principle. In view of Black's comments about the size of the group and the value of narrowing the scope of libel, his opinion suggested rather that the traditional test of individual injuries added concreteness and discipline to prosecutions for libel. As soon as one gets into the libel of groups, the remarks get more and more general, the target becomes larger and more diffuse, and it becomes that much harder to argue that anyone in particular has been libeled. If someone went on national television and made disparaging remarks about blacks in general, it would be absurd, say, to let the Reverend Jesse Jackson go into a court in Chicago, seeking personal damages.[30] Once the connection to individual injuries is lost, the charge of libel becomes so vague that it may be nothing more than arbitrary warrant for cutting off speech that is critical of certain groups.

First, as to the matter of confining libel to the test of individual injuries, it is worth trying to see what that argument can or cannot establish. It would clearly establish that a suit for personal damages would be highly inappropriate as a form of remedy for the problem posed in *Beauharnais*. Certainly, it would be hard to show special damages[31] or injuries to an individual, and so a civil suit in these

---

[29] *Id.* at 273.

[30] It may be as unworkable, in this respect, as the suit brought by the Mexican-American Anti-Defamation Committee against the makers of Frito corn chips. A television advertisement for Frito Banditos had a cartoon character represented in the stereotype of a Latin American, with sombrero, mustache, and accent. The Anti-Defamation Committee claimed that the advertisement reinforced a harmful stereotype of the Mexican-American, and it sought $100 in punitive damages for every Chicano in the United States. See New York Times, 1 January 1971, p. 31, col. 6.

[31] On the more precise meaning of "special damages," see Terwilliger v. Wands, 17 N.Y. 54, 60 (1858), where Judge Strong mentioned, by way of example, "the

cases would be either clumsy or inapt. That the injuries are hard to demonstrate through the conventional tests of a civil suit, however, would not establish that there are no injuries, that there is no such thing as the libel of a group, or that no serious injuries may arise for the separate members as a result of being stigmatized as a group.

The question is whether there is not some plausibility in the argument made by Justice Frankfurter (and David Riesman)[32] that it is indeed possible to be libeled through a group, that a libel directed at a group may defame no less because it is directed at the group as a whole, that, in fact, it may defame even more, because it sweeps with a broader brush. There are data that confirm the vigor and widespread presence of racial and religious stereotypes.[33] When blacks were commonly turned away from hotels and other public accommodations—the black middle class and professional people as well as the poor and uneducated—one may seriously wonder whether the clerks behind the counters were responding to these people as individuals or whether they were responding largely to a category into which these people had been thrust, and in which they had been stigmatized as a group. The Frankfurter-Riesman argument would be impossible to reject unless one were also willing to reject the proposition that certain minority groups in this country have in fact suffered injuries in the past as a result of racist stereotypes that have been perpetuated in the public mind. Unless one is prepared to reject that proposition, one cannot reject group libel out of hand.

It is precisely because group libels sweep with a broader brush that they can be that much harder to avoid; there are some groups from which an individual cannot disengage himself. As Frankfurter

---

loss of a marriage, loss of hospitable gratuitous entertainment, preventing a servant or bailiff from getting a place, the loss of customers by a tradesman," and so on. It is worth noting, too, as a partial counter to Black's argument, that after the advent of libel as a separate tort, special damages became pertinent only when the words were not actionable in themselves or clearly defamatory in nature. *Cf. id.* at 57; see 8 HOLDSWORTH, HISTORY OF ENGLISH LAW 365 (1926).

32 See note 8 *supra*.

33 See, *e.g.*, ALLPORT, THE NATURE OF PREJUDICE (1954); BETTELHEIM & JANOWITZ, DYNAMICS OF PREJUDICE chs. 2–3 (1950), and for a more recent work that reprints the older study and adds some later material, see their SOCIAL CHANGE AND PREJUDICE, esp. ch. 1 (1964); *cf.* also CAMPBELL, WHITE ATTITUDES TOWARD BLACK PEOPLE 109–10 (1971).

remarked at one point in his opinion, it may be hard to deny the assumption that may have been held by the Illinois legislature, that:[34]

> a man's job and his educational opportunities and the dignity accorded him may depend as much on the reputation of the racial and religious group to which he willy-nilly belongs, as on his own merits. This being so, we are precluded from saying that speech concededly punishable when immediately directed at individuals cannot be outlawed if directed at groups with whose position and esteem in society the affiliated individual may be inextricably involved.

There is a major difference between groups of an almost primordial nature and organizations of a more voluntary nature, like political parties and trade associations, from which it may be possible to withdraw. It is not quite as easy to "contract out" of one's race or even one's religion, and for that reason it can be far harder then to evade the force of the libel. And so there is some point, too, in Frankfurter's argument that the law in Illinois was limited to groups of a less voluntary nature—groups defined by "race, color, creed, or religion"—and that the law goes only as far as it intends to go when it covers only these groups, which have been the objects traditionally of the fiercest loyalties and the fiercest calumnies. That is to say, it may be possible for the law to strike at the most serious sources of the problem without spilling over, as Justice Black had feared, to affect groups like political parties; and in that case, it may be possible to limit the effects of the law in restricting speech that is more conventionally political.[35]

It may be hard to make a precise connection in any case between the suffering of a harm and any particular publication that might have helped to sustain (or create) a climate of prejudice from which injuries may arise. In the nature of things, the lines of causation here cannot be drawn with exactness between particular events, and many of the harms that result from the defamation of groups may not crop up until years after the fact. The lines of connection may be impossible to chart empirically, and yet reasonable men understand that the connections exist. From the standpoint of protecting people either from psychological assaults or material injuries, there

---

[34] 343 U.S. at 263.

[35] On this point, see Frankfurter, *id.* at 263 n.18.

is a real difference between a society in which leaflets like Beauharnais's are encouraged until they flourish, and a society in which publications of this sort are not given the sanction of respectable opinion.

In this respect, the problem of proving cause and injury—and justifying punishment—is not much different from what it is in other areas where social policy is supported by legal penalties. For example, if someone claimed moral objections and refused to pay that part of his federal income tax that went into the support of a woman on welfare who kept having illegitimate children, he would be open to penalties that are far more severe than the fine that was leveled at Beauharnais.[36] And yet, the refusal of one taxpayer to pay his taxes could not possibly cause a reduction of one cent in the support of any welfare recipient, and even if a handful of taxpayers succeeded in opting out, the effect would still not be noticeable to others.[37] Which is to say, then, a dissenting taxpayer who does not want to be implicated in a style of life he finds deeply offensive, may nevertheless be punished, even though it could not be proved that his withdrawal of funds would cause injury to any specific person. Of course, it hardly needs stating that the concern of public policy in this case is with the injuries that may be suffered in the aggregate if others were encouraged to act upon this precedent. Similarly, in the case of Beauharnais, the concern is with the injuries that may occur in the aggregate when more people are circulating leaflets that resemble Beauharnais's and when the ideas represented by Beauharnais come to be regarded as more respectable and plausible.

To restate the case, one could argue in response to Justice Black that the problem of proving injury and justifying punishment was

---

[36] For the failure to pay one's income tax on the appropriate date without a reasonable excuse or justification, the law stipulates a fine equal to the amount of the unpaid tax plus 5 percent of the first month, and 5 percent for each additional month that the tax remains unpaid, up to a level of 25 percent of the original tax. 26 U.S.C. § 6651(a).

[37] Mancur Olson's analysis in *The Logic of Collective Action* (1965) would bear directly on this argument. The courts conceded the same point indirectly in the early cases on "standing." See, *e.g.*, Frothingham v. Mellon 262 U.S. 447 (1923), where the Court denied a taxpayer standing to sue on the grounds that any one person's tax payments would represent such a minute fraction of the whole that one's "support" of any program would be largely a fiction, and one's degree of injury, then, as a result of being compelled to support a program, would be virtually insignificant.

no harder in group libel than it was in many other areas of our law, where we have routinely accepted punishment for behavior that is nowhere near as malevolent as the activity involved in *Beauharnais*. But beyond that, one could argue that the problem of proving injury is not strikingly different from what it is even in the case of individual libels. Even where there has been no doubt about the identity of the person being libeled, the courts have recognized that it is probably beyond their means to establish in any rigorous sense a causal connection between the words that were uttered and the behavior that produced the injuries. There is an important difference between the evidence that the courts have been willing to accept in these cases as proof of injury stemming from libel[38] and the kind of evidence that social scientists typically demand as a basis for rejecting or preserving hypotheses at a known level of statistical significance.[39]

The logic of the matter really goes back to the original understanding of words that were in themselves libelous or defamatory and the rationale that lay behind the creation of libel as a separate tort. Since the latter part of the seventeenth century, one could recover damages for libel without the need to prove special damages, as one had to do in cases of slander. The result, as Holdsworth commented, was that the "publication of written defamation was regarded as a wrong to reputation from which damage could be presumed," and that that "naturally tended to make the insult a more prominent element in the tort than the damage."[40] Furthermore, "once the libel was proved, the defendant was shown to be a wrongdoer, and the plaintiff could recover damages because the commission of such a wrong implies damage."[41] It is worth recalling that the evidence of a material injury has not been the only test for defamation or the inflicting of a harm, and the discovery of libel has turned even more importantly on our ability to recognize the kinds of expressions that defame by their very meaning or function. What we are brought back to, in other words, is the question that is common to both the libel of individuals and groups, the question of what standards identify those uses of language that

---

[38] See Tex Smith v. Godfrey, 102 N.Y. S.2d 251 (N.Y. Co. 1951), and Ellsworth v. Martindale-Hubbel Law Directory, 68 N.D. 425 (1938).

[39] A good review may be found in MOSER, SURVEY METHODS IN SOCIAL INVESTIGATION ch. 5 (1958).

[40] 8 HOLDSWORTH, note 31 *supra*, at 365. [41] *Ibid.*

are defamatory in nature. And it is that question into which, ultimately, everything else resolves itself.

That question also applies to the second part of Black's argument: that group libels are too much like the stuff of political speech, too close to matters of public, rather than merely private, dispute, and they can be restricted only at the peril of closing off speech that is authentically political. But individual libels are not necessarily more easily identified than group libels, either in knowing the targets of the libel or in assessing the degree of injury. One does not get around the problem of vagueness by restricting the law to individual libel. And if Black's dominant concern were with restraints on political speech, it should be remembered that any political speech is involved in attacks on individuals just as much as on groups, and a good deal of it concerns character as well as policy. One thinks of the attacks on American presidents—the charges of corruption, racism, and murder, satires that are obscene even by current standards. As we have noted, too, the Supreme Court has enlarged the scope of political comment to take in the "public figure," in addition to the public official, and it has reduced the zone of privacy that has been claimed in the past even by political figures. As Mr. Justice Stewart has put it, somewhat tartly: "A candidate who . . . seeks to further his cause through the prominent display of his wife and children can hardly argue that his qualities as a husband or father remain of 'purely private' concern."[42] To confine libel then to individuals is not to confine it to an area that is necessarily more personal and less public, and it does nothing to avoid the problem of restricting political speech.

There was a critical tension in Black's argument. If he had been truly committed to an absolutist position in protecting all political speech, the logic of his commitment should have moved him to reject individual libels as well. And in fact, ten years later, he did just that. He brought his position to a point of apparent consistency by declaring himself in opposition to all libel laws as incompatible with the character of the First Amendment.[43] I say "appar-

[42] Monitor Patriot Co. v. Roy, 401 U.S. 265, 274 (1971).

[43] See *Justice Black and First Amendment "Absolutes": A Public Interview*, 37 N.Y.U.L. Rev. 549 (1962). For an expression of this view in his formal opinions, see New York Times v. Sullivan, 376 U.S. 254, 293–97 (1964); also, Rosenblatt v. Baer, 383 U.S. 75, 94 (1966) (concurring and dissenting); Curtis Publishing Co. v. Butts, 388 U.S. at 170–72 (1967) (dissenting); Monitor Patriot Co. v. Roy, 401 U.S. at 278 (1971) (separate opinion).

ent consistency," because there was a flaw in the structure of his thought, which gave rise to some strange paradoxes. Despite everything Black was later to say about libels, he was still willing throughout his career to restrict speech of the clearest political import; and the curious part is that the grounds he was content to accept in these cases were virtually identical with the grounds that were decisive in *Beauharnais*. To show what those grounds were, it is necessary to look more closely at the issues that separated the two main dissents in this case.

III. The Third Man: Enter the Jackson Dissent

Initially, at least, it might have appeared that Justice Jackson, in dissent, was preparing the kind of framework that could support the conviction of Beauharnais (as, to some extent, he was). He began with a rather carefully drawn statement against the "incorporationist" position, or the view that the Fourteenth Amendment had "incorporated" the first eight amendments and made them binding on the states. Jackson had no doubt that the First Amendment applied with full stringency against the federal government, and he thought it was a matter of some significance that the Court had never sustained a federal criminal libel statute.[44] But while he conceded that the Fourteenth Amendment imposed some limits on the capacity of the states to regulate speech, he was more persuaded now, with Holmes and Brandeis, that the "liberty" protected against the states "may be accepted with a somewhat larger latitude of interpretation than is allowed to Congress."[45] That latitude had to be larger, he was convinced, because the responsibilities of the two governments were not really comparable in the protection of those substantive interests that were threatened most directly by the misuse of speech. The criminality of defamation, for example, was predicated on the "power either to protect the private right to enjoy integrity of reputation or the public right to tranquillity."[46]

> Neither of these are objects of federal cognizance except when necessary to the accomplishment of some delegated power, such as protection of interstate commerce. When the Federal Government puts liberty of press in one scale, it has a very

[44] 343 U.S. at 288–90.

[45] Gitlow v. New York, 268 U.S. 652, 672 (1925), quoted in 343 U.S. at 291.

[46] 343 U.S. at 294–95.

> limited duty to personal reputation or local tranquillity to weigh against it in the other. But state action affecting speech or press can and should be weighed against and reconciled with these conflicting social interests.

Therefore, it did not follow for him that, because Congress could not have enacted this group libel statute, the state of Illinois might not.[47] And it was clear to him that the limitations imposed on the states had never foreclosed the power to enact criminal libel statutes.[48]

If the Fourteenth Amendment offered a wider latitude to the states, however, it still imposed some basic tests for the states in the regulation of speech, and Jackson was not satisfied that those tests had been met in this case. Among the authorities that he found critical here were Fox's Libel Act of 1792, which permitted the jury to determine whether a publication was libelous, and Lord Campbell's Libel Act of 1843, which allowed truth to be proved as a defense. The American precedent came in *People v. Croswell*,[49] where Justice Kent ruled on appeal that the trial court was obliged to submit the libelous character and intent of the article to the decision of the jury, which had to be permitted then to decide the questions of both law and fact.[50] In *Beauharnais*, however, the libelous character of the publication had been decided by the judge as a matter of law. Evidence as to the truth of the charges contained in the pamphlet, as well as explanations bearing on the motives of the defendant, were all ruled out of the trial and in that way barred from the purview of the jury.[51]

A second point of objection for Jackson arose over the "clear and present danger" test, the one addition that the Court had made in the past to the restraints that many of the states had adopted for themselves in the regulation of speech.[52] His concern was that

47 See *id.* at 288.

48 *Id.* at 292.

49 3 Johns. Cas. 337 (N.Y. 1804).

50 The significance of this case is considered more fully by Berns, *Freedom of the Press and the Alien and Sedition Laws: A Reappraisal*, 1970 Supreme Court Review 109, 150–59.

51 343 U.S. at 300.

52 See *id.* at 298. As Jackson phrased it, "where expression, oral or printed, is punished, although it has not actually caused injuries or disorders but is thought to have a tendency to do so, the likelihood of such consequence must not be remote or speculative."

speech had been punished in this case without any effort, on the part of either the judge or the jury, to consider the context in which the speech occurred. No evidence had been taken of any injuries, or any breach of the public peace; nor had there been any attempt made to weigh the potential for violence or the imminence of any injuries to specific persons. "The leaflet," said Jackson, "was simply held punishable as criminal libel *per se* irrespective of its actual or probable consequences."[53]

The two points were accurate as far as they went; the only question was whether they went far enough. The truth of the publication was indeed excluded from the inquiry of the trial, but in the nature of the case one wonders how the test of truth could ever have been more than a gesture without consequence. In the law of defamation, the test of truth has usually proceeded in a framework in which the statement, if it is defamatory, is presumed to be false, and the burden of proof is given over to the defendant. Moreover, the requirement has been that the truth be proved by the defendant in exacting detail; that it be proved directly about the plaintiff, and not merely about the accuracy of any secondary account concerning the plaintiff or his reputation; and that it be proved in every respect that is at all relevant to the charges.[54]

In the case of Beauharnais, his charges had to be proved true of the whole group at which they were leveled. It was possible, of course, that Beauharnais could have cited some statistics in support of his views; and he could have shown, very likely, that the rate of illegitimacy was indeed higher in black areas, as were the rates for murder and other serious crimes. In this respect the defense might have claimed that Beauharnais was saying nothing very different in substance from the things that many social scientists had reported;[55] and it might have been argued, in addition, that when

---

[53] *Id.* at 302.

[54] See GREGORY & KALVEN, CASES AND MATERIALS ON TORTS 1019 *et seq.* (2d ed. 1969). The editors call particular attention to Sharpe v. Stephenson, 34 N.C. 348 (1851), which contained this headnote: "In an action of slander . . . for charging that the plaintiff had criminal intercourse with one A. at a particular time and place, the defendant cannot justify by showing that she had such intercourse with A. at another time and place." For a criticism of this view, see Courtney, *Absurdities of the Law of Libel and Slander*, 36 AM. L. REV. 552, 563 (1902).

[55] As a more recent account, *e.g.*, on the problem of crime, see Wilson, *Crime in the Streets*, 5 PUBLIC INTEREST 26 (1966).

statements of this kind are made about whole groups or collectivities, they are understood to be general statements, which carry an implicit sense of exceptions.

The comparison, however, is not fully satisfying. There are important differences that are not to be discounted in the way the material is treated in the hands of a scholar and the way it is used by a Beauharnais. Scholars may vary widely in their degree of scholarly care, but they are almost universally cautious about qualifying their remarks, and if for no better motive than to guard themselves against obvious criticisms, they can usually be depended on to say something about the limits of generality in the analyses they are offering. With the material involved in *Beauharnais*, a scholar would be likely to have warned that the data he was reporting about blacks described the characteristics of an aggregate; that it was hazardous to draw inferences about individuals from the statistical profile of a population; and that there was of course some overlap among populations, so that there were classes of whites who had higher crime rates than blacks as a group, and many blacks who had never been implicated in a crime.

Beauharnais's leaflet was not designed for reflection so much as action, and it is hard to abstract this piece of writing, if not from the circumstances, then at least from the prospect of action. Beauharnais was not saying, after all, that one ought to look at the particular black who moves in next door as an individual with his own merits, to accept him if he seems likely to make a decent neighbor but to be cautious generally about the overall quality of blacks who move in elsewhere in the neighborhood. Beauharnais's counsel, rather, was a counsel of resistence—to all blacks, to any black who moved into a white neighborhood—and it had to be premised then on assumptions about blacks as a group that were fully as sweeping, and as lacking in equivocation, as the nature of the resistance he was urging. To have made his conviction hinge, therefore, on his success in proving the "truth" of his charges against blacks was to condition his acquittal on something he had no prospect of accomplishing. No one realized this better than Justice Jackson. Although he was willing to overturn the conviction because the matter of truth had not been submitted to the jury, Jackson conceded that, in his own estimate, "this defendant [did not stand] even a remote chance of justifying what impresses me, as it did the trial court, as reckless and vicious libel":[56]

> A publication which diffuses its attack over unnamed and impersonal multitudes is likely to be harder to justify than one which concentrates its attack on named individuals, but the burden may properly be cast on an accused and punishment follow failure to carry it.

The burden was to be cast upon the accused even though, apparently, he had no chance of carrying it. One would think that a conclusion of this kind would have appeared sufficiently paradoxical that it would have raised a serious question about the substance of the reasoning that supported it.[57] For the very nature of the publication that made it impossible for Beauharnais to prove its truth also made it reckless or inappropriate to submit the matter of truth to the jury. One can think of few things worse than having a jury pronounce on the "truth" of Beauharnais's charges, with all the solemnity and authority of the legal process. It would be quite as bad as if Beauharnais had charged that Negroes, as a race, are less intelligent than whites; as if he had then submitted, say, the writings of Arthur Jensen[58] as support for his views; and as if the jury had then been invited to arbitrate the dispute that has gone on in recent years between Jensen and his scholarly critics.[59] These are not the kinds of questions that we typically trust to the judgment of juries. They are not at all like the question of assessing the intentions or credibility of individuals, where the circumstances of the case have been reconstructed in some detail, and where the nature of the judgment depends more heavily on the sense of mature people who have some experience in the world. The questions involved here are questions about the nature of evidence and generalization and the

---

[56] 343 U.S. at 300, 301.

[57] In a similar vein, Roscoe Pound once warned against the dogmatic insistence on the test of truth in those instances when it was evident that the truth of the publication could not be proved, and when the insistence on forming a jury to try the matter of truth comprised the greatest obstacle to the use of injunctive relief in cases of defamation. See Pound, *Equitable Relief against Defamation and Injuries to Personality*, 29 HARV. L. REV. 640, 656–57, 664–65 (1916).

[58] See, *e.g.*, Jensen, *How Much Can We Boost IQ and Scholastic Achievement?*, 39 HARV. EDUC. REV. 1 (1969).

[59] For some responses by Jensen's critics, see *id.* at 273 *et seq.* (and for Jensen's reply in turn, *id.* at 449).

logic of propositions. They may not all be resolved in a definitive way by the philosophers and social scientists who have been addressing them, but they are questions nevertheless that require some professional competence, and they cannot be given up simply to the intuition of laymen. Therefore, one could be justified in refusing to submit these questions to the "decision" of the jury. And if it becomes impracticable, as it was in this case, to litigate the truth of the publication, then there is something to be said in addition for avoiding the use of the courtroom as a political forum. If Beauharnais had been allowed to make use of his trial to offer "evidence" against blacks—even when the issue could not have had a bearing on the outcome of the trial—we would have come rather close to a political use of the courts, much in the way that the Nazis turned the courtrooms of Weimar into public theaters, where they could advance the attack on their political enemies.[60]

The case for submitting the truth of the publication to the jury becomes far more equivocal, then, as it comes under closer examination (and as it is viewed more closely, it also illumines something more about the peculiar nature of group defamation). Justice Jack-

---

60 There are precedents in cases virtually indistinguishable from libel where the truth—even though it was published for legitimate ends—was not accepted as a justification. In Brent v. Morgan, 221 Ky. 765, 766 (1927), the defendant had placed a sign in his show window that read: "Notice. Dr. W. R. Morgan owes an account here of $49.67." The plaintiff sued both for libel and the invasion of privacy. He was awarded damages. The court held that truth was a defense in libel suits, but not in actions for privacy.

Now there may be grounds for holding to a distinction between the defamation that occurs through false charges and the public embarrassment (and, conceivably, defamation) that is caused by an accurate report; but the two are often hard to distinguish. In recent years, there has been more skepticism about the invasion of privacy as a tort, and the scope for privacy actions has been narrowed now by the same decisions that have contracted the possibilities for libel prosecutions. See Kalven, *Privacy in Tort Law—Were Warren and Brandeis Wrong?*, 31 LAW & CONTEMP. PROB. 326 (1966); see also text *supra*, at notes 15–17. I feel, however, that we would still like to uphold the plaintiff in *Brent v. Morgan*, and if so, we would seem to be conceding in principle that, in certain contexts not yet precisely defined, some things are so insulting or harmful—inflict such hurt—that there should be no justification for publishing them, even if they contained a residue of truth. This is the rationale behind the old view that truth alone is not sufficient to justify publication; that one must show, in addition, good motives or the absence of malice. See Andrew Hamilton's argument for the defense in People v. Croswell, 3 Johns. Cas. 337, 355 (N.Y. 1804). See also Harnett & Thornton, *The Truth Hurts: A Critique of a Defense to Defamation*, 35 VA. L. REV. 425 (1949). If that argument be plausible in regard to individuals, it is plausible, too, for group defamation, which may take the form of political pornography, and inflict embarrassment on the innocent to an even greater degree.

son reflected that equivocation himself to some extent, and so it seems fair to say that his dissent really came down more importantly on his second point, the application of the clear and present danger test. That explains, more than anything else, why Justice Black could not have joined Jackson's opinion (and why Jackson, in turn, could not have joined his). With the clear and present danger test, one must consider whether the words used are likely to bring about a substantive evil that the state has a right to prevent; and to do this one must pay close attention to the peculiar details and circumstances of each case.[61] For Black this was a form of empiricism run wild. In most instances the danger test would dissolve into a mere exercise in "balancing" the claims of speech against other social interests, and if one believed, with Black, that there were fundamental liberties involved, then these were not things to be "balanced" away from case to case. From the time Black finally declared himself for an "absolutist" position in the protection of First Amendment rights, he became equally adamant in rejecting the danger test and its preoccupation with "balancing."[62] In the same way that he would refuse later even to look at the motion picture in cases involving censorship of the movies,[63] he feared a movement away from strict grounds of principle as soon as the judgment was thrown open to more and more details of the case. He did not care to know, then, any more than he had to know in order to dispose of the case, and what he had to know, he thought, was very limited. If he could only identify the case, if he could determine, for example, that he was dealing most essentially with a problem of political speech, then that was all he had to know.

---

[61] It bears saying, though, that in the earliest applications of the clear and present danger test, the relation between the words or publication and the substantive evil they were thought to be threatening could be rather remote. See Schenck v. United States, 249 U.S. 47 (1919); Abrams v. United States, 250 U.S. 616 (1919), along with the dissent by Holmes, joined by Brandeis, at 624–31. *Cf.* the refinement of the danger test in the language of Judge Learned Hand in Masses Pub. Co. v. Patten, 244 Fed. 535 (1917) and Justice Harlan in Yates v. United States, 354 U.S. 298, 321 (1957).

[62] See Black, *The Bill of Rights and the Federal Government,* in CAHN, ed., THE GREAT RIGHTS, 41, and especially 55 ff. (1963); Adamson v. California, 332 U.S. 46, 89–92 (1947) (dissenting); Barenblatt v. United States, 360 U.S. 109, 134, and especially 143–44 (1959) (dissenting).

[63] See Kingsley Int. Pictures Corp. v. Regents of New York, 360 U.S. 684, 690 (1959); see also Black's comment, in Curtis Publishing Co. v. Butts, 388 U.S. 130, 171 (1967).

That was a position, however, that most of his colleagues were never able to accept. (There is a serious question whether Black really held to it consistently himself, except in dissent.) Their reluctance to follow him was not without reason, for the approach was deceptively formulistic and never quite as simple as it appeared. In *Beauharnais*, Black was able to classify the leaflet under the heading of political speech, and he was willing to protect it on that basis, because it had the form, in part, of a petition; it was addressed to the mayor of Chicago. But as Jackson pointed out, the leaflet also contained a coupon to be clipped for the sake of taking out a membership in the White Circle League and sending in a contribution.[64] And so it might have been quite as tenable to argue that the leaflet was an advertisement or a solicitation, as much as it was a petition. For all one could tell, the address to the mayor might have been added largely for dramatic or rhetorical effect, and as Jackson suggested, one could not be allowed to save an otherwise scurrilous publication merely by cloaking it as a petition.[65]

Justice Black's scheme for the protection of political speech could resolve itself, then, into a formal exercise, which turned largely on the way one came to describe an event that might have been described in any of several ways. It had the appearance of a more impartial or objective method, which depended on a simple act of description rather than any exercise of judgment. And yet it is clear that Black did not proceed simply by describing the case to himself and then recording the decision that the description entailed. It is probably more accurate to say that the descriptive label he finally pinned on the case reflected his reading of the circumstances, his sense of the facts that were more "essential" in defining the character of the case, and to an important extent it also reflected his judgment on the issues. And so when Black encountered varieties of speech and assembly that seemed to him far less justified in their context—like the wearing of black arm bands in school to protest the Vietnam war,[66] or the holding of demonstrations in front of

[64] 343 U.S. at 301.

[65] *Ibid.*

[66] Tinker v. Des Moines School Dist., 393 U.S. 503 (1969), and see *id.* at 520, where Black tries to distinguish his judgment in *Tinker* from his concurrence in the decision of the Court in West Virginia Bd. of Educ. v. Barnette, 319 U.S. 624 (1943), in which he seemed to agree at the time with the majority that a flag salute was not merely "conduct" but a form of expression that was covered by the First Amendment. See 319 U.S. at 643–44.

Mayor Daley's home[67]—he was quite capable of declaring that these were not matters of speech at all, but matters merely of "conduct," which were not of course protected by the First Amendment.[68] He could reach these decisions without betraying a sign of reservation, despite the fact that the expression and assembly involved in these cases were unmistakably political in their nature. It was, to put it mildly, a rather paradoxical view, and it could produce at one moment this paradoxical expression: "The First and Fourteenth Amendments . . . take away from government, state and federal, all power to restrict freedom of speech, press, and assembly *where people have a right to be for such purposes.*"[69]

IV. The Decisive Role of Chaplinsky

Justice Jackson was undoubtedly right to avoid the kind of mechanical approach that Justice Black held out, for he recognized that it really offered no alternative to the necessity of looking separately at the facts of each case. But in making the danger test the critical point on which his dissent turned, Jackson also clarified the grounds of his difference with Frankfurter and the majority opinion. For despite the use, in part, of language that was associated with the danger test, it was not the danger test that was decisive in the opinion of the Court.

Justice Frankfurter did mention the history of race riots in Illinois, and he did not think it unreasonable for the Illinois legislature to conclude that "[i]n many of these outbreaks utterances of the character here in question . . . played a significant part."[70] He noted that the Supreme Court of Illinois had characterized the words prohibited in the statute as those "liable to cause violence and disorder," and in his view that paraphrased "the traditional justification for punishing libels criminally, namely their 'tendency to cause breach of the peace.' "[71] In these passages, Frankfurter seemed to be writing in the tradition of group libel that came down from

---

[67] Gregory v. Chicago, 394 U.S. 111, 113 (1969) (concurring opinion).

[68] See *id.* at 124; Cox v. Louisiana, 379 U.S. 536, 577 (1965); Giboney v. Empire Storage & Ice Co., 336 U.S. 490, 502 (1949).

[69] 379 U.S. at 578. (Emphasis in original.)

[70] 343 U.S. at 259.

[71] *Id.* at 254.

King v. Osborn,[72] with its emphasis on the incitement to a breach of the peace and the danger of injury to identifiable persons.[73]

If we apply those standards in an exacting way, it is evident that they did not really fit the circumstances in *Beauharnais*. The leaflets in *Beauharnais* were handed out in downtown Chicago in a patently nonselective way; they were not distributed in an area that was undergoing racial transition or that might have been tense already with racial conflict. There was no evidence, then, of a potential for violence that might have been ignited by the systematic spread of this literature. As far as one could tell, the leaflets could not be connected with any breach of the peace, or for that matter, with any other act of an illegal nature; and so, if the danger test had been applied in any strict sense, Beauharnais could never have been convicted.

Frankfurter's opinion did indeed cover the incitement to a breach of the peace, but very clearly, also, it was not confined to the danger test—and that, precisely, was the point of Jackson's disagreement. Frankfurter's opinion was based on the understanding of certain words or expressions that were defamatory in themselves—words that by their very utterance were likely to inflict injury. And if they did not inflict injury in themselves, they might incite to a breach of the peace or, at the very least, they would degrade the climate of civility and make future harms more likely.[74] The

[72] 94 Eng. Rep. 425 (1732).

[73] In *Osborn*, a publication charged that Jews who were recent arrivals from Portugal, and who were living near Broad Street in London, had burned a Jewish woman to death when she bore a child out of wedlock by a Christian man. It was alleged further that these acts of retribution occurred frequently. As an apparent result of these stories, which were spread by publication, Jews were assaulted and beaten in various parts of the city, and the peace was actually breached. The Court observed that, in contrast to an earlier case where the targets of the defamation were not clearly known [King v. Alme & Nott, 91 Eng. Rep. 790 (1700)], here "the whole community of the Jews are struck at." 94 Eng. Rep. at 425.

[74] It is curious that by Jackson's own account, the danger test would have been satisfied for him if Beauharnais's leaflet had "caused injury to any individual Negro, such as being refused living quarters in a particular section, house or apartment, or being refused employment." 343 U.S. at 302. Yet, these were not injuries that would have been detectable necessarily by the time of the trial, and they were rather beyond the scope of the danger test as it was strictly and narrowly applied. They were closer to the kinds of injuries described earlier, which may be quite delayed in their occurrence, because they arise out of a climate of prejudice. And, as we noted before, it may be impossible to establish a connection between the injury that is suffered and the particular publications that have sustained the climate

authority he relied on for this understanding was the old *Chaplinsky* case,[75] and the key passage he cited there was the most memorable in Justice Murphy's opinion.[76]

> There are certain well-defined and narrowly limited classes of speech, the prevention and punishment of which have never been thought to raise any Constitutional problem. These include the lewd and obscene, the profane, the libelous, and the insulting or "fighting" words—those which *by their very utterance inflict injury* or tend to incite an immediate breach of the peace. It has been well observed that such utterances are no essential part of any exposition of ideas, and are of such slight social value as a step to truth that any benefit that may be derived from them is clearly outweighed by the social interest in order and morality.

As sometimes occurs with cases viewed over a distance of many years, the opinion rings with a firmness that the case itself may lack. Chaplinsky was a member of the Jehovah's Witnesses, and on a busy Saturday afternoon he was distributing literature attacking all religion as a "racket" (except, presumably, his own). A complaint was made to Bowering, the city marshal, who explained that Chaplinsky was acting within his legal rights. At the same time, he warned Chaplinsky that the crowd was getting restless. Somewhat later, a disturbance occurred on the street, and Chaplinsky was led away by a traffic officer. Heading toward the station, Chaplinsky and the officer met Bowering, who was on his way to what he thought was the scene of a riot. The marshal repeated at that moment the warning he had made to Chaplinsky earlier. With that, Chaplinsky allegedly called Bowering a "racketeer" and said that he was "a damned Fascist and the whole government of Rochester are Fascists or agents of Fascists."[77] Chaplinsky was charged with a verbal assault on Bowering, and he was convicted under a state law proscribing insults in a public place.

---

of prejudice. See text *supra,* at notes 34–36. The very fact, though, that Jackson conceded a possible connection between Beauharnais's pamphlet and harms of a more distant nature, should have been enough in itself to concede the plausibility of Frankfurter's case.

[75] Chaplinsky v. New Hampshire, 315 U.S. 568 (1942); for Frankfurter's reliance on this case, see 343 U.S. at 255–58.

[76] 315 U.S. at 271–72. (Emphasis added.) Murphy leaned heavily on this passage in CHAFEE, FREE SPEECH IN THE UNITED STATES 149 (1941), and this reliance was the subject of critical comment in KALVEN, note 7 *supra,* at 49–50.

[77] 315 U.S. at 569.

It is far from clear that we would consider the same words actionable today when directed against a policeman, who might be in the class, after all, of a public official.[78] In some respects, that may be a measure of our own callousness, of how much more it takes today to pass the threshold we have established for serious verbal assaults. Yet there may be room to argue, even today, that the police are not less deserving of the protections of civility in a public place than ordinary citizens are, and there are some verbal assaults that are so provocative and malicious that we would not want to protect them merely because they are directed at the police. But if there may be more uncertainty over the way in which we would dispose of the case today, the principles of *Chaplinsky* stand on firmer ground, and they have established some points of durable import for the regulation of speech in the public streets. For one thing, the case established that certain forms of speech or expression may constitute an assault in themselves, even if they are not accompanied by overt acts that involve a physical assault. It reminded us that, traditionally, "assaults" have not required bodily contact. In that sense, the case helps to remind us, too, that there is in fact such a thing as psychological injury, which may be quite as grave—and as much of a concern in the eyes of the law—as an assault on one's body or a broken leg. When these points were taken together, *Chaplinsky* suggested in a rather compelling way that one had a claim to be protected from an unprovoked assault (including a verbal or psychological assault) when one ventured into a public place.[79]

---

[78] *Cf.* Mr. Justice Powell, concurring, in Lewis v. New Orleans, 408 U.S. 913 (1972).

[79] In interpreting the statute involved in *Chaplinsky*, the Supreme Court of New Hampshire declared that no words were "forbidden except such as have a direct tendency to cause acts of violence by the persons to whom, individually, the remark is addressed." Later it added: "The statute, as construed, does no more than prohibit the face-to-face words plainly likely to cause a breach of the peace by the addressee, *words whose speaking constitutes a breach of the peace by the speaker*." Quoted in 315 U.S. at 573. (Emphasis added.) For the sake, apparently, of avoiding the notion that someone may be punished for "mere" words, the Court sought to assimilate the words themselves to an act of violence, and it managed that largely by importing language that suggested a near certain connection between the utterance of the words and the outbreak of violence.

All of this was based, of course, on the assumption that most people would be moved to violence by certain classes of "fighting words," an assumption that may be highly problematic in any case, even though people may uniformly take of-

That, of course, is not all there was to *Chaplinsky*, but it does suggest the features that made *Chaplinsky* such a durable case. In a manner that was far more satisfying than any other decision, *Chaplinsky* was able to account for the grounds on which we would be justified in calling the police, for example, to order a crowd to "move along" or disperse in cases where nearly everyone would agree that the crowd should, in decency, be dispersed, even though only speech was involved. Consider two hypothetical cases, which approximate incidents we have already experienced. In the first case, a crowd gathers all night before the house of the first Negro family to move into the neighborhood. No violence arises; no rocks or bottles are thrown. The crowd merely stands there, chanting in a low tone, and as it stays on through the night, it makes almost no sound at all. There is no breach of the peace, or even anything that fits our usual notion of a public disturbance. The crowd simply stands in silence through the night, intimidating by its presence.

In the second case, a young black child or a group of black children are on their way to school as part of the first cohort of blacks in a previously all-white school. As they walk along, they are followed by a larger crowd of whites who shout epithets and do everything in their power to harass and intimidate the children, short of using violence. Or, as in the first case, the crowd may say very little or nothing; it takes care to avoid anything that might resemble a disturbance of the peace, and it tries instead to work its intimidation largely through its presence alone.

In both cases, the crowds refrain from violence, and so it might be said that they are engaged in peaceable assembly, or, at their most unruly, in a form of public protest. For despite the fact that harassment is aimed at private individuals, these acts cannot be dismissed as mere private quarrels with no political significance, and no claim therefore to the status of political speech. The purpose of these acts was to have a larger effect on the character of the community by keeping blacks out. In pursuing these forms of intimidation outside the law, the object was to discourage blacks from exercising

---

fense at the words. The understanding that the courts—and many commentators—have seemed anxious to avoid is that the inference of injury is being made from the words themselves, and from nothing more. Professor Kalven pursued much the same kind of exercise when he said, in explaining the *Chaplinsky* case, that "a certain class of face to face epithets are regulatable per se because they are, so to speak, per se freighted with a clear and present danger." KALVEN, note 7 *supra*, at 49–50.

rights that are theirs in the law, or to frustrate the ends of a public policy that seeks to bring down the barriers to racial integration.[80]

For the most part, then, these acts would have been peaceful, they would have been comprised mainly of speech or expressive gestures; they would have had a dimension that was clearly political, and finally—but perhaps most important of all—one could not have pretended that they were punishable because they were likely to provoke the victims to a breach of the peace. Realistically speaking, the chances were rather remote that either the children on the way to school, or the family inside the house, would take the initiative in assaulting the crowd. We clearly strain the limits here of the old fiction that the law may touch these cases only because it is necessary to forestall private acts of reprisal.[81] If the law can reach these cases, it must be because we recognize that there is something in the nature of the words or gestures themselves that constitutes an assault. No government that would call itself a decent government would fail to intervene in these cases and disperse the crowd, and it will not do, at those times, to slough off the matter of justification and say that we are simply "balancing" one right against another, or giving more weight to the interests of those who appear to be outnumbered. The metaphor of "balancing" explains nothing here, first, because it says nothing about the standards we use to measure and balance, and second, because it implies that the claims we are balancing here are equally plausible or that they are of a comparable order of dignity.

That is to say, "balancing" tends to suggest an intuitive and, possibly, idiosyncratic judgment, which might come out just as defensibly on one side as the other. But there can be no such parity for the claims involved in these cases. The rights of the crowd in

---

80 An argument might be made that there is still a sensible distinction to be drawn in these cases between the home of a public official and that of a private citizen. Yet, as we have shown, that argument would be weakened by the fact that the distinction between the official and the private citizen has already been blurred in the law; and on the other hand, it is not clear that we would wish to withhold these protections even from public officials. In Justice Black's view, even a public official like Mayor Daley had some right to enjoy the privacy of his home as a "sacred retreat" from the clamor of demonstrators. See *Gregory* v. *Chicago*, 394 U.S. 111, at 125.

81 For a fuller discussion of the subject, see Wade, *Tort Liability for Abusive and Insulting Language*, 4 VAND. L. REV. 63 (1950).

the street cannot really stand on the same plane as the rights of the family inside the house or the children on the way to school. One set of rights is incontestably more fundamental than the other, and the matter goes far beyond the privileges of citizenship or the differences that may arise in liberality between an authoritarian and a democratic regime. The claims involved here are the claims, as we have suggested, that any government is obliged to respect if it is to be regarded as a decent or legitimate government. We are dealing in this instance with the things that governments have an obligation to render to both citizens and noncitizens alike, and when we speak in this way in a language that is not textured by the gradations of privilege or the sense of discrimination among polities, we are speaking of rights that come closer to the level of natural rights. No government may stand back and allow a man to be run down and lynched in the public streets. No government may stand by and let a local mob take matters into its own hands, destroying all the shops, say, of Jewish merchants (as occurred, for example, in Germany during the notorious Kristallnacht in 1938), or, as in the case of the crowd outside the house, discouraging blacks from making use of the liberty that is theirs to secure property where they can and live where they choose. No government may hold back in these instances and properly claim the allegiance of its citizens, for if we may use an older phrase, it would have shown itself at that moment to be destructive of those ends for which governments are instituted. It would have defaulted then on the first obligation of government as it was understood by the men who framed the Declaration of Independence: to protect its subjects from lawlessness in the taking of their lives, the abridgment of their liberty, or the destruction of their property.

Depending on the circumstances, of course, one may be justified in taking a human life, or restricting both liberty and property, but the point is that it does have to be justified: it cannot be done in a lawless way, without reasons or justifications that can be given under the discipline of lawful procedure.[82] What Lincoln said, then, in explaining the grounds of objection to lynching may apply with equal force to other kinds of lawlessness that visit punishment in

---

[82] On the question of "natural rights," see Brown, *Inalienable Rights*, 64 PHILOSOPHICAL REV. 192 (1955), and also Hart, *Are There Any Natural Rights? id.* at 175.

this way without the constraint of procedure. As he warned in his famous speech to the Young Men's Lyceum:[83]

> When man take it in their hands today, to hang gamblers, or burn murderers, they should recollect, that, in the confusion usually attending such transactions, they will be as likely to hang or burn some one, who is neither a gambler nor a murderer [as] one who is; and that, acting upon the example they set, the mob of tomorrow, may, and probably will, hang or burn some of them, by the very same mistake. . . . [T]he innocent, those who have ever set their faces against violations of law in every shape, alike with the guilty, fall victims to the ravages of mob law.

A trial, with its formal rationality, may not always produce a verdict that is substantively rational or just,[84] but with its stricter controls on the presentation and assessment of evidence, it is likely to be far more accurate in the long run than any random procedure in making distinctions between the innocent and the guilty. To recognize no distinctions of that kind, to be willing, in principle, to let the innocent suffer with the guilty, must be the mark of a polity that is disordered in a fundamental way. For no government could claim to call itself a decent or lawful government in the most basic sense if it were not committed to recognizing, in the first instance, the differences that separate the innocent and the guilty, the decent and the corrupt.

All this goes beyond, of course, any facts that arose in *Chaplinsky*. But the questions here are the questions that must, of necessity, arise if one merely follows out the implications of *Chaplinsky*. In principle, that case ran far more deeply than suspected, and it was tied up with the things that are necessary to any decent society.

As I have tried to show, the validity of *Beauharnais* turned most decisively on the argument in *Chaplinsky*. The question whether *Beauharnais* is good law may thus depend on the question whether *Chaplinsky*, at this moment, is itself good law. *Chaplinsky* has now been seriously threatened—if, indeed, it has not been undermined—

83 Address before the Young Men's Lyceum of Springfield, Illinois (27 January 1838) in 1 COLLECTED WORKS OF ABRAHAM LINCOLN, 108–15, at 110–11 (Basler ed. 1953). For an excellent analysis of this address, see JAFFA, CRISIS OF THE HOUSE DIVIDED ch. 9 (1959).

84 See RHEINSTEIN, ed., MAX WEBER ON LAW IN ECONOMY AND SOCIETY l–li, 59, 63–64 (1954); ARKES, BUREAUCRACY, THE MARSHALL PLAN, AND THE NATIONAL INTEREST 352 *et seq.* (1972).

by the decision of the Court in *Cohen v. California*[85] and a series of recent cases that have been controlled by the judgment in *Cohen.*[86] I cannot treat *Cohen* here in its proper fullness, but I can pick out those parts of the opinion that presented the most radical challenge yet to the premises on which *Chaplinsky* rested, for they provided a critical test of the grounds on which a case like *Beauharnais* would have to be defended.

V. Cohen and the Problem of Chaplinsky

In April 1968, Paul Robert Cohen was visiting the Los Angeles County Courthouse, and as he went through the corridors of this public place he wore a jacket that bore the inscription "Fuck the Draft." He was arrested, and subsequently convicted, on a state law that prohibited, among other things, "maliciously and willfully disturb[ing] the peace or quiet of any neighborhood or person . . . by . . . offensive conduct . . . or us[ing] any vulgar, profane, or indecent language within the presence or hearing of women or children.[87]

In reversing the conviction, Justice Harlan assumed at the outset that he was dealing with a class of speech that was presumptively "political."[88] That was a considerable leap from the premises of *Chaplinsky*, and once the shift in presumptions was made, a new burden was placed on the kind of evidence that was needed for conviction. The Court was not disposed now to assume, without the benefit of supporting evidence, that Cohen had shocked the sensibilities of those who saw him or that his words were likely to have led to the outbreak of violence. Not only was it necessary to show now that someone had in fact taken offense at Cohen's sign, but it had to be demonstrated also that the one who had been offended had been "powerless to avoid" Cohen and his jacket.[89] Gone was the sense that came out of *Chaplinsky*, that one had some right to be protected against a verbal assault, or the knowing infliction of a psychological shock, when one entered a public place. The burden was now on the side of the potential victim rather than

---

85 403 U.S. 15 (1971).

86 See Gooding v. Wilson, 405 U.S. 518 (1972); Rosenfeld v. New Jersey, 408 U.S. 901 (1972); Lewis v. New Orleans, 408 U.S. 913 (1972); Brown v. Oklahoma, 408 U.S. 914 (1972).

87 403 U.S. at 16 n. 1.

88 *Id.* at 18–19.

89 *Id.* at 22.

the assailant; it was now apparently more reasonable to ask the auditors to turn away or to make some effort to avoid the offensive speech—something that is not always easy to do in public streets or buildings—rather than to ask the speaker to accept some restraints on his behavior in public.

The understanding of injury was narrowed to the most personal and immediate terms, and to accomplish that, the meaning of *Chaplinsky* also had to be narrowed. In Justice Harlan's hands, the scope of *Chaplinsky* was reduced to cover face-to-face encounters and "those personally abusive epithets which, when addressed to the ordinary citizen, are . . . inherently likely to provoke violent reaction."[90] But the danger of a violent reaction was only one-half of the formula in *Chaplinsky:* what Harlan left out here was the understanding of "words . . . which by their very utterance inflict injury," even without inciting a breach of the peace.[91] The question of the immediate danger was, of course, a prominent test in these cases of insults and "fighting words," because the context was often as important as the words in establishing the overall meaning of the act. But when the danger test is made the exclusive test in these cases, the emphases will be placed even more heavily on the personal encounter rather than the offense, and the results may often be unfortunate.

For example, let us suppose that instead of Cohen we had someone with a jacket saying "Fuck the Jews." Let us suppose further that, like Cohen, he is in a courthouse, or perhaps in a line at the Internal Revenue Service, where he has an appointment to consider his tax returns. Most of the people around him are probably there on business that leaves little freedom for rescheduling, and so if they are standing in line somewhere behind the person with the jacket, waiting to take up the question of their taxes, they may not feel they can afford to leave the line if they happen to take offense at the jacket. Now it is conceivable that, within the terms of Harlan's opinion, we would be able to reach this case. In relation to Cohen's

90 *Id.* at 20.

91 That the holding in *Chaplinsky* does indeed extend much farther has been been recognized most recently by Mr. Justice Powell in his dissenting opinion in *Rosenfeld*. Writing, as it were, against the line of argument emerging from the *Cohen* case, Powell pointed out that "*Chaplinsky* is not limited to words whose mere utterance entails a high probability of an outbreak of physical violence. It also extends to the willful use of scurrilous language calculated to offend sensibilities of an unwilling audience." 408 U.S. at 905.

statement about the draft, Harlan thought that "No individual actually or likely to be present could reasonably have regarded the words on appellant's jacket as a direct personal insult."[92] But for any Jew who is present, it is plausible that the sign "Fuck the Jews" could be taken as a "direct personal insult"; and since the rule embraces any individual "actually or likely" to be present, it allows the authorities to anticipate that any Jew who enters the room is likely to feel personally affronted.

The assumption that Jews are likely to enter the room may be quite problematic or speculative and, for that reason, a rather weak peg on which to hang a prosecution. By insisting on the test of a direct personal assault, Harlan leaves out the possibility that someone may take offense at this statement about Jews even though he is not himself Jewish and cannot be the object then of a direct personal assault. If there is a cause of action in this case, it must arise from the nature of the words themselves; and if there is a valid interest to be asserted, it can only be an interest in preserving the climate of civility, regardless of whether the ingredient of a personal insult is present. That becomes even clearer with a statement like "Fuck the Draft," which attacks only an impersonal institution and does not single out any particular persons for ridicule. To come forward at this point and ask someone to remove his jacket, one would have to take seriously the notion that there truly is something like a climate of civility, which is important in itself, and which can be degraded only with costs that are by no means trivial.[93]

With Harlan's opinion in *Cohen*, the Court resolved for the first time that the preservation of civility was simply not substantial enough as an interest of the state to warrant any restrctions on speech that had even the slenderest pretense of being "political." There could be no room for claims of civility because Harlan's

[92] 403 U.S. at 20.

[93] There is a danger here of confusing the issue of principle with the question of the particular penalty that is applied. The issue of principle would be established if it were conceded that the authorities would be acting with propriety if they merely asked Cohen to remove his jacket in a public place. Everything after that amounts simply to a dispute over the reasonableness of the penalty. In other words, one may accept in principle the restraints on certain kinds of speech, and yet at the same time one may prefer that Cohen be given a warning or request in the first instance, rather than that he be subjected to an immediate arrest, or, if he refused to remove his jacket, that he be given a light fine or some penalty far less severe than the one that was prescribed in this case, which was thirty days in jail.

opinion denied at its root that there was any longer such a category as profane or libelous speech. Speaking of the profanity on Cohen's jacket, Harlan asked, "How is one to distinguish this from any other offensive word?" Surely the state would not have a right "to cleanse public debate to the point where it is grammatically palatable to the most squeamish among us"; and yet he saw no way to avoid that result once one conceded the right to restrain offensive speech, for there was "no readily ascertainable general principle" by which one could draw a distinction.[94] Which is to say, there was no reasonable way of distinguishing the profane and defamatory from forms of speech that were either neutral or inoffensive. It was all, in the final analysis, a matter merely of personal taste: "One man's vulgarity," said Harlan, "is another's lyric," and it was precisely "because governmental officials cannot make principled distinctions in this area" that the Constitution left these "matters of taste and style so largely to the individual."[95] What Harlan denied no less was the existence of any standards for identifying offensive speech, because the offensiveness of the words depended entirely on the subjective feelings of the people who heard them.

There was a slight, but telling, discord, though, in Harlan's argument between the case he was forced to make for the radically subjective nature of all offensive and defamatory words, and the assumptions that led him into the case and defined his initial break from *Chaplinsky*. As I have noted, Harlan had begun by turning the presumptions in *Chaplinsky* around: instead of presuming that profane or defamatory speech was beneath constitutional protection, he presumed that the speech was protected and that the burden of proof lay with those who would restrict it. The speech acquired a new claim to protection because it was seen to be "political," and it was seen to be political because it was assumed now by Harlan that the jacket was presenting an argument over public policy. According to Harlan, what Cohen was doing with his jacket was "asserting [a] position on the inutility or immorality of the draft."[96]

The properly irreverent question is, what precisely did Cohen mean when he said "Fuck the Draft," that the draft was "inutile," or that it was "immoral"? One wonders if some point might be served in pointing out that "Fuck the Draft" may not mean either

---

[94] *Id.* at 25.

[95] *Ibid.*

[96] *Id.* at 18.

one of those things, and that very probably it meant neither. The profanity on the jacket, like most expressions that have acquired the status of swear words, had a certain grossness to it that was an important part of its meaning and of the purpose for which it was used. By its nature, it lacked the precision of analytic prose, particularly when it was applied to questions of public policy, where it mocked through its gross lack of relevance. But was this not, in fact, what Justice Murphy had in mind when he wrote in *Chaplinsky* of utterances that were "no essential part of any exposition of ideas" and which were "of such slight social value as a step to truth"[97] that they might be restrained, with no serious harm, for the sake of preserving other values that were at least as important, and perhaps even more compelling, for a civil society?

All one could safely infer from Cohen's jacket was that, for some reason his language was incapable of disclosing, Cohen strongly condemned the draft. But it was evident, even when *Chaplinsky* was decided, that profane and defamatory statements were usually charged, as Justice Harlan put it, with "emotive" meaning, and that they were capable of conveying a powerful sense of likes and dislikes, approval and condemnation. *Chaplinsky*, though, suggested that these statements conveyed nothing of substance that could not be conveyed in some other way. Since it was possible to express the same substance in another manner, it did not seem to threaten the free flow of ideas to require avoidance of the grosser forms of profanity and defamation, out of some respect for the sensibilities of others in a public place.[98]

---

[97] 315 U.S. at 572.

[98] Chief Justice Burger saw fit to point out recently, in Paris Adult Theatre I v. Slaton, 413 U.S. 49, 67 (1974), that the " 'live' performance of a man and woman locked in a sexual embrace at high noon in Times Square [would not be] protected by the Constitution because they simultaneously engage in a valid political dialogue." The case could be presented in a "purer" form if the action took place on the steps of the capitol and the dialogue were removed, so that we would have a problem of "symbolic speech." In either event, one cannot read Chief Justice Burger on this point without receiving the impression that his words were directed at Justice Harlan's opinion in *Cohen*. Within the terms of Harlan's opinion, there was no principled way of reaching a situation of this kind. As long as there is a residue of political significance in the act, it would have a claim to be protected as symbolic expression, and the burden would fall to passersby to avert their eyes. And yet, the Court would probably feel obliged to restrain this "expression," and it is Murphy's opinion in *Chaplinsky* that explains the grounds on which it would be justified in doing that.

VI. Group Libel: The Reach and Uses of a Concept

Nathan Lerner[99] notes that when the Council of Europe was considering a statute on the defamation of groups, a question arose on the point of separating the incitement to hatred from incitement to a breach of the peace. It was argued by the Italian representative, Januzzi, that the two were really very separate:[100]

> These [incitements to a breach of the peace] are not factors that must be taken into consideration as contributory to the offence of incitement to hatred, inasmuch as that offence might equally well exist without violence, insult or breach of *ordre public* or of the peace. . . . Incitement [to hatred] is, thus, an independent offence at law which might be accompanied by such others as violence, threats, insults, breach of *ordre public*, but which nevertheless must have its own special characteristics, its own objective consistency, its own criminal intent.

For all practical purposes, that understanding underlay the decision of the Court in *Beauharnais*, and it may explain why the concept of group libel still holds a special usefulness in our law today, although group libel statutes have virtually disappeared. Experience suggests that, even in the absence of statute, we may have to re-create the concept. There are important parts of our public policy today that are hard to understand or justify on any grounds other than group libel. Beyond that, there are frequent occasions in the preservation of public order where the concept of group libel may be especially apt, and where the alternative standards for restraining speech may suffer serious defects in principle. Examples will make my point.

Title VIII of the Civil Rights Act of 1968 made it unlawful:[101]

> (a) To refuse to sell or rent after the making of a bona fide offer, or to refuse to negotiate for the sale or rental of, or otherwise make unavailable or deny, a dwelling to any person because of race, color, religion, or national origin.
>
> (b) To discriminate against any person in the terms, conditions, or privileges of sale or rental of a dwelling, or in the provision of services or facilities in connection therewith, because of race, color, religion, or national origin.

---

99 *International Definitions of Incitement to Racial Hatred*, 14 N.Y. L. Forum 49 (1968).

100 Quoted *id*. at 53.

101 42 U.S.C. § 3604.

> (c) To make, print, or publish, or cause to be made, printed, or published any notice, statement, or advertisement, with respect to the sale or rental of a dwelling that indicates any preference, limitation, or discrimination based on race, color, religion, or national origin, or an intention to make any such preference, limitation, or discrimination.

The act provided an exemption for dwellings that were owned and occupied by single families, but after 31 December 1969 the exemption would continue only if these houses were sold or rented:[102]

> (A) without the use in any manner of the sales or rental facilities or the sales or rental services of any real estate broker, agent, or salesman, or of such facilities or services of any person in the business of selling or renting dwellings . . . and (B) without the publication, posting or mailing, after notice, of any advertisement or written notice in violation of . . . this title. . . .

According to the 1960 census (the census that was available to Congress at the time), dwellings owned and occupied by single families accounted for nearly 62 percent of the total dwelling units in the country.[103] Yet Congress was willing to exempt this class of private dwellings from the act and preserve the owners in their right of private choice—including the right to discriminate on grounds of race, religion, and nationality—on condition, however, that any discrimination that occurred should indeed remain private. Those who would discriminate would not be allowed to implicate others in their private discriminations by making use of brokers and advertising, and they would not be allowed to further their private ends through the use of public media.

It may appear on the surface that the law has settled for a prudential compromise, but it has created a paradoxical situation that raises serious questions of principle. On the one hand, it has declared that certain private acts of discrimination will still be considered legitimate. On the other hand, it has withdrawn from individuals the freedom of expression they would require in order to make effective use of their rights. And, if it is true that, as far as the law is concerned, these private acts of discrimination are in no way unlawful, then on what grounds could Congress justify condemning freedom

---

[102] 42 U.S.C. § 3604.

[103] 1 U.S. Census of Housing, 1960 1-1 (1963).

of expression that forms a necessary extension of lawful private rights?

It could be argued that Congress was seeking only to insure that holders of property would not bring to the level of "public" practice a convention that public policy has condemned in principle. If, however, the practice is indeed offensive in principle, what is the justification for the exemption that the law has allowed? So long as that exemption continues, is not the exercise of private discrimination legitimate as far as the law is concerned?

As an alternative, one might be tempted to fall back, as the government has most recently, on a distinction that has been accepted in the law between "commercial" speech and other subjects of expression.[104] I cannot here treat the issue with the fullness it deserves. The distinction was resisted very early by the American Civil Liberties Union, and it has been used all too casually over the past thirty years to restrain speech that merely happened to be bound up with the prospect of buying and selling. But the problem here, as before, should turn on the question whether the activity or business is itself lawful. If the end is legitimate—and if one does not seek to encourage harm or vice as a means of furthering one's own trade or self-interest—then the speech that supports any lawful occupation must be presumed to have at least as much of a claim to protection as the speech employed by the partisans of political or religious movements. The speech may be found objectionable, of course, on other grounds (if, for example, it is broadcast from an inappropriate place in the public streets), but the standards used to restrain this kind of speech need not be any less exacting or justifiable than the standards used to restrain other forms of legitimate speech.

If we object, then, to the practice of individuals in advertising the terms of their private discriminations—even as we leave their right to discriminate unchallenged in the law—it must be because we find this kind of advertising objectionable in itself. And in that

104 The Government took this line of argument when the Fair Housing Act was tested for the first time in its provision on discrimination in advertising. See United States v. Hunter, 324 F. Supp. 529 (D. Md. 1971), *aff'd* 459 F.2d 205 (4th Cir. 1972), *cert. denied*, 409 U.S. 934 (1972); see also Holmgren v. Little Village Community Reporter, 343 F. Supp. 510 (N.D. Ill. 1971) (advertising an intention to discriminate on the grounds of "national origin"). In arguing for the distinction between commercial and other forms of speech, the principal authorities relied on were Valentine v. Chrestensen, 316 U.S. 52 (1942), and Breard v. Alexandria, 341 U.S. 622 (1951).

event, the proscription established by law must be defended on its own, independent rationale. The grounds of objection to this kind of public advertising are identical with the objections in the past to common signs saying, "No Irish Need Apply," "Whites Only," "Gentiles Only," or, to take a sign that was seen only a short time ago in Roanoke, Virginia, "No Syrians, Jews, or dogs allowed." If we have found these signs offensive, it is because of the embarrassment or hurt they have caused through the public demeaning of a whole group. The point is that one could accept the right of private individuals to preserve their own standards of private choice, and yet object to this cavalier willingness to inflict public insult. The two issues are separate, and to recognize their separateness is to recognize that our aversion to discriminatory advertising has its own foundation, quite apart from any other harm that may result from discrimination itself, and that our objections, at their root, rest on group libel grounds.

From those instances in lower courts in which judges have made use of *Beauharnais* as a precedent[105] it would appear that the most essential points in Justice Frankfurter's opinion have been fairly well understood. The decisions have not been uniformly perceptive, but they have recognized at least that the "danger test" was not necessary to the judgment in *Beauharnais*, and that speech could be punishable even if it did not raise the prospect of overt violence.[106]

For Mr. John Pemberton, Jr., of the American Civil Liberties Union, such cases are only proof of the mischief that *Beauharnais* is capable of perpetuating.[107] In his view, speech should be punishable only when it threatens an immediate breach of the peace. That standard should be fully adequate, he has argued, to any legitimate interest that the state might have in checking the abuse of speech, and more precisely to the point, it would serve just as well in those places where the courts have been tempted to make use of *Beauharnais*. His bête noire is *Chicago v. Lambert*,[108] in which an appellate court in Illinois relied very heavily on *Beauharnais*. The facts of *Lambert* made *Beauharnais* pale by comparison.

---

105 See, *e.g.*, Chicago Real Estate Board v. City of Chicago, 36 Ill.2d 530 (1967); *cf.* Kasper v. Brittain, 245 F.2d 92 (6th Cir. 1957); Carroll v. Princess Anne County, 247 Md. 126 (1967), *rev'd* 393 U.S. 175 (1968).

106 See esp. 36 Ill.2d at 553.

107 Pemberton, note 9 *supra*, at 33.

108 47 Ill. App.2d 151 (1964).

The case involved eight members of the American Nazi party who picketed a movie theater in downtown Chicago where a film featuring Sammy Davis, Jr., was being shown. The eight men appeared in front of the theater at the height of the evening rush hour with placards and leaflets advertising a "correspondence course" for blacks. "Niggers!" the leaflet read, "You Too Can Be A Jew. . . . It's Easy: It's Fun . . . Sammy-the-Kosher-Coon Shows You How. . . . In Ten Easy Lessons. . . ." "In Just Minutes A Day!" it said, "Be One of us Chosen People . . . Here's some of the Things You Learn: Jewish customs and traditions such as how to force your way into social groups, how to be obnoxious and arrogant, how to throw orange peels around in a professional Jewish manner . . . How to make millions cheating widows and orphans . . . How to Hate-Hitler and get people believing he killed six millions of us even though we are all over here living it up on the dumb Christians."[109] There was more of the same. It was, on the whole, a pamphlet of rare edge and viciousness.

Within a matter of fifteen minutes, in the heavy rush hour traffic, a crowd of about two hundred gathered around the small band of marchers. Complaints were heard in the crowd, particularly from blacks and Jews, and men were seen in different places picking up objects to use as weapons. The police sergeant on the scene was informed by another patrolman that a crowd was gathering on Lake Street and that it was likely to try to break up the march. The sergeant had approached Lambert, the leader of the self-proclaimed Nazis, and urged him to have his group disperse. Lambert refused. In the meantime one officer went to observe the group forming on Lake Street and found about forty to sixty people who were not to be constrained. They told him, as he testified later, that they would not leave until something had been done about the marchers. At the theater the tension seemed to be mounting. The marchers were again asked to disperse, again they refused. This time they were arrested.

In the exchange between the policeman and the crowd on Lake Street, there was as much a question as a threat. Either directly or indirectly, the question put to the police was: "Do we really have to do these things, do we really have to work ourselves up to the point of violence and make serious moves toward taking the law

---

109 *Id.* at 154.

into our own hands before the police can do anything about these men?" And, pursuing the same question from the other side, if there were no clear grounds for an arrest before the situation grew menacing, what was there in the mere willingness of a crowd to assemble and take up weapons that provided any clearer warrant for the arrest of these men? Here, as in other cases,[110] the insistence on waiting for the first signs of violence works with a clear antilibertarian effect: it conditions the rights of the speaker on the sufferance of a hostile audience. The speaker becomes a hostage then to the first rock that is thrown, or to the first heckler who cares to instigate a fight and stir a commotion in the audience. Under the conditions of a crowd, it may often be hard to remove scattered hecklers without bringing on the very disturbance that the police are trying to avoid (and which the hecklers may be trying to create). And so it may be all too easy, under the formula of the danger test, to deprive the speaker of his audience and make a mockery out of his right to speak.[111]

Not only is the danger test, in this sense, highly questionable as a libertarian device, but it teaches the worst lessons that a regime of law could possibly teach. It suggests that, before citizens can expect the law to protect them or to vindicate their interests, they must be prepared themselves to use violence outside the law. More than that, it encourages the private use of force, as it did in the case of Lambert, for the purpose of inducing the authorities to make an arrest. All things considered, that rather alters our sense of the bases on which arrests ought to be made. One cannot help wondering, then, why Mr. Pemberton and others would find this situation so much more desirable than having the law step in earlier and respond to the offense itself, rather than let matters hinge upon the reaction of the crowd.

The answer seems to be that, as high as the cost may be in principle, it is a price they are nevertheless willing to pay for the sake

---

110 See, *e.g.*, Feiner v. New York, 340 U.S. 315 (1951).

111 *Cf.* Terminiello v. Chicago, 337 U.S. 1, 16, 22 (1949), where the police made arrests in the crowds, both inside and outside the hall, before they were forced finally to remove the speaker from the rostrum. Instead of subjecting the rights of the speaker to the tolerance of a partly hostile audience, the police tried first to deal with the hecklers and the violence where they could, but they were compelled also to judge the nature of the words used by the speaker, in the context in which they were used, as a measure of his own intentions and responsibility.

of avoiding an alternative they regard as far worse in principle: that it may be legitimate to restrict speech by judging the content of the speech itself. The point is frequently made on the libertarian side that one does not trust judges or policeman—or anyone else—to make decisions about the kind of speech that is so lacking in substantive value that it falls beneath constitutional protection. At the root, there is still a tendency to believe that the law has no standards in these cases that are anything but hopelessly subjective, and that therefore there can be no way of restraining Lambert and his neo-Nazi band without imperiling all speech and writing of a critical nature.

The premise itself is misconceived. The meaning of words cannot be so arbitrary and subjective. There may, of course, be borderline cases that are difficult to judge. But there are borderline judgments to be made in all kinds of cases, including murder, assault, and rape. Even though the injuries are unambiguous in these cases, they cannot be enough in themselves to determine the verdict. Whether a killing is a murder or a "justifiable homicide" will depend, by definition, on the case that could be made in justification. It will become necessary then to consider matters of intention and provocation, and these things can be judged only by reading the circumstances of the case. But the facts of the case, as we know, are not always so unequivocal. Testimony may be in conflict, key points of mitigation may not be fully documented, and so a decision, when it is finally made, may have to rest on an educated hunch—an estimate of character or an exercise of conjecture, which may be quite as slippery and "subjective" as anything one is likely to encounter in cases of speech or verbal assault.

Not all murders present borderline cases; neither do all cases of speech. There are some speech cases, like *Lambert*, that are far more unambiguous, and far easier to judge, than some cases of murder and many cases of rape. Our standards for recognizing a verbal assault or an act of defamation are no more uncertain than the standards we have for the recognition of other kinds of assaults. If anything, the language itself may present a measure of intention that is even more precise and reliable than the measures that are available to us in other cases. The fact that mistakes may be made at times in judging matters of speech can no more stand as an argument against the law than the mistakes made by juries in cases of murder and assault can establish the essential injustice of having laws on murder and assault. The most disturbing part of the libertarian argument is not that it promises to let quite a lot of degrading speech flourish, but that it denies, in principle, the very possibility of judging. If it is impossible to judge the content of Lambert's pamphlet, it is impossible to judge anything; if there are no grounds on which one could distinguish between the decent and the indecent in cases like *Lambert*, then there are no grounds on which one could make distinctions of that kind in any other area of our public policy.

Unlike *Beauharnais*, there was not the thinnest pretense in *Lambert* that the leaflet was presenting either an argument or a petition. That it was very much political, however, in its intention and effect, is something that cannot be denied. It can only press one to consider, in a more sober way, whether it is possible to claim protection for anything that has political relevance, no matter how distant it may be from the substance of argument, and how unrelievedly malicious it may be in its character. Without passing judgment on the leaflet itself, there is no defensible way for the law to touch Lambert and his group, and it is not clear that *Cohen v. California* would offer any help. There was nothing here to support a direct personal assault. The leaflet was ostensibly aimed at Sammy Davis, Jr., but Davis himself was not even in Chicago at the time. Besides, the attack on Davis was the most transparent formal device, a vehicle for a much larger purpose of defamation that the court was very quick to recognize. The evident purpose of the pamphlet was to defame blacks and Jews, and it was obviously understood in that way by many blacks and Jews who were present, despite the fact that they were never mentioned personally in the leaflet.

It is at least somewhat revealing that the court in Illinois leaned initially on the danger test and the breach of the peace, but as it sought to justify its decision, it moved away from standards that put more emphasis on the reactions of the bystanders than on the responsibility of the marchers. The justification began to turn, in other words, on the nature of the leaflet, and as the court came over to the view that the danger of violence was really inherent in the words that were used, the opinion of the court came rather near to the language of the statute in *Beauharnais*:[112]

> Persons may express their feelings on matters of public interest but actions calculated to asperse and degrade other persons

[112] 47 Ill. App.2d at 161.

> because of their race or religion can and do provoke breaches of the peace, violence, riots or other public disturbances. . . . A mere reading of the leaflet refers to Negroes and Jews as people possessing various criminal tendencies, unchastity and degrading sexual inclinations, all of which are "fighting words" liable to cause violence and disorder between the races.

There is a measure of irony in the fact that the court could find itself filling out a rationale along the lines of group libel in the same year that the Illinois legislature repealed the statute on group defamation that had formed the basis for the prosecution in *Beauharnais*. But with ironies of this kind, important lessons are often taught. In this case, the lesson is that there is a class of problems in the law that the concept of group libel is precisely fitted to address and that courts may be compelled, enduringly, to apply the logic of the concept even if all the statutes on group libel should vanish from the books.

VII. The Flight from Legal Restraint

Even if this understanding is correct, it is possible to argue that it would be better not to deal with these problems of defamation through the formal instruments of the law. The intervention of the government carries the portents of censorship, and rather than take that risk, it would be better, in this view, to search for voluntary restraint and rely on informal processes of negotiation. It might be argued, for example, that even without the help of the government a great deal of offensive material is already screened from the public media. Ethnic and religious associations have often been quite effective in having material censored when members of their groups have been portrayed in foolish or defamatory stereotypes. The Italian-American Civil Rights League has managed to have a number of commercials removed from television, including one done for Alka Seltzer that had a man saying, "datsa somma spicy meatball." More significant, the League succeeded in having the words "Mafia" and "Cosa Nostra" expunged from a series on the FBI that was carried by the American Broadcasting Company.[113] Not long after that, Jewish groups brought pressure on the Columbia Broadcasting System over a series called "Bridget Loves Bernie." Both Orthodox and Reform rabbis took the lead in this movement

[113] N.Y. Times, 24 March 1971, p. 4, col. 3.

to have the program taken off the air because of the heavy use of Jewish stereotypes and because the show treated intermarriage in a favorable light.[114]

In Chicago, two years earlier, an alliance of community action groups withdrew petitions they had filed with the Federal Communications Commission to deny a renewal of broadcast licenses to WBBM-TV and WBBM radio. The withdrawal came after an agreement was reached between the stations and the community action groups for what was described as "upgraded community broadcast services." According to the report in the *New York Times*, the stations agreed, on their part, to advise the community groups of job openings as soon as they became available, to open business accounts in two weeks with Chicago firms owned by blacks, and "to meet with the community groups regularly over the next three years to discuss policies and programming; to screen advertising for demeaning references to ethnic or racial groups."[115]

There is little reason to doubt that private groups in our society can be quite effective in protecting their interests and screening material from the media, without the help of government. But instead of weakening the case for legal restraints, this state of affairs only sharpens the problem. For it is plain that the choice is not between restraint and free expression. It is between two kinds of restraint, one carried on outside the law by private groups, and another administered by the government and carried out under the authority of law. Between these two kinds of restraint it is by no means clear that we should choose the informal, as though it were somehow more benign and less coercive for being outside the law.

From these examples, it is apparent that a system of extralegal censorship may move well beyond matters of racial and religious defamation to reach ideas of a more contentious political nature. Instead of operating in a precise and limited way, they have worked with diffuse and uncontained effects. All this was understood with notable clarity by the Supreme Court when it addressed the same problem in a slightly different form some ten years ago. In *Bantam Books v. Sullivan*,[116] the Court dealt with the Rhode Island Commission to Encourage Morality in Youth, an organization that was

---

114 N.Y. Times, 7 February 1973, p. 79, col. 1.

115 N.Y. Times, 3 March 1971, p. 8, col. 2.

116 372 U.S. 58 (1963).

charged by the legislature to educate the public about obscene materials that could tend to the corruption of young people. As a part of its responsibilities, the commission was "to investigate and recommend the prosecution of all violations" of the laws on obscenity.[117] The commission had no formal powers of prosecution, but when it "advised" a distributor that certain books or magazines had been found objectionable for young people under the age of eighteen, a prudent distributor did not have to be told twice. Field agents would be sent out to the various retailers, where they would pick up all the unsold copies, and the books would then be returned to the publisher. As one distributor testified, there was a strong incentive to act immediately on the receipt of the notice, "rather than face the possibility of some sort of a court action against ourselves, as well as the people that we supply."[118]

A group of publishers finally pressed a suit and charged that the commission was engaged in a scheme of censorship without the usual safeguards of the legal process.[119] In writing for the Court, Mr. Justice Brennan acknowledged that the commission had been limited to "informal sanctions," but the record amply showed that the commission had set out to suppress publications that were considered "objectionable" and that it had succeeded rather thoroughly in its aims. "We are not the first court," he said, "to look through forms to the substance and recognize that informal censorship may sufficiently inhibit the circulation of publications to warrant injunctive relief."[120]

The distributors had been free, of course, to disregard the warnings of the commission in the sense that, if they had refused to comply, they would have violated no law. But threats of prosecution were not to be lightly disregarded, especially when they came from a body that apparently enjoyed such a close relation to agencies of the government. As Mr. Justice Brennan remarked, one had to be naive to credit the assertion of the State that "these blacklists are in the nature of mere legal advice, when they plainly serve as instruments of regulation independent of the laws against obscenity":[121]

> Herein lies the vice of the system. The Commission's operation is a form of effective state regulation superimposed upon

[117] *Id.* at 60. [118] *Id.* at 63. [119] *Id.* at 60–61, 64.

[120] *Id.* at 67, and see also note 7 on the same page for further references on the problem of "informal censorship."

[121] *Id.* at 68–70.

> the State's criminal regulation of obscenity and making such regulation largely unnecessary. In thus obviating the need to employ criminal sanctions, the State has at the same time eliminated the safeguards of the criminal process. Criminal sanctions may be applied only after a determination of obscenity has been made in a criminal trial hedged about with the procedural safeguards of the criminal process. The Commission's practice is in striking contrast, in that it provides no safeguards whatever against the suppression of nonobscene, and therefore constitutionally protected, matter. It is a form of regulation that creates hazards to protected freedoms markedly greater than those that attend reliance upon the criminal law.

The fact that this system of censorship went on outside the law, without the direct use of legal penalties, did not make it, for that reason, any more gentle or liberating. On the contrary, it produced a form of restraint that was far more stringent in its effects than anything one was likely to have accomplished if one had been forced to work under the discipline of a formal statute. Without the need, as a matter of course, to face a challenge in court and justify its decisions, the commission could get along fairly well with standards that were rather gross and unarticulated. Publications were listed simply as "objectionable," without any further word of explanation.[122] The attorney general of Rhode Island conceded in his oral argument that several of the books listed by the commission would not have met the Supreme Court standards defining obscenity.[123] And while that point might not have been as significant as it was made out to be, it was nevertheless true that a system designed for the purpose of restricting materials from a youthful audience was having the effect, in this case, of suppressing publications for the state as a whole, for adults as well as adolescents.[124] The system worked in an unconstrained way and could reach publications that the authorities would have been powerless to forbid if they had been compelled to work their will through an explicit statute.[125] Altogether, the experience seemed to bear out Mill's admonition that, for the true libertarian, there were worse

122 *Id.* at 71.

123 *Id.* at 64.

124 See Mr. Justice Brennan's argument on the point, *id.* at 71.

125 As a forerunner of the *Bantam Books* case, where the censoring body in question (the Watch and Ward Society of Boston) had an even more remote relation to the formal agencies of government, see American Mercury v. Chase, 13 F.2d 224, esp. at 225 (D.Mass. 1926).

things to be dreaded than the acts of the public authorities: there was the need for protection, too, "against the tendency of society to impose by other means than civil penalties, its own ideas and practices as rules of conduct."[126]

In that sense, the *Bantam Books* case had the advantage of setting several things in order that apply just as well to the defamation of groups as to other problems in the regulation of speech. It suggested, for example, that one may still share the concerns of the libertarian, even as one regards the defamation of groups as a fit object of restraint, which deserves to be treated with the most solemn and formal processes of the law. The two concerns are not necessarily in conflict, and they may be reconciled by the way in which one chooses, finally, to place one's presumptions in the enforcement of the law. One might be resolved, for example, to eradicate every sign and vestige of group defamation, and one may presume then, even in all doubtful cases, that it is better to arrest and convict. On the other hand, our aim may be to reach only the most egregious cases, where the offense is unambiguous. In that event our presumptions would be turned around. Instead of presuming in favor of prosecution, we would presume now, in all doubtful cases, that we ought to let the matter go. The change may seem slight, but the difference may be profound as far as the consequences are concerned. The shift in presumptions creates a different structure of action, in which the bias is placed in favor of one set of outcomes and the burden of proof is given over to the other side.

In this case the presumptions could be set in favor of free expression, and the burden of proof could be placed on the side of those who would restrict speech. Without too much difficulty, the police can be coached to hold back on these matters and to act only when they have an unmistakable case. There is evidence that the police are responsive to cues of this sort from their superiors.[127] And in those situations where a judgment has to be made about the intentions of a speaker, we could encourage the police to be even more circumspect. We could take a leaf from the "stop and frisk" cases and caution the police to wait for those "specific and articulable facts" which, when combined with the "rational inferences

---

126 *Mill*, note 10 *supra*.

127 See, *e.g.*, WILSON, VARIETIES OF POLICE BEHAVIOR (1968).

from those facts," could reasonably justify their decision if the matter were reviewed in court.[128]

By arranging the presumptions and incentives in this way, we could preserve an active arena of public discourse, while at the same time allowing ourselves to reach the most odious cases of group defamation, or the cases that are so public and offensive that they cannot be avoided. Again, there is no need to overreach ourselves. It is quite enough if we confine ourselves to the most obvious cases, which raise the clearest issues of principle. For in doing that, we would demonstrate once again that it is indeed possible to judge; and when we judge, as we would here, with all the force and attention of public authority, we would hold up an example to others that goes well beyond the matter of group libel. We would encourage confidence in the discipline of judging itself, and we would encourage others to make judgments as well, not simply on group defamation, but on other matters that raise questions about propriety and decency and the obligations that individuals may have to one another.

VIII. A Framework for Regulation

We should expect, of course, that mistakes in judgment will be made, as they are made in other areas of adjudication. The question, though, is whether the mistakes can be kept at a tolerable level, and for that, there are certain structures that are better than others. That is to say, there are certain structures in which mistakes, when they occur, are more likely to be isolated and less likely to be raised to a level of principle.

The beginnings of this argument were put forward by Justice Jackson in his dissent in *Beauharnais*. Jackson had rejected so-called incorporationist theory of the Fourteenth Amendment. He argued that "the powers of Congress and of the States over [libel] are not of the same dimensions, and that because Congress probably could not enact this law [on the defamation of groups] it does not follow that the States may not."[129] He thought that a single standard was

---

128 The phrases are drawn from Terry v. Ohio, 392 U.S. 1, 21, 22 (1968). See *id.* at 5–6, 22–23, for a recitation of the facts that were able to satisfy the formula in this case. *Cf.* also the facts in Terminiello v. Chicago, 337 U.S. 1, 13–22, esp. at 16, 22 (1949) (Jackson, dissenting), which could have satisfied this test and upheld the decision of the police.

129 343 U.S. at 288. See also text *supra,* at notes 44–46.

inappropriate in restricting both the states and the federal government because the responsibilities of the two were quite different in protecting those rights that were threatened most directly by the abuse of speech. As Jackson argued, the criminality of defamation was "predicated upon power either to protect the private right to enjoy integrity of reputation or the public right to tranquillity." In contrast to the states, the federal government had only a very limited duty to protect either personal reputation or local tranquillity.[130] For these reasons," said Jackson, "I should not, unless clearly required, confirm to the Federal Government such latitude as I think a State reasonably may require for orderly government of its manifold concerns."[131]

A few years later, in his dissent in the *Roth* case,[132] Justice Harlan recalled Jackson's argument in *Beauharnais* and took it a few steps further. Applying it now to the problem of obscenity, Harlan wrote:[133]

> Not only is the federal interest in protecting the Nation against pornography attenuated, but the dangers of federal censorship in this field are far greater than anything the States may do. It has often been said that one of the great strengths of our federal system is that we have, in the forty-eight States, forty-eight experimental social laboratories. . . . Different States will have different attitudes toward the same work of literature. The same book which is freely read in one State might be classed as obscene in another. And it seems to me that no overwhelming danger to our freedom to experiment and to gratify our tastes in literature is likely to result from the suppression of a borderline book in one of the States, so long as there is no uniform nation-wide suppression of the book, and so long as other States are free to experiment with the same or bolder books.

In a similar way, we would expect that the enforcement of restraints on group defamation would vary widely among different states and localities in this country. In some places, it may not appear to be a very serious problem, while in other places, like Chicago and New York, it may seem to be a far more urgent matter, and the authorities may be inclined to enforce the law with greater

130 343 U.S. at 294, 295.

131 *Id.* at 295.

132 Roth v. United States, 354 U.S. 476 (1957).

133 *Id.* at 505–06; see also Harlan in Smith v. California, 361 U.S. 147, 169 (1959).

stringency. It is entirely possible that in some cases, as Justice Harlan suggested, the authorities, in their earnestness, will suppress "borderline" publications. That it may happen at all is something we can only regret; but these are errors, nevertheless, that we can live with. Thirty years ago, when *Chaplinsky* was decided, we were a great deal more vigorous than we are today in the regulation of obscenity, as well as other forms of offensive speech. Yet few people doubted at the time that, in the world of 1942, the United States held out, along with Britain, the example of healthy democracies, where civil liberties were generally protected and the range of political dissent could be rather wide. Even today, in Britain, the courts have been far sterner than their American counterparts in the treatment of libel, and as recently as the mid-sixties, the Labour Government secured the passage of a statute on racial defamation, at a time when the matter was being regarded in the United States as a relic of a benighted past.[134] And yet it would be hard to assert that the public discourse of politics is any less vigorous or substantive in Britain than it is in the United States. Nor has anyone been able to argue that these restraints on speech have had such an inhibiting effect on political expression that the alternatives presented by the parties in Britain have been in any degree narrower, or less significant in their reach, than the alternatives that have been offered by the American parties.

All things taken together, it is hard to believe that we would lose our character as a constitutional democracy if a number of cities and towns suddenly took a harder line on the matter of racial and religious defamation, or if a policeman, say, in Chicago, moved a shade too quickly one day and took an anti-Negro speaker off a public corner. One has the sense, somehow, that we can survive occasional errors of that sort without impairing the basic character of this regime or absorbing flaws that reach to the level of principle. Or at least, one might say, we could survive those mistakes more easily than we could survive the consequences of making no judgments at all, or professing no recognition of any standards by which one could ever hope to judge.[135]

---

134 For an account of the background and nature of the British Race Relations Act of 1965, see Dickey, *English Law and Race Defamation,* 14 N.Y. L. FORUM 9 (1968).

135 At the time of this writing, the Supreme Court has taken a line of argument that is virtually identical to the one marked out here, as it has moved to give

IX. Conclusion

If for no other reason, it would usually be wise to show somewhat more modesty in one's aims if one were at all aware of the limits of one's analysis. In our case, the boundary of the argument is marked by the "Jabberwocky" problem. That is, we can usually identify rather clearly the words that are established in our language as terms of defamation and insult; but what would we do in a case where the words are arrayed in such a context that the language serves a defamatory function, even though the words themselves are literally innocent or meaningless? In Lewis Carroll's "Jabberwocky," one can tell rather easily just which words are the nouns, which the verbs and adjectives, even though the words themselves are literally nonsense: " 'Twas brillig and the slithey toves did gire and gimble in the wabe." (It was, after all, the "toves" that did "gire and gimble" in the "wabe.") Might something similar be done in a conscious way to employ innocent words, but with the purpose of achieving a defamatory effect? In Florida, in 1950, George Smathers managed the very difficult task of defeating the incumbent, Claude Pepper, in the Democratic primary for United States senator. In the course of the campaign, Smathers delivered these remarks to a rural audience in the Florida panhandle:[136]

> Are you aware that Claude Pepper is known all over Washington as a shameless extrovert? Not only that, but this man is reliably reported to practice nepotism with his sister-in-law, and he has a sister who was once a Thespian in New York. Worst of all, it is an established fact that Mr. Pepper, before his marriage, practiced celibacy.

Here we may decide, with Aristotle, that we would be wise not to push our principles to the limits of their logic. It is enough, as

---

more latitude to state and local governments in the regulation of pornography. See, *e.g.*, Miller v. California, 413 U.S. 15 (1973), and Paris Adult Theater I v. Slaton, 413 U.S. 49 (1973). And of course, what can be argued in this vein about pornography would apply just as well to the problem of group defamation. It is notable in this respect that the Court, in framing its decision on pornography, returned to the old *Roth* case and to the reliance that was placed there, originally, on *Chaplinsky*. See 413 U.S. at 20–21. In fact, it is hard to read the opinions of the Chief Justice in these cases without discerning some intention on the part of the majority to firm up precedents that had grown seriously weaker in cases like *Cohen v. California*.

136 Quoted in Buckley, McCarthy and his Enemies 304 (1954).

we have said, if we reach only the most egregious cases, the cases that raise the deepest concern, and which call out in the most urgent way for the response of a decent society. If we can live with mistakes borne of an excess of diligence, we can live, too, with certain borderline violations. In the end we must agree after all with Holmes—if only we had the leave now to recall him in a voice slightly gentler than his own—that the law does all it needs to do when it does all it sensibly can.